Johann Albrecht Bengel

Gnomon of the New Testament

Johann Albrecht Bengel

Gnomon of the New Testament

ISBN/EAN: 9783741103117

Manufactured in Europe, USA, Canada, Australia, Japa

Cover: Foto ©ninafisch / pixelio.de

Manufactured and distributed by brebook publishing software (www.brebook.com)

Johann Albrecht Bengel

Gnomon of the New Testament

GNOMON

OF

THE NEW TESTAMENT

BY

JOHN ALBERT BENGEL.

NOW FIRST TRANSLATED INTO ENGLISH.

WITH

ORIGINAL NOTES EXPLANATORY AND ILLUSTRATIVE.

REVISED AND EDITED BY

REV. ANDREW R. FAUSSET, M.A.,
OF TRINITY COLLEGE, DUBLIN.

VOL. I.

"TO GIVE SUBTILTY TO THE SIMPLE, TO THE YOUNG MAN KNOWLEDGE AND DISCRETION. A WISE MAN WILL HEAR, AND WILL INCREASE LEARNING; AND A MAN OF UNDERSTANDING SHALL ATTAIN UNTO WISE COUNSELS."—PROV. 1. 4, 5.

EDINBURGH:
T. & T. CLARK, 38, GEORGE STREET.

MDCCCLXXIII.

PRINTED BY MURRAY AND GIBB,
FOR
T. & T. CLARK, EDINBURGH.

LONDON, ... HAMILTON, ADAMS, AND CO.
DUBLIN, ... JOHN ROBERTSON AND CO.
NEW YORK, . . . C. SCRIBNER AND CO.

OF

THE NEW TESTAMENT

BY

JOHN ALBERT BENGEL.

ACCORDING TO THE EDITION ORIGINALLY BROUGHT OUT BY HIS SON,

M. ERNEST BENGEL;

AND SUBSEQUENTLY COMPLETED BY

J. C. F. STEUDEL.

WITH CORRECTIONS AND ADDITIONS FROM THE ED. SECUNDA OF 1759.

VOLUME I.

CONTAINING THE AUTHOR'S PREFACE, THE NOTES ON
ST MATTHEW, TRANSLATED BY

REV. JAMES BANDINEL, M.A.,

OF WADHAM COLLEGE, OXFORD.

AND THE NOTES ON ST MARK, TRANSLATED BY

REV. ANDREW ROBERT FAUSSET, M.A.,

TRINITY COLLEGE, DUBLIN.

SEVENTH EDITION.

EDINBURGH:
T. & T. CLARK, 38, GEORGE STREET.

MDCCCLXXIII.

1631
13/1540

EDITOR'S PREFACE.

It is quite superfluous to write in praise of the Gnomon of Bengel. Ever since the year in which it was first published, A.D. 1742, up to the present time, it has been growing in estimation, and has been more and more widely circulated among the scholars of all countries. Though modern criticism has furnished many valuable additions to our materials for New Testament exegesis, yet, in some respects, Bengel stands out still " facile princeps" among all who have laboured, or who as yet labour, in that important field. He is unrivalled in felicitous brevity, combined with what seldom accompanies that excellence, namely, perspicuity. Terse, weighty, and suggestive, he often, as a modern writer observes, " condenses more matter into a line, than can be extracted from pages of other writers."

This condensation of style requires that the reader should have his attention always on the alert, and never presume that any remark is without point. Bengel's parallel references to Scripture are never common-place and superficial, and ought to be in all cases looked for, as being often equivalent to an able and lengthened comment. His use of italics, for the most part, has relation to the *ipsissima verba* of the text or context. Deeply imbued with a holy reverence for *all* the Written Word, he employs quotations of it in a way which opens out to the diligent student new and rich mines of thought in the Sacred Volume. The notes are not to be read isolated from their connection: they form a continuous thread, guiding the earnest and prayerful reader through the pleasant pastures of the Word, and by the still waters of comfort.

In the passages which form the subject of controversy between Calvinists and Arminians, Bengel takes the view adopted by the latter, and in this respect I do not concur with him. But whilst he thus gives an undue prominence, as it would seem to me, to the responsibility and freedom of man in these passages, yet, in the general tenor of his work, there breathe such a holy reverence for God's sovereignty, and such spiritual unction, that the most extreme Calvinist would, for the most part, be unable to discover to what section of opinions he attached himself, and as to the controverted passages would feel inclined to say, " Quum talis sis, utinam noster esses."

If all were able to read Latin notes fluently, it would not be desirable that Bengel's powerful language should be diluted by transfusion into another tongue. But as there are many who read Latin imperfectly, to whom much of Bengel's meaning is lost,—and as there are still more who cannot read Latin notes at all, and yet are diligent Bible-students,—I trust that the religious public will consider that a debt is due to the spirited publishers of the present work. Three able scholars—Rev. J. Bandinel,[1] M.A., of Wadham College, Oxford, Rev. James Bryce, late of Aberdeen, and Rev. Dr Fletcher, Head Master of the Grammar School, Wimborne, Dorsetshire,—have, along with myself, executed the translation with all possible pains and accuracy. The Rev. James Bandinel has translated the Preface, and Notes on St Matthew ; Rev. J. Bryce has translated from Romans to Hebrews inclusive ; and Rev. Dr Fletcher from James to Revelation inclusive; and my portion of translation has been from Mark to Acts inclusive. I have revised carefully and edited *the whole*, and hold myself responsible for the substance of all that is in the present work, even in those parts not translated by me, but only corrected, and where the language is, generally speaking, that of my fellow-translators.

I have introduced additional notes of three kinds: I. Brief

[1] Author of " Sermons," Devotional and Practical," " Lufra," and " Milton Davenant."

notes explanatory of Bengel's meaning, where, avoiding diffuseness, he falls into the opposite error, "Brevis esse laboro, Obscurus fio." II. Where he differs from the Received Text, I have given the authorities, viz. MSS. Versions and Fathers on both sides, leaving the decision to the reader, except where I have thought the probabilities on one side decided. III. Where Bengel gives differences of Greek synonyms, I have stated what I conceive to be the true distinctions, by a comparison of Bengel's views with those of able writers of more recent date.

As to the second class of notes, affecting the Greek Text, it is remarkable how Bengel, with intuitive sagacity, discerned the high value of the Vulgate, and laid hold of the true principle of textual criticism, so generally now recognised, whereby the few ancient authorities are preferred to the numerous MSS., etc., which support the "Textus Receptus." It is true the passages in question are few, yet the more firmly that we uphold the plenary inspiration of all Scripture, the more does it become us to seek by all legitimate means to make the closest approximation possible to the very words of the Sacred Autographs.

The Edition of the Gnomon which the present Translation follows, is that brought out originally by Ernest Bengel, the son of J. Albert Bengel, our author, and subsequently revised by J. C. F. Steudel.[1] The initials E. B. mark the notes of Ernest Bengel; *V. g.* mark the notes extracted from the German Version of the Gnomon; *Harm.*, those from the Harmony of the Evangelists; *Not. Crit.*, those from the "Notulæ Criticæ" (Appar. crit. Ed. ii. p. 4, No. 14); ED., my own original notes; (J. B.), the notes of the Translator of St Matthew: B. G. V., Mr Bandinel's translation from the German Version, and B. H. E., those from the Harmony.

The technical terms and figures, which recur so frequently in

---

[1] Several misprints in this Edition I have corrected from the 2 Ed. quarto, published at Tubingen, 1759; also misprints in the Latin translation of passages extracted from the German Version, I have corrected by the help of the German original.

the Gnomon, are not a mere empty parade of scholastic terminology to confound the unlearned, but are really notes condensed into a word, to save periphrasis and attain brevity. The reader will do well to consult the Appendix at the end, which explains fully the force of these terms. The sketch of the life of Bengel (in the 5th Vol. of this translation), drawn up by me, partly from that written by Ernest Bengel, partly from other sources, will, I trust, be read with interest by all who revere devoted piety, combined with profound scholarship.

May He, for whose glory this work was originally written, bless the present translation of it, to the promotion of sound Scripture-criticism and practical edification among the many in England who have heretofore been deprived of the benefit of it by the language in which it was veiled!

I append an Index, First, of the MSS. quoted by me in the notes. They are all uncial, *i.e.* written in capitals, not in cursive characters; the latter being of comparatively modern date. Secondly, an Index of the Versions, all of a date as early as about the first five centuries, and some of them as far back as the second century—centuries before our oldest Greek MS. They follow literally not only the *words*, but for the most part the very *order*, of words of the Greek text. They are, therefore, an accurate reproduction of the Greek text of the MSS. which they *then* used. It is strikingly confirmatory of the correctness of the *few* old MSS. we have, as contrasted with the *host* of modern MSS. on which the received text is based, that, the more fully we have restored the genuine text of the Versions (as in the Vulgate by the Amiatinus Codex; the pre-Jerome Latin by the Vercellensis MS.; and the Syriac by the Curetonian MSS.), the more does *their* text agree with that of the *old Greek* MSS. in our possession, rather than with the more recent MSS. and the received text. Thirdly, the Fathers of the first four centuries quote nearly all the Greek text, as they *then* had it. Even though *some* quotations be from mere memory, yet others must be trustworthy, viz. where they *expressly* and avowedly quote the words, in such a way, that the *point of their argument* rests on the *verbal* accuracy of their quotation. The old MSS. differ often among themselves; but this very difference makes their witness, where they all agree, the more forcible against the received text. Their differences are a surer test of genuineness, than the suspicious universal agreement of the multitude of modern MSS.: the agreement of the latter is probably the result of their mutually *copying one another*, the disagreements being in course of time removed, so as to present the uniform text, which is found in the Constantinopolitan MSS. The "threefold cord" of the restorers of the true text—such as Lachmann, Tischendorf, and Tregelles, of whom Bentley and Bengel were, in some degree, forerunners—is the agreeing testimony of three classes of independent witnesses, the *oldest* Greek MSS., the oldest Versions, and the earliest Fathers.[1]

ANDREW ROBERT FAUSSET, M.A.
Formerly Sch. and Sen. Classical Moderator, Trin. Coll.,
Dubl., Editor of Terence, Homer's Iliad, I.-VIII.
Livy, I-III., now Stipendiary Curate of
Bishop Middleham, Co. Durham,
July 1, 1857.

[1] The Edition of Tischendorf referred to in this work is that of Leipsic, 1849. Recently he has published an Edition, in which he goes back to many of the readings of the more modern MSS. and of the Rec. Text. It is argued, that some older readings than those of the oldest extant MSS. may be preserved in the modern MSS. It is true that thay *may*. But the question is, can we find any *satisfactory test* of such readings? Is it not better to aim at that which is, in a great degree, positively attainable, viz. the text as it stood in the 4th century (at latest, and probably much earlier), rather than *conjecture* as to a text, which we have now no solid means of establishing, viz. that of the autographs themselves? Tischendorf has perplexed the question by bringing in quotations of authorities comparatively modern and void of weight. I have, therefore, adhered rather to the *few oldest* authorities given in Lachmann; adding, however, the very ancient Syriac, Memphitic or Coptic, and Thebaic or Sahitic Versions, which Lachmann does not notice. A fault also in Tischendorf, which I have avoided, is his not referring to the precise passages of the authors whom he quotes. The Edition of Lachm. which I use is that of Berlin 1842, in 2 vols. 8vo.

GREEK MSS.

A = the Alexandrine MS.: in Brit. Museum: fifth century: publ. by Woide, 1786–1819: O. and N. Test. defective.
B = the Vatican MS., 1209: in Vat. libr., Rome: fourth cent.: O. and N. Test. def.
C = Ephræmi Rescriptus: Royal libr., Paris: fifth or sixth cent.: publ. by Tisch. 1843: O. and N. T. def.
D = Bezæ, or Cantabrig.: Univ. libr., Cambridge: fifth cent.: publ. by Kipling, 1793: Gospels, Acts, and some Epp. def.
Δ = Claromontanus of Paul's Epp.: Roy. libr., Paris: eighth cent.: marked D by Tischend.: Λ by Lachm.
E = Laudianus: Bodl. libr., Oxford: seventh or eighth cent.: publ. 1715: Acts def.
G = Boernerianus: Elect. libr., Dresden: ninth cent.: publ. by Matthæi, 1791: Paul's Epp. except Hebrews.
H = Coisliniana fragmenta: Roy. libr., Paris: Paul's Epp. def.: sixth cent.: publ. by Montfaucon.
P and Q = Guelpherbytana: libr. Wolfenbuttel: Gospels def.: sixth cent.: publ. by Knittel, 1763.
T = Borgiana: Veletri: part of John: fourth or fifth cent.: publ. by Georgi, 1789.
Z = Dubliniensis rescr.: Trin. Coll., Dublin: Matthew def.: sixth cent.: publ. by Barrett, 1801.

SECONDARY AUTHORITIES.

L = Cod. Reg., Paris, of the Gospels: the text akin to that of B: edited by Tisch.
X = Cod. Monacensis, fragments of the Gospels.

Δ = San Gallensis: in the libr. of St. Gall: the Greek and Latin of the four Gospels. It and G. Boernerianus of Paul's Epp. are severed parts of the same book.

B = Cod. Basilianus (not *the* B. Vaticanus): Revelation: in the Vatican: edited by Tisch., who assigns it to the beginning of the eighth century.

VERSIONS.

a = Vercellensis of the old 'Itala,' or Latin Version before Jerome's, probably made in Africa, in the second century: the Gospels.
b = Veronensis, do.
c = Colbertinus, do.
d = Cantabrigiensis, do.: the Gospels, Acts, and 3d Ep. John
e = Laudianus, do.: Acts.
f = Claromontanus, do.: Paul's Epp.
ff = Sangermanensis, do. do.
g = Boernerianus, do. do.
h = Primasius in Apocalypsin.
F = Fuldensis MS. of Jerome's Vulgate: done at the request of Damasus, Pope of Rome, 383.
V = Do., corrected by Victor, Bishop of Capua.
L = Laurentianus or Amiatinus. These three I do not specially quote, except very occasionally, where they mutually differ, but simply quote 'Vulg.' in general, as correctly given by Lachmann from these MSS. in his Greek Test.
Memph. = the Memphitic, or Coptic Version from Egypt: third cent.: publ. by Wilkins at Oxford, 1716.
Theb. = the Thebaic, or Sahidic do.: publ. by Woide and Ford, from MS. Alex. at Oxford, 1799.

Syr. = the Peschito Syriac Version : second cent. : publ. and corrected by Cureton, from MS. of fifth cent.

Later Syr. = a second Syriac Version, by Polycarpus, in A.D. 508.

FATHERS.

Irenæus (of Lyons, in Gaul : born about 130 A.D., and died about the end of the second century). The Editio Renati Massueti, Parisinæ, a. 1710.

Origen (born about 186 A.D., died 253 A.D., a Greek father : two-thirds of the N. Test. are quoted in his writings). Ed. Vinc. Delarue, Paris. 1733, 1740, 1759.

Cyprian (in the beginning and middle of the third century : a Latin father). Ed. Steph. Baluzii, Paris. 1726.

Hilarius Pictavensis (a Latin father : died 368 A.D.) Ed. Maurinorum, Paris. 1693.

Lucifer of Cagliari (a Latin father : died about 370 A.D.) J. Dom. et Jac. Coletorum, Venctæ, 1778.

JOHN ALBERT BENGEL'S

GNOMON

OF

THE NEW TESTAMENT,

IN WHICH,

FROM THE NATURAL FORCE OF THE WORDS,
THE SIMPLICITY, DEPTH, CONSISTENCY,[1]
AND SAVING POWER
OF THE DIVINE REVELATION THEREIN CONTAINED
IS INDICATED.[2]

---

[1] "CONCINNITAS — SENSUUM CŒLESTIUM," literally, "The symphonious harmony—of the heavenly meanings —(I. B.)

[2] "Indicatur."—In allusion to, and explanation of the title *Gnomon*.— See Preface, sect. vii., and note.—(I. B.)

THE AUTHOR'S PREFACE.

WRITTEN AT THE COLLEGE OF HERBRECHTINGEN, 20TH MARCH A.D. 1742, AND AFTERWARDS REVISED.

SUMMARY.

I. The WORD OF GOD, written in the books of the Old and New Testaments, is the greatest of all His gifts.
II. It should be rightly handled.
III. *Commentaries* were not necessary in primitive times.
IV. How far they are useful in later times.
V. The *several ages* of Scriptural Exegesis distinguished.
VI. The origin of the *present* work.
VII. The title, "*Gnomon Novi Testamenti,*" explained; with some account of the author's object and design.
VIII. *Suggestions* as to how to distinguish the pure and genuine Text of the New Testament, and to combine it prudently with the *Textus Receptus.*
IX. The "CRISIS" of *Gerard von Maestricht* examined.
X. The Text carefully revised, the foundation of the present *Exegesis.*
XI. And the same Text *divided* into Sections, and correctly punctuated.
XII. The *Style* of the Apostolic Writings vindicated from misrepresentation.
XIII. The Books of the New Testament reduced into Synoptical Tables.

XIV. The inherent *force of words* considered; especially of the *Greek* words, and that with due regard to *Hebraism*.
XV. The *feelings* [affectus, *mental affections*] and *tone of mind* [mores, ἤθη, *manners*] of the Sacred Writers considered.
XVI. The various methods of Annotation derivable from these considerations.
XVII. Previous writers are seldom cited in the present work.
XVIII. What has been contributed in the present work especially towards the elucidation and illustration of each of *the Gospels*?
XIX. What towards that of the *Acts* and *Epistles*?
XX. The Apocalypse again treated of: Dr *Joachim Lange's* agreement and disagreement with the author's views thereon: the *Ordo Temporum*.
XXI. The *Author's Orthodoxy*.
XXII. His desire to assist those also, who do not understand *Greek*.
XXIII. The *Style* employed in the present work.
XXIV. The *Technical* Terms introduced.
XXV. The *usefulness* and *moderate size* of the Gnomon.
XXVI. Concerning the Author's *German* Interpretation of the New Testament.
XXVII. An exhortation to the *constant and diligent* study of Holy Scripture.

GRACE AND PEACE BE MULTIPLIED TO THE CHRISTIAN READER.

I.

THE word of the living God, which formed the rule of faith and practice to the primitive patriarchs, was committed to writing in the age of Moses, to whom the other prophets were successively added. Subsequently, those things which the Son of God preached, and the Paraclete spake through the apostles, were written down by them and the evangelists. These writings, taken together, are termed "*Holy Scripture;*" and, how great soever is their dignity and value, are, in conjunction with this very title of theirs, their own best encomium; for they are called "*Holy Scripture,*" because they contain the utterances of God, and constitute the LORD's own Book. "The word of our God," exclaims the prophet, "shall stand for ever."—(Isaiah xl. 8.) "Verily, I say unto you," says the Saviour Himself, "Till heaven and earth pass, one jot or one tittle shall in no wise pass from the law, till all be fulfilled."—(Matt. v. 18.) And again, "Heaven and earth shall pass away; but My words shall not pass away."—(Ibid. xxiv. 35.) The Scriptures, therefore, of the Old and New Testaments, form a most sure and precious *system* of Divine testimonies. For not only are the various writings, when considered separately, worthy of GOD, but, also, when received as a whole, they exhibit one entire and perfect body, unencumbered by excess, unimpaired by defect. The Bible is, indeed, the true fountain of wisdom, which they, who have once actually tasted, prefer to all mere compositions of men, however holy, however experienced, however devout, or however wise.[1]

II.

It follows, therefore, that those who have been intrusted with such an inestimable gift, should make a right use of it. Scripture itself teaches what that use is, namely, to *perform* it. In order to perform it, we require knowledge, knowledge which is open to all who possess rectitude of heart.[2]

III.

Myriads of annotations were not written in the Church of the Old Testament, although the measure of light vouchsafed was far more scanty then than now; nor did learned men think, that the Church of the New Testament required to be immediately laden with such helps. Every book, when first published by a prophet or an apostle, bore in itself its own interpretation, clear by its inherent light, being accommodated to the then existing state of things. The text, which must have been continually in the mouth of all, and read by all, maintained itself its own perspicuity and integrity. The saints did not employ themselves in diligently selecting the berries, as if the other portions of Holy Scripture were fit only for the pruning-hook; nor did they occupy their time in accumulating the encumbrances of commentaries. They had the Scriptures [and they found them all-sufficient]. The unlearned could refer for oral instruction, to those who were learned in the Old and New Testaments.

---

[1] *We may add;* They who have not tasted it, give the precedency *before it to all compositions of mere men, however profane, however vain, however wanton, however foolish.* "Hinc illæ lacrymæ."

[2] *Comp.* Ps. xxv 14, Matt. xi. 25, John vii. 17; 1 Cor. ii. 14. *For there is not one of those,* who possess rectitude of heart, *that will allow the saving power of those passages to be snatched from himself by any hermeneutic arts whatever*

IV.

Writings and commentaries are chiefly available for the following purposes : to preserve, restore, or defend the purity of the *text ;* to exhibit the exact *force of the language* employed by any sacred writer ; to explain the *circumstances* under which any passage was uttered or written, or to which it refers ; to remove *errors* or abuses which have arisen in later times.—The first hearers required none of these things. Now, however, it is the office of commentaries to effect and supply them in some measure, so that *the hearer of to-day, when furnished with their aid, may be in a condition similar to that of the hearer in primeval times who made use of no such assistance.* There is one point in which the moderns have an advantage over the ancients, namely, that they can interpret the prophecies more clearly by the subsequent event. Whatever things, of whatsoever kind, individual readers themselves derive from the study of Holy Scripture, they can and ought all to communicate to each other, especially by word of mouth, and also by written compositions ; in such a manner, however, *as neither to diminish, supersede, or interfere with,* the perpetual use of Scripture itself.

V.

Scripture is the foundation of the Church : the Church is the guardian of Scripture. When the Church is in strong health, the light of Scripture shines bright ; when the Church is sick, Scripture is corroded by neglect ; and thus it happens, that the countenance of Scripture and that of the Church, are wont to exhibit simultaneously, the appearance either of health, or else of sickness ; so that it comes to pass that the treatment of Scripture corresponds, from time to time, with the condition of the Church. That treatment has had various ages, from the earliest times, down to the present day. The first may be called *Native* or natural ; the second, *Moral ;* the third, *Dry ;* the fourth, *Revived ;* the fifth, *Polemic, Dogmatic, Topical ;* the sixth, *Critical, Polyglott, Antiquarian, Homiletic.* That mode, therefore, of examining, expounding, elucidating, and illustrating Scripture which is offered by Scripture itself, has not as yet prevailed to any great extent in the Church. Our rankly-abundant discrepancies of opinion, our dulness of sight in interpreting prophecy, prove this beyond all question. We are called upon, then, to advance further, till we arrive at such a proficiency in the study and treatment of Scripture, as is worthy of *men* and of *kings*, and corresponds with sufficient closeness, to the perfection of Scripture itself. Men must, however, be prepared for this by passing previously through the ordeal of difficulties.[1] The history and description of those ages, would furnish fitting matter for an accurate and useful treatise; but other things are more necessary in this place.

VI.

Whosoever desires to render any help in interpreting Scripture, should examine himself, and ascertain by what right he ventures to do so. As far as I am concerned, I did not apply my mind to writing commentaries from any previous confidence in myself; but unexpectedly, by little and little, under the Divine guidance, I have been led on to the present undertaking. The nature of my public office, which imposed on me for more than twenty-seven years, the duty of expounding the Greek New Testament to studious youth, induced me in the first instance to make some observations [on that Sacred Volume]. As their number increased, I determined to commit them to paper, and, at the suggestion of a certain venerable Prelate,[2] to put the finishing hand to them. Exegesis was accompanied by revision of the text; in revising the text for the interpretation of the Apocalypse, I was led on to investigate successively different various readings. The harmony of the Evangelists, commenced in the mean time, and the Exegesis of the Apocalypse, produced the Ordo Temporum. Now all these having been in turn carefully examined, are corrected, filled up, and blended together in the same Exegesis

---

[1] *Whatever to the contrary those 'literati' may think, who, relying on their own powers alone, suppose, that nothing is effected towards the understanding of Scripture by* trials *and by* prayer *but all by mere* meditation. It is TROUBLES [vexatio] THAT GIVE UNDERSTANDING.

[2] Christopher Zeller, prelate of Lorch.—(I. B.)

of the New Testament. I shall have, therefore, to repeat some things which I have already said, concerning each of these writings, and to add some remarks, which are entirely new, so that this work, now reduced to a single whole, may be rendered more complete and unassailable, by the addition of this preface,[1] armed, as it were, to the teeth.

VII.

I have long since given the name of GNOMON, a modest, and, as I think, appropriate, title, to these *Exegetical Annotations*, which perform only the office of an *Index*;[2] and, I should have chosen the term *Index*, as the title of my work, but for the misconception which would have arisen, in the minds of most persons, from the ordinary and technical use of that term [*i.e.*, a *Registry or Table of Contents*]. It is, in short, my intention, briefly to *point out*, or *indicate*, the full force of words and sentences, in the New Testament, which, though really and inherently belonging to them, is not always observed by all at first sight, so that the reader, being introduced by the straight road, into the text, may find as rich pasture there as possible. The Gnomon points the way with sufficient clearness. If you are wise, the text itself teaches you all things.[3]

VIII.

Human selections of sayings and examples, taken from Scripture, have their use; the study, however, of the Sacred Volume, should not end here; for it should, both as a whole, and in its several parts, be thoroughly studied and mastered, especially by those who are occupied in teaching others. In order fully to accomplish which, we ought to distinguish the clearly genuine words of the Sacred Text, from those which are open to doubt or

---

[1] *Prologus galeatus*, lit. "Helmeted" Prologue. A prologue, in which a person defends himself against the opponents of a book. Thus, Jerome calls the preface to his edition of Holy Scripture.—See *Riddle*.—(I. B.)

[2] In the sense of pointer or indicator, as of a sun-dial, etc.—(I. B.)

[3] In the original the last sentence is expressed by the following distich,
Nonnihil Indicii satis est in Gnomone factum:
Omnia te Textus, si sapis, ipse docet.—(I. B.)

question, from the existence and authority of various readings, lest we should either pass by, and thus fail to profit by the words of the apostles, or treat the words of copyists as if they were those of the apostles. I have endeavoured to furnish such a text, with all care and fidelity, in my *larger edition* of the Greek New Testament, published at Tubingen, and in the *smaller* one published at Stuttgardt. Both of them appeared in the year 1734: and the small one was republished, with a new *prologue* (*admonition*) in the year 1738, and lastly, entirely revised, in the year 1753.—For, I considered it my duty not to suppress, but, on the contrary, publish before my death,[1] those things which the experience of a long intervening period, had supplied. Those who desire either to know, or to state, what *my Revision* contains, on any passage, must refer to one of these editions, and not to any other. He who has been accustomed to the first of the smaller editions, will easily, and advantageously, observe the differences in the latter edition. The New Testament, as revised by me, has come to be considered as one edition with this Gnomon, just as if they had been published in one volume. This will appear more clearly in the progress of the present preface, especially in the eleventh Section. My recension has obtained the approval of many; some of whom have partially adopted it in translations.[2] It has, however, met with some impugners, especially *two*: for Andreas Buttigius'[3] pre-

[1] During his last illness he was occupied in correcting the proof-sheets of his German Version of the New Testament, and the preface he had written for the Old Testament Gnomon of his son-in-law, Ph. D. Burk.—(I. B.)

[2] In 1745 when the authorized Danish version was revised by order of the King of Denmark, the text of Bengel was preferred as the standard, for that purpose.—(I. B.)

[3] Andreas Buttigius brought out an edition of the Greek New Testament in 1737—entitled

'Η καινή διαθήκη. Novum Testamentum Græcum, ita adornatum ut textus probatarum editionum medullam, margo variantium lectionum in suas classes distributarum, locorumque parallelorum delectum exhibeat, curante Andrea Buttigio. Lipsiæ ex officina Weidmaniana. MD.CC.XXXVII.

Le Long subjoins it to his *Editiones Bengelii*, with the following observations—

Jungimus præcedentibus merito hanc editionem, quæ nil nisi iterata est textûs Bengeliani editio, quod ipse, quamvis in rubro Bengelii nomen silentio prætermissum sit, in præfatione fatetur editor. Textus idem est, sed more

face agrees for the most part with my views, and, where it differs, I have given the explanations in the Prologue, which I have just mentioned. What, however, others have said upon individual readings, we shall examine in their proper places. To those two, therefore (whose names I need not mention on the present occasion),[1] I have put forth two defences. One was printed in German, with the Harmony of the Evangelists, A.D. 1736, at Tubingen, and afterwards, in a separate and more convenient form, in Latin, with some additions, A.D. 1737, at Leyden. In this, I showed that I had not acted *timidly;* in the other, that I had not acted with temerity. That other, was written in answer to an attack upon truth, exceedingly prejudicial in the case of the ignorant, and inserted A.D. 1739, in the New Tubingen Miscellany.[2] It was reprinted in a separate form the same year, and again at Ulm, A.D. 1745. The *former* defence has become now nearly obsolete: for, he against whom it was directed, has made the " *Crisis Mastrichtiana,*" so far as he has corrected it, entirely conformable to my views; and the learned Lilienthal[3] states, in his Bibliotheca Exegetica, pp. 1263, 1264, what is the opinion entertained by others, of the matters in dispute, between us. So much the more, therefore, do I wish that they who are desirous of avoiding temerity, yet of ascertaining the truth, would carefully examine my *second* Defence. All, at least, by whom I know that pamphlet to have been read, acknowledge that I have exerted myself laboriously, and in a religious spirit, to obtain a pure text of the New Testament. And that very society, in

consueto in versiculos distinctus et bipartitis columnis inscriptus. Variantes lectiones a majori editione mutuo sumptæ sunt, appositis notis valoris earum, et tabula, quâ signa ipsa explicantur. Loca parallela editor ex eodem opere descripsit.—Bibliotheca Sacra, Pt. I., cap. 11., sec. I., § 62, n. 7.—(I. B.)

[1] The first of these was J. J. Wetstein, Bengel's great critical rival—the other an anonymous writer, probably John George Hager, M.A. of Leipsic, whose attack was inserted in "Early Gathered Fruits."—See p. 12, f. n. 1. —(I. B.)

[2] A periodical publication, entitled, *New Literary Notices from Tubingen.* —(I. B.)

[3] MICHAEL LILIENTHAL, a Lutheran divine, a learned historian and philologist, and an able writer, born in 1686 at Liebstadt, in Prussia, member of the Academy of Berlin, and honorary professor of that of Petersburg: he established himself at Königsberg, where he was pastor and professor up to the time of his death, which occurred in 1750.—(I. B.)

whose name my censor previously acted, has not, as far as I know, though repeatedly challenged by me to do so, brought forward, in "*The Early Gathered Fruits*"[1] one single instance, in which I have altered, by innovation, even a syllable of the Sacred Text.[2] This silence furnishes the desired proof of admitted truth. Part of my Defence is reprinted in the present work, at the commencement of my annotations on the Apocalypse.

Most learned men entirely neglect the *spirit*, and, consequently, do not treat even the *letter* rightly. Hence it arises, that up to the present time, the most confused and contradictory opinions prevail, as to the mode of deciding between conflicting readings, and on the method of combining such decision with the Received Text. One relies on the antiquity, another on the number of Manuscripts, nay, even to such an extent, as to exaggerate their number: one man adduces the Latin Vulgate, another the Oriental Versions: one quotes the Greek Scholiasts, another the more ancient Fathers: one so far relies upon the context (which is truly the surest evidence), that he adopts universally the easier and fuller reading: another expunges, if so inclined, whatever has been once omitted by a single Ethiopic —I will not say translator, but—copyist: one is always eager to condemn the more received reading, another equally determined to defend it in every instance. *Not every one who owns a harp can play upon it.*[3] We are convinced, after long and careful consideration, that every various reading may be distinguished

---

[1] The following remarks had occurred in a journal bearing that name (No. 4 of the year 1738).

"If every bookmaker is to take into his head to treat the New Testament in this manner, we shall soon get a Greek text totally different from the received one. The audacity is really too great for us not to notice it, especially as such vast importance, it seems, is attached to this edition. Scarcely a chapter of it has not something either omitted, or inserted, or altered, or transposed. The audacity is unprecedented."—(I. B.)

[2] With some exceptions, in the Apocalypse, a book peculiarly circumstanced, he had not admitted into the text a single syllable, which had not been already embodied with it in printed editions. This is accounted for, and explained afterwards.—See Section X. of this Preface.—(I. B.)

[3] "Non omnes, qui citharam habent, sunt citharœdi." This proverb is of very ancient date. It is quoted by Varro, who died B.C. 28, in his treatise *de Re Rustica*, lib. 11, cap. 1.—(I. B.)

and classified, by due attention to the following suggestions (*Monita*):—

1. By far the more numerous portions of the Sacred Text (thanks be to GOD) labour under no variety of reading deserving notice.

2. These portions contain the whole scheme of salvation, and establish every particular of it by every test of truth.

3. Every various reading ought and may be referred to these portions, and decided by them as by a normal standard.

4. The Text and Various Readings of the New Testament are found in Manuscripts and in Books printed from Manuscripts, whether Greek, Latin, Græco-Latin (concerning which I have expressed the *same* opinion in my Apparatus Criticus,[1] pp. 387, 642 [Second Edition, pp. 20, 319, 320], as Ludolf Kuster[2] has of the *Boernerian*,[3] the most important of them in

[1] "Patria eorum est Britannia."—App. Crit. p. 20.—(I. B.)

[2] Ludolf Kuster reprinted Mill's Greek New Testament, with alterations at Rotterdam, 1710.—(I. B.)

[3] The CODEX BOERNERIANUS derives its name from Dr CHRISTIAN FREDERICK BOERNER, to whom it once belonged: it is now deposited in the royal library at Dresden. It contains St Paul's Epistles, with the exception of that to the Hebrews, and is written in Greek and Latin; the Latin, or old ante-Hieronymian version being interlined between the Greek, and written over the text, of which it is a translation. Semler supposed that the Latin was written since the Greek; but Professor Matthæi, who published a copy of this manuscript, suggests that the uniformity of the handwriting, and similarity in the colour of the ink, evince, that both the Greek and Latin texts proceeded from the same transcriber. It frequently agrees with the Codex Claromontanus. The time when this manuscript was written, has not been determined with precision. That it is ancient, appears (says Michaelis) from the form of the characters, and the absence of accents and marks of aspiration. It seems to have been written in an age when the transition was making from the uncial to small characters; and, from the correspondence of the letters *r*, *s*, and *t* in the Latin version, to that form which is found in the Anglo-Saxon alphabet, Bishop Marsh infers, that this MS. was written in the west of Europe, and probably between the 8th and 9th centuries. Kuster, who first collated this MS., supposed it to be British; Doederlein, Irish. The learned reviewer of Matthæi's edition of this MS., in the Jena Literary Gazette, decides that it could only be written in Germany or France; because, in the margin, many passages are noted *contra* γνωδισκαλκον, apparently because they are contradictory to the opinion of Gottschalk, a celebrated monk, who disputed concerning predestination, in the 9th century, but whose tenets excited little attention, except in those two

his preface to the New Testament), Syriac, etc., Latinizing Greek, or other languages, the clear quotations of *Irenæus*, etc., according as Divine Providence dispenses its bounty to each generation. We include all these under the title of *Codices*, which has sometimes as comprehensive a signification.

5. These codices, however, have been diffused through Churches of all ages and countries, and approach so near to the original autographs, that, when taken together, in all the multitude of their varieties, they exhibit the genuine text.

6. No *conjecture* is ever on any consideration to be listened to. It is safer to bracket [*tutius seponitur*] any portion of the text, which may haply appear to labour under inextricable difficulties.

7. All the codices taken together, should form the *normal standard*, by which to decide in the case of each taken separately.

8. The *Greek* Codices, which possess an antiquity so high, that it surpasses even the very variety of reading, are very few in number: the rest are very numerous.

9. Although versions and fathers are of little authority, where they differ from the Greek Manuscripts of the New Testament; yet, where the Greek Manuscripts of the New Testament differ from each other, those have the greatest authority, with which versions and fathers agree.

10. The text of the Latin Vulgate,[1] where it is supported by the consent of the Latin Fathers, or even of other competent witnesses, deserves the utmost consideration, on account of its singular[2] antiquity.

countries. The writer in question thinks it probable that this MS. was written by Joannes Scotus, who lived at the court of Charles the Bald, King of France, and was the most celebrated opponent of Gottschalk. The MS., however, could not have been written later than the 9th century; for, in the beginning of the 10th, the Gottschalk dispute had lost all its importance. There is a transcript of this MS. in the library of Trinity College, Cambridge, among the books and MSS. left by Dr Bentley, who probably procured it for his intended edition of the Greek Testament. Professor Matthæi published a copy at Meissen, in Saxony, in 1791, in quarto, which was reprinted at the same place in 1818, also in quarto.—(I. B.)

[1] The Latin Vulgate was corrected with the help of ancient Greek MSS., then in existence, by Jerome, in the fourth century, from a version, known as the *Vetus Itala*, supposed to have been executed in the second century. —(I. B.)

[2] Singular is here used in its strictest sense, q. d. *unique*.—(I. B.)

11. The *Number* of witnesses, who support each reading of every passage, ought to be carefully examined : and to that end, in so doing, we should separate those Codices which contain only the *Gospels*, from those which contain the *Acts* and the *Epistles*, with or without the *Apocalypse*, or those which contain that book alone; those which are *entire*, from those which have been mutilated; those which have been collated for the Stephanic[1] *edition*, from those which have been collated for the Complutensian,[2] or the Elzevirian,[3] or any obscure edition; those which are known to have been *carefully collated*, as, for instance, the Alexandrine,[4]—from those which are not known to have been

[1] The Stephani (called in French *Etiènne*, or *Estiènne*, in English Stephens) were the most famous and learned printers of their day. Henry Stephens had three sons, Robert, born A.D. 1503; Francis, and Charles. Robert had also a son named Henry, born A.D. 1528. They were persecuted at Paris by the Sorbonne, and ultimately forced to fly to Geneva, in 1552. Robert published his first edition of the Greek New Testament in 1546, a second in 1549, and a third in 1551, to which his son added another in 1569.—(I. B.)

[2] *i.e.*, The Sixth Volume of the Complutensian or Alcalá Bible, so called from Alcalá, in Spain, where it was printed. The full title of the work is, "Biblia Sacra Polyglotta, complectentia Vetus Testamentum, Hebraico, Græco, et Latino Idiomate; Novum Testamentum Græcum et Latinum; et Vocabularium Hebraicum et Chaldaicum Veteris Testamenti, cum Grammaticâ Hebraicâ, nec non Dictionario Græco; Studio, Operâ et Impensis Cardinalis Francisci XIMENES de Cisneros. Industriâ Arnaldi Gulielmi de Brocario artis impressoriæ magistri. Compluti 1514, 1515, 1517. 6 Vols. Folio." It cost the Cardinal Ximenes 50,000 ducats.—(I. B.)

[3] Printed at Leyden, at the celebrated Elzevir press. The first edition appeared in 1624, the second, which is considered the best, in 1633. The Elzevir text claimed to itself, *par excellence*, the title of *Textus Receptus;* a phrase, however, which is not always confined to that recension. In the preface to the edition of 1633, occurs the arrogant assertion : "*Textum*, ergo habes nunc ab omnibus *receptum;* in quo nihil immutatum aut corruptum damus."—(I. B.)

[4] The CODEX ALEXANDRINUS, now in the British Museum, a manuscript of the fourth or fifth century. A facsimile of it has been published by G. Woide, 1786. This codex consists of four folio volumes; the three first contain the whole of the Old Testament, together with the Apocryphal Books, and the fourth comprises the New Testament, the first Epistle of Clement to the Corinthians, and the Apocryphal Psalms, ascribed to Solomon. It was sent as a present to King Charles I., from Cyrillus Lucares, a native of Crete, and Patriarch of Constantinople, by Sir Thomas Rowe, Ambassador from England to the Sublime Porte, in the year 1628.—(I. B.)

carefully collated, or which are known to have been carelessly collated, as for instance the Vatican MS.,[1] which, otherwise, would be almost without an equal.

12. And so, in fine, *more* witnesses are to be preferred to fewer; and, which is *more important*, witnesses who *differ* in country, age, and language, are to be preferred to those who are closely connected with each other; and which is *most important of all*, *ancient* witnesses are to be preferred to modern ones. For, since the original autographs (and they were written in Greek), can alone claim to be the well-spring, the amount of authority due to codices, drawn from primitive sources, Latin, Greek, etc., depends upon their nearness to that fountain-head.

13. A reading, which does not allure by too great facility, but shines with its own native dignity of truth, is always to be preferred to those which may fairly be supposed to owe their origin to either the carelessness or the injudicious care of copyists.

14. Thus, a corrupted text is often betrayed by *alliteration*, *parallelism*, or the convenience of an *Ecclesiastical* Lection,[2] especially at the beginning or conclusion of it; from the occurrence of the same words, we are led to suspect an *omission*; from too great facility, a *gloss*. Where a passage labours under a manifold variety of readings, the *middle*[3] reading is the best.

15. There are, therefore, *five* principal *criteria*, by which to determine a disputed text. The *Antiquity* of the witnesses, the *Diversity* of their extraction, and their *Multitude;* the apparent *Origin* of *the corrupt* reading, and the *Native* colour of the *genuine* one.

[1] The CODEX VATICANUS, No. 1209, in the Vatican Library at Rome, a manuscript of the fourth or fifth century. No accurate collation of it has yet been published. Originally this MS. contained the entire Greek Bible, including both the Old and New Testaments. At present the Old Testament wants the first forty-six chapters of Genesis, and thirty-two Psalms; and the New Testament wants the latter part of the Epistle to the Hebrews, and also the whole of the Epistles to Timothy, Titus, and Philemon, and the entire Book of Revelation.—(I. B.)

[2] *i.e.*, a portion of Scripture appointed to be read in any Church Service. —(I. B.)

[3] " Ubi non modo duplex, sed multiplex occurrit lectio, *media* est optima. Ex hâc enim unâ tanquam ex centro discessum est in ceteras," etc.—App Crit., p. 17.—(I. B.)

16. When these Criteria all concur, no doubt can exist, except in the mind of a sceptic.

17. When, however, it happens that some of these Criteria may be adduced in favour of one reading, and some in favour of another, the critic may be drawn sometimes in this, sometimes in that direction; or, even should he decide, others may be less ready to submit to his decision. When one man excels another in powers of vision, whether bodily or mental, discussion is vain. In such a case, one man can neither obtrude on another his own conviction, nor destroy the conviction of another; unless, indeed, the original autograph Scriptures should ever come to light.

18. It is not the best style of criticism, which may be resolved into the following shape,—" Erasmus, and the Stephani, and almost all the printers, have printed it *thus : thus*, therefore, it must remain, even to the end of time, without the minutest variation. Monuments of antiquity, as far as they support this reading, are to be admitted; as far as they call it in question, with however universal consent, they ought to be rejected." We must speak the truth : this is a most summary and unsatisfactory kind of criticism, and entirely unworthy of men who have reached years of discretion. It encourages an obstinate and credulous attachment to the more received text, and a perverse and jealous distrust of ancient documents. They who declare that, without such support as this, the safety of those portions of the sacred text, which are free from all variation, and, consequently, of Scripture and Christianity itself, would be *endangered*, are themselves *dangerous* thinkers, and know not the meaning of faith. We have recorded in our Apparatus[1] (p. 401 ; *i.e.*, Ed. ii., p. 35, Obs. xix.) the most just judgment of Calovius,[2] far removed from the typographical superstition,

---

[1] sc "Modernos Graecos codd. quorum integritatem asserimus, non esse praecise editiones Graecas neotericas, hujus vel illius opera divulgatas, seclusis codicibus manuscriptis antiquioribus et probatioribus: sed respici hic universos cod. Graecos et manuscriptos et typis editos. Crit. sacr., p. 492."—(I. B.)

[2] Abraham Calovius, a celebrated Lutheran divine, one of the ablest opponents of the Socinians. He was born at Morungen, in Brunswick, A.D. 1612: studied at Königsberg and Rostock, and became successively Professor at Königsberg, Rector at Dantzic, and Professor of Theology at Wittemberg, where he died, 1686.—(I. B.)

which some at the present day entertain. Even before the invention of printing, Scripture was entire; nor has Divine Providence, ever watchful over Holy Scripture, bound itself down to the typography of the sixteenth century, the era, within whose narrow limits, the whole of the text defended by these zealots, was collected and defined.

19. We maintain, however, the purity and integrity of nearly the whole of the *printed text*, not because it has gained authority by its prevalent use, but because it excels in those *Criteria* which we have here laid down; and we rejoice that such is the case.

20. The text of the Greek New Testament, which was printed by Frobenius,[1] and, after Luther's death, by the Stephani and Elzevirs, differs frequently from Luther's version; as may be seen, by referring to the *table* of passages from the New Testament, added to the Hebrew, Greek, and German Bibles, published at *Züllichau*.[2] It is allowable, however, to embrace the genuine text with delight, wherever it agrees with that of *Luther*. We ought, indeed, laying aside all party feeling, to seek for an entire and unadulterated text; which many, however, disgraceful though it be, care less for than a patched glove.

21. It would be highly desirable to produce an edition of the Greek Testament, in which the text itself should in every in-

---

[1] Frobenius, or Froben, was a famous German printer. He was a great friend of Erasmus, and printed his works, as also some of the fathers, Jerome, Augustin, etc.—(I. B.)

[2] Muthman and Steinbart had agreed to publish at Züllichau, a German original Bible, with the Greek New Testament, according to Bengel's revision, annexed, and had announced their intention, in proposals dated 1st Oct. 1738: but they were so violently attacked from various quarters, respecting this appendage, that they changed their purpose, and, instead of the text of Bengel, chose that of Reineccius. By the appearance, however, of Bengel's defence, the alarm was so far allayed, that they applied to him to compose, for their work, a tabular index, displaying, in parallel columns, the more important variations between the text of Luther, the Greek text of Reineccius, and that of Bengel. This table was very serviceable in showing the correctness of Bengel's revisions; so that none could help seeing, that they supported Luther's version much more closely, than did the readings, which had hitherto been most commonly adopted.—(I. B.)

stance clearly exhibit the genuine reading, and leave not a single passage in dispute. The present age, however, cannot accomplish this; and the more nearly any one of us has approached to primitive genuineness, so much the less does he obtain the assent of the generality.

22. I have determined, therefore, in the meanwhile (until a fuller measure of light be vouchsafed to the Church), to construct as genuine a text as possible, by a judicious selection from approved *editions*. In the *Apocalypse alone*,[1] I have introduced some readings here and there from *MSS.* [as opposed to printed *editions*], the reason of which I have frequently stated.

23. Some *very few* passages, however, of the *Textus Receptus*, I have separated by brackets from the rest of the text, as being either doubtful or corrupt; and thus they are noticed as such in the text itself, without any injury to truth.

24. These passages being excepted, and only for a while, as it were, sequestrated, even the unlearned may rely firmly on, and use for his salvation, the whole of the *rest* of the text.

25. On the other hand, some most precious readings, drawn out from their previous obscurity, are recognised as *genuine*, to the advantage and increase of truth.

26. Readings which are not to be found in the *Textus Receptus*, whether equally probable or evidently genuine, should not be introduced immediately into the text itself, but indicated in the margin, especially if they are not supported by many codices.

27. This [marginal] indication of readings may be accurately exhibited, if the various marginal readings be divided into classes. For every various reading (so far as the question can be decided at any particular time) must have claims, which are either equal, superior, or inferior to those of its rivals, and this again, with either a greater or less amount of marked difference. All readings, therefore, firm, plausible, or doubtful,—whether placed in the text or the margin, may be reduced analytically to five degrees, though I consider it an ascertained fact, that otherwise [if minutely defined, *just as in the relative magnitude of the*

---

[1] See Section X.

stars, etc.] they are innumerable. I have therefore denoted these degrees by the Greek letters, α, β, γ, δ, ε.

No one, I conceive, can be so obstinately hostile, or so slavishly devoted to the more received text, as to object to these suggestions *(Monita)*. Some of them are more fully explained hereafter, with the addition of examples, in various parts of the epistle to the Romans, that of St James, and the Apocalypse. I do not, however, advance anything new. I have always entertained and expressed the same views. Theophilus a Veritate[1] says, that *the warnings, which the learned have found it necessary to give against my edition of the New Testament, are well known.*— See his *Beleuchtung,* p. 27. I suppose he means those *learned men,* to whom I replied in my Second Defence. I wish, therefore, that he would weigh it carefully, and also refer to and examine my edition with regard to those charges, which he brings against me in p. 58, and at the end of p. 64. He will then discard the exception, which he employed in declaring his candour towards me. I do not think that I need or ought to defend myself very laboriously for the future, lest I should seem to prize inadequately the support of those men, distinguished by their piety, zeal, orthodoxy, and literary eminence, who defend me by their well-known judgments and vindications, and repel and vanquish those who are otherwise disposed, whilst I remain quiescent. And now I will rather proceed to show the real value of those guides, whom most men follow.

IX.

In the year 1711, there appeared at Amsterdam, together with the Greek New Testament, the CRISIS OF GERARD VON MAESTRICHT,[2] in which he undertook to decide every various

---

[1] Count Zinzendorf had made a translation of the New Testament, and had issued printed specimens of it, in which he acknowledges that he had availed himself of Bengel's revised Greek text as his principal standard for the work. This acknowledgment provoked a great outcry against the Count's new version, especially through a publication entitled Theophili a Veritate, or Biblical Scandal, given by Zinzendorf.—(I. B.)

[2] The title in full was Η ΚΑΙΝΗ ΔΙΑΘΗΚΗ, NOVUM TESTAMENTUM,

reading by *Forty-three Critical* CANONS. This *Crisis* received the highest tributes of praise from the learned, not only in Germany, as from J. G. Baier,[1] in his dissertation on the Use and Abuse of the Various Readings of the New Testament (p. 18, etc.), but also in other countries, as from the Englishman, Anthony Blackwall,[2] in his "Sacred Classics Defended and Illustrated,"—(pp. 6, 17, etc.) I have shown, however, in my Apparatus, pp. 440, 441, 442 [Ed. ii., pp. 76, 77, 78], that the *Crisis*, taken *as a whole*, is far removed from the truth; and when, in the year 1735, that same *Crisis* reappeared at Amsterdam, with a few alterations, I instituted a second examination of it in my former Defence, already mentioned. s. s. xxvi., xxx., xxxiii., xxxvii. It is right that they, who place reliance on the *Crisis*, should examine my Apparatus and Defence.[3] In that Defence, published in Latin, I added these words: "We shall, at a future time, *examine* those celebrated forty-three *Canons* of Gerard von Maestricht, singly, in order, modestly, and truly." Now, I almost repent of my promise, and would gladly be spared the trouble of such an examination at the present day, as I know that there are some who will like this work of mine the more, the less that it contains of the Crisis. But, since *many are still caught by those Canons*, and I do not know of a more suitable occasion for discussing them than the present, I will do so at

---

post priores Steph. Curcellaei, tum et D.D. Oxonensium labores; quibus parallela Scripturæ loca nec non variantes lectiones ex plus C. MSS.— Codd. et antiquis versionibus collectae exhibentur.—Accedit tantus locor: parall: numerus, quantum nulla adhuc, ac ne vix quidem ipsa profert praestantiss: Editio Milliana; variantes praeterea ex MSº. Vendobonensi; ac tandem Crisis perpetua, qua singulas variantes earumque valorem aut originem ad XLIII Canones examinat G.D. T. M.D. cum ejusdem Prologomenis, et Notis in fine adjectis. Omnium Indicem quaere ad calcem Praefationis Amstelaedami, ex Officina Wetsteniana cIɔIɔ CCXI. The text was that of the Elzevir Editions.—(I. B.)

[1] John William Baier, son of the distinguished writer of the same name, was born in 1675, and died in 1729: he was a Lutheran divine, and learned Philologist of the Academy of Altorf.—and author of many learned works.—(I. B.)

[2] Anthony Blackwall.—See 1st. fn. to Section XI.—(I. B.)

[3] It forms number IV. of the Appendix or Fourth Part of the App. Crit.: Ed. II. It is thus entitled there: "*Defensio Prior*, excusa cum *Harmonia Evangelistarum*, Germanice, *Tubingae*, A. 1736, et Latine, scorsum, commodius paullo auctior, A. 1737. *Lugduni Batavorum*.— (I. B.)

once, quoting the Canons themselves in full (by which I shall assuredly obtain the favour of those who admire them), accommodating my observations to both editions of the *Crisis*, endeavouring to be both easy and brief, and taking heed not to lose sight of becoming moderation, amongst the thorns [*i.e.* whilst employing *pointed* arguments] which are required to arouse some persons from sleep.

Canon 1. Various Readings, as all must admit, result from the *negligence, carelessness, haste,* or *foul play* of transcribers. A *Various Reading* is, in our opinion, a departure of a transcriber from Scripture, or from the meaning of the author whom he transcribes. This general description recognises every departure from the original, even that of the least letter, as a various reading. It would be better to refer the former sources of various readings rather to error, the latter one to design, which may therefore be considered as a various reading. For not every *departure* from Scripture involves necessarily a *departure* from the *mind* of the author : which by far the greater part of these Various Readings (*in the Oxford Edition of the New Testament,* A.D., 1675,[1] *and thence in the Amsterdam Edition*), nay, I may venture to say, three-fourths of them, will prove to demonstration.

Observation on the above. We acknowledge this to be true, with the caution (which will be given when we consider the eighth Canon) concerning the *meaning* or mind of the sacred writer. These remarks, however, do not furnish any criterion by which to give the preference to one reading of a passage over

---

[1] Dr John Fell, Bishop of Oxford, published in 1675, a small edition of the Greek New Testamant, with the various readings at the foot of the page, with the authorities by which they were supported; those taken from Curcellaeus, of course, had only the abbreviation of his name as their authority. Besides MSS., the margin contains citations from the Coptic (Memphitic) and Gothic versions. Bishop Fell gave the readings of some MSS. previously uncollated, and in his appendix, he added what has been called the Barberini collection of various readings from twenty MSS. This collation was found by Poussin in the Barberini library at Rome; and he published it at the end of a Catena on St Mark, in 1673. In it the MSS. are not cited separately, but merely *so many* as agreeing in any particular reading. The collation had been made by Caryophilus of Crete, about fifty years before.—(I. B.)

another. Never, to my remembrance, is this canon cited by the author in his margin, although, like many others, it deserves the name rather of an *observation*, than a *Canon*.

2. Transcribers have frequently erred, through carelessness, fancying, when repetitions of words occurred either in the same or in the following verse, that they had transcribed the preceding or the succeeding words. Hence have arisen *omissions*, or else *variations*, the intervening or following word or sentence having been left out. The same thing might arise when a copy is made from dictation.

A good Canon, and one which ought to be frequently employed, but one which has seldom been employed by the author. It ought to have been adduced, for example, in favour of the marginal readings in Luke x. 11, and 1 John ii. 23.

3. Hence also arise sometimes *interpolations*, or the repetition of a word or sentence, which ought only to occur once, when the transcriber's eye has fallen again upon the same word or sentence, or has passed over any thing.

A good Canon, which ought to be frequently employed, but has seldom been employed by the author. The cause of error, which is mentioned in it, produces not only interpolations, but also changes of words. It ought, therefore, to have been adduced, for example, in support of the marginal reading in 2 Pet. ii. 2.

4. Transcribers frequently made a mistake, or introduced a various reading, when they had written a word before that which preceded it, and were unwilling to erase it lest they should impair the beauty of the Manuscript. Hence has arisen the *transposition* of words which ought not to produce a various reading, if the sense remain uninjured. The same thing has happened, when they had *omitted* a word, which they were afterwards unwilling to insert.

A true observation : but we must determine from other sources which reading is genuine.

5. Transcribers had frequently read a sentence, and having forgotten the original word or words of the text, substituted an *equivalent*, or *almost equivalent* word or phrase, or some *other*, or omitted it altogether, and have afterwards been unwilling to change, erase, or supply it, lest they should blot the copy. This

must not be considered as a various reading, nor is the text to be altered on such a ground.

When *equivalent* phrases occur, this observation does not enable us to determine, which is that of the original autograph, which that of the Greek copyist or paraphrast, nor does it distinguish an omission from an addition.

6. Transcribers have often been guilty of changing or omitting single *letters*, especially those consisting of only one *member* ;[1] also of interchanging *syllables*, which resembled each other in sound (an alteration which frequently occurs in transferring proper names from one language to another); and as these changes frequently left the sense intact, they were unwilling to correct them for fear of marring the neatness of the copy. This again ought not to be considered as a Various Reading, but as a neglect of the transcriber. Such must also be our decision, when *changes* have occurred in the instance of *tenses, moods, verbs, cases, genders,* etc.

This observation touches indeed the origin of the variation, but not so as to arrive at a solution of it.

7. Transcribers have often been guilty of omitting, adding, or varying *particles, pronouns, adverbs, prepositions,* etc.,—a malpractice which has frequently occurred also in the case of *compound verbs.*—This, however, does not constitute, nor ought it to be considered, a various reading : A thousand, and a thousand times has this error been committed.

The same remarks apply to this, as to the Canon immediately preceding.

8. That reading which, whether by addition, subtraction, or mutation of words, or even by variety of construction, does not *alter the sense* of the passage, is not (even though it be found in three or four MSS.), to be considered as a various reading, nor even allowed a hearing, in opposition to the very many other MSS. of good or better mark. For we are not bound, in such a case, to prefer the various reading to the received text.

When you have once exceeded the number of *three or four* MSS. (which we shall consider when examining Canon 11),

---

[1] Such for example as *ι*.—(I. B.)

this observation does not in any case give the preference to one reading over another. It must also be remarked, that those instances are few indeed, where addition, subtraction, or mutation leave the *sense* precisely the same. If I perceive no difference, it is, perchance, perceived by another: if I see it not to-day, I may have seen it yesterday, or I may see it to-morrow. If there be no difference as to doctrine, there may be as to elegance, simplicity, emphasis, connection, or some kind of parallelism.

9. *A single manuscript* does not establish a various reading, because it argues merely the carelessness of the transcriber, especially in the case of omission; provided only that the received reading is according to the analogy of the faith,—otherwise, Canon 22 comes into play.

In Canons 9–12, and 40–43 (compare his Prolegomena n. 108), our author treats of the *number* of manuscripts. But, in the first place, the *antiquity* and *diverse origin*[1] of MSS. is

[1] "Bengel," says Tregelles, " clearly observed the difference existing in MSS. and versions, so that he saw that in a general manner they belonged to two different *families*. The one embraces the most ancient documents whether MSS. or versions, the other comprises the greater part of those that are more recent. It was thus that a ground-plan of a division into Alexandrian and Byzantine families was laid down: these were termed by him, African and Asiatic."

Bengel thus expresses himself in his App. Crit. Ed. II , pp. 425, 426,—

" 1. Codices, Versiones, et patres in duas discedunt familias, Asiaticam, et Africanam.

" 2. Ex Africana est cod. Al. pæne solus; (quia codices Africani fere deleti sunt), at quamlibet multis par: cum versione Æth. Copt. Lat. Ex Asiatica ceteri fere testes. Latinæ versioni subordinantur cod. Græcolatini et Latinizantes.

" 3. Lectio familiæ Africanæ semper antiqua est, sed tamen non semper genuina: præsertim ubi aberratio in proclivi erat.

" 4. Codices Asiatici, quamvis multi, exiguum sæpe pondus habent: nulla præsertim antiqua versione stipati.

" 5. Africana lectio sæpius excessum Asiaticum redarguit: Asiatica lectio interdum medetur hiatui Africano.

" 6. Consensus plurium vel certe præcipuorum testium ex utraque familia magnum est genuinæ lectionis criterium.

" 7. Præclarum esset adjumentum, si duo testes, insignis codex Græcus, et insignis aliqua versio, sumerentur: quorum consensio primum, deinde discrepantia non ipsam quidem ubique decisionem daret, sed tamen iter ad

of more importance than their *number*, which he adopts indiscriminately; and, in the second place, he leaves the very number in great obscurity and confusion—in one instance, supposing that there are in support of a reading many MSS., where there are few or scarcely any—in another instance, that there are few, when in reality there are a sufficient number, or more, or even very many in its favour. For most of the codices (a list of which is prefixed to his Canons) contain only the Gospels, a few the Acts and Epistles, a very few the Apocalypse; in addition to which they are occasionally imperfect, not examined with equal care, collated with editions which are at variance with each other; but our author is accustomed to attribute to the reading of his margin only the MSS. expressly cited in the margin, whilst he ascribes almost all the remaining MSS. (which he enumerates) in such a manner to his text, as though he supposed it to be supported by *hundreds* of MSS., even in the case of the Apocalypse.

The second edition of the "*Crisis*" rightly denominates this a *manifest and great error;* and the formula, therefore, concerning *hundreds* of MSS., etc., has been expunged; but the rest of its tenor remains unaltered. So much the more necessary, therefore, is it to warn those, who fancy that this Crisis has been now purged of all its errors. Anthony Blackwall has committed a similar error in his "Sacred Classics Illustrated," p. 594, where he has cited a hundred and twenty MSS. on Acts ii. 24, and 1 John iv. 3; though, before his time, not so many as forty MSS. had been collated for the Acts and Epistles of St John; and he has also mistaken the sixteen MSS. of Stephens (for I suppose he would have it read thus, not *sixty*),

eam paulatim patefaceret. Duo huiusmodi testes debebant, 1. totum complecti N. T.; 2. antiquitate excellere; 3. et de lectionibus eorum liquido constare. Ex versionibus nulla est, quæ cum *Latina* conferri possit. Nam etiam Syriaca diversis temporibus est adornata : et de ceteris abstrusioribus multa sunt ambigua. Latina versio est ex familia Africana : cui si unus aliquis codex Græcus Asiaticus jungi posset, plus esset facilitatis. Nunc quum ejusmodi nullus præsto est, Alexandrinus tantisper adsciscendus venit. Huic unum Vaticanum opponi passim video : sed id judicium vanum esse, ostendi in Gnom."—(I. B.)

which embrace different parts of the New Testament, for MSS. of *the whole New Testament*, pp. 600, 617, 618, 636. In the Oxford Excerpts,[1] which Maestricht has subjected to his *Crisis*, one, two, three, or four MSS. are often said to have a reading, which is in reality supported by many witnesses. With Maestricht himself, the reading of the text, however weak, can never lose—that of the margin, however genuine, can never gain—the cause.

As far as the *Ninth Canon* is separately concerned, in cases where the number of MSS. is small, a single MS. may make a various reading; nay, as in the case of Erasmus's[2] edition of the Apocalypse, a single MS. has been known to sustain the whole text. The greater, however, that the number of MSS. is, the more rarely can a single MS. support a Various Reading with any show of probability. Maestricht has, however, frequently mentioned only one MS. when in reality there are many. This Canon is cited, for instance, on Matt. xxvi. 35, and Mark ix. 40, though the marginal reading in those passages is supported not merely by *one* MS., but by *nearly all*. In Rev. iii. 12, all the MSS. known, and all the editions printed before Beza,[3] have ναῷ; those, therefore, who have compared the MSS., have not indicated any various reading in this place. In Beza's edition λαῷ was substituted for ναῷ by an error of the press: Beza

---

[1] "Wetstein and Smith, publishers and printers at Amsterdam—in the year 1711 had brought out an edition of the Greek Testament, in which a selection of the various readings [called by Bengel *Excerpta Oxoniensia*] given by Mill and Küster were repeated; and at the end an attempt was made to repudiate the greater part of them, as not worthy of notice by means of the application of certain canons of Gerard von Mäestricht, the editor."— TREGELLES.—(I. B.)

[2] Erasmus's first edition of the Greek New Testament appeared 1st March 1516. For the Apocalypse he had but one mutilated MS., borrowed from Reuchlin, in which the text and commentary were intermixed almost unintelligibly. And thus he used here and there the Latin Vulgate for his guide, re-translating into Greek as well as he could. This was the case with regard to the last six verses, which, from the mutilated condition of his MS., were wholly wanting.—(I. B.)

[3] Theodore Beza, the successor of Calvin at Geneva, was born at Vezelay, in France, A.D. 1519.—His first edition was published at Geneva in 1555, and was repeated in 1576. A third appeared in 1582, a fourth in 1589, and a fifth in 1598.—(I. B.)

observed, and subsequently corrected, the mistake: one Huiss, however, who collated the Codex Alexandrinus with a copy of Beza's edition printed with the mistake λαῷ, noted ιαῷ as a various reading of the Codex Alexandrinus. On which ground Maestricht has by this Canon condemned the reading ιαῷ, as if it were found in only *one* MS., though it is really found in *all*, and is undoubtedly the true reading. These mistakes could not have been committed by Maestricht, unless his Crisis, taken as a whole, were erroneous. The last words of this Canon, "provided the Received Text," etc., needlessly imperil the reading of the Received Text.

10. Nor should *two Codices* establish a Various Reading, in opposition to the reading received and published and of sound sense: since it merely argues the carelessness of two transcriptions, executed by two transcribers, or perhaps by the same hand. This holds good, more especially in the case of omission, when it is generally sufficient to say, "it has been left out."

This Canon is cited on Rev. xiv. 1 and xvii. 4, though the marginal reading of those passages (which refutes the mistake introduced by Erasmus, and received by the Stephani and so many others) is supported not by merely *two*, but by *all* Manuscripts. And yet there are those, who dare to limit the exercise of Divine Providence in preserving the integrity of the New Testament exclusively to the Stephanic Press, and cease not to bring the charge of audacity against all, who endeavour to employ earnestly and reverently, for the common edification, all the helps, which Divine Providence has vouchsafed to the age in which they live.

11. Nor should *three or four* MSS. establish a Various Reading (especially in the case of an omission) in opposition to twenty or more MSS.

This Canon is cited, for example, at Luke xiii. 35; but the marginal reading in that passage is supported, not by *three or four*, but by very many witnesses, and those too of high character. Thus in Matt. ii. 11 and xxviii. 19, the marginal reading is supported, not by merely *three or four* MSS., but by so many, that the reading of the Text is not firmly supported by the testimony even of *one*.

Where Mill[1] (says Maestricht in the last section of his prolegomena) *adduces many Manuscripts, Versions, or Fathers, there, by a slight change in the number of Codices, three or four may, for example, be increased to six or seven : but not even that number ought to establish a various reading, in opposition to a hundred* (Ed. ii., *the vast majority of*) *other* MSS. *or witnesses.* We have already spoken of his " hundred" or " vast majority." The difference is very trifling between *three* or *four* and *six* or *seven :* but the difference is in reality far greater, as any reader may learn, by comparing Maestricht's marginal readings with our Apparatus Criticus, on any disputed passage.

12. A *great number of MSS.* (twenty or more, for example), establishes beyond question the common reading of the Textus Receptus, provided it be of sound sense. This holds good especially in the case of omission.

A *Reading " of sound sense," generally received* before the invention of printing, or even from that time forward, is confirmed by a just number of MSS. ; but, from various causes, a just number may consist sometimes of more, sometimes of fewer MSS.: and the antiquity of witnesses, together with the diversity of their origin, is of more weight than their mere number.

13. The Various Readings adduced by Stephen Courcelles[2] must not be admitted as Various Readings, because he does not indicate the Codices from which they are obtained, or whether they are obtained from MSS. or from printed copies. They may even be considered as a single Codex.

I have spoken of Stephen Courcelles in my Apparatus Criticus, p. 440 (Ed. ii., p. 76).[3] Maestricht expresses his *astonish-*

[1] John Mill, D.D. A learned divine. Born at Shap, Westmoreland, 1645. Entered as Servitor of Queen's College, Oxford, 1661. Became Rector of Blechington, Oxon., 1681, Principal of St Edmund's Hall, 1685, and Prebendary of Canterbury, 1704. He died 1707, the same year in which his edition of the Greek New Testament, which had occupied him for thirty years, was published.—(I. B.)

[2] Stephen Courcelles, known also as Stephanus Curcellaeus, was born at Geneva, A.D. 1586. He became a follower of Arminius. After residing some time in France, he settled at Amsterdam, where he succeeded Episcopius as Divinity professor. He died, A.D. 1658. He was an able writer, and a great linguist.—(I. B.)

[3] sc. Courcelles has seldom admitted anything into his margin, which has

ment, in his Notes on 1 Cor. vi. 5, that Courcelles should *alone* have been cited by the Oxford Editors, although Mill was in possession of thirty Manuscripts. It escapes him, therefore, that such things occur frequently, as, for example, on Matt. v. 48, and James ii. 18. Those even, who are devoid of the sense of sight, may ascertain, by the touch, that the Oxford Excerpts, which Maestricht has subjected to his Canons, are utterly unsuitable to them; and also that he has not collated the *editions* with proper care. For he imagines that Courcelles is cited alone, or almost alone, where Courcelles quotes the text of printed *editions*, and sometimes the best text, as in Rom. vii. 6, 1 Peter ii. 21, and Rev. xxii. 15.

14. Even the most ancient *versions*, when differing from editions and Manuscripts, should not establish a Various Reading, as neither should printed books; but they rather show the carelessness of the translator, or the corruptness of the copy, which he employed. The first *Complutensian* Edition, that of 1514, being extremely exact, and printed from various MSS. (resembling even in its type the ancient MSS. of Scripture), is of nearly as great authority as an actual Manuscript: on which account its various readings are indicated in the Oxford edition of 1675.

What may be the weight of *Versions*, where they *agree* with editions and Manuscripts, with some of them at least, we do not learn from this Canon. They certainly far surpass in antiquity the Greek MSS. which we at present possess, and scarcely ever agree in supporting a manifestly corrupt reading. They are therefore of the very greatest weight where the Greek MSS. differ from each other. The Oxford margin cites a single Coptic *version*, with some Gothic fragments, and that only to the Gospels. This is a great defect. Nor, again, should *printed* books be denied the privilege of establishing a various reading,

not already been given by the first editors, or Grotius. Wherever he has introduced anything new, he may be supposed to have obtained it from the MSS. which he mentions in his preface. He placed, however, his conjectures not in the *Margin*, but in the *Appendix*, certainly in his first edition, and distinguished them from various readings. He is, therefore, very unjustly accused of having placed them on a footing of equality, or mixing them together.—(I. B.)

where it is ascertained that their editors made use of Manuscripts. The author of the Canons approves of the *Complutensian* edition; but he very frequently rejects its best readings.

15. From the *character of the Manuscripts* we must observe the character of the transcribers and their transcriptions, whether they are accustomed to err by omission, or by addition. See also Canons 30 and 31.

This *character* does little towards the actual Decision; since that never depends on the character of one MS.

16. But if other words, or changes of words, inflexions, etc., occur in the parallel passages of the other Evangelists, as distinguished from the Evangelist whose text is under consideration, it is probable, that the various reading has crept in from thence.

This Canon has nothing different from Canon 24.

17. *Citations by the Fathers* of the Text of the New Testament ought seldom to establish a Various Reading, because, quoting as they frequently do from memory, they often employ not the very words,[1] but such as are equivalent to them.

There is not a single citation from *the Fathers* in the Oxford Margin: this 17th Canon therefore, and the three that follow it in this Crisis, remain dormant. The Fathers too are seldom cited even in the Notes: another great defect. For though, where the Fathers differ from the MSS., their words are not to be pressed, yet where the MSS. differ from each other, those MSS. have the greatest weight, which agree with the Fathers: and the more ancient the Fathers are, the greater weight is due to their support. It is frequently difficult to ascertain, what was the reading of the text, which the Fathers employed: it is often clear beyond question. The distinction is explained in the Apparatus Criticus, pp. 389, 390 (Ed. ii. p. 23).

18. Thus the Fathers frequently omit, what does not bear upon their present purpose.

In such a case, no man of sense will reject what the Fathers omit.

19. The Fathers also, from slip of memory, ascribe sometimes to one writer, what really belongs to another.

---

[1] For some very interesting information on this and kindred subjects, see H. WESTCOTT *on the Canon of Scripture*, pp. 154-169.—(I. B.)

No genuine reading has ever yet sustained injury from any such slip of memory.

20. The Fathers also very frequently quote passages, which are not anywhere to be found.

Let your reliance in each case depend upon the quoter.[1]

21. Those which are considered as real Various Readings by the Critics, and which alter the sense,—are not to be examined or decided by these Canons: but their origin, their cause, and their character are to be examined and discovered: to which investigation the reader is directed by the twenty-third Canon.

This is a methodical scholium, not a Canon.

22. A Reading which is *absurd*, and which is convicted of absurdity by the context, either immediately preceding or following, must be rejected.

A Reading, which is manifestly *absurd*, has seldom the support of more than one MS.: so that this Canon is superfluous. Sometimes the absurdity is not in the MS. itself, but in the misquotation from it (*e.g.* Matt. xviii. 20, collated by Mill), or in the mistranslation of a various reading, as in Matt. xxi. 32, where according to the Cambridge MS.,[2] in opposition to the interpretation of others, *the Pharisees repented of believing.*— Often also that Reading is really absurd, which does not appear so; that Reading not really absurd, which does appear so. Amongst the twelve Canons, with which Pfaff[3] concludes his dissertation on the Various Readings of the New Testament, the eighth is remarkable, " A Reading, which appears at first sight

---

[1] "Fides semper esto penes citantem"—a similar phrase to that of Pliny, "Penes auctores sit fides"—which Cooperi Thesaurus renders, "I reporte mee to the authoures whether it be true or no. As for the truth thereof I refer you to the authoures."—(I. B.)

[2] The CODEX BEZÆ, or CODEX CANTABRIGIENSIS, is a Greek and Latin MS., containing the greater part of the four Gospels and the Acts of the Apostles. It is deposited in the Public Library of the University of Cambridge, to which it was presented by the celebrated Theodore Beza, in 1581. It is conjectured to have been written in the sixth or seventh century. A fac simile was published in folio by Kipling, at Cambridge, in 1793.—(I. B.)

[3] Christopher Matthew Pfaff, D.D., a learned Lutheran divine, was born at Stuttgard in 1686, Professor of Divinity at Tubingen in 1717, and died in 1760 —(I. B.)

absurd, is not to be immediately rejected, nor one, which carries with it an obscurity of style: for such Readings are not wont to be manufactured."

23. See the Notes.

See the Apparatus Criticus; for there we have considered these Notes, as far as was necessary.

24. Whenever the origin of the Various Reading is known, the Various Reading itself generally falls to the ground: as for instance, when an expression or a sentence has been introduced from one Gospel into the parallel passage of another, which was not an uncommon practice, with the view of making the accounts of the different Evangelists consistent with each other.

A remarkable Canon. It should have been adduced in favour of the marginal reading in Luke iii. 19, etc., and also in other parts of the New Testament as well as the Gospels, as *e.g.* in Eph. v. 9.

25. A gloss.[1]

This is contained in Canon 35, to which the Reader is therefore referred.

26. Transcribers have, frequently, for the sake of brevity omitted words, which they considered as *superfluous*, or *unnecessary*, especially where the omission did not change or disturb the sense. Such omissions must not be admitted as Various Readings, but imputed to the audacity of the transcribers.

Omission is generally the result of chance, seldom of design, as Hauber[2] rightly judges, whose criticism in other respects agrees with the spirit of this Canon, as we have observed on Acts xv. 34. By what means, however, omissions are to be distinguished from additions, the author of the *Crisis* does not indicate: so that the matter is left still in uncertainty.

27. On the other hand, when the *meaning* of a passage appeared to the transcribers *elliptical, obscure,* or imperfect, they frequently supplied the noun, verb, or pronoun, etc., from the context. This also is audacity.

---

[1] "Glossema." The meaning is, that where Canon 25 is cited in the Crisis, the author considers the reading in question a *gloss.*—(I. B.)

[2] Eberhard David Hauber, a learned Lutheran divine of the last century, was author of " Harmonie der Evangelisten."—(I. B.)

VOL. I.　　　　　　　　　　　　　　　　C

This is also contained in Canon 35, to which the reader is therefore referred.

28. It frequently occurred, that when transcribers had changed a previous expression, verb, number, case, or tense, being unwilling to erase what they had written, and thus blot the copy, they have adhered to their mistake throughout the whole passage. Innumerable examples of such continuous alteration occur.

The principle of this Canon is identical with that of the fourth, to which the reader is therefore referred.

29. The Reading of the Received Text is to be the more effective.

The genuine reading is always the *most effective:* but efficiency, the companion of native simplicity, must be distinguished from that false colouring so pleasing to the Greeks. Thus, in Matt. xxiii. 8; 2 Cor. viii. 8; Rev. xi. 17, this Canon, though brought by Maestricht in defence of the Text, fights bravely in support of the marginal reading.

30. Every Manuscript usually omits something.

An useless Canon. It is clearly contained in Canon 9.

31. Every Manuscript usually adds something.

A Canon of the same value.

32. Differences of punctuation (or commas and full stops placed differently), as well as the conjunction or division of words, which occur in MSS., do not amount to a diversity of reading, because in ancient MSS. the text is frequently unpunctuated, and the words run into each other. Hence have frequently arisen the *fusion* of two words into one, or the *division* of one word into two. But this belongs rather to the interpreters and explainers of the text, than to criticism.

This is not a Canon at all.

33. An omission or variation has frequently occurred, when the *construction* of a verb or preposition might be *equally* applied *to the words farther off*, or *to the nearer words*. Transcribers have frequently erred from this cause.

As far as *Variation* is concerned, this Observation does not determine, which is the genuine Reading. We have already spoken of *omission*, when considering the twenty-sixth Canon

34. Refer also the number or numbers of the Canons, which

are affixed to this (sc. the thirty-fourth) Canon, to the immediately preceding Reading, and from that Canon, or those Canons, deduce the value of that Reading.[1] The author rightly calls this a *Monitum*. It is not a Canon.

35. Transcribers have frequently wished to express something more clearly than it stands in the Received Text. Such readings must not be too hastily adopted. This error has very often occurred. These should generally be considered as glosses.

This Canon is by far the most excellent; but our author has neglected to employ it, where it was most wanted, *e.g.* Mark vii. 2, and Acts x. 21; xxiii. 9: nay, he has too often adduced the opposite Canon 26, instead of it, as in Matt. iv. 12, and Mark xii. 32. Greek copyists have often interpolated 'Ο Ἰησοῦς and other words, especially at the beginning of an ecclesiastical lection. There is much weight in what Reineccius[2] says, in the preface to his tetraglott[3] New Testament,—" The great importance of the matter in hand demands the utmost attention and circumspection, lest any of the words of God should be rejected amongst the scholia of men, or any of these words of men be circulated, as the words of God." And dangerous as it is to take away, it is still more dangerous to add anything, as I have shown in my Apparatus, Part I., section 21 (Ed. ii. p. 17): wherefore I consider it essential to inculcate also this,—" A bland facility of style, adopted by many transcribers, but those only of modern

---

[1] *i.e.*, when this Canon is cited, such is the course to be pursued. See note on Canon 25.—(I. B.)

[2] Christian Reineccius was born in Saxony, A.D. 1668. He studied at the Universities of Rostock and Leipsic. He afterwards became Rector of the Gymnasium and Councillor of the Consistory at Weissenfels. He died A.D. 1752. He was a man of great learning and wrote many works.—(I. B.)

[3] The full title of the work is—Biblia Saera Quadrilinguia Veteris Testamenti Hebraici, cum versionibus e regione positis, utpote versione Græca LXX Interpretum ex codice manuscripto Alexandrino, a J. Ern. Grabio primum evulgata—Item versione Latina Sebast. Schmidii noviter revisa et textui Hebraeo accuratius accomodata, et Germanica beati Lutheri, ex ultima beati viri revisione et editione 1544–45, expressa. Adjectis textui Hebraeo Notis Masorethicis et Graecae Versioni Lectionibus Codicis Vaticani; notis philologicis et exegeticis aliis, ut et summariis capitum ac locis parallelis locupletissimis ornata. Accurante M. Christ. Reineccio. Lipsiæ, 1750. 3 vols. folio. Hartwell Horne speaks of it in high terms.—(I. B.)

date, is frequently the sign of a reading, that has been tampered with: brevity of style, together with antiquity of witnesses, is indicative of a genuine text." The men of this generation are so averse, and, in their own opinion, religiously opposed to condemning glosses, that there is considerable danger, lest many should reject the genuine text of the New Testament in very important passages, from a desire to amend it, and hear and follow any of Maestricht's Canons, rather than this *golden* one. But, though it be of little use, to warn writers, many of whom give themselves little space for thinking,[1] each sensible reader should exercise more caution and prudence in his own quiet nook.

36. *Changes* of tenses, cases, moods, numbers, and degrees of comparison, occur so frequently in executing a copy, that this cause has given rise to the great majority of Various Readings. This may be referred also to Canon 6, except that the present is stricter.

This observation also does not enable the reader to decide between two readings of the same passage.

37. Something is frequently omitted in a Manuscript, because the transcriber thought that it had been already sufficiently expressed, either actually in the passage itself, or in the context.

Transcribers have often erred from this cause, especially the more learned ones.

See my remarks on Canon 26, as this differs nothing from that.

38. When any Various Readings are discovered or observed, let not any of them be introduced into the Text, but let the Reading of our printed copies remain intact, especially that of the Comptutensian or Stephanian editions. The Various Reading should be indicated in the Notes of the Commentator.

This is not a Canon enabling the reader to decide on a controverted text: the author calls it a ' *Monitum*.'

39. When the text of the printed editions exhibits no Various Reading, but yet there appears a difficulty in the meaning, on account either of the language, or the subject,— the question is

---

[1] But on that very account, so much the greater license in judging.—E. B.

one rather for the commentator to expound and reconcile, than for the critic to decide.

My last observation applies to this also. There are, however, many important Readings, no trace of which is to be found in Maestricht's Edition. See my Apparatus, p. 142 (Ed. ii. p. 78), where I have drawn attention to Mark x. 14, and other passages.

40. This Canon indicates,[1] that Various Readings may be found in the greatest part of those MSS. which have hitherto been discovered and collated.

In no instance, that I am aware of, has this Canon been cited by the author; though it might have been cited very frequently, very usefully, and very rightly, in favour of the marginal Reading. And, instead of it, he cites *passim* Canons 41, 42, 43, nay, 12, 11, and 10, nay even 9. In not a single instance, does the author of the Crisis ascribe the true number of manuscripts to a genuine Reading, whether of the Elzevir Text (which happens to be that, which he employs) or of the Margin. But, in every case, where it is in the Text, he claims for it too many MSS., where in the Margin too few.

41. This Canon indicates, that an equal number of MSS. may support the Published and the Various Reading.

This Canon might frequently have been employed with advantage; but it is seldom adduced. It is cited, indeed, *ex. gr.* on Matt. xxvi. 74; but there the MSS. with the greatest unanimity, support the marginal Reading.

42. This Canon indicates, that the third part of the MSS. known to us, say thirty or more than thirty, may support the Various Reading.

Frequently in this work is that accounted only a third part of the MSS. which is in reality a far greater number, as in Matt. xvii. 14; Mark vi. 33; Luke viii. 43; Acts xxiv. 20; Gal. v. 7; Phil. i. 23.

43. This Canon lastly indicates, that a fourth or lesser part of the MSS. known to us, say twenty or less than thirty, may support a Various Reading.

In fine, that is frequently in this work accounted as only

[1] For this and the two following Canons, see notes on Canons 25 and 34. —(I. B.)

the fourth part, or even less, which is so far from being less, that it is really much greater, e.g., Acts xx. 28, and xxi. 15.

Such being the case, it is evident, what little value can be attached to that examination of Various Readings on Matt. xxv., which the author of the Crisis has given as a specimen, in his Prolegomena, Nos. 94-98. Nothing ought to be more severely examined than *Rules;* for all other things depend upon them. This Crisis, then, which we have been examining, (1) rests upon an utterly false number of MSS.; (2) passes by the most important witnesses to the genuine Text; (3) applies its Canons to passages, where they are not applicable, and neglects to apply them, where they were of the most value, etc. I do not wish to injure the reputation of a distinguished man: his Crisis is, however, "an unsatisfactory defence of the more received text, where sound, and a vast hindrance to its purification, where corrupt." Oh that they, who follow this Crisis, like an unreasoning herd, would at length awake, so as to use their own senses. They, who treat the whole subject of criticism with contempt (provided they do not do so, from contempt of the Divine Word itself), are far more endurable, than those, who esteem the critic's vocation highly, yet both exercise it ill themselves, and keep others in ignorance, or lead them into error. Here also "overweening confidence is the principal means, by which a bad cause is defended, and eked out."

Daniel Whitby[1] also has laid down certain *Rules* in his examination of the Various Readings of Mill (Preface, fol. 8), quoted by *J. G. Carpzov*[2] in his preface to the critical commen-

---

[1] Daniel Whitby, D.D., was born A.D. 1638, at Rushden or Rusden, in Northamptonshire; admitted at Trinity College, Oxford, 1653, elected Scholar 1655, and Fellow 1664. He became Prebendary of Salisbury in 1688, and Precentor in 1672.

He obtained also the Rectory of St Edmund's Church, Salisbury. He died 1726. He was a man of great learning and untiring industry. In his last days he became an Arian. He wrote numerous works, amongst which was "A Paraphrase and Commentary on the New Testament," in the first volume of which is to be found his "*Examen variantium lectionum Johannis Millii in Novum Testamentum.*"—(I. B.)

[2] John Gottlob Carpzov (known also as J. G. Carpzovius), was born at Dresden 1679, and died 1767.—(I. B.)

tary of Rumpaeus.¹ As far as these rules treat of the value of ancient authorities, they are excellent: but the author does not always decide rightly in the case of particular passages of the N. T. He frequently blames Mill with justice, but, as often happens, falls himself into the opposite extreme. From not observing this distinction, many, who admire Whitby, make a bad use of him. To use him rightly, you should always hear the other side, *i.e.* Mill. We have made some remarks also on Whitby, in our Apparatus, pp. 443, 787, 788 (Ed. ii., pp. 79, 498, 499), and in our Second Defence. Very lately, *Charles Gottlob Hofman*² has published eight Canons, of considerable merit, on Pritz's³ Introduction to the Study of the New Testament, cap. 29. The substance of these Canons, as well as that of others by different authors, is contained in the MONITA, which we have given in Section VIII.

X.

All good men will, I trust, acknowledge the principles of my revision to be unassailable. And though, in some of the most difficult passages, opposite conclusions may be drawn from those principles—yet in the case of by far the greater number of various readings, a clear and unhesitating decision may be arrived at by their means. For although I have reserved to myself the liberty of changing my opinion, it has seldom required to be changed. Some such instances will be easily found in this Gnomon by those who think it their interest to find them.

Most of the Readings, however, which we approved formerly, we still maintain. The Text of my Revision (which must again and again be asserted, in opposition to unfounded suspicions), adheres, *without the change of a single letter*, in the Apocalypse

---

[1] Justus Wesselus Rumpaeus, a Lutheran divine of the last century, must not be confounded with Rumphius, the Dutch botanist.—(I. B.)

[2] Charles Gottlob Hoffmann, a Lutheran divine, and learned Philologist, born 1703. died 1774.—(I. B.)

[3] John George Pritz (called also Pritius), a learned Lutheran divine, was born at Leipsic in 1662, died at Frankfort in 1732.—(I. B.)

to the most and best MSS., in the other Books of the N. T. to the best printed editions. But the *Exegesis* (which is the subject at present principally under consideration), is based, and that rightly, upon the *genuine* Reading, as far as it can be ascertained up to the present time, whether I have placed that Reading in the Text or the Margin: which was what I undertook to show in Sections VIII and IX. On the other hand, a true Exegesis will show, that the selection of an edition of the Greek New Testament, with a text correctly revised, is not a question of mere curiosity.

XI.

There is great advantage in distinguishing, without dividing, the text into greater and smaller sections, which was first made clear by Anthony Blackwall,[1] and his laborious editor, Christopher Wollius.[2]—See Sacred Classics, Vol. II. Part ii., chap. i. With that view I have, in my edition, distinctly marked the beginnings of the greater Sections, whilst leaving the Sections themselves continuous, and unbroken. I have revised with great care the full stops, colons, commas, accents, and breathings (concerning which I have made some very essential remarks in my annotations on Rev. i. 5), according to the meaning of the words themselves. Many editors promise these things, few perform them. Hence, as I fancy, it arises, that no reliance is now placed even on the word of one, who affirms it with truth. He who has fairly observed, in the daily use of my edition, the greater and lesser divisions (examples of which are to be found in the sixth section of the Preface to my small edition of the

---

[1] Anthony Blackwall, an elaborate and learned writer, was born in Derbyshire, 1674, and educated at E. College, Cambridge, where he took his degree of M.A. in 1698. Soon afterwards, he became master of the Free School, Derby, and in 1772 of the Grammar School, Market Bosworth. He became Rector of Clapham, Surrey, in 1726, and died 1730. The work here alluded to, is, "The Sacred Classics Defended and Illustrated; or an Essay proving the Purity, Propriety, and True Eloquence of the Writers of the New Testament." 2 vols. 8vo, 1727-1731.—(I. B.)

[2] Christopher Wollius, a Lutheran divine, and philologist, born at Leipsic 1700, died 1761.—(I. B.)

Greek New Testament) will perceive that this statement
has not been made without reason, and will, I trust, derive
thence very great advantage. I should be unwilling, however,
that any one should estimate my edition of the Greek New
Testament from that which has been printed in imitation of it
beyond the limits of Wirtemburg :[1] for the verses are very
differently disjoined and conjoined in that edition from what
they are in mine. We scarcely ever give a different punctuation
in the present work from that which we have given before :
sometimes, however, we have done so, and drawn attention to
the fact, as in the remarkable passage, Rom. viii. 31.

XII.

The first requisite for making a Commentary is a knowledge,
and appreciation of *the style*, employed by the writers of the New
Testament. On this subject there has long existed a great diversity
of opinion, and *John Lamius*[2] has collected and digested much
information regarding it, in his book on the Learning of the
Apostles. We shall say what is necessary. The wisdom of
GOD employs a style undoubtedly worthy of GOD[3] even when

---

[1] The edition here alluded to is that brought out in 1737, at Leipsic, by
Andreas Buttigius. See p. 10, f.n. 3.—(I. B.)

[2] Giovanne Lami, Professor of Ecclesiastical History in the University of
Florence, and keeper of the Recordi Library, born in 1697, died 1770, was
a scholar of great research, and author of many learned works.—(I. B.)

[3] " Some appear to disparage the style of Scripture, as barbarous. Some
apologize for it, as the work of illiterate and unlearned men. Surely these
notions are false and dangerous. The diction of Scripture, it is true, is not
the language of any other composition in the world. The Greek of the New
Testament is not the Greek of Xenophon, Plato, or Demosthenes. It is a
language of its own. And we need not scruple to affirm, that in precision of
expression, in pure and native simplicity, in delicacy of handling, in the
grouping of words and phrases, in dignified and majestic sublimity, it has no
rival in the world. The more carefully it is studied, the more clearly will
this appear. 'Nihil otiosum in sacra Scriptura' (Origen). Every sentence
—we might almost say, every phrase—is fraught with meaning. As it is in
the Book of Nature, so is it in the pages of Holy Writ. Both are from the
same Divine Hand. And if we apply to the language of Holy Scripture, the
same microscopic process, which we use in scrutinizing the beauties of the

by means of His instruments He accommodates Himself to the grossness of our perceptions. It is not, however, our part arrogantly to define, but humbly to believe what is worthy of God, 1 Cor. ii. 1, and xiv. 21. The holy men of God, both in the Old and New Testaments, exhibit, not only an exact knowledge of the Truth, but also *a systematic arrangement of their subject, a precise expression of their meaning, and a genuine strength of feeling.* Beyond these three requisites nothing need be desired. The result of these three qualifications was, that the writers of the New Testament, however unlearned, wrote always in a style becoming their subject, and, raised far above the technical rules of Greek Rhetoricians, produced an eloquence truly natural, and devoid of all study after mere effect. We shall describe these characteristics one by one, indicating at the same time what has been observed concerning them in the present work.

XIII.

The *arrangement* of subjects, contained in each book, is exhibited in the several *Tables*, which I have prefixed to each of them; not merely with the view of assisting the reader's memory, but that I might also show the plan of the sacred writer, as accurately as possible. Any one, who has impressed those tables upon his mind, will perceive their utility. No one would have wished for an argument of each chapter, at its commencement. The division of the New Testament into chapters, now in use, was made in the dark ages, after the selection of portions for ecclesiastical readings, which frequently therefore run on from one chapter into another. That division frequently separates things which are closely connected, and joins together things which are really distinct. The arguments of the chapters, therefore, are more rightly to be sought for in the tables,

natural world, and which reveals to us exquisite colours, and the most graceful texture in the petals of a flower, the fibres of a plant, the plumage of a bird, or the wings of an insect, we shall discover new sources of delight and admiration in the least portions of Holy Writ."—CHRISTOPHER WORDSWORTH.—(I. B.)

already mentioned, which do not preserve that division. Where the divisions given in the tables are rather large, subdivisions (but not too many in number), are supplied in the notes. The tables at once utterly confute the ignorance, in some cases impious, of those who maintain that the Apostles gave immediate utterance to whatever chanced to occur to them, without any plan or design. In the Works of GOD, even to the smallest plant, there is the most entire symmetry: in the Words of GOD there is the most systematic perfection, even to a letter.

XIV.

It is the especial office of every interpretation, to exhibit adequately the force and signification of the words which the text contains, so as to express every thing which the author intended, and to introduce nothing which he did not intend to express. The two chief excellences of a good style are depth, and ease (*facilitas*). They are seldom combined in the case of human authors: and, as each man writes himself, so do others seem to him to write also. He, who himself weighs every word, is in danger (when studying the work of another) of fancying here and there, that he discovers a meaning which the author did not design; he, who writes with less precision himself, interprets the words of others too vaguely. In the Divine Scriptures, however, the greatest depth is combined with the greatest ease (*facilitas*); we should take care, therefore, in interpreting them, not to force their meaning to our own standard; nor, because the sacred writers are devoid of anxious solicitude, to treat their words as if employed without due consideration. The Divine language far, very far, surpasses all human elegances of courtly style.

God, not as man, but as God, utters words worthy of Himself. Deep and lofty are His thoughts: His words, which flow from them, are of inexhaustible efficacy. In the case also of His inspired interpreters, although they may not have received human instruction, their language is most exact. The expression of their words corresponds exactly with the impression of the things in their minds; and it is so far from being beneath the comprehension of those who hear it, that, rather, they seldom attain to its entire meaning. The Apostles frequently deduce conclusions, more weighty than the world itself, from an epithet, from a grammatical accident, or even an adverb, as we have shown in our Apparatus, Part. I., Section I. Chrysostom interprets the particle καί with emphatic precision in the writings of St Paul, and he, as well as the other fathers, render many other things in a similar manner, as we have remarked upon his book on the Priesthood, §§ 136, 441. It is right to follow these traces. In this spirit Luther says, *The science of theology is nothing else, but Grammar, exercised on the words of the Holy Spirit;*[1]—a sentiment which has often been repeated since then by other theologians. This observation involves the examination of *emphatic expression*, in which the original signification of the words sometimes increases, sometimes decreases in intensity. Many modes of expression were *emphatic* in Greek, which are not so in German, as, for example, the employment or omission of the personal pronouns, seldom omitted by us, frequently so by the Greeks; middle verbs, too, which are unknown in German or Latin, but which are distinctively expressed in Greek: and verbs simple or compound, such as γινώσκω[2] and ἐπιγινώσκω,[2] which are expressed by one word in Latin or German, but which are different words in Greek; and the article, which has no existence in Latin.

On the other hand, it frequently happens, that the *apparent* exceeds the *real* emphasis, as οὐ μή[3] with the subjunctive; as in the verb ἐκβάλλω,[4] as in the preposition ἐντός,[5] as in the com-

---

[1] "*Nil aliud esse Theologiam, atque Grammaticam, in Spiritus Sancti verbis occupatam.*"—(I. B.)

[2] γινώσκω = *to know, to be aware of*, etc. For a full explanation of all the meanings and shades of meaning of the simple and compound verbs, see Schleusneri Lexicon in voc., where the first occupies five, and the latter two columns.—(I. B.)

[3] οὐ μή a double negative frequent in classical as well as Scriptural Greek. With Fut. Indic. it *forbids*: with the Subjunctive, it *denies;* but, in Ecclesiastical Greek, often less emphatically. See Buttman, Matthiæi, Kühner, etc., on the subject.—ED.

[4] ἐκβάλλω = lit. *to cast forth,* often no more than "*to put forth.*" —ED.

[5] ἐντός = *within*, often used in a weaker sense, than the literal.—ED.

pounds ἐκπειράζω,[1] ἐκπορνεύω, ὑπεναντίος, ὑποδείκνυμι, κ.τ.λ.., the meaning of which does not in the Septuagint differ from that of the simple verbs, from which they are derived. Any degree whatever of acquaintance with the Greek New Testament is useful and laudable : but they, who are less expert therein, frequently see false instances of emphasis, seize on them with eagerness, and publish them abroad, whilst they pass by those which are genuine. This renders it the more necessary that we should all help each other in turn. Even dull eyes can make use of light for the chief purposes of life : but he, who has a peculiarly strong sight, perceives many things more accurately than others do. Thus is it also in Scripture : all see [or may see] as much as is necessary to salvation, but the clearer that the believer's sight is, the greater is his profit and delight : and that which one believer once sees, others who of themselves saw it not, are, by his direction, enabled to perceive. I have exposed the fallacy of many instances of supposed emphasis, brought forward by other writers; many others I have passed over in silence : genuine instances, which offer themselves spontaneously, I have not neglected. If, however, I should be thought to dwell at times too minutely, and too long, upon these matters, I shall be readily acquitted by those who have observed the *perpetual analogy* of accurate and universally self-consistent expression, which pervades alike every portion of Scripture.

In order to weigh precisely the force of the words, it is essential to observe the Hebraism with which the language of the Greek New Testament is tinged. It is beyond question, that the Apostles and Evangelists were accustomed to speak and write in such a style as was especially suited to the Hellenizing[2] Jews resident in Asia and elsewhere, who had introduced the spirit of the Hebrew language into their ordinary Greek

---

[1] For the convenience of those readers who are unacquainted with Greek, it may be as well to explain that ἐκπειράζω and the words which follow are derived, respectively, from πειράζω, *to tempt ;* πορνεύω, *to debauch* or *prostitute ;* ἐναντίος, *over against ;* δείκνυμι, *to show.*—(I. B.)

[2] *i.e.* those who from having resided for some generations in countries where Greek was the common medium of intercourse, spoke that language (with some idiomatic peculiarities) as their mother tongue : they are spoken of in Acts vi. 1, as " *Hellenists,*" which E. V. renders " *Grecians.*"—(I. B.)

discourse, and to whom the Greek translation of the Old Testament (which Hebraizes to a very great degree) was evidently familiar,—that translation, which acted in subservience to the Divine design of making the Greek language the vehicle of the Divine Word. The Apostles and Evangelists, therefore, were right in introducing into the style of the New Testament whatever peculiarities of idiom existed in the translation of the Old Testament, or in the spoken Greek of the Hellenizing Jews: and the more familiar that the reader of the Greek New Testament is with the Septuagint, and the Hebrew Syntax, the greater proficiency will he attain to in his sacred studies. The Paraclete conferred the most copious facility of speaking languages on the holy men who wrote the Scriptures of the New Testament: but it was necessary that they should descend to the level of their immediate auditors and earliest readers. If any of the Apostles were sent to-day to Barbarians or Greeks, he would (wisely, as I think) employ the most rugged tongues of the Barbarians, or the present vernacular Greek, however corrupt it be. The style of the New Testament has, in different passages, phrases which agree with the most approved Greek writers, even where you would least expect it. But the whole and perpetual spirit of the language employed by the writers of the New Testament is distinctively Hebraizing, and differs in this respect decidedly from the style of other Greek authors, though here and there resemblances are to be found; nor is this to be wondered at, since the volume of the New Testament is so small when compared with the vast mass of profane Greek writings; besides that even these authors have sometimes let fall expressions which might not altogether please them, and which are eagerly caught at by philologists of much reading, and compared with the style of the Greek New Testament. See also my notes on John vi. 37, and xii. 6; and Rev. xi. 5.

Such being the case, I have not had far to go to explain the language of the Greek New Testament, for I have generally found an explanation close at hand. Thus, for example, in any passage of the Epistle to the Romans, I have compared it first with the immediate context, then with the remainder of the Epistle, then with the other Epistles of St Paul, then with the Greek Fathers, who, being themselves Greeks, studied both the

Greek New Testament and the ancients; lastly, and that very rarely, with profane authors. Where passages of the Old Testament are cited in the New, I have given in full the words of the LXX., especially those from which the New Testament differs, that the comparison might be the more easy. Where any difficulty has been experienced as to the interpretation of words in the New Testament, which occur also in the Septuagint, I have compared them with the corresponding expressions in the original Hebrew:[1] by which method I have ascertained the true meaning of τροποφορεῖν,[2] ἑτοιμασία,[3] κεφαλὶς βιβλίου,[4] κ.τ.λ.

I have endeavoured, indeed, to introduce into these annotations, as many explanations and illustrations as can be derived from the LXX. No one will expect to find in the Gnomon what can be obtained from a Grammar or Lexicon of the Greek Tongue. Sometimes, however, when anything of moment is involved, or when others labour under a hallucination, we descend to such matters.

XV.

Earth produces nothing which can be compared with holy feelings.[5] They comprehend, however, what the Greeks call τὰ ἤθη,[6] which we are obliged to express in Latin by the less suit-

---

[1] *i.e.* where there is any doubt or difficulty about the meaning of a word used by any of the writers of the New Testament (whether in a quotation from the Old Testament, or in any other case), which word is used also by the LXX., Bengel has examined the passages of that version in which it occurs, and compared it in each instance with the Hebrew word for which it stands.—(I. B.)

[2] See Gnomon on Acts xiii. 18, 19.—(I. B.)

[3] See Gnomon on Ephes. vi. 15.—(I. B.)

[4] See Gnomon on Heb. x. 7.—(I. B.)

[5] The words of the original are—"Cum *affectibus* sanctis, quod comparari possit, terra nihil alit."—(I. B.)

[6] Every student of Aristotle has probably shared the difficulty which Bengel frankly acknowledges. Twining, in the notes to his translation of the Poetics, says, "The word, ἦθη, taken in its utmost extent, includes *everything* that is *habitual* and *characteristic;* but it is often used in a limited sense, for the *habitual temper* or *disposition.*" It might be para-

able word "*Mores*."¹ The *Feelings*, absolutely so called, are vehement: the "*Mores*" are calmer feelings quiet and composed. I would recommend the reader to peruse on this subject, Quintilian VI. 2: for the whole disquisition cannot be introduced into this Preface.² The styles of the writers of the New Testament have, in common with all other styles, their own peculiar Subjects, Feelings, and "*Mores*." Every one treats of the Subjects; those who are wiser and endued with spiritual experience pay due regard to the Feelings; the "*Mores*" (let me say it without offence), have been almost entirely lost sight of, except that the *Modesty*³ of Scripture has been sometimes mentioned. And yet these "*Mores*" pervade in a wonderful manner all the discourses and epistles of the New Testament, forming a certain continual recommendation⁴ of him who acts, speaks, or writes, and realizing in a pre-eminent degree the "*Decorum*."⁵ We phrased here by "Moral sentiments," "Subjective moral principles," or expressed *chemically* as "Moral principles held in solution," or rendered, perhaps, "Moral tone;" but none of these phrases are the exact counterparts of the original.—(I. B.)

¹ The word *Mores*, when used as it is by Bengel in the present passage, is as impossible to render as the expression which it is intended to represent: the expression "*Les moeurs*," with the force which it frequently has in French *philosophical* writings, comes probably as near to it as any modern phrase. Montesquieu (Esprit de loix xix. 16), says, "Il y a cette différence entre les Loix et les Moeurs, que les Loix reglent plus les actions du Citoyen, et que les Moeurs reglent plus les actions de l'homme. Il y a cette différence entre les Moeurs et les Manieres que les premieres regardent plus la conduite interieure; les autres l'exterieure." I give this, however, rather as an illustration than an explanation.—(I. B.)

² I cannot, however, forbear quoting the following passage:—"Quare in iis quæ verisimilia esse volemus simus ipsi similes eorum, qui verè patiuntur, affectibus; et a tali animo proficiscatur oratio, qualem facile judicem volet. An ille dolebit, qui audiet me, cum hoc dicam, non dolentem? Irascetur, si nihil ipse qui in iram concitat, idque exigit, simile patietur? Siccis agenti oculis lacrymas dabit? Fieri non potest. Nec incendit nisi ignis, nec madescimus nisi humore, nec res ulla dat alteri colorem quem ipsa non habet. Primum est igitur, ut apud nos valeant ea quæ valere apud judicem volumus, afficiamusque antequam afficere conemur. Quint. VI. 2, § 3.—(I. B.)

³ See the Gnomon on Acts ii. 30, and Rom. i. 26.—(I. B.)

⁴ See Aristotle on the πίστις ἠθική, Rhet. I. 2, §§ 3, 6, II. 1, § 6, etc.—(I.B.)

⁵ DECORUM, the neuter of the adjective *Decorus, a, um*; derived from the

have dropped something on this subject in our App. Crit. p.
372 (*i.e.* Sect. 1 of the Introduction to the Criticism of the New
Testament, Ed. II., pp. 4, 5), and more in our Harmony of the
Four Evangelists, pp. 57, 103, 111, 214, 216, 242, 278, 281,
282. (Ed. II., A.D. 1747, pp. 56, 69, 171, 183, 340, 342, 380,
382, 451, 454, 455): but in the present work I have bestowed
fuller consideration on the "*Mores*" as well as the Feelings.
These "*Mores*" are for the most part of such a kind, that you
can more easily reach them by a perception of the heart than by
a circuit of words. And this will be a principal reason why our
Commentary may be considered frequently too subtile, frequently
too frigid. I doubt not, however, that those who have by degrees become accustomed to it will agree with me in my admiration of the language of the sacred writers. The painter by the
most delicate stroke of his brush, the musician by the swiftest
touch of fleeting notes, exercises the highest skill of his art: and
in the perfection of anything whatever, those minute particulars
which escape the ears and eyes of the ignorant and unrefined,
bestow the most exquisite delight on those who are capable of
appreciating them,—a delight springing from the very root and
essence of the thing itself. Such is the case with Holy Scripture. Let each one, then, take in what he is capable of re-

---

impersonal verb DECET, *it becomes*, or *is becoming*: used in the sense of
Aristotle's ΤΟ ΠΡΕΠΟΝ, which signifies that which is *becoming*, *proper*,
or *suitable*, to the *person, character, office, condition,* or *circumstance,* under
consideration.—(I. B.)

"Id, quod Græcè πρέπον dicitur, decorum dici Latinè potest; hujus vis ea
est, ut ab honesto non queat separari."—Cic. Off. 1. 27.—(ED.)

"Caput artis est," says Quinctilian, "decere." "The first principle of
art is to observe decorum." No one should ever rise to speak in public,
without forming to himself a just and strict idea of what suits his own age
and character; what suits the hearers, the place, the occasion; and adjusting the whole train and manner of his speaking on this idea. All the
ancients insist much on this. Consult the first chapter of the eleventh book
of Quinctilian, which is employed wholly on this point, and is full of good
sense. Cicero's admonitions in his Orator ad Brutum, I shall give in his
own words, which should never be forgotten by any who speak in public:
"Est Eloquentiæ, sicut reliquarum rerum, fundamentum, sapientia; ut
enim in vita, sic in oratione nihil est difficilius quam quod deceat videre,"
etc.—*Blair*, Lecture XXVII.

See also Explanation of Technical terms in voc.—(I. B.)

ceiving, and abstain from meddling with what he is unable to comprehend.

XVI.

There are many classes of those who undertake to illustrate the Sacred Books by Commentaries: and it sometimes happens that they despise each other's plans and love only their own. For my part, I do not act exclusively as a Paraphrast, a Grammarian, a Scholiast, an Antiquary, a Logician, a Doctrinal Expositor, a Controversialist, or an Inferential Commentator; but I take *all* these characters by turns, without stint or distinction. Each of these indeed has its own use: when that use is carried too far it degenerates into abuse: and this abuse may again be remedied by a just estimation and judicious employment of all the means at our disposal. I do not pass by without notice decisions, the authority of which has been generally received (*Dicta Classica*); I do not ignore difficulties which are the subject of wide discussion; but I examine with equal care the rest of Scripture, which is equally worthy of consideration. In each individual case I employ that kind of annotation which the part or passage under consideration may require to exhibit its force, to explain its words and phrases, to draw attention to the habit of mind of those who speak or of those whom they address, to bring out the true or refute the false doctrine, to elicit those maxims of piety or Christian prudence which are involved or suggested by the sacred text, to examine quotations from the Old Testament, occurring in the New, and other parallel passages,—or to indicate the weight, and unravel the connection of the arguments employed by the sacred writer. And all these things are laid before the reader in such a manner, as to give him the opportunity and inducement to pursue the train of thought further himself. At each separate annotation the GNOMON must be supposed to say " *The Text runs thus*, not otherwise. *This*, and no other, is the noun; *this*, the verb; *this*, the particle; *this*, the case; *this*, the tense; *this* is the arrangement of the words; *this* is the repetition or interchange of words; *this,* the succession of arguments; *this,* the emotion of the minds, etc."

XVII.

He who comprehends the intention of this work, will not expect to find differences of opinion carefully enumerated and laboriously refuted, with the names of their advocates and the titles of their works. It is expedient indeed that some should undertake that office, and deduce the history of Scriptural interpretation from century to century; few, however, possess the opportunity or the capacity for performing such a task; though there are many who can search out and bring together many particulars for the general advantage. It is better, however, for the weak to be wholly ignorant of opinions which are in themselves foolish, and would scarcely enter into the mind of any one, than to have them recorded in connection with the passages to which they refer [even though in each instance they be carefully and successfully refuted]. We should fare badly, if, in order to ascertain the royal road of truth, it were necessary for us to obtain an accurate knowledge,[1] and make a personal survey of all the tracks which lead away from it.—In fact, the true interpretation is more frequently buried than assisted by a multitude of conflicting opinions. I have, however, guarded the reader against some erroneous interpretations of modern date, without either naming the authors or quoting their words. The reader who is unacquainted with them will not perceive the allusion, nor is it necessary that he should do so; whereas, he who is acquainted with them will understand what I mean. I touch also upon some rather probable interpretations as yet little discussed; and where my own opinion might appear paradoxical, I support it by the consent of others, especially the ancients.

[1] "In numerato habere," Quint. VI. 3, iii., "*To have in readiness.*"—ED. Said to be an expression of Augustus. The phrase originally refers to "*numeratum* argentum"—*i.e.* money *paid down*—actually *counted out.*—See Andrews, Ainsworth, Riddle, etc.—(I. B.)

XVIII.

Nothing is more frequent in commentaries than the title "*Harmonia Evangelica.*" Under this title, however, I have felt it necessary to produce something exceedingly different from the generality of compositions which have hitherto appeared with this name. The basis of my Harmony is the recognition of the fact that there were Three Passovers, and Three only, between our Lord's Baptism and His Ascension,—a fact frequently acknowledged by the ancients, and of late years by Timotheus Philadelphus;[1] though most writers of recent date lay down a greater number of Passovers. I have combined and arranged the Four Gospels in accordance with the determining standard of the Three Passovers in my Harmony of the Four Evangelists, published first, A.D. 1736, and again with emendations, A.D. 1747: and the consideration of the separate Gospels in the present work is intimately connected with that treatise. I will, therefore, quietly repeat the points, which are most necessary for my purpose.

1. The Nativity of our Lord cannot be placed later than two months before the death of Herod the Great.

2. The death of Herod the Great cannot be placed sooner or later than the month of February, in the third year before the Dionysian Era.[2] This is proved by the eclipse of the moon, mentioned by Josephus, and the events, which he relates, as

---

[1] Author of a work, published in 12mo, at Stuttgard, A.D. 1728, and entitled—

"Grundveste der wahren Kirchen."

Bengel, in the Preface to his Exposition of the Apocalypse, says—"All the systems we have of the Apocalypse may be divided into these six classes; of each of which I will subjoin one example—1. Some go in a *metaphysical* and *theosophical* way; for instance, *Timotheus Philadelphus.*"—(I. B.)

[2] The Dionysian Era, now in general use, so called from Dionysius Exiguus, a native of Scythia, who published his chronological system about the year 532. He is considered to have placed the birth of Christ four years too late; so that to obtain the exact number of years which have at any time elapsed since that event, we must add four years to the date of the current year.—(I. B.)

having happened between that phenomenon and the Passover of that year.

3. The fifteenth year of the reign of Tiberius cannot begin before the month Tisri,[1] of the twenty-seventh year of the Dionysian Era.

4. Our Lord, when He was about thirty years old, was baptized, and, after forty days, tempted of the Devil, some time before the Passover of the twenty-eighth year of the Dionysian Era.

5. In that same year, and no other, could the Temple have been said to have been forty-six years in building.—See John ii. 20.

6. Our Lord was crucified in the thirtieth year of the Dionysian Era; for this particular year, and not one of the years 29, 31, or 32, had the Passover at the end of the week: but the year 33 is too late, and is refuted by all the opinions of the Ancient Church.

7. Therefore the whole course of events recorded, from the Passover mentioned in John ii., to that mentioned in John xviii., is included in the 28th, 29th, and 30th years of the Dionysian Era.

This makes three, and only three Passovers.

These statements, if taken singly, may possibly appear to leave the matter in doubt: but, when taken together, they are clear and unquestionable; and necessarily prove, that there were only three Passovers.

My Harmony has found a most courteous opponent in Hauber,[2] of whose present opinions on the subject, I am entirely ignorant: but certainly, in his great work, which is entitled *Deutsche Original Bibel* (German Original Bible), he has adopted the main features of my Harmony, adding his own view of the details. And very lately Walchius,[3] in his observations

---

[1] The month Tisri comprehended part of September and October, though corresponding nearly with the latter. —(I. B.)

[2] See f.n. 1, p. 39.—(I. B.)

[3] John Ernest Immanuel Walchius was born at Jena in 1725, and attained to a high station in the University there. In 1749 he published at Jena his "*Einleitung in die harmonie der Evangelisten.*" He died in 1778.— (I. B.)

on the Life of our Lord Jesus Christ, frequently finds fault with me; but neither of them has brought into play the chronological mainsprings of the Gospels.

The Gospel chronology has been studiously treated of, in our day, by Campegius Vitringa,[1] Peter Allix,[2] Count Camillus de Sylvestris,[3] Nicasius,[4] J. J. Hottinger,[5] C. G. Hoffman,[6] Leonard Offerhaus,[7] etc. These all differ widely from each other, but if you compare them together, and abridge them into one, you will find, that, whatever truth is contained in any of them, confirms, at times against their will, the ternarian hypothesis (that, namely, which supposes three Passovers, and three only): nor can they, who pretend four, not to say more Passovers, avoid doing violence to those chronological data so emphatically laid down by the Evangelists themselves. The quaternarian hypothesis, (that, namely, which supposes four Passovers), doubles, or even trebles, with manifest inconvenience, the long series of passages from the fourth to the thirteenth chapters of St Matthew (repeated in the parallel passages of St

---

[1] Campegius Vitringa, a learned Protestant divine, born in Friesland 1659, died 1722, became successively Professor of Oriental Languages, Divinity and Sacred History, at Franckaer.—(I. B.)

[2] Peter Allix, a learned French divine, born at Alençon 1641, was successively minister of the Protestant Church at Rouen, and at Charenton. At the revocation of the edict of Nantes, he retired to England, where he became Canon of Windsor, and Treasurer of Salisbury Cathedral. He died in 1717.—(I. B.)

[3] Count Camillus de Sylvestris, a learned writer, was born at Padua in 1645, studied at Rovigo, and became honorary member of most of the Universities of Italy. He died in 1719.—(I. B.)

[4] The writer apparently intended is Claud Nicaise, born at Dijon in 1623, and died at Velay in 1701. He took orders in the Roman Church, and became a learned Philologist and Archæologist.—(I. B.)

[5] John James Hottinger, eldest son of the celebrated John Henry Hottinger, was born at Zurich in the sixteenth century, published various works in 1706, 1708, 1720, etc., and died in 1735.—(I. B.)

[6] See f.n. 4, page 39.—(I. B.)

[7] Leonard Offerhaus, a celebrated scholar, was born at Ham, in Westphalia, in 1699. In 1720, he gave the first earnest of his future celebrity in a disputation on the public and private life of our Lord. He died at Groningen in 1779, after having filled for more than half a century the chair of eloquence and history there with distinction.—(I. B.)

Mark and St Luke), the identity[1] of which is recognised by the Three Passover system. The ternarian hypothesis admits, in the history of merely a very few months, the principle of *chronological transposition*,[2] either in Matthew, or in Mark and Luke, especially the two latter, and that with great advantage: the quaternarian, under the appearance of order, introduces *confusion*. Lightfoot, in his Chronicles[3] of the Old and New Testament (although he advocates the four Passover system), labours advisedly to show, that chronological transpositions occur in the Gospels and other parts of Scripture. The ternarian hypothesis agrees exactly with the seventy weeks of Daniel, and with the Lessons from Moses and the Prophets, read in the synagogues on Sabbath and Holy days—lessons which are clearly and frequently alluded to by the Evangelists; and it attributes to the Saviour's course a suitable rapidity:[4] the quaternarian hypothesis obliterates all these things. A fuller demonstration of these points is to be found in my Harmony, sect. 12, and Ordo Temporum, ch. 5. Hence, I with justice draw the following conclusion,— *Whosoever places more than three Passovers between the baptism and ascension of our Lord, his labour on the Gospels, as far as it relates to a Harmony of them, and to the life of our Saviour, ought to be considered utterly vain and held in little honour, by all who do not swallow error as readily as truth.* The GNOMON refers the reader, here and there, to the Harmony framed on the basis already mentioned, and to the *Ordo Temporum*, which

---

[1] And singleness [as opposed to the series being regarded as twofold or threefold.]—ED.

[2] "*Trajectio*," as for example in the accounts of our Lord's temptation, in one of which there must be a chronological transposition.—(I. B.)

[3] The works referred to are, "Chronicle and Harmony of the Old Testament, with Notes,"—and, "Harmony, Chronicle and Order of the New Testament. The Text of the Four Evangelists methodized, the Story of the Acts of the Apostles analyzed, the Order of the Epistles manifested, the Times of the Revelation observed, all illustrated with a variety of observations, etc."—(I. B.)

[4] "Cursuique Salvatoris celeritatem convenientissimam tribuit"—*i.e.* does not represent the time of our Lord's Ministry as having been longer than it really was; represents Him as reaching His goal with sufficient fleetness. A metaphor taken from the race-course. Cf. 1 Cor. ix. 24, 25, etc.—(I. B.)

render the remaining consideration of the Gospels so much the easier. The Harmony has a table (a Monotessaron[1] as it were), compiled from all the Evangelists; but the GNOMON exhibits the separate Gospels in the tables, severally accommodated to them.

XIX.

The Acts of the Apostles are intimately connected with the Epistles, especially those of St Paul, and are principally illustrated by them. In the Epistles, our annotations are not confined to those portions which are more abundantly full of doctrine: but they are carried on equally throughout, and are almost perpetual. The sum and series of events is given in the *Ordo Temporum,* cap. 6.

XX.

The principles, upon which we have treated the Apocalypse, are stated in the *annotations* to that book, as well as in the *Prœmium* prefixed to it. For as our exposition of it exists separately in German, so is it also added at the end of this work. The celebrated theologian, Dr Joachim Lange,[2] has lately issued a *critical examination* (*Beurtheilung*) of the German edition : and Frederick Eberard Rambach, has added it to W. Sherlock's[3]

---

[1] It is subjoined to the end of the Harmony, and occupies twenty-five pages.—(I. B.)

[2] Joachim Lange was born in 1670, in the territory of Brandenburgh. He was a distinguished theologian, philologist, and historian, of the Academy of Halle. He died in 1744.—(I. B.)

[3] William Sherlock, D.D., Dean of St Paul's, must not be confounded with his son, Thomas Sherlock, Bishop of London, nor with Dr Richard Sherlock, author of "The Practical Christian." He was born in Southwark about 1641, educated at Eton, and thence removed to Peterhouse, Cambridge, 1657. He became Rector of St George's, Botolph Lane, London, in 1660 ; after which he was made successively Prebendary of St Pauls, Master of the Temple, Rector of Therlfield, Hertfordshire, and in 1691 Dean of St Pauls. He died A.D. 1707. He was a learned divine, a clear, polite, and forcible writer, and an eloquent preacher.—(I. B.)

"Preservative against Popery," which he has translated into the vernacular tongue, under the title of "*Mantissa*[1] *Apocalyptica.*" The "*Critical Examination*," however, coincides with what the author has said on the subject in his Latin *Commentary* on *the Glory of Christ.* I have thought it expedient, therefore, to take the present opportunity, to examine the principal sinews of his commentary, and reply to his "Critical Examination." As soon as I heard of the appearance of that "Critical Examination," I determined to yield to truth, if established by that most accomplished commentator, with no less delight than that with which I should defend it, if found on my own side. Having made myself master of the treatise, I found some things culled from my work and touched upon, which either pleased or displeased this author. I in my turn will explain, in what portion that distinguished man has delighted me by his assent, or by his dissent invited me to reconsider my opinion; and as he has exercised the greatest courtesy towards me, so will I maintain the greatest respect towards an old man, whose hospitality I shared in 1713, and whose friendship I have enjoyed ever since.

1. He disagrees with me especially concerning *the Beast*, and *the Whore.*—See pp. 371–405.

Answer.—There is, I grant, a great difference between them: but in what that difference really consists, we have considered in our annotations on Revelation xiii. 1.

2. He infers thence (referring the reader to his former commentaries), that I, no less than Vitringa, am generally mistaken in the interpretation of the Seven *Seals*, and Seven *Trumpets*, and, therefore, of the whole *book.*—See p. 405.

Answer.—My interpretation of the Beast and the Whore, being vindicated, reciprocally supports, and is supported by the remaining portions of my exposition. There are many things, of which the "Critical Examination" has given plausible explanations (pp. 371, sqq., 394, sqq., 400, sqq.), but they do not interfere with me; for I myself acknowledge them as true. A discussion of the matters in dispute would have been much more desirable. I find, however, something which astonishes me. I had examined in my book, pp. 500–504, the main features of the Apocalyptic system set forth by Dr Lange, mentioning the

[1] *Mantissa*, a Tuscan word: *a make-weight*, and so, *a gain.*—Ed.

author by name, and I had written there these words—"*Whosoever seeks the truth, should most diligently examine this.*" And yet, he is entirely silent on the whole of that my examination, nor does he even touch upon pp. 107, 108, 123, 124, 214, 215, 285, 295, and by far the greater part of those, which I had collected in the seventh section of my Preface. He says, that he has read the book through : otherwise, I should have thought it clear, that he had only gleaned some portions of it in a cursory manner. I indeed desire, that those passages, referred to above, should be considered as entirely and formally reasserted on the present occasion : for they presuppose that I had carefully examined the commentaries of this distinguished author, and diligently avoided the errors which he refutes in Vitringa. Besides which, I have temperately stated in my annotations on the Apocalypse, contained in the present work, what is the nature of that distinguished man's interpretation on the *Seals*, the *Trumpets*, and the other parts, where it possesses any *sinew*.—See the Notes on iv. 1, etc.

3. He thinks (p. 406), that I have placed the commencement of the *three woes*, especially of the *third woe*, too early.

I have answered this objection in the Notes on Rev. viii. 13.

4. He agrees with me, on *the Two Witnesses*, the *Great City*, and the *Kingdom*.—See pp. 406, seqq.

5. He approves of my exposition of ch. xii., as far as regards the future : as far as regards the past he does not (p. 408) approve of it.

Concerning the past, see my Notes on xii. 5.

6. He cordially adopts (pp. 409-421) my views on the *Conversion of the Nations*, the *Future Millennium* (though he only admits *one*) and the *First Resurrection*. And in this part especially, he has freed the prophecy from the *Equuleus Hermeneuticus*,[1] which he so frequently speaks of. He seeks, however, to vindicate the consistency of the language, used in Scripture concerning the last times (which are described both as bad and good), by asserting a twofold advent of Christ ; conceiving, that

[1] *Equuleus Hermeneuticus*—A quaint expression signifying literally "An instrument of torture applied to the interpretation of prophecy." The *Equuleus* was so called from its being shaped like a horse.—(I. B.) *The interpreter's rack.*—ED.

the bad will be before the first of these two advents, the good in the Millennium (see his commentary on the Apocalypse, p. 239): although that consistency cannot be maintained (if we are to retain our belief in the unity of Christ's advent), except by supposing *two periods of a thousand* years each, concerning which, see my Notes on Rev. xx. 4.

7. He says (p. 421), that he cannot understand what I have said on *the other periods of time*, compared with that of a thousand years.

He has forgotten the results of my exposition (pp. 127, 644, etc.), obtained by a correct analysis of the different periods. Those, who acknowledge the accuracy of this analysis, perceive that the examination of prophecy is especially necessary for the present age (cf. *Beurtheilung*, pp. 409, 410): those who do not acknowledge the accuracy of that analysis, float about [without chart or compass] in a long expanse of ages: for that hypothesis, which is chiefly maintained by the Theologian of Halle, involving the notion, that the forty-two months of the *Beast* denote three and a half common years, defers those three and a half years, and the subsequent flourishing state of the Church, two centuries and more.—See *Erklärung Offenbarungs*, pp. 503, 504. Were such an expectation well-founded, it would be more profitable as yet to meditate upon other points, and to give our attention to those prophecies, which refer to the present time.

8. The venerable theologian has condescended to quote long passages from my book concerning those chapters, in which he finds that I agree with him, and justly declares the *victory* of truth.—See p. 422. That it is not, however, an examination of my whole work, the heads just mentioned clearly show: for they deal with very few chapters of the Apocalypse, and leave the remainder almost untouched. He was at liberty to take his own course in the matter; but it is the reader's interest to know that I have treated there of many other subjects, such as *The Flux of things from the Invisible to the Visible, and their Reflux from the Visible to the Invisible; the difference of the Seven Angels, Churches, Seals, Trumpets, Phials; the Division of the Septenaries into Fours and Threes; the Progress of affairs from East to West*, etc. On account of the subjects so ably handled by the venerable divine in question, I should not myself have published an exposition of the

Apocalypse, had I not felt sure that somewhat had trickled from the inexhaustible fountain of Apocalyptical Wisdom into my channel, which it became my duty to communicate to the world at large.

9. With singular kindness he declares his opinion (p. 428), that I may be able to produce something towards interpreting the prophecies of the Old Testament. He adds, however, and I acknowledge it, that my system requires to be more carefully finished off. By the assistance of the Apocalypse, which is *not sealed*, Daniel who was *sealed*, and the other prophets, who described the *mystery of* GOD, will be laid open. But those particulars, which he thinks I ought to retract, will never prevent the true comparison of that book with the prophecies of the Old Testament.

10. I am the more firmly convinced of this by my *Ordo Temporum*, which he so warmly welcomed. That compendium has an intimate connection with both my expositions of the Apocalypse, having been published between the two, exhibiting, as it does, one chain of historic and prophetic periods, perpetually intertwined with each other.

I have evoked all my εὐπείθεια and docility, that I might be ready even now to abandon with a good grace any error which the *aged interpreter* should prove me to have adopted. I find myself unable, however, without flattery, which I know him to abhor, to change my opinion: and, if such be the will of God, I will hereafter submit for his consideration some observations, in the German language, which we have both of us made use of, together with the Latin. *For there is a just, and shortly to be satisfied expectation, of certain things, by which the application of prophecy to our age will be rendered more distinct, and a facility be afforded of combining many useful things in one composition.* We both search sincerely for truth: his affection for me, and my reverence for him, are augmented instead of being diminished, by the candour of the one, and the forbearance of the other. Nor is our very disagreement on the interpretation of certain chapters without its advantage: for in proportion as our adherence to our several opinions, where they differ, is the more unbending, so much the more ought our agreement on other points to induce the spectators of this most friendly contest to examine the whole matter in question; and whosoever shall consider the arguments of this veteran interpreter to be satisfactory in this instance, will be the less easily terrified by the attacks of others on my Apocalyptical views. The matter will become clearer hereafter as I had said [1] in sec. xv. of the Preface to the work under consideration. In the meantime I wish from my heart, that the Theologian of Halle in his Biblia Parenthetica, or any other subsequent commentaries, may by the grace of God be enabled to explain, in accordance with the Divine meaning, these portions of prophecy. And I wish, since so many depend on his authority, that, after considering the matter more maturely, as far as his precious hours permit, he would declare *whether he wishes to be considered by a more enlightened posterity, as the assailant or supporter* of those parts of my system, which he has condemned in his *Beurtheilung*. I am not influenced in this matter by any spirit of ambitious contention, but by the gravity and urgency of the matter. He will deserve as well of the Church by writing a single sentence, as a volume on this question. I shall feel no shame at the triumph of truth. In conclusion, I will put forward a thing, which alone will be sufficient to decide the matter: his too eager interpretation of the half-hour,[2] for a millennary period (firmly established in its proper place), has plainly introduced the whole system, of which the Theologian of Halle is so strenuous a defender. If that interpretation falls to the ground, this system will yield to truth.

The opinions, which *others* have expressed with regard to my commentary on this book, are exceedingly various. With some, I shall scarcely be able to redeem, by my other labours, the blame which they consider me to have incurred by my prophetical researches. Some are said to be dissatisfied with my calculations: they seek, forsooth, mathematical *prae-excellence*[3] and soar far above our humble path: for we are satisfied with the rudiments

---

[1] " A greater degree of knowledge awaits posterity. To them much that is now made little account of will serve for a foundation on which to build more; much that is now current will no longer pass; and many proofs that to most men seem not sufficient now, will then be more than enough."— Loc. cit. *Robertson's Translation.*—(I. B.)

[2] See Rev. viii. I.—(I. B.)

[3] In the original,—" Sublimitatem videlicet mathematicam quærunt."— (I. B.)

of Arithmetic, provided the *fractions* be carefully observed. Many others, nay by far the greater number, laying aside the labour of investigation, proceed with greater ease and celerity, and fancy that they are riding in port, when in reality they are at sea with their eyes shut. Let them consider well what they are about; Truth is of too noble a nature to force herself upon the notice of mankind. I have nothing new to say on her behalf. I still employ this defence; *Pray, place the Holy Scripture before you on the desk of your heart, and acquaint yourself with the* WHOLE *matter, before you arrive at a decision.* " Happy is he, that speaketh in the ears of them, that will hear."—Ecclesiasticus xxv. 9.

XXI.

No one has as yet called my *orthodoxy* in question. Whoever has examined my writings, must acknowledge that I have followed Scripture, not only in doctrines, but even in words, with a religious exactness, which even to good men seems scarcely removed from superstition. For I consider, that no aberration from the line of Truth laid down in Scripture, however slight, is so unimportant, but that the full and simple recognition of the Truth, corresponding with the knowledge of God, expressed according to His direction, and agreeable to His glory, is to be preferred to it.—Truth is one; [incapable of diminution, or division] and consistent with itself in its greatest, and in its least parts. It is the reader's duty, therefore, to think well of me, until I am proved guilty of error by some one who does not err himself in accusing me. It too frequently happens, that one man attributes to another a pernicious opinion, which both equally abhor, and thus by a short and hasty assertion places a stumbling-block in the way of a thousand others. What I consider the reader's duty, what my own, in such a case, I have declared in sect. xiii. of the preface to my German Exposition of the Apocalypse.

XXII.

Those, who have learnt, or are learning Greek, cannot fail to derive great advantage from the present work. I wish, however, to be of service also to other lovers of truth. And they will see, that I have endeavoured to hinder them, as little as possible, by the introduction (at times necessary) of Greek words. For I have prefixed the Greek words of the text, without the Latin, to those annotations only, which are of a merely verbal class; whereas I have introduced the Latin, as well as the Greek, where they concern the subject: in some instances, the Latin words are put instead of the original Greek, in some instances added to explain it. The Latin words of the text have been taken from the Vulgate and other translations, or employed now for the first time to express those of the original, and they are generally put in that case, which the Latin context requires, although it be different in the original Greek:—and I have selected such words and phrases, as, even with some derogation from pure Latinity, would render the native force of the Greek, as closely as possible.[1]

XXIII.

In the rest of my language, throughout this work, I have used that form of Latin expression, which seemed best suited to this kind of commentary, without either too rude a contempt or too servile a devotion to Latinity, which is frequently violated by those who profess to cultivate it most fondly, to the extreme disgust of those who are at all really acquainted with classical Latin.[2]

[1] I have, when it seemed advisable, put the Greek words where Bengel had put only Latin, and in every case where it was possible to do so, I have given an English translation of the Greek words even when no translation is given by Bengel. In these cases I have derived, as elsewhere, great assistance from Bengel's own German version of the New Testament, which I succeeded in obtaining after a long search. In these as well as other instances, it has been my endeavour to render the word, phrase, or particle, not as I should render it, but as Bengel would have done. I have also added interpretations to the Hebrew words, etc., cited by Bengel, where he has omitted to do so, and in every instance I have selected those renderings which appeared most in accordance with Bengel's own meaning and intention, without the slightest regard to the opinions of other commentators.—(I. B.)

[2] In the original,—" Qui aliquid vernaculæ latinitatis olfecerunt."—(I. B.)

XXIV.

Technical terms[1] occur throughout this work, such as *Anthypophora, Apodioxis, Asyndeton,* ἓν διὰ δυοῖν, *Epiphonema, Epitasis, Ethopoeia, Hypallage, Litotes, Mimesis, Oxymoron, Ploce,* Περιθεραπεία καὶ Ἐπιθεραπεία, *Prosopopœia, Sejugatio, Zeugma,* etc.: in which cases, the reader must be warned, not to pass by without consideration an annotation, reduced to a compendious form by technical terms, but more useful than he supposes: as for example that on John x. 27, 28. Especial advantage, however, is obtained from a consideration of the *oratio concisa,* or *semiduplex* derived from the Hebrew style, and the χιασμὸς, which is of the greatest service in explaining the economy of the whole epistle to the Hebrews. The Index contains examples of both figures. It would have taken too much space to have expressed such things in every instance by a periphrasis. Those, therefore, who are at fault with any figure, must seek for its meaning elsewhere. The Annotations are written either in the person of the author (*i.e.* of him, whose words are contained in the text), or in that of the commentator.

XXV.

Where there is any difficulty, I am sufficiently diffuse: for the most part, however, I am brief, *because* the subject is frequently plain and easy, especially in narratives,—*because* I usually introduce observations illustrative of many passages, not in every passage to which they apply, but in the first which occurs,—*because* I have already treated elsewhere of many things, which it was unnecessary to repeat here (See Sections

---

[1] I have endeavoured to get rid of them wherever I could do so consistently with conciseness and accuracy, as they often serve only to encumber the text, and would, I fear, remind the general reader of the Bourgeois Gentilhomme's astonishment at finding that he had been all his life speaking prose.

A full explanation of all the technical terms which occur in the course of the work is given in the Appendix to the last volume.—(I. B.)

viii., xix., xxi.),—*because* many things, which relate to the division, connection, and punctuation of the Text, may be discovered by merely looking at the Text itself, or my revision of it (See Sect. xi.),—*because* those things, which regard the Analysis of each book, are clearly set forth in *the tables* prefixed to them, and cannot be easily repeated in the notes (See Sect. xiii.),—*because* I usually declare the simple truth, without a labyrinth of many opinions (See Sect. xvii.),—*because* many things are compressed into small compass by the aid of technical terms (See Sect. xxiv.). Hence it comes to pass, that this volume, though intended to illustrate the whole of the New Testament, is small in size, and less in weight, than many commentaries on single books of the New Testament. I have not thought it necessary to subjoin *Practical applications*, "*usus*," as they are termed, to each chapter; for he who submits himself to the constraining influence of Divine Love in the search after Divine Truth, imbibes from the Divine Words, when he has once perceived their meaning, all things profitable for salvation, without labour, and without stimulus. They, however, who read rightly, that is to say, so as carefully to weigh all things, and are simply occupied with the Text, instead of being led away from it, will find some assistance, we trust, from this work, in arriving at the full meaning of Scripture, and more especially with regard to those matters, which we have spoken of in sect. iv. Nor will the *Indexes* at the end of the work be without their use. I will not add more, either in commendation, or excuse of my work. I will only make this one request to you, Reader;—if you should ever meet with an exegetical commentary on the whole New Testament, or any part of it, beside which our GNOMON *appears* to you superfluous, compare the two works together on a *single* portion or chapter, *e.g.* Matthew xxiv.; Acts xiii.; Romans xii.; Hebrews xii.; 1 Peter iii.; or Revelation x.; and then, and not till then, form your judgment. I must mention in this place Philip David Burk,[1] who has not only greatly assisted me, both

---

[1] This individual (author of the Gnomon to the twelve minor prophets, published at Heilbronn in 1753, and at present pastor of the Church of Markgrüningen, and special superintendent of the neighbouring parishes) has revised this second edition of the Gnomon of the New Testament, has added the author's latest labours from his manuscript sheets, carefully ex a-

by neatly transcribing my Apocalyptical Treatise, Ordo Temporum, and Gnomon, and by his dexterity in making researches and solving difficulties, so that I have been enabled to explain many things with more facility, than I otherwise should have done;—but who has also become so fully acquainted with my thoughts and feelings, by the daily intercourse of many years, that he is fully competent to answer in my stead as ἰσόψυχος,[1] on various subjects, if applied to even after my departure by those who will perhaps take a greater interest in them then, than they do now.

XXVI.

In the Preface to my Larger Edition of the New Testament, I thought it advisable to divide my Exegetical Notes so, as to explain philological questions in Latin, practical matters in German. I have since found that the one class of subjects could not be separated from the other, without great difficulty and inconvenience: and I have therefore joined them together in this Gnomon. It is consequently less necessary for me to hurry the publication of the German work, which I have in contemplation: for I have determined to bring out in German,[2] annotations on the whole New Testament, suited more exclusively for *mere* edification. What may be the progress, what the result of this undertaking, whether I live or sleep,—I commit to GOD. As to the rest, I should not now venture to commence any new work of length. Many examples have lately occurred of

---

mined, and introduced through the work many valuable annotations from the Clavicula which the New Prologue to the New Testament had promised : he now commends this work to the grace of God and the kind and careful consideration of the Christian reader.—26th February 1759.—*Note to the Edition of* 1759.

The *Clavicula Novi Testamenti*, literally *Little Key of the New Testament*, is published as number XIII. of the Appendix or fourth Part of the Second Edition of the Apparatus Criticus.—(I. B.)

[1] ἰσόψυχος—from ἴσος *equal*, and ψυχή, *soul—i.e.*, one whose soul is *equivalent* to my own.—(I. B.)

[2] This German version of the New Testament with annotations suited *rather for mere* edification, was published at Stuttgard A.D. 1753, shortly after his death.—*Note to the Edition of* 1759.

men, who, after a life spent in literary avocations, have been overtaken by imbecility. Whatsoever remains to me and my contemporaries of life or strength, I recognise as a debt overdue, and I adopt the words of David—"*Grant that I may recover myself, before I go hence, and be no more.*"

XXVII.

The multifarious *abuse*, or I should rather say nefarious *contempt* of Holy Scripture has, in our days, reached its climax, and that not only with the profane, but even with those, who in their own opinion are wise, nay spiritual. The ΓΕΓΡΑΠΤΑΙ, "It is written," wherewith the Son of GOD Himself, in His single combat with Satan, defeated all his assaults, has come to be held so cheap, that those, who feed upon Scripture *whole and alone*, are considered to dote or to want soul. Thus will the *False Prophet*, at his coming, find the gates standing open. And well-intentioned writers too emulously produce practical treatises, prayers, hymns, soliloquies, religious tales. Singly, they may be exceedingly useful: but the mass of them when *taken together*, draws away many from the BOOK OF GOD, that is the Scripture, which in itself combines, in the utmost plenitude and purity, all that is serviceable to the soul's health. Let those, who prove all things that are best, preserve the Heavenly Deposit, which God, by writings gradually increasing in clearness and explicitness, has given, not in vain, from the time of Moses down to that of the Apostles. Then, if any one thinks, that he has received from this work of mine any aid towards the saving treatment of Scripture, let him employ it for the glory of God, for his own edification and that of others,—and pray for a blessing upon me.

END OF THE AUTHOR'S PREFACE.

TRANSLATOR'S NOTE.

N.B.—I have very great pleasure in acknowledging my obligations to the following very valuable works, from which I have translated, copied, abridged or compiled many of the Foot-notes appended to The Author's Preface and The Commentary on St Matthew.

DICTIONNAIRE Historique, Critique, Chronologique, Geographique et Literal DE LA BIBLE. CALMET. 4 vols. 4to. Geneva, 1730.

BIBLIOTHECA SACRA. LE LONG. 4 vols. 4to. Halle, 1781.

CHRISTOPHORI SAXII ONOMASTICON LITERARIUM, sive NOMENCLATOR HISTORICO-CRITICUS. 7 vols. 8vo. Maestricht, 1790.

DICTIONNAIRE UNIVERSEL, HISTORIQUE, CRITIQUE, et BIBLIOGRAPHIQUE. Neuvième Edition. 20 vols. 8vo. Paris, 1810.

A Memoir of the Life and Writings of JOHN ALBERT BENGEL. By the Rev. JOHN CHRISTIAN FREDERICK BURK, translated from the German by ROBERT FRANCIS WALKER. 8vo. London, 1837.

An Introduction to the Critical Study and Knowledge of the Holy Scriptures. By THOMAS HARTWELL HORNE. Ninth Edition. 5 vols. 8vo. London, 1846.

The Life and Epistles of St Paul. LEWIN. 2 vols. 8vo. London, 1851.

CYCLOPÆDIA BIBLOGRAPHICA. DARLING. London, 1854.

It would be wrong to mention this admirable work without acknowledging the promptitude and courtesy with which Mr Darling has allowed me the use of his valuable and extensive library.

TREGELLES on the Printed Text of the NEW TESTAMENT. London, 1854.

THE NEW TESTAMENT OF OUR LORD AND SAVIOUR JESUS CHRIST in the Original Greek, with Notes. By CHR. WORDSWORTH, D.D. Part I.—The Four Gospels.—4to. London, 1856.

Wherever I have derived my information or remarks from other quarters, I have acknowledged them specifically, except where they have been furnished from private sources or are the result of my own studies.—(I. B.)

GNOMON OF THE NEW TESTAMENT.

The name of *New Testament* is sometimes given to that collection of sacred writings, in which the New Testament, strictly so called, is described. What the New Testament, strictly so called, really is, we have explained in our notes on Matthew xxvi. 28. This collection may be divided into two parts, one of which contains the writings of the Evangelists and Apostles, whilst the other consists singly of the Apocalypse of Jesus Christ. The former exhibits firstly, the history of our Lord from His coming in the flesh, to His ascension into heaven; secondly, the external and internal history of the Church, as constituted by the apostles after the ascension. In the latter, a revelation, which stands entirely alone, teaches us the future history of Christ, the Church, and the whole world, even to the consummation of all things. In brief, there are the Evangelists, the Acts and Epistles of the Apostles, and the Apocalypse. The connection and relation which exist between these various writings, afford a satisfactory proof of their perfection. We have shown in our *Ordo Temporum*, at about what time each of them was written.

ANNOTATIONS

ON THE

GOSPEL ACCORDING TO ST MATTHEW.

THE Evangelists contain the rudiments of the New Testament.—(See John xvi. 12.[1]) Concerning their authority,[2] see Ephes. iv. 11; and 1 Peter i. 12. They are four in number—two of them, namely John and Matthew, were themselves apostles, and took part, therefore, in the things which they relate: the other two, Mark and Luke, afford, in their own persons, an example of faith, having derived their sure and accurate knowledge of the Gospel from others. Mark, however, presupposes the existence of Matthew, and, as it were, supplies his omissions; Luke does the same for both of them; John for all three. Matthew, an apostle wrote first,[3] and thus established an authority for both Mark and Luke. John, also an apostle, wrote last,[4] and con-

---

[1] The Evangelists, from the earliest days of Christianity, were reckoned to be *four;* very many pseudo-evangelists, whose writings were not in consonance with the pure faith, having been rejected. Those, who choose to apply the four cardinal rivers of Paradise, and many such-like fourfold types, especially that one which has the sanction of hoar antiquity, viz., the Lion, Ox [or *calf*], Man, and Flying Eagle [the Cherubim, Rev. iv. 7], as typical of the fourfold Gospel, are entitled to have the credit of the suggestion, whatever amount of credit is due. If you desire an exact definition of an EVANGELIST, my definition would be a holy man of GOD, who publicly, and with an irrefragable testimony, sets forth to men a history of Jesus Christ, either by word of mouth or in writing.—*Harm. Ev.,* Ed. ii., p. 34, etc.

[2] "*In which they are inferior to the Apostles and Prophets, but superior to Pastors and Teachers.*"—*Harm.,* p. 35.

[3] "*A fact, which is evident from this, that the title ἡγεμών, expressed by Luke once, ch. iii. 1, but never by the rest, is, in the history of the passion, continually assigned by Matthew to Pilate.*"—*Harm.,* p. 37.

[4] "*And yet, as is plain from his ch. v. 2, John did not defer writing till so late as after the destruction of Jerusalem.*"—*Harm.,* p. 38.

firmed to mankind, more fully, the works of Mark and Luke, already sufficiently firm in themselves.[1] Matthew wrote especially to show the fulfilment of the Old Testament Scriptures, and to convince the Jews. Mark produced an abridgement of Matthew, adding at the same time many remarkable things which had been omitted by his predecessor, and paying particular attention to the noviciate of the apostles. Luke composed a narrative of a distinctly historical character, with especial reference to our Lord's office as Christ. John refuted the impugners of His divinity. All which is recorded by either of these Four, was actually done and said by Jesus Christ. But they severally drew from a common treasury those particulars, of which each had the fullest knowledge, which corresponded to his own spiritual character, and which were best suited to the time when he wrote, and to the persons whom he primarily addressed. Chrysostom, at the commencement of his second homily on the Epistle to the Romans, says,—*Moses has not prefixed his name to the five books which he wrote. Nor have Matthew, John, Luke, nor Mark, to the Gospels written by them. Why so? Writing, as they did, for those who were present, it was not necessary for them to indicate themselves, being also present.*

The term GOSPEL has several significations, which, though cognate, are not identical. (1.) The *Good News* itself concerning Jesus Christ, which was communicated by Jesus Christ Himself, His forerunner, His apostles, and other witnesses, first to the Jews, then to the whole human race. (2.) The whole office and system of propagating that Good News, either by preaching or writing: in which sense, for example, we find the expression "*my Gospel,*" sc. that of Paul, in 2 Timothy ii. 8.

---

[1] "*Although there is a generally prevalent, but not well enough established opinion, that Matthew wrote in the eighth year after the Ascension, Mark in the tenth, Luke in the fifteenth, and lastly John, in the thirty-third.*"—*Harm.*, p. 37.

[2] Moreover, if you join together the testimonies of John and Matthew, and also those of Mark and Luke, you will have the full range of the whole conversation, acts, and words of Jesus Christ, the beginning, progress, and end, as also all the alternations [vicissitudines], which one may observe, in the disciples, in the people, in His adversaries, and, owing to the different treatment these needed, in the Saviour Himself, if only you pay attention to method.—*Harm.*, pp. 38, 39.

(3.) By a still further metonymy,[1] the written remains of those who have committed the Gospel narrative to writing. If you wish, in Greek, to name at once the four books, which Tertullian styles *the Gospel Engine* (*Evangelicum Instrumentum*), you ought in strictness to make use of the singular number, and say, τὸ κατὰ Ματθαῖον, κατὰ Μάρκον, κ.τ.λ. Εὐαγγέλιον (the Gospel according to Matthew, according to Mark, etc.[2]), not in the plural (τὰ κ.τ.λ.. Εὐαγγέλια, the Gospels), except perhaps for the sake of brevity. For the subject of all four is one and the same; though treated in one manner κατὰ Ματθαῖον, *i.e.*, *as far as Matthew is concerned, according to Matthew, by Matthew*, as Matthew treated it; in another manner κατὰ Μάρκον: etc.—Cf. κατὰ, Acts xxvii. 7, fin.—Nevertheless, as in Genesis, the first word which occurs is *Bereschith* (which was afterwards adopted as the title), so the first word written by Matthew was βίβλος, *Book*, or *Roll* (see Gnomon on Matthew i. 1); by Mark ἀρχή, the *Beginning* (see Gnomon on Mark i. 1), and so on. The appellation, however, of Gospel, as a title for the book itself, occurs in the most ancient fathers. By the same authorities, Matthew is said to have written his Gospel in Hebrew. Why should he not have written the same work, the same without the slightest variation, in Greek as well as in Hebrew, even though he did not, strictly speaking, translate it from the one language into the other?—Cf. Jeremiah li. 63, xxxvi. 28, and the annotations of Franzius[3] on that passage (De Interp. S.S., p. 504); see also La Vie de Madame Guion,[4] pt. ii., p. 229.—We now proceed to give the following

[1] See explanation of technical terms. See also Horne's Introduction, vol. ii., pp. 454–461.—(I. B.)

[2] *i.e.*, There is but *one* Gospel, with a *fourfold* aspect.—ED.

[3] Franzius, Wolfgang, D.D., a Lutheran divine. Born 1564. Educated at Frankfort-on-the-Oder, and afterwards removed to Wittemberg, where, in 1598, he was appointed Professor of History, and afterwards of Theology. Died 1628. He wrote, besides other works, *Tractatus de Interpretatione S. Scripturarum*.—(I. B.)

[4] Her life is said to be written by herself, but believed to have been compiled from her papers by the Abbé de Brion. Quérard says of her, in *La France Littéraire*, "Guyon (Mme. Jeanne-Marie Bouvieres de la Mothe) celebre par sa mysticité et plus encore par la dispute qu'elle fit naitre entre Bossuet et Fenelon sur le quietisme: née á Montargis en 1648, morte a Blois le 9 Juin, 1717.—(I. B.)

SYNOPSIS

OF THE

GOSPEL ACCORDING TO ST MATTHEW.

I. *The Nativity, and the matters immediately following.*
    α. The Genealogy: . . . Ch. i. 1–17
    β. The Generation: . . . 18–25
    γ. The Magi: . . . ii. 1–12
    δ. The Flight and Return. . 13–23

II. *Our Lord's Entrance on His Ministry.*
    α. John the Baptist: . . iii. 1–12
    β. The Baptism of Jesus: . . 13–17
    γ. His Temptation and Victory. . iv. 1–11

III. *The deeds and words, by which Jesus proved Himself to be Christ.*
    α. At Capernaum: . . 12–16
      Where must be remarked,
      1. His Preaching, . . 17
      2. The Call of Peter, Andrew, James, and John, . . . 18–22
      3. His Preaching and Healing, the conflux of Multitudes, . 23–25
      4. The Sermon on the Mount, . v.–vii.
      5. The Leper, . . . viii. 1–4
      6. The Centurion and his servant, 5–13
      7. Peter's mother-in-law, . 14, 15
      8. Many sick persons. . . 16, 17
    β. The voyage across the sea; the two individuals warned concerning following Christ; the command exercised over the wind and the sea: the devils migrating from men into swine. . 18–34

γ. Again at Capernaum,
   1. The Paralytic, . . Ch. ix. 1–3
   2. The call of Matthew, Intercourse with Sinners defended, . 9, 10–13
   3. Fasting, . . . 14–17
   4. The girl dead, and, after the healing of the woman who had an issue of blood, restored to life, . 18–26
   5. The Two Blind Men, . 27–31
   6. The Demoniac; . . 32–34
   7. Our Lord goes through the cities and villages, and commands labourers to be prayed for, . . 35–38
   8. He sends and instructs labourers, x. 1–42 and preaches Himself: . xi. 1
   9. John's message to our Lord: 2–6
   10. Our Lord praises John, denounces woe against the refractory cities, invites those that labour: . 7–30
   11. The ears of corn rubbed: . xii. 1–8
   12. The withered hand healed: 9–13
   13. The Pharisees lay snares: Jesus departs: . . . 14–21
   14. The Demoniac is healed: the people are amazed: the Pharisees blaspheme: Jesus refutes them, . 22–37
   15. He rebukes those who demand a sign, . . . 38–45
   16. He declares who are His, . 46–50
   17. He teaches by Parables, . xiii. 1–52
δ. At Nazareth, . . 53–58
ε. At other places
   1. Herod, after the murder of John, hearing of Jesus, is perplexed: Jesus departs, and is sought by the people, xiv. 1–13
   2. He heals; and feeds five thousand: 14–21
   3. The sea voyage, and cures in the land of Genesareth, . 22–36

a	*c* 4. Unwashen hands;	Ch. xv.	1–20
	5. The woman of Canaan;		21–28
	6. Many sick healed;		29–31
	7. Four thousand fed;		32–38
	8. In the coasts of Magdala, those who demand a sign are refuted;	39–xvi.	4
	9. The warning concerning leaven,		5–12

IV. *Our Lord's Predictions of His Passion and Resurrection.*

α. The First Prediction.
    1. The preparation by confirming the primary article, that Jesus is the Christ: . . . 13–30
    2. The Prediction itself delivered; and the interference of Peter rejected. 21–28

β. The Second Prediction.
    1. The Transfiguration in the Mount; silence enjoined; . . xvii. 1–13
    2. The Lunatic healed; . 14–21
    3. The Prediction itself; . 22, 23
    4. The Tribute-Money paid; . 24–27
    5. Who is the greatest? . xviii. 1–20
    6. The duty of forgiving injuries. 21–35

γ. The Third Prediction.
    1. The Departure from Galilee; xix. 1, 2
    2. The question concerning Divorce; 3–12
    3. Kindness to little children, . 13–15
    4. The Rich Man turning back; 16–22
        And thereupon discourses,
            On the Salvation of the Rich, 23–26
            On the rewards of following Christ, 27–30
            On the Last and the First. xx. 1–16
    5. The Prediction itself; . 17–19
    6. The request of the sons of Zebedee; humility enjoined. . . 20–28

a V.   7. The two Blind Men cured.

V. *The Events at Jerusalem immediately before the Passion.*

α. Sunday:
1. The Regal Entry, . . Ch. xxi. 1–11
2. The Cleansing of the Temple; 12–17

β. Monday:
The Fig-tree. . . 18–22

γ. Tuesday. Occurrences—
A. In the Temple:
1. The Interference of the Chief Priests,
  i. Repulsed,
    a. By the Question concerning John's Baptism, . 23–27
    b. By two Parables:
      (1) The Two Sons, . 28–32
      (2) The Vineyard, . 33–44
  ii. Proceeds to lay snares for Him. 45–46
2. The Parable of the Marriage Feast: . . . xxii. 1–14
3. The Questions of our Lord's Adversaries—
  i. Concerning Tribute, . 15–22
  ii. ——— the Resurrection, 23–33
  iii. ——— the Great Commandment: . . . 34–40
4. Our Saviour's question in return concerning David's Lord, 41–46
His warning concerning the Scribes and Pharisees, xxiii. 1–12
His denunciation against them, 13–36
And against the city itself:— 37–39
B. Out of the Temple.
The Discourse concerning the Destruction of the Temple and the End of the World. . xxiv. xxv.

a VI. *The Passion and Resurrection.*
  A. The Passion, Death, and Burial.
    a. Wednesday.
      α. Our Lord's Prediction,   Ch. xxvi. 1, 2
      β. The Deliberation of the Chief
        Priests,   .   .   3–5
      γ. The agreement of Judas, of-
        fended at the anointing of our
        Lord, to betray Him.   .   6–16
    b. Thursday.
      α. By Day;
        The Passover prepared.   .   17–19
      β. At Evening.
        1. The Betrayal indicated,   20–25
        2. The Lord's Supper.   .   26–29
      γ. By Night.
        1. The offence of Peter and the
          Disciples foretold;   .   30–35
        2. The Agony in Gethsemane;   36–46
        3. Jesus is taken, forbids the
          employment of the sword,
          rebukes the crowd, is de-
          serted by His disciples: 47–56
        4. Is led to Caiaphas: false wit-
          nesses are unsuccessful: con-
          fesses Himself to be the Son
          of God: is condemned to die:
          is mocked.   .   .   57–68
        5. Peter denies; and weeps.   69–75
    c. Friday.
      α. The Passion consummated.
        i. In the Morning.
          1. Jesus is delivered to Pilate.   xxvii. 1, 2
          2. The death of Judas.   3–10
          3. The kingdom of Jesus:
            His silence.   .   11–14
          4. Pilate; warned in vain by
            his wife releases Barabbas,

				and delivers Jesus to be crucified. . .	15–26

    5. Jesus is mocked and led forth.   27–32
   ii. The Third Hour.
    The Vinegar and Gall: the Cross: the Garments divided: the Inscription on the Cross: the two Thieves: the Blasphemies. .   33–44
   iii. From the Sixth to the Ninth hour: the Darkness: the Desertion. . .   45–49
  β. The Death.
   The Vail Rent, and the great Earthquake. . .   50–53
   The Centurion wonders: the Women behold.   54–56
  γ. The Burial. .   57–61
 d. Saturday.
  The Sepulchre guarded,   62–66
B The Resurrection:
 α. Announced to the Women.
  1. By the Angel, .   xxviii. 1–8
  2. By the Lord Himself, .   9, 10
 β. Denied by His Enemies, .   11–15
 γ. Shown to His Disciples. .   16–20

ST MATTHEW.

CHAPTER I.

1. Βίβλος Γενέσεως,—*the Book, or Roll, of the Generation*) A phrase employed by the LXX. in Genesis ii. 4 and v. 1. The books of the New Testament, however, being written at so early a period, abound with Hebraisms: and the Divine Wisdom provided, that the Greek version of the Old Testament should prepare the language, which would be the fittest vehicle for the teaching of the New. This title, however, *the genealogy*,[1] refers, strictly speaking, to what immediately follows (as appears from the remainder of the first verse), though it applies also to the whole book, the object of which is to prove that Jesus is the Christ, the Son of David, etc., [*in whom, as being the promised Messiah, the prophecies of the Old Testament have received their fulfilment. Hence it is that from time to time the evangelist frequently repeats the formula,* " That it might be fulfilled."—Vers. Germ.] See ver. 20, and ch. ix. 27, etc. For Scripture is wont to combine with genealogies the reasons for introducing them. See Gen. v. 1 and vi. 9.—'Ιησοῦ Χριστοῦ, *of Jesus Christ*) The compound appellation, JESUS-CHRIST, or CHRIST-JESUS, or the simple one of CHRIST, employed by antonomasia,[2] came into use after the Pentecostal descent of the Holy Spirit. The four Gospels, therefore, have it only at their commencements

---

[1] *Recensio Ortûs. Tabulæ recensionis* was an expression applied to the Censor's Register. *Ortus* signifies both origin by descent and birth. —(I. B.)

[2] See Appendix on this figure. The substitution of an appellative term of designation, instead of a proper name.—ED.

VOL. I.   F

and conclusions, the other writings everywhere.—See Notes on Rom. iii. 24 and Gal. ii. 16. Comp. ver. 16 below.—υἱοῦ Δαυίδ,[1] υἱοῦ 'Αβραάμ, *the Son of David, the Son of Abraham*) Our Lord is called the Son of David and the Son of Abraham, because He was promised to both. Abraham was the first, David the last of men to whom that promise was made; whence He is called the Son of David, as though David had been His immediate progenitor.—(See Rhenferd[2] Opera Philologica, p. 715.) Both of these patriarchs received the announcement with faith and joy (See John viii. 56; and Matt. xxii. 43). Each of those mentioned in the following list was acquainted with the names of those who preceded, but not of those who came after him. Oh, with what delight would they have read this genealogy, in which we take so little interest! An allusion is here made by anticipation to the three *Fourteens* (afterwards mentioned in the 17th verse), of which the first is distinguished by the name of Abraham, the second by that of David, whilst the third, commencing, not like the others with a proper name, but with the Babylonian Captivity, is crowned with the name of Jesus Christ Himself: for the first and the second Fourteen contain the promise, the third its fulfilment. The narration, however, in the first verse goes backward from Christ to David, from David to Abraham. And so much the more conveniently is Abraham put here in the second place, because he comes on the scene immediately again in the following verse. St Mark, however, in the opening of his Gospel, calls Jesus *the Son*, not of *David*, but of *GOD*, because he begins his narration with the baptism of John, by whom our Lord was pointed out as the Son of God. Thus each of these evangelists declares the scope of his work in the title. The former part of this verse contains the sum of the New Testament—the latter part, the recapitulation of the Old.

[1] E. M. Δαβίδ.—This variation occurs all through, and will not therefore be noticed again. Bengel alway writes Δαυίδ.—The Exemplar Millianum always has Δαβίδ.—Tregelles and Tischendorf prefer Δαυίδ.—Lachmann, Δαυείδ.—Wordsworth also writes the word Δαυίδ.—(I. B.)

[2] James Rhenferd, a celebrated Oriental scholar, born at Mulheim, in Westphalia, 1654. Educated at the College of Meurs, in the Duchy of Cleves. Rector of the Latin College in Francker, 1658; removed to Amsterdam 1680. Professor of Oriental languages at Francker, 1683. Died 1712.—(I. B.)

2. 'Αβραάμ, *Abraham*) St Matthew, in enumerating our Lord's ancestors, adopts the order of *descent* (though he employs that of ascent in ver. 1), and begins also from Abraham, instead of Adam, not however to the exclusion of the Gentiles (cf. xxviii. 19), since in Abraham all nations are made blessed.—καὶ τοὺς ἀδελφοὺς αὐτοῦ, *and his brethren*) These words are not added in the case of Abraham, Isaac, or Jacob, though they also had brethren, but only in that of Judah: for the promises were restricted to the family of Israel.

3. καὶ τὸν Ζαρά, *and Zara*) the twin-brother of Pharez.—ἐκ τῆς Θάμαρ, *of Thamar*) St Matthew, in the course of his genealogy, makes mention of women who were joined to the race of Abraham by any peculiar circumstance. Thamar ought to have become the wife of Shelah (see Gen. xxxviii. 11, 26), and Judah became by her the father of Pharez and Zara: Rahab, though a Canaanitess, became the wife of Salmon: Ruth was a Moabitess, yet Boaz married her. The wife of Uriah became the wife of David.

4. Ναασσών, *Naasson*) Contemporary with Moses. The silence regarding Moses preserved throughout this pedigree is remarkable.

5. τὸν Βοὸζ ἐκ τῆς 'Ραχάβ, *Boaz of Rahab*) Some think that the immediate ancestors of Boaz have been passed over; but it stands thus also in Ruth iv. 21: nor can the first *Fourteen*, the standard of the two others, admit of an hiatus. More correct is their opinion, who maintain that, in such a length of time, some of the ancestors mentioned lived to a great age. The definite article, τῆς, placed before the proper name 'Ραχάβ, shows that Rahab of Jericho is here meant; nor does the orthography of the word 'Ραχάβ interfere with this hypothesis: for both 'Ραάβ (Raab or Rahab) and 'Ραχάβ (Rachab) are written for רחב. See Hiller's[1] Onomasticon Sacrum, p. 695. The Rahab of Jericho was very young when she hid the spies (Josh. vi. 23): she outlived, however, Joshua and the elders (Ibid. xxiv. 29, 30); and her marriage with Salmon must have taken place still later, as it is not mentioned in that book, though

---

[1] Matthew Hiller, a Lutheran divine and learned Orientalist, born at Stuttgard, 1646. Successively Professor at various universities with great reputation. Died 1725.—(I. B.)

it is recorded that she dwelt in Israel (See Josh. vi. 25). In Ruth i. 1, the earliest times of the Judges seem to be meant, so that the verb שָׁפַט (which might otherwise be supposed redundant) may have an inceptive[1] force, as in like manner מָלַךְ[2] often signifies *he took the kingdom*, or *began to reign*: and Naomi must have gone into Moab, before the Moabite domination mentioned in Judges iii. 12. Rahab might therefore have been, as she actually was, the mother of Boaz. He did not marry Ruth till he was far advanced in life (see Ruth iii. 10); and their grandson, Jesse, was very old (see 1 Sam. xvii. 12, 14), when he became the father of David.—Cf. concerning Jehoiada, 2 Chron. xxiv. 15.

6. Δαυίδ δὲ ὁ βασιλεὺς, *but David the King*) The appellation ὁ βασιλεὺς (*the King*), has been omitted by some early editors, but wrongly.[3] The kingship of David is twice mentioned here, as is the Babylonian captivity afterwards. The same title is understood, though not expressed, after the names of Solomon and his successors, as far as ver. 11. David is, however, called especially *the King*, not only because he is the first king mentioned in this pedigree, but also because his throne is promised to the Messiah. —See Luke i. 32.

7. ἐγέννησε, *begat*) Bad men, even though they are useless to themselves in their lifetime, do not exist in vain; since by their means the elect even are brought into the world.

8. Ἰωράμ δὲ ἐγέννησε τὸν Ὀζίαν, *but Joram begat Josiah*) Ahaziah (who is the same as the Joahaz of 2 Chron. xxi. 17, and xxii. 1), Joash, and Amaziah (mentioned in 1 Chron. iii. 11, 12), are here passed over: so that the word ἐγέννησε (*begat*) must be understood *mediately*[4] instead of immediately: as frequently happens with the word υἱός (*son*), as in the first

---

[1] Bengel means, that שָׁפְטוּ הַשֹּׁפְטִים (translated in the E. V. *the Judges ruled*, marg. *judged*) ought to be rendered *the Judges began to judge*, so as to indicate with greater exactness the date of the event, at the commencement of the era of the Judges.—(I. B.)

[2] מָלַךְ יִמְלֹךְ.—(1) *to reign, to be king*; (2) *to become king*, 2 Sam. xv. 10, xvi. 8; 1 Kings xiv. 2.—GESENIUS.—(I. B.)

[3] B, the best MSS. of Vulg., the Memph. and Theb. and Syr. Versions omit ὁ βασιλεὺς. But Δac agree with Rec. Text and Beng. in retaining the words.—ED.

[4] *i.e.*, There being mediate or intervening persons.—ED

verse of this chapter, where our Lord is called the Son of
David, who was His remote ancestor. In like manner Joram is
here said to have begotten Josiah, who was his great-grandson,
—that is to say, he was his progenitor. Thus, by referring to
1 Chron. vi. 7, 8, 9, we find, that six generations are left out in
Ezra vii. 3, between Azariah and Meraioth. St Matthew
omitted the three kings in question, not because he was ignorant
of their having existed (since the whole context proves his
familiar acquaintance with his subject), but because they were
well known to all: nor did he do so with any fraudulent intention, since, by increasing the number of generations, he would
have confirmed the notion that the Messiah must have already
appeared. Nor did he omit them on account of their impiety,
for he has mentioned other impious men, as *e.g.* Jechonias, and
him with especial consideration, and he has passed over several
pious ones. But, as in describing roads and ways, it is necessary to be especially careful with regard to those points where
they branch off in different directions, whereas a straight road
may be found without any such direction, so does St Matthew
in this genealogy point out with particular care those who have
had *brothers*, and who, in contradistinction to them, have propagated the stem of the Messiah. He has indeed carried this so
far that, having a reason[1] for not naming Jehoiakim, he has
assigned his *brothers* to his only son; whilst he has passed over,
without inconvenience, Joash, who was the only link[2] in his
generation, together with his father and son. Furthermore, as
in geography the distances of places from each other are, without any violence to truth, described sometimes by longer, sometimes by shorter stages,—so is it with the successive steps of
generations in a pedigree; nor is the practice of Hebrew gene-
alogists an exception to the general custom in this matter. The
writers of the New Testament are accustomed also rather to
imply than assert circumstances already well known on the
authority of the Old Testament, and not liable to be mistaken,
employing a brevity as congenial to the ardour of the Spirit, as

[1] See Jer. xxii. 30.—(I. B.)

[2] In the original, "qui unica sui temporis scintilla fuerat."—(I. B.)
"The only spark in his generation to prevent the line being extinguished."
—Ed.

desirable on other grounds.—See Gnomon on Acts vii. 16. Oziah was previously called Azariah, but by the omission of one Hebrew letter (י, R) his name becomes Oziah.

11. Ἰωσίας δὲ ἐγέννησε τὸν Ἰεχονίαν, *But Josiah begat Jechoniah*) Many transcribers both in ancient and in modern times, and those principally Greeks, have inserted *Jehoiachim* here, because, firstly, the Old Testament had that name in this situation, and secondly, the number of fourteen generations, from David to the Babylonian captivity, given by St Matthew, seemed to require the insertion. *Jehoiachim*, however, must not be inserted: for history would not suffer Jehoiachim to be put without his brothers, and brothers to be *thus* given to *Jechoniah*, who had none. Some have sought for *Jehoiachim* in St Matthew's first mention of Jechoniah; Jerome[1] has done so especially, when answering Porphyry's[2] objections to this verse on the ground of the hiatus. No transformation, however, will produce Jechoniah (in the LXX. Ἰεχονίας) from the Hebrew יהויקים, the Ἰωακείμ (Joakim) of the LXX., so as to make them one and the same name: nor have we any more reason for supposing that Jehoiachim and Jechoniah are intended by the repetition of the former, than that two separate individuals are intended by the repetition of Isaac's name; and so on with the other names in the genealogy. The same Jechoniah is twice introduced under his own name: he was descended from Josiah through Jehoiachim, whose name is omitted. St Matthew calls Jechoniah's uncles his *brothers* (cf. Gen. xiii. 8), and that with great felicity; for *Zedekiah* came to the throne after the commencement of the captivity, to the exclusion of the sons of Jechoniah, whom he succeeded, and who, though his nephew, was born eight years before him. The brothers, therefore, of Jehoiachim, of whom Zedekiah was chief,

---

[1] One of the most celebrated Fathers of the Christian Church, born of Christian parents at Stridon, on the borders of Pannonia and Dalmatia, in the year 331. Educated at Rome under the best masters. After travelling through France, Italy, and the East, he adopted the monastic life in Syria in his 31st year. He died A.D. 422.—(I. B.)

[2] A Platonic philosopher, born at Tyre, A.D. 223. Studied under Longinus and Plotinus. He was a man of great talent and learning, and one of the most able opponents of Christianity. He died in the reign of Diocletian.—(I. B.)

who is expressly called the *brother* in 2 Chron. xxxvi. 10, and 2 Kings xxiv. 17, instead of the *uncle* of Jechoniah, are appropriately mentioned *after* Jechoniah as his brothers.[1]—ἐπὶ τῆς μετοικεσίας, *about the time of the migration*[2]) The preposition ἐπί, which is contrasted with μετὰ (*after*) in the twelfth verse, is also employed sometimes to denote the immediate sequence of that, during or about the time of which something else takes place.— See Gnomon on Mark ii. 26. The Hebrew præfix ב has the same force in Gen. x. 25. The birth of *Jechoniah* was followed immediately by the *removal to Babylon,*—which is called by the LXX. both ἀποικεσία (*the emigration*), and μετοικεσία (*the migration, immigration, or sojourning*); the former with reference to Palestine, the latter with reference to Babylon.—Βαβυλῶνος, *of Babylon*) *i.e. to,* or *into* Babylon. In like manner ὁδὸς Αἰγύπτου, in Jer. ii. 18, signifies *the way into Egypt*.

12. μετὰ, *after*) sc. after he had migrated to Babylon.—Σαλαθιὴλ δὲ ἐγέννησε τὸν Ζοροβάβελ, *but Salathiel begat Zorobabel*) *i.e.,* was the progenitor of; Pedaiah being the son of the former, and father of the latter. St Luke (iii. 27) mentions another Salathiel and Zorobabel, father and son, who must have lived about the same time with these.[3]

13. Ἐγέννησε τὸν Ἀβιούδ, *begat Abiud*) This is the same as Hodaiah,[4] who was in like manner descended from Zorobabel, through several intervening ancestors (see 1 Chron. iii. 19, 24), as *Hiller* explains in his Syntagmata, pp. 361, sqq., where he shows, that the Jews acknowledged the genealogy in the said passage of Chronicles to be that of the Messiah: nor, indeed, was it necessary that any other genealogy should have been carried further down there than that of the Messiah. There can, therefore, be no doubt but that the passage in question was

---

[1] *Irenæus*, 218, writes, "Ante hunc *Joachim* (Joseph enim Joachim et Jechoniæ filius ostenditur, quemadmodum et Matthæus generationem ejus exponit)." So M Cod. Reg. Paris of 9th century, and U Cod. Venetus of same date, in opposition to the ancient authorities, insert Ἰωακείμ.—ED.

[2] sc. to Babylon.—(I. B.)

[3] *D. Crusius explains the causes of this fact l. c. p.* 369, 370, *showing that the Zorobabel of Luke was a prince of Juda, and the associate* (σύζυγον) *of Joshua in the restoration, whereas the Zorobabel of Matthew was a private individual.*—E. B.

[4] Or *Hodajah*, as in Bengel.

particularly well known to the Jews; and there was, consequently, the less need that St Matthew should repeat it *in extenso*. In this generation, then, concludes the scripture of the Old Testament. The remainder of the genealogy was supplied by St Matthew from trustworthy documents of a later date, and, no doubt, of a public character.

16. Τὸν ἄνδρα Μαρίας, *the husband of Mary*) This turn of the genealogical line is evidently singular;[1] and in this place, therefore, I must advance and substantiate several important assertions.

I. *Messias or Christ is the Son of David.*
This is admitted by all.—See Matt. xxii. 42, and Acts ii. 30.

II. *Even in their genealogies both Matthew and Luke teach that Jesus is the Christ.*
This is clear from Matt. i. 16, and Luke iii. 22.

III. *At the time when Matthew and Luke wrote the descent of Jesus from David had been placed beyond doubt.*
Both Matthew and Luke wrote before the destruction of the Temple of Jerusalem, when the full genealogy of the house of David, preserved in the public records, was easily accessible to all: and our Lord's adversaries did not ever make any objection, when Jesus was so frequently hailed as *the Son of David*.

IV. *The genealogy in St Matthew from Abraham, and that in St Luke from the creation of man, to Joseph the husband of Mary, is deduced, not through mothers but fathers, and those natural fathers.*
This is evident in the case of all those ancestors, whose names St Matthew and St Luke repeat from the Old Testament. Wherefore it is not said, whether Ruth had been the wife of Mahlon or Chilion; but Obed is simply said to be the son of his real father Boaz by Ruth [though his legal father was Mahlon. —See Ruth iv. 10, etc.] From Abraham to David the same ancestors are evidently mentioned by both Matthew and Luke: so that there can be no doubt but that both Evangelists intend not mothers but fathers, and those, fathers by nature, from David to Joseph. Thus, in the books of Kings and Chronicles, as often soever as the *mother* of a king is mentioned alone, it is a sign that he whom her son is said to have immediately succeeded was his natural father.

[1] 'Singularis,' *i.e., unique.*—(I. B.)

V. *The genealogy in Matthew from Solomon, and that in Luke from Nathan, is brought down to Joseph, not with the same, but with a different view* [respectu, *relation, regard.*]

This is clear from the preceding section.

VI. *Jesus Christ was the Son of Mary, but not of her husband Joseph.*

This is evident from Matt. i. 16.

VII. *It was necessary that the genealogy of Mary should be drawn out.*

Without the genealogy of Mary, the descent of Jesus from David could not be proved, as follows from what has just been said.

VIII. *Joseph was for some time reputed to be the father of the Lord Jesus.*

The mystery of the Redeemer's birth from a virgin was not made known at once, but by degrees; and, in the meanwhile, the honourable title of marriage was required as a veil for that mystery. Jesus, therefore, was believed to be the Son of Joseph, for instance, after His baptism, by Philip (John i. 45); in the time of His public preaching, by the inhabitants of Nazareth (Luke iv. 22; Matt. xiii. 55), and only a year before His Passion by the Jews (John vi. 42). Many still clung to this opinion even after our Lord's Ascension, and up to the time, therefore, when, a few years subsequently to that event, St Matthew wrote his gospel.

IX. *It was therefore necessary that the genealogy of Joseph also should in the meanwhile exist.*

It was necessary that all those who believed Jesus to be the Son of Joseph, should be convinced that Joseph was descended from David. Otherwise they could not have acknowledged Jesus to be the Son of David, and consequently could not acknowledge Him to be the Christ. When therefore the angel first appeared to Joseph, and commanded him to take unto him his wife, he called him (ver. 20) the *son of David:* because, forsooth, the Son of Mary would for a time have to bear that name as if derived from Joseph. In like manner, not only was Jesus in truth the first-born (Luke ii. 7, 23) of His mother, but it behoved also that He should be reputed to be the first-born of Joseph· those, therefore, who are called the *brethren* of Jesus, were His first cousins, not His half-brothers. It is needless to attempt, as some have done, to prove the consanguinity of Joseph and Mary from their marriage: for even if David be their nearest common ancestor, St Matthew's object is attained. St Matthew then has traced the genealogy of Joseph, but still so as to do no violence to truth: for he does not say that Jesus is the Son of Joseph, but he does say that He was the Son of Mary; and in this very sixteenth verse he intimates, that this genealogy of Joseph, which had its use for a time, would afterwards become obsolete. Mary's descent from David was equally well known at that time, as appears from St Luke.

X. *Either Matthew gives the genealogy of Mary, and Luke that of Joseph; or Matthew that of Joseph, and Luke that of Mary.*

This clearly follows from the preceding sections.

XI. *The genealogy in Matthew is that of Joseph; in Luke, that of Mary.*

St Matthew traces the line of descent from Abraham to Jacob: he expressly states that Jacob *begat* Joseph, and expressly calls Joseph the husband of Mary. Joseph therefore is regarded throughout this genealogy as the descendant of those who are enumerated, not on Mary's account, but on his own. Matthew, indeed, expressly contradistinguishes Joseph from Mary as the son of Jacob; but in St Luke, by a less strict mode of expression, *Heli* (Luke iii. 23) is simply placed after *Joseph*. Since, then, Joseph is described in Matthew as *actually* the son of Jacob, St Luke cannot mean to represent him as *actually* the son of Heli. The only alternative which remains, therefore, is to conclude that he is the son of Heli, not in his own person, but by virtue of another, and that other his wife. Mary, then, is the daughter of Heli. The Jewish writers mention a certain מרים בת עלי, *Mary, the daughter of Heli*, whom they describe as suffering extreme torments in the infernal regions.—See Lightfoot[1] on Luke iii. 23, and Wolfius[2] on Matt. i. 20. St Luke

---

[1] John Lightfoot, D.D. Born in Staffordshire, 1602. Educated at Christ Church, Cambridge. One of the Assembly of Divines during the Commonwealth. In 1648 was made Master of Catherine Hall, Cambridge, and served the office of Vice-Chancellor: and died in 1675. He excelled in rabbinical learning.—(I. B.)

[2] John Christopher Wolfius, a learned Lutheran divine, pastor and Pro-

does not, however, *name* Mary in his genealogy; for it would have sounded ill, especially to Jewish ears, had he written " Jesus was the Son of Mary, the daughter of Heli, the son of Matthat," etc.—on which account he names the husband of Mary, but that in such a manner that all may be able to understand (from the whole of his first and second chapters), that the *name* of Mary's husband stands for that of Mary herself.

XII. *That in St Luke is the primary, that in St Matthew the secondary genealogy.*

When a genealogy is traced through female as well as male ancestors, any descent may be deduced in many ways from one root; whereas a pedigree, traced simply from father to son, must of necessity consist only of a single line. In the genealogy, however, of Jesus Christ, Mary, His mother, is reckoned with His male ancestors, by a claim of incomparable precedence. In an ordinary pedigree ancestors are far more important than ancestresses. Mary, however, enters this genealogy with a peculiar and unrivalled claim, above that of every ancestor whatever of the whole human race; for whatever Jesus derived from the stock of man—of Abraham, or of David—that He derived *entirely* from His mother. This is the One Seed of *Woman* without *Man*. Other children owe their birth *partly* to their father, *partly* to their mother. The genealogy of Mary, therefore, which is given in St Luke, is the primary one. Nor can that of Joseph, in St Matthew, be considered otherwise than secondary, and merely employed for the time, until all should become fully convinced, that Jesus was the Son of Mary, but *not* of Joseph. St Matthew mentions Jechoniah, although he is passed by in the primary genealogy.—See Jer. xxii. 30; and cf. Luke i. 32, 33.

XIII. *Whatever difficulty yet remains regarding this whole matter, so far from weakening, should even confirm our faith.*

The stock of David had, in the time of Jesus of Nazareth, dwindled down to so small a number (see Rev. xxii. 16), that on this ground also the appellation " *Son of David*" was used by

fessor of Oriental Languages at Hamburgh. Born 1683. Died 1739. Author of Bibliotheca Hebræa, Curæ Philologicæ et Criticæ in Novum Testamentum.—(I. B.)

Antonomasia[1] for " The Messiah." And that family consisted so exclusively of Jesus and His relatives, that any one who knew Him to belong to it could not fail, even without the light of faith, to acknowledge Him as the Messiah, since the period foretold by the prophets for His manifestation had already arrived, and none of our Lord's relations could be compared with Himself. Our Lord's descent, therefore, from the race of David, as well as His birth at Bethlehem, were less publicly known; nay, rather He was in some degree veiled, as it were, by the name of *Nazarene*, that faith might not lose its price.[2]—See John vii. 27, 41, 42. And thus men, having been first induced on other grounds to believe that Jesus was the Messiah, concluded, on the same grounds, that He must be the Son of David.—See Matt. xii. 23. The necessary public documents, however, were in existence, whence it came to pass, that the chief priests, though employing every means against our Lord, never questioned His descent from David. Nay, even the Romans received much information concerning the Davidical descent of Jesus.—See Luke ii. 4. Of old the facility with which His descent could be traced, showed Jesus to be the Son of David: now the very difficulty of so doing (caused as it is by the destruction of Jerusalem, and all the public records which it contained), affords a proof, against the Jews at least, that the Messiah must long since have come. Should they acknowledge any other as the Messiah, they must ascertain his descent from David in precisely the same manner that we do that of Jesus of Nazareth. As light, however, advanced, the aspect of the question has not a little changed. Jesus was called, on various occasions, " *The Son of David*," by the multitude (ch. xii. 23, xxi. 9), by children (xxi. 15), by the blind men (ix. 27, xx. 30), by the woman of Canaan (xv. 22): but He never declared to His disciples that He was the Son of David, and they, in their professions of faith, called Him, not " The Son of David," but " The Son of God." He invited, also, those who called Him the Son of David, to advance further.—

---

[1] The substitution of an appellative designation for a proper name.—ED. See explanation of technical terms in Appendix.—(I. B.)

[2] " *Ut pretium fidei maneret.*" Faith was allowed to remain attended with seeming difficulties, at the cost of surmounting which, men were appointed to attain to it.—ED.

See xxii. 42, 43, and ix. 28. In the first instance our Lord's descent from David was rather a ground of faith, afterwards it became rather an obstacle to faith. No difficulty can now be a hinderance to them that believe.—See 2 Cor. v. 16. Jesus is *the root and the offspring of David, and the bright and morning star*.[1]

XIV. *Matthew and Luke combine ulterior objects and advantages with the genealogy.*

If the Evangelists had merely wished to show that Mary and also Joseph were descended from David, it would have been sufficient for their purpose, had they, taking the genealogies as they exist in the Old Testament for granted, commenced at the point where these conclude, namely, with Zorobabel, or at any rate with David himself, and traced the line through Nathan or Solomon down to Jesus Christ. St Matthew, however, begins further off, viz. with Abraham, and descends through David and Solomon. St Luke, on the other hand, ascends to Nathan and David, and thence beyond Abraham to the first origin of the human race. Each of them, therefore, must have had at the same time a further object in view.

St Luke, as is evident at first sight, makes a full recapitulation[2] and summary of the lineage of the whole human race, and exhibits with that lineage the Saviour's consanguinity to all Gentiles, as well as Jews: St Matthew, writing to the Hebrews, begins with Abraham, thus reminding them of the promise which had been made to that Patriarch. Again, St Luke simply enumerates the whole series, through more than seventy steps, without addition or comment: whereas St Matthew, besides several remarkable observations which he introduces in particular cases concerning the wives and brothers of those whom he mentions, and the Babylonian Captivity, divides the whole series into three periods; and, as we shall presently consider, enumerates in each of these periods fourteen generations. And hence, also, we perceive the convenience of the *descent* in Matthew, and the *ascent* in Luke: for in this manner the former was enabled more conveniently to introduce those observations and divisions; the latter, to avoid the stricter word ἐγέννησε, *begat*, and

[1] Rev. xxii. 16.—(I. B.)

[2] See explanation of technical terms in voc. ANAKEPHALAEOSIS. The word is used by Quintilian.—(I. B.)

take advantage of the formula ὡς ἐνομίζετο, *as was supposed*, and in an exquisite manner to conclude the whole series with God.—ὁ λεγόμενος Χριστός, *who is called Christ*) St Matthew is dealing with the Jewish reader, who is to be convinced that *Jesus is the Christ*, by such means as His genealogy. And accordingly he here and there [throughout his Gospel] expresses and establishes what the other Evangelists take for granted. The force of the name *Christ* recalls especially the promise given to *David* concerning the *Kingdom* of the Messiah : and the force of the name *Jesus* recalls especially the promise given to Abraham concerning the *Blessing*.[1]

17. Πᾶσαι οὖν αἱ γενεαὶ, κ.τ.λ., *So all the generations*, etc.) An important summing up (*ingens symperasma*),[2] the force of which we exhibit by the following positions.

I. *St Matthew introduced this clause with the most deliberate design.*

The Messiah was really descended from David through Nathan: the genealogy, however, in Matthew, descends from David through Solomon to Joseph. Therefore, those who already knew that Jesus was not the Son of Joseph, paid little heed to Joseph's pedigree ; St Matthew, therefore, traces this genealogy in such a manner as to be serviceable to all who either believed that Jesus was the Son of Mary, but not of Joseph, or thought that He was the Son of Joseph also, and so to lead both classes to *Christ, the Son of David*.

II. *St Matthew makes three fourteens.* We exhibit them in the following table :

1. Abraham.	David.	Jechoniah.
2. Isaac.	Solomon.	Salathiel.
3. Jacob.	Rehoboam.	Zorobabel.
4. Judah.	Abijam.	Abiud.

[1] The Greek Χριστός, and the Hebrew משיח, means Anointed, *i.e.*, King. Jesus is the proper name of our Lord: [the] *Christ* is a surname [cognomen], implying His office. The ancients were expecting the Christ, before the birth of Jesus : when Jesus had been born, a demonstrative proof was given that this very Jesus is the Christ ; and when that demonstration of His being the Christ was subsequently made more widely known, the appellation, *Jesus Christ*, became the prevalent one.—*Vers. Germ.*

[2] See Appendix on the figure *Symperasma*.—E.D.

5. Pharez.	Asa.	Eliakim.
6. Hezrom.	Jehoshaphat.	Azor.
7. Aram.	Jehoram.	Sadoc.
8. Aminadab.	Ahaziah.	Achin.
9. Naasson.	Jotham.	Eliud.
10. Salmon.	Ahaz.	Eleazar.
11. Boaz.	Hezekiah.	Matthan.
12. Obed.	Manasseh.	Jacob.
13. Jesse.	Amon.	Joseph.
14. David.	Josiah.	JESUS, who is called CHRIST.

III. *St Matthew, therefore, lays down three periods.*

St Luke enumerates every step, ascending even to GOD. Yet, so far from counting the steps in each period, he does not divide his genealogy into periods at all: St Matthew, however, distinguishes three periods,—the first from Abraham to David, the second from David to the captivity, the third from the captivity to Christ; and in each of these periods, as we shall presently see, he mentions fourteen steps.

IV. *St Matthew reduces each period to fourteen generations.*

Matthew does not mention all the ancestors of Joseph who occur in the direct line, and yet he reduces those whom he does mention to a set number. Some seek here a division into *sevens*; the Evangelist, however, does not mention sevens, but fourteens. Again, he does not bring these fourteens together into a sum total, for he does not say, that they amount in all to 40, 41, or 42: nor is it our business to do so. As in the reigns of the kings of Israel, the last year of the preceding is frequently reckoned as the first of the succeeding sovereign, so must we admit that St Matthew has acted on the same principle, since the fact itself leaves no doubt of the case. Thus David undoubtedly is both the last of the first fourteen, and the first of the second fourteen. He is reckoned in the first; for it would otherwise comprise only thirteen generations. He is reckoned in the second, because as the first begins *inclusively* from Abraham, and the third *inclusively* from Jechoniah, so must the second begin *inclusively* from David. Jechoniah, however, is not reckoned in the same manner as the last of the second fourteen, because the fourteen generations, which commence with David, are counted not to Jechoniah, but to the Babylonian captivity. Vallesius[1] (p. 454) thinks Jechoniah, as it were, a double person; you might assert that with greater correctness of David.

V. *In each case, his object was to prove that Jesus was truly called, and was, the Christ.*

He proceeds in a marked manner from the name *Jesus* to the surname *Christ*, in verses 16, 17, 18; and he marks the *dissimilarity* in the character of the periods, and the *equality* in the number of the generations. That dissimilarity, and that equality, whether taken apart or together, tend to the one object of proving *Jesus* to be the *Christ*, as we shall immediately perceive.

VI. *The three periods are dissimilar to each other.*

If St Matthew had merely intended to compose a genealogy, he might have omitted all this *Congeries*[2] of names, or at any rate, have confined himself to the mention of proper names, and said, " From Abraham to David," " from David to Jechoniah," " from Jechoniah to Jesus." Instead of so doing, however, after the other matters preceding, he says, " *to the Captivity;*" and again, " *From the Captivity* to Christ." The land-mark, limit, standing-point, therefore, of the first period is David, of the second the Captivity, of the third Christ. The first period, then, is that of the Patriarchs; the second, that of the Kings; the third, for the most part, of private individuals.

VII. *This dissimilarity strikingly proves that Jesus is the Christ.*

The different heads under which St Matthew reduces the three periods, show, that the time at which *Jesus* was born, was the time appointed for the birth of the Christ, and that Jesus Himself was the Christ. The first and the second *fourteen* have an illustrious commencement; the third has one, as it were, blind and nameless. Hence is clearly deduced, and brilliantly shines forth, the end and goal of the third, and all the periods, namely, *the* CHRIST. The first period is that of promise, for in it Abraham stands first, and David last, to each of whom the

---

[1] Vallesius, or Vallès, Francis, a native of Spain, physician to Philip II. He wrote a treatise, " De iis quæ scripta sunt physice in libris sacris, sive de sacrâ philosophiâ."—(I. B.)

[2] See Appendix on this figure. The enumeration of the parts of a Whole.—ED.

promise was given; the second is that of adumbration, by means of the Davidical sovereignty, and the fact that it is considerably shorter than either of the others, furnishes a reasonable ground for expecting that the kingdom of David, as fulfilled in Christ (see Luke i. 32), will be far more glorious hereafter, and more lasting. The third period is that of expectation. The most distinguished personages in the first period are Abraham and David, who stand respectively first and last in it. The most distinguished personage in the second period is the same David, who is now found standing first. The first name which occurs in the third period is that of Jechoniah, so called also in 1 Chron. iii. 17, who was *bound* with chains, to whom no heir was promised of his throne; nay, further, against whom, as well as against his uncle and father, all other woes were denounced (Jer. xxii. 11, 18, 25), so that, though he was not actually without offspring, yet, as a warning to posterity, he should be written ערירי, *childless* (Jer. xxii. 28, 30), without, that is to say, an heir to his throne; and it was with reference to these *three* kings that the earth was invoked *thrice*, "O earth, earth, earth, hear the word of the Lord" (*Ibid.* ver. 29). Hence it arises that, when stating the boundary between the second and third *fourteens*, St Matthew does not name Jechoniah; but, instead of so doing, mentions the Babylonian Captivity. Much additional weight accrues to this argument from the words of Jeremiah; for in the time of Moses, midway between Abraham and David, a covenant was made with the people of Israel, which was abrogated about the time of the captivity of Jechoniah.—See Jer. xxix. 1, xxxi. 31; Heb. viii. 8, 13. In the times of Abraham and David, Christ was promised; after the time of David, the Davidical sovereignty, which was overthrown at the Babylonian Captivity, did not last so long as the preceding period, that, namely, between Abraham and David. Then, indeed, it was that a new covenant was promised, the author and surety whereof should be Christ. The state, therefore, of the Jewish nation after the Captivity, could not but tend to, and end in *the Christ*. In the Psalms, and other predictions delivered during the time of the Kings, the sacred writers, as the march of prophecy moved onward, generally *compared* the present with the future; whereas, after the Babylonian Captivity, they *contrasted* the one with the other, whilst contemplating the future as coming nearer and nearer their own times.¹

VIII. *St Matthew makes the three periods equal with each other.*
This is evident from his repeating the number FOURTEEN three times with the utmost deliberation.—See Section IV.

IX. *He makes up both the third and the second Fourteens by omitting several links in the pedigree: in the first, however, he makes no such omission.*

In the second period, he, after Jehoram, passes over Ahaziah, Joash, and Amaziah, and, after Josiah, he leaves out Jehoiakim: in the third period, after Salathiel, he omits Pedaiah. Nor, indeed, was Zorobabel the immediate father of Abihud; for, whereas his sons are *Mesullam* and *Hananias,* each of these two names differs from *Abihud.* Hiller enumerates *nine* links omitted after Zorobabel, and shows that Hodaiah and Abihud are the same individual. The descendants of David from Solomon to Hodaiah are enumerated in 1 Chron. iii. 5, 10–24. Now, since neither the second nor the third *Fourteen* consist in themselves of exactly fourteen generations, the first must of necessity have that number: for otherwise the number Fourteen, by which the three periods are arranged and represented as equal, would be without any foundation in fact, and the number *fifteen,* or some greater still, would have to be substituted for it. Fourteen generations are clearly enumerated in the Old Testament from Abraham to David.—See 1 Chron. i. 34, ii. 1, 4–15. Whence Rabbi Bechai² says, that King David was the fourteenth from Abraham, according to the number of the letters of his name דוד, which make fourteen.³ In early ages men generally became fathers at a more advanced period of life, than they did in later times. Hence it is that the first *Fourteen* stands on its own foundation, the second is produced by a less, the third by a greater omission. And though some generations, with

---

¹ The original runs thus: "In psalmis et in aliis prophetiis regum tempore latis sermo fere per *comparationem* status præsentis et futuri incedebat: sed post migrationem Babylonis potius per *oppositionem* incedit, futura prospiciens subinde propius."—(I. B.)

² Rabbi Bechai. There were two Rabbis of the name of Bechai; one flourished about 1100, the other about 1290; both were natives of Spain.—see Dr. Rossi.—(I. B.)

³ Sc. ד = 4, ו = 6, ד = 4: therefore ד + ו + ד = 14.—(I. B.)

which we are already acquainted from the Old Testament, are in St Matthew passed over and left to be understood, the Evangelist has not omitted in the New Testament a single generation, which was subsequent to those that are mentioned in the Old: and in the Old Testament, not a single generation is omitted. The first *Fourteen*, therefore, is so in fact, the second and third are so in form.

X. *The number of generations which St Matthew omits, accords with the numbers which both he and St Luke mention.*

Between Jehoram and Abihud, St Matthew omits in all *fourteen generations*, see Sect IX.; and though he only mentions three *Fourteens* for the sake of the number of the periods from Abraham to Christ, he nevertheless implies, in accordance with his system, that there were really four.[1] In this way Matthew has by implication, from Abraham to the *birth* of Christ, fifty-five generations. St Luke expressly enumerates fifty-six generations to the time when Jesus was *thirty years* of age. They therefore agree.

XI. *The equality of the Fourteens is not fulfilled in the actual number* XIV., *by which they are distinguished.*

The Talmudists are fond of reducing the proximate numbers of different things to actual equality. Lightfoot has collected examples of this in illustration of the present passage, and they afford a satisfactory reply to the Jews, when they sneer at the *Fourteens* of St Matthew. He defends, however, somewhat too slackly the actual truth of the *Fourteens*. What James Rhenford adduces on this passage is far more to the purpose, viz., that the fifteen generations before Solomon, and the fifteen after him, were so enumerated by the Jews, as to correspond with the days of the increasing [waxing] and waning moon. But this

---

[1] The words in the original are, "Omnino XIV. *generationis* inter *Joram* et *Abihud* prætermittit Matthæus, § ix. Concinneque ab Abraham ad Christum tessaradecadas, tribus pro numero periodorum expressis, *quatuor* tamen innuit." The meaning is, that though St Matthew mentions thrice fourteen as the number of generations, he means that there were three *periods* of fourteen generations, and implies, that to make up the number of *actual* generations, another *Fourteen*, or fourteen generations more, must be added, q.d. the Fourteens of generations *expressly* mentioned by St Matthew are periods of *Fourteen ages;* to make up the sum total of actual generations, the number Fourteen, which is the normal regulator of the system, must be brought into play once more. Cf. § § Sqq.—(I. B.)

line of argument also is somewhat weak. St Matthew did not follow any technical[1] or masoretic[2] aid to the memory, or anything else of the kind. For what great purpose could it serve to retain in the memory the names and number of these ancestors, in preference to those which are omitted, or to adopt a method never before employed in the many genealogies and other important chapters of the Old Testament, for impressing them more fully on the minds of the Jews, who retained them in their memory accurately enough of themselves. But if he had wished to secure the integrity of this enumeration by a kind of Masora, it would have been better for the purpose to have made one sum of all the generations. In the last place, it would have ill suited the grave character of an apostle and evangelist, first to enumerate the generations as suited his own convenience, and then admire the equality of the *Fourteens*. The number *Fourteen* is not mentioned for its own sake, but for the sake of something else: it is not an end, but a means to obtain an end of greater importance.

XII. *The Equality here intended is Chronological.*

The apostles, looking back from the New to the Old Testament, have great regard to the *fulness of the times;* and the Jews are wont to describe the chief divisions of chronology by numbers of generations, as, for example, in Seder Olam.[3] St Matthew, therefore, skilfully propounds to the reader a Chronology under the garb of a Genealogy, combining both in this summary. The particle οὖν (*therefore*) has an inferential, and the article αἱ[4] (*the*) a relative force, indicating that those identical generations are intended, which have been just enumerated

---

[1] Mnemonicum—subsidium," *i.e.* anything resembling a *memoria technica.*—(I. B.)

[2] *Masora* means *tradition.* The Masoretes continued the labours of the Talmudists, whom they imitated in counting the words and letters of the Old Testament, finding imaginary mysteries in the very letters as well as words of Scripture; stating, also, such minute particulars as, which was the central word and letter of the whole, etc., etc. They have thus afforded us a guarantee for the accuracy of the Hebrew text, even though we have extant no Hebr. MS. older than the 12th century. The Masoretes flourished from the 6th to the 11th century.—ED.

[3] כדר עילם, a chronological work of high reputation amongst the Jews.—(I. B.)

[4] Definite Article, nominative plural. feminine.—(I. B.)

in the preceding verses. Each clause, moreover, of this verse has the word γενεαί (*generations*), both in the subject and predicate. In the subject it corresponds with the Hebrew תֹלְדֹת,[1] as in Genesis xxv. 12, 13; but in the predicate it corresponds with the Hebrew דּוֹר,[2] and has a chronological force, as is evident from the addition of the numeral *fourteen;*—Cf. Gen. xv. 16. In the Greek there is an instance of *Antanaclasis,*[3] one Greek word performing the part of two Hebrew ones: so that we may paraphrase the verse thus—*All those genealogical generations, therefore* (never mind the tautology), reduced for the sake of method to fourteen, *are* actually *fourteen chronological generations,*—from Abraham to David, etc. Such being the case, we perceive a sufficient cause for St Matthew's reducing to such numbers the genealogy, which would have been in itself much plainer without such an enumeration. Well does Chrysostom[4] say, that St Matthew enumerates generations, times, years, and lays them before the hearer as subjects for further investigation. —See Chrys. Hom. iv. on St Matthew. Let us, however, consider wherein the chronological equality consists. It does not consist in the number Fourteen which is employed in all the three periods for the sake of method; see Sect. XI.: nor in the *years of generations* in the *Fourteens* taken separately; for in the first *Fourteen* the generations are, for the most part, much longer than in the second and third: but it consists in the periods themselves. Consider the following scheme:—

[1] תֹּלֵדוֹת f. pl. (from the root יָלַד)—(1.) *generations, families, races.* GESENIUS.—(I. B.)

[2] דּוֹר m.—(1) *an age, generation* of men. GESENIUS.—(I. B.)

[3] See Appendix: the same word put twice, but in a twofold sense.—ED.

[4] JOHN CHRYSOSTOM was one of the most distinguished Fathers of the Ancient Church. To his wonderful eloquence he owed the name of *Chrysostom,* or *the golden-mouthed,* by which he is generally known; and his Commentaries on Scripture are replete with learning, piety, and practical power. He was born at Antioch, A.D. 354, of heathen parents. After studying rhetoric under Libanius, he embraced Christianity, and was ordained a reader in his native city. Having entered on the monastic life, he spent four years in the Desert; but, returning to Antioch, was ordained deacon in 381, and priest in 386; he became Bishop of Constantinople in 397. He died in exile in 407.—(I. B.)

ANNO MUNDI
- 1946 Birth of Abraham.
- 2016 The *Promise*, I. [characteristic of the first period].
- 2121 Death of Abraham.
- 2852 Birth of David.
- 2882 David becomes *King*, II. [characteristic of the second period].
- 2923 Death of David.
- 3327 Birth of Jechoniah.
- 3345 Jechoniah *Bound*, III. [characteristic of the third period].
- 3939 Birth of *Christ*.
- 3969 Baptism of Christ.

Now, in the first place, take the sum of the years in each *Fourteen*, and divide them by fourteen, which is the *number of generations*, and you will obtain the length of the single *generations* in each period: so that, in the first period, a generation will contain sixty-two, in the second, thirty-three, and in the third, forty-two years. The mean length will be about forty-six years: this, however, I will not press. Take, in the second place, which is more to the purpose, the nine hundred and twenty-three years from the promise given to Abraham till the birth of Christ, and divide them by *three*, which is the *number of the periods*: the *mean* length of the periods will not come up to that of the first, will exceed that of the second, but will agree admirably with that of the *third*. The third therefore stands as the primary period (to which the two others are subservient), between the excess of the first and the defect of the second, which mutually compensate each other. And the Evangelist has acted as geographers do, who, when wishing to express the distance between two cities, enumerate the stations interposed between them, in such a manner, that they add to one stage the paces which they take from another, and thus produce more conveniently the real total without any violence to truth. In fact, the Evangelist has done that, which every chronologer does, when he enumerates the years in his canons so as to absorb the excesses and defects of the months and days. In short, the years of the first and second period, taken together, are exactly double those of the third period. On the same principle, Moses has reduced the times of *Isaac, Jacob, Levi, Kohath, Amram, Moses,* which might have exhibited more or fewer genealogical generations in this or that family, to *four* chronological generations, or four centuries, those years only being omitted, in which *Levi, Kohath,* and *Amram* became parents. It is difficult to represent in words the design of Moses or Matthew; nor can the interpretation of such a matter appear, at first sight, otherwise than crude and harsh : if, however, it be frequently pondered upon, the acerbity will disappear.

XIII. *The chronological equality of the three periods, is a proof that Jesus is the Christ.*

There is a perpetual analogy between the periods of time, defined by Divine Wisdom; and these three most important periods correspond remarkably with each other. From the Captivity *to Christ,* are Fourteen generations, says St Matthew; just as Gabriel, when revealing to Daniel the seventy weeks, said, that the city should be built ["in seven weeks, and threescore and two weeks from the going forth of the commandment"] *unto the Messiah* the Prince.—See Dan. ix. 25. And St Matthew had that same system of times in his mind. The Captivity, the revelation which was vouchsafed to Daniel, the Return, the actual commencement of the Seventy Weeks, are separated by short but remarkable intervals. From that point downwards, the Seventy Weeks, throughout their long course, accompany this the last *Fourteen,* until *Christ* completes both, and the *Fourteen* before the Weeks. The Seventy Weeks consist of less than 560 years, as I have shown in the *Ordo Temporum,* and comprise about twelve generations, each of them (as we have observed in Section IX.) being about forty-six years in duration. It behoved that Christ should come *within* the Seventy Weeks. The expectation of Israel, therefore, could not be delayed for *more* than fourteen generations after the Captivity.

XIV. *The dissimilarity of the three periods, and the equality of the Fourteens, when taken together, confirm this important conclusion still more, by a cumulative argument.*

If any one will compare together, and combine what we have said in the Seventh and Thirteenth Sections, he will perceive that these two arguments reciprocally strengthen each other. The first and second periods were far more glorious than the third, which could not therefore fail to have the conclusion most desired, after so long a cessation of both the Promise and the Kingdom.[1]

In the *Treatise on the birth of the Lord* JESUS, *published* A.D. 1749, *by Dr S. J. Baumgarten*,[2] *in the name of the Academy of* Halle, my *Gnomon* is openly assailed in three places.

In the *first* place, after refuting the opinion of William Reading, who concluded from the right of Jesus Christ to the Jewish kingdom, that Joseph had had no sons before his birth, he says (p. 20), that I *appear to maintain the same view*. I however only showed (p. 10, Sec. IX.) that Jesus must have been reputed to be the first-born of Joseph, just as much as He was reputed to be his Son. I said nothing there concerning His right to the kingdom.

The *second* passage, which occurs soon afterwards, runs thus:—"They double and wonderfully increase the difficulty, who consider that Phaidaiah has been passed over by St Matthew, so as to make Zorobabel the grandson of Salathiel, and the great grandson of Jechoniah; a view which has found favour with many interpreters, although Phaidaiah is expressly called (1 Chron. iii. 18, 19) the brother of Salathiel, and the son of Jechoniah. This opinion, however, is far more tolerable than that put forward by *Matthew Hiller*, in the third chapter of his dissertation on the true meaning of the words which composed the inscription on our Lord's Cross (*Syntagmata Hermeneutica*, pp. 361–363). Bengel, however, in the eighth and fourteenth pages of his Gnomon, has gone still further, declaring that the Abiud of Matthew is the same with the Hodaiah or Hodauihu mentioned in 1 Chron. iii. 24, as the tenth from Zorobabel. By which immense leap, he has so far pleased himself, as seriously to think that Matthew has purposely and

---

[1] " Post tantam promissionis regnique pausam," *i.e.* after the voice of prophecy had been so long silent, the royalty of David's throne remained so long in abeyance.—(I. B.)

[2] A Lutheran divine, historian, and philologist of the Academy of Halle; born 1706; died 1756. His works were very numerous.—(I. B.)

deliberately passed over an entire Fourteen, which is made up of these nine descendants of Zorobabel, of the father of the same Phaidaiah, of three descendants of Joram, and of the father of Jechoniah, and that this is not without mystery for the construction of the three periods of time, which he then computes according to his own pleasure. We will give his own words. 'Between Jehoram and Abiud, St Matthew omits in all *fourteen generations*; see section IX.; and though he only mentions three *fourteens* for the sake of the number of the periods from Abraham to Christ, he nevertheless implies, in accordance with his system, that there were really four.'[1]

" Greatly and sadly do we fear lest the credit of Holy Scripture should be brought into danger by this fictitious systematizing,[2] a danger not to be averted by any distinction between implied or expressed meaning. Even if the Book of Chronicles expressly mentioned Abiud, this hypothesis would still be inadmissible (since many men have undoubtedly borne the same name); and it will appear utterly inexcusable to any one who carefully considers with himself, both what tortures must be employed to transform Abiud into Hodaiah, and also how very much the divine credit of the Book of Chronicles must be imperilled, if it be laid down (the only argument by which the conjecturers support their improbable opinion), that no genealogy is carried further in that book, than the genealogy of the Messiah, of which the writer of Chronicles must certainly have been ignorant without a special revelation."

What follows in the *Programm*[3] has nothing to do with me. To the objections quoted above, I reply :

(1.) I have computed the three periods of *time*, not *according to my own pleasure*, but from the observations which occur in the text of St Matthew. For the first and second periods are

---

[1] See § x., and footnote.—(I. B.)

[2] " Ficta concinnitate," alluding to Bengel's use of the cognate adverb, "concinnè." See § x., and footnote.—(I. B.)

[3] " *Programm*" (Programma) must not be confounded with " *Programme;*" it is used here in a peculiar and technical sense, and signifies, " *An introductory dissertation, generally on some religious or classical subject, read by the Rector, Sub-rector, or some Professor of a German University, at the commencement of their lectures.*—(I. B.)

divided by "David, *the King*," who, in the mere genealogy of Ruth iv. 22, is not called "the king:" the second and third are divided by the *Babylonian Captivity*, which is not a generation, but an epoch. Dr Baumgarten's *Programm* itself (p. 24) does not differ much from this.

(2.) I am more doubtful now than I was formerly whether St Matthew has passed over Jehoiakim: it is certain, however, that he has passed over three generations, viz., Ahaz, Joash, and Amaziah; and my Gnomon suggests one reason, his *Programm* another, why the Evangelist should have passed over these three rather than any others. It ought, therefore, to be carefully considered, whether the observations which are made in that *Programm* against the other generations, which have also been omitted, do not bring the credit of the sacred writers into danger. The *Programm* also lays it down (p. 18) that six generations are omitted in Ezra vii. 3.

(3.) Whether it was one man, called indiscriminately Hodaiah and Abiud, or whether two individuals are represented respectively by these names, Hiller has assuredly demonstrated that the meaning of both is the same, whose modes of eliciting the truth[1] many would find serviceable, if they would condescend to employ them.

(4.) I now, however, acknowledge that Hodaiah and Abiud were distinct individuals; but I am induced to do so by the single argument, that the nearer Abiud is to Christ, the farther he must be from the ancient times of the Chronicles, and of Hodaiah himself. I have nowhere said that the genealogy of the Messiah or Joseph is carried farther in Chronicles than the other genealogies, neither have I had any cause for so saying.

(5.) The number of Fourteen generations which Hiller has specified as being omitted by St Matthew, received a certain additional appearance of probability from their accordance with the three *Fourteens* of generations mentioned by the Evangelist.

(6.) Where the *Programm* in question abruptly concludes with those words of mine concerning St Matthew, there the Gnomon goes on immediately to say, "St Luke expressly enume-

---

[1] "Fidiculis," alluding to the invidious term applied by Baumgarten to Bengel's modes of proving the identity of Abiud and Hodaiah.—ED.

rates fifty-six generations from Abraham to the time when Jesus was thirty years of age. They agree, therefore." On considering this passage, it will, I think, become evident, that the antithesis between the words "*implied*" and "*expressed*" is perfectly harmless; and that the apparent difference in the numbers of generations mentioned by the two evangelists can be satisfactorily reconciled by means of those which St Matthew has omitted.

(7.) If St Matthew has omitted rather fewer generations, this does not detract from the remainder of my explanation.

(8.) Since the *Programm* (p. 13) touches on the passage in Luke iii. 23, we shall offer some observations also on it. In these words, ὢν, ὡς ἐνομίζετο, υἱὸς 'Ιωσὴφ, τοῦ 'Ηλεί, κ.τ.λ. (being, as was *supposed, the son of Joseph, which was the son of Heli, etc.*), Baumgarten expunges the comma after ἐνομίζετο (*was supposed*), so as to make "ὡς ἐνομίζετο υἱὸς 'Ιωσὴφ (*as was supposed the son of Joseph*) a parenthesis; though the word ἐνομίζετο (*was supposed*) belongs rather, without any diminution of truth, to the whole genealogy, as I have shown in the present work. I remark by the way—on the passage in question, that, when our Lord is said to have been *about thirty years* of age, some latitude is ascribed to the year xxx. by the word ὡς (*about*), so that there may have been an excess, or rather a defect, of some *days*, without detriment to the precise number of thirty years. Baumgarten, however, in his Church History, Sec. i. p. 105, introduces *some few* years above thirty: a license which is quite unallowable, since in this manner the most important calculations of time which occur in the evangelists, are put entirely out of joint. Scripture records many and various ages of men, and introduces odd numbers of years, such as 21 and 29, although they approach very nearly to round numbers, such as 20 and 30. We ought not, therefore, to imagine that the most important of all, namely, the age of Jesus, can have been left in doubt.

The third passage occurs at p. 26, and runs thus:—"They who attempt to produce any other equalization or comparison of these periods, seek to serve unwisely the interests of a good cause, which is not benefited by crude and harsh fancies, such as Bengel himself confesses that his own opinion (of the chronology which he imagines to be concealed in this genealogy, and to be conducive to the exposition in his Gnomon) must appear at first sight. We at least have not experienced that which he thought would be the case, namely, that it would grow less harsh by being more frequently thought over; for though we have read it again and again at least ten times, and thought it over diligently, it has by this process become more and more repugnant to us: in fact, we are clearly convinced, that whatever is by means of arithmetical operations made out of the numbers which we meet with in the sacred history, ought not to be attributed to the sacred writers, and cannot be referred to their meaning, unless we wish to excel even Jewish ingenuity by our cabalistic sagacity."

Others have followed and added to this censure. For at Leipsic there has appeared both a certain academical exercise and the revision of an academical exercise, in which these words are applied to me,—"He almost surpasses the fabrications of Jews and Cabalists, since he introduces his raw fancies into the sacred chronology." But I return to the Hallian censure. The author of that censure should take care lest the last words which I have quoted from it strike the sacred writer himself, whose meaning is placed at a far greater distance above mere accommodation to Jewish tastes than the *Programm* either acknowledges or permits to be acknowledged. If, however, another sufficient interpretation be given, I will willingly give up my own. It has not happened to the author of the Programm to find my opinion grew, upon consideration, less harsh: it does, however, happen to others, who weigh well my notes on ver. 16, 17. For, in fact, I am neither the only one nor the first who have asserted that the Evangelist propounds a chronology under cover of the genealogy. I have already cited Chrysostom, at p. 30. I must add Daniel Chamier,[1] who says that thrice fourteen chronological ages are intended by the

---

[1] A French Protestant writer of considerable ability, born in the sixteenth century.

He was appointed in 1612 Professor of Divinity at Montauban, and during the siege of that town by Louis XIII., was killed by a cannon-ball in 1621. He is supposed to have had great part in composing the Edict of Nantes.—(I. B.)

genealogical steps, which were really more numerous than those mentioned. See by all means his Panastratiæ Catholicæ, vol. iii. b. 18, ch. 2. Very lately also John Frederick Fresenius has produced a commentary on the thrice fourteen generations of Matt. i., which not only exists in a separate form, but has also been inserted by his brother with equal advantage into his fifth pastoral collection from John D'Espagne.[1] The very *Programm* itself employs words which accommodate themselves to my opinion in spite of their author; for at p. 24 he says,— " By the gradual evolving of the Divine promise,[2] the complete time which had elapsed from GOD's entering into covenant with Abraham was divided into three periods, nearly equal in length, if you reckon that length by ages of men." He is right in employing the word *Ages* (*Aetates*); for the equality consists properly in the number of ages intimated by the number of generations expressed; whereas the actual number of generations, some of which are expressed and some omitted, is somewhat larger than that of those which are expressed. Such being the case, the numbers stated in Holy Scripture invite the diligent reader to *arithmetical calculations*, nor can they safely be treated with contempt where they accord with the matter under consideration. The Hebrews frequently express numbers of years by generations. Away with *Jewish Ingenuity!* away with *Cabalistic Sagacity!* Christian research will rightly endeavour, if not to attain to, at least to follow after, the *sagacity* of the Evangelist, mentioned in the *Programm* (p. 25.) It may easily be supposed that the *Programm*, delivered on a solemn occasion in a celebrated spot, must have found many more readers than this my explanation. I trust, however, that it may confer some little advantage on some few readers: and it is better to induce even one man to search after truth, than to estrange many from a single trace of it, however slight.

18. Τοῦ δὲ Χριστοῦ ἡ γέννησις οὕτως ἦν, *The generation, however, of*

[1] John d'Espagne lived in the 17th century.
He wrote, besides other works, Essay des merveilles de Dieu l'harmonie des temps, published at Geneva, 1671.—(I. B.)

[2] " *Promissionis Divinæ Gradatione*," literally, " *By the Gradation of the Divine Promise*," i.e. by the several stages of its evolution to fulfilment.

110   ST MATTHEW I. 18.

Christ was on this wise) By this most ancient reading[1] the text refers to ver. 17, and the advent of the Messiah, expected for so many generations, is declared and exhibited (exsertè demonstratur) to the reader. Thus, too, the words, ἐγεννήθη, (*was generated*), and γέννησις, (*generation*), refer mutually to each other. The particle δὲ (*however*) subserves both references. In like manner, the name "JESUS" is repeated in ch. ii. 1, from ch. i. 25. In later ages, most of the Greek copyists have added Ἰησοῦ[2] (the genitive case of Ἰησοῦς, *Jesus*) before Χριστοῦ (the genitive case of Χριστός, *Christ*), according to which reading, the expression would refer with less force to either the first or sixteenth verse indifferently. It was the CHRIST whom Mary had in her womb by the Holy Ghost, and whom Joseph, *afterwards*, by the command of the angel, called JESUS. Elegantly, and in accordance with the order of events, the name JESUS is reserved till ver. 21, 25.—Cf. Gnomon on Luke ii. 11. The word γέννησις (*generation*) includes (ver. 18–25) both the Conception (cf. γεννηθὲν, *conceived*, ver. 20) and the Nativity (cf. γεννηθέντος, *having been born*, ii. 1). For ver. 18 contains the introductory statement (*propositionem*)[3] of those matters which follow, to which, also, the οὕτως (*thus*, or *on this wise*) refers: and the conjunction γάρ (*for*) commences the handling of the subject (*tractationem*), which corresponds with the introductory statement. —Cf. the use of γάρ in Heb. ii. 8.[4] The particle οὕτως guards us from thinking, on account of the preceding genealogy, that Joseph was the natural father of Jesus.—μνηστευθείσης γάρ τῆς

---

[1] In Matt. i. 18, we know how it was read in the second century from Irenæus, who (after having previously cited the words, "*Christi autem generatio sic erat*") continues, "*Ceterum potuerat dicere Matthæus, Jesu vero generatio sic erat; sed prævidens Spiritus Sanctus depravatores, et præmuniens contra fraudulentiam eorum, per Matthæum ait: Christi autem generatio sic erat.*"—(C. II. lib. iii. 16, 2.) TREGELLES.—(I. B.)
PZ and Rec. Text read Ἰησοῦ Χριστοῦ, which, therefore, Lachmann prefers. B, and Origen 3, 965*d* read Χριστοῦ Ἰησοῦ. But Iren. 191, 204, and *a b c d* Vulg. read only Χριστοῦ, which Tischendorf prefers.—ED.
[2] Such is the reading of E. M., viz., τοῦ δὲ Ἰησοῦ Χριστοῦ, κ.τ.λ.—(I. B.)
[3] *Propositio* and *Tractatio* are terms regularly used by Bengel in his Introductory Synopses in the technical and rhetorical sense.—ED.
[4] Lachmann omits γάρ with B'Z*abc* Vulg. Iren. 204. Tischendorf, with less weight of authorities, retains it, viz., of the oldest, I'*d*.—ED.

μητρὸς Αὐτοῦ Μαρίας, *For after His mother Mary had been betrothed*) The LXX. render the Hebrew ארש (*to betroth*) by μνηστεύομαι in Deut. xx. 7, etc.—πρὶν ἢ συνελθεῖν αὐτούς, *before they came together*) Joseph had not yet even brought Mary home (see ver. 20); but in these words, and the more firmly on that account, the *commercium tori* is specifically denied, in order to assert her pregnancy by the Holy Spirit. Nor does the expression, πρὶν ἢ (*before*), imply that they came together after our Lord's birth.—εὑρέθη ἐν γαστρὶ ἔχουσα ἐκ Πνεύματος Ἁγίου, *she was found with child of the Holy Ghost*) There can be no doubt but that Mary disclosed to Joseph (perhaps when he proposed to consummate their marriage) the sacred pregnancy, which she had concealed from every one else.—ἐκ, *of*) The expression ἐκ Πνεύματος Ἁγίου (*of the Holy Spirit*) occurs again at ver. 20. See, also, John iii. 6.

19. δίκαιος, *just*[1]) It is disputed in what sense this epithet is applied to Joseph. The thing is clear. Joseph wished to put away Mary, and he also wished to put her away privately. The Evangelist indicates the cause of both wishes. Why did he wish to do it *privately*? Because he was unwilling to publish the matter, and exact the penalty which the law permitted in the case of women guilty, or suspected, of adultery, and thus to make an example of one, whose sanctity he had in other respects so greatly revered. But why did he wish to put her away at all? We learn from the context. Because he was *just* (*justus*), and did not think it reputable (*honestum*) to retain as his wife one who appeared to have broken her conjugal faith. His thoughts were many and conflicting; his mind was in doubt. St Matthew expresses this with great beauty, by a phraseology somewhat ambiguous in this its brevity; for Greek participles may be resolved into the corresponding verbs with the conjunctions *although, because,* or *since*: [and μὴ θέλων, therefore, may be rendered either *although he was unwilling, because he was unwilling,* or *since he did not wish*]. Elsewhere δίκαιος is sometimes found with the signification of *yielding* and kind, as *in-*

---

[1] In Bengel, "*justus,*" which, as well as the original, δίκαιος, signifies, and is translated, either *just* or *righteous*, as the case may require. In Bengel's own German version, it is rendered in the present instance GERECHT, which is equally ambiguous.—(I. B.)

justus[1] (which signifies primarily *unjust* or *unrighteous*) with that of severe.—παραδειγματίσαι, *to make an example of*) Thus the LXX. in Num. xxv. 4, have—Παραδειγμάτισον αὐτοὺς τῷ Κυρίῳ, κατέναντι τοῦ ἡλίου, *Make an example of them to the Lord before the sun:* where the expression is used of persons executed by hanging. The simple form, δειγματίζειν, occurs in Col. ii. 15: for both δεῖγμα and παράδειγμα [from which the verbs are respectively derived] denote that which is exhibited as a public spectacle.—λάθρᾳ, *privily*) *i.e.* without a public trial, without even a record of the reason on the writing of divorcement. Two witnesses were sufficient.—ἀπολῦσαι *to put her away*) fearing to take her.

20. ἰδοὺ, *behold*) He was not left long in doubt.[2]—κατ' ὄναρ, *in a dream*) Dreams are mentioned also in Acts ii. 17, in a quotation from the Old Testament. With this exception, St Matthew is the only writer of the New Testament who has recorded *dreams*; viz., one of Pilate's wife, ch. xxvii. 19; one of the Magi, ch. ii. 12; one of Joseph, in this passage; a second in ch. ii. 13; a third in ch. ii. 19; and a fourth in ii. 22. This mode of instruction was suitable to those early times of the New Dispensation.[3] —αὐτῷ, *to him*) In the first instance, Gabriel was sent to Mary, afterwards the remaining particulars were revealed to Joseph. Thus all things were made sure to both of them.—Ἰωσὴφ, *Joseph*) In visions, those to whom they are vouchsafed are generally addressed by name, as if already well known [to the speaker].— See Acts ix. 4, 10, and x. 3, 13.—παραλαβεῖν, *to take unto thee*) sc. to the companionship of life and board, under the *name* of wedlock: on which ground the angel adds the words, τὴν γυναῖκά σου (*thy wife*).—Μαριάμ, *Mary*) This termination was more usual in early times (from the example of the Hebrew and the LXX.) than the Greek form Μαρία, which soon, however, prevailed. St Matthew, therefore, uses Μαριάμ here, in the angel's address, for the name of our Lord's mother; but Μαρίας [the genitive case of the Greek form Μαρία] when speaking of her (ver. 16, 18) in his own person; and in like manner, he employs the Greek form

---

[1] Ex. gr. Virg. Ecl., "Injusta noverca."—Ed.

[2] Thus God guides His own, and teaches them at the right time, what they have to do.—B. G. V.

[3] Shortly after men prophesied concerning Christ; as also Christ Himself acted the part of an interpreter of their prophecies.—*Vers. Germ.*

when mentioning other women of the same name. And St Luke does mostly the same. *Miriam*, according to Hiller, signifies *Rebellion*, sc. of the Israelites in Egypt. Scripture teaches us to look to the etymology of the name, not of Mary, but of JESUS.—τὸ γὰρ ἐν αὐτῇ γεννηθέν, *for that which is conceived in her*) The *foetus*, as yet unborn, is usually spoken of in the neuter gender.—Cf. note on Luke i. 35.

21. Τέξεται, *shall bring forth*) The word σοι (*to thee*), which is added (Luke i. 31) concerning Zachariah, is not introduced here ;[1] —καλέσεις, *thou shalt call*) By the use of the second person singular, the duties and obligations of a father are committed to Joseph. St Matthew records more particulars than the other evangelists regarding him ; afterwards, when men had become acquainted with the truth, the first place is given (in Luke i. 31) to Mary.—Ἰησοῦν, *Jesus*) Many names of the Messiah were announced in the Old Testament ; but the proper name "JESUS" was not expressly announced. The meaning and force of it are, however, proclaimed everywhere, namely, SALVATION ; and the name itself was divinely foretold in this passage before our Lord's birth, and in Luke i. 31, even before His conception. The name יֵשׁוּעַ (*Jeshua*), which occurs in Neh. viii. 17, is the same as יְהוֹשׁוּעַ or יְהוֹשֻׁעַ (*Jehoshua*, commonly called Joshua): both of which are rendered Ἰησοῦς (*Jesus*) by the LXX. And in so far, learned men have been right in declaring that the name *Jesus* contains the Tetragrammaton, [יהוה] or ineffable name of God.—See Hiller's Syntagmata Hermeneutica, p. 337, where the name of *Jesus* is thus interpreted, HE WHO IS *is* SALVATION : yea, the angel interprets it ΑΥΤΟΣ ΣΩΣΕΙ (*He shall save*), where Αὐτὸς (He) corresponds with the Divine Name.—Cf. Gnomon on Heb. i. 12. Nor does the name *Jehoshua* differ from the original, *Hoshea* (See Num. xiii. 16) in any thing else, except the addition of the Divine Name, which transforms the name from a prayer, *Save* (*Salva*), into an affirmation, *Jehovah Salvation*. And, since the name *Emmanuel* mentions GOD most expressly together with SALVATION, the name *Jesus* itself, the force of which, the Evangelist of the Old Testament, *Isaiah* (whose own name signifies the same thing) clearly indicates by the synonym *Emmanuel*, requires much more the mention of the Divine Name :

[1] *i.e.* Because our Lord was not the child of Joseph.—(I. B.)

for *Emmanuel* and *Jesus* are equivalent terms.—See notes on vv. 22, 23. Nay, even if the ʼ in יְשׁוּעַ be considered as merely the sign of the third person, still, as is frequently the case with Hebrew names, "GOD" must be understood, and here with especial force.—Αὐτὸς, *He*) The pronoun αὐτὸς, in the nominative, is always emphatic; here it is peculiarly so. In the oblique case, it is frequently a mere relative.—σώσει, *shall save*) As often, therefore, as the words, "to save," "Saviour," "salvation," "salutary,"[1] occur with reference to Christ, we ought to consider, that the name of JESUS is virtually mentioned.—τὸν λαὸν Αὐτοῦ, *His people*) sc. Israel, and those who shall be added to the fold of Israel.[2]—Αὐτοῦ, *His*) and at the same time God's.—Cf. ch. ii. 6.

22. Τοῦτο δὲ ὅλον, γέγονεν ἵνα, *But the whole of this came to pass, that*) The same phrase occurs in ch. xxvi. 56. There are many particulars, in which St Matthew observes that the event announced by the angel corresponded exactly with the prediction of Isaiah. (1.) A virgin pregnant and becoming a mother; (2.) A male child (Cf. Rev. xii. 5); (3.) The Nomenclature of the child; (4.) The Interpretation of the Name.—ἵνα πληρωθῇ, *that it might be fulfilled*) The same phrase occurs in ch. ii. 15, 17, 23, iv. 14, viii. 17, xii. 17, xiii. 35, xxi. 4, xxvii. 9, 35. Those things *have been fulfilled* in Jesus, not only which He performed Himself (and which might therefore appear to the unbelieving to be open to suspicion), but those also which were done to Him by others. Wherever this phrase occurs, we are bound to regard and recognise the character and dignity of the Evangelists, and (however dull our own perception may be in the matter) to believe that they mention an event, not merely corresponding [accidentally] with some ancient prophecy, but one which in consequence thereof, and agreement therewith, could not have failed to occur at the commencement of the New Dispensation, on account of the Divine Truth which was pledged to its fulfilment. The evangelists, however, frequently quote pro-

---

[1] *Salutare*—conducive to *health*, whether of *body* or *soul*: it is frequently difficult, sometimes impossible, to give at once the full and exact force of these words in an English translation.—(I. B.)

[2] The gathering in of the Gentiles to the Church was at that time a mystery even to the angels.—*Vers. Germ.*

phecies, the context of which must, at the time that they were first delivered, have been interpreted of things then present, and that, too, according to the Divine intention. But the same Divine intention, looking forward to remote futurity, so framed the language of prophecy, that it should apply with still greater specialty to the times of the Messiah. And this hidden intention (some portion of which the learned observe to have oozed out even to the Jews) the apostles and evangelists, themselves divinely taught, teach us: and we are bound to receive their statements concerning the fulfilment of prophecy in a teachable spirit, on account of the correspondence between the predictions which they adduce, and the events to which they apply them. This is enough for the defence of the Evangelists, until any one is led to acknowledge their authority on other grounds. Their sincerity is clearly evidenced by the fact, that they have amplified, as far as possible, the number of prophecies relating to the Messiah, and therefore the labour (delightful indeed!) of proving[1] that Jesus is the Christ. The Jews, on the other hand, endeavour as eagerly to turn aside in any other direction whatever, everything which the prophets have predicted concerning Christ, so that it is wonderful that they still believe that there either is, or ever will be, a Messiah.—διὰ τοῦ προφήτου, *by the prophet*) St Matthew quotes the *prophets* with especial frequency, to show the agreement between the prophecies and the events which fulfilled them: the other Evangelists rather presuppose that agreement.[2]—λέγοντος, *saying*) This should be construed with προφήτου (*prophet*); see ch. ii. 17. Isaiah is not mentioned by name. The ancients were studious readers; there was less need, therefore, in those times, to cite books and chapters.

23. Ἰδοὺ ἡ παρθένος ἐν γαστρὶ ἕξει καὶ τέξεται Υἱὸν, καὶ καλέσουσι τὸ ὄνομα Αὐτοῦ Ἐμμανουήλ—*Behold the virgin shall have in her womb* [or *conceive*], *and shall bring forth a Son, and they shall*

---

[1] The onus probandi.—ED.

[2] SS. Mark and Luke have at times noted down these prophecies, which our Lord himself quoted; but they have been more sparing of their own spontaneous appeals to the Old Testament, since they were looking forward to readers becoming now continually more and more established in the Christian faith. John, the last of the Four, added one or two prophecies, and their subsequent fulfilment.—*Harm.*, p. 49.

call his name Emmanuel.—The LXX. render Isaiah vii. 14, thus —Ἰδοὺ ἡ παρθένος ἐν γαστρὶ λήψεται Υἱόν, καὶ καλέσεις κ.τ.λ.—*Behold the virgin shall conceive in her womb a Son, and thou shalt call,* etc.—ἰδού, *Behold!*)—a particle especially adapted for pointing out a *Sign.*—See Isa. vii. 14.—ἡ παρθένος, *the virgin*) In the original Hebrew, the word employed is הָעַלְמָה;[1] and עַלְמָה denotes *a virgin*;[2] whether you derive it from עָלַם,[3] so that it may be one who has *escaped the notice of* man,[4] who has not been *known* by man (cf. ver. 25, and Luke i. 34), for נֶעְלָם (*to be hidden, to lie hid, to escape the notice of*), and יָדַע (*to know,* etc.), are opposed to each other, both in their general signification, as in Lev. v. 3, 4, and also in this special one: or whether עַלְמָה (the verb cognate with which the Syriac translator has employed to represent ἤκμασεν[5] in Rev. xiv. 18), signify ἀκμαία, *in the flower of her age.* The Hebrew article ה (*the*), prefixed in the original to the word under consideration (concerning which article cf. Gnomon on ch. xviii. 17), points out a particular individual visible on the mirror of Divine prescience. For the prophet is speaking of a *Sign,* and introduces it by the word "*Behold,*" and then immediately addresses the Virgin herself, with the words, Thou shalt call, etc. Isaiah indicates, in the first instance, some woman who lived at the time, and whose natural fecundity was considered doubtful, who, from a virgin, was to become a mother, and that of a son: she, however, as the sublimity of the prophet's words clearly show, was a type of that Virgin, who, still a virgin, brought forth the Messiah; so that the force of the *Sign* was twofold, applying to that which was close at hand, and to that which was far distant in the future.—See Alexander More.[6]

---

[1] הָעַלְמָה is עַלְמָה with the article prefixed.—(I. B.)

[2] "The ancient version, which gave a different rendering, did so for party purposes, while the LXX., who could have no such motive, render it *virgin* in the very passage where it must, to their minds, have occasioned a difficulty." S. P. Tregelles.—(I. B.)

[3] עָלַם *to hide, to conceal:* the Niphal of which is נֶעְלָם—*to be hidden, to lie hid.*—(I. B.)

[4] "Quæ latuit virum."—(I. B.)

[5] ἤκμασεν, *is fully ripe.*—(I. B.)

[6] Alexander More (or Morus) was born A.D. 1616, at Castres, in the south of France, where his father, a Scotchman by birth, was Principal of a Protestant college. He was a man of considerable talents and great attain-

The virginity of our Lord's Mother is not fully proved by the words of the prophet taken alone; but the manifestation of its fulfilment casts a radiance back on the prophecy, and discloses its full meaning.—Υἱόν, *a Son*) sc. the Messiah, to whom the land of Israel belongs.—See Isa. viii. 8.—καλέσουσι, THEY *shall call*) Both the Hebrew and the LXX. have "Thou shalt call," *i.e.*, "THOU *Virgin-Mother*."—"THOU *shalt call*," occurs also in ver. 21, addressed to Joseph: whence is now substituted "THEY *shall call*," *i.e.*, all, thenceforth. The angel says to Mary, in Luke i. 28, *The Lord is with* THEE. Not one or the other of His parents however, but all who call upon His name, say, "*with* us."—Cf. Luke i. 54.—Those words deserve particular attention in which the writers of the New Testament differ from the LXX., or even from the Hebrew.—τὸ ὄνομα, *the name*) This does not mean the name actually given at circumcision, but yet the true name (cf. Isa. ix. 5), aye, the proper name too, by which he is *called*, even by his parents (cf. Isa. viii. 8), and which is even especially proper to Him, inasmuch as it is synonymous with the name *Jesus*.—See an example of synonymous names in the note on ver. 8. Many of the faithful actually address the Saviour by the name of EMMANUEL, as a proper name, though it would have been less suitable in Jesus to call Himself *God-with-us*.—ὅ ἐστι μεθερμηνευόμενον, Μεθ' ἡμῶν ὁ Θεός—*which is, being interpreted, God with us*). This interpretation of a Hebrew name shows, that St Matthew wrote in Greek. Such interpretations subjoined to Hebrew words show that, the writers of the New Testament do not absolutely require that the reader of Holy Scripture should be acquainted with Hebrew. The Son of Sirach also uses the word μεθερμηνεῦσαι (*to interpret*) in his preface. The name *God-with-us*, in itself, so far as it involves an entire assertion, is not necessarily a Divine name (See Hiller Onomasticon Sacrum, p. 848); and it was, therefore, given also to a boy who was born in the time of Isaiah; and the same is the case with the name *Jesus*: but in the sense in which each of them applies exclusively to Christ, it signifies Θεάνθρωπος or *God-Man*. For the union of the Divine and human natures in Christ is the

ments. He became professor of Greek at Geneva when only twenty years of age, and successively occupied other professorial chairs there and elsewhere. He died at Paris in 1670.—(I. B.)

foundation of the union of God with men, nor can any one consider the latter apart from the former, especially when treating of the birth of Christ.

24. Ἐποίησεν, *did*) sc. without delay.—ὡς κ.τ.λ., *as*, etc.) Hence the command of the angel and the performance of Joseph are described in the same words in this passage, and in ch. ii. 13, 14, and 20, 21.—παρέλαβε τὴν γυναῖκα αὐτοῦ, *took unto him his wife*) sc., with the same appearance to those without, as though they lived together according to common custom.

25. Καὶ, *and*) St Matthew says "*and*," not "*but*." He took her, *and* knew her not: both by the command of the angel.— οὐκ ἐγίνωσκεν αὐτὴν, ἕως οὗ, *knew her not until*) It does not follow from this ἕως (*until*) that he did so afterwards. It is sufficient however, that her virginity should be established up to the time of her delivery. With regard to the remainder of her married life, the reader is left to form his own opinion. The angel did not expressly forbid Joseph to have conjugal intercourse with her: but he perceived such a command to be implied by the very nature of the case.—ἕως οὗ ἔτεκε τὸν υἱὸν, *until she brought forth the Son*) A very old Egyptian version has only these words, without the addition of "*her first-born:*[1] according to which reading, the address of the angel, the declaration of the prophet, and the act of Joseph [in naming Him as the angel directed] are expressed in words which exactly correspond together.—sc., "*She shall bring forth a son, and thou shalt call his name Jesus*,"— "*She shall bring forth a Son, and they shall call his name Jesus,*" —*She brought forth* ΤΟΝ Υἱὸν, ΤΗΕ *Son, and he* [Joseph][2] *called His name Jesus.* The article ΤΟΝ (the) has a relative value here, and refers to ver. 21 with the same meaning, "*until she brought forth* ΤΗΑΤ *Son.*" The same reading is found in Codex Barberini I. (by which name we suppose the celebrated Vatican MS. to be intended in this place), and we have assured ourselves that beyond doubt such must have been originally that of the Latin Vulgate. For Helvidius,[3] and Jerome in the com-

---
[1] The disputed words are found in E. M. Tregelles favours the omission. —(I. B.)

[2] See Text v. 25, "*He* called his name Jesus."—ED.

[3] A famous Arian disciple of Auxentius. He lived in the fourth century.— (I. B.)

mencement of his book against him, thus quote the words of St Matthew—*et non cognovit eam, donec peperit filium suum, i.e., and he knew her not till she brought forth her Son;* but more commonly they quote thus *donec peperit filium, i.e., until she brought forth (a or the) Son,* without the addition of either *suum (her)* or *primogenitum (first-born)*; nor can it be argued, that they have in these instances intended to abridge the text, since Jerome in one place thus quotes the passage in full, " *Exurgens autem—accepit uxorem suam et non cognovit eam, donec peperit filium: et vocavit nomen ejus Jesum,*" *i.e., But on rising from sleep —he received his wife, and knew her not until she had brought forth [the] Son: and he called His name Jesus.*[1]

Both these writers, after a long dispute upon this passage of St Matthew, seek for a fresh argument grounded on the appellation πρωτότοκος, *first-born,* not from this passage of St Matthew, but solely from Luke ii. 7. If the Codex Barberini 1., and the Coptic version already mentioned, obtained this reading from Greek MSS., their testimony is on that ground of great weight; if, on the other hand, they obtained it from Latin sources, they greatly corroborate the genuine reading of the very ancient Latin version. The words αὐτῆς τὸν πρωτότοκον, " *her first-born,*" appear to have been introduced into St Matthew, from the parallel passage in St Luke already cited: and the very idea of the *Son of a Virgin,* implies that He must have been the firstborn in a pre-eminent and strictly singular manner. [Such as He is expressly declared to be in Luke ii. 7, *Vers. Germ.*]

In some passages our criticism takes a different view of matters from what it did formerly. Yet no one can fairly accuse me of inconstancy; for I do not confine myself to those views, which have gained acceptance by long usage (though I do not reject such assistance where truth requires it): but I proceed to draw forth, by degrees, from their concealment, those things which have been buried out of sight.

Ἐκάλεσε, *he called) i.e.,* Joseph did so; as we learn from ver. 21.

[1] BZ. Memph. Theb. *b.c.* read only υἱόν (without the article or the words following). D*d.* and Vulg. read as the Rec. Text. Lachmann and Tischendorf follow the former reading, as resting on the weightiest authorities.—ED.

CHAPTER II.

1. 'Ἐν Βηθλεὲμ τῆς Ἰουδαίας, *in Bethlehem of Judaea*) It is thus distinguished from Bethlehem of the Zabulonites, mentioned in Josh. xix. 15.—'Ἡρώδου, *of Herod*) *i.e.* Herod the Great, a native of Ascalon, a foreigner by descent, the sceptre being just on the point of departing from Judah. Amongst his sons[1] were Archelaus, mentioned in ver. 22, the Herods Antipas and Philip, mentioned in the 14th chapter of St Matthew and the 23d of St Luke, and Aristobulus, the father of Herod Agrippa, who is mentioned in Acts xii.—ἰδοὺ, *behold*) This particle frequently points to a thing unexpected. The arrival of the Magi at Jerusalem had not been announced.—Μάγοι, *Magi*) Μάγος occurs frequently in the Septuagint version of Daniel for the Hebrew אשף, and signifies with the Persians a *wise man* or a *philosopher*. St Matthew considers it sufficient to denote them

---

[1] The following genealogy of the Herodian Family, extracted from Lewin's Life of St Paul will be useful to the student:—

THE FAMILY OF THE HERODS.

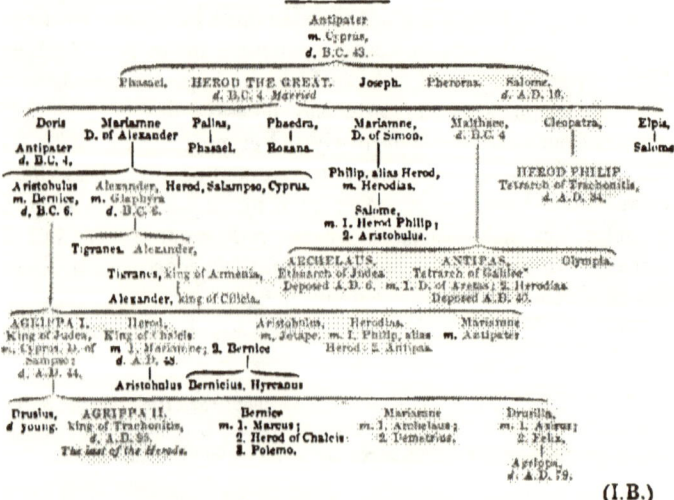

(I.B.)

by this their condition; he does not define either the rest of their dignity or their number, nor whether or no they had ever been addicted to curious arts, nor in what part of the East they were born; by which last omission he intimates the unrestricted universality of this great salvation. Magus is a word of ambiguous signification and of wide extent in the East. These Magi appear to have been descendants of Abraham, but not of Jacob; for the name of Magi does not apply to Jews, and the mention of gold and frankincense directs our attention to Isa. lx. 6, where he speaks of the coming in of the Gentiles, so that in this place already are seen the preludes of the Messiah being received rather by the Gentiles than by His own people. (See Luke iv. 26, etc.) *The King of the Jews*, they say, not, *our king*, showing thereby that they were not themselves Jews. If you make two classes, the one of those who received, the other of those who rejected our Lord, and observe the variety of men on either side, you will be able to draw many useful observations from the whole of the New Testament.—ἀπὸ ἀνατολῶν, *from the East*) cf. ch. viii. 11. The north and the south occur in Greek only in the singular number. The east and the west occur also in the plural. The *rationale* of this is clear: when we look either due north or due south, our eyes are always turned toward one precise spot, the North or South Pole, which is not the case when we look eastward or westward, since there is no stationary point of east or west longitude.—παρεγίνοντο, *arrived*) After He had received the name "JESUS," and, consequently after His circumcision.¹—εἰς Ἱεροσόλυμα, *at Jerusalem*)

---

¹ Nay even we have no reason to doubt, that the *arrival* of the Magi, and the *flight* into Egypt, which was intimately connected with it, took place after His παράστασις, *presentation*, as recorded in Luke ii. 22, 23. And, moreover, this very order of events, whereby the παράστασις in the temple, the arrival of the Magi, and the departure to Egypt, are in continuous succession, affords us most useful consequences. For 1) the poverty of Jesus' parents, (a fact, which is proved by their sacrifice in accordance with the law, Lev. xii. 6, 8, concerning those unable to make the more costly offering) was relieved by the Fatherly providence of GOD, through the gifts of the Magi, so that they were thereby supplied with the means of livelihood during their exile.—2.) We may observe the various features of Propriety ["Decorum"] which characterise this series of events. First of all Jesus, as being the First-begotten, was presented to the Lord: then next, the first-fruits of the

It was natural to suppose, that the metropolis would be the place where the truth would be most easily ascertained, and they conceived, no doubt, that the King had been born there.

2.) Ποῦ, *where?*) They are so sure of the *event* and the *time*, that they only ask *where?* The Scribes only knew the *place.* It was incumbent on them to learn the time from the Magi, or to avail themselves of the opportunity of learning it. The knowledge of time and of place are both necessary in this instance.—ὁ τεχθεὶς βασιλεύς, *He who is born king*) They affirm His birth as having already taken place, and His right to the kingdom combined with it, and contrary to their expectation, find it to be a subject of terror to Herod. One is said to be *born,* who from His *very birth* is King. As in the Septuagint version of 1 Chron.

Gentiles presented themselves to Jesus Himself. In His παράστασις He was Himself made manifest to the Israelites of Jerusalem, and a short while afterwards to the Gentiles also. We may conjecture, from the words of the Magi, in which they draw the conclusion as to the birth of the King of the Jews, from the Star which they had seen, and also from the age of the little children slain by Herod, in accordance with the time which he had ascertained from the Magi—that the star was seen by them at the time of Christ's conception, and that it was by it their long journey was directed; so that at the time most suitable, namely after the lapse of six months from the nativity, they arrived and paid their adorations.—3.) Simeon foretold of Jesus, that He was to be a Light to lighten the Gentiles, immediately subjoining the statement as to the Cross. Both truths were to His parents, at the time of presentation, as a communication strange, and such as they had not heretofore realised; therefore it was not till afterwards, though not long afterwards, that the one prophecy began to be fulfilled by the arrival of the Magi, the other by the flight into Egypt.—4.) The presentation was made in the temple on that very day of the week, which was subsequently called *the Lord's day.*—5.) It is most easy to understand how it was that the King of the Jews remained unknown, all along from His birth to His presentation in the temple, to King Herod, inasmuch as that king was at the time aged, sick, torn with anguish on account of his sons, and hated by the Jews, and did not become known to him sooner than through the Magi. In fact, it was similarly that Herod the Tetrarch heard nothing of the miracles which Jesus performed before the beheading of John, notwithstanding the length of the interval from the beginning of the Lord's miracles.—6.) If you place the departure into Egypt before the παράστασις, you must suppose the former to have been accomplished wholly in the winter : but the true order of events leads to the inference which is more in accordance with suitability of seasons, viz. that the flight occurred at the approach of spring, and the return at the spring season itself.—*Harm,* p. 53, 55, 56.

vii. 21, we read οἱ ταχθέντες ἐν τῇ γῇ, *who were born in the land.*— τῶν Ἰουδαίων, *of the Jews*) The name of *Jews* after the Babylonian Captivity included all the children of Israel, being opposed to Greeks or Gentiles. Whence it is given also to Galileans in Luke vii. 3; John ii. 6; Acts x. 28, etc. The Jews, however, or Israelites, called Christ *the king of Israel*, the Gentiles *the king of the Jews.* See ch. xxvii. 29, 37, 42; John i. 50, xii. 13, xviii. 33.—εἴδομεν γὰρ κ.τ.λ., *for we have seen*, etc.) Prognostics both true and false occur, especially in the case of nativities.— Αὐτοῦ τὸν ἀστέρα, *His star*) His own. In proportion as the Magi were better acquainted with the ordinary course of the stars, so much the more easily were they able to appreciate the character of the extraordinary phenomenon, and the reference of the star which was seen to this King who was born. What was their principle in either case, who can now decide? The star was either in itself new, or in a new situation, or endued with a new or perhaps even a various motion. Whether it still exists or be destined to appear again, who knows? The Magi must have undoubtedly had either an ancient revelation from the prophecies of Balaam, Daniel, etc., or a new one by a dream, cf. ver. 12.—[1]The Magi are led by a star; the fishermen by fishes, to the knowledge of Christ. Chalcidius,[2] in his Commentaries on Plato, has mentioned a tradition concerning this star.— ἐν τῇ ἀνατολῇ, *in the East*) They mean to indicate the quarter from whence they have come; for the article τῇ shows that the east country is intended. These words should therefore be construed with εἴδομεν (*we have seen*), for whilst they were in the east they had seen the star to the west, over the geographical situation (clima) of Palestine. See ver. 9.—προσκυνῆσαι Αὐτῷ, *to worship Him*) The verb προσκυνεῖν (*to worship*) in the New Testament as well as with profane authors, governs mostly a dative, though it sometimes admits an accusative. The Magi acknowledged Jesus as the *King of Grace,* and as their Lord. See Luke i. 43. All things must however be interpreted

---

[1] The methods of Divine revelations not unfrequently are disclosed only to those to whom they are vouchsafed.—*Vers. Germ.*

[2] He flourished in the third or fourth century, and wrote a commentary on the Timæus of Plato. Considerable doubt exists as to his religious opinions.—(I. B.)

according to the analogy of these beginnings. It was certainly not on any political grounds, that after having undertaken and performed so long and arduous a journey, and being so soon about to return home, they worshipped[1] a King distant and an infant, and that too without paying the same homage to Herod: nor did Herod (in ver. 8) profess an intention of paying Him political homage. That the Magi actually did *worship* Him, we learn from ver. 11.

3. Ἐταράχθη, *was troubled*) The king, now seventy years old, might be troubled all the more easily, because the Pharisees, a short time before, had foretold (as we learn from Josephus, Antiquities xvii. 3), that the kingdom was about to be taken from the family of Herod. The trouble of the king is a testimony against the carelessness of the people. If Herod fears, why do not the Jews inquire? why do they not believe?—πᾶσα, *all*) sc. πόλις, *the city*[2]—μετ' αὐτοῦ, *with him*) The people, who had been long accustomed to the king, followed his lead. Men are frequently overset by the sudden announcement of even good tidings.

4. Πάντας, *all*) i.e., all who were in Jerusalem at that time.—ἀρχιερεῖς, *chief priests*) The writers of the New Testament seldom speak of ἱερεῖς, *priests*, but generally of ἀρχιερεῖς, *chief priests*. This word had distinct significations in the singular and plural number: the singular ὁ Ἀρχιερεύς signifies *the High Priest*; the plural ἀρχιερεῖς, either with or without the definite article, signified those priests who were more nearly related to the High Priest, and had from that circumstance greater influence than the rest.—See Acts iv. 6.—γραμματεῖς τοῦ λαοῦ, *scribes of the people*) With the LXX. γραμματεύς (*scribe*) corresponds to the Hebrew שֹׁטֵר;[3] in which sense τοὺς γραμματεῖς τοῦ λαοῦ (*the*

---

[1] The verb προσκυνέω signifies either religious worship, civil homage, or any other lowly manifestation of extreme respect. Cf. the various meanings of the English word "*worship*."—(I. B.)

[2] Which had been so long standing in a posture of expectation, awaiting the Messiah's coming.—*Vers. Germ.*

[3] i.e. שֹׁטֵר *a scribe* (LXX. γραμματεύς, γραμματοεισαγωγεύς); hence from the art of writing having been especially used forensically, a magistrate, prefect of the people: specially שֹׁטְרִים is used of the prefects of the people of Israel in Egypt, Ex. v. 6-19, and in the desert, Num. xi. 16 (used of the seventy elders), Deut. xx. 9. etc., etc.; magistrates in the towns of Palestine,

scribes of the people), occurs in 1 Macc. v. 42, cf. also Deut. xx. 5. They render also ספר¹ by γραμματεύς. And that signification suits also the present passage, where a Theological Reply is spoken of. The *scribes of the people* are spoken of in contradistinction to the *chiefs of the priests*: and were private men or doctors, well versed in the Scriptures; cf. note on ch. xxii. 35.—ἐπυνθά- νετο, *inquired.* ΄ He ought to have done so before.—ποῦ ὁ Χριστὸς γεννᾶται, *where Christ is born*) He makes the question of the Magi his own. The present tense of the verb γεννᾶται (*is born*), accords with the general expectation of the coming of the Messiah, which prevailed at that time.

5. Βηθλεέμ, *Bethlehem*) The knowledge which the scribes, who do not go themselves, have derived from their ancestors, is of service to the Magi, who are seeking for Christ.—οὕτω γὰρ γέγραπ- ται διὰ τοῦ προφήτου, *for thus it is written by the prophet*) This reason was alleged by the council ; but St Matthew has stamped it with his approval.

6. Καὶ σὺ Βηθλεέμ κ.τ.λ., *and thou Bethlehem*, etc.) The passage referred to is in Micah v. 2, thus rendered by the LXX., καὶ σὺ Βηθλεέμ ὁ οἶκος Εὐφραθᾶ, ὀλιγιστὸς εἶ τοῦ εἶναι ἐν χιλιάσιν Ἰούδα· ἐκ σοῦ μοι ἐξελεύσεται, τοῦ εἶναι εἰς ἄρχοντα τοῦ Ἰσραήλ. On which passage see Hallet's Notes.² Let the following be accepted as a paraphrase of both the Prophet and the Evangelist. *And thou Bethlehem Ephrata*, or *district in the tribe of Judah*, art *small*, להיות, *to be,* in other words, *inasmuch as thou art* (*quæ sis*) (consult on ל Noldii³ Concordantiæ Particularum, p. 458), *among*

Deut. xvi. 18, etc., etc. ; used of the superior magistrates, Prov. vi. 7.— *Gesenius.*—(I. B.)

[1] *i.e.* סֹפֵר *a scribe*, Psalm xlv. 2, Ezra ix. 2, 3; specially (*a*) the king's scribe; 2 Sam. viii. 17, xx. 25 ; 2 Kings xii. 17, xix. 2, xxii. 3, 4 ; (*b*) a military scribe who has the charge of keeping the muster-rolls, Jer. xxxvii. 15, lii. 25; 2 Kings xxv. 19 ; (*c*) in the later books a person skilled in the sacred writings, γραμματεύς, 1 Chron. xxvii. 32 ; Ezra, vii. 6, etc., etc.; or סָפַר (1) *a scribe*, a royal scribe accompanying a satrap or governor of a province, Ezra iv. 8, 9, 17, 23 ; (2) γραμματεύς—one skilled in the sacred books, Ezra vii. 12, 21.—*Ibid.*—(I. B.)

[2] JOSEPH HALLET, a dissenting minister, born at Exeter, 1692 ; died 1744.—(I. B.)

[3] CHRISTIAN NOLDIUS, author of " Concordantiæ Particularum Hebræo- Chaldæorum," was an eminent Dutch divine, born 1626, died 1683.—(I. B.)

the thousands of Judah, if this dignity which is not otherwise to be despised, and which far exceeds thy proportion and measure, be compared with that dignity exclusively thine own, by virtue of which thou art *by no means the least*, but altogether the greatest among the princes and thousands of Judah, sc., *that from thee shall go forth for Me*, להיות, *one who is to be (qui sit) the Ruler in Israel*. A similar mode of expression occurs in 2 Sam. vii. 19; Isaiah xlix. 6. The greater honour obscures and absorbs the less.—γῆ 'Ιούδα, *a land of Judah*. The *land* or district is put by *Synechdoche*,[1] for the township, as in Luke ix. 12, fields for cantons: *Judah* was the tribe of the Messiah. Both words supply the place of Ephrata in the Hebrew. The LXX. have in Joshua xv., either between ver. 58 and 59, or between ver. 59 and 60, the following passage: Θεκὼ καὶ 'Εφραθά· αὔτη ἐστὶ Βηθλεέμ κ.τ.λ.—*Theko and Ephrata, which is Bethlehem*, etc. If this passage (instead of having fallen out of the Hebrew text from coming between two which have the same ending), be redundant in the Septuagint, it affords a proof, that, at the time when the land of Canaan was divided amongst the tribes of Israel, Bethlehem was not even reckoned among the cities; Cf. John vii. 42. It must, however, have been so reckoned as early at any rate as the reign of Rehoboam, as we learn from 2 Chron. xi. 6. Micah addresses it in the masculine gender, with an implied reference to אלפים, *thousands, families*, Cf. אלפי, ἡ χιλιάς μου, *my thousand*, i.e., *my family*, in Judges vi. 15. Wherefore St Matthew, after putting ἐλαχίστη, *least*, in the feminine gender (to agree with γῆ, *land*, understood), mentions, instead of the thousands themselves, the princes of thousands (for אלף *a thousand, family*, etc., and אלוף, *a chief, leader*, etc., are cognate words) over whom he places one prince (ἡγούμενον), even Christ: nor does he so much give the preference to this city or thousand over the other cities or thousands of Judah, as to the Prince who came forth thence, over the other Princes of Thousands.—ἐκ σοῦ ΓΑΡ ἐξελεύσεται, FOR *from thee shall go forth*) The LXX., as we have seen, have, from the Hebrew ἐκ σοῦ ΜΟΙ ἐξελεύσεται, *from thee shall go forth* FOR ME, a reading which is followed by the Codex Basiliensis

---

[1] See Explanation of Technical Terms in Appendix.—(I. B.)

β,¹ and the Aldine reprint of Erasmus' first edition.² Others combine both readings thus, ἐκ σοῦ ΓΑΡ ΜΟΙ ἐξελεύσεται—FOR *from thee shall go forth* FOR ME.³ The pronoun ΜΟΙ (*to*, or *for*, ME) evidently represents God the Father, speaking of Christ as His Son.—See Luke i. 32, and Cf., ver. 13. But the conjunction γαρ (*for* or *because*) points out the *birthplace* of Christ more significantly. The word γεννᾶται, shall be *born* (*nascetur*), which occurs in ver. 4, is synonymous with the ἐξελεύσεται, *shall go forth*, of the present passage. The יצא of the Hebrew; the derivative of which מוצאה (rendered by the LXX., ἔξοδοι, *goings forth*) ought also to be understood of birth or generation, and that from everlasting: Cf. מוצא in Job xxxviii. 27, and Numbers xxx. 13. The LXX. render צאצאים more than once by τέκνα, *children*.—ἡγούμενος ὅστις ποιμανεῖ, *a prince who shall shepherd*) In 1 Chron. xi. 2, concerning David, the LXX. have σὺ ποιμανεῖς τὸν λαόν Μου, τὸν 'Ισραήλ· καὶ σὺ ἔσῃ εἰς ἡγούμενον ἐπὶ τὸν λαόν Μου τὸν 'Ισραήλ, *thou shalt shepherd My people Israel, and thou shalt be for a prince over My people Israel*. Concerning the expression *to shepherd*, see Ps. lxxviii. 71, 72. It is indeed a word worthy the kingly office, and at the same time according with the pastoral youth of David at Bethlehem. By the word ποιμανεῖ (*He shall shepherd*) the evangelist includes also and condenses the third [fourth] verse of the chapter of Micah already cited, where the LXX. have the same expression.—τὸν λαόν Μου, MY *people*) which corresponds with the expression in Micah, Μοί ἐξελεύσεται, *shall go forth for* ME, *i.e.*, GOD.—τὸν 'Ισραήλ, *Israel*) The article is added to the name of a man, when put for that of a people. *Israel*, *i.e.*, all the tribes of Israel. In the subsequent narrative no further mention occurs of Bethlehem, so that it may be doubted whether our Lord ever returned thither.

7. Λάθρα, *privily*) lest anything should transpire. This argues insidious designs on the part of Herod.—ἠκρίβωσε, *enquired dili-*

---

¹ A MS. in the Basle Library, entitled there B. vi. 25; but designated as β by Bengel, for the sake of convenience.—See App. Crit., p. 90.—(I. B.)

² See Tregelles on the printed text of the Greek New Testament, pp. 19-26.—(I. B.)

³ The only *very* ancient authority for γὰρ μοι ἐξελ. is C. Theodoret and the Armen. Vers. follow it; but Z (and probably B) and D, and Vulg. omit μοι.—ED.

gently) even to the smallest particle of time. Hence we perceive the craft of Herod,[1] and the simplicity of the Magi.—φανομένου, *appearing*) The Present Tense. Herod enquired the time at which the star which was now visible, had first become so.[2]

8. 'Εξετάσατε ἀκριβῶς, *enquire diligently*) others read ἀκριβῶς ἐξετάσατε,[3] diligently enquire.[4] The variation is of no consequence, especially as it occurs in the words of Herod. Let us pass by such things without comment. The same phrase occurs in the Septuagint Version of Deut. xix. 18 [where we read "καὶ ἐξετάσωσιν οἱ κριταὶ ἀκριβῶς," " and the judges shall enquire diligently."] —ἐπὰν δὲ, *but if*)[5] The use of the particle gives an antithetical force to the succeeding words.—See Luke xi. 22, 34. Herod did not accept the intelligence of the Magi as true, though he considered it as possible ; it is not, therefore, to be wondered at that he did not immediately go with them to worship.

9. Οἱ δὲ ἀκούσαντες, τοῦ βασιλέως, *But when they had heard the king*) The king ought rather to have heard and assisted *them*. The Magi, however, obtained the answer which they desired.[6]— καὶ ἰδοὺ ὁ ἀστήρ, κ.τ.λ, *and, lo, the star*, etc.) During the whole of their journey, they had not seen the star.—ἐλθὼν, *having come*) It may be conjectured, from the use of this verb, that the star

---

[1] So great enmities did that monarch indulge in and foster, although he did not esteem as a fable the doctrine concerning Christ, but was by this time aware of the time and place of His nativity.—*Vers. Germ.*

[2] In the original the passage stands thus—" Præsens tempus, quo conspici cœpta esset stella, *quæ appareret*, quaesivit Herodes." This is evidently a misprint for—" Præsens. Tempus quo conspici cœpta esset stella, *quæ appareret*, quaesivit Herodes."
In his German Version Bengel renders the passage "*und vernahm von ihnen die Zeit, da der Stern erschienen,*" i.e. "*and ascertained accurately from them the Time when the Star appeared.*" In his Harmony he renders it— "*und erlernte mit fleis von ihnen wann der Stern erschienen wäre,*" i.e. "*and learnt with diligence from them, when the star made its appearance.*"—(I. B.)

[3] This is the reading of E. M.—(I. B.)

[4] BC (corrected later) D *abc*, Vulg. read with Beng. ἐξετάσατε ἀκριβῶς. The reading of Rec. Text is without very ancient authority.—Ed.

[5] Engl. Vers. *And when.*—(I. B.)

[6] Nor were they at all affected by the torpor and apathy of the scribes or of the Jews.—*Vers. Germ.*

was subject to the guidance of an intelligent cause.—Cf. ἐλθὼν, in ver. 8.

10. Ἰδόντες, κ.τ.λ., *when they saw*) It must have been night.—τὸν ἀστέρα, *the star*) Both Scripture and the star show them the time and the place: Scripture, indeed, indicates the time with some latitude, in accordance with the general way in which the expectation of the Messiah's coming then universally prevailed.

11. Εἶδον, *they saw*) Sweetly is expressed the increase and progress of their joy from that of seeing the star to that of seeing the KING Himself. The inferior reading, εὗρον[1] (*they found*), corresponds with the words of Herod, "Enquire diligently, and when ye have *found*," etc. But the star, by becoming *stationary*, spared the Magi the labour of enquiring. They did not so much *find* as *see*. - Cf. Luke ii. 17, 20, 26, 30.—προσεκύνησαν Αὐτῷ, *they worshipped Him*) Mary was not an object of worship to the Magi. If she had been conceived without sin, as the greater portion of the Roman Church has now decided, why should she not then have been worshipped as well as now? for she was then already the Mother of the King, who was to be worshipped.—τοὺς θησαυροὺς αὐτῶν, *their treasures*) or *receptacles of treasures*. The Hebrew אצר, which is rendered by the LXX. θησαυρὸς in Prov. viii. 21, etc., signifies a storehouse, a repository, even a portable chest or casket.—προσήνεγκαν, *they offered*) as to a King. They were not offended by His present poverty.—χρυσὸν, καὶ λίβανον, καὶ σμύρναν, *gold, and frankincense, and myrrh*) from the productions of their own country. There was a prediction concerning gold and frankincense in Isaiah lx. 6. These first fruits showed that all things were to belong to Christ, even in the mineral and vegetable kingdoms, etc.—See Haggai ii. 8.

12. Χρηματισθέντες, *being warned of God*) sc. either each of them separately, or all of them through one of their number. Thus they had wished or prayed: for χρηματισμὸς signifies an oracular answer, [and an answer implies a preceding question.] The same word occurs at ver. 22.—μὴ ἀνακάμψαι, *not to return*) They had therefore thought of doing so.—ἀνεχώρησαν, *they departed*) by a road, which led in another direction.

---

[1] BCDa read εἶδον. bc, Vulg. and Rec. Text, with less authority, εὗρον.—ED.

13. Ἐγερθείς, *rising*) i.e. immediately.—τὸ παιδίον, *the child*) Greater regard is paid to Him than to His mother.[1]—ἕως ἄν, κ.τ.λ., *until*, etc.) Thus the faith of Joseph was exercised; all things were not revealed to him at once; he was to await the time of returning [till it should please God to direct him to do so]: nor did the angel speak to him in the meanwhile.—Ἡρώδης, *Herod*) of whom Joseph appears to have hoped well from the discourse of the Magi.

14. Νυκτός, *by night*) The benefit of night is great in times of persecution.

15. Λέγοντος, *saying*) This must be construed with τοῦ προφήτου, *the prophet*, and so also in ver. 17.—ἐξ Αἰγύπτου ἐκάλεσα τὸν υἱόν Μου, *out of Egypt have I called my Son*) Thus Hosea xi. 1, in the original Hebrew, though the LXX. render it, ἐξ Αἰγύπτου μετεκάλεσα τὰ τέκνα αὐτοῦ, *out of Egypt have I called for (summoned) his children*. Aquila,[2] however, renders it ἀπὸ Αἰγύπτου ἐκάλεσα τὸν υἱόν Μου, *From Egypt have I called* [him] *My son*. The meaning of the passage in Hosea is, "Then when Israel was a child, I loved him: and from the time that he was in Egypt, I called him my son." This is evident from the parallelism of either clause. And the expression, "*from the land of Egypt*," occurs in the same sense in Hosea xii. 9, and xiii. 4; and from the Egyptian era, Israel began to be called *the son of God*; see Exod. iv. 22, etc. And God is always said to have *led forth*, never to have *called*, His people *out of Egypt*. In like manner, St Matthew also, when interpreting the passage of the Messiah, and that, too, of Him when a child, connects the quotation with His sojourn *in*, rather than His return *from*, Egypt.—Cf. Isa. xix. 19. Jesus, from His birth, was the Son of God; and immediately after His nativity, He dwelt in Egypt. It behoved, however, that the Messiah, as well as the people, should return from Egypt into the land of promise, for the same reason, viz., because God loved each of them, and called him His Son. The

---

[1] And it is rather towards the name and kingdom of Christ, than towards any power external to Christ, that the world bears a grudge.—*Vers. Germ.*

[2] A native of Sinope, in Pontus, of Jewish descent, who flourished in the second century of the Christian æra. Having renounced Christianity, he undertook to execute a new translation of the Hebrew Scriptures into Greek. —(I. B.)

sojourn of Christ in Egypt was the prelude to the Christianization of that country; see Deut. xxiii. 7. In the first ages of Christianity, the Egyptian Church was greatly distinguished: perhaps it will be so again hereafter: cf. Isa. xix. 24, 25. Concerning the double fulfilment of the single meaning of a single prophecy, cf. Gnomon on ch. i. 22. In short, God embraced in one address, as with one love, both the Messiah Himself, in whom is all His good pleasure, and His people for His sake. The Messiah resembles His people in His adversity; His people resembles the Messiah in its prosperity. *The head and the body are the whole Christ.* Moreover, when His people was in Egypt, Jesus Christ was there also in one of those patriarchs who are enumerated in ch. i. 4.—Cf. Heb. vii. 10.

16. 'Ενεπαίχθη, *was mocked*) Such was the king's impression, entirely at variance with the spirit of the Magi. They did, however, hold the royal authority at nought in comparison with the Divine. Herod did not know what might be doing [and he, therefore, became anxious and infuriated].— ἀποστείλας, *having sent*) sc. murderers, and that suddenly.— ἀνεῖλε, *he slew*) This was a sin crying to Heaven for vengeance; cf. ver. 18.—πάντας, *all*) "Of whom," says Feu-Ardent[1] on Irenæus iii. 18,—"Christ, whilst yet Himself a child, consecrated fourteen thousand as martyrs, by the unutterable cruelty of Herod, as the Ethiopians record in the Liturgy left to them by St Matthew, and the Greeks preserve in their calendar."—τοὺς παῖδας, *the boys*) not girls; cf. Exod. i. 16.—ἀπὸ διετοῦς, *from two years old*) The adjective is put in the masculine, as τριετοῦς in 2 Chron. xxxi. 16; cf. the Hebrew original. κατὰ τὸν χρόνον, κ.τ.λ., *according to the time*, etc.) The time indicated by the Magi was, perhaps, a little beyond a year: and Herod laid down, therefore, two years as the limit of massacre.

18. Φωνὴ ἐν Ῥαμᾶ ἠκούσθη, θρῆνος καὶ κλαυθμὸς καὶ ὀδυρμὸς πολὺς, Ῥαχὴλ κλαίουσα τὰ τέκνα αὐτῆς· καὶ οὐκ ἤθελε παρακληθῆναι, κ.τ.λ.— *A voice was heard in Rama, lamentation and weeping and much mourning: Rachel bewailing her children, and would not be comforted*, etc.) The passage is thus rendered by the LXX., Jer.

---

[1] FRANÇOIS FEU-ARDENT, a Cordelier, was born at Coutance in 1541, became Doctor of the Sorbonne in 1576, and died at Bayeux in 1610. He published an edition of Irenæus, with an original commentary, in 1575.—(I. B.)

xxxi. (xxxviii.) 15:—Φωνὴ ἐν 'Ραμᾶ (Cod. Alex. ἐν τῇ ὑψηλῇ) ἠκούσθη θρῆνου καὶ κλαυθμοῦ καὶ ὀδυρμοῦ· Ραχηλ ἀποκλαιομένη ἐπὶ τῶν υἱῶν αὐτῆς· καὶ οὐκ ἠθέλησε παρακληθῆναι, κ.τ.λ.—*A voice was heard in Rama (Cod. Al. on high) of lamentation and weeping and mourning: Rachel bewailing herself on account of her sons, and would not be comforted,* etc.—ἠκούσθη, *was heard*) so that it reached the Lord. Jeremiah both prefixes and subjoins, *Thus saith the Lord*.—θρῆνος καὶ κλαυθμὸς καὶ ὀδυρμὸς πολὺς,[1] *lamentation and weeping and much mourning*) The LXX. have θρῆνου καὶ κλαυθμοῦ καὶ ὀδυρμοῦ, *of weeping, and of lamentation, and of mourning.* The original Hebrew, however, is נהי בכי תמרורים—*lamentation, weeping of bitternesses,* (*i.e., lamentation and bitter weeping*). The shorter[2] reading of St Matthew, supported by so many versions, viz.,[3] κλαυθμὸς καὶ ὀδυρμὸς πολὺς, *weeping and much mourning*, agrees with this so as to express the Hebrew plural תַּמְרוּרִים, *bitternesses*, by the Greek epithet πολὺς, *much*. I used to suspect that the translators who omitted θρῆνος καὶ, *lamentation and*, had done so from the poverty of their language: but you might, with equal justice, say that the Greek copyists added these words from the LXX., from not duly weighing the force of the adjective πολὺς, *much*, which is not found in the LXX.

The Hebrew words[4] and accents[5] declare the matter more gradually (rem gradatim magis declarant), and exhibit successively,

---

[1] In his Apparatus Criticus, Bengel writes, in loc.:—

"18 (—9ρῆνος καὶ) *Æth. Arab. Copt. Lat.* (et inde *Barb. I.* vel etiam *Cypr.* et *Colbert.* n. 2467). *Pers. Syr.* ex inopiâ synonymorum; *Hieron.* nescio an *Justinus Martyr.* Extat non solum apud LXX., sed etiam in Hebræo." He then goes on, " Inopia synonymorum laborasse," etc., as in the Gnomon, and concludes by referring the reader to that work.—(I. B.)

[2] E. M. has the longer reading.—(I. B.)

[3] So BZ*abc* Vulg. Hilary, 613. D is the only very ancient authority for the 9ρῆνος καὶ of the Rec. Text.—ED.

[4] "Sermo."—(I. B.)

[5] "The design of the accents in general is, to show the rhythmical members of the verses in the Old Testament text. But, as such, the use is twofold—viz., *a*. To show the logical relation of each word to the whole sentence; *b*. to mark the tone syllable to each word. In respect to the former, they serve as signs of *interpunction;* in respect to the latter, as signs of the tone or accent. . . . The use of the accents as signs of *interpunction* is somewhat complicated, since they serve not merely *to separate* the members of a sentence, like our period, colon, and comma, but also as marks of connection."
—*Gesenius*, Heb. Gr. sec. 15, *q v.*—(I. B.)

—(1.) Shrill grief indefinitely: her who mourns, and those whom she mourns, (2.) refusing the consolation offered to her; and the cause why she refused it.—The thirty-first chapter of Jeremiah is prospective to a great degree of the times of the New Testament; and so does this passage refer to this event in the New Testament history, whether Jeremiah regarded at the same time the Babylonian Captivity or not; a greater and less event of distinct periods may correspond with the single meaning of a single prediction, until the prophecy is exhausted.—'Ραχήλ, *Rachel*) put antonomatically for the individual daughters of Rachel and other mothers, who thus had *sons of pangs* [Benoni]. —Cf. Gen. xxxv. 18. The sons of *Rachel* are named: the sons of other mothers are understood at the same time, as in 1 Cor. x. 1, the Gentiles are also included under the fathers of the Jews. The infants of Bethlehem might also be called " sons of Rachel," on account of the tomb of Rachel mentioned in Gen. xxxv. 19, as being near that town: just as the Samaritans (John iv. 12) called Jacob their father, because they lived in the same place where he had formerly dwelt. But *Rama* did also belong to the tribe of Benjamin (see Josh. xviii. 25), who was the son of Rachel. It is quite conceivable that the assassins despatched so suddenly by Herod to Bethlehem, may have proceeded *even as far as Rama*, as the towns were very near together: see Judg. xix. 2, 9, 13; Ezra ii. 21, 26: from which circumstance Jeremiah, a priest from the land of Benjamin, pointed it out as the limit of the massacre.—κλαίουσα, *weeping*) *i.e.*, κλαίει, *weeps*, a Hebraism.—οὐκ ἤθελε παρακληθῆναι, *refused to receive consolation*) A phrase which expresses intense grief.—οὐκ εἰσί, *they are not*) Thus, in the S. V. of Gen. xlii. 36, we read 'Ιωσὴφ οὐκ ἔστι, Συμεὼν οὐκ ἔστι, *Joseph is not, Simeon is not*); and in 1 Kings xx. 40, οὗτος οὐκ ἦν, *he was not*) in the Hebrew איננו, *he is not*, in the singular number used distributively. The mothers mourn each especially their own, or even their only sons; for even only children would, in this case, be expressed in the plural number: the slaughtered infants were of two years old, or a little under, so that a single mother could not easily be deprived of more than one. The event was accurately foretold. Others refer the singular number to the Messiah, whom they suppose the women to have imagined slain, or mourned as banished.

20. Εἰς γῆν Ἰσραήλ, *into the land of Israel*) Joseph was allowed to choose the *town* or *district*, but not the *country* of their abode; since it behoved that Emmanuel should come to years of manhood (adolescere) in His own *land*.—τεθνήκασι, *they are dead*) The plural concisely signifies, that Herod is dead, and that there are not any others who entertain evil designs.[1]—οἱ ζητοῦντες τὴν ψυχήν, *who sought the life*) literally, *who sought the soul.* A phrase employed by the LXX.

22. Βασιλεύει, *is reigning*) Archelaus was reigning, whether with or without the name of king.—ἐφοβήθη, *was afraid*) Anxious about the child, fearful lest Archelaus should emulate his father's hatred.—ἐκεῖ, *thither*) The Hebrew שמה, *thither*, is frequently rendered ἐκεῖ by the LXX.—ἀπελθεῖν, *to depart*) Mary and Joseph also, without doubt, had previously dwelt at Nazareth.—εἰς τὰ μέρη, *into the parts*) From hence may be inferred the poverty of Joseph, who had not a fixed abode which he could return to as a matter of course.—τῆς Γαλιλαίας, *of Galilee*) This did not prevent attentive souls from knowing the real birthplace of Christ.

23. Ἐλθὼν κατῴκησεν εἰς, *he came to and took up his abode at*) [E. V., *he came and dwelt at*], *i.e.*, he came to dwell at, or he dwelt at. The same mode of expression occurs at ch. iv. 13. Thus, in Gen xiii. 18, the LXX. have ἐλθὼν κατῴκησε περὶ τὴν δρῦν, *he came and dwelt by the oak*.—Ναζαρέτ, *Nazareth*) In Hebrew, נצרת. The final ה is rendered in Greek by Τ.—Ναζωραῖος, *a Nazarene*) Our Lord spent His private life—that is, by far the greatest portion of His years—in the town of Nazareth, from whence the surname of Nazarene was given to Him in the common speech of men, whether devoted or hostile to Him, and in the title on the cross. This is what the prophecy here cited by St Matthew had long ago intimated. Some seek for the whole force of this prediction in an allegorical interpretation of the etymology of the word Nazareth; and this indeed should clearly be sought for in נזר, *a diadem*, etc., not from נצר, *to keep or hide*,[2] which Jewish animosity employs maliciously; for the Hebrew צ (Tzade)

---

[1] What a vast host of enemies rising against Christ, from then till now, has perished utterly.—B. G. V.

[2] See Prov. vii. 10, where a harlot is spoken of as נצרת לב, *subtle* of heart. —(I. B.)

is always rendered by the Greek Σ (Sigma), whereas the Greek z (Zeta) universally corresponds to the Hebrew ז (Zayin), as it does also in the word Ναζωραῖος. This rule is universal, which no one can rightly oppose without bringing forward examples to the contrary. Consider what the sound and learned Hiller says on this subject, Syntagm. hermen. p. 347, etc., and Onom. Sacr., pp. 695, 701, 893; and compare his remarks with I. H., a Seelen,[1] medit. exeg., p. 632. This belongs to the etymology of the name Nazareth; it does not, however, establish the allegory. For neither is there any reason why we should ascribe the character of a Levitical Nazarite to Christ (see Matt. xi. 19), nor why we should think that the scope of the prophecy is exhausted by any signification of the word NZR, נזר.

It was predicted by Micah, that Christ should go forth from Bethlehem: *Bethlehem*, בֵּית לֶחֶם, signifies *house of bread*, and Christ is the Bread of Life. But who would have said that the prophecy of Micah was fulfilled by Christ being the bread of life? We know that the town where Christ was born was intended by the prophecy; in like manner, the town where He grew up; and the common surname which thence arose was indicated by the prediction, " Ναζωραῖος κληθήσεται," " *He shall be called a Nazarene:*" and therefore the particle ὅτι[2] is prefixed by the evangelist, as is the custom in citing testimonies. Although at what time that prophet flourished by whom this prediction was uttered; whether the town of Nazareth, of which no other mention occurs in the Old Testament, was then of any account or not; whether that prophet was himself a Nazarene, and deposited this remarkable verse at Nazareth, or whether he left it to posterity, conveyed by word of mouth alone, or also committed to writing,[3] whence St Matthew obtained it, who knows? what signifies it to know? In heaven, some stars illumine

---

[1] JOHN HENRY A SEELEN, an historian and philologist of the Academy of Lubeck, born in the year 1688. He published his *Meditationes Exegeticæ* at Lubeck, 1732.—(I. B.)

[2] The literal meaning of ὅτι is *that*; but in cases like the present it has, by the Greek idiom, merely the force which inverted commas have in English. —(I. B.)

[3] For the prophets have uttered many things which were not inserted in their public writings.—B. G. V.

either hemisphere, some both, some have various risings and settings; on earth, rivers sometimes withdraw themselves from the sight of men, until by hidden ways they reach the place where they again burst forth. Thus the Divine Oracles are dispensed with admirable variety; a singular example of which is afforded by the passage in St John, concerning the three who bear witness in heaven, of which the Eastern Church was for many ages in ignorance, whilst the Western and African Churches maintained it always, though not everywhere. This prediction, indeed, *He shall be called a Nazarene*, was not known or understood by most persons; otherwise Galilee and Nazareth itself would not have been so much despised (see John i. 47, and vii. 52). And, rightly, many have long since denied that this verse exists in the Scriptures of the Old Testament. Its condition, therefore, is the same as that of the prophecy of Enoch, introduced at length by St Jude into the Scriptures of the New Testament, and thus stamped with the seal of inspiration; the same as that of the apothegm, which, though delivered by our Lord, does not occur in the Gospels, but is quoted by the mouth of St Paul, and the pen of St Luke, Acts xx. 35. Nor have the Jews any ground of accusation, because anything is quoted in the New Testament which does not exist in the Old; for they relate many ancient things which equally are not to be found there. Where lay hid the Proverbs of Solomon from ch. xxv. 1; the prophecy of Azariah (2 Chron. xv. 2, etc.); the epistle of Elijah (2 Chron. xxi. 12), until they were inserted in the books of the Old Testament, many ages after they were delivered? Certainly, there was no sufficient reason why St Matthew should frame[1] this, if it had been a perfect novelty in his own time. By such a proceeding, he would have more injured than advantaged the whole Christian cause. He had sufficiently numerous examples of prophecies fulfilled in Jesus of Nazareth without this. Those who interpret this important verse more vaguely, so as to make out that it is contained here or there in the Scriptures of the Old Testament, in truth take away one from the ancient

---

[1] *i.e.*, It would serve no purpose to insert this prediction, if it had been a mere figment.—(I. B.)

prophecies; whereas those who consider τὸ ῥηθὲν (*that which was uttered*), "*He shall be called a Nazarene*," to have been expressly uttered of old, recognise a homogeneous portion of the entire testimony of prophecy, and thus in truth maintain the integrity and defend the simplicity of Scripture (Cf. Calovius's Biblia Illustrata, and Rus's[1] Harmonia Evangelistarum, p. 284). *WHO* was to have the surname of *Nazarene*, is not added in the verse: for wherever anything occurs in the prophecies which is not foreign to the Messiah, that should be understood of the Messiah, although there be no express mention of His name. It is, however, probable that more words than these two may have existed together with them in a very short prediction. The long concealment of this monument of antiquity was agreeable to the manner of Christ's private life, spent in the retirement of *Nazareth*, and calculated to try the faith of saints, and condemn the falsehood of sinners. (See John i. 46, etc., and vii. 41, etc.)

Now that we have proved that the peculiar and primary force of the name *Nazarene*, is to be found in the town itself of *Nazareth*, we proceed to lay down as a corollary, that the etymology of the country, and surname of Christ thence derived, is not unimportant. Christ, the Son of David the Bethlehemite, was not called a Bethlehemite: therefore, in the etymology of the town of Bethlehem, a mystery is not equally sought for. Christ was called a *Nazarene*. This was indeed effected by the discourse of men; but not without the overruling providence of God. It was not by mere accident that Pilate inscribed categorically, in the three cardinal languages, *Jesus, King of the Jews*, and retained what he had written: it did not by mere accident happen that Pilate at the same time inscribed "THE NAZARENE," and that others, both before and after, used the expression with reference to our Lord. The names, "JESUS," "CHRIST," "EMMANUEL," etc., intimate, that that which is implied by their sound is actually being exhibited: you would rightly deny that the surname, "*Nazarene*," alone should be

---

[1] JOHN REINHARD RUS, a learned Lutheran divine of the eighteenth century. The title of the work is "Harmonia Evangelistarum, ita adornata, ut investigatâ, sedulò textus cohærentiâ, nullus versus, sive trajiciatur, sive pretereatur sine brevi ac succinctâ explicatione, quæ justi commentarii loco esse queat." Jenæ 1727-1730.—(I. B.)

without a mystical meaning : נֵזֶר, *a diadem*, is the token of a king's head, and נצרה is, according to Hiller, a town which *crowns* the summit of a mountain; the name, therefore, of Nazarene, may thus be expressed in German, "Zu Cronberg hat der Gecrönte gewohnet,"—"*The crowned one hath dwelt on the summit of a hill.*"—See Ps. cxxxii. 18. The names of places are frequently put for the thing itself which is signified : we pass by the *Veronenses, Placentini, Laudiceni*, of the Latins. The meaning of Scripture is deeper : Simon the Canaanite was also called Zelotes, both from his country and his distinguishing virtue.—See Matt. x. 4, and Luke vi. 15. See especially Is lxiii. 1.

CHAPTER III.

1. Ἐν ταῖς ἡμέραις ἐκείναις, *in those days*) In the Evangelistaries[1] this formula merely denotes the commencement of an extract: but in the Gospels it has a more definite meaning. In the present case it signifies, "whilst Jesus was dwelling at Nazareth." —See ch. ii. 23.[2] An interval of time is denoted between the events last recorded and those now mentioned, not short, yet not remarkable for any great change.—παραγίνεται, *cometh*) This word is pleasantly repeated at ver. 13 : the LXX. frequently introduce it in the present tense.—κηρύσσων, *preaching*) sc. loudly. The expression in ver. 3, φωνὴ βοῶντος (*the voice of one crying*), agrees with this. The words ὁ βαπτιστής, *the Baptist*, and κηρύσσων, *preaching*, declare the two parts of John's office.—ἐν τῇ ἐρήμῳ, *in the wilderness*) See ver. 3.

2. Μετανοεῖτε, *repent ye*) A lovely word (see verses 8, 11), im-

---

[1] The Evangelistaria were selections of ecclesiastical readings from the Gospels.—(I. B.)

[2] At the time that John entered on his public life, Joseph was probably no longer in the land of the living. Therefore, in the words of the text, the reference is to Him, of whom it was said by the prophets, *He shall be called a Nazarene*. Jesus sojourned at Nazareth from His return out of Egypt up to the time of John's entrance on his ministry.—*Harm.*, p. 63.

plying *change your disposition*, put on a disposition royal, heavenly, worthy the kingdom of heaven.¹ Thus Jesus Christ Himself, thus His apostles commenced their preaching: thus the Lord commanded John to write at the commencement of the Apocalypse.—ἡ βασιλεία, *the kingdom*) See Gnomon on ch. iv. 17.—τῶν οὐρανῶν, *of the Heavens*) expressed in the plural number agreeably with the Hebrew שמים.² This phrase ἡ βασιλεία τῶν οὐρανῶν, *the kingdom of the Heavens*,³ is peculiar to Matthew, who employed it that he might cure the Jews, for whom he was writing, of the notion of an earthly kingdom.

3. Οὗτος, κ.τ.λ., *this*, etc.) There are many circumstances recorded in the New Testament, which had been predicted in the Old.—γαρ, *for*) The reason why it was necessary that John should thus arise at that time (as is described in verses 1, 2), was, that it had been so predicted.—φωνή, κ.τ.λ., *a voice*, etc.) See Gnomon on Luke iii. 4. "*A voice*," i.e., "*it is a voice.*" —βοῶντος, *of one crying*⁴) i.e., of John. An analogous phrase occurs in Rom. x. 15, viz., οἱ πόδες τῶν εὐαγγελιζομένων, *the feet of them that preach.*—ἐν τῇ ἐρήμῳ, *in the wilderness*) Not in the temple, or the synagogues. Some construe this passage thus, "*Prepare ye in the wilderness*, etc," because the accents⁵ in the original Hebrew of Isaiah require it to be so construed there. But if such had been the evangelist's meaning, he would subsequently have expressed, in equivalent terms, the parallel phrase בערבה, *in the desert*.⁶ As the passage stands, the expressions, "*preaching in the wilderness*," in ver. 1, and "*a voice of one crying in the wilderness*," in ver. 3, correspond with each other. It comes to the same thing: for where there is the voice, there

¹ In the original, "regnum *cœlorum*," "the kingdom *of the heavens*."—See f. n. 3, infra.—(I. B.)
² See Genesis i. 1., etc.—(I. B.)
³ E. V., "*The Kingdom of Heaven.*" I have generally rendered it thus, as being a phrase more familiar to the English reader.—(I. B.)
⁴ "Clamantis"—*crying out*, uttering with a loud voice—not *weeping.*—(I. B.)
⁵ See p. 132, f. n. 5.—(I. B.)
⁶ In Isaiah xl. 3, the passage stands thus: "The voice of him that crieth in the wilderness, Prepare ye the way of the LORD, make straight in the desert a highway for our God;" where the phrases, *in the wilderness*, and *in the desert*, are in parallelism to each other.—(I. B.)

also are the hearers who are commanded to prepare the way, and there is the Coming of the Lord. St Matthew, also, in ch. iv. 15, contains something different from the Hebrew accents.—Cf. Gnomon on Heb. iii. 7.—τὴν ὁδόν, *the way*) There is one primary way, and this includes many *tracks*, τρίβους.—Κυρίου, *of the Lord*) The Hebrew יהוה, *Jehovah*, for which the Hebrews of later ages substituted אדני, *Adonai*, is rendered by the LXX. Κύριος, *Lord*. In this passage Christ is intended. The appellation Κύριος, *Lord*, when applied to Christ in the New Testament, has various meanings, according to the variety of circumstances, times, and speakers. In passages quoted from the Old Testament it frequently corresponds to the names יהוה and אדני, of which the one expresses His majesty as the Son of God, the other, His glory also as the Messiah. Men amongst whom He walked addressed Him thus with various purport, according to the various extent of their faith. From that time forward, the apostles, and the faithful in general, frequently employed this appellation with reference to His dominion and authority over His own followers, and over all things beside, even in His state of humiliation,[1] but rather in His state of exaltation: in which cases the pronoun "*my*" is sometimes added, which is never joined with the tetragrammaton יהוה.—εὐθείας) *straight*.

4. Αὐτὸς δὲ ὁ Ἰωάννης, κ.τ.λ., *And the same John*, etc.) A remarkable description. Even the dress and food of John preached, being in accordance with his teaching and office. Such as should be that of penitents, such was always that of this minister of penitence.—Cf. Gnomon on ch. ix. 14, and xi. 18.—ἀπὸ τριχῶν καμήλου, *of camels' hair*) His dress was mean,[2] and rough,

---

[1] "Exinanitionis;" literally, *of being emptied out:* a phrase of frequent occurrence, suggested by the words in Phil. ii. 7, ἑαυτὸν ἐκένωσε. *He emptied Himself*—rendered in E. V., made *Himself of no reputation*.—(I. B.)

[2] "Parabilis." It is curious to see the changes which took place in the meaning of this word. In classical Latin, it signified (1) procurable, (2) easy to be procured, (3) ordinary, cheap, not costly, mean.—(See Ainsworth, in voc.) In the middle ages, as we learn from the *Glossarium Manuale ad Scriptores Mediæ et Infimæ Latinitatis*, it had a very different signification. *The abbreviator of Du Cange* writes thus: " PARABILIS. Testamentum Perpetui Episcopi Turonensis: *Equum meum Parabilem, et mulum quem elegeris do, lego.* Equus forte qui Gallis dicitur *Cheval de parade*, ad pompam, ad apparatum."—(I. B.)

and coarsely woven.—Cf. Mark i. 6.—καὶ ζώνην δερματίνην περὶ τὴν ὀσφὺν αὐτοῦ, and a girdle of skin around his loins) Thus the LXX. in 2 Kings i. 8, of Elijah, καὶ ζώνην δερματίνην περιεζωσμένος τὴν ὀσφὺν αὐτοῦ, and girt around his loins with a girdle of skin. The girdle of John, like that of Elijah, was not of leather, but of skin rudely dressed. It is not without object that Scripture records the dress of many saints, of the Baptist, and of Jesus Christ Himself.— τροφή, food) We gather the nature of his drink from Luke i. 15. —ἀκρίδες, locusts) In Lev. xi. 22, the LXX. render חגב (an animal which the Jews were permitted to eat), by ἀκρίς, locust.—μέλι ἄγριον, wild honey) flowing spontaneously.—See 1 Sam. xiv. 25. —Locusts might sometimes fail.

5. Πᾶσα, all) i.e., from all parts.

6. Ἐβαπτίζοντο, received baptism) The verb is in the middle voice.—ἐξομολογούμενοι, confessing) The preposition ἐξ denotes that they confessed their sins freely and expressly, not merely in the ear of John. A true confession mentions even individual sins (as formerly in the case of sin-offerings), although it does not enumerate them one by one. It holds the just mean between the lax abuse of a general formula and the narrow strictness of auricular confession. Thus it relieves the soul. At the Baptism of Repentance men confessed their sins, at the Baptism of Christ they confessed Christ.

7. Πολλούς, κ.τ.λ., many, etc.) of whom some adhered to their purpose of receiving the baptism of John; some, deterred by his just denunciations, appear to have gone back. By far the greater number did not come at all.—See ch. xxi. 25, and Luke vii. 30. —τῶν Φαρισαίων καὶ Σαδδουκαίων, of the Pharisees and Sadducees) Differing sects.—αὐτοῖς, to them) i.e., to the Pharisees especially, but also to the people, before baptizing them.—See ver. 11, and Luke iii. 7. It frequently occurs, that words are mentioned after the act which they accompany or precede.—See 2 Sam. i. 16, 15.—γεννήματα, broods) Various families.—ἐχιδνῶν, of vipers) This is said in opposition to their boasting of their descent from Abraham.—τίς, κ.τ.λ., who? etc.) As though he had said, "You appear to be showing the way to others, but who showed it to you?" He implies that wrath was in store for them; that there was, close at hand, a means of escaping it, but that the Pharisees and Sadducees were strangers to it.—ὑπέδειξεν, hath showed)

The compound verb has the same meaning as the simple δείκνυμι. He approves of their coming, but with an important condition.— φυγεῖν, *to flee*) sc. by baptism.—ἀπὸ τῆς μελλούσης ὀργῆς, *from the wrath to come*) which they will incur, rejecting the kingdom of Heaven by their impenitence. That same wrath is afterwards spoken of, in 1 Thess. i. 10, as τῆς ἐρχομένης, *which is coming*. At the same time, the error of the Sadducees in denying the resurrection is refuted. That wrath was to come upon them at the destruction of Jerusalem and the last Judgment.

8. Ποιήσατε, *produce*—καρπὸν ἄξιον, *worthy fruit*) Origen remarks, that in St Matthew worthy fruit is required in the singular number from the Pharisees and Sadducees; whereas, in St Luke, worthy fruits are required in the plural number from *the people*. I do not myself see what difference it makes in the matter. The singular καρπός, *fruit*, is often used collectively; and in the preaching of St John it may be opposed to *barrenness*: in the plural number, it implies *fecundity*. Men are here represented as trees; and the fruit is, therefore, their repentance.—τῆς μετανοίας, *of repentance*) Construe these words with καρπόν.[1] Thus, in Acts xxvi. 20, we read ἄξια τῆς μετανοίας ἔργα.—μετάνοια, *repentance*, is an entire change of character,[2] and a renunciation of all that is evil, by which renunciation we wish that evil void or undone.

9. Μὴ δόξητε, *think not*) The verb δοκῶ, *to appear or imagine* (in the same manner as φάσκω, *to allege or suppose*, the particle ὡς, *as*; and the Latin expressions, præ me fero, *to profess;* ostendo, *to declare;* puto, *to suppose;* videor, *to seem;* apparet, *it appears;* species, *appearance*), sometimes denotes a thing which is true, and at the same apparent; sometimes an empty appearance, which any one presents to himself or others. And thus the meaning in this passage is, "You may indeed say this, in some degree, with truth, but you must not plume yourselves upon it."[3]

---

[1] Bengel would apparently render the passage thus: *worthy fruit of repentance;* and so in the passage immediately cited from the Acts, *worthy works of repentance.* E. V. has, in the one passage, *fruits meet for repentance;* in the other, *works meet for repentance.*—(I. B.)

[2] This scarcely expresses the original " *transmutatio mentis.*" Ainsworth gives us the first signification of MENS—" *That part of the rational soul which is the seat of natural parts and acquired virtues.*"—(I. B.)

[3] There is nothing that men will not rake together, especially self-

—λέγειν, *to say*) i.e. with safety.—τὸν Ἀβραάμ, *Abraham*) as there is no lack of his posterity.—λέγω γὰρ ὑμῖν, *for I say unto you*) A most solemn formula, employed by a great man, on an occasion of the highest importance.—Cf. Gnomon on ch. v. 18.—δύναται, *is able*) The Jews supposed that they *could not* fall utterly away. —ἐκ τῶν λίθων τούτων, *from these stones*) and from any other material, as He produced Adam from the clod. God is not tied to the law of succession in the Church.—τούτων, *these*) The stones to which John pointed were perhaps those which had been placed there in the time of Joshua, that they might be for a testimony that the people of Israel had crossed the river Jordan, and entered the Land of Promise, and that they owed the land, not to themselves, but to God. The words sound like a proverbial expression, as well as those in Luke xix. 40.—τέκνα, *children*) i.e. according to the spirit. They were indeed children according to the flesh, who are called nevertheless broods of vipers.

10. Ἤδη δὲ, *but now*) Placed in opposition[1] to μελλούσης, *which is to come*, in ver. 7.—καὶ, κ.τ.λ.., *also*, etc) Where grace manifests itself, there also is wrath shown to the ungrateful. It is not only *possible* that you should be punished, but *also* punishment is nigh at hand.—τὴν ῥίζαν, *the root*) The axe was aimed not merely at the branches, but at the root itself.—τῶν δένδρων, *of the trees*) i.e. the Jews (see Luke xiii. 7–9), in comparison with whom the Gentiles were mere stones.—κεῖται, *lies*) Although the blow has not yet begun to be struck.—ἐκκόπτεται, *is being cut down*) The present tense is used, to show that there will be no delay.—πῦρ, *fire*) See Heb. vi. 8.

11. ὑμᾶς, *you*) John, therefore, did not exclude the Pharisees from baptism.—ἐν ὕδατι, *in water*) The conclusion of the verse corresponds with this part of it. John, however, depreciates not so much his baptism as himself. And again, in this place alone, is that *fire* mentioned in contradistinction to *water*, whereas the Holy Spirit is mentioned in every case.—εἰς μετάνοιαν, *for repentance*) This portion of the verse corresponds with ver. 12.—δὲ, *but*) The contrast does not apply only to those who confer, but to

justiciaries, in order to claim God as their own, even after they have rejected repentance toward God.—*Vers. Germ.*

[1] In ver. 7 he spoke of the wrath of God as *future*, as yet *to come*; he now speaks of it as already *present*, or close at hand.—(I. B.)

those also who receive baptism (See Acts i. 5, *but ye shall be baptized with the Holy Ghost*), and also to the different times.—ὀπίσω μου, *after me*) It was fitting that John should be born a little before the Messiah.—ἐρχόμενος, *that cometh*) sc. immediately; see ver. 13.—ἰσχυρότερός μου, *mightier than I*) One whom you ought to fear and to worship, rather than me, who am feeble. John teaches, both here and in ver. 12, that his power is not great; whereas that of Christ, as God, is infinite.[1] He does not say directly, "Messiah cometh after me," but expresses it by a paraphrase more obscurely, and yet more augustly. John, moreover, said this at the time when he possessed the greatest power; see Acts xiii. 25.—βαστάσαι, *to bear*) As a servant bears the shoes, which his master has either called for, or commanded to be taken away.—Cf. Psa. lx. 8.—Αὐτὸς, *He*) Believe on Him: see Acts xix. 4.—ὑμᾶς, *you*) sc. as many as shall receive Him.—βαπτίσει, *shall baptize*) i.e. *abundantly impart*; see Titus iii. 6; Acts ii. 3, 4, 17, and x. 44; and shall thereby show Himself the *mightier*. The Holy Spirit and fire have the greatest power.—ἐν, κ.τ.λ., *in*, etc.) This was the difference between John and Christ; see John i. 33.—Πνεύματι Ἁγίῳ, *the Holy Ghost*) See Gnomon on Luke iii. 16.—καὶ πυρὶ, *and with fire*) St Luke has these words, though St Mark has not: even, therefore, were the reading doubtful in St Matthew, there would be no danger;[2] it is certain, however, that he also wrote καὶ πυρί. The Holy Spirit, with which Christ baptizes, has a fiery power, and that fiery power was manifested to the eyes of men; see Acts ii. 3.

12. οὗ, *whose*) This, and Αὐτοῦ, *His*, being placed emphatically thrice, shows the power of Christ. οὗ—αὐτοῦ is a Hebraism. —τὸ πτύον, *the fan*) i.e. the Gospel.—ἐν τῇ χειρὶ Αὐτοῦ, *in His hand*) even now. The whole of John's harangue, and therefore the commencement of the Gospel, agrees entirely with the last clause of Old Testament prophecy, in Mal. iii. 19–24, where the connection of things from Moses to the conclusion of ancient prophecy, and thence to Christ's forerunner and Christ Himself,

---

[1] A power, which there is no one who shall not experience, either exercised for salvation, or else in terrible vengeance.—*Vers. Germ.*

[2] Orig. 4, 131e, 132c, Iren. 321, Cypr. 1l1l. Vulg. have καὶ πυρί. It is only some more recent uncial MSS. (ESV in Tischend. Gr. Test.) and Syr. of Jerus., which have omitted the words.—ED.

and the day of His universal judgment, is exquisitely and solemnly declared.—Αὐτοῦ, *His*) Neither His forerunner, nor any of His apostles, had this fan in the same manner as the Lord Jesus Himself. The consolation of His ministers in their weakness is, "The Lord will do it." Their wrath, though void of strength, is not vain.—τὴν ἅλωνα Αὐτοῦ, *His threshing-floor*) The wayfarers are in the threshing-floor, the conquerors in the garner.[1]—Αὐτοῦ, *His*) See Heb. iii. 6.—καὶ συνάξει τὸν σῖτον Αὐτοῦ εἰς τὴν ἀποθήκην, *and will gather His wheat into the garner*) Αὐτου, *His*, must either be omitted or construed with ἀποθήκην, *garner*;[2] cf. Matt. xiii. 30, τὸν δὲ σῖτον συναγάγετε εἰς τὴν ἀποθήκην Μου, *but gather the wheat into My garner*. The Same is Lord of the *wheat* as of the *garner*: the Same of the *garner* as of the *threshing-floor*. See Luke iii. 17.—ἄχυρον, *chaff*) The chaff is held of no[3] account.[4]—πυρὶ, *with fire*) Every one must be either baptized with fire here, or burned with fire hereafter: there is no other alternative.—ἀσβέστῳ, *unquenchable*) See therefore that your sins be first blotted out. In Job xx. 26, the LXX. have πῦρ ἄκαυστον, *incombustible fire* [*i.e.* fire that cannot be burnt out] *shall consume the ungodly*: or, rather, from the Cod. Alex., ἄσβεστον, unquenchable, *unextinguishable* (which word would otherwise not be found in the LXX.), so as to render נָפַח לֹא אֵשׁ, *fire which can never be extinguished*.

14. Διεκώλυεν, *forbade*) John had not yet known that this was the Messiah. He had known, however, that the Messiah was close at hand, and that He would come to his baptism, and be indicated by a clear sign; see John i. 33. In the meanwhile, as soon as he sees Jesus, from that sympathy by which he had been moved in the womb, and from His most gracious aspect, he judges that this candidate for baptism must be the Messiah, and skilfully declares his conviction by a previous protest.[5] See

---

[1] One cannot well express in English the contrast implied in the very rhythm of Bengel's Latin, "In *area* sunt viatores, in *horreo* victores."—ED.
[2] "Which Luther has rightly done."—Not. Crit.
[3] Cf. Gnomon on chap. xIII. 40.—(I. B.)
[4] Although at times it is not unlike the wheat.—*Vers. Germ.*
[5] By this protest, precaution was becomingly taken, on the part of Providence, that the humiliation wherewith Christ condescended to undergo baptism, should not prove at all derogatory to His dignity.— *Vers. Germ.*

Luther's Kirchen Postille, on this passage, Fest. Epiph., Part II., ed. Spen., ff. 95, 96.—*ἐγώ, I*) It is probable that John himself had not been baptized: see Luke i. 15, fin.—*χρείαν, need*) For it is elsewhere the part of the greater to baptize, of the less to be baptized, and to come on that account to one who baptizes.— *ὑπὸ Σοῦ βαπτισθῆναι, to be baptized by Thee*) sc. with Thy baptism of the Spirit and of fire. If either of us is to be baptized by the other, I am he.—*Σὺ ἔρχῃ; comest Thou?*) sc. seeking to be baptized.

15. "Ἄφες, *permit*) He courteously reduces John to silence. The word *ἀφίησιν, he permits*, at the end of the verse, refers to this.— *ἄρτι, now*) sc. without delay, this once.—*οὕτω, thus*) as I have come to thee.—*πρέπον, becoming*) That, which did not to John appear becoming, was in reality especially so, because it was righteous. The propriety which is manifested in all the counsels and works of God, claims our attention and admiration. See Heb. ii. 10, vii. 26. The discourses and actions of Christ are pre-eminently conspicuous for that propriety, which, so well expressed by the Evangelists, affords a proof that they wrote under the impulse of the Holy Spirit, since it could not have been the product of human genius, however exalted.— *ἡμῖν, to us*) Our Lord speaks as if He were not yet fully known by John. It becomes *Me*, as the principal; *thee*, as the minister. In the mind of Jesus it might also have this sense, " It becomes Me and My Father that I should fulfil all righteousness." See v. 17, and cf. Heb. ii. 10.—*πληρῶσαι, to fulfil*) all righteousness. This is effected, not by John and Jesus, but by Jesus alone, who undertook that very thing in His baptism; whence the appellation, " *baptism*," is transferred also to His passion, Luke xii. 50.— *πᾶσαν δικαιοσύνην, all righteousness*) i.e. all the component parts of righteousness; and therefore this part also, the earnest of the other greater parts. In accordance with the *particular* view of righteousness, it would seem that John should be baptized by Jesus: in accordance with the *universal* compass of righteousness, the matter was inverted. Jesus uttered the words here recorded,

Subsequently, by reason of the sign which, in accordance with the promise of God, was added after the baptism, John was so much the more confirmed and fitted for bearing testimony of Jesus being the Son of God.—*Harm.*, p. 146.

instead of that which others who were baptized, being sinners, confessed concerning their *sins*. Such a speech suited none save the Messiah Himself. In matters even the most humble, the Son of God watches over the right of His own majesty. See John xiii. 7, seqq., xiv. 30, xviii. 5, xx. 36.—τότε, *then*) sc. forthwith.

16. Ἀνέβη εὐθύς, *went up immediately*) There was nothing to detain Him longer. Thus also He rose immediately from the dead.—ἰδού, κ.τ.λ., *lo*, etc.) A novel and great occurrence.—Αὐτῷ, *to Him*) This implies far more than if the Evangelist had said "*above Him.*"—οἱ οὐρανοί, *the heavens*) in the plural number.

16, 17. Καί, κ.τ.λ., *and*, etc.) A most glorious manifestation of the Holy Trinity, and a proof of what occurs when we are baptized, since Christ was not baptized for Himself. And He received the Holy Spirit to baptize us with. See John i. 33.—ὡσεὶ περιστεράν, *like a dove*) See Gen. viii. 10, 11.

17. Φωνή, κ.τ.λ., *a voice*, etc.) A most open manifestation of God, such as those recorded in Acts ii. 2, 3; Exod. xix. 4, 9, 16, xl. 34, 35; Num. xvi. 31, 42; 1 Kings viii. 10, 11, xviii. 38.—οὗτός ἐστιν, *This is*) St Mark and St Luke record that it was said, "Σὺ εἶ," "*Thou art.*" St Matthew has expressed the meaning. The words, "οὗτός—εὐδόκησα," occur again in xvii. 5. Faith assents, declaring, "Thou art the Son of God," as in xvi. 16.—ὁ, *the*) The article introduced twice has great emphasis.—Υἱός, *Son*) See John i. 18, and iii. 16 —ἀγαπητός, *beloved*) This might appear to be a proper name (cf. ch. xii. 18), so as to produce these two predications : (1.) This is *My Son*; (2.) He is *the Beloved*, in whom I am well pleased. It is clear, however, from Luke iii. 22, that *Beloved* is an epithet. Love is something natural, because *This* is the *Son*; good-pleasure, something, as it were, additional, because He *does* the things which please the Father. He is the Beloved, the only one; He shares not the Father's love with another.—ἐν ᾧ, *in whom*) The preposition ἐν, *in*, indicates especially the object, and then also the cause of the Father's *good-pleasure*. The Son is of Himself the object of the Father's good-pleasure, and in the Son, all persons and all things. A phrase of the LXX.; cf. Gnomon on Col. ii. 18.—εὐδόκησα, *I am well pleased*) The verb εὐδοκῶ, *to be well pleased*, and the noun

εὐδοκία, *good-pleasure*, are employed when one is pleased either by what one has, or does ones's self, or by that which another has or does. Both parts of this notion agree with the present passage concerning the good-pleasure of the Father in the Son; for there is an eternal στοργή (*natural affection*) towards the only-begotten, a perpetual graciousness towards the Mediator, and in Him towards us, the sons of reconciliation. In ch. xvii. 5, are added the words, "Αὐτοῦ ἀκούετε," "*Hear Him*;" for then He was about to speak of His passion: now they are not added; for, at the commencement of His ministry, He only taught that which the Father spake, "*This is My Son.*"

CHAPTER IV.

1. Τότε, *then*) sc. on His baptism.—ἀνήχθη, *He was led up*) sc. towards Jerusalem, by an inward impulse.—εἰς τὴν ἔρημον, *into the wilderness*) a wilder part than that mentioned in ch. iii. 1.—ὑπὸ τοῦ Πνεύματος, *by the Spirit*) sc. the Holy Spirit; see ch. iii. 16.—πειρασθῆναι, *to be tempted*) This temptation is a sample of our Lord's whole state of humiliation (exinanitionis), and an epitome of all the temptations (not only moral, but still more especially spiritual), which the devil has contrived from the beginning.—ὑπὸ τοῦ Διαβόλου, *by the Devil*) The LXX. generally render the Hebrew שטן, *Satan* or *Adversary*, by Διάβολος, *Devil* or *Accuser*: only in 1 Kings xi., and there twice or thrice, they translate it Σατάν, *Satan*.

2. Νηστεύσας, *when He had fasted*) no doubt by virtue of His baptism. Fasting implies also abstinence from drink.—ἡμέρας, *days*) In these days, during this retirement, matters of the greatest importance passed between God and the Mediator.—τεσσαράκοντα, *forty*) A celebrated measure of time, also, in the lives of Moses and Elijah. But the condition of Moses, when without food, was one of glory; that of Christ (which is more to be wondered at), one of humiliation. An angel brought food to Elijah before his fast commenced; many angels ministered to Christ after His fast ended. Jesus passed forty days before He

appeared in public: forty days, as if for the sake of preparation before His ascension.—ὕστερον, *afterwards*) up to this point it had not been so much a temptation as a preparation for it: cf. the beginning of the following verse.—ἐπείνασι, *He hungered*) *Hunger is a very bitter temptation*; *thirst* He experienced in His passion. This temptation may be compared with that which is described in Gen. iii.: the Tempter employed the same arts; but that cause, which the first-formed pair of the human race had lost, Christ restored.

3. Προσελθὼν Αὐτῷ, *having come to Him*) sc. in a visible form. The Tempter watched his time.[1]—ὁ πειράζων, *the tempter*) who did not wish it to be known that he was Satan: yet Christ at the conclusion of the interview, and not till then, calls him, in ver. 10, Satan, after that Satan had plainly betrayed his satanity, *i.e.*, pride, his peculiar characteristic. Thus, by Divine skill, He defeated his infernal skill. The tempter seems to have appeared under the form of a γραμματεύς, *scribe*, since our Lord thrice replies to him by the word, γέγραπται, "*It is written*."— εἰ, *if*) Thus also, in ver. 6, Satan both doubts himself, and endeavours to produce doubt, to take away that which is true, to teach that which is false. He solicits our Lord, stating that hypothetically, which had been (iii. 17) declared categorically from heaven.—εἰπί, κ.τ.λ., *command*, etc.) The tempter acknowledges that He who is the Son of God must be Almighty.— οἱ, κ.τ.λ., *these*, etc.) *i.e.*, that some one of these stones become bread [or *a loaf*]: see Luke iv. 3, [where it is, "Command *this stone* (sing.) that it be made bread."]—λίθοι, *stones*) *q. d.*, "You are in the wilderness, which has hard stones, but no bread." Nay, on very different grounds shalt thou become convinced, O Tempter, that this is the Son of God. Soon will He commence the work of thy destruction. See Luke iv. 34, 41.

4. Γέγραπται, *it is written*) Jesus does not appeal to the Voice from heaven: He does not reply to the arguments of the Tempter: against those arguments He employs the Scripture alone, and simply cites its assertions. He declines to state

[1] Our Lord spent that season of the year in the wilderness, in which the nights are longer, the wild beasts more ravenous, the weather more inclement, and when there was no means of obtaining food either from trees or herbs.—See *Harm. Evang.* 149.

whether He be the Son of God or not. When addressing mankind, our Lord seldom quoted Scripture, but said, "*I say unto you.*" He says that only in answer to Satan, "*It is written;*" *i.e.*, "Whoever I am, I assuredly keep to that which is written." All the statements which He thus advanced were in themselves indisputable: and yet He keeps to that, "*it is written.*" By doing which, He declares that He is the Destined One who should fulfil Scripture; and at the same time shows the high authority of Scripture itself, irrefragable even to Satan.—οὐκ ἐπ' ἄρτῳ μόνῳ ζήσεται ἄνθρωπος, αλλ᾽ ἐπὶ παντὶ ῥήματι ἐκπορευομένῳ διὰ στόματος Θεοῦ, *Man shall not live by bread alone, but by every word that proceedeth out of the mouth of God*) The LXX. (Deut. viii. 3) prefix the definite article ὁ to ἄνθρωπος (*man*), and repeat after Θεοῦ (*of God*) ζήσεται ὁ ἄνθρωπος (*shall man live*). Even in the wilderness, the Israelites had felt the force of these words. The sixth chapter of the same book is cited in ver. 7 and 10: so that the two paraschae,[1] ואתחנן and עקב, contain the three sayings propounded to the Israelites in the wilderness, and in the wilderness employed by Christ as a sword against the tempter. At the same season of the year[2] at which Moses had uttered them, Jesus employed these sayings against the tempter.— ζήσεται, *shall live*, etc.) Jesus had experienced this during these forty days. It is equally easy to live without bread, or to make bread out of stone. This is truly αὐτάρκεια,[3] *constant tranquillity of mind* (*præsens animi quies*), to require nothing besides *life*. Jesus knew that He should live.—ἄνθρωπος, *man*. He does not

---

[1] The Pentateuch is divided into 50 or 54 *Paraschioth*. or larger sections, according as the Jewish lunar year is simple or intercalary; one of which sections was read in the synagogue every Sabbath-day. This division many of the Jews suppose to have been appointed by Moses; but it is by others attributed, and with greater probability, to Ezra. These paraschioth were, as in the instances referred to by Bengel, called by the Hebrew words with which they happened to begin; they were further subdivided into smaller sections, termed *Siderim*, or orders.—(I. B.)

[2] GRESWELL gives, as the date of our Lord's being led up into the wilderness (v. 1), Sebat 28, Jan. 24, Fer. 1 (*i.e.* Sunday); and of Satan's coming to Him (v. 3), Veader 9, Martii 5, Fer. 6 (*i.e.* Friday).—See his *Harmonia Evangelica*.—(I. B.)

[3] Literally, *self-sufficingness*—a word which sometimes signifies independence, at other times has the force of entire contentedness.—(I. B.)

reply to the tempter with reference to the appellation, "Son of God," but speaks as if one of many, who were bound to the Written Word. And already in the time of Moses, Divine Wisdom had expressed all this testimony in those words with which the Saviour was to smite the tempter. Jerome says, "Propositum erat Domino humilitate Diabolum vincere, non potentiâ,"—" *The Lord had determined to overcome the Devil, not by power, but by humility.*"—ἐπὶ παντὶ ῥήματι ἐκπορευομένῳ διὰ στόματος Θεοῦ, *by every word that proceedeth out through the mouth of God*) Thus in Psalm lxxxix. (lxxxviii.) 34, the LXX. have, concerning a Divine promise, τὰ ἐκπορευόμενα διὰ τῶν χειλέων Μου —*the things which proceed out through My lips*. Cf. concerning vows: S. V. of Num. xxx. 13, and Deut. xxiii. 23: Cf. also Jer. xvii. 16, and Num. xxxii. 24.—*That which goeth forth out of the mouth* (exitus oris), is put by Metonomy for *that which is uttered by the mouth.*—διὰ στόματος, *through the mouth*) and, therefore, *from the heart*.

5. Τότε, *then*) St Matthew describes the attempts of Satan in the order of time in which they were made; see Gnomon on verses 8, 10: St Luke observes a gradation in the places, and mentions successively (iv. 1, 5, 9) the desert, the mountain, the temple; which change of order, not only harmless but beneficial, is a proof that the one evangelist did not copy from the other. Perhaps, also, the tempter assailed our Lord with something of the third temptation before the second, and appeared in various disguises.—παραλαμβάνει, *taketh along with him*[1]) An abbreviated mode of expression[2] for *he takes and leads*. The same word is used with the same force, in ver. 8. St Luke, iv. 9, 5, uses the words ἤγαγεν, *led* [Him],—ἀναγαγὼν, *leading* [Him] *up*. A marvellous power was granted to the tempter, until our Lord says to him, in ver. 10, "Depart." "It is not to be wondered at," says Gregory, "that Christ should permit Himself to be led about by the Devil, since He permitted Himself to be crucified by the Devil's members." Satan tempts everywhere.—Cf. on the change of place, Num. xxiii. 13, 27. Christ was tempted everywhere, in all places where afterwards He was to exercise

---

[1] See Blomfield in loc.—(I. B.)
[2] See Appendix on Concisa Oratio.—ED.

His office.—εἰς τὴν ἁγίαν πόλιν, *into the holy city*) where an angelic guard might have seemed especially to be expected.—ἐπὶ *upon*) Our Lord was as truly on the pinnacle, and on the mountain, as He was in the desert.—πτερύγιον, *pinnacle*) to which the ascent was far more easy than the descent from it. What this pinnacle was, antiquarians doubt.[1] Christ was tempted by height and depth.

6. Γέγραπται, *it is written*) A most specious temptation, which appears to quote Scripture appositely. There is no doubt but that Satan must have often felt the force of this saying, from the protection which the angels extended to the godly against him.—ὅτι—περὶ σοῦ καὶ ἐπὶ, κ.τ.λ.) *He shall give his angels charge concerning thee, and in their hands they shall bear thee up, lest at any time thou dash thy foot against a stone.* The LXX. render Ps. xci. (xc.) 11, 12,—ὅτι—περὶ σοῦ, τοῦ διαφυλάξαι σε ἐν πάσαις ταῖς ὁδοῖς σου ἐπὶ, κ.τ.λ., *He shall give his angels charge over thee, to keep thee in all thy way: they shall bear thee up in their hands, lest thou dash thy foot against a stone.* The fraud of Satan consists rather in false application, than in omission.—ἐπὶ χειρῶν, *in their hands*) That is, they shall guard Thee with great circumspection.—λίθον, *a stone*) i.e., one of those of which the Temple was built. The tempter applies the psalm speciously.

7. Πάλιν γέγραπται, *it is written again*) Although Satan retorted the phrase, "It is written," Jesus does not suffer it to be forcibly taken from Him as something trite, but employs it three times. Scripture is to be interpreted and reconciled by Scrip-

---

[1] τὸ πτερύγιον. The article τό indicates something single of its kind; and, therefore, πτερύγιον cannot mean a porticus or corridor; nor would there be any special *eminence* in πτερύγιον so understood. It rather signifies the apex of the *fastigium*, αἴτωμα, or tympanum of the Temple. Cf. the use of the word (τὸ πτερύγιον τοῦ ἱεροῦ), also τοῦ ναοῦ, by *Hegesippus* (in *Euseb.* ii. 23, and *Routh*, R.S. i. 210, 339), in his account of the martyrdom of St James. There, also, it is evidently a pointed eminence; and it would seem that a person there standing, would be visible and audible to a large concourse of people, such as we may suppose collected in the court of the Israelites."—*Wordsworth* in loc. "The general opinion, that our Lord was placed on *Herod's royal portico*, described Jos. Ant. xv. 11, 5, is probably right. That portico overhung the ravine of Kedron from a dizzy height."—*Alford* in loc. Various other suppositions have been speciously supported and illustrated. —(I. B.)

ture.—οὐκ ἐκπειράσεις, κ.τ.λ.) *thou shall not tempt*, etc.—Thus the LXX. in Deut. vi. 16. According to the usage of those interpreters, ἐκπειράζω is not a word of stronger signification than πειράζειν.—Jesus, however, means, "It is not Mine to provoke God by tempting Him."—Κύριον, *the Lord*) This is put as a proper name.

8. Πάλιν, *again*) This was the third and last conflict, as is evident from the expression "*Depart*," ver. 10.—ὄρος, *a mountain*) A new theatre of temptation.—δείκνυσιν, *shows*) To His eyes those things which the horizon enclosed: the rest, perhaps, by enumeration and indication. Satan is a subtle spirit.

9. Δώσω, *I will give*) But the Son is the heir of all things, and whatever authority Satan possessed on account of man's defection from God, that, Christ, *stronger than he*,[1] took from him, not by compact, but by conquest. What the devil could not persuade Christ to do in his temptation, that he will effect by his vassal the Beast, see Rev. xiii. 2. And what he offered to Christ, he will give to that adversary of His, viz., *the kingdoms of the world*.—ἐὰν, κ.τ.λ., *if*, etc.) Vast pride, to offer all the kingdoms of the earth as a gift, in return for one act of adoration acknowledging that gift.[2] Without doubt, he appeared in an august form.

10. Ὕπαγε, *depart*) "*Get thee behind Me, Satan*," said the Lord to Peter, when he took Him and endeavoured to dissuade Him from undergoing His passion; thus commanding Peter to retire into the proper place of a disciple, *i.e.*, behind Him. But to Satan He said, Depart, Satan: go, not *behind* Me, but plainly *from* Me.—Σατανᾶ, *Satan*) *q.d.* "Thou hast tried to discover who I am, and I tell thee who thou art." He calls the tempter, when he wished to appear specially gracious to Him, *Satan*.[3]— Κύριον—προσκυνήσεις, κ.τ.λ., *Thou shalt worship the Lord thy God, and Him only shalt thou serve*) In Deut. vi. 13, the LXX. have Κύριον—φοβηθήσῃ, κ.τ.λ., *Thou shalt fear the Lord*, etc. Jesus substitutes *worship* aptly for *fear*.—Cf. ver. 9.—μόνῳ, *only, alone*)

[1] Luke xi. 21, 22.—(I. B.)

[2] "What the angel did not permit John to do, that the tempter demands of Jesus, the Lord of all (Rev. xxii. 8, 9)."—*Vers. Germ.*

[3] For he had plainly showed, by his pride, that he was Satan.—*Vers. Germ.*

Thus the LXX. have it, who have inserted μόνος; also in Gen. iii. 11, 17, without doing violence to the meaning.

11. "Αγγελοι, *angels*) Who had probably witnessed the contest. Cf. 1 Cor. iv. 9; 1 Tim. iii. 16.—διηκόνουν, *ministered*) Undoubtedly, by doing that which was then necessary, sc. bringing Him food.—Cf. 1 Kings xix. 5, 6.

12. 'Ακούσας δὲ ὅτι, κ.τ.λ., *but having heard that,* etc.) The name of Jesus is expressed in ver. 17. It is not expressed in ver. 12,[1] because this passage, verses 12–16, when taken in connection with what precedes it, intimates in what manner John made room for the Lord. But in ver. 17, etc., is described the actual commencement of the Lord's preaching, in which is included the vocation of the two pairs of brothers. Wherefore, in ver. 18, ὁ 'Ιησοῦς, *Jesus*, is again understood, but not expressed.—παρεδόθη, *was delivered up*) sc. to confinement in prison (*in custodiam*).— See ch. xi. 2. As John decreased, Jesus increased.[2]—ἀνεχώρησεν,

---

[1] So BC*DZ Memph. Vulg. (MS. Amiat.) Orig. 3, 502c, 4, 161c. Rec. Text with fewer very ancient authorities, viz., *Vulc*. Hil. 620. reads ὁ 'Ιησοῦς. —ED. E. V. renders it, " *Now when Jesus had heard.*"—(I. B.)

[2] Most fittingly the imprisonment of John is mentioned as it were in passing, and the death of the same, in chap. xiv. 3, not as (when) the fact *occurred*, but as (when) it *reached* the ears of Jesus. And yet a long interval cannot have elapsed between the beginning of John's imprisonment and the report of it reaching Christ. In John iii. 24, the Baptist was not yet imprisoned, but yet he was on the point of ' decreasing,' ver. 29, 30. And not even at chap. iv. 1 is mention made of his imprisonment; and at chap. v. 35 he is no doubt said " to HAVE BEEN ('was') a burning and shining lamp," but it does not follow from this, that he, at that time, when Christ asserted this of him, was already confined in prison (for not even in that state did he altogether cease to be a burning and shining lamp). In fact, John is mentioned in the past tense (John v. 35), in respect to the fact that the Jews had already become sated and weary of the joy which they had derived from John, and The True Light, Jesus Christ, by His infinite splendour, had all but eclipsed John, who was, at it were, but a wax-light lamp. Besides, we must take into account, that the Saviour foreknew the imprisonment and subsequent death impending over John. Therefore the latter must have been cast into prison almost six months after the commencement of his public ministry, about Pentecost, and about a full year elapsed from that time till his death. They who maintain that more than three Passovers intervened between our Saviour's baptism and His death, must of necessity assign two years to John's imprisonment, which is less suitable to the general requirements of the case. For John ought rather to have passed

he departed) The same verb occurs, ch. xiv. 13, from a similar cause.[1]—εἰς τὴν Γαλιλαίαν, *into Galilee*) and, indeed, into that part of Galilee which was farthest from Herod and the prison of John. St Matthew speaks of the whole of Galilee in opposition to Judea, where the temptation had taken place. Jesus then came forth from private into public life.[2]

13. Ναζαρέτ, *Nazareth*) where He had hitherto resided.— παραθαλασσίαν, *which is upon the sea-coast*) See vv. 15, 18. A place much frequented.

15, 16. Γῆ Ζαβουλὼν καὶ γῆ Νεφθαλείμ, ὁδὸν θαλάσσης πέραν τοῦ Ἰορδάνου Γαλιλαία τῶν ἐθνῶν, ὁ λαὸς ὁ πορευόμενος[3] ἐν σκότει εἶδε φῶς μέγα, καὶ τοῖς καθημένοις ἐν χώρᾳ καὶ σκιᾷ θανάτου, φῶς ἀνέτειλεν αὐτοῖς, *The land of Zabulon, and the land of Nephthalim, by the way of the sea, beyond Jordan, Galilee of the Gentiles; the people which walketh in darkness saw great light; and to them which sat in the region and shadow of death light is sprung up*) The LXX. thus render the passage in Is. viii. 23 and ix. 1 :[4] χώρα Ζαβουλὼν, ἡ γῆ Νεφθαλείμ, καὶ οἱ λοιποὶ οἱ τὴν παραλίαν, καὶ πέραν τοῦ Ἰορδάνου Γαλιλαία τῶν ἐθνῶν. Ὁ λαὸς ὁ πορευόμενος ἐν σκότει, ἴδετε φῶς μέγα· οἱ κατοικοῦντες ἐν χώρᾳ καὶ σκιᾷ θανάτου φῶς λάμψει ἐφ᾽ ὑμᾶς,—*Country of Zabulon, the land of Nephthalim, and ye the rest who inhabit the region situated by the sea, and bounded by*[5] *the Jordan, thou Galilee of the Gentiles! Thou people which walketh in darkness, behold ye a great light: ye who dwell in the country and shadow of death, a light shall shine upon you.* The two verses are in Isaiah most closely connected together, on which ground the Evangelist takes part of the topography from over the scene quickly, even including his imprisonment. The One Great Prophet, Jesus, passed the principal part of His appointed time alone in His Office.—*Harm.*, p. 183, 184.

[1] Our Lord now departed on account of the imprisonment, He afterwards did so on account of the death, of the Baptist.—(I. B.)

[2] Viz., that of Galilee.—(I. B.)

[3] E. M. καθήμενος.—(I. B.)

[4] This is the Hebrew notation. In the LXX., the Vulgate, and the English Version, the extract is contained in Isaiah ix. 1, 2.—(I. B.)

[5] I have rendered πέραν *bounded by*, instead of *beyond*, in accordance with the remarks which immediately follow on the עבר of the original Hebrew. I may add in illustration, that Liddell and Scott say of πέρα and πέραν, "They are, no doubt, the dative and accusative of an old substantive—ἡ πέρα = πεῖραρ, πεῖρας, πέρας, *end, boundary.*"—(I. B.)

the former [to explain the application of the latter]. Many of the apostles were from this region. See Ps. lxviii. 28; Acts i. 11, ii. 7.—γῆ, *land*, and λαὸς, *people*, are placed in opposition.—ὁδόν, the *way*) The LXX. render דרך (*way*) by ὁδόν (*way*). We must here understand κατά, *by*. The exactness of the prophetical topography is marvellous, minutely accurate both in latitude and longitude.—Θαλάσσης, *of* the *sea*[1]) See ver. 18.—πέραν τοῦ Ἰορδάνου, *beyond the Jordan*) The Hebrew עבר,[2] rendered in the present passage by the Greek πέραν (*beyond*), is used with reference to a boundary considered in reference to, not only the farther side, but the hither side also.—Γαλιλαία τῶν ἐθνῶν, *Galilee of the Gentiles*) Galilee, though inhabited by Israelites, was conterminous to the Gentiles, especially as far as the tribes of Zabulon and Naphthali were concerned.—See Hiller's Onomata Sacra, p. 816. Galilee, previously to the time under consideration, was behind Judaea in the cultivation of sacred learning: the citadel of the Levitical worship was at Jerusalem: the Jews therefore ought to have acknowledged our Lord more readily than the Galilaeans, to whom a compensation is now made for their previous disadvantages.

16. Ὁ πορευόμενος, *that walketh*) There is here a threefold ascending climax.[3]

First Clause.	Second Clause.
The people that Walketh	And on those sitting
In Darkness	In the Region and Shadow of Death,
Hath seen a Great Light.	A Light hath arisen.

It is worse to *sit, detained*, in darkness, than to *walk* in it.[4]—εἶδε, *hath seen*—φῶς, *a Light*[5]) No one is saved except he be illuminated [by that Light]. See Acts xiii. 47.—καὶ τοῖς καθημένοις,

---

[1] Sc. of Galilee.—(I. B.)
[2] Commonly, *The region beyond.*—(I. B.)
[3] *i.e.* The three expressions used in the latter clause of this sentence are respectively stronger than those used in the former clause.—(I. B.)
[4] Unfortunately for this remark, there is no very ancient authority for πορευόμενος. All the oldest MSS. and versions, Vulg., etc., read καθήμενοις. Lachm. and Tischend. do not even notice the former reading.—ED.
[5] "Which illumines the whole world."—B. G. V.

κ.τ.λ., *and to those sitting*, etc.) The LXX. in Ps. cvii. (cvi.) 10, have καθημένους ἐν σκότει καὶ σκιᾷ θανάτου, *sitting in darkness and the shadow of death*. The verb *to sit* aptly denotes a sluggish solitude.—χώρᾳ καὶ σκιᾷ, *region and shadow*) one thing expressed by two words.[1] The natural situation of the country was low, and such was also its spiritual condition.—ἀνέτειλεν αὐτοῖς, *hath risen upon them*) In the original Hebrew it is נגה, *shines, upon them.* This increased force of expression corresponds with the epithet μέγα, *great*, in the preceding clause.

17. Ἤρξατο, *began*)[2] A word of frequent occurrence. It indicates the commencement of an action to be often repeated, or of one deliberate and ample, or even of long continuance.—ἡ βασιλεία, *the kingdom*) It is an example of elegance in the Divine style, that first the kingdom should be said to have come in the abstract, then the King or Messiah in the concrete. The former mode of expression suits the hidden beginnings, the latter the triumphant consummation, [of the Gospel Dispensation].—Cf. Gnomon on Luke i. 35, and 2 Thess. ii. 3.—ἡ βασιλεία τῶν οὐρανῶν, *the kingdom of the Heavens*) i.e., the kingdom of God (cf. ch. v. 3, with Luke vi. 20); for it is called also thus by St Matthew, sometimes, as his book proceeds, and is always thus denominated in the other books of the New Testament,[3] e.g. Acts i. 3, xxviii.

[1] In the original, ἓν διὰ δυοῖν. See Explanation of Technical Terms.—(I. B.)

[2] "Jesus had indeed begun to teach in the schools at Nazareth before He had come thence to Capernaum (see Luke iv. 16), but now raising His voice, He betook Himself to κήρυγμα also, or *proclaiming* the kingdom of GOD. The King Himself acted as His own herald."—B. H. E., p. 190.

[3] *The Kingdom of the heavens*, *Repentance*, and *the Gospel*, are three terms which are found most frequently, not only in St Matthew, but also in SS. Mark and Luke; but never in the Gospel of John. But the latter propounds the same truths substantially by very graceful modes of expression. He no doubt uses the phrase, *the Kingdom of God*, in accordance with the custom of the rest of the Evangelists, but only in the conference with Nicodemus; indicating that same truth by implication, when Jesus is described as the *Son of God*, as *the Life*, as *the Light*, as *the Bridegroom*, as He *into whose hands* the Father hath given *all things*, to whom He hath committed *power over all flesh*, as also *all judgment*; who, in fine, is *to draw all men to Himself*, and such like declarations. John intimates *Repentance*, when he urges on us *the birth from above*, the need of *coming to Jesus*, and *having faith* in Him, etc. That which he delights in terming *the Testimony*, is the same thing

31, and Rom. xiv. 17. The *Metonomy* by which Heaven is substituted for God, is of frequent occurrence, and very suitable to the first times of the Gospel.—See ch. iii. 2. By the expression, "*The Kingdom of the Heavens*," which is almost peculiar to the books of the New Testament, the hope of an earthly kingdom was cut away,[1] and all were invited to Heavenly things. It is thus called with a regard to its final consummation.—See Luke xxi. 31, and Acts i. 3.

18. Θάλασσαν τῆς Γαλαλαίας, *Sea of Galilee*) See verses 15, 23.—Σίμωνα, *Simon*) Simon, the first who followed on this occasion, was the first to remain.

19, Δεῦτε, *come ye*) This word has the force of calling combined with the idea of the present moment; see xi. 28, xxi. 38, etc. This is evident from the singular δεῦρο, *hither*.—ποιήσω, κ.τ.λ., *I will make*, etc.) The authority of Jesus Christ [is here asserted].—ἁλιεῖς, *fishers*) See Jer. xvi. 16.

20. Εὐθέως, *straightway*) A promptitude and quickness in following our Lord is denoted in James and John, in ver. 22, where εὐθέως occurs again. The same quickness is denoted in ver. 19, in the case of Peter and Andrew, by the word Δεῦτε, whether you read εὐθέως or not. In the very ardour of doing their daily work, they received the call. Thus also Matthew ch. ix. 9, blessed moment!—ἠκολούθησαν, *they followed*) Ingenuously, without any immediate stipulation concerning reward.—See ch. xix. 27.

21. Μετὰ Ζεβεδαίου, *with Zebedee*) They were therefore youths: their father Zebedee being still in his prime, and both their parents alive. John lived seventy years longer. James was the first of the apostles who died; John survived him a long time.[2]—καταρτίζοντας, *adjusting for work*) This word is said of a vessel or tool, which is either prepared for work or repaired after work. The first meaning is more suitable to this passage. The sons of Zebedee, as well as those of Jonas, on more than one occa-

as *the Gospel*. These his variations of phraseology are calculated to edify the attentive reader, provided only that we do not fasten wholly on the mere words, but admit their power to pervade the inmost recesses of the heart.—*Harm.*, p. 190, 191.

[1] "Præcidebatur."—(I. B.)

[2] These two are more frequently joined together in the New Testament than Peter and Andrew.—B. G. V.

sion, abandoned the work in which they were respectively engaged with the greatest promptitude and obedience.

23. Καὶ περιῆγεν, κ.τ.λ., *And Jesus went about*, etc.) Thus, also, clearly in ch. ix. 35.[1]—κηρύσσων, *preaching*) His teaching in the synagogues was public, but His preaching more public still.—See ch. x. 27, and xi. 1; comp. also Luke viii. 39; John iii. 2, 4.—τὸ εὐαγγέλιον, *the Gospel*) The chief teaching of Christ was the Gospel: the other things which He taught concerned only the removing impediments [to its saving reception].—τῆς βασιλείας, *of the kingdom*) sc. of God. In Holy Scripture God is the perpetual object of contemplation.—πᾶσαν, *every*) No one sick or dead, whom Jesus met, remained in sickness or death.—νόσον, *disease*) νόσος signifies *a disease* of the whole body: μαλακία, *an infirmity* of any particular part, attended with pain: βάσανος (ver. 24), *a torture*, or malady accompanied by excruciating pain: μάστιξ (Luke vii. 21), *a scourge*.—ἐν τῷ λαῷ, *among the people*) Among the people of Israel: and it was among *the people*, [*i.e.*, in public,] that, as the sick were promiscuously brought to Him, even those were healed whose disease was a matter of public notoriety; see John ix. 8, and Acts iii. 10. But in the case of miracles of later times, men, or dumb images, to whom they are pretended to have happened, are thrust forth from some obscure nook or other by collusion.

24. Ἀπῆλθεν, *went out thence*) sc. afar.—ἀκοή, *fame*) The LXX. frequently render שְׁמוּעָה[2] by ἀκοή.—Συρίαν, *Syria*) The province of which Palestine was considered a part.—προσήνεγκαν Αὐτῷ, *they brought unto Him*) Even the Syrians did so.—τοὺς κακῶς ἔχοντας, *those who were ill*)[3] The miracles of Jesus Christ were performed for the good[4] of men.—See John vi. 2; Matt. xi. 5; Acts

---

[1] See also Mark vi. 6; Acts x. 38, etc. It was by this system that He, in so short a ministry, benefited a vast multitude of men by His teaching and miracles; thereby He the more trained His disciples; and, moreover, produced this effect, that men, so far from being weary of Him, even from time to time conceived the stronger yearning desire after Him.—*Harm.*, p. 235, 236.

[2] שְׁמוּעָה and שֵׁמַע prop. *that which is heard*: hence (1), *a message, tidings*, whether joyful or sorrowful, especially a message sent from God: hence (2), *i q. instruction, teaching doctrine*; (3), *rumour*.—GESENIUS.—(I. B.)

[3] "*Male habentes.*"—(I. B.)

[4] *Salutem*, health or salvation—i.e, they were [with rare exceptions]

x. 38.—δαιμονιζομένους, *possessed with devils*) The sick and the possessed are frequently mentioned together.—See Acts v. 16.

25. "Οχλοι, *multitudes*) The plural is used on account of the various places from which they came.—Δεκαπόλεως, from *Decapolis*)[1] situated on both sides of the Jordan. Samaria is not mentioned in this enumeration.—πέραν, *beyond*) i.e., ἀπὸ τῆς πέραν —*from the* country *beyond*.

CHAPTER V.

1. 'Ἰδών, *seeing*) sc. afar off.—ὄρος, *mountain*) and moreover the higher part of the mountain. There He prayed and selected His apostles; see Mark iii. 13–19; Luke vi. 12–16. Afterwards he came half way down the mountain; and, as He was coming down with His disciples, He met the people coming up, and *sat down* there to teach; see note on Luke vi. 17.[2] A mountain, as being a lofty part of the earth, and thereby nearer to heaven, is best suited for the most holy actions.—προσῆλθον Αὐτῷ, *came unto Him*[3]) The close admittance and docility of recent disciples.

2. 'Ἀνοίξας, κ.τ.λ., *having opened, etc.*) A beginning studiously made is great part of a great matter. In commencing narrations of great and deliberate affairs, Scripture uses the phrases,

---

miracles of mercy, the effect of which was to improve the condition of those on whom they were performed.—(I. B.)

[1] The region called Decapolis comprehended the ten cities of Scythopolis: Hippos, Gadara, Dios, Pella, Philadelphia, Gerasa, Canatha, Capitolias, and Abila.—*W. Hughes.*—(I. B.)

[2] The night, which is mentioned in Luke vi. 12, *succeeded* to [followed immediately after] miracles, as appears from Mark iii. 10, and *preceded* miracles, according to Luke vi. 18. What is said in the beginning of Matt. v. is suited to the even-tide, which put a close to both classes of miracles, viz., *Seeing the multitudes, He went up into a mountain:* the day following will thus claim to itself the rest of His proceedings, viz., *When He was set* (seated), *i.e.*, after the cures recorded in Luke, which he had performed standing,—*His disciples came unto Him.*—*Harm.*, p. 242.

[3] Not only the twelve.—B. G. V.

He turned his shoulders, He moved his feet, He raised his eyes, He opened His mouth. See Acts x. 34. Here the fountain began to pour forth water. Cf. Matt. xiii. 35.—*ἐδίδασκεν, He taught*) He instructed by doctrine, by consolation, by exhortation, by precept.—*αὐτοὺς, them*) the disciples. For He addresses these, in the hearing of the multitudes;[1] see vii. 28. The Evangelists have transcribed at full length two discourses of our Lord, as models of all the rest; the one delivered publicly at the commencement of His ministry, that namely which we are now considering; the other privately at its conclusion, recorded in John xiii.–xvi. Our Lord's object in the present discourse is to teach true righteousness (see Isa. lxiii. 1): and He also declares at the same time, that He came to establish the Law and the Prophets, and exposes the spurious character of the righteousness of the Scribes and Pharisees. In the exordium, there is firstly, ver. 3, 4, a sweet invitation to the fellowship of true righteousness, and therein of blessedness; secondly, ver. 13, 14, to the communication of it to others. From ver. 17 to vii. 12, there is a treatise, the end of which corresponds with the beginning, even to a word. The conclusion of this discourse, firstly, ch. vii. 13, 14, points out the gate of righteousness; secondly, ch. vii. 15, 16, warns against false prophets, who go themselves, and lead others, into all kinds of error;[2] and thirdly, vii. 24, 25, exhorts us to fulfil these precepts of righteousness. The impression produced by the Heavenly Teacher's discourse on those who heard Him, is described in the two last verses of the same chapter.

3. Μακάριοι, *blessed*) This initial word, so often repeated, indicates the object of Christ's teaching.[3] By means, however, of striking paradoxes, blessedness is proposed not only by itself, but inasmuch as, *in Christ now present*, it is within the reach of all who are capable of receiving Him. There were some such amongst our Lord's auditors, though undistinguished by the eye of man (see ch. ix. 36, 37, xi. 28; Isa. xxix. 19), although

[1] [He, however, addressed the latter also at the same time; v. 17.—V. g.]
[2] In alia omnia ducentibus et euntibus—literally, "leading and going into all other things"—sc. other than the strait gate.—(I. B.)
[3] The first word of this discourse announces its whole scope: a great blessedness is here p'aced before us by the Lord.—See Heb. ii. 3.— B. G. V.

compared with the rest they were not many in number: for the
epithet *blessed* frequently implies both the excellence and rarity
of a thing (as in Ecclus. xxxi. 8), from which the expressions,
theirs, they, etc., exclude those otherwise disposed: cf. Luke vi.
24, 25, 26, where the *woes* are denounced. Seven however of
the μακαρισμοί, or *predications of blessedness,* are *absolute,* declaring the condition of the godly, as far as regards themselves;
two are *relative,* having respect to the conduct of men towards
them. In both cases the *kingdom of heaven* is placed first, as
embracing the whole of the beatitudes. All are enumerated in
a most beautiful order. With these may be compared the
matter and order of the eight woes, which are denounced
against the Scribes and Pharisees, in ch. xxiii. 13–16, 23, 25,
27, 29. In both cases mention is made of the *kingdom of
heaven,* here ver. 3, there ver. 13; of *mercy,* here ver. 7, there
ver. 23; of *purity,* here ver. 8, there ver. 25; and of *persecution,* here ver. 10, 11, and there ver. 29, 30: and undoubtedly
the other clauses may also be respectively compared with each
other. In the *subject,* the saints are described as they are *now*
in *this life;* in the *predicate,* as they will be *hereafter* on *that
day*: see Luke vi. 25, 23. Our Lord, however, frames His
words in such a manner, as at the same time to intimate the
blessedness of *individual* saints already commencing in the present life, and to signify prophetically the blessedness of the holy
people, which will hereafter be theirs also upon *earth:* see ver. 5.
—οἱ πτωχοί, *the poor*) A vocative, either expressly or such in
meaning (cf. ver. 11, and Luke vi. 20). Nor does the pronoun
αὐτῶν, *theirs,* oppose this view. Cf. Gnomon on xxiii. 37. *Poverty*
is the first foundation. *He is poor,* who has it not in his power
to say, *this is mine;*[1] and who, when he has anything for the
present, does not devise what he will have for the future, but
depends on the liberality of another. The riches which are dis-
claimed by such poverty, are either spiritual or natural, and are
either present or absent. Such cardinal and fundamental virtues
are despised by the world: whereas those which the world admires as such, are either no virtues, or false ones, or merely the
offshoots and appendages of Christian virtues.—πνεύματι, in

---

[1] *i.e.,* Has nothing which he can call his own.—(I. B.)

spirit) *i.e.* in their inmost self. This word is to be understood also in the following passages as far as ver. 8, where the words τῇ καρδίᾳ, *in heart*, occur.— ὅτι, *because*) Each kind of blessedness which is predicated corresponds with the previous description of [the character or condition which is] its subject,[1] and is taken, either (1.) from *the contrary* (for the works of God, 2 Cor. iv. 6, vii. 6, xii. 9, are effected in the midst of their contraries);[2] or (2.) regulated by a law of benignant retribution or exact conformity.[3]—ἐστιν, *is*) sc. already. The present in this verse, and the future in those which follow, mutually imply each other.— ἡ βασιλεία τῶν οὐρανῶν, *the kingdom of heaven*, literally, *the kingdom of the heavens*),[4] which, promised in the Old Testament, is actually conferred by the Messiah.

4 and 5. Οἱ πενθοῦντες, κ.τ.λ.) *they that mourn*, etc.—οἱ πραεῖς, κ.τ.λ., *the meek*, etc.) Most of the Latins transpose these verses, and certainly the third and fifth verses correspond with each other. *Blessed are the* POOR *in spirit, for theirs is the kingdom of* HEAVEN ; *blessed are the* MEEK, *for they shall inherit the* EARTH. עָנִי = πτωχός, *poor*, עָנָו = πραΰς, *meek*, especially in Ps. xxxvii. 11, where the inheritance of the earth is spoken of, and ibid. ver. 14. But this does not interfere with our order of the verses; for ver. 4 is subordinate to ver. 3, and ver. 6 to ver. 5.[5] *Mourning* has a

---

[1] Sc. of the present state of the subject. Ex. gr. " Blessed are they that *mourn :* for they shall be *comforted.*"—ED.

[2] In the original, " in mediis contrariis," the full force of which it is difficult to give by a single phrase. Bengel's meaning is best obtained by a reference to the texts which he gives.—(I. B.)

[3] In the original, "a talione benigna proximave convenientiâ," where *talio* (talion) is used in a sense cognate with its original derivation from *talis, such*, but unknown (as far as I am aware) to classical usage. It is one of those peculiar adaptations of words frequently occurring in Bengel, and sanctioned (in its principle) by no less an authority than Horace.—See his Ars Poetica, ver. 47, 48. For an example of Bengel's meaning, cf ver. 7, 8 of this chapter.—(I. B.)

[4] This expression, *the kingdom of the heavens*, marks the commencement of the discussion (tractatio) in this verse, as it also marks the close of the discussion in ver. 10.—*Vers. Germ.*

[5] For the arrangement, whereby the beatitude of οἱ πραεῖς comes before that of οἱ πενθοῦντες, there are Dac Vulg. Orig. 3, 740d, Euseb. *Canon.* Hilary 621d, 622a. For the arrangement of the Rec. Text, οἱ πενθ.—οἱ πραεῖς, there are of very old authorities Bb.—ED. By the word αὐτοί it is

more widely extended signification than sorrowing for *one's own sins*. See Gnomon on 1 Cor. v. 2.

4. Παρακληθήσονται, *shall be comforted*) The future tense indicates promises made in the Old Testament, and now to be performed; see Luke xvi. 25, and 2 Thess. ii. 16. The poor and the meek are joined together in ver. 3, 5, as in the frequently-occurring עני ואביון, *poor* and *needy*, cf. also ch. xi. 29.

5. Οἱ πραεῖς, *the meek*) Those are here named for the most part, whom the world tramples on.—πρᾷος is connected with the Latin *pravus*, which has frequently the meaning of *segnis*, slow, sluggish, etc.—κληρονομήσουσι, *shall inherit*) the future. The meek are seen everywhere to yield to the importunity of the inhabitants of the earth; and yet they shall obtain possession of the earth, not by their own arm, but by inheritance, through the aid of the Father: cf. Rev. v. 10. In the mean time, even whilst the usurpation of the ungodly continues, all the produce of the earth is ordered for the comfort of the meek. In all these sentences, blessedness in heaven and blessedness on earth mutually imply each other. See Ps. xxxvii. (xxxvi.) 11,—Οἱ δὲ πραεῖς κληρονομήσουσι γῆν, καὶ κατατρυφήσουσιν ἐπὶ πλήθει εἰρήνης, *But the meek shall inherit the earth, and shall delight themselves in the abundance of peace*. This is, indeed, the subject of that whole Psalm; see ver. 3, 9, 22, 29, 34.

6. Οἱ πεινῶντες καὶ διψῶντες, κ.τ.λ., *who hunger and thirst*, etc.) who feel that of themselves they have no righteousness by which they may approve themselves either to God or man, and eagerly long for it. Faith is here described, suitably to the beginning of the New Testament.—τὴν δικαιοσύνην, *righteousness*) Our Lord plainly declares Himself here to be the author of righteousness. That which is signified here is not the right (*jus*) of the human, but of the Divine tribunal. This verse is the centre of this passage, and the theme of the whole sermon. Our Lord does not say, *Blessed are the righteous*, as he presently says, *Blessed are the merciful*, etc.; but, *Blessed are they that hunger and thirst after righteousness*. Pure righteousness will become their portion in due time. (See 2 Pet. iii. 13; Is. lx. 21.)—χορτασθήσονται, *they shall

implied that the contraries to these beatitudes shall be the portion of those oppositely disposed.—*Vers. Germ.*

ST MATTHEW V. 7–11. 165

be filled) with righteousness; see Rom. xiv. 17. This was the meat of Jesus himself: see John iv. 34; cf. Matt. iii. 15. This satisfying fulness He proposes to His followers in the whole of this sermon, and promises and offers them in this very verse.

7. Ἐλεήμονες, *the merciful*) The Greek word ἔλεος, *ruth*, from which ἐλεήμονες is derived, corresponds to the Hebrew חֶסֶד,[1] and does not refer merely to miserable objects.

8. Οἱ καθαροὶ τῇ καρδίᾳ, *the pure in heart*) Ceremonial purity is not sufficient. Jesus requires, and teaches, the virtue of the heart. Purity of heart includes both chastity and freedom from the other defilements of sin.—τὸν Θεὸν ὄψονται, *shall see God*) A clear knowledge of God is promised even now, but in words which will be more literally fulfilled in life eternal: see 1 John iii. 2, 3, 6; cf. concerning the opposite to purity, 1 Thess. iv. 5.

9. Εἰρηνοποιοί, *peacemakers*) They who make all lawful peace between those who are at variance, at discord, or at war.—υἱοί, *sons*) How great is this dignity!—Θεοῦ, *of God*) who is the God of peace.—κληθήσονται, *shall be called*) i.e., shall be in name and in reality.

10. Οἱ δεδιωγμένοι, *they who endure persecution*) In the next verse, δεδιωγμένοι signifies, Those who have offered themselves to undergo persecution. Our Lord already announces the treatment which He and His followers will receive from the world. He unfolds this truth, however, gradually. He speaks of His *yoke* in ch. xi. 29; of His *cross* in xvi. 24. By comparing Mark viii. 34, and Matt. x. 38, it appears that He speaks of His *cross* to His disciples alone.—ἕνεκεν δικαιοσύνης, *for righteousness' sake*) In the next verse, He says, *for My sake*; cf. ch. x. 39, 42, xvi. 25, xviii. 5, xix. 12, 29.

11. Ὀνειδίσωσιν, *shall revile*) sc. in your presence: understand ἄνθρωποι, *men*. They inflict *insult* by words, *persecution* in fact. —ὑμᾶς, *you*) Jesus speaks sometimes in the first person plural of Himself, and mankind, taken collectively, when the matter treated of is one plainly external (see John xi. 7), or when He speaks as one unknown (see ch. iii. 15, John iv. 22); but mostly

---

[1] חֶסֶד . . (1) in a good sense, *zeal* towards any one, *love*, kindness, specially (*a*) of men amongst themselves, *benignity*, *benevolence*, as shown in mutual benefits; *mercy*, *pity*, when referring to those in misfortune : Gen. xxi. 23; 2 Sam. x. 2. LXX. often ἔλεος.—GESENIUS.—(I. B.)

uses the second person, to signify that He is not on a par with others. See ver. 12, 13, 20; John vi. 49, x. 34, xiv. 9, xx. 17. —εἴπωσι, *shall say*) sc. in your absence.

12. Χαίρετε, *rejoice*) Joy is not only a feeling, but also a duty of the Christian (see Phil. iv. 4); and in adversity, the highest grade and very nerve of patience.—ἀγαλλιᾶσθε, *be exceeding glad*) so that others also may perceive your joy.—ὅτι, κ.τ.λ., *because*, etc.) You may therefore rejoice on account of your reward.—ὁ μισθὸς, *the reward*) sc. *of grace*. The word *Reward* implies something further beyond the beatitudes, which spring from the very disposition of the righteous. Therefore it is said, *Rejoice.*—τοὺς προφήτας, *the prophets*) who, by bearing witness to Christ, have encountered hatred (see Acts vii. 52), whose reward you know to be great. Persecution has not occurred only in the case of barbarous nations whilst they were being converted to the Gospel, but always in the times of both the Old and New Testament: see 1 John iii. 12, 13.

13, 14. Ὑμεῖς, *you*) sc. the first disciples and hearers of the Messiah. Salt and light are, in nature, things essential, and of widest use. Frequently in Scripture the same thing is first declared by metaphorical expressions, that our attention may be excited; and then, when we have not understood it as we ought, and in the meanwhile have perceived our blindness, it is disclosed in plain words.—τῆς γῆς, *of the earth*).—τοῦ κόσμου, *of the world*) The earth of itself is without salt, the world without light.— ἐὰν, κ.τ.λ., *if*, etc.) It is not affirmed in this passage, that salt does lose its savour; but it is shown what, in such a case, would be the lot of the Salt of the earth.—μωρανθῇ, *should lose its savour*) Galen,[1] in his observations on Hippocrates, explains μεμωρωμένα (the perf. pass. part. of this verb) by τὰ ἀναίσθητα, *i.e., which have no feeling;* in Mark ix. 50, we find ἄναλον γένηται, *become saltless.* It is the nature of salt to have and to give savour; and to this savour are opposed saltlessness, want of taste, value lost.— ἁλισθήσεται, *shall it be salted*) Impersonal. Neither can the salt

---

[1] Hippocrates, the greatest physician of antiquity, was born at the island of Cos in the 80th Olympiad, and flourished during the time of the Peloponnesian War. Galen, second only to Hippocrates, was born at Pergamus, in the Lesser Asia, about the year 131.—See ENCYCLOPÆDIA BRITANNICA. —(I. B.)

(see Mark, cited above) nor the earth be seasoned from any other source.—ἔξω, *out of doors*) far from any household use.—καὶ, *and*) sc. *and* therefore.—καταπατεῖσθαι, *to be trodden under foot*) There is nothing more despised than one who wishes to be esteemed divine, and is not so.[1]—ὑπὸ τῶν ἀνθρώπων, *by men*) i.e., by all who come in its way. This is the force here of the article τῶν.

14. [2] Ὄρους, *a mountain*) Appositely, cf. ver 1. Concerning the thing itself, see Rev. xxi. 10.

15. Καίουσι, *do they light*) Impersonal. οἱ καίοντες, *those who light* must be understood, cf. vii. 16.—ὑπὸ, *under*) i.e. behind. In Luke viii. 16, we find ὑποκάτω, *underneath*.

16. Ἔμπροσθεν τῶν ἀνθρώπων, *before men*) sc. all men.—ὅπως, *in order that*) The force of this particle does not so much refer to the verb ἴδωσιν (*they may see*) as to δοξάσωσι (*may glorify*).—ὑμῶν—ἔργα, *your works*) Your works, not yourselves. The light, not the candle.[3]—τὸν Πατέρα ὑμῶν, *your Father*) Who has begotten you like unto Himself. In the whole of this address, the Son shows God to us as our Father, and that more richly than all the prophets of old.

17. Μὴ νομίσητε, *Do not think*) An elliptical mode of speech by Metonomy of the Consequent.[4] Do not think, fear, hope, that I am a teacher like those teachers to whom you have been accustomed, and that I, like them, shall set aside the law. He who thinks the former, thinks also the latter.—ἦλθον, *I have come*) Our Lord, therefore, existed before He came upon earth, which is implied also in ch. viii. 10, by εὗρον, *I have found.*—καταλῦσαι, *to destroy, to abrogate*) To the compound verb, καταλύειν, *to unloose or dissolve*, is opposed πληροῦν, *to fulfil;* to the simple verb λύειν, *to loose*, combined with διδάσκειν, *to teach*, is opposed ποιεῖν, *to do*,

---

[1] The mere man of the world is not so much disgraced by his vanity as is such a one.—*Vers. Germ.*

[2] By the words οὐ δύναται, it is implied that there is no need of a constrained feigning to be what we are not; so also, a light or lamp, provided it is not stifled, *cannot but* shine.—*Vers. Germ.*

[3] So there follows [That men may See] *Your Father;* not yourselves: comp. ch. vi. 2.—*Vers. Germ.*

[4] The *consequent*—that I, like them, shall set aside the law: the *antecedent*—that I am a teacher like those to whom you are accustomed.—(I. B.)

or *perform*, joined with the same verb διδάσκειν: from which the relative force of the words appears; those are said of the whole law, these of the separate precepts. καταλύειν, *to unloose*, and λύειν, *to loose*, both signify to render void.¹—τὸν νόμον ἢ τοὺς προφήτας, *the law or the prophets*) Many of the Jews esteemed the prophets less than the law. They are joined also in ch. vii. 12.—πληρῶσαι, *to fulfil*) By My deeds and words, to effect that *all things should be fulfilled* which the law requires. See the conclusion of the next verse.² The Rabbins acknowledge that it is a sign of the Messiah to fulfil the whole law.

18. ’Αμὴν, *Amen, verily*) Jesus alone employed this word at the commencement of His addresses, to give them greater force and solemnity. No apostle did so. Wagenseil,³ in his Sota, p. 379, says, that this word had sometimes with the Jews the force of an oath. And wherever חי אני (*I, living*) occurs in the Hebrew, the Chaldee Paraphrast has אנא קים, *I, constant:* and קים, *to confirm*, etc., is found there passim for ישבע, *to swear*. See Louis le Dieu on this passage; and Kimchi interprets אמן, *amen*, itself by קים, *stability*.⁴

In the New Testament, however, it is not, strictly speaking, an oath : for it corresponds with ναὶ, *yea*, and ἀληθῶς, *truly;* cf. Luke xi. 51, xxi. 3, with Matt. xxiii. 36, and Mark xii. 43. It is, however, a most grave asseveration, exclusively suitable to Him who asseverates by Himself and His own truth, and from the dignity of the Speaker, is equivalent to an oath, especially when it is uttered twice, sc. "*verily, verily :*" see note to John i.

---

¹ The Latin verb *soleo*, which is used in this passage, represents the Greek λύω far more fully and accurately than any English word can. καταλύω is also more adequately rendered by *dissolvo* than by any English word.—(I. B.)

² He was not the founder of a new law ; but, by His own obedience, Himself fulfilled the law, and showed how it should be fulfilled by His disciples.—*Vers. Germ.*

³ John Christopher Wagenseil was born at Nuremberg in 1633, and educated at the University of Altdorf, where he was appointed Professor of History in 1667, and of Oriental Languages about 1675. He died in 1705. The full title of the work referred to in the text is, Sota, hoc est liber Mixlenicus de uxore adulterii suspecta, una cum libri ex Jacob excerptis Gemaræ, versione Latina et commentario perpetuo, in quo multa sacrarum literarum ac Hebræorum Scriptorum loca explicantur.—(I. B.)

⁴ *Firmitas, stabilitas, duratio.*—BUXTORF.—(I. B.)

52. The Hebrew word is preserved in all languages.[1]—λέγω ὑμῖν, *I say unto you*) This formula, frequent and peculiar to the Lord, possesses the highest authority, and denotes frequently a matter declared by Him, which, for special reasons, is neither written expressly in the Old Testament, nor can be clearly proved from any other source, but is first produced by Himself from the secret treasuries of wisdom and knowledge, so that the assent of the hearers may rest on His sole affirmation, and the dull in heart may be deprived of all excuse for the future. The prophets were wont to say in the third person, נאם,[2] *saith the Lord*; the apostles, *It is written*; but Christ, in the first person, *I say unto you*; see ver. 20, 22, 26, 28, 32, 34, 39, 44, ch. vi. 2; John iii. 3, xiv. 12, 25, etc. Cf. notes on John iv. 21, and xiv. 25. St Paul, when again and again compelled to speak in the first person, takes especial care not to trench on the Divine prerogative. See Rom. xii. 3; 1 Cor. vii. 6. *Faith* is the correlative of this, "*I say unto you*," and by this formula is, suitably to that time (*pro modo illius temporis*), placed, as it were, as the foundation on the very threshold of the New Testament. Christ seldom quotes passages of Scripture, and not except for some special reason: He befittingly rests on His own authority.—ἕως ἂν παρέλθῃ, *until pass away*) The verb, παρέλθῃ, leaves undetermined the manner of the end of the world.—ὁ οὐρανὸς καὶ ἡ γῆ, *Heaven and earth*) The whole system of nature.—ἰῶτα, *jot*) *iota, yod.* Yod, the smallest and most elementary letter in the Hebrew alphabet, and one in which Keri and Kethib[3] very fre-

---

[1] And it (the Hebr. *amen*) ought to be retained in translation, as in the end, so also in the beginning of sentences. The same principle holds good of other Hebrew words.—*Not. Crit.*

[2] "נאם . . *to mutter, to murmur, to speak in a low voice;* specially used of *the voice of God*, by which oracles were revealed to the prophets. By far the most frequent use is of the part. pass. constr. in this phrase, נְאֻם יְיָ, נְאֻם אֵל, נְאֻם יהוה. 'The voice of Jehovah (is);' or (so) hath Jehovah revealed. Thus the prophets themselves were accustomed either to insert in the discourse, like the Lat. *ait, inquit Dominus*, Am. 6: 8, 14; 9: 12, 13, or to add at the end of a sentence."—*Gesenius.*—(I. B.)

[3] QERI AND KETHIBH.
"The margin of the Hebrew Bible exhibits a number of various readings of an early date, called קְרִי (*to be read*), because, in the view of the Jewish critics, they are to be preferred to the reading of the text, called כְּתִיב (*written*). Those critics have therefore attached the vowel signs, appropriate

quently differ, so that it almost appears to be indiscriminately absent or redundant. In the course of the Hebrew Scriptures, 66,420 yods are numbered. The Greeks frequently write the *iota* below, or omit it altogether.—κεραία, *a tittle*) An appendage to a portion of a letter, a mark by which one letter is distinguished from another, as ב, Beth (B), from כ, Kaph (K), or ר, Resh (R), from ד, Daleth (D), or one sound from another, as a vowel point or an accent; in short, anything which in any way belongs to the signification of the Divine will, or assists to declare that signification as revealed in the law.—οὐ μή, *a double negative*) οὐ μή always has a subjunctive, and its emphasis ought not to be stretched too far; cf. ver. 20, 26.—οὐ μὴ παρέλθῃ, *shall not pass away*) From hence may be inferred the entireness of Scripture; for, unless the Scripture were entire, it could not be entirely fulfilled.—ἀπὸ τοῦ νόμου, *from the law*) Understand and supply, " or from the prophets." The smallest portion of the law is contrasted with the whole world.—ἕως ἄν, κ.τ.λ., *until*, etc.) For righteousness shall dwell in *new Heavens and a new Earth.* See 2 Pet. iii. 13.—πάντα, *all particulars*) sc. of the law. Observe the contrast between this and μίαν, *one*, in the next verse.[1]—γένηται, *be fulfilled*) They have been fulfilled, and they are being fulfilled by Jesus Christ, [not only in Himself, but] even in Christians: they had not been fulfilled before His coming.

19. Λύσῃ, *shall break*) The antithetical word to this is ποιήσῃ, *shall do*, which occurs further on in this verse. The Scribes, who thought themselves " *great*," were in the habit of breaking them. The same verb, λύω, occurs in John vii. 23, and x. 35.—τούτων, *of these*) those, namely, which follow in ver. 22, 28, etc.—τῶν ἐλαχίστων, *of the least*) These precepts, " *Thou shalt not kill,*" etc., are not essentially the least, for in them the whole law is con-

to the marginal reading, to the consonants of the corresponding word in the text; *e.g.* in Jer. xlii. 6, the text exhibits אִן, the margin אִם־לֹא. Here the vowels in the text belong to the word in the margin, which is to be pronounced אִם־לֹא; but in reading the text אִן, the proper vowels must be supplied, making אֵן. A small circle or asterisk over the word in the text always directs to the marginal reading."—*Gesenius*, Heb. Gr. Sect. 17.— (I. B.)

[1] In the original, " Antitheton, *unum*, in v. seq." I have endeavoured in this, as in other instances, to give such a rendering as shall convey Bengel's meaning to the general reader.—(I. B.)

tained. But they are so only inasmuch as, when rightly explained, they regulate even the most subtile affections and emotions of the soul, and the slightest movements of the tongue, and thus, when compared with other precepts, appear to men to be the least.—ἐλάχιστος, *least*) Referring to the preceding ἐλαχίστων. An instance of *Ploce*.[1] As we treat the Word of God, so does God treat us; see John xvii. 6, 11; Rev. iii. 10. "*A little*" signifies "*almost nothing*," whence "*the least*" comes to mean "*none at all*" (for they considered anger, for instance, as of no consequence whatever); cf. in ver. 20, "*ye shall not enter.*" ἐλάχιστος has a different force in this passage from that which ὁ μικρότερος (*the least*) "*in the kingdom of heaven*" has in ch. xi. 11. —ἐν τῇ βασιλείᾳ τῶν οὐρανῶν, *in the kingdom of heaven*) which cannot endure the presence of the unrighteous.—ποιήσῃ καὶ διδάξῃ, *shall do and teach*) The same order of words occurs in Acts i. 1.—ποιήσῃ, *shall do* them, sc. all; for it is not lawful to break or neglect even *one* of them.—οὗτος, *this* man, *he*) A pronoun used emphatically. Comp. with this use of οὗτος, ch. vii. 21 (Latin Version[2]); Luke ix. 24; John vii. 18.—μέγας, *great*) All the commandments are of *great* account to him, especially in their full compass[3] (see ver. 18); therefore he shall be called *great*.

20. Ἐὰν μὴ περισσεύσῃ ἡ δικαιοσύνη ὑμῶν, *except your righteousness shall exceed*) Our righteousness, even though it should satisfy, could never *exceed*, the requirements of the law; but the Scribes and Pharisees thought that theirs did so. We are bound to surpass their righteousness. Cf. the force of περισσεύσῃ (*abound*, or *exceed*), with that of περισσὸν (*more than others*, *exceeding the general standard*), in ver. 47. We must surpass both Pharisees and publicans: see ver. 48.—ὑμῶν ἡ δικαιοσύνη, *your righteousness*) The pronoun, ὑμῶν (*your*), being placed first, is opposed with

---

[1] See Appendix. The same word employed twice: in the first instance, expressing the simple idea of the word itself; and in the second, an attribute of it.—ED.

[2] See Gnomon on vii. 21, and notes.—(I. B.) The Vulgate, referred to, thus renders the οὗτος, etc., which *abc* Hil. and Cypr. read, but which BZ omit, "Qui facit voluntatem patris, etc., *ipse* intrabit," etc.—ED.

[3] "Præsertim in complexu suo,"—i.e. when considered with reference to all that they involve, as explained by our Lord in this discourse, v. 21, etc.—(I. B.)

greater emphasis to the righteousness of the Scribes and Pharisees.[1] Others read ἡ δικαιοσύνη ὑμῶν.[2] That righteousness is intended, of which specimens are given in ver. 19, 22, 23. This language does not make void the righteousness of faith; but the language of Jesus Christ before His ascension, keeps, as it were, the mean between Moses and the apostles.—πλεῖον τῶν γραμματίων, κ.τ.λ., *more than the Scribes,* etc.) *i.e.* πλεῖον τῆς δικαιοσύνης τῶν γραμματίων, κ.τ.λ., *more than the righteousness of the Scribes,* etc.—τῶν γραμματίων, *of the Scribes*) Our Lord does not command the righteousness of His followers to be greater than the righteousness of Moses, as if the law of Moses had been imperfect, which promised life to those who performed it, and was (see Rom. vii. 12, 14) just, holy, good, and spiritual; but greater than the *righteousness* (which word, however, is elegantly omitted) *of the Scribes and Pharisees,* who observed ceremonial and legal, but neglected moral righteousness. The *Pharisees* urged traditions; the *Scribes,* or *Karaei,*[3] the letter, which was written, and constantly read out. It seemed to be especially the part of the Scribes *to teach* : of the Pharisees *to do.* Our Lord does not name Moses; but He says impersonally, *It has been said.*—οὐ μὴ εἰσέλθητε, *ye shall not enter*) See ch. xviii. 3; John iii. 5; 1 Cor. xv. 50.

[1] Which was esteemed in those days as superlatively good.—*Vers. Germ.*
[2] Lachm. and Tischend., with the oldest MSS. Vulg., etc., read ἡ δικαιοσύνη ὑμῶν. For the order ὑμῶν ἡ δικ. there are of good, though later authorities, only L Δ.—ED.
[3] Bengel's words are, "*scribæ* sive *karæi,* literam, quæ erat scripta et lectitabatur ;" where "*scripta erat*" (was written) refers to "*scribæ*" (scribes), derived from the Latin verb *scribo, to write* : and *lectitabatur* (*was constantly read out*) refers to "*karæi,*" derived from the Hebrew verb קָרָא, of which Gesenius says, "(4) *to recite, to read aloud* (from the signification of crying out,—see No. 1) anything, with an acc., Exod. xxiv. 7; Josh. viii. 34, 35; 2 Kings xxiii. 2; also בְּסֵפֶר קָרָא, *to read* what is written *in a book.* . . . Neh. viii. 8, 18, ix. 3; Isa. xxxvii. 14. seqq. . . . Hence generically *to read,* Deut. xvii. 19; 2 Kings v. 7, xix. 14."

The *Karaites,* a sect which existed before the destruction of the Temple of Jerusalem, have been called *the Protestants of Judaism.* Their name is derived from the Hebrew קָרָאִים, which signifies, according to Calmet, " people perfected in the study of Scripture; people attached to the text, and to the letter of Scripture." They are, of course, diametrically opposed to the Rabbinists, who zealously maintain the Rabbinical traditions. For an account of their history and tenets, see *Milman's History of the Jews,* and *Calmet* in voc.--(I. B.)

21. Ἠκούσατε, *ye have heard*) From public readings, to which you have given your assent. In the New Testament the teachers are referred to their reading of the law, the people to their hearing of it. See John xii. 34; Rom. ii. 13, 18.— ὅτι ἐῤῥέθη, *that it has been said*) An impersonal form of speech, to which is elegantly opposed, *I say*. Moses said it truly; the interpreters of Moses said it with altered meaning: the hearers did not distinguish the meaning of Moses from that of his interpreters. The name of Moses occurs, but with a less forcible contrast, in ch. xix. 8, 9, sc. *Moses permitted, but* [*I*] *say unto you*, where *I* is not expressed in the original, for there is no contention between Moses and Christ: the Jews had departed from both Moses and Christ. The language of Christ does not exceed the law of Moses (see ch. vii. 12); for concupiscence, proscribed in ver. 28, is also prohibited by the law: see Rom. vii. 7. He however restores the truths which the Scribes had taken from the law, and clears away the falsehoods which they had added; see ver. 43. The phrase, "*But I say*," is an antithetic formula, by which Christ, as if Moses had never existed (for the servant gives place to his Lord), orders all things simply, not in the guise of a Legislator or Interpreter, but as the Son declaring the will of His Father: see ch. vii. 21, and cf. ch. iii. 17. The law is perfect: whatever the Saviour prohibits or commands in this passage, the law had previously prohibited or commanded: it judges the secrets of the heart (see Rom. vii. 14); but on account of the hard heart of the people, it more frequently expresses outward acts. Therefore the Lord says, "*But I say unto you*," not, "*Moses however said unto you*." The Jews were in many things otherwise circumstanced in the time of the Pharisees than in the time of Moses.—τοῖς ἀρχαίοις, *to them of old time*[1]) sc. the fathers in the time of Moses. The Scribes wished to appear to be in conformity with the ancient and primitive rule. Antiquity should be maintained, but it should be genuine antiquity.[2]

[1] E. V. *by* them of old time.—(I. B.)

[2] In fact, it was not in the time of Moses, and to the ancients ["to them of old time"], that the rather lax interpretation of the law was set forth, but in the time of the Scribes and Pharisees, and to the men of that age. The Scribes themselves were the persons who crusted over with the plea of anti-

—ὑμῖν, *to you*) This word is antithetic[1] to τοῖς ἀρχαίοις, from whence it is evident, that τοῖς ἀρχαίοις (*antiquis*) is not in the ablative, but in the dative case; and the construction is more easy if we render the passage thus, "*it was said* TO *them of old time*, than thus, "*it was said* BY *them of old time*."—οὐ φονεύσεις, *thou shalt not kill*) Our Lord begins with the clearest precept.—τῇ κρίσει, *to the judgment*) The Hebrew דין, rendered κρίσις, was the inferior tribunal existing in the several towns, and consisted of twenty-three judges, who had the power of life and death. The dative, τῇ κρίσει, signifies, *as far as belongs to*[2] *the judgment*, or municipal tribunal: in like manner, in the next verse τῷ συνεδρίῳ signifies *as far as belongs to the Sanhedrim*: for ἔνοχος, *criminal*, is here used absolutely.

22. Πᾶς, κ.τ.λ., *every one*, etc.) This is opposed to the lax rule[3] of the Scribes.—ὁ ὀργιζόμενος, *who is angry*) either with a lasting feeling or a sudden emotion.—τῷ ἀδελφῷ αὐτοῦ, *with his brother*) This appellation shows the unworthiness of anger.—εἰκῆ, *without a cause*) This gloss[4] evidently betrays its human origin.[5] He who is angry *without a cause* is superfluously angry: not even the Pharisees taught that it was lawful to be angry *without a cause*. Even if there be a cause for being angry, there ought to be no anger. *God also forbids us to hate even with cause, in that He commands us to love our enemies.*—Tertullian de Spectaculis, ch. xvi. On the other hand, the magistrate, in killing those who ought to be killed, does rightly, and yet it is never said, *Thou shalt not kill without a cause.*—ἔνοχος ἔσται τῇ κρίσει, *shall be criminal as far as belongs to the judgment or municipal*

quity their own innovations, as generally happens in religious controversies, or when morals are being corrupted.—*Vers. Germ.*

[1] See Explanation of technical terms in Appendix.—(I. B.)

[2] In the original, "*quod ad judicium attinet*," where in the phrase, "quod attinet," generally rendered "*with respect to*," "*as regards*," etc, *attinet* seems to have its own more peculiar and precise force of *pertains*; —and to signify, "is the province of." "comes under the jurisdiction of ;"—a meaning which appears to coincide with Bengel's observations on the next verse.—(I. B.)

[3] In the original "sanctione," a somewhat peculiar expression.—(I. B.)

[4] "Which Luther rightly omitted."—*Not. Crit.*

[5] It is retained by E. M.—(I. B.) B Vulg. Origen, omit it, and Lachm. and Tisch. read accordingly. But Dabc Iren. 242, 247, Cypr. 306, Lucf. 121, and after ὀργιζομ., Iren. 165, Hilary 128 (625) retain εἰκῆ.—ED.

tribunal) *i.e.* he is a murderer. Cf. ver. 21.[1] As he who looks upon a woman to lust after her is an adulterer, so *he that hateth his brother* (1 John iv. 15) *is a murderer.* This verse does not indicate three degrees of human or temporal punishment; for neither was it the part of the municipal tribunal and the Sanhedrim to punish the emotion of anger or the utterance of Raca, nor was the valley of the son of Hinnom the place for any punishment, much less for any punishment inflicted by any other power than that of the municipal tribunal or the Sanhedrim, still less for punishment on account of the abusive epithet of Fool. The judgment, therefore, and the council, are assigned to the emotion of anger and the utterance of Raca, as to the first and second degree of murder, deserving the first and second degree of punishment in hell: and the fiery Gehenna[2] is appropriately assigned to the third degree of murder, the abusive epithet of Fool, and indicates a more fiery punishment in hell. There is, therefore, a metonymy of the consequent for the antecedent. " He is criminal as far as belongs to the tribunal," etc.; signifying, he is a murderer in the first, second, and third degree. Civil guilt denotes spiritual guilt, both as to the fault and the punishment.—εἴπῃ, *shall say*) in his heart or with his lips once or continually.—'Ρακά, *Raca*) A Hebrew word, frequently used by Hebrews according to Lightfoot, the force of which no Greek word expresses. It denotes a sort of middle term between anger and the appellation of Fool.[3] Chrysostom on this passage says, that Raca denotes in Syriac the same as " *thou*," uttered contemptuously: others derive it from the Syrian

---

[1] For whatever is repugnant to meekness and love, is a principle rising up against life, and so breathes the spirit of murder.— *Vers. Germ.*

[2] " γέεννα— גיא (*vallis*), גיא חנם *Hinnom*, the valley at the foot of Moriah, and in which Siloa flows (*Jerome* on x. 28), on the east of Jerusalem, desecrated by the idolatrous fires of Moloch (Jer. vii. 31; Isa. xxx. 33), and called *Topheth*, from *Tuph*, the tympanum used to drown the cries of children there immolated."— *Wordsworth* in loc.

" Josiah therefore polluted it (2 Kings xxiii. 10); and thenceforward it was the place for casting out and burning all offal and the corpses of criminals; and therefore its name, ἡ γέεννα τοῦ πυρός, was used to signify the place of everlasting punishment."— *Alford* in loc.—(I. B.)

[3] Dreamy indolence (oscitantia) was the reproach usually meant to be conveyed by it, or else a headlong and hasty mode of action.— *Vers. Germ.*

"Ρακ," *he spits*. An old English Version renders it *Fie*. Light persons are called רֵיקִים in Judges ix. 4, xi. 3; 2 Chron. xiii. 7; and κενός, *empty or vain*, is thus used in James ii. 20. Reproof should reach even the trivial expressions and common manners of mankind, and that specifically; see ver. 34, 35, etc.; 1 Cor. xv. 32; James ii. 3, iv. 13.—τῷ συνεδρίῳ, *the Sanhedrim*) or Great National Council of seventy-two Judges, which was held at Jerusalem, and decreed the more severe punishments.—Μωρέ, *thou fool*) A most harsh taunt denying common sense, without which a man is incurable and utterly deplorable; cf. μωρανθῇ in ver. 13, and the note upon it. The LXX. used the word μωρός very sparingly, the Son of Sirach frequently.—ἔνοχος ἔσται εἰς τὴν γέενναν τοῦ πυρός, *he shall be criminal for the fiery Gehenna*) An elliptical mode of speech[1] for, *so that he may be consigned to the fiery Gehenna*—sc. the valley of the Son of Hinnom, where carrion and carcases lie unburied, and at length are burnt. The word γέεννα, *Gehenna*, does not occur in the Septuagint; in the New Testament it is used by St Matthew, St Mark, St Luke, and St James; but not by either St John, St Paul, St Peter, or St Jude. Hiller (in his Onomata Sacra, p. 811) derives it from the Hebrew גֵּי הַנִּי, *the Valley of Lamentation*. Concerning the fire of that valley, see Jer. vii. 31, 32, etc.—εἰς, etc., is used with the same force as in the expression εἰς κόρακας, *to the ravens*.[2]

23. Ἐὰν οὖν, κ.τ.λ., *if therefore*, etc.) Reconciliation is not said to be only then necessary, for the word ἐκεῖ, *there*) indicates that you ought to have *remembered* it before; but the meaning is, Whatever you are doing, even if you have already undertaken the best and most holy and most necessary matter, leave everything until you have been reconciled to your brother: see Eph. iv. 26. They sin who do not make it up with their brother, until they are just about to receive the Holy Supper. Yet reconciliation is especially necessary, and an examination of the conscience especially imperative on those who are about to perform the most solemn act of devotion.—ἐπί, *to*) For it was the

---

[1] See, on the Locutio Concisa, Appendix.—ED.

[2] A phrase used by the Greeks to denote not only the disgrace of the gallows, but the still greater one of remaining unburied.—*Liddell and Scott*.—(I. B.)

part of the priest to offer *on* the altar, and afterwards occurs the expression, *ἔμπροσθεν τοῦ θυσιαστηρίου*, *before the altar.*—καὶ ἐκεῖ μνησθῇς, *and there rememberest*) The word of God portrays the most hidden secrets of the human heart. In the performance of a sacred rite, the remembrance of offences arises more naturally, than in the noise of human affairs.—ἔχει, *hath*) as having been offended [by thee].

24. Ὕπαγε, πρῶτον, *go thy way, first*) placed antithetically to τότε ἐλθών, *then having come*,—διαλλάγηθι τῷ ἀδελφῷ σῷ, *be reconciled to thy brother,*) that thou mayest be reconciled to God.—ἐλθών, *coming*) not *returning;* for the first going being in vain is not reckoned.

25. Ἴσθι εὐνοῶν, *be friendly*) Seek kindly feeling by showing it yourself.—τῷ ἀντιδίκῳ, *with the adversary*) to whom you owe money.—Cf. ver. 26. The language is parabolical, it applies principally to an adversary who entertains grave animosity even beyond death.—ταχύ, *quickly*) The pride of the human heart is slow in deprecation and satisfaction.—ἐν τῇ ὁδῷ, *in the way*) sc. to the tribunal.—μετ' αὐτοῦ, *with him*) The plaintiff used himself to apprehend the defendant.—σε παραδῷ, *deliver thee*) Great is the power of the adversary. God, as Judge, prosecutes the demand of him who pleads for justice.—φυλακήν, *ward*) where thou thy whole self wilt be the pledge of payment for the debt.

26. Ἕως ἄν, *until*) The debtor is left to himself; see ch. xviii. 34. It is strange that the expression, ἕως ἄν, should have been urged by those, who hence infer the possibility of payment, rather than τὸν ἔσχατον κοδράντην, *the last* farthing.—τὸν ἔσχατον, *the last*) Thus does Divine justice exact everything, not a single farthing more or less than you owe.[1]—κοδράντην, *quadrantem*) Substantives which express foreign articles are very frequently transferred from one language to another, instead of being translated.[2]

27. Ἐρρέθη, *it has been said*) Murder and adultery are equally

---

[1] O the vain and most deceitful persuasion of the old man, whereby he supposes that God will only lightly exact the debts due to Him. Nay, unless remission interpose so as to remove utterly one's countless faults, the uttermost avarice of man does not exercise as great rigour, as the divine justice justly and deservedly maintains.—*Vers. Germ.*

[2] The *quadrans*, the fourth part of an asse, about a farthing and a half of our money.—(I. B.)

sins against our neighbour, and so is revenge, and therefore the words, τοῖς ἀρχαίοις, *to them of old time*, are not expressed but understood in ver. 27, 31, 38, 43, from ver. 21. They are, however, expressed in ver. 33, where our Lord treats of oaths, and, therefore, of our duty to God.

28. Ὁ βλέπων, *that looketh*) Refer to this expression the right eye mentioned in the next verse.—πρὸς, *to*) This particle determines the character of the looking.—ἤδη, *already*) by that very act.

29. Ὁ δεξιὸς, *the right*) The right, strictly speaking in the case of the hands, is most useful and most precious, thence also, it is mentioned in the case of the eyes, feet, etc.—See Zech. xi. 17; Exod. xxix. 20.—σκανδαλίζει, *is a stumbling-block to*) so that you should see wrongly; as in the case of your *hand*, so that you should act wrongly.—ἔξελε αὐτὸν, *pluck it out*) not the eye absolutely, but the eye which is a stumbling-block, *i.e.*, make all things hard to thyself, until it cease to be a stumbling-block to thee. Not the organ itself, but the *concupiscence* which animates the eye or hand is meant: for this is the soul of the eye where that organ proves a stumbling-block; in like manner as soon afterwards the body is said for the [whole] man [soul as well as body]. He who, where his eye proves a stumbling-block, takes care not to see, does in reality blind himself. On the other hand, a man might pluck out his material eye, and yet cherish concupiscence within. A similar mode of expression occurs in Coloss. iii. 5, where the apostle says—*Mortify, therefore, your members which are upon the earth; fornication*, etc. A negative maxim is frequently expressed by affirming the opposite.—See ver. 39, 40, and ch. vi. 17.—βάλε, *cast*) with earnestness. The expression βληθῇ, *be cast*) in the next verse has reference to this.— συμφέρει, *it is profitable*) to thy salvation. Not only is it not hurtful, but also it will be glorious.—ἀπόληται, *should perish*) True self-abnegation is not of less amount than the loss of an eye, etc.: and it is so necessary that it is better to be deprived of an eye itself, than to sin with the eye, unless the sin may be separated from the eye. An eye which is actually plucked out, as in the case of a martyr, will be restored in the resurrection.—ἓν τῶν μελῶν σου, *one of thy members*) Many, indeed, have been destroyed by neglecting the mortification of one member, as, for example,

the gullet.—ὅλον τὸ σῶμά σου, *thy whole body*) If one member sin, the whole man sins and pays the penalty.—γέενναν, *hell*) of eternal fire.—See ch. xviii. 8, etc.

30. Χεὶρ, *hand*) The matter proceeds from sight to act.

31. Ὅς ἂν ἀπολύσῃ, *whosoever shall put away*) They held divorce to be an arbitrary matter.[1]—ἀποστάσιον, *a divorce*) i.e. a writing of divorcement. A metonymy which occurs in ch. xix. 7, and is also employed by the LXX.

32. Λόγου, *for the cause*) The Hebrew דָּבָר corresponds to the Greek λόγος in the sense of a *cause*, why anything may be rightly done.[2]—ποιεῖ αὐτὴν μοιχᾶσθαι, *makes her to commit adultery*) sc. by other nuptials into which the divorce permits her to enter.—ἀπολελυμένην, *one that has been divorced*).

33. Ἀποδώσεις, *thou shalt render*)[3] Perjury therefore is the non-performance of promises attested by an oath. Christ, therefore, especially forbids promissory oaths, since men *by* them asseverate concerning future things, none of which is in their power, see ver. 36. The human oaths concerning which Moses gives regulations, or which holy men have sworn, have more frequently reference to confirming, more rarely to promising, and in fact more persons perjure themselves with regard to future, than past matters. Wherefore the Romans prudently preferred binding with oath their magistrates at the conclusion, rather than at the commencement of office.—ὅρκους, *oaths*,) sc. things promised by oath.

34. Μὴ ὀμόσαι ὅλως, *not to swear at all*) The ὅλως, *at all*, extends this prohibition to swearing truly as well as falsely: it does not, however, universally prohibit all true swearing. The right employment of oaths is not only like divorce permitted but clearly established by the law, nor is it here abolished by Christ; see ver. 17. But the abuse of oaths was extremely frequent with the Jews of that age, to the destruction of their legitimate use, as is clear from the forms of swearing cited in

---

[1] δότω does not indicate a command but a permission. [*He may give.*] They seemed to think Moses had nothing in view save the observance of certain formalities.—*Vers. Germ.*

[2] These words, παρεκτὸς λόγου πορνείας, apply also to the following clause καὶ ὃς ἐὰν ἀπολελ. γαμ, and are to be supplied in it.—*Vers. Germ.*

[3] E. V. "Thou shalt perform."—(I. B.)

this passage; nor did they think him guilty of perjury who called only *creatures* to witness in his oath, however falsely he might swear. See Samuel Petit,[1] *Variae Lectiones*, ch. xvi. The following decree of the Jews is to be found in Elle Schemoth Rabba,[2] section 44, *As heaven and earth shall pass away, so shall the oath pass away which calls them to witness.* There is clearly, however, a prohibition, whilst the prevalent[3] abuse of oaths is forbidden, and their true use restored. Many of the ancient Christians received this command simply and literally, and so much the more readily declined the heathen oaths which they were commanded to take. See however, Rev. x. 6; Jer. xxiii. 8; Is. xlv. 23, the last of which passages refers to Christian times. On the contrary, there is now-a-days a great danger lest a very small proportion of the number that are made be true, and of the true a very small proportion necessary, and of those that are necessary a very small proportion free, fruitful, holy, and joyful. Many are employed for show, for calumny, for silencing just suspicions.—ἐν, *by*) That which is sworn by is offered in pledge: it should therefore be in the power of him who swears. He who swears wrongly (ver. 34, 36) is guilty of sacrilege. Therefore, in this sense a man ought not to swear by God, because, in case of his swearing falsely, he pledges himself to renounce God. This, however, it is not in his power to do. But we must swear in that manner which is sanctioned in the Divine law itself, so that our oath should be an invocation of the Divine name. Even the customary formula, *So help me God*, is not to be taken in the former but in the latter sense, so that the emphasis should fall upon the word GOD. This interpretation is at any rate favourable to him who swears, and makes the matter rather easier.—τῷ οὐρανῷ, *by heaven*) How much greater is their sin who swear by God Himself!—Θρόνος, *throne*) How great is the majesty of God! God is not enclosed by heaven, but His glory is especially manifested there.

[1] A celebrated scholar, born at Nismes in 1594, studied at Geneva, raised at an early age to the Professorship of Theology and of Greek and Hebrew in that city. Died 1645. A man of vast and profound erudition.—(I. B.)

[2] *i.e.* "Mystical Commentary on Exodus," a rabbinical work in high estimation among the Jews.—(I. B.)

[3] "Grassatus," a word used of a fiercely raging epidemic.—(I. B.)

35. Εἰς, *upon*) There is a difference between this and ἐν (*by*)[1] used in the last verse. The Jews were accustomed to pray for all blessings upon Jerusalem. The meanings of the formula therefore was—*So may the city be in safety, as*—*So may it light upon the city, as*[2]—πόλις, *the city*) the royal abode.—τοῦ[3] Μεγάλου Βασιλέως, *of that*[4] *Great King*), (see Ps. xlviii. 2), *i.e.* of the Messiah whom (ver. 34, 35) heaven and earth obey. It is not unbecoming in Him to speak thus of Himself. See ch. ix. 38, and xxii. 43.

36. Κεφαλῇ, *head*) Their sin is still graver who swear by their life or their soul.—μίαν τρίχα λευκὴν ἢ μέλαιναν ποιῆσαι, *to make one hair* [thereof] *white or black*) The dye of human art is not real whiteness or blackness. Not merely is a single hair, but even the colour of a single hair, beyond the power of man.

37. Ὁ λόγος ὑμῶν, *your conversation*) your daily ordinary speech. ναὶ, ναί. οὒ, οὔ, *yea, yea ; nay, nay*) Let " *yea,*" or, " *it is,*" be employed to affirm what is true,—" *Nay,*" or, " *it is not,*" to deny what is false.[5] Cf. Gnomon on 2 Cor. i. 17, 18, and James v. 12.—περισσὸν, *exceeding, that which exceeds*) Excess is faulty.— ἐκ τοῦ πονηροῦ, *of evil*); the word is here in the neuter gender, [and signifies evil in the abstract] : see ver. 39.

38. Ὀφθαλμὸν, *an eye)* sc. Thou shalt require. In Exod. xxi. 24, the LXX. have ὀφθαλμὸν ἀντὶ ὀφθαλμοῦ, ὀδόντα ἀντὶ ὀδόντος, *eye for eye, tooth for tooth*. The *lex talionis* was most suitable for punishments, as in the greater injury, murder, and in the less, theft, so also in that which stood midway between them. See Lev. xxiv. 20. Mutilation was frequent in punishments without reference to the principle of the *lex talionis;* why then should it not be used to carry out that principle itself ? Cf. Jud. i. 7.[6] Penalties would avail more, if human judgment did not depart

---

[1] E. V. renders both words "*by*"—sc. " by Heaven," " by Jerusalem," etc.—(I. B.)

[2] Perhaps it may refer to the Jewish custom of praying with the face towards Jerusalem, Daniel vi. 10.—ED.

[3] The article has a magnifying force.—*Not. Crit.*

[4] *Magni illius regis.* E. V. renders it " of the Great King."—(I. B.)

[5] Lit. Let the "*It is*" of fact be also the "*It is*" in your words : let the "*It is not*" of fact be also the "*It is not*" in your words.—ED.

[6] What had been prescribed to the magistrate, that the Scribes allotted to private vengeance.—B. G. V.

so far from the wisdom, the equity, and the severity of the Divine law.

39. Μὴ ἀντιστῆναι, *not to resist*) The infinitive is governed by λέγω, *I say*, as in Rev. xiii. 14. To resist evil is to return injury for injury.—ἀλλ᾽, *but*) Our Lord gives examples of private, legal, and political wrong, ver. 39, 40, 41.—ῥαπίσει, *shall smite*) elsewhere ῥαπίζειν is *to strike with rods*, but in this passage as the cheek is mentioned, it means to smite with the open hand.—τὴν δεξιάν σου σιαγόνα, *the right cheek*) or the left either. See Luke vi. 29. An instance of *Synedoche*.[1]—στρέψον, *turn*) It is sometimes advisable to do so literally.[2] The world says, on the other hand, Assert thy courage by a duel. Those who are able ought ere this to have made a stand against this evil, this disgrace of the Christian name, and to have given all diligence that they might do so effectually. One man who becomes a murderer by a duel involves a whole camp in his guilt. Many, so far dilute and extenuate the lessons here given by the Saviour, that they slide down to a level with the righteousness of the Scribes and Pharisees, or even below it.

40. Χιτῶνα, *the tunic*) or inner garment.—ἱμάτιον, *the vest*) or outer robe. These are inverted in Luke vi. 29. (Cf. in the same chapter, ver. 44, with Matt. vii. 16, for a similar inversion in the case of the grapes and the figs.) The sense remains the same; sc. *Give up both*. The ἱμάτιον was more precious than the χιτών. See Mark xiii. 16.—σου, *thine*) by right.

41. Ἀγγαρεύσει) A word of Persian origin.[3] They who travelled on the public business could press a person into service. See Vriemoet on this passage.[4]

---

[1] See Explanation of Technical Terms in Appendix.—(I. B.)

[2] Spiritual prudence will teach the children of GOD, *when* they ought to do so. The words of Christ are not words belonging to the mere human and natural life, but to the eternal life. What seems folly to the world, appears in a quite different light in the eternal Life.—*Vers. Germ.*

[3] "Ἄγγαρος, a Persian word for a royal courier, who had authority to press horses, etc. into his service in execution of his mission. The word אנגריא (*angaria*) (whence *avania* and *avanie* in Ital. and Fr.) is used in the Talmud for any forced work. Connected with this is the Hebrew אגרת (*iggereth*), a letter."—*Wordsworth* in loc.—(I. B.)

[4] Emo-Lucius Vriemoet, born at Embden, in Friesland in 1699, became Professor of Oriental languages and Hebrew antiquities at Francker, and

42. Αἰτοῦντι, *to him that asketh*) who wishes you to give to him gratuitously, even though he do not ask with the best claim.—δίδου, *give*) as God does; see Luke xi. 10.—τὸν θέλοντα, *him that would*) even though he does not venture to beseech thee vehemently.—μὴ ἀποστραφῇς, *turn not thou away*) although you have a specious pretext for so doing.

43. Τὸν πλησίον, *Thy neighbour*) Gataker[1] in his Adversaria miscellanea posthuma, ch. x. f. 527, remarks, that in Sophocles and Aristotle, all men are indiscriminately called οἱ πέλας.[2]—μισήσεις τὸν ἐχθρόν σου,[3] *thou shalt hate thine enemy*) The Jews abused the precept which had been given in reference to certain accursed nations, as in Deut. xxiii. 7; for they had also been commanded to love even their enemies. Christopher Cartwright[4] cites decrees of the Jews concerning the hatred of enemies.—See Book 2; Mellif. Heb. ch. 1.

44. Ἀγαπᾶτε, *love ye*— εὐλογεῖτε, *bless ye*—καλῶς ποιεῖτε, *do ye good to*—καὶ προσεύχεσθε ὑπέρ, *and pray ye for*) Here are four clauses, the second and third of which are wanting in some of the ancients—the second in the Vulgate, the third in Tertullian,[5] De Patientia, ch. vi. Four clauses ought, therefore, to be read, although the third is almost contained in the first, and the second in the fourth by *Chiasmus*:[6] on which account St Luke transposes them.[7] In ver. 46, the verb ἀγαπάω, *to love*, occurs again,

published many learned works on these subjects. He died in 1764.—(I. B.)

[1] Thomas Gataker was born in London 1574; became Preacher of Lincoln's Inn in 1601, Rector of Rotherhithe 1611, and died 1654. He was one of the most learned theologians of his time. He subscribed the Covenant, but declared in favour of Episcopacy, and during the Commonwealth preferred the Presbyterians to the Independents. His works are many and various.—(I. B.)

[2] *i.e.* neighbours.—(I. B.)

[3] A most vile gloss.—B. G. V.

[4] Christopher Cartwright, a learned English divine; born 1602; died 1658. The work here cited is Mellificium Hebraicum, sive observationes ex Hebræorum antiquiorum monumentis desumptæ.—(I. B.)

[5] Quintus Septimius Florens Tertullianus, a native of Carthage, where he became a Presbyter, the earliest of the Latin fathers, flourished in the third century.—(I. B.)

[6] See explanation of technical terms in Appendix.—(I. B.)

[7] Vulg. Memph. Versions, Orig. 4,329c; 351a; Cypr. 248, 260, 319, IIil.

and in ver. 47, the word ἀσπάσησθε, *salute,* corresponds with εὐλο-γεῖτε in the present verse.—τῶν ἐπηρεαζόντων ὑμᾶς, *them which despitefully use you*) ἐπήρεια, [the substantive from which the verb ἐπηρεάζω is derived] signifies an injury inflicted, not for the benefit of the injurer, but for the damage of the injured party.—See my notes to Chrysostom on the Priesthood, p. 429. It is, therefore, a sign of extreme hatred. A striking contrast. Pray for such persons as these: obtain by your prayers blessings for those, who take blessings from you.

45. Ὅπως γένησθε, *that ye may become*) When they love their enemies, they become His sons [but] in such a manner as [not to contravene the fact], that they already previously have Him for their Father.[1] An instance of *Ploce*:[2] Sons become sons, as disciples become disciples.—Cf. John xv. 8. Thus, the God of Israel became the God of Israel; 2 Sam. vii. 24. Great is God's condescension in not disdaining to invite His sons to imitate Him. ὅτι, κ.τ.λ., *for,* etc.) Such is the principle upon which the Father is to be imitated. As God treats and rules us, so ought men to treat and rule each other.—τὸν ἥλιον Αὐτοῦ, *His sun*) A magnificent expression. He both made the sun and governs it, and has it exclusively in His own power.—ἀνατέλλει, *maketh to rise.*—βρέχει, *raineth, sendeth rain*) It is the part of piety to speak of natural things as received from God, rather than to say impersonally, *It rains, it thunders.*—See ch. vi. 26, 30; Job xxxvi. 27, 28, and chapters xxxvii.–xli.; Ps. civ., etc. Franzius urges this strongly in his treatise on the Interpretation of Scripture, pp. 83, 632. Rain is a great blessing.

46. Τίνα μισθὸν, *what reward*) God seeks in us an occasion for giving us a reward.—τελῶναι, *publicans*) who refer all things to gain; but have none in Heaven.

47. Ἐὰν ἀσπάσησθε, *if ye salute*) contrasted with, *bless ye,* etc., in ver. 44. The very verb ἀγαπάω, *to love,* is repeated in ver.

---

303 omit εὐλογεῖτε τ. καταρωμένους ὑμᾶς, καλῶς ποιεῖτε τοῖς μισοῦσιν ὑμᾶς. Dcd Lucif. insert these words with Rec. Text (which, however, has τ. μισοῦντας.)—ED.

[1] *i.e.* He first loves them, and is their Father already; but they become His sons, and prove their sonship afterwards, when they love their enemies, even as He loved them when still enemies.—ED.

[2] See Appendix.—ED.

46 from ver. 44; but as the heathens do not also bless and pray, the verb to *salute* is put here instead of either blessing or praying.—τοὺς ἀδελφοὺς ὑμῶν, your brethren [1]—ἐθνικοί, *the heathen*) The Publicans regard their own interest, the Heathens perform also offices of kindness towards their connections and friends, and more especially towards their *blood relations*. In ver. 46, therefore, the example of the Publicans is cited; in ver. 47, that of the Heathens.—τί περισσόν, *what remarkable thing*) [2] such as befits the sons of God.[3]

48. Ὑμεῖς, *you*) In honourable contradistinction to them.— τέλειοι, *perfect*) sc. in love towards all.[4]

CHAPTER VI.

1. Προσέχετε, *take ye heed*) The hortatory address,[5] πρόσεχε σεαυτῷ, *take heed to thyself* was familiar to the early Christians; since the Hebrew השמר [6] (which occurs so frequently in Deuteronomy), was thus rendered by the LXX.—τὴν δικαιοσύνην,[7] ὑμῶν, *your righteousness*) This depends upon μὴ ποιεῖν, *not to do*.[8]—δικαιοσύνην, *righteousness*) The treatment of the subsequent divisions relating to almsgiving, prayer, and fasting, exhibits such an exact analogy that from a comparison of them it becomes evident, that the

---

[1] The margin of Beng. Ed. π and Vers. Germ. prefer φίλους to ἀδελφούς: But not so the larger Edition of α. 1734. Lucifer reads *amicos*, also of second rate Uncial MSS. L Δ. But the oldest MSS. and Vulg. ἀδελφούς, fratres.—ED.

[2] E. V. *What do ye more than others?*—(I. B.)

[3] He who does nothing but what is customary ought to stand in fear (*soll in Sorge stehen*.)—B. G. V.

[4] See Col. iii. 14.—(I. B.)

[5] Celeusma, from the Greek κέλευσμα—properly an exhortation to any work; especially of sailors: Either the cry of sailors for encouraging one another, or a beating of time to the rowers.—See RIDDLE.—(I. B.)

[6] E. V. Take heed, etc.—See Deut. xii. 13, etc.—(I. B.)

[7] E. M. τὴν ἐλεημοσύνην.—(I. B.)

[8] i.e. τὴν δικαιοσύνην is the accusative after μὴ ποιεῖν—so that the passage must be rendered "*Take heed that ye do not your righteousness*," etc.— (I. B.)

warning contained in this verse does not apply solely and exclusively to the first division, but has the force of a general proposition. The design of the whole discourse is to teach true righteousness; (see ch. v. 6, 10, 20, and vi. 33); and this reading accords with that design. Others read ἐλεημοσύνην,[1] *almsgiving*.[2] *Righteousness* is the whole (cf. Gnomon on ch. v. 6), three divisions of which follow immediately; viz., *almsgiving*, as being our especial duty towards our *neighbour*—*prayer*, as occupying the same position with regard to *God*—*fasting*, as holding the same place with reference to *ourselves*. These three relations, to God, to ourselves, and to our neighbour, are frequently enumerated in Holy Writ; see Rom. ii. 21, 22–vii. 12–xiv. 17; 1 Cor. vi. 11–xiii. 5, 6, 13; Eph. v. 9; 1 Tim. i. 13; Tit. i. 8–ii. 12; Heb. xii. 12, 13.— Διαθῆναι, *to be seen as a spectacle*) Theatre and hypocrite[3] (spoken of in the next verse) are words of cognate meaning.

2. Μὴ σαλπίσῃς ἔμπροσθέν σου, *do not sound a trumpet before thee*) This affected and insolent ostentation of actually sounding a trumpet is not inconsistent with the practices of hypocrites among the Jews of that age: cf. ver. 5, 16. The poor would be easily summoned by a trumpet: hypocrisy, therefore, employs it as a means of display.—οἱ ὑποκριταί, *the hypocrites*) *Hypocrisy* is the combination of actual vice with apparent virtue, by means of which a man deceives either himself or others.—ἀμήν, *assuredly*) our Lord [by virtue of His essential and proper divinity] knows the secrets of the Divine counsels.—ἀπέχουσι τὸν μισθὸν αὐτῶν, *they have their reward*[4]) An example of metonymy of the antecedent for the consequent, *i.e.* they will not receive any reward hereafter at the hands of their Heavenly Father; see ver. 1.

3. Μὴ γνώτω ἡ ἀριστερά, κ.τ.λ., *let not thy left hand know*, etc.) So far from holding a trumpet, let it not even know what thy right hand doeth. Do not thou even consider over again the good that thou doest.

---

[1] See f. n. [7] to last page.—(I. B.)

[2] BDabc Vulg. Hilary read δικαιοσύνην. But Z supports ἐλεημοσύνην, the reading of the Rec. Text.—ED.

[3] The word originally signifies *one who answers*, thence, *one who takes part in a dramatic dialogue*, thence, *one who assumes a feigned character*.—(I. B.)

[4] Which consists in the praise of men.—B. G. V.

ST MATTHEW VI. 4–7. 187

4. 'Εν τῷ κρυπτῷ, *in secret*) The godly shine, but shine in secret.
—ὁ Πατήρ σου, *thy Father*) John Despagne observes, that to employ the possessive pronoun of the first person singular, and say, "*My Father*," is the exclusive privilege of the Only Begotten; but "*Thy Father*" is said *to* the faithful also; FATHER, or OUR *Father*," *by* the faithful; see John xx. 17.—ἐν τῷ κρυπτῷ, *in secret*) He is Himself in secret, and performs His works in secret, and approves most those things which are done in secret. The whole essential being of things, has its existence in secret.—ἀποδώσει, *shall reward*) This word, without the addition of Αὐτὸς (*Himself*), expresses a reward awarded by God and not man. This reward is sure: see ver. 1. The Αὐτὸς (*Himself*), appears to have been inserted here, and the ἐν τῷ φανερῷ (*openly*) in ver. 4, 6, 18, from a fear that the words might have otherwise been rendered, "Thy Father, who seeth that, shall reward thee in secret." [2]

5. Φιλοῦσιν, κ.τ.λ., *they love*, etc.) and, therefore, make a practice of doing so.—ἐν ταῖς γωνίαις, *in the corners*) sc. where the streets meet.—ἑστῶτες, *standing*) in order that they may be the more conspicuous.

6. 'Εν τῷ κρυπτῷ, *in secret*) God both *is*, and *sees*, in secret.

7. Μὴ βαττολογήσητε, *use not vain repetitions*) Gattaker has collected from antiquity many persons called Battus, celebrated for their stammering, and thence for their frequent repetition of the same word (tautologia), and deriving their name from that circumstance. Hesychius[3] renders βαττολογία by ἀργολογία (*idle talking*), ἀκαιρολογία (*unseasonable talking*): he says, "βατταρίζειν appears to me to be derived from an imitation of the voice," etc., and he explains βατταρισμὸι by φλυαρίαι.[4] It is clear, therefore,

---

[1] In the original, "Pii lucent sed latent."—(I. B.)
[2] Rec. Text has αὐτός with D. But BLZabc Vulg. Memph. Versions, and Cyprian omit it. So also ἐν τῷ φανερῷ added in Rec. Text with abc, is omitted in BDZ Vulg. Memph. Versions.—ED.
[3] Hesychius. There were several distinguished men of this name. The individual here intended was a celebrated grammarian and lexicographer of Alexandria, who lived somewhere about the fourth century.—(I. B.)
[4] βατταρισμὸς signified either originally *stuttering*, or derivatively *idle prating*: φλυαρία, *silly talk, nonsense, foolery*. It is used also in the plural. The kindred adjective φλύαροι is rendered *tattlers* in 1 Tim. v. 13, and the cognate participle φλυαρῶν, *prating* in 3 John 10 by the Eng. Ver.—(I. B.)

that βαττολογεῖν means the same here which πολυλογία (*much speaking*) does immediately afterwards, sc. when the same things are repeated over and over again, as is the case with stammerers, who endeavour to correct their first utterance by a second.—ὥσπερ οἱ ἐθνικοί, *as the heathen do*) In all things the practice of hypocrites is to be avoided, in prayer that also of the heathen.—ἐν τῇ πολυλογίᾳ αὐτῶν, *in their much speaking*) *i.e.* whilst they say many words. They think that many words are required to inform their deities what they want of them, so that they may hear and grant their requests, if not at the present, at some future time. Cf. on the other hand, "*your Father* KNOWETH," etc., ver. 8. The same word, πολυλογία (*much speaking*) occurs in the S. V. of Proverbs x. 19. Ammonius[1] says, μακρολόγος is one who utters *many words* concerning *few things*, πολυλόγος, one who utters *many words* concerning *many things*. Christ commands us to utter *few words*, even when praying for *many things;* see ver. 9–13.—εἰσακουσθήσονται, *shall be regarded.* The Hebrew ענה, *to answer*, is rendered by the LXX. εἰσακούειν. God answers substantially;[2] see ch. vii. 7.

8. Πρὸ κ.τ.λ., *before,* etc.) We pray, therefore, not with the view of instructing, but of adoring, the Father.

9. Οὕτως, *thus*) *i.e.* in these words, with this meaning; sc. with a short invocation of the Father, and a short enumeration of the things which we require. To have truly prayed *thus*, is sufficient, especially in meaning, one portion being employed at one time, another at another, to express our desires; and *thus* also *in words*. For this formula is given in opposition to much speaking, has words best suited to the things which they express, a most perfect arrangement, and a fulness combined with brevity, which is most admirable; so that the whole discourse may be said to be contained in it. The matter of this prayer is the basis of the whole of the first epistle of St Peter; see Gnomon on 1 Peter i. 3.—Πάτερ, *Father.* An appellation by which God is never *addressed* in the Old Testament: for the examples which

---

[1] Ammonius the grammarian must not be confounded with the author of the *Ammonian Sections.* He was a native of Alexandria, and flourished in the fourth century. The work here alluded to is his treatise *De differentia dictionum.*—(I. B.)

[2] In the original "Deus respondit solide."—(I. B.)

Lightfoot has adduced, are either dissimilar or modern, and prove no more than that the Jews spoke of God as their Father in Heaven, a formula to which Christ now gives life. The glory of the faithful in the New Testament is thus *to pray*. In this place is laid the foundation of praying in the name of Christ: see John xvi. 23. He who is permitted to address God as his Father, may ask all things from Him in prayer.—ἡμῶν, *our*) The children of God individually pray for all His children collectively: but even *their* prayers are, by this little word *our*, declared to be more acceptable when offered in common: see ch. xviii. 19.— ὁ ἐν τοῖς οὐρανοῖς, *which art in the Heavens*) *i.e.* Maxime et optime[1] (*Almighty, and All-good*); see ch. vii. 11. Shortly afterwards we find in ver. 10.—ἐν οὐρανῷ, *in Heaven*; nor is it without cause that the number[2] (which is elsewhere frequently used promiscuously, as in ch. xxii. 30, and xxiv. 36), varies in so short a passage as the present: οὐρανός (in the singular number), signifies here that place, in which the will of the Father is performed by all, who wait upon Him; οὐρανοί (in the plural) signifies the whole Heavens which surround and contain that one as it were lower and smaller Heaven: cf. note on Luke ii. 14.—ἁγιασθήτω, *hallowed be*) The petitions are seven in number and may be separated into two divisions, the former containing three petitions which relate to the Father, " Thy *Name*, Thy *Kingdom*, Thy *Will*," the latter containing four which concern ourselves. In the former we declare our filial affection subscribing to the right, the dignity, and the good pleasure of God, after the manner of the angelic chorus in Luke ii. 14: but in the latter we both sow and reap. In both divisions is expressed the struggle of the sons of God from Earth to Heaven, by which they as it were draw down Heaven to Earth. The object of the first petition is the sanctification of our Divine Father's Name. God is holy: *i.e.* He is God. He is sanctified therefore, when He is acknowledged and worshipped and celebrated as He really is. The mood[3]

---

[1] The mode in which the ancients addressed the Supreme God.—(I. B.)

[2] *i.e.* οὐρανός Heaven in the singular—οὐρανοί heavens in the plural.—(I. B.)

[3] *i.e.* all the three verbs are in the same mood, the Imperative, and have the same *precatory* force. It is scarcely necessary to remind the general reader that the Imperative Mood *intreats* as well as commands.—(I. B.)

in ἁγιασθήτω (*hallowed be*), has the same force as in ἐλθέτω, *come* and γενηθήτω (*be done*): it is, therefore, a prayer and not an express doxology.

10. 'Ελθέτω—γενηθήτω κ.τ.λ., *come—be done*, etc.) Tertullian has transposed these two petitions for the sake of his plan. For in his book on prayer, after he has treated of the petition, "*Hallowed be Thy name*," he says, "ACCORDING TO THIS FORM, we add, '*Thy will be done in the heavens and on the earth.*'" And he then refers the coming of God's kingdom to the end of the world.—ἡ βασιλεία Σου, *Thy kingdom*) See Gnomon on ch. iv. 17, and Rev. xi. 15, 17. The sanctification of God's name is as it were derived from the Old Testament into the New, to be continued and increased by us; but the coming of God's kingdom is in some sort peculiar to the New Testament. Thus with these two petitions respectively, Cf. Rev. iv. 8, and v. 10.—τὸ θέλημα Σου, *Thy will*) Jesus always kept His Father's will before His eyes, for His own performance and for ours. See ch. vii. 21, xii. 50.—ὡς, κ.τ.λ, *as*, etc.) "It will be the part of the pastor to admonish the faithful, that these words, 'as in heaven so on earth,' may be referred to each of the (three) first petitions as, 'Hallowed be Thy name, as in heaven so on earth,' also, 'Thy kingdom come as in heaven so on earth,' in like manner, 'Thy will be done as in heaven so on earth.'"—ROMAN CATECHISM.[1] The codices however which in Luke xi. 2 omit the words, "*Thy will be done*," omit also the words, "*As in heaven so on earth.*"—ἐν οὐρανῷ, *in heaven*) We do not ask that these things may be done in heaven: but heaven is proposed as the normal standard to earth—earth in which all things are done in different ways.[2]

11. Τὸν ἄρτον, *the bread*) sc. nourishment of the body; see ver. 19, etc., 25, etc., from which it is evident that the disciples were not yet raised above the cares of this life. This short

---

[1] sc. that, issued under the sanction of the Council of Trent.—(I. B.)

[2] In the original "in quâ aliter alia fiunt omnia."—Lit.: "in which all things are done, some one way, some another."—*i.e.* The unvarying uniformity of Heaven, which conforms itself undeviatingly to the Divine Will, should be the standard by which to correct the multiform variety of Earth, the infinite diversities of which are none of them in strict accordance with that Will.—(L. B.)

petition is opposed to the much speaking of the heathen, mentioned in ver. 7, which principally referred to the same object;[1] and it is placed first amongst those petitions which refer to ourselves, because the natural life is prior to the spiritual. Every want of ours is cared for in this prayer.—ἡμῶν, *of* or *belonging to us*) *our*, sc. earthly. But the spiritual bread is the bread of God, *i.e.* that which is [given] by God, and [cometh forth] from God.—ἐπιούσιον, *daily*) This adjective is derived ἀπὸ τῆς ἐπιούσης, *from the following day*, and is composed of ἐπί and ἰοῦσα.[2] For from εἰμί, *to be* (from which also comes περιούσιος) or from οὐσία, *essence* or *private property*, would be composed, ἐπούσιος, in the same manner as ἐπουράνιος, etc.: since although ἐπί does not always lose the ι in composition before a vowel, it does lose it in ἔπεστιν, as also in ἔπειμι from which this adjective must be originally derived according to this hypothesis. Our heavenly Father gives each day what is needed each day. Nor is it necessary that He should give it before. This His paternal and providential distribution suggests the expression ἐπιούσιος, *for the coming day*. The continuance, therefore, of our indigence, and of God's fatherly beneficence as from year to year, so from day to day, is denoted by this phrase. Cf. 2 Kings xxv. 30.—λόγον ἡμέρας ἐν ἡμέρᾳ αὐτοῦ, *the proportion for the day on its day*. Cf. Acts vi. 1, διακονία καθημερινή, *daily ministration*. *The bread*, as a whole, is appointed us for all our days; but the "*giving*" of it is distributed through the several days of our life, so as to take place each day. Both these ideas are expressed by the word ἐπιούσιος. What was necessary for the support of my life on any particular day, needed not to be given me on the day before that, but on that very day; and what was necessary on the following day, was given soon enough on that day, and so on. The sense therefore of ἐπιούσιος extends more widely with regard both to the past and the future, than that of "*crastinus*," *to-morrow's*.—σήμερον, *to-day*) In Luke xi. 3, we find τὸ καθ' ἡμέραν, *day by day*. Day by day we say and pray, "*to-day*." Our confidence and contentedness (αὐτάρκεια)[3] are thus expressed. Thus in James ii. 15, we have ἐφήμερος

---

[1] viz. the cares of this life.—ED.
[2] The feminine of ἰών, the participle present of εἶμι *to go*.—(I. B.)
[3] See p. 150 and f.n. 3.—(I. B.)

τροφή, *daily food.* Cf. also Prov. xxx. 8. Thus was manna given.

12. Καὶ, *and*) The three remaining petitions regard the commencement, progress and conclusion of our spiritual life in this world; and those who utter them confess, not only their own need, but also their guilt, their peril, and their difficulties. When these have been removed, God is all in all to them, by virtue of the three first petitions.—ὀφειλήματα, *debts*) In ver. 14 we find παραπτώματα, *lapses.* In Luke xi. 4, we have ἁμαρτίας, *sins.* Cf. Matt. xviii. 24.[1]—ὡς, *as*) Before it was "AS *in heaven,* so *on earth,*" now it is "so *in heaven* AS *on earth.*"

13. Μὴ εἰσενέγκῃς ἡμᾶς, *Lead us not into*) Temptation is always in the way: wherefore we pray, not that it may not exist, but that it may not touch or overpower us.—See ch. xxvi. 41; 1 Cor. x. 13.—ἀλλὰ, *but*) The sixth and seventh petitions are so closely connected that they are considered by many as forming only one. —ῥῦσαι, *deliver*) See 2 Tim. iv. 18.—ἀπὸ τοῦ πονηροῦ, *from the evil one*) *i.e.,* from Satan.—See ch. xiii. 19. 38.

Ὅτι σοῦ ἐστιν ἡ βασιλεία καὶ ἡ δύναμις καὶ ἡ δόξα εἰς τοὺς αἰῶνας. Ἀμήν, *For thine is the kingdom, and the power, and the glory, for ever and ever. Amen*) This is the scope of the Lord's Prayer, that we may be taught to pray in *few* words (ver. 8), for the things which we *require ;* and the prayer itself, even without the doxology, involves the praise of God in all its fulness (summam laudis Divinae imbibit). For our Heavenly Father is sanctified and glorified by us, when He is invoked as our Heavenly Father, when things of such magnitude are asked of Him alone, when to Him alone all things are referred. We celebrate Him, however, in such a manner as should content those who are fighting the fight of their salvation in a foreign land. When the whole number of the sons of God *shall have reached* their goal, a simple (mera) doxology will arise in Heaven, *Hallowed be the name of our God. His kingdom has come: His will has been done. He has forgiven us our sins: He has brought temptation to an end: He has delivered us from the evil one. His is the kingdom, and*

---

[1] We ought not merely in general to pray for deliverance from guilt contracted by our sins; but whoever offends God in this or any other peculiar manner, is bound also specially to acknowledge and pray for deliverance from such offences, and so to give Him the honour due to Him.—V. g.

the power, and the glory, for ever and ever. Amen. A prayer was more suitable than a hymn, especially at the time in which our Lord prescribed this form to His disciples. Jesus was not yet glorified: the disciples as yet scarcely comprehended the full extent of these petitions, much less the amount of thanksgiving corresponding thereto. In fine, no one denies that the spirit of the whole clause is pious and holy, and conformable to the doxologies which frequently occur in Scripture: but the question is whether the Lord prescribed it in this place in these words. Faithful criticism regards little, in doubtful passages, what may happen to be the reading of the majority of Greek MSS. now extant, which are more modern and less numerous than is generally supposed: the question under consideration is rather, what was the reading of the Greek MSS. of the first ages, and therefore of the spring itself, *i.e.* the first hand.[1] The Latin Vulgate, which is certainly without this clause, stands, and will continue to stand, nearest in antiquity to the spring: but the force of its testimony is not appreciated till after long experience. In this passage, however, Greek witnesses, few indeed, but those of high authority, support the reading of the Vulgate. I wish what *I have said on this subject* in my Apparatus[2] to be carefully considered.[3] Nothing has occurred since I published that work

---

[1] BDZa*bc* Vulg. Memph. Origen, Cypr. (who adds "Amen") omit the doxology. Orig. Nyssen, Cyril, Maximus all omit it in giving expressly an explanation of the prayer. So all the Latin Fathers. It rather too widely separates ver. 12 and 14, which are connected together. Moreover Jesus was not yet glorified when He gave the prayer: it therefore was hardly *then* appropriate. It was probably added *after* the kingdom had been founded by the Holy Ghost on Pentecost. Ambrose *de Sacram.* vi. 5 implies that the doxology was recited by the priest alone, as a response ($\dot{\epsilon}\pi\iota\phi\dot{\omega}\nu\eta\mu\alpha$) after the people had repeated the Lord's prayer. Alford, from 2 Tim. iv. 18 where similarly $\dot{\rho}\dot{\upsilon}\sigma\epsilon\tau\alpha\iota\ \dot{\alpha}\pi\dot{o}\ \pi o\nu\eta\rho o\tilde{\upsilon}$ is followed by the doxology, argues that some such way of ending the prayer existed at that time.—Ed.

[2] He has devoted more than eight pages to the subject: See App. Crit. pp. 101-109.—(I. B.)

[3] E.B. and those who have adopted his text, add here "especially § x. on this passage." It runs thus:—

De tota re, lector judicet.

Prætermisit clausulam Lutherus, in Agendis Baptismi, eisque renovatis; in Tract. de Decalogo, symbolo Apost. et oratione Dominica; in Catechismo utroque, et Hymno: ubi etiam *Amen* cum Hieronymo ad rogationes refert

to weaken the arguments which I there brought together on this
point, whereas something has occurred to confirm them very
greatly: I allude to a passage in Enthymius, who flourished at
the beginning of the twelfth century. For when inveighing
against the Bogomili[1] for not using this clause, he does so only
on the ground that it was an addition of the Fathers, calling it
τὸ παρὰ τῶν θείων φωστήρων καὶ τῆς ἐκκλησίας καθηγητῶν προστεθὲν ἀκρο-
τελεύτιον ἐπιφώνημα, *The choral conclusion added by those who were
the divine illuminators and guides of the Church.* La Croze,[2]
relying on this testimony, clearly prefers in this passage the
Latin to the Syriac version; see his Histoire du Christianisme
des Indes, p. 313. One thing ought to be considered again and
again: the more that any one diminishes the authority of the
Vulgate on this passage, so much the more does he injure his
own cause if he maintains the genuineness of that most important passage in 1 John v. 7: for it at present rests solely on the

non ad clausulam, quanquam in Homil. ad. capp. v. vi. vii. Matth. eam
tractat. Appendicem eam esse persuadent nobis rationes § ix. collectae; quanquam margo noster in suspenso rem reliquit, dum rationes fuissent expositae:
et plane pro appendice habet *Brentius; Hunnius* vel pro *appendice* vel pro
epilogo, cujus moderationem recte sequentur, qui nil certi secum hic possunt
constituere. Liberum saltem est privatim vel Matthæi receptam, vel Lucæ
lectionem in orando sequi: quin etiam publice, in choro cœnobiorum Wir-
tembergicorum, et alibi hodienum prætermitti solita est clausula. Cavendum
vero, ne idiotæ intempestivis de hâc clausulâ sermonibus perturbentur. Hâc
quoque in re et veritati et paci inserviendum est. " Sincera crisis," etc., as
in the Gnomon Ed. MDCCLIX, which is followed in this translation.—(I. B.)

[1] The BOGOMILES were a sect of heretics which arose about the year
1079. Their founder was Basilius, a monk, who was burnt at Constantinople
in the reign of Alexius Comnenus. He maintained that the world and all
animal bodies were formed, not by the Deity, but by an evil demon who had
been cast down from heaven by the Supreme Being. Hence that the body
was only the prison of the soul, and was to be enervated by fasting, contemplation, etc., that the soul might be gradually restored to its primitive
liberty. Marriage therefore was to be avoided. Basilius also denied the
reality of Christ's body, which he considered to be only a phantom, rejected
the law of Moses, and maintained that the body on its separation by death
returned to the malignant mass of matter, without possibility of a future resurrection to life and felicity.—See *Mosheim.*—(I. B.)

[2] MATHURIN VEYSSIERE DE LA CROZE, a distinguished Oriental scholar,
born at Nantes in 1661. In the course of his life he abjured Romanism, and
died at Berlin in 1739.—(I. B.)

single testimony of the Latin Interpreter, and rests upon it firmly.

14. Γὰρ, *for*) referring to the twelfth verse. See of how much account it is to forgive our neighbour. Of the seven petitions, one alone, the fifth, has a certain condition or restriction, *as we also*; the reason of this is, therefore, added in the present verse.

15. Τὰ παραπτώματα αὐτῶν, *their trespasses*) The copies which omit these words, elegantly intimate that the sins of men against us, if compared with our sins against the Father, will vanish away. Some Latin writers omit also the words τοῖς ἀνθρώποις, *men*.

16. Ὅταν νηστεύητε, *when ye fast*) Fasting also ought to be of great account with us; it is not a part of the ceremonial law.— ἀφανίζουσι, *they disfigure*) By neglecting the daily attention to the person of washing and anointing. An exquisite oxymoron, ἀφανίζουσι, φανῶσι.[1]

17. Ἄλειψαι—νίψαι, *anoint—wash*) Both verbs are in the middle voice; [the meaning therefore is] anoint and wash alone (solus *unge* et *lava*). It was customary for the Jews to be anointed on feast days.[2]

18. Τῷ Πατρί, *to thy Father*) sc. thou mayest be known.

19. Ὅπου, *where*) i.e. on earth. This has a causative force,[3] being equivalent to *because there*.[4]—βρῶσις, *corrosion*) This word, in opposition to *moth*, expresses *rust*, and every evil quality by which anything can become useless.—καὶ κλέπτουσι, *and thus steal*.

21. Θησαυρὸς ὑμῶν—καρδία ὑμῶν,[5] *your treasure—your heart*) Others read θησαυρός σου—καρδία σου, *thy treasure—thy heart*.[6] The objects which are mentioned in ver. 22, 23 (consequentia)

---

[1] *i.e.* a play upon these words, ἀφανίζω being the privative transitive formed from φανῶ, *to appear*.—(I. B.)

[2] The sense is, Abstain from all rather severe exercises.—V. g.

[3] Aetiology. See Appendix.—Ed.

[4] Such is the principle of the life of not a few men, that they seem to exist in the world only for the purpose of amassing an abundance of earthly possessions.—V. g.

The particle δὲ in ver. 20 indicates that both cannot at the same time stand together.—V. g.

[5] Thus E. M.—(I. B.)

[6] Θησαυρός σου—καρδία σου is the reading of Bab*c* Vulg. Memph. Theb.

are in the singular, those which are mentioned in ver. 19, 20 (antecedentia), with which this verse is connected, are in the plural number. The plural therefore must stand in this verse. The singular, "*thesaurus tuus*," "*thy treasure*," easily crept into the Latin Vulgate, and was convenient to the Greeks for ascetic discourses. The treasure which YOU collect is called in Luke xii. 34 ὁ θησαυρὸς ὑμῶν, YOUR *treasure*.—ἔσται, *will be*) sc. in heaven or in earth respectively.

22. Ὁ ὀφθαλμός, *the eye*) This is the subject of the proposition.[1] —ἐὰν οὖν, *if therefore*) The particle οὖν (*therefore*) agrees exactly with the scope of the passage, and has been easily left out by some who have understood it, though they omitted it.[2] We will not linger on such matters.—ἁπλοῦς, *single, simple*) The word simplicity never occurs in the sacred writings in a bad sense. ἁπλοῦς signifies here simple and good, singly intent on heaven, on God. Here is an antithesis between ἁπλοῦς, *single*, in this verse, and δυσί, *two*, in ver. 24. That which is propounded figuratively in ver. 22, 23, is declared in plain words in the following verses.—φωτεινὸν, *full of light*) As if it were all eye.

23. Πονηρὸς, *evil*) sc. shifting, double, inconsistent, imbued with self-love.—τὸ φῶς, *the light*) which the lamp should give.— τὸ σκότος, *the darkness*) How great darkness must be the darkness of the whole body![3]—πόσον, *how great*) As great as the body.

Cypr. 239, 303. The change to Sing. from Plur. ver. 20, is perhaps to imply that the heart of each *individually* is to be given to God.—ED.

Such is the reading supported by Bengel in his German Version, where he writes, "*Denn wo dein Schatz ist, da wird auch dein Herz seyn.*" "*For where* THY *treasure is, there will* THY *heart be also.*" He explains *dein Schatz* (thy treasure) by "Thy possession (*dein Gut*), on which thy Anxiety is set night and day." In his App. Crit he supports the reading of the Received Text, and speaks of σου as having crept in from the next verse.— (I. B.)

[1] Not as in E. V. "THE LIGHT *of the body is the eye,*" but "THE EYE *is the light of the body.*"—ED.

[2] *i.e.* Those who omitted the word actually when copying in the text must have supplied it mentally when reading it.—(I. B.)

Οὖν is the reading of B; *b* has *enim*; ac Hil. 520 omit it.—ED.

[3] In the original the passage runs thus—

"*Tenebræ* totius corporis, quantæ erunt tenebræ!" and then proceeds, "Singularis *tenebra*, veteribus non ignotus, a multis Theologis in loco adhibitus, sæpius conveniret simplicitati hermeneuticæ."—(I. B.)

24. Κυρίοις, *masters*) God and Mammon in sooth act as master to their servants, but in different ways.—δουλεύειν, *to serve*) i.e.[1] *to be a servant of.*—ἢ γάρ, *for either*) Each part of this disjunctive sentence has καί (*and*) with a consecutive force, viz. The heart of man cannot be so free as not to serve *either* God *or* a creature, nor can it serve them both at once;[2] for it either still remains in enmity with God or it takes God's part. In the one case, *then* (καί) it cannot but love Mammon; in the other, *then* (καί) it cannot but despise Mammon. This statement may be inverted, so that the clause referring to the laudable state of mind may precede the other. Cf. ver. 22, 23. Attachment and a desire to please are consequent upon either servitude. See ver. 21.—Θεῷ δουλεύειν, *to serve God*) Which is described in Luke xii. 35, 36.[3]—μαμωνᾷ, *Mammon*) Mammon does not only mean affluence, but external goods, however few. See ver. 25.[4] Augustine[5] tells us, that both in Phœnician and Chaldee *mammon* signifies gain.

25. Μὴ μεριμνᾶτε, *take no care for*) The disciples had left all things which could be the source of care to them.—τῇ ψυχῇ, *the soul*) The soul is supported by food in the body, which itself lives on food: the body alone is covered by raiment.—καὶ τί πίητε, *and what ye drink*) This has been easily omitted by copyists, or is easily understood (subauditur) by us. The 31st verse requires the express mention of *drinking* rather than the

---

[1] With one's full powers.—V. g.

[2] Although very many think themselves thoroughly versed in this art of combining both.—V. g.

[3] The servants of Mammon, in obedience to their natural instincts, hate Him, who alone is good.—V. g.

[4] Yea, even the commonest necessaries of life. Comp. ver. 32. But if even such a service of Mammon, as affects the mere necessaries of life, is opposed to the service of GOD, what then are we to suppose it to be *to serve* GOD. It is this: to be borne towards Him with the full tide of love, and with uninterrupted regard.—V. g.

[5] AURELIUS AUGUSTINUS, one of the most celebrated fathers of the Western Church, was born at Tagasta, in Africa, in 354. His mother Monica was a holy Christian woman: his father a heathen, in which religion he was educated. His early career, though one of extreme brilliancy, was disfigured by profligacy. At length, however, he embraced Christianity; was baptized by St Ambrose, Bishop of Milan, in 387; ordained priest in 391; and consecrated in 395 Bishop of Hippo, where he died in 430.—(I. B.)

present, for in it the careful are introduced as themselves speaking, whereas in the present verse our Lord speaks in His own person.[1]—ἡ ψυχὴ—τὸ σῶμα, *the soul—the body*) Both of which God gave and cares for. See the latter part of ver. 30.[2]

26, 28. τὰ πετεινὰ τοῦ οὐρανοῦ—τὰ κρίνα τοῦ ἀγροῦ, *the fowls of the air—the lilies of the field*) which men do not take care of, often in fact destroying them; as for example the ravens, mentioned in Luke xii. 24.[3]

26. Οὐδὲ συνάγουσιν, *neither do they collect*) as for example by purchase, for the future.[4]—ὑμῶν, *your*) He says *your*, not *their*.— μᾶλλον, *more*) *i.e.* you more excel as sons of God, than other men do, or than you who indulge in such care (anxiety) consider. The word μᾶλλον, therefore, is not redundant. In this verse, the argument is from the less to the greater; in ver. 25, from the greater to the less.

27. Τίς—ἐξ ὑμῶν, *which—of you*) A mode of speaking frequent with Christ, full of majesty, and yet suited for popular use.— ἡλικίαν, *stature*) See Gnomon on Luke xii. 25, 26.—πῆχυν, *a cubit*) So as to become of gigantic height.

28. Πῶς αὐξάνει, *how they grow*) sc. to a great height.—οὐ κοπιᾷ, *they toil not*) *Toil* is remotely, *spinning* intimately connected with procuring raiment, as *sowing* and *reaping* are with food.

29. Λέγω, *I say*) Christ truly knew the dress of Solomon.— ὡς, *as*) sc. *is clothed*, or *is*.—ἓν, *one*) any one, not to say a whole garland.[5]—τούτων, *of these*) The pronoun is used demonstratively.

30. Δὲ, *but*) Used *epitatically*.[6] Garments are objects of comeliness, as well as necessity. The mention of the *lilies*

---

[1] *ab* Vulg. Hil. Bas. Epiph. Jerome (who says, however, it was added in some MSS.) omit ἢ τί πίητε. But BC, Orig. 1,711*d* Memph. read the words. Rec. Text has καὶ instead of ἢ, the reading of the oldest authorities.—ED.

[2] There is nothing so small and insignificant, which His omniscience neglects, ver. 32.—V. g.

[3] The ant (Prov. vi. 6) is an example, which we may apply as an antidote to slothfulness; the birds of heaven, to anxious cares.—V. g.

[4] "Into barns:" or even into other repositories of food, as we may see instanced in other animals.—V. g.

[5] Kings were wont to wear white robes; but these are surpassed by the whiteness of the lilies.—V. g.

[6] See Append. on Epitasis. It implies some word or words added to a previous enunciation to give augmented force.—ED.

with the verb περιβάλλεσθαι, *to be arrayed*, refers to the former; that of *grass* with the verb ἀμφιέννυσθαι, *to be clothed*, to the latter notion.—χόρτον, *grass, blade*) as for example that of growing wheat.—See ch. xiii. 26. An instance of *Litotes*.[1]— σήμερον ὄντα, *which to-day is*) i.e., which endures for a very short time.[2]—αὔριον, *to-morrow*) After a short interval, the grains having been thrashed out, the straw serves for the fire.—κλίβανον, *the oven*) To heat it.—See Lyranus.[3] Pliny[4] says, "rinds beaten from the flax are useful for ovens and furnaces."—B. 19, ch. 1. It is not said, into the fire, as in John xv. 6 (cf. 1 Cor. iii. 12), but into the oven. Not, therefore, for the sake merely of being burnt, but of some utility.—ἀμφ ἐννυσιν, *clothe, dresseth*) The dress is properly that without which the body is naked: grass, although it has no external clothing, yet, because it is not naked, but is covered with its own surface, is itself its own dress, especially in its highest and flowering part, of which it is divested when it dries up.—πολλῷ μᾶλλον, *much more*) In this life few attain to the adornment of Solomon, not to mention that of the lilies; our Lord's words, therefore, regard the certainty, not the degree of adornment: but in the life to come we shall be more adorned than the lilies. We ought not, however, altogether to reject adornment in things, however perishable.—ὀλιγόπιστοι, *O*

[1] See explanation of technical terms in Appendix.—(I. B.)

[2] E. B. quotes here C. W. Lüdecke, "At Pentecost all these regions are clad in green verdure; but when the south wind suddenly arises, in 24 hours, or two or three days at most, there is nothing that does not become white and blanched."

[3] The individual thus denominated was NICOLAS DE LYRE, so called from the place of his birth, a small village in Normandy. He is supposed by some to have been of Jewish extraction: he was born in the thirteenth century: he assumed the habit of the Franciscan order in 1291. He was a man of great learning, and especially versed in Hebrew: he wrote several treatises in defence of Christianity against the Jews, and a series of Postills or small commentaries on the whole of the Bible. He died in 1340. He was known in the schools by the surname of *Doctor utilis*. So great was the effect of his labours, that it gave rise to the proverb, "Si Lyra non lyrasset, Lutherus non saltasset," *i.e.* "If Lyre had not played on the lyre, Luther would not have danced."—(I. B.)

[4] CAIUS PLINIUS SECUNDUS, commonly called the elder Pliny, born, it is supposed, at Verona, about A.D. 23; died A.D. 79. He was a man of indefatigable study, and, though holding high offices in the state, published, besides other works, a natural history in thirty-seven books.—(I. B.)

ye of little faith) Want of faith was clearly unknown and abhorred by Christ; for He had known the Father. He teaches faith in this passage.[1]

32. Πάντα γὰρ ταῦτα, κ.τ.λ., *for all these things*, etc.) and nothing else.—τὰ ἔθνη, *the gentiles*) the heathen nations. The faithful ought to be free from the cares, not only of the covetous among the heathen, but of all heathens; many, however, in the present day fall short of the heathen in this matter.[2]—ἐπιζητεῖ, *seek after*) as though a difficult matter. This word is followed by the simple verb ζητεῖτε, *seek ye*.—οἶδε γὰρ ὁ πατὴρ ὑμῶν ὁ οὐράνιος, *for your Heavenly Father knoweth*) An argument from the omniscience, the goodness, and the omnipotence of God.—ὑμῶν, *your*) sc. who is your Father in a pre-eminent degree in preference to the heathen.[3]

33. Ζητεῖτε, *seek ye*) the kingdom which is nigh at hand, and not difficult of acquisition.—πρῶτον, *first*) He who seeks that first, will soon seek that only.—βασιλείαν, *kingdom*.—δικαιοσύνην, *righteousness*) Heavenly meat and drink are opposed to earthly, and thus also raiment; and, therefore, St Luke in his twelfth chapter leaves *raiment* to be understood at ver. 29, and *righteousness* at ver. 31, although *righteousness* also *filleth*; see ch. v. 6.[4]—αὐτοῦ, *his*) sc. righteousness.—See the note on Rom. i. 17.—ταῦτα, *these things*) An instance of Litotes.[5]—προστεθήσεται, *shall be added unto*) These things are a προσθήκη or *appendage* of the life and body (see ver. 25); and still more so of the kingdom (see Luke xii. 32).

---

[1] This is the only mode of address, which Jesus employed, when wishing to censure the disciples: chap. viii. 26, xiv. 31, xvi. 8.—V. g.

[2] In the original, "At multi hodie non eam, quam gentes, habent αὐτάρκειαν." Bengel in Gnomon on ch. iv. 4 defines αὐτάρκεια as "*Præsens animi quies.*" See p. 150 and f.n. 3.—(I. B.)

[3] In the original all this is expressed by two words, "*præ ethnicis.*"—(I. B.)

[4] Sc. "Blessed are they that hunger and thirst after RIGHTEOUSNESS, for they shall be FILLED." See also Gnomon in loc.—(I. B.)

[5] The word used in the original is ταπείνωσις, concerning which John Albert Burk says, in his Explanation of the Technical Terms employed in the Gnomon—

"LITOTES, Μείωσις, Ταπείνωσις, EXTENUATIO, quæ singulæ in Gnomone passim allegantur, vix ac ne vix quidem differunt."

For explanation and examples, see Appendix.—(I. B.)

34. Ἡ αὔριον, κ.τ.λ., *the morrow*, etc.) A precept remarkable for *Asteismus*,[1] by which care, though apparently permitted on the morrow, is in fact forbidden altogether; for the careful make present cares even of those which are future, wherefore, to put off care is almost the same as to lay it aside. There is also a personification of the morrow (cf. Ps. xix. 2): "*the day*," says our Lord, (*not you*) "*shall take care*." He who has learnt this, will contract his cares at length from the day to the present hour, or altogether unlearn them.—μεριμνήσει ἑαυτῇ,[2] *shall take care for itself*) A *Dativus Commodi*,[3] as in ver. 25, μὴ μεριμνᾶτε τῇ ψυχῇ —μηδὲ τῷ σώματι, κ.τ.λ., *take no care for your* LIFE—*nor yet for your* BODY, etc.—ἀρκετὸν, *sufficient*) God indeed distributes our adversity and prosperity, through all the periods of our life, after a wonderful manner, so that they temper each other.—ἡ κακία, *the evil*) *i.e.* the sorrow; therefore there were no cares in the beginning.—κακία, though originally meaning *badness* (*wickedness*), signifies here *sorrow*; just as the Hebrew טוב (ἀγαθός, *good*) means joyful in Prov. xv. 15.—αὐτῆς, *thereof*) Although it be not increased by the sorrow of either the past or the coming day.

CHAPTER VII.

1. Μὴ κρίνετε, *Judge not*) *i.e.* without knowledge, charity, or necessity. Yet a dog is to be accounted a dog, and a swine a swine; see ver. 6.

---

[1] *i.e.* For skilfully conveying a stern truth in such a manner as not to repel, offend, or startle the hearer: in the original, "monitum mire ἀστεῖον."—(I. B.) See on Asteismus in the Append.—ED.

[2] The Ed. Maj. regarded ἑαυτῇ as a less reliable reading than τὰ ἑαυτῆς. But Gnom. Ed. 1 (1742 A.D.) and Marg. Ed. 2, and Vers. Germ. prefer ἑαυτῇ.—E. B.

Sollicitus erit *sibi ipse*. Vulg.

BGLabc Vulg. Cypr. 210, 307, Hil. 635, read μεριμνήσει ἑαυτῆς. Rec. Text has τὰ ἑαυτῆς, evidently a correction to introduce the more usual construction of μεριμνάω with the accusative.—ED.

[3] See explanation of Technical Terms.—(I. B.)

2. Ἐν ᾧ μέτρῳ, *with what measure*) The principle of the *lex talionis*.[1]

3. Ἐν τῷ ὀφθαλμῷ, *in the eye*) In that part of the body which is the most noble, the most delicate, and the most conspicuous.—ἐν τῷ σῷ, *in thine own*) See Rom. ii. 21, 23.

4. Πῶς, *how?*) *i.e.* How is it fitting for you to do so?

5. Διαβλέψεις, *thou shalt see beyond*) now that the beam has been taken *out of the way*, and no longer interposes itself between you and your brother's eye, and that your own is relieved of the incumbrance. He who, having first corrected himself, seeks to correct another, is not a perverse judge.[2]

6. Μὴ δῶτε, *give not*) Here we meet with the other extreme; for the two extremes are, to judge those who ought not to be judged, and to give holy things to the dogs. Too much severity and too much laxity.[3]—κυσί, χοίρων, *dogs, swine*) Dogs feed on their own filth, swine on that of others. See Gnomon on 2 Pet. ii. 22; Phil. iii. 2. The holy and dogs are put in opposition to each other in Exod. xxii. 30;[4] a dog is not a wild beast, but yet it is an unclean animal.—ὑμῶν, *your*) An implied antitheton.[5] *That which is holy* is the property of GOD; pearls are the secret treasures of the faithful, intrusted to them by GOD.—ῥήξωσιν, *rend*) This also appears to refer to the swine.[6]—ὑμᾶς, *you*) From whom they expected something else, husks, etc.

[1] So it is not hard to judge, what retribution hereafter each one is likely to have.—V. g.

[2] For what man is there, who does not gladly allow a straw [thorn] to be extracted from his finger, not to say from his eye, by a skilfully applied hand? The principle is the same as in the gnat and the camel, chap. xxiii. 24.—V. g.

[3] This admonition especially has regard to our daily conversation. When such things are set before them in public, such persons lightly pass over them.—V. g.

[4] This is the Hebrew notation. In the Septuagint, Vulgate, and English Version it is reckoned as the thirtieth. It runs thus—"And ye shall be HOLY men unto me; neither shall ye eat any flesh that is torn of beasts in the field: ye shall cast it to the DOGS."—(I. B.)

[5] Sc. between *you* and *swine*.—(I. B.)

[6] Swine attack the pearls with their feet, the saints with their tusk. A well-disposed man is more than once apt to suppose, that what seems sacred and precious to him, ought to seem so to others also, until he learns, by experience of the contrary, to act with more caution.—V. g.

7. Αἰτεῖτε, *ask*) Ask for gifts to meet your needs.—ζητεῖτε, *seek*) sc. the hidden things which you have lost, and return from your error.—κρούετε, *knock*) sc. ye who are without, that ye may be admitted within. See 2 Cor. vi. 17, fin. *Ask, seek, knock*, without intermission.[1]

8. Πᾶς, *every one*) that asketh, even from man, much more from God.

9. ῎Η, An interrogative particle, corresponding to the Latin *an*.[2]—ἐξ ὑμῶν, *of you*) Parables are especially popular, when they are addressed *ad hominem*.—ἄνθρωπος, *a man*) One, that is, who is not clearly devoid of humanity.[3]—ἄρτον, *bread*) A stone, which is useless for food, resembles outwardly a loaf or roll. A snake, which is noxious, resembles a fish. A child can more easily do without fish than bread, and yet he obtains even a fish by asking for it. Fishes were given then to children, as apples are now.—μὴ λίθον, *a stone?*) Lat. *num lapidem*, [such must be the force of μή[4] in this place]; for the parent, when asked, will not refuse to give either bread or a stone.

11. Ὑμεῖς, *you*) Christ rightly excepts Himself, and no one else.[5]—The ὑμεῖς here refers to ἐξ ὑμῶν, *of you*, in ver. 9.—πονηροί, *evil*) An illustrious testimony to the doctrine of original sin. Cf. *the evil one*,[6] vi. 13. The Panegyric of Gregory[7] Thau-

---

[1] Never cease, I pray thee, Reader, to turn such a promise to thy advantage, as often soever as the opportunity presents itself.—V. g.

[2] The second part of a disjunctive interrogation.—ED.

[3] The arrangement of the words in the original brings this idea strongly out.—(I. B.)

[4] The interrogative particle, which expects a negative answer.—" He will not give a stone, will he?"—ED.

[5] *What man of you*, ver. 9, implies that all but Himself are included in His words.—(ED.)

[6] Men who are devoid of a godly disposition imitate him.—B. G. V.

In the original the expressions used are, *Malus, malitiam, male audit*.— As the first of these = *the Evil One*, I have rendered the others so as to correspond with it.—(I. B.)

[7] GREGORY, surnamed THAUMATURGUS, or the wonder-worker, was born at Neo-Cæsarea, in Cappadocia. He was originally a heathen, and highly educated, in the learning of the ancients. He afterwards embraced Christianity, and studied under Origen. Having taken orders, he was ordained Bishop of his native city about 239. He died between 264 and 271. He was a man of high attainments and great piety. Several valuable

ınaturgus (p. 20, 146), has a similar confession of the *evilness* of human nature, with an emphasis rare in that age. Man is addressed as *evil* in the Scriptures. See ch. x. 17, and John ii. 25.[1] It is wonderful therefore that Holy Scripture should have ever been received by the human race. Bread and fish are good things; man is evil, prompt to commit injury.[2]—οἴδατε, *ye know*) Distinguishing bread from a stone, etc. It is wonderful that this *understanding* (intelligentiam) has remained in us. We are so evil. Cf. Job. xxxix. 17[3] with the preceding verses. —ἀγαθὰ, *good things*) both harmless and profitable things.[4]—τοῖς τέκνοις ὑμῶν, *to your children*) especially when they ask you.— ὁ ἐν τοῖς οὐρανοῖς, *which is in the heavens*) In whom there is no evil.— τοῖς αἰτοῦσιν, *to them that ask*) sc. His children ; for where true prayer begins, there is Divine sonship.

12, οὖν, *therefore*) The sum of all that has been said from the beginning of the chapter. He concludes [this portion of the discourse], and at the same time returns to ch. v. 17. The conclusion corresponds with the commencement. And we ought to imitate the Divine goodness, mentioned in ver. 11.—θέλητε ἵνα ποιῶσιν, *ye would that they should do*) " *Ye would:*" this is pointedly said (notanter): for men often do otherwise [than what ye would that they should do]. We are not to follow their example. Sc. by benefiting, not injuring.—οἱ ἄνθρωποι, *men*) The indefinite appellation of *men*, frequently employed by the Saviour, already alludes to the future propagation of His teaching throughout the whole human race.—οὕτω, *thus*) The same things in the same way: or *thus*, as I have told you up to this point.—οὗτος, *this*) The law and the prophets enjoin many other things, as for example the love of God : but yet the law and the prophets also tend to this as their especial scope, viz.

---

works of his are still in existence ; that alluded to here, is his Panegyric on his master Origen, edited by Bengel, A.D. 1722.—(I. B.)

[1] E. B. and the later editions add Matt. xvi. 23, Rom iii. 4, etc. —(I. B.)

[2] It is in fact wonderful that a human father, when his son asks him for a fish, does not offer him a serpent.—V. g.

[3] Where the Vulgate has—Privavit enim eam Deus sapientiâ nec dedit illi *intelligentiam*—and E. V. " Because God hath deprived her of wisdom, neither hath He imparted to her *understanding*."—(I. B.)

[4] And therefore also the Good Spirit Himself. V. g.

whatsoever ye would, etc., and he who performs this, performs all the rest more easily: see ch. xix. 19.

13. Εἰσέλθετε, *enter ye in*) Make it the object of your constant and earnest endeavours (Id agite) really to enter.[1] This presupposes that they are attempting to walk on the narrow way. Observe the antithetical relation between " εἰσέλθετε," " *enter ye in*" [in the first], and " οἱ εἰσερχόμενοι"—" *they which go in*" [in the last clause of this verse].—στενῆς, *strait*) sc. of righteousness.—πύλη, *the gate*) This is put before *the way;* the gate therefore in this verse signifies that, by which a man begins in any manner to seek for the salvation of his soul; as in the next verse the gate is that, by which true Christianity is received.—ἀπάγουσα, *which leadeth away*) from this short life. So also in the next verse.—πολλοί, *many*) See 2 Esdras ix. 15, 17.—οἱ εἰσερχόμενοι, *they which go in*) There is no need that they should find it, for they spontaneously fall into destruction. Cf. v. 14.—δι' αὐτῆς, *through it*) sc. the gate.

14. Ὅτι στενή, κ.τ.λ., *because straight*, etc.) Many read τί στενή, κ.τ.λ.,[2] HOW *straight*, etc., as in the S.V. of 2 Sam. vi. 20, where מה[3] is rendered by τί—sc. τί δεδόξασται σήμερον ὁ βασιλεὺς Ἰσραήλ.—HOW *glorious was the king of Israel to-day!* But there the expression is ironical.—The true reading is undoubtedly,[4] ὅτι πλατεῖα—ὅτι στενή, κ.τ.λ.—BECAUSE *broad*—BECAUSE *straight*. Thus in 1 Kings xxi. 15, כי[5] (rendered ὅτι by the LXX.) occurs twice.—ὅτι οὐκ ἔστι Ναβουθαὶ ζῶν, ὅτι τέθνηκε : *For, Naboth is not alive, but dead.*[6] The last כי has the force of *but;* and is thus rendered

---

[1] Into life, into the kingdom of heaven.—V. g.

[2] Lachm. reads τί στενή, with B corrected by a second hand, CLΔ *bc* Vulg. Syr. Cypr. But Tischend. ὅτι, with B corrected by the first hand, X, Orig. 3, 527*b*, and Memph. T/ for ὡς is a Hellenistic idiom, Ps. viii. 1, where for the LXX. ὡς θαυμαστόν other versions have τί μέγα. The τί may be a gloss on ὅτι taken with the positive, as it is often with superlatives, intensively (ὅτι πλεῖστος, etc.) : so in Plato ὅτι τάχυς, *valde celeriter*. However Bengel makes ὅτι, as before πλατεῖα, so to be repeated before στενή in the sense *sed*, 'but.'—ED.

[3] *What*, or *how*.—(I. B.)

[4] Thus also E. M.—(I. B.)

[5] For a full account of this word and its meanings, see Gesenius's Lexicon in voce.—(I. B.)

[6] Literally—" *Because* Naboth is not living, *because* he has died.—(I. B.)

by the LXX. in Dan. ix. 18, and 2 Chron. xx. 15. See also Heb. viii. 10, 11.[1]—*αὐτὴν, it*) sc. the gate. Cf. the commencement and conclusion of ver. 13.

15. Προσέχετε, *beware of*) There are many dangers: therefore we are frequently warned.—See ch. vi. 1, xvi. 6, xxiv. 4; Luke xii. 1, 15, etc.—δὲ, *but*) Whilst you are endeavouring yourselves to enter, beware of those who close the gate against you. See ch. xxiii. 13.—ψευδοπροφητῶν, *false prophets*) whose teaching is different from that of true prophets. See ch. v. 17. [comp. ver. 12. *He who works iniquity, however he may prophesy in the name of Christ* (ver. 22), *is nevertheless a false prophet. In our day, they who delight in casting against others the taunt of being Pharisees and false prophets, are themselves that which they lay to the charge of others.*—V. g.]—ἐνδύμασι προβάτων, *in sheep's clothing*) *i.e.* in such clothing as they would wear if they were sheep.

15, 16. Οἵτινες ἔρχονται—ἐπιγνώσεσθε αὐτούς, *who come—ye shall know them*) a very similar passage occurs in Luke xx. 45–47.[2]

16. Ἀπὸ[3] τῶν καρπῶν αὐτῶν, κ.τ.λ., *from their fruits*, etc.) This declaration is solemnly repeated at ver. 20.—καρπῶν, *fruits*) The fruit is that, which a man like a tree puts forth, from the good or evil disposition which pervades the whole of his inward being. Learning, compiled from every quarter, and combined with language, does not constitute fruit; which consists of all that which the teacher puts forth from his heart, in his language and conduct, as something flowing from his inner being, like milk, which the mother gives from her own breast: see ch. xii. 33, 34, 35. This is the true force of ποιεῖ, *produces*, in ver. 17–19: cf. ver. 21, 23, 24, 26. It is not his speech alone which constitutes the true or the false prophet, but his whole method of *leading*[4] himself, and others with him, by the one or the other

---

[1] Εἰς τὴν ζωὴν is the expression used of the future life of blessedness: for the present life is not life at all.—V. g.

[2] True judgment looks to the *inward* character of persons and things ["*inwardly* they are ravening wolves"].—V. g.

[3] However the margin of Ed. ii. of N. Test. more readily allows the omission of this particle than the larger edition.—E. B.

Bab Hil. 1245 read ἀπό: but c Lucif. ' ex,' Vulg. ' a.'—ED.

[4] See ver. 14, "*leadeth*."—ED.

road or gate to life or death (see ch. xv. 14, 13); whence it arises that doing and saying are closely connected in ch. v. 10. The fruits indeed are the tokens (Gnorismata) or evidence of the truth or falsehood of the prophet, and therefore also of the doctrine set forth by the prophet. The doctrine, therefore, is not the fruit by which the prophet is known; but it is the form of the true or false prophet which constitutes him the one or the other, and is itself known from its fruit. The goodness of the tree itself is truth and inward light, etc; the goodness of the fruit is holiness of life. If the fruit consisted in doctrine, no orthodox teacher could be damned or be the cause of another's destruction.—See Schomer,[1] Theol. Moral. p. 252.— *ἀπὸ ἀκανθῶν, of thorns*) although their berries resemble grapes, as the heads of thistles do figs. In Luke vi. 44 the same comparison is differently turned, for *ἄκανθα, the thorn*, and *βάτος, the bramble*, are very closely allied. *The grape* therefore (σταφυλή) is denied to each of them. Certain *thorns* (ἄκανθαι) also have large shoots:[2] figs therefore can be denied to them as well as to thistles.

19. Δένδρον, *a tree*) The allegory is continued.

21. Οὐ πᾶς, κ.τ.λ., *not every one*, etc.) for all in some manner say, and shall say so; see ver. 22, and cf. Luke ix. 57, 59, 61.— *ὁ λέγων, that saith*) Put in opposition to ὁ ποιῶν, *that doeth*: cf. 1 Cor. ix. 27, xiii. 1, 2.—Μοι, *unto Me*) The meaning is, "*unto Me* and My Father;" and again, "*My Father's Will* and Mine." —Κύριε, *Lord*) Jesus acknowledged that this Divine appellation was due to Him. Many, even men of high rank, called Him LORD: He called no one so, not even Pilate.—ὁ ποιῶν, κ.τ.λ., *he that doeth*, etc.) There is an *antithesis* between this and οἱ ἐργαζόμενοι (*that work*), in ver. 23.—τὸ θέλημα, κ.τ.λ., *the will*, etc.) sc. that which I preach, the righteous will, which is declared in the Law: cf. v. 19.—τοῦ ἐν οὐρανοῖς,[3] *which is in heaven*[3]) No one, therefore, who is contrary to God will enter heaven.—ἀλλ' ὁ

---

[1] JUSTUS CHRISTOPHER SCHOMER, a celebrated Lutheran divine, was born at Lubeck in 1648, and died in 1693, professor of Theology at Rostock. In 1690 he published his celebrated work, *Theologia Moralis sibi constans*, quoted in the text.—(I. B.)

[2] *i.e.*—resembling figs in some measure.—(I. B.)

[3] The word is in the plural number.—(I. B.)

ποιῶν τὸ θέλημα τοῦ Πατρός Μου τοῦ ἐν οὐρανοῖς,[1] οὗτος εἰσελεύσεται εἰς τὴν βασιλείαν τῶν οὐρανῶν,[1] *but he that doeth the will of My Father which is in Heaven,*[1] *he shall enter into the kingdom of Heaven*[1]) These last words,[2] "ipse intrabit in regnum coelorum,"[1] "*he shall enter into the kingdom of heaven,*" are found in that most ancient authority, the Latin Vulgate,[3] and from it in both Hebrew editions[4] of St Matthew, in the Anglo-Saxon Version,[5] in Jerome, and in Lupus,[6] Ep. 84, and, perhaps from another version, in Cyprian. The copyists of later times, slipping from οὐρανοῖς to οὐρανῶν, have omitted the clause. In antithetical passages of this character, the sacred writers frequently employ the figure entitled *Plenus Sermo*.[7]

22. Πολλοί, *many*) even of those, perhaps, whom posterity has canonized and commanded to be accounted blessed and saints; many, certainly, of those who have had rare gifts, and have shown at times a good will (see Mark ix. 39), who apprehend the power and the wisdom, but not the mercy of God.—ἐροῦσι, *shall say*) flattering themselves in their own persuasion. Many souls will retain the error, with which they deceive themselves, even up to that day:[8] [*A miserable expectation, previously, is theirs: an awful judgment, subsequently!*—V. g.] see ch. xxv. 11. Hence may be illustrated the doctrine of the state after death. In the Judgment all things will at length be made known: see Rom.

[1] The word is in the plural number.—(I. B.)
[2] They are not found in E. M.—(I. B.)
[3] See p. 14, f. n. 1.—(I. B.)
[4] See Le Long, Bibliotheca Sacra, pt. II. Sect. 1, §§ 4, 5, 6; and Bengel's App. Crit. pt. I. Sect. 32, Obs. 6.—(I. B.)
Vulg. *abc* Cypr. Hil. add "ipse intrabit in regnum coelorum:" they moreover must read αὐτὸς *ipse*, not as Beng. has it, *hic*, οὗτος. BZ and most of the oldest authorities omit the clause.—ED.
[5] Supposed to have been executed in the eighth century. See *Hartwell Horne*, vol. II. Pt. I. chap. 3, Sect. iii. § 4.—(I. B.)
[6] LUPUS SERVATIUS (or SERVATUS), a native of France, and disciple of the celebrated Aldric, who sent him to Fulda to study the Holy Scriptures under the famous Rabanus Maurus. He became Abbot of Ferriere A.D. 842, and distinguished himself both as a scholar and a theologian. His character stands high both as a man and an author.—(I. B.)
[7] *i.e.* give the *words in full*, even though any reader might have readily supplied them.—ED.
[8] Sc. the day of judgment.—(I. B.)

ii. 16; 1 Cor. iii. 13.—*ἐν ἐκείνῃ τῇ ἡμέρᾳ, on that day*) that great day, in comparison with which all previous days are nothing.— Σῷ, Thy) The emphasis and accent fall upon this word in each of the three clauses: Thy, sc. that of the Lord.—*προεφητεύσαμεν, we have prophesied*) We have openly proclaimed the mysteries of Thy kingdom. Add also: We have written commentaries and exegetical observations on books and passages of the Old and New Testament, we have preached fine sermons, etc.—*δαιμόνια, devils*) It is not said *διαβόλους*, because *διάβολος* is only used in the singular number.[1]

23. Τότε, κ.τ.λ., *then*, etc.) although they had not thought so before.—*ὁμολογήσω, I will profess*) sc. openly. Great was the *authority* evinced by this saying: see ver. 29.—*οὐδέποτε, κ.τ.λ.., never*, etc.) although you cite My *Name*.—*οἱ ἐργαζόμενοι, κ.τ.λ.., that work*, etc.) Not even then will their iniquity have been changed.[2]—*ἀνομίαν, iniquity*) how much soever they may boast of the *Law*.[3] Unbelief exclusively damns (Infidelitas proprie damnat); and yet in the Judgment the Law is rather cited; see ch. xxv. 35, 42; Rom. ii. 12, because the reprobate, even then, when they see Christ visibly manifest, will not comprehend the true nature of faith.

24. Ὁμοιώσω, *I will liken*) In ver. 26 it is, *he shall be likened*. God refers salutary things[4] to Himself; He removes evil things[5] from Himself; cf. ch. xxv. 34, 41.—*φρονίμῳ, prudent*) True prudence spontaneously accompanies true righteousness; cf. ch. xxv. 2.

25. Καί—καί—καί—κ.τ.λ., *and—and—and—etc.*) In the last days of a man and of the world, temptations throng together to the attack (*concurrunt*), sc., *rains* on the roof, *rivers* at the base,

---

[1] Sc. with its technical meaning: for *διάβολος*, in its original sense of *accuser*, may be used indiscriminately in all three numbers.—(I. B.)

[2] He means that our Lord will address them as even then working iniquity with hearts still unconverted. —(I. B.)

[3] There is a play upon the words *ἀνομία*, the state or conduct of those who are without law, and *ὁ νόμος*, the Law, on which they self-righteously and delusively relied.—(I. B.)

[4] *i.e.* things connected with salvation, as ex. gr. the building on the rock. —Ed.

[5] As ex. gr. the building on the sand; therefore it is here, "*he shall be likened*," not "*I will liken*."—Ed.

winds at the sides [of our spiritual edifice].[1]—ἡ βροχὴ, *the rain*) The presence of the *article* denotes that the rain will not be deficient.—προσέπεσον, *fell upon*) *i.e.* to try its power of endurance. In ver. 27, we have προσέκοψαν, *beat upon*, as though at random and without object.

26. Ὁ ἀκούων, *he that heareth*) He who neither *hears* nor *does*, clearly does not build at all.—ἐπὶ τὴν ἄμμον, *on the sand*) which frequently looks like the rock, but is not of the same consistence.

27. Καὶ ἦν ἡ πτῶσις αὐτῆς μεγάλη, *and great was the fall of it*) It was great indeed, for it was entire. We see, from the present example, that it is not necessary for all sermons to end in a consolatory strain.

28. Συνετέλεσεν, *concluded*) The Lord did nothing abruptly: see ch. xi. 1, xix. 1, xxvi. 1.—ἐξεπλήσσοντο, *were astonished*) The attractions of true teaching are genuine; those of profane, futile. You may wonder, perhaps, why our Lord did not in this discourse speak more clearly concerning His own Person. But (1) He explained His teaching so excellently, that from thence His auditors might judge of the excellence of the Prophet who thus taught; (2) His person had been already[2] sufficiently declared; (3) in the discourse itself, He sufficiently intimates who He is, namely, "*He that cometh*,"[3] *i.e.*, the Son of God, the Judge of all; see ch. v. 11, 17, 22, vii. 21–27.

29. Ὡς ἐξουσίαν ἔχων, *as one having authority*) They could not withdraw themselves away.[4] It is the mark of truth to constrain minds, and that of their own free will. See examples of our Lord's *authority* (ἐξουσία) in the Gnomon on ch. v. 3, 18–20, vii. 22, 23, and also viii. 19, and John vii. 19.—γραμματεῖς,[5] *scribes*)

---

[1] All kinds of judgments are here intimated; but especially the last judgment. It is indeed scarcely that the righteous man *is saved*, yet however he is saved [1 Pet. iv. 18].—V. g.

[2] *e.g.* Matt. iii. 17.—(I. B.)

[3] See ch. xi. 3.—(I. B.)

[4] *They felt the majesty of the Teacher, and the power of His word.*— V. g.

[5] The argin of Edit. A.D. 1753 regards the fuller reading, οἱ γραμματεῖς αὐτῶν καὶ οἱ Φαρισαῖοι, as almost equal in probability to this shorter one.— E. B.

Lachm. adds the words with C corrected by the first and second later

to whom the people were accustomed, and who had no *authority*.

CHAPTER VIII.

1 Ἠκολούθησαν, *followed*) They did not immediately leave Him.

2. Λεπρὸς, *a leper*) The most grievous diseases were leprosy (cf. with this passage 2 Kings v. 7), paralysis (cf. Mark ii. 3 with ver. 6) and fever (see ver. 14). It is probable that the leper[1] had listened to our Lord's discourse from a distance.—ἐὰν, κ.τ.λ., *if*, etc.) the leper does not doubt our Lord's power, but he humbly rests the event upon His will alone. Faith exclaims, *if Thou wilt*, not, *if Thou canst*; see Mark ix. 22.—δύνασαι, *Thou canst*) At the commencement of His ministry, the chief object of Faith was the omnipotence of Jesus. This faith the leper might have conceived from His discourse.

3. Τὴν χεῖρα, *His hand*) to which the leprosy, that would have polluted others, was compelled to yield.—θέλω, *I will*) corresponding to, *If thou wilt*. A prompt echo to the matured faith of the leper. The very prayer of the leper contained the words of the desired reply. The expression, *I will*, implies the highest authority. Our Lord performed His first miracles immediately, that He might not appear to have had any difficulty in performing them: but after He had established His authority, He frequently interposed a delay salutary to men.

4. Μηδενὶ, *to no one*) sc. before you have gone to the priest, lest the priests, if they had heard of it before, should deny that the leprosy had been really cleansed; sc. to *no one* of those who had not witnessed the miracle.—σεαυτὸν, *thyself*) not by means of another.—εἰς μαρτύριον, *for a testimony*) See John v. 36. Thus

hand, *ac* Vulg. Hil. 640, Euseb. ἀποδ. 27b : *b* also, adding αὐτῶν. However the weighty authority of B is against the additional words.—ED.

[1] *Whose cure Matthew places, in the correct order, between the Sermon on the Mount and the cure of the centurion's servant.*—Harm., p. 252.

the LXX. use the word μαρτύριον in Ruth iv. 7.[1] The priests did not follow our Lord: He sends the leper to them from Galilee to Jerusalem: He was much in Galilee at that time.—αὐτοῖς, *to them*) that a testimony might be exhibited to them of the Messiah's presence, and of His not derogating from the law, and that they too might thus be enabled to give testimony to these facts.

5. Προσῆλθεν Αὐτῷ ἑκατόνταρχος, *There came unto Him a centurion*) The centurion did not actually come to Him in person; nor would our Lord have praised him, as He did just afterwards, in his presence.—See ver. 10, and cf. ch. xi. 7. Others, indeed, were praised by our Lord in their presence, but not until after previous humiliation, and not so singularly and in comparison with others as the centurion is here praised in contradistinction to *all Israel*. And the same reverence, which induced the centurion to declare himself unworthy that our Lord should come under his roof, prevented him from going to Him in person.—See ver. 8, and Luke vii. 7, 10.[2] He appears to have come out of his house in the first instance, but to have gone back before he had reached our Lord. The will, therefore, on his part was held in Divine estimation as equivalent and even preferable to the deed: and this estimation is nobly expressed by St Matthew in the sublime style of a divine rather than a human historian. Jesus and the centurion conversed truly in spirit.

6. Λέγων, *saying*) cf. ch. xi. 3, and Luke xiv. 18.—παραλυτικός, *a paralytic*) Paralysis is a disease difficult to Physicians.

7. Ἐλθών, *coming*) In His Divine wisdom, our Lord puts forth those addresses by which He elicits the profession of the faithful, and thus as it were anticipates them: which is the reason why men of those times received a swifter, greater, and more frequent effect from heavenly words than they do now. He declares Himself ready to come to the *centurion's servant*. He does not promise that He will do so to the *nobleman's son*. By

---

[1] Sc. καὶ τοῦτο—ἦν μαρτύριον ἐν Ἰσραήλ.—E. V. And this was a testimony in Israel.—(I. B.)

[2] D. Hauber *has fully proved*, in den harmon. Anmerk. p. 72, *that the history here given in Matthew is one and the same as that in Luke*.—Harm. p. 265.

each method. He arouses faith, and shows that He is no respecter of persons.

8. Στέγην, *roof*) Although not a mean one, cf. Luke vii. 5. There were others whose reverence did not prevent them from seeing and touching the Lord, see ch. ix. 18, 20. The same internal feeling may manifest itself outwardly in different modes, yet all of them good.—εἰπὲ λόγῳ, *command by word*) Thus does the centurion declare his belief that the disease will yield to our Lord's command. Some few copies have rather more carelessly, εἰπὲ λόγον,[1] *say the word.*—ἰαθήσεται, *shall be healed*) The centurion replies by this glorious word: our Lord had said modestly, " θεραπεύσω," *I will cure.*[2]—ὁ παῖς μου, *my boy*) A kinder mode of speech than if he had said ὁ δουλός μου, *my slave*.

9. Καὶ γὰρ ἐγὼ, *for I also*) Reason might object, " The slave and the soldier hear the command without difficulty; not so the disease." The wisdom of faith, however, shining forth beautifully from the military abruptness with which it was expressed, does away with this objection, and regards rather those considerations which confirm, than those which might destroy (frangant) hope; those, namely, which arise from the supreme dominion and jurisdiction of Christ, who issued His injunctions to the sea, and the winds, and diseases; see ver. 26; Luke iv. 39. HE commands: the thing is done. The centurion can command soldier and slave, but not disease; the Lord, however, can order the disease, and that more easily, humanly speaking, than the will of man, who is frequently rebellious.—ἄνθρωπός εἰμι ὑπὸ ἐξουσίαν, *I am a man under authority*) He does not say, *I am a military officer*, but since he is obliged

---

[1] BCbc Orig. 4,278d and Vulg. read λόγῳ. Rec. Text, without good authority, has λόγον.—ED.

[2] The word used by the centurion was confined to the notion of healing, and cognate with that which denoted a physician: that employed by our Lord had also the signification of *attending upon*, and was cognate with one which denoted an *attendant*. Bengel's remark applies not to our Lord's meaning, but to the *mode* in which He expressed it.—(I. B.)

[3] Tittmann, Syn. ii., distinguishes the words thus: θεραπεύω ἰάομαι differunt ut nostra: (Germ.) *helfen* et *heilen*. θεραπεύεσθαι ἀπὸ τῶν ἀσθενειῶν, ἰᾶσθαι τοὺς ἀσθενοῦντας, i.e. θεραπεύομαι refers to the *infirmities* cured, ἰᾶσθαι to the *persons* cured. Θεραπεύω seems to me to mean, to *treat a case, to tend, to minister to*: ἰᾶσθαι, to *heal*.—ED.

to mention that others are subject to him, he says with great delicacy,¹ *I myself am subject.* There is also a concealed antithesis,² sc. Jesus is supreme Lord, *souverain.*—ὑπὸ—ὑπ᾽, *under*—*under*) Such persons are at present called subalterns.

10. Ἐθαύμασε, *wondered*) Faith and unbelief were both the objects of Christ's wonder; see Mark vi. 6. Our Lord praises His friends warmly, where there is an opportunity for so doing. See ch. xi. 7, xv. 28, xxv. 35, xxvi. 10; Luke vii. 44, xxi. 3.—ἐν τῷ Ἰσραήλ, *in Israel*) sc. the people of Israel. Neither the centurion nor the woman of Canaan were of Israel; but with regard to the latter, our Lord may seem to have given a higher testimony, because she came openly from the coasts of the Gentiles, whereas the former had dwelt in Israel: and the centurion himself anticipated that objection (id occupavit), when he declared himself to be unworthy, and interposed the elders of the Jews between himself and our Lord.—τοσαύτην, *so great*) especially as the centurion had had much less intercourse with our Lord [than His brethren according to the flesh]. His faith was an example and earnest of the faith by which the Gentiles would surpass the Jews.—πίστιν, *faith*) From this first mention of faith in the New Testament, we may gather that *faith* (as well as *unbelief*) is in both the understanding and the will, being the result of deliberation and free choice.³ See the concordances on the word πείθω.⁴ Of all the virtues evinced by those who came to the Lord, He is wont to praise faith alone. See ch. xv. 28; Luke vii. 50.⁵—οὐδὲ—εὗρον, *I have not found*) though I have come to seek it.

11. Πολλοί, *many*) who, being not Jews, are similar to the centurion. This is intended to awaken the emulation of the

---

¹ Προθεραπεία, *anticipatory precaution;* lest his mention of soldiers being under him should offend against humility, he puts first the mention of his being himself under the authority of others. See Append. on the figure.—ED.

² See Explanation of Technical terms in Appendix.—(I. B.)

³ *Deliberation* being the province of the *Understanding; Free Choice*, the offspring of the *Will.*—(I. B.)

⁴ πείθω, *to persuade*, etc., the verb from which πίστις, *faith* is derived.—(I. B.)

⁵ *In proportion to the greatness of humility, is the greatness of faith.*—See ver. 8, and Luke xvii. 5-10.—V. g.

Jews.—*ἀπὸ ἀνατολῶν, from the east*) see ch. ii. 1,—*from the east and from the west;* an euphemism for "from the Gentiles."—*ἥξουσι, shall come*) A prophecy: they shall come in spirit [and by faith.—V. g.]—*μετὰ, together with*) see Heb. xii. 23.[1]—*ἐν τῇ βασιλείᾳ, in the kingdom*) sc. in this life, and in that which is to come.

12. Οἱ δὲ υἱοὶ τῆς βασιλείας, *but the children of the kingdom*) i.e. nearest heirs to the kingdom. The same title is employed with another meaning in ch. xiii. 38.—*σκότος, darkness*) Whatever is *without* the kingdom of God is outer: for the kingdom of God is *light,* and the kingdom *of light.* That darkness will envelope not only the eye, but also the mind, with the grossest obscurity. —*ἐξώτερον, outer*) the unbeliever has internal darkness in himself already, and obtains, therefore, external darkness also as his fitting home. And the nearer that any one might have approached [to the Divine presence], so much the further will he be cast forth into the depths of darkness.—*ἐκεῖ, there*) at length [even though not here and now]. Without the brilliant scene of the feast [the marriage supper so often mentioned].— *ὁ*) a remarkable article, used emphatically.[2] In this life, grief is not yet really grief.—*κλαυθμὸς, weeping*) Then will weep heroes now ashamed to weep, from grief at the good they have lost, and the evil they have incurred. Oh horrible sound of so many wretched beings! how far more blessed to hear the sounds of heaven!—See Rev. xiv. etc.—*βρυγμὸς τῶν ὀδόντων, gnashing of teeth*) from impatience and bitterest remorse, and indignation against themselves, as being the authors of their own damnation.[3] Self-love, indulged on earth, will then be transformed into self-hate, nor will the sufferer be ever able to depart from himself. Nor is this weeping and gnashing of teeth combined with darkness only, but also with fire, etc.; see ch. xiii. 42, 50; Luke xiii. 28. Another exposition is, the soft will weep, the stern will rage. The same phrase occurs in Acts vii. 54.[4]

---

[1] With the Fathers in the faith, Heb. xi. 9—V. g.

[2] As though this were the true ideal of sorrow—the normal standard of suffering—the archetypal reality of agony.—(I. B.)

[3] As also from a spiteful and malignant feeling against others, to whom they enviously grudge the salvation which those others have obtained. Comp. Ps. cxii. 10.—V. g.

[4] Sc. they gnashed upon him [Stephen] with their teeth.—(I. B.)

13. Ὡς ἐπίστευσας, *as thou hast believed*) A bountiful concession.

14. Πενθεράν, *mother-in-law*) Peter had not long before married a wife, and they are guilty of a mistake who paint him with white hair;[1] for all the disciples were young, and had a long course to perform in this world; see John xxi. 18.[2] This must be well kept in mind in every Evangelical History.[3]—πυρέσσουσαν, *sick of a fever*) in the actual paroxysm.

15. Διηκόνει Αὐτῷ, *waited upon Him*) She performed the duty of the house-mother (mater-familias), as a joyful sign of her entire restoration to health. St Mark and St Luke mention the disciples as preferring the request in favour of Peter's mother-in-law, and therefore add—διηκόνει αὐτοῖς, *she waited upon* THEM, sc. the Lord and His disciples. St Matthew mentions only the Lord, and therefore wrote Αὐτῷ. The erroneous reading, αὐτοῖς, has been introduced from the other Evangelists.[4]

16. Ὀψίας, *evening*) of that day on which so much had been said and done. Diseases are wont to be more oppressive at eventide.—τὰ πνεύματα, *the spirits*) i.e. the devils.—λόγῳ, *with a*

---

[1] Although it is not improbable that he was older than the other disciples.—B. H. E. p. 257.

[2] You may gather that concerning Judas Iscariot from Ps. cix. 8, 9; Zebedee and Salome, the parents of James and John, were likewise both still living.—B. H. E. p. 258.

[3] For whoever will carefully weigh the youthful age of the disciples, and their original family connections and former condition, will readily make allowances for several errors which were committed by them in their state of discipleship, and, having regard to this consideration of the time, he will not require from them more than is reasonable, and so will find himself extricated from not a few difficulties.—*Harm.* l. c.

[4] Those who are anxious to avoid *Transpositions*, maintain the opinion, that the mother-in-law of Peter was delivered from a fever more than once. But in the case of sick persons healed by the Saviour, the danger that impended over them was not from the return of their disease, but from some greater evil. Nor did the Lord warn the mother-in-law of Peter, as He did others, on that head: and if she had been attacked by fever anew, it would have happened at a most brief interval after the former cure, and therefore in that case the disciples, who were as yet but novices, might have doubted, along with others, whether the fever (a disease liable to alternations and intermissions more than all other diseases) had been really and completely removed.—*Harm.* p. 257.

word[1]) by that *alone*.[2]—πάντας, *all*) without exception : some men are said to have a healing power in the case only of certain special diseases.

17. Ὅπως πληρωθῇ, *that it might be fulfilled*) It behoved that the Physician of the soul should also remove bodily complaints from those who came in His way.[3] In this manner also, therefore, was fulfilled the prophecy of Isaiah. Body and soul together form one man : the corrupting principle of both soul and body is one [namely sin]; *one* and the same aid was given to both by this great Physician, as the case required.—ἔλαβε, *took*) *i.e.* removed from us.

18. Ἀπελθεῖν, *to depart*) Thus Jesus sought repose, and gave to the people time to bear fruit from His teaching, and kindled their interest in Himself for the future.

19. Εἷς γραμματεύς, κ.τ.λ., *one Scribe, etc.*) Out of so great a multitude, this man alone exhibits such an emotion. Yet he seems to have been fond of comfort, a Scribe less hardy than the fishermen. The Scribes came often to tempt our Lord.

19–21. Εἶπεν, *said*) The doctrine of Jesus Christ is clearly opposed to the natural will of man. He wisely sent away those who endeavoured to follow him wrongly or unseasonably; see Mark v. 18. Those who showed a hesitation in following Him, He commanded to follow Him. He treated the Scribes in one way, the disciples in another; see Luke ix. 57–62.—Διδάσκαλε, *Teacher*[4]) Jesus did not address those as Rabbi and Lord, who were called so by human law or custom, but he was deservedly addressed as such by them. See Mark v. 35; John iii. 2, iv. 49; Matt. viii. 6. The apostles addressed their hearers as *brethren* and *fathers :* our Lord never did so.

20. Καὶ λέγει αὐτῷ ὁ Ἰησοῦς, κ.τ.λ., *and Jesus saith unto him, etc.*) Our Lord does not repulse this man, but he proposes a condition by which to correct the view with which he made the offer respecting comfort or wealth, or even the power of working

---

[1] That such is Bengel's meaning is clear from his German Version, where he renders it "*mit einem wort.*" E. V. has "By His word."—(I. B.)

[2] "Solo," *i.e.* without using any other means.—(I. B.)

[3] And of whom the extraordinary numbers are from time to time noticed, Matt. iv. 23, ix. 35, 36 (Luke iv. 21), xii. 15, xv. 30, xxi. 14.—*Harm*, p. 259.

[4] E. V. Master.

miracles.—ὁ Υἱὸς τοῦ ἀνθρώπου, *the Son of man*) See Gnomon on ch. xvi. 13.—οὐκ ἔχει, κ.τ.λ., *hath not, etc.*) O admirable poverty and endurance, combined with perpetual pilgrimage.[1]

21. Μαθητῶν, *of the disciples*) of those, namely, who were not always present.

22. Τοὺς νεκρούς, *the dead*) An expression urgently commanding the man to follow Him, and therefore embracing many things. Both *the dead who are to be buried*, and *the dead who are to bury them*, must come under consideration. The dead who are to be buried, are without doubt those literally dead, whether the father of this disciple was already then dead or old, and near to death, and with only this one son. Cf. Tobit xiv. 12. *The dead who bury*, or those to whom the burial of the dead should be left, are *partly* those who are also about to die, mortals bound to the law of death (cf. Rom. viii. 10), as distinguished from the hope of a better life—that hope, however, being not altogether taken away. The appellation is to be limited by the context: as in Luke xx. 34, they, who nevertheless are capable of being saved, are called the children of this world; so they are called dead, who are more fit for burying than for announcing the kingdom of God. As in ch. ix. 24, the girl is called *not dead*, who soon shall live (cf. John xi. 4), so they are called dead, who soon shall die.[2] In the time of pestilence, the dead are buried by those who soon themselves die. Nor is the case very different with successive generations of mortals in the course of ages. *Partly*, they are already dead: and with regard to them the expression is hypothetical, with this meaning—Do thou follow Me, and leave the burial of the dead to the dead themselves; *i.e.* Let the dead, as far as you are concerned, remain unburied. A similar mode of expression occurs in Exod. xxi. 14, *Let the murderer be taken from the altar: i.e. let him be slain, even if he has fled to the altar*. The appellation, therefore, of *the dead who bury*, is abrupt, and suitable to a com-

---

[1] Neither had He a house of His own, nor a fixed dwelling anywhere, Mark i. 45. The Scribe regarded it as an easier matter than it really was, to follow Him whithersoever He was going.—*Harm.*, p. 269.

[2] The dead are in their lasting home, and the mourners are not far off from the same, but continue wandering all around it, until they themselves also enter it.—See Eccles. xii. 5.—V. g.

mand which could brook no delay—a command which had sacred grounds, and flowed from the divine perception of the Saviour. We ought to surrender ourselves wholly and immediately.—τοὺς ἑαυτῶν, *their own*) sc. relatives. See Gen. xxiii. 4. It was the duty of this disciple to deny his father.[1]

23. Τὸ πλοῖον, *the vessel*) The article refers by implication to ver. 18. Jesus had a moving school: and in that school His disciples were instructed much more solidly than if they had dwelt under the roof of a single college, without any anxiety or temptation.

24. Σεισμὸς μέγας, *a great tempest*) The faith of the disciples was greatly exercised by these maritime perils.—καλύπτεσθαι, *was covered*) the danger reached the highest pitch: then came the succour.—ἐκάθευδε, *slept*) No fear fell on Jesus. Nay, in ver. 26, He marvelled at the fear of men, even in the utmost peril. He slept, wearied by the various labour of the day.

25. Σῶσον, *save*) An abrupt prayer.—ἀπολλύμεθα, *we perish*) It is a proof of candour in the disciples to have recorded their own weaknesses: this was not, however, difficult to them, since after the coming of the Paraclete they had become other men.

26. [2]Δειλοί—ὀλιγόπιστοι, *fearful—of little faith*) Synonymous terms. Cf. Mark v. 36. Our Lord does not find fault with the disciples for their importunity in disturbing His rest, but for their timidity.[3]—τότε, *then*) Jesus calmed first the minds of His disciples, then the sea.—ἐπιτίμησε, *rebuked*) Satan probably had ruled in this tempest.

27. Ὑπακούουσιν Αὐτῷ, *obey Him*) Cf. Mark i. 27. The winds and the sea acknowledge no other control.[4]

28. Γεργεσηνῶν,[5] *of the Gergesenes*) *Gerasa* (said for *Gergescha*)

---

[1] The winds and the sea, on this occasion, sooner obeyed the will of Christ than did men.—*Harm.* 269, 270.

[2] Καὶ λέγει, *And He saith*) Being not at all discomposed or agitated.—V. g.

[3] In the whole life of Christ, never is there any fear of any creature evinced in all the incidents which occurred to Him.—V. g.

[4] In the original, "Venti et mare alias libera."—Bengel is very fond of the adverb "*alias*," and frequently employs it emphatically.—(I. B.)

[5] This reading, which Michaelis supposed to rest on the mere conjecture of Origen, is estimated by the Margin of Beng. more highly in this passage than in the parallels, Mark v. 1, and Luke viii. 26.—E. B.

BCΔ, Syr. (Peschito) and Harcl. (txt.) Syr. read Γαδαρηνῶν. Lachm.

and *Gadara* were neighbouring cities.[1] See Hiller's *Onomata Sacra*, pp. 807, 812.—ἐκ τῶν μνημείων, *from the tombs*) The possessed avoid human society, in which the exercises of piety flourish. Invisible guests also *have their dwelling* in sepulchres (See Mark v. 3); those which are malignant, especially, I believe in the sepulchres of the impious.—παρελθεῖν, *pass by*) not even pass by.

29. Τί ἡμῖν καὶ σοί, *what have we to do with Thee?*) A formula of declining interference or intercourse. See S. V. 1 Kings xvii. 18; Judges xi. 12; 2 Kings iii. 13. They confess in this address their despair and horrible expectation, and at the same time they seem to add, " we desire to have dealings, not with Thee, but with men liable to sin."—Υἱὲ τοῦ Θεοῦ, *Son of God*) Men seeking aid addressed Him with confidence as *the Son of David*; devils with terror, as *the Son of God*.—ὦδε, *hither*) The devils claimed, as it were, some right in that place, and especially over the swine in that place.—πρὸ καιροῦ, *before the time*) This may be construed either with ἦλθες, *hast Thou come*, or with βασανίσαι, *to torment*, or with both. Jesus came indeed when the world was ripe for His coming, and yet sooner than the enemy desired. Thus in Rom. v. 6, we read Χριστὸς—κατὰ καιρὸν—ἀπέθανε, IN DUE TIME *Christ died*.—βασανίσαι, *to torment*) It is torment for the devils to be without the bodies of man or beast, which they ardently desire to possess, that they may thereby, for the time being, extinguish that fire with which they are always burning. See ver. 31. This was a prelude to their being hereafter placed in subjection under the feet of Jesus.

30. Χοίρων, *of swine*) The owners of the swine were either heathens dwelling among the Jews, or Jews greedy of gain.

31. Παρεκάλουν, *besought*) It is one thing to ask in an ordinary way (in which manner natural men, and even devils, have been

reads Γεργεσηνῶν with *bcd* Vulg. Hilar. 645, and D apparently (its Latin having this reading). Γεργεσηνῶν has but second-rate authorities, LX. etc. Memph. Goth. The variety probably arose from the parallel passages being altered from one another. Tregelles (Printed Text of N. T. p. 192) has shown Origen, iv. 140, Γερασηνῶν, does not refer to Matthew exclusively, but to the Gospel *narration* generally. It proves the name was sometimes read Γαδαρηνοί, sometimes Γερασηνοί, and that Γεργεσηνοί was *not a then known* reading, but was his mere conjecture.—ED.

[1] See Bloomfield's Greek Testament in loc.—(I. B.)

ere now able to obtain something[1]), and another thing to pray in faith. Even Satan himself sometimes obtains his request, as we learn from the first chapter of Job.—*εἰ, κ.τ.λ., if*, etc.) They perceived already that they must change their abode.—*ἐπίτρεψον ἡμῖν, κ.τ.λ., suffer us*, etc.) The mischief should be ascribed to the devils, not to the Lord; and who would compel Him to hinder the devils?

32. *Ἀπῆλθον, they were come out*) Our Lord performed one miracle by which He inflicted punishment on a tree, namely, a fig tree; another on swine; another on men buying and selling in the temple. A specimen of future vengeance. His other miracles were full of grace; and even in these benefit was produced, as, for example, in the present case, a road rendered safe, a region freed from spirits to which it was liable, by their being driven into the sea, the possessed liberated, an excessive quantity of animal existence removed which was forbidden to be eaten, and in this case liable to be possessed by devils. And the Gergesenes were guilty, and deserved to lose the herd. The circumstance shows indisputably the right and the authority of Jesus.—*ἀπέθανον, died*) It seems that a possessed brute cannot live long. That men who are possessed do not thus perish immediately, is an especial mercy of God.

33. *Οἱ βόσκοντες, they who fed*) Although they were not professedly herdsmen by occupation.—*ἔφυγον, fled*) The devils could not overtake them.

34.[2] *Παρεκάλεσαν, they besought*) Those who are held fast by concern about their property, more easily and readily repel than pursue. Even avarice is timid. Or perhaps they besought our Lord with no evil feeling.[3] See Luke v. 8.[4]

---

[1] Comp. Mark v. 10, 12.—E.B.

[2] Πᾶσα ἡ πόλις, *the whole city*) Such great commotion do earthly interests cause!—V. g.

[3] At all events, though the Gergesenes besought Him with such a request, as did also their neighbours the Gadarenes, yet He left behind a leading one of those who had been possessed (Luke viii. 35, viz. the man whom the men of the city had found "sitting at the feet of Jesus, clothed, and in his right mind") as a preacher of the Gospel to them. This one may have been a Gadarene, and the other a Gergesene.—*Harm*. p. 274.

[4] Where Peter, from humility instead of malignity, exclaims, "DEPART FROM ME, for I am a sinful man, O Lord."—(I. B.)

CHAPTER IX.

1. Διεπέρασε, *He crossed over*) Being asked to do so by the Gergesenes. The Lord does not force His blessings on the unwilling.¹—ἰδίαν, *His own*) sc. Capernaum, exalted by this inhabitant.

2. Προσέφερον Αὐτῷ, *they brought to Him*) Many such offerings were made to the Saviour, and they were pleasing to Him.—τὴν πίστιν αὐτῶν, *their faith*) i.e. of him who was borne, and of them who bare him.—θάρσει, τέκνον, *Son, be of good cheer*²) "Neither thy sins nor thy disease shall stand in thy way." Thus, at ver. 22, θάρσει, θύγατερ, *daughter, be of good comfort*. "*Be of good comfort*;" neither thy sins shall prevail against thee, nor thy disease. Thus also, "*Be of good comfort, daughter*," in ver. 22. —ἀφέωνταί σοι, *are forgiven thee*) Without doubt, great was the sense of great sins in that man.³—σοι has here both emphasis and accent, but in ver. 5 the same words are repeated after the manner of a quotation, and σοι or σου is enclitic.⁴

3. Εἶπον ἐν ἑαυτοῖς, οὗτος βλασφημεῖ, *said within themselves, this man blasphemeth*) Blasphemy is committed when (1.) things unworthy of God are attributed to Him; (2.) things worthy of God are denied to Him; (3.) when the incommunicable attributes of God are attributed to others.

4. Εἰδὼς, *knowing*) Besides many Greek codices, which Mill first began to notice on this passage, the Gothic version and the margin of Courcelles reads thus.—ἰδὼν⁵ appears to have been in-

---

¹ And by that very fact He excited in men the more ardent desires after Him, inasmuch as He did not make too long delays in the one place.—*Harm.*, l. c.

² The word used by Bengel is "*confide*," which is repeated each time in the remarks which follow.—(I. B.)

³ This was the principal benefit, by occasion of which chiefly the thoughts of the men present there were thrown open and made manifest, ver. 3, 8. —*Harm.* p. 276.

⁴ Never had that voice been heard put forth in this way, from the time that the earth had borne men on it.—V. g.

⁵ Lachmann reads ἰδὼς with B, Goth Vers. and probably a. Dbc and Rec. Text read ἰδὼν. Vulg. "*Cum vidisset.*"—ED.

troduced by some persons from ver. 2. St Mark and St Luke have ἐπιγνοὺς in the parallel passages. Thus too we find εἰδὼς in ch. xii. 25.—ὑμεῖς, *you*) The pronoun is expressed for the sake of emphasis.[1]

5. Τί γάρ, *for which?*) In itself either is the sign of Divine authority and power; and the connection between sin and disease is in itself most close: the power which removes both is one. According to human judgment, it is easier to say, "*Thy sins are remitted;*" and he who can say "*Arise,*" which appears greater, can also say this, which appears less.

6. Εἰδῆτε, *ye may know*) This word also breathes *authority*.[2]— ἐπὶ τῆς γῆς, *on earth*) This is exclusively the place where sins are committed and remitted. Earth was the scene of Christ's works from the beginning.[3] See Prov. viii. 31; cf. the two clauses in Ps. xvi. 3; see[4] Jer. ix. 24; John xvii. 4; Luke ii. 14. I have, says He, all authority in heaven, much more on earth; see ch. xvi. 19, xxviii. 18.[5] This speech savours of a heavenly origin.—ἐξουσίαν, *authority*) The argument from power to authority holds good in this passage.—λέγει, *He saith*) A similar change of person between the protasis and apodosis occurs in Num. v. 20, 21, and Jer. v. 14.

8. Ἐξουσίαν τοιαύτην, *such authority*) sc. to heal and save (see ver. 6), and that close at hand in the *man* Jesus Christ.—τοῖς ἀνθρώποις, *to men*) so long afflicted with sin.[6] An expansive expression (lata oratio), as in ver. 6.[7] They rejoiced that there was one of the human race endued with this authority.

[1] Often one, whilst he is arraigning others for their sins, is sinning himself. And indeed the most heinous sins can be committed even in the *heart* alone.—V. g.

[2] Bengel just below translates ἐξουσίαν (rendered in E. V. *power*) by "*authority,*" and refers to it by anticipation.—(I. B.)

[3] Nay more, it is the wrestling arena between sin and grace.—V. g.

[4] E. B. inserts here "Gen. vi. 5," which has been adopted by the later editions.—(I. B.)

[5] We also in our turn may now say: Seeing that He had that power, when sojourning on the earth, why should He not also have the same, now that He has been raised from the dead and taken up into heaven? Acts v. 31.—V. g.

[6] A *Dativus Commodi.*—V. g. *i.e.* for *the good of* men.—ED.

[7] Beng. seems to me, not to take ἀνθρώποις as Engl. V., "God who had given such power *to men*," but, as the Dative of advantage, "Who had be-

9. Ματθαῖον, *Matthew*) A Hebrew by nation, and yet a publican. In St Mark and St Luke, he is called Levi.[1] It is possible that Matthew did not like the name which he had borne as a publican.—καθήμενον, *sitting*) actually employed in the business of his calling. And yet Matthew followed. A great miracle and example of the power of Jesus. A noble instance of obedience[2] [*productive of eternal joy.*—V. g.]

stowed such power (in the person of *the man* Christ Jesus) *for the benefit of men*, so long afflicted as they had been with sin. Thus the meaning of Bengel's "lata oratio, uti v. 6" is, that the words "on earth," in ver. 6, imply the same *wide range* of the Saviour's power for the good of men as ἀνθρώποις here.—ED.

[1] J. D. Michaelis, Einleitung T. ii. p. m. 932, etc., conjectures that Levi was the chief of the publicans, and Matthew his subordinate assistant. But it is not likely that either Matthew, consistently with his modesty, would have omitted to record the obedience of Levi to the Lord's call—Levi being, by the hypothesis, Matthew's principal and also host at the large entertainment given on the occasion—or that Mark and Luke should have omitted the call of Matthew, who was more distinguished than Levi on account of his apostleship. It is no objection, that Matthew is not mentioned by the men of Nazareth, Matt. xiii. 55, among the four sons, *i.e.* sister's sons of Mary: for not even Levi (who in Mark ii. 14 is explicitly made the son of Alpheus) is reckoned among those four. What suppose we say that Levi, or Matthew, was the son of Alpheus, though not by Mary, but by a different wife, and so connected with the Saviour by no tie of blood. At all events, the very etymological root of the names seems to establish the identity of the persons. For לוי (Levi) is from לוה *adhered, attached to*, and מתי or מתני (Matthew) is from the Arab. word מתה, *he formed a tie of connection* or *propinquity*. Moreover: in the same way as Saul, from that period of time in which, after being solemnly set apart to the work of preaching, he gained over Sergius Paulus as the first-fruits of his mission, and so became superior to Barnabas, was distinguished by the name of Paul, even by Luke himself (Acts xiii. 2, 9): so also Levi (Luke v. 27), from the moment in which by solemn election he was enrolled among the Apostles, obtained the name of Matthew even in Luke (c. vi. 15). These considerations will enable the reader to decide the question.—E. B.

[2] This may be supposed to have been the series of the events: Matthew a short while before went to Jesus as a publican, and even then, at that early time, beyond all that he could have conceived, was called to the apostolic office, Matt. v. 1, Luke vi. 15 (comp. Num. xi. 26): whereby is evinced the extraordinary clemency of the Saviour towards this publican, thus selected out from the rest of his fellows. He was present, as an apostle freshly-appointed, at the Sermon on the Mount: where there is no doubt but that the words, *Do not even the publicans the same?* recorded by Matthew him-

10. Ἐν τῇ οἰκίᾳ, *in the house*) Cf. ver. 28; or, if you take it of Matthew's house, Mark ii. 15; Luke v. 29. Matthew appears in this feast to have bid adieu to his former companions,[1]

self, ch. v. 46, made the deepest impression on his mind. He did not, however, on that very day commence following the Lord daily, but had still some occupation in levying taxes, therein without doubt being observant of that righteousness which is commanded in Luke iii. 13. There was, on the part of the Jews, a great abhorrence of publicans, even though they were themselves Jews; and it is to this abhorrence that the Saviour adapted His language, Matt. xviii. 17. However, the publicans were not altogether excluded from the temple, whether they had the same degree of access to it open to them as the Pharisees had, or an access more remote: Luke xviii. 13. John admitted the publicans to baptism, on condition that, in the discharge of their office, they would allow themselves to be stirred up to the duty of justice; nay more, not even did the Saviour command them altogether to leave their employment, but to "make to themselves friends of the Mammon of unrighteousness," Luke xv. 1, xvi. 1, 9. Neither Christ nor His forerunner were bound by the Jewish traditions, which excluded publicans from church-communion. And besides, it is probable that the Jews, from malice against Christ, subsequently established more severe enactments as to publicans. Accordingly Matthew, being called to the apostleship, and not as yet at that time ordered to leave the receipt of customs, may have discharged this duty up to the time that he was called to follow Jesus. But if Matthew did the same as Zaccheus, before his conversion, he was in duty bound to make amends to those whom he had defrauded on the same principle as Zaccheus, or even to compare and make up all accounts whatever with the other publicans. *Jesus*, therefore, *when he saw him sitting at the receipt of custom, saith, Follow Me.* And he arose and followed Him. Independently of the general crowd of hearers and disciples, coming to Him and going away from time to time, Jesus admitted certain *followers* to daily intimacy (Luke ix. 59, xviii. 22; Acts i. 21), and twelve apostles, *i.e.* extraordinary messengers of the kingdom of heaven. Peter and Andrew, James also, with John, were made *followers* before that they were made *apostles*: Matthew was called to the *apostolic* dignity sooner than he was admitted to the intimacy of daily following the Lord, although not even this could have been put off for long, and in matter of fact was not delayed for *more than a few days.* At all events, he was not present in the journey to the country of the Gergesenes, who perhaps knew him well as a publican; but he may have been a spectator of the other acts of the Lord at Capernaum previous and subsequent to that journey. Even though he were ever so much behind the other apostles in following Christ: yet he followed soon enough for attaining the object proposed, as an apostle, Acts i. 21.—*Harm.* 281, etc.

[1] He seems also hereby to have afforded them an opportunity of going to the Lord, such as would hardly have been given to so great a number of such characters at any other time. Shortly after, Matthew came to know the

nor does he call the house any longer his own.—τελῶναι καὶ ἁμαρτωλοί, *publicans and sinners*) who had sinned grievously against the sixth and seventh [seventh and eighth] commandments.—συνανέκειντο, *sat down together with*) Kind and condescending was the intercourse of Jesus.[1]

11. Τοῖς μαθηταῖς, *to the disciples*) The Pharisees acted in an oblique manner, with cunning, or at least with cowardice; to the disciples they said, Why does your Master do so? to the Master, Why do your disciples do so? see ch. xii. 2, xv. 2; Mark ii. 16, 18.—διατί, κ.τ.λ., *why, etc.*) The sanctity of Jesus was held in the highest esteem by all, even His adversaries. See Luke xix. 7.

12.[2] Χρείαν, *need*) χρεῖαι, *needs*, are to be seen everywhere.—[3]κακῶς, *ill*) Such is indeed the case with sinners.[4]

13. Πορευθέντες, *having gone*) sc. into the synagogue, where you may refer to Hosea [sc. vi. 6.] Our Lord often said to those who were not His own,[5] "πορεύου," "*depart*," see John viii. 11. His style of quoting the Scriptures is full of suitableness and majesty, and different from that of the apostles; for He does it in such a manner as not Himself to rest upon, but to convince His hearers by their authority; and He employs it

---

glory of Jesus by His acts, and especially by the raising of Jairus' daughter, ch. ix. 19; and he was sent forth, at no long interval afterwards, with the rest of His apostles: on which occasion he has called himself *Matthew the publican*, ch. x. 3; and, from the deepest sense of gratitude (as is natural), has recalled to remembrance with what marvellous speed grace transferred him from his state as a publican (ch. xviii. 17) to an Apostolic embassy which was distinguished by miracles.—*Harm.* p. 282.

[1] For whose sake the banquet was given, to which, without any command on His part, publicans and sinners came. Therefore the objection of the Pharisees, even looking at it in a mere external point of view, was void of all justice.—V. g.

[2] Jesus, as a faithful master, brings help to his disciples.—V. g.

[3] Dost thou feel infirmity (οἱ κακῶς ἔχοντες), as opposed to strength (οἱ ἰσχύοντες)? In that case betake thyself to the Physician, and seek His help.—V. g.

[4] In the original, "Sic sane habent peccatores." There is a play here on the word *habent*, sc. χρείαν ἔχουσιν—κακῶς ἔχοντες.—(I. B.)

[5] In the original "Alieniores,"—an expression which is used several times by Bengel in the course of this gospel, and which it is easier to understand than to translate.—(I. B.)

more towards His adversaries than towards the disciples who believed on Him.—μάθετε, *learn ye*) ye who think that ye are already consummate teachers.—ἔλεον θέλω, *I will have mercy*) A few read with the LXX. in Hos. vi. 6, with whom the other words in this passage agree, ἔλεος θέλω.[1] The LXX. more commonly use τὸ ἔλεος in the neuter, as in Hos. vi. 4. Sometimes, however, ὁ ἔλεος, like the ancient Greeks. Is. lx. 10, lxiii. 7; Dan. i. 9, ix. 20; Ps. ci. 1; 1 Macc. ii. 57, iii. 44; and especially in the minor prophets, Jonah ii. 9; Mic. vi. 8 (which passage is also parallel with the evangelist), Ibid. vii. 20; Zech. vii. 9; Hos. xii. 6. Thus ὁ ἔλεος occurs in the present passage, in Matt. xii. 7, xxiii. 23; Tit. iii. 5; Heb. iv. 16; but τὸ ἔλεος occurs frequently in St Luke, St Paul, St James, St Peter, St John, and St Jude; and in Mic. vii. 18, the LXX., have θελητὴς ἐλέους ἐστίν, *He is a willer of mercy*. We have here an axiom of interpretation, nay, the sum total of that part of theology which treats of cases of conscience. On *mercy*, cf. ch. xxiii. 23. The word θυσίαν, *sacrifice* (victimam), is put synecdochically.[2] It is an act of *mercy* to eat with sinners for their spiritual profit.[3]— ἦλθον, *I have come*) sc. from heaven.—καλέσαι, *to call*) Such is the mission, such the authority of Christ.—ἁμαρτωλούς, *sinners*) The word is purposely and emphatically repeated by our Lord. Cf. ver. 11.

14. Τότε, *then*) At the time of the Feast.[4]—προσέρχονται Αὐτῷ, *come to Him*) of set purpose.—οἱ μαθηταὶ Ἰωάννου, *the disciples of John*) They were half-way between the Pharisees and the disciples of Jesus, and appear on this occasion to have been instigated by the Pharisees.[5]—Cf. Luke v. 33.—Σοῦ μαθηταί, *Thy*

---

[1] So BC corrected later, D. This is the Hellenistic form, as τὸ πλοῦτος, τὸ ζῆλος, found in LXX. and oldest MSS. of N. T. for ὁ πλοῦτος, ὁ ζῆλος. Rec. Text has ἔλεον, the classic form.—ED.

[2] A part for the whole of positive performances.—ED.

[3] So far ought you to be from despising repentance; for repentance is in fact the curing of the soul.—V. g.

Καὶ οὐ θυσίαν) This is one portion of the rigorous observance of those things, which are contained in the Law.—V. g.

[4] It was also the day of the public fasts, as it appears, which were celebrated not by the enactment of divine Law, but according to the private will of certain individuals.—*Harm.*, p. 283.

[5] For Matthew in this passage mentions the disciples of John; Mark (ch. ii.

disciples) They proceed modestly, and do not enquire concerning John or Jesus Himself.

15. Καὶ, *and*) Our Lord replies calmly and cheerfully: He draws joyful parables from the garments and the wine (which were being employed in the Feast) to condemn the sadness of those who questioned Him.—οἱ υἱοὶ τοῦ νυμφῶνος, *the children of the bridechamber*) The companions of the bridegroom.[1] Parables and riddles are suited to feasts and nuptials, and are employed to illustrate this nuptial period.[2]—πενθεῖν, *to mourn*) Mourning and fasting are joined together.—ἐλεύσονται, *shall come*) He means His departure, which should take place at a future period.—καὶ τότε, *and then*) Neither before nor after.[3]—νηστεύσουσιν, *they shall fast*) necessarily and willingly.[4]

16. Οὐδεὶς, *no one*) Our Lord chose, as His disciples, men who were unlearned, fresh and simple, and imbued with no peculiar discipline.—See ch. xv. 2; cf. Gnomon on Luke vii. 20. The old raiment was the doctrine of the Pharisees; the new, that of Christ.—αἴρει, *taketh away*) both itself and more.—αὐτοῦ, *his*) The word is here in the masculine gender.[5]—χεῖρον σχίσμα γίνεται, *the rent becomes worse*) Therefore, there was before some rent. A ragged garment, altogether ragged, is intended.

17. Ἀσκοὺς, *leather bottles*) which were used instead of casks. The old bottles are the Pharisees; the new, the disciples; the wine, the Gospel.—ἀπολοῦνται, *will perish*) So that they can neither hold that, nor any other wine henceforward.—ἀμφότεροι, *both*) masculine, as τίς in ch. xxiii. 17.

18) mentions the same persons in company with the Pharisees; Luke mentions the Scribes and Pharisees.—*Harm.* l. c.

[1] The Bridegroom Himself, if you except the forty days in the wilderness, is nowhere recorded as having fasted.—V. g.

[2] Bengel means to say, the period when our Lord was with His disciples.—(I. B.)

[3] Bengel means, neither whilst the Bridegroom was with the Church on earth, nor when the Church should be with the Bridegroom in heaven.—(I. B.)

[4] This is the very characteristic aspect of Christianity: At one time is the nuptial and festive season; at another time, the season for fasting and sorrow.—V. g.

[5] Rosenmüller more naturally refers αὐτοῦ to ῥάκους, "pannus impexus a vestimento vetustate contrito aliquid aufert." Beng. seems to take αὐτοῦ with πλήρωμα, as "the portion put in *by him* to fill up the rent."—ED.

18. Προσεκύνει, *worshipped*) Although in outward appearance Jairus was greater than Jesus.—ἐτελεύτησεν, *is dead*) Thus he said from conjecture, or after he had received intelligence of his daughter's death, whom he, in the great strength of faith, had left at the point of death.—See Mark v. 23.—ἐλθών,[1] *coming*) cf. John iv. 47.

20. Γυνή, *a woman*) Eusebius[2] narrates that the statue of this woman and of the Lord healing her was still in existence in his time.—H. E., Bk. vii., c. 17.—ὄπισθεν, *from behind*) sc. out of modest humility.—τοῦ κρασπέδου, *the hem* or *fringe*) See Num. xv. 38, S. V. Our Lord performed even that part of the law. There is no valid argument from the dress which our Lord then wore to the efficacy of relics.

21. Τοῦ ἱματίου Αὐτοῦ, *His garment*) The woman, from the sense of her own impurity, acknowledged the absolute purity of Jesus. —σωθήσομαι, *I shall be made whole*) The expression in ver. 22—σέσωκέ σε, *hath made thee whole*—sweetly replies to this thought.[3]

22. Θύγατερ, *daughter*) She was, therefore, not advanced in years.[4]—ἡ πίστις σου σέσωκέ σε, *thy faith hath placed thee in a state of health or salvation*[5]) Our Lord was wont to say thus to those who, of themselves, as it were drew the health of their body and soul to themselves;[6] see Luke vii. 50, xvii. 19, xviii. 42; by which

---

[1] Lachm. with BCDabcd Vulg. Hil. reads εἰς, and with BLUabc Vulg. ('accessit') προσελθών. Tischend. has εἰσελθών; Beng. and Griesb. εἰς ἐλθών. Both these last two readings are equally tenable, as the letters are not separated in different words in MSS.: CDXΔ support either reading. Matth. often uses εἰς as אֶל = τις; ch. viii. 19, xix. 6.—ED.

[2] A celebrated ecclesiastical historian; born about A.D. 267; became Bishop of Cæsarea in Palestine, A.D. 313 or 315; and died A.D. 338 or 340. —(I. B.)

[3] It is to a wonderful degree profitable to do simply, and without roundabout methods, whatever the spirit of faith and love teaches; ch. xxvi. 7.— V. g.

[4] Our gracious Saviour did not at all censure her on the ground that she neglected to offer a prayer to Him, and as it were stole help from Him.— V. g.

[5] E. V. Thy faith hath made thee whole.—(I. B.)

[6] In the original, "qui salutem corporis et animæ ad se ultro quasi attraxere"—"*attraxere*," "*by their own instrumentality;*" "*ultro,*" "*of their own accord.*" See Reff.—(I. B.)

words He shows that He knew the existence and **extent of their faith**; He praises and confirms their faith; He ratifies the gift, and commands it to remain; and at the same time intimates, that if others remain without help, unbelief is the only cause.[1]

23. Τοὺς αὐλητὰς, *the flute-players*) It was the custom to employ flutes at funerals, especially those of the young.—τὸν ὄχλον, *the crowd*) See Luke vii. 12.

24. Ἀναχωρεῖτε, *depart*) That is, you are not needed here. Our Lord proceeds without hesitation[2] to perform the miracle, cf. ch. xiv. 19.—οὐ γὰρ ἀπέθανε τὸ κοράσιον, *for the damsel is not dead*) Jesus said this before He entered where she was lying dead. The dead all live to God; see Luke xx. 38; and the girl, on account of her revival, which was to take place soon, quickly, surely, and easily, was not to be numbered amongst the dead who shall rise hereafter, but amongst those that sleep.— κατεγέλων Αὐτοῦ, *they laughed Him to scorn*) This very circumstance confirmed the truth of both the death and the miracle. They seem to have feared the loss of their funeral dues.

25. Ἠγέρθη, *she was raised*) Jesus raised the dead from the bed, from the bier, from the grave; in this instance, in Luke vii. 14; in John xi. 44. It would be inquisitive to speculate concerning the state of the souls which had been separated for a short time.

26. Ἡ φήμη, *the fame*) see ver. 31.—τὴν γῆν ἐκείνην, *that land*) St Matthew, therefore, did not write this book in *that land*. See ver. 31, ch. xiv. 34, 35, iv. 25.

27. Τυφλοὶ, *blind men*) Many blind men received faith, and afterwards sight. Without doubt they sought for sight, more especially on the ground that, being alive at that time, they might see the Messiah; and they did see Him with joy incredible.—ἐλέησον ἡμᾶς, *have mercy upon us*) An expressive formula, containing a confession of misery, and a prayer for free mercy. Even those who are without have employed this

---

[1] It more than once happened, that a person came to know that he had faith only when the Saviour announced the fact to him, and not before.— V. g.

[2] In the original, "certus ad miraculum accedit"—a phrase which loses half its force in the translation.—(I. B.)

form of prayer.¹—υἱὲ Δαυίδ, *son of David*) that is, Christ. See ch. i. 1 and xxii. 42.²

28. Ἐλθόντι, *when he was come*) They persevered in praying.—δύναμαι, *I am able*) The object of faith.

29. Κατὰ, *according to*) He says this by way of affirmation, not of limitation.—γενηθήτω, *let it be done*, or *let it become*) corresponding with the Hebrew יְהִי.³

30. Ἀνεῴχθησαν, *were opened*) The same verb is used also in the case of ears, Mark vii. 34, 35, and of the mouth, Luke i. 64.—ἐνεβριμήσατο, *straitly charged*) perhaps lest an opportunity might be given to the Pharisees. Cf. ver. 34.⁴—ὁρᾶτε, *see*) A word used absolutely; for neither does the following imperative depend on this.

32. Προσήνεγκαν Αὐτῷ, κ.τ.λ., *they brought to Him*, etc.) One who could scarcely come of his own accord.

33. Ἰσραήλ, *Israel*) In the nation in which so many wonderful things had been seen.

34. Ἐν τῷ ἄρχοντι, *through the prince*) The Pharisees could not deny the magnitude of our Lord's miracles; they ascribe them, therefore, to a great author, though an evil one.⁵

35. Τῆς βασιλείας, *of the kingdom*) sc. of God.—πᾶσαν, κ.τ.λ., *every*, etc.) sc. of all who were brought to Him.

36. Ἐσπλαγχνίσθη, *He was moved with compassion*) The disposition of Jesus was most fruitful in works of mercy.⁶—ἐσκυλμένοι,

---

¹ For instance, the woman of Canaan, the father of the lunatic, the ten lepers, etc.—V. g.

² It was distressing to them, that, though living at that very time, in which the Son of David, who had been so long looked for, was living in the world, they were yet not permitted even to see Him.—V. g.

³ Used in the celebrated passage, Genesis i. 3, "And GOD said, '*Let there be Light:*'—and *there was* Light."—(I. B.)

⁴ It would have been better for them to have obeyed His injunction of silence: and yet their conduct is not without affording us means of inferring, how great is the effect which the power of Christ has on those who have experienced it.—V. g.

⁵ At a subsequent period they even more wantonly poured out bitter remarks of this kind. Yet, however great their wickedness, they were at least more clear-sighted than those, who acknowledge the reality of neither demons, nor demoniacal possession, nor expulsion.—V. g.

⁶ It was a striking work of mercy to bring wretched souls to a state of spiritual soundness by praying or teaching.—V. g.

tired out) walking with difficulty; a word especially suitable to this passage, concerning which see the Gnomon Mark v. 35. The reading, ἐκλελυμένοι, is clearly deficient in authority.[1]—ἐρριμμένοι, *cast down*) i.e. lying down. A further step in the path of misery,[2] and yet such a condition is already the prelude of approaching help. Cf. concerning the harvest, John iv. 35.—ὡσεὶ πρόβατα μὴ ἔχοντα ποιμένα, *as sheep not having a shepherd*) Cf Num. xxvii. 17, S. V.—ὡσεὶ πρόβατα οἷς οὐκ ἔστι ποιμήν, *as sheep for whom there is not a shepherd.*—ποιμήν is properly *a shepherd of sheep*. Concerning sheep, cf. ch. x. 6.

37. Ὁ μὲν θερισμὸς, κ.τ.λ., *The harvest indeed*, etc.) He repeated the same words[3] to the Seventy; see Luke x. 2.—θερισμὸς, *harvest*) i.e. in the New Testament, for in the Old Testament it was the time for sowing. See John iv. 35, 36. And again, the present time is the season of sowing; the end of the world the harvest.—πολὺς, *plenteous*) See ch. x. 23.—ἐργάται, *labourers*) Fit persons to whom the work should be entrusted.

38. Δεήθητε, *pray ye*) See of how great value prayers are. The Lord of the harvest Himself wishes Himself to be moved by them. More blessings, without doubt, would accrue to the human race, if more men would, on men's behalf,[4] meet the ever ready will of GOD. See Gnomon on 1 Tim. ii. 3. The reaping and sowing is for our advantage. The Lord Himself exhorts us to entreat Him. He prevents us, that He may teach us to prevent Him.[5] (Cf. John xvi. 5.) And forthwith,

---

[1] E. M. ἐκλελυμένοι.—(I. B.)

BCDabc ('vexati') Vulg. Hil. read ἐσκυλμένοι: d. 'fatigati.' Rec. Text has ἐκλελυμένοι, evidently a marginal gloss to get rid of the strange expression, ἐσκυλμένοι. Σκύλλω Th. σκῦλον, *torn off skin*, as *exuviæ* from *exuo*. Here, worn out, as tired sheep, with the φόρτια of the Pharisees.—ED.

[2] In this condition properly are those, who are destitute of the knowledge of Christ.—V. g.

[3] After the lapse of a year.—B. H. E. p. 288.

[4] Those who are nearer to God praying in behalf of those who are further removed from Him.—V. g.

[5] *Prevent* is here used in the old Engl. sense of *anticipate, be before another in doing a thing;* as in the Book of Common Prayer, "*Prevent* us, O Lord, in all our doings with thy most gracious favour." God would have us also, *as it were*, prevent Him, or be the first to ask those things, which He really knoweth and willeth to give us before we either desire or ask them, Isa. xli. 21, xliii. 26.—ED.

whilst He is commanding us to pray, He implants the desire, to which it is He too that hearkens. See ch. x. 1. These same persons who are commanded to pray [for labourers], are presently appointed labourers themselves (ibid.)—Κυρίου, *the Lord*) see ch. x. 1, xiii. 37. Christ is the Lord of the harvest.— ὅπως ἐκβάλλῃ,[1] *to send forth*) ἐκβάλλειν[2] does not always imply force, as it does in ver. 33.

CHAPTER X.

1. Καί, *and*) This is clearly connected with the end of ch. ix., as the repeated mention of *sheep* indicates. He sends, before He is greatly entreated to do so.—προσκαλεσάμενος, *having called to Him*) solemnly.[3] All did not hear and see all things together.—τοὺς δώδεκα μαθητάς, *the twelve disciples*)[4] In the following verse they are called *the twelve apostles*. Matthew the *apostle* calls them *apostles* once, sc. in the present passage, where they

[1] E. M. ἐκβάλῃ.—(I. B.)

[2] See Author's Preface, Sect. xiv. and footnotes.—(I. B.)

[3] This is that remarkable embassy or mission, to which the Lord appeals in Luke xxii. 35. He sent forth the Seventy also without purse, scrip, and shoes, Luke x. 4. But in Luke xxii. 35 He is speaking not of the Seventy, but of the Apostles. We have the return of the Apostles recorded in Mark vi. 30, Luke ix. 10. In the intervening period, the Lord is represented more than once as having had the disciples present with Him, Matt. xii. 1, 49, xiii. 10; Mark vi. 1. I feel well persuaded, that no considerable portion of that time elapsed, without the Saviour having had present with Him at least some of His Apostles, as witnesses of those most important things, which He during that time both spake and performed. Nor even was the whole body of the Apostles long away from Him; comp. ver. 23. Meanwhile they returned one after the other: in which way it may have happened that *some* individuals out of the Twelve are named οἱ δώδεκα ; or even it may have been that, coming and going from time to time, they took their turns with the Lord, when making His journeys, until at length it was the privilege of them all to be with Him together again. It seems indeed to be tacitly intimated in Luke ix. 10, that their actual return took place somewhat earlier, their narration or report of their proceedings following subsequently more than once.—*Harm.*, p. 292.

[4] The election of whom as Apostles, the sacred writer takes for granted as having taken place before the sermon on the mountain.—V. g.

are first *sent* forth; St Mark does so once (vi. 30), and that when they just returned from that *mission;* John, the apostle, never does so; for in ch. xiii. 16 he uses the word in its general, not its particular meaning; St Luke does so in his Gospel particularly, but only on occasions, and those the same as Matthew and Mark, or *subsequently*, for other weighty reasons: see Luke vi. 13, ix. 10, xi. 49, xvii. 5, xxii. 14, xxiv. 10. For they were, during the whole of the period which the Gospels embrace, *disciples, i.e. scholars*, and are therefore so called. But, after the advent of the Paraclete, in the Acts and Epistles they are never called disciples, but apostles. In the Acts, those only are called *disciples*, who had either *learnt with* the apostles, or were then *learning from* the apostles, and were apostolic men, and the seed of all Christian posterity; see Acts vi. 1, xxi. 16. After which last passage the word disciple does not occur again in the New Testament: but they are called *brethren, Christians, believers* (fideles), *saints*, etc.—ἔδωκεν, κ.τ.λ.., *He gave*, etc.) The apostles made gradual progress. Great is the *authority* of conferring authority.[1]—αὐτοῖς, *to them*) The disciples, when in the Lord's presence, were employed in miracles only to a certain extent, as in ch. xiv. 19 and xvii. 27; but they did not themselves perform miracles (see ch. xvii. 18), unless when sent forth by Christ (see Luke x. 17), or after the departure of Christ; see John xiv. 12.—πνευμάτων, *of spirits*) i.e. against *spirits.*—ἀκαθάρτων, *unclean*) A frequent epithet: sometimes they are called πνεύματα πονηρά, *evil spirits.*—θεραπεύειν, *to heal*) sc. in His name: see ch. ix. 35.

2. Τὰ ὀνόματα, *the names*) Scripture, in enumerations of this kind, preserves an accurate order. See Gen. xlviii. 20; Num. xii. 1; and, "Noah, Daniel, and Job," in Ezek. xiv. 14, 20. Therefore the plan which is observed in the list of the apostles, princes of the kingdom of Christ, is of far graver import than any precedence of the kings of the world (as, for example, Peter is named *first*, not without an indication of rank):[2] nor is there

---

[1] *i e. His* great authority is evinced in the fact of His being able to give *them* authority to do all these miracles.—ED.

[2] In the original, "non sine indicio ordinis." In the notes to his German Version he says, on the words "*Der erste,*" "the first," *In der That war* SIMON *den andern überlegen: wiewel das der Stuhl zu* ROM *nichts angehet.*"

anything fortuitous in it. It is not said, "*Bartholomew, Peter, Jude, John, Andrew, Matthew*," etc.: and the four, as it were, *locations* of them, are deserving of observation:—

(I.) Matthew x. 2.	(II.) Mark iii. 16.	(III.) Luke vi. 14.	(IV.) Acts i. 13, 26.
1. Simon,	1. Simon,	1. Simon,	1. Peter,
2. And Andrew,	2. And James,	2. And Andrew,	2. And James,
3. James,	3. And John,	3. James,	3. And John,
4. And John,	4. And Andrew, (See also Ib. xiii. 3.)	4. And John,	4. And Andrew,
5. Philip,	5. And Philip,	5. Philip,	5. Philip,
6. And Bartholomew,	6. And Bartholomew,	6. And Bartholomew,	6. And Thomas,
7. Thomas,	7. And Matthew,	7. Matthew,	7. Bartholomew,
8. And Matthew,	8. And Thomas,	8. And Thomas,	8. And Matthew,
9. James the son of Alphaeus,	9. And James the son of Alphaeus,	9. James the son of Alphaeus,	9. James the son of Alphaeus,
10. And Lebbaeus,	10. And Thaddaeus,	10. And Simon Zelotes,	10. And Simon Zelotes,
11. Simon the Canaanite,	11. And Simon the Canaanite,	11. Judas the brother of James,	11. And Judas the brother of James;
12. And Judas Iscariot.	12. And Judas Iscariot.	12. And Judas Iscariot.	12. Matthias.

The first and the third arrangements enumerate them by pairs, the second singly, the fourth mixedly. The first and third arrangements correspond generally to the time of their vocation, and the conjunction of the apostles in twos; the second, to their dignity before our Lord's passion; the fourth, to their dignity after His ascension. All the arrangements may be divided into three quaternions, none of which interchanges any name with either of the others.[1] Again, Peter stands always first in the first quaternion, Philip in the second (cf. John i. 42, 44, xii. 22), James the son of Alphaeus in the third; though, within their several quaternions, the other apostles exchange their relative position [in the different lists]. The traitor stands always last.

"SIMON *was in reality superior to the other* [apostles], *though that* [fact] *does not in any way concern the See of* ROME."—See Gnomon below on $\pi\rho\tilde{\omega}\tau o\varsigma$.— (I. B.)

[1] *i.e.* No one of the three quaternions allows a name found in it to be exchanged for a name found in one of *the other* two quaternions; though the names are varied as to their order *in the same* quaternion by the different writers.—ED.

The plan of the first and third quaternions is contained in what I have just said: in the second, Matthew places himself modestly after his[1] Thomas, thus proving himself to be the writer of the book; for both Mark and Luke put Thomas after Matthew, although St Luke, after the confirmation of Thomas's faith (John xx. 27, 28), puts him, in the Acts, even above Bartholomew, and associates him with Philip. From the first quaternion we have the writings of Peter and John; from the second, that of Matthew; from the third, those of James and Jude, or Thaddeus. St John has not enumerated the apostles in his Gospel, but he has done so by implication in the Apocalypse; see Rev. xxi. 19, 20, and my German, Exposition of it.—πρῶτος, *first*) On the primacy of Peter, see Luke viii. 45, ix. 32; John i. 42; Matt. xvi. 16; John xxi. 15; Acts i. 15, ii. 14, viii. 14, x. 5, xv. 7. He was, however, first *among* the apostles, not placed *over* the apostles: *in* the apostolate, not *above* it. What is this to the Pope of Rome? Not more than to any other bishop; nay, even less.—ὁ λεγόμενος Πέτρος, *who is called Peter*) A surname which became afterwards better known.[2]

3. Ὁ τοῦ Ζεβεδαίου, *the son of Zebedee*) To distinguish him from James the son of Alphaeus.—ὁ τελώνης, *the publican*) A humble confession of the Evangelist concerning himself. He does not call Peter, Andrew, etc., *the fishermen:* but he does call himself *the publican.*

Λεββαῖος, *Lebbaeus*) According to Hiller, Thaddaeus, derived from the Chaldee תד, *bosom*, and Lebbaeus, from the Hebrew לב, *heart*, are synonymous terms, and denote a *man of much heart:*[3] see Onomata Sacra, p. 123. So *Thomas* means the same thing as *Didymus.* Those copies[4] which have in this passage only Λεββαῖος, are supported by the list of the apostles which

---

[1] "Thomam suum," *his* Thomas. *i.e.* his associate in the lists; Matthew and Thomas being placed together in all of them.—(I. B.)

[2] *i.e.* better known than the *name* "Simon," which he had received at his circumcision.—(I. B.)

[3] "Hominem pectorosum," lit. in classical Latin, a man of broad, large, or high breast.—(I. B.)

[4] The reading of E. M. is "καὶ Λεββαῖος ὁ ἐπικληθεὶς Θαδδαῖος."—(I. B.)

So the margin of Bengel's larger Ed., though in the text there stood Θαδ-

Cotelerius[1] has published with the apostolical constitutions, and by Hesychius in the article Ἰαρα.[2] As this reading is shorter and *middle*,[3] it appears to be the right one. Some persons having appended the disputed clause from the parallel passage of Mark as a gloss, others introduced it into the text from the same source. Their reading considers *Thaddaeus* as a *surname*, and *Lebbaeus* as the *name* of this apostle: His *name*, however, in reality was *Judas* the brother *of James*: but he was called *Lebbaeus* by name, as it were to distinguish him from Judas Iscariot.[4]

δαῖος. The first Ed. of the Gnomon gives the palm to the shorter reading, Λεββαῖος. So marg. of Ed. 2 and Vers. Germ., leaving it however to the decision of the reader, whether the words ὁ ἐπικληθεὶς Θαδδαῖος are to be accepted or rejected. Michaelis, in his Einleitung, T. ii., p. m. 1687, etc., shows, by many proofs, that Judas the brother of James is the same as Thaddeus and Lebbeus, and was called among the Syrians Adai or Adæus.— E. B.

[1] COTELERIUS, alias JEAN BAPTISTE COTELIER, born at Nismes in 1627, was one of the most eminent critics of modern times. As a mere child, he was considered a prodigy of learning; and he sustained this reputation at the Sorbonne, where he took the degree of Batchelor. In 1667 the great Minister Colbert selected him, together with the celebrated Du Cange, to examine and catalogue the Greek MSS. of the Royal Library. The able manner in which he performed this task procured him, in 1676, the Professorship of Greek in the Royal College at Paris. His labours were many and valuable. He died in 1686.—(I. B.)

[2] The passage referred to does not really occur under "Ιαρα, but under 'Ιάκωβος, which is by mistake placed out of its alphabetical order. The article on "Ιαρα consists of a single line, viz. 'Ιαρα αἷμα ἢ μοῖρα.

Then follow immediately the words referred to by Bengel: 'Ιάκωβος 'Αλφαίου. ὁ καὶ Θαδδαῖος καὶ Λευί, παρὰ τῷ Μάρκῳ, παρὰ δὲ τῷ Ματθαίῳ Λεββαῖος. παρὰ δὲ Λουκᾷ, 'Ιούδας 'Ιακώβου.

In the note on Hesychius (Ed. Lugd. Bat. 1776), vol. xi. col. 10, are these words—

Nullus dubito quin diversos hic confuderit Glossæ hujus insititiæ auctor, ex male intellecto Veteris cujusdam Scriptoris apostolicorum nominum laterculo, qualem ex MS. codice Bibliothecæ Regiæ protulit Cotelerius ad lib. ii. *Constitut. Apostol.* c. 63, p. 264, ed. Cleric.—(I. B.)

[3] "Media." See Author's Preface, viii. 14. and footnote in voc.—(I. B.)

[4] Lachm. with Bc Vulg. reads Καὶ Θαδδαῖος. Tischend. with D and MSS. in August. reads Καὶ Λεββαῖος. *ab* have Judas. Mill attributes the reading Λεββαῖος here to some one wishing to call attention to the fact, that Mark and Luke call Matthew Λευί, *Levi*. It seems hard to account for the introduction of such a reading, if not genuine: and yet the weight of autho-

4. Ἰσκαριώτης, *Iscariot*) so called from the village of Iscariot in the tribe of Ephraim, as Jerome says on the beginning of Isaiah xxviii. Louis de Dieu, on Acts i. 16, says, "In the Æthiopic language, I find אִשְׂכָּבָה for *a bag or pouch to carry money in*: for thus the translator has rendered τὸ γλωσσόκομον (*the bag*) in John xii. 6, and xiii. 29.—Hence may be derived, without any impropriety, אִישְׁכַּרְיוּתָא (Iscariota), ὁ ἔχων γλωσσόκομον, *he who hath the bag.*—ὁ καὶ, *who also*) The word *also* implies that Judas was best known and most easily distinguished by *the betrayal.*—παραδοὺς, *betrayed*) By the mention of his treason, it is silently intimated that Matthias, whom St Luke mentions by name in the Acts, was his successor in the apostolate.

5, 6. Ὁδὸν—πόλιν—οἶκον, *way—city—house*) The apostles were sometimes obliged to tread the roads of the Samaritans in their journeys;[1] but there was the less need for them to enter their cities, and stay there, because the Lord had preached to them in His journey (see John iv.), and the apostles also were afterwards to come to them. The first of these injunctions regards this first legation; most of the rest apply equally to the whole office of the apostolate, to which the twelve are introduced on the present occasion; cf. ver. 18. Our Lord gave nearly the same commands to the seventy disciples; Luke x. 1–11.

6. Πρόβατα, *sheep*) See ch. ix. 36.—ἀπολωλότα, *lost*) He uses this expression in preference to *led astray*: cf. ch. xviii. 12, 14. The apostles would find sufficient occupation in attending to these.—Ἰσραήλ, *Israel*) from which the Samaritans had departed.

7. Πορευόμενοι, *as ye go*) Answering to πορεύεσθε (*go ye*), in ver. 6.—κηρύσσετε, *preach ye*) Here were the disciples going forth like students in theology, who practise the rudiments of the ministry and perform the functions of curates, and afterwards return to receive further instruction.[2]—ἤγγικεν, *is at hand*) This

rities are for Καὶ Σαδδαῖος here, which otherwise might well be a transcriber's or harmonist's correction from Mark iii. 18; Λεββαῖος, as the less open to suspicion of transcribers' corrections, being accounted as the genuine reading. Jerome calls him τριώνυμος, *triple-named;* so that in his day Lebbeus must have been a recognised name either here or in Mark, as well as Thaddeus and Judas.—ED.

[1] Inasmuch as Samaria was situated between Judea and Galilee.—V. g.

[2] They themselves, in fact, were as yet destitute of perfect knowledge of Jesus Christ, who not until afterwards instructed them more distinctly con-

was to be the burden and sum of their discourses;[1] cf. Mark vi. 12.

8. Ἀσθενοῦντας—δαιμόνια, *sick—devils*) An ascending gradation: cf. ver. 1, where the highest grade is put first.—δωρεὰν, *gratuitously*) This is not inconsistent with the conclusion of ver. 10. Hire is due for labour, but miracles and gifts of grace ought not to be sold.

9. Μὴ κτήσησθε, κ.τ.λ., *do not procure*, etc.) Thus they were taught apostolic contentedness.[2] They were permitted to use what they already possessed, but not to procure any thing new.—χρυσὸν—ἄργυρον—χαλκὸν, *gold—silver—brass*) i.e., money, large or small.—εἰς τὰς ζώνας, *into your girdles*) which served also for purses.

10. Πήραν, *scrip*) in which bread and other articles of food were kept; see Mark vi. 8.—μηδὲ ῥάβδον, *nor staff*) In Mark vi. 8, we read "*but one staff*." He who had no staff, was not to care about procuring one, for our Lord says "do not procure;" he however who possessed a staff, might take it with him, for convenience, not defence.—ἄξιος γὰρ ὁ ἐργάτης, κ.τ.λ., *for the labourer is worthy*, etc.) On the other hand, the hire is worthy of the labourer.—τροφῆς, *food*) This word includes all the articles which are enumerated in ver. 9, 10.

11. Ἐξετάσατε, *search out*) sc. by asking others, and by spiritual examination. The godly are easily discovered by the godly, and in like manner the ungodly by the ungodly.— ἄξιος ἐστι, *is worthy*) sc. of being your host.—κἀκεῖ μείνατε, *and there remain*) sc. in the house of that man, until you leave the

---

cerning His passion, death, and resurrection. In the meantime, their preaching, confirmed as it was by very many miracles, prepared the minds of men, so as that they subsequently, without difficulty, yielded themselves up to obey Him, on His advent among them, of whom the hope had been presented to them by this preparatory announcement. Comp. ver. 23.— *Harm.*, p. 293.

[1] Which exhorted to repentance.—V. g.

[2] "Sic didicere αὐτάρκειαν apostolicam." The word αὐτάρκεια, implies not merely the patient endurance of penury or privation, but such a state of mind and habit of acting and judging as would actually render the individual sufficiently fed, clothed, etc., and fully satisfied with that which would not meet the exigencies of another. The sense of *Independence*, so frequent in the classical writers, is not wholly abandoned.—(I. B.)

city.¹ A change of houses might have the appearance of fastidiousness.²

12. Ἀσπάσασθε, *salute*) i.e. say שלום, *peace*, mentioned in ver. 13, *i.e.* salvation. Our Lord adopted formulæ and ceremonies already observed, but He elevated them to a higher use.

13. Ἐὰν μὲν, κ.τ.λ., *if indeed*, etc.) i.e. if they receive you.—ἐλθέτω—ἐπιστραφήτω, *let it come—let it return to*) The imperative may here be taken in its strict sense. *If you pray for it, let it come. If you are not unwilling, let it return.* So bear yourselves, that [in the one case] it may come [upon the house], that [in the other] it may return [to you]. Impart your salutation to them with ready good-will, or take it back to yourselves.³—ἡ εἰρήνη ὑμῶν, *your peace*) sc. that of which you are the messengers.—ἐὰν δὲ, κ.τ.λ., *but if*, etc.) contrary to your expectation.—πρὸς ὑμᾶς ἐπιστραφήτω, *let it return to you*) By a testimony of duty performed, and an increase of tranquillity and spiritual power. That which has once gone forth from the wealth of God, has not gone forth in vain, but assuredly finds some one whom it may reach. A consolation for ministers who appear to themselves to produce no edification. The Lord says to them thus, "They have despised it; have it yourselves."⁴

14. Ὅς ἐὰν, *whosoever*) whatever householder or magistrate.—ἐξερχόμενοι, *when ye depart*) The ignorance of men was not yet invincible. At present, in a greater multitude of labourers and hearers, it is not necessary to depart.⁵—ἤ, *or*) If you should

---

¹ A distinguishing privilege was thereby granted to those who were their "first-fruits" in each city.—V. g.

² In the original, "potuisset præbere speciem hominum delicatorum," where it is difficult to find an exact equivalent to "delicatorum:" though one is naturally reminded of Luke vii. 25, q. v.—(I. B.)

³ This was, as it were, a prelude to the loosing and binding (c. xviii. 18).—V. g.

⁴ In his German Version he says, "you must not distress (*kränken*) yourselves. That which others reject becomes thereby a greater blessing to you."—(I. B.)

⁵ Beng. seems to mean, There was not then, as yet, the invincible ignorance of men to contend with, that there is now: it was wilful unbelief; and in such a case it was their duty not to waste time, as the spiritual labourers were few, but to depart. In our day, on the other hand, where the numbers of both spiritual labourers and their hearers are many, it is not the duty of the former to depart, though many *wilfully* harden themselves, for there are

not be admitted into any house of the city.—*χονιορτόν, dust*) Because punishment (ver. 15) would overtake the very dust of the *land* trodden by the feet of the impious, from which the apostles would wish to be altogether free; see Acts xiii. 51; cf. Matt. xviii. 6; Mark vi. 11. That seeing your determination, they may know it has been said to them as *a testimony against them.* The action combined with the word moves both spectators and auditors; see Neh. v. 13.—*τῶν ποδῶν, your feet*) This depends upon *ἐκτινάξατε, shake off from.* Guilt is supposed to adhere to the feet or shoes; see 1 Kings ii. 5. Therefore the apostles ought to declare, by shaking the dust from their feet, that the fault of those who did not listen has been removed from them.

15. *Ἀνεκτότερον, more tolerable*) Therefore it is worse *not to believe the Gospel*, than to imitate the men of Sodom; see ch. xi. 22, 24. There appears to be an hypallage, viz.: that city shall, on the day of judgment, undergo a heavier punishment than the land of Sodom and Gomorrha either endured of old, or shall receive at the judgment. If merely a brief[1] repulse shall be so heavily punished, what shall be their fate who resist more obstinately.

16. *Ἰδοὺ, behold*) Behold is frequently used for pointing out a thing which is present.—*ἐγὼ, I*) your Lord. Do not hesitate. I give you a safe conduct.—*πρόβατα, sheep*) unarmed.—*ἐν μέσῳ, in the midst*) not *into* the midst, for you are already among wolves.—*λύκων, of wolves*) who will be unwilling that the *lost sheep*, mentioned in ver. 6, be brought back; cf. ch. vii. 15, concerning false prophets, although here the appellation "*wolves*" has a wider signification.—*γίνεσθε, become ye*) In exhortations this word is frequently used rather than *ἔστε, be ye.* Go forth as such, and show yourselves to be so.—*ὡς οἱ ὄφεις, as serpents*) The godly often appear to the ungodly as serpents, and thus

---

others who labour under ignorance, and it is the minister's duty to labour to overcome that ignorance, which, though invincible in itself, can be overcome by the Spirit of God.—ED.

[1] In the original, "Si perbrevis repulsa tam graviter punietur:" where "*perbrevis,*" "*very short,*" does not imply that the impenitence and unbelief of the persons indicated was of short continuance, but that their actual refusal to receive the Gospel occupied only the same time as the *brief* visit of the Apostles whom they rejected.—(I. B.)

vanquish the old serpent.—καί, *and*) Thus David was at the same time prudent and simple towards Saul,[1]—ἀκέραιοι, *without horn*) hoof, tooth, or sting; both actively and passively harmless. Many words of this kind have at the same time both an active and a passive signification; cf. Gnomon on Rom. xvi. 19.

17. Προσέχετε δὲ ἀπὸ τῶν ἀνθρώπων, *but beware of men*) The expression used in the last verse, "Be ye wise," is now explained; and the force of the injunction is extended,[2] for the word *men* is of general signification; cf. John ii. 24.[3]—συνέδρια—συναγωγαῖς, *councils—synagogues*) The councils, where the chief men assemble; the synagogues, where the people also resort.—ἐν ταῖς συναγωγαῖς, *in the synagogues*) They will consider the action so holy, that it may be performed even in the *synagogue*, which is put in opposition to *the council*; see ch. xxiii. 34.—μαστιγώσουσιν, *they shall scourge*) Hard things are foretold, yet they were actually endured by the apostles, and even by our Lord Himself.

18. Δὲ, *but*) The particle is here used epitatically,[4] to denote a further step in the subject announced.—ἀχθήσεσθε, *ye shall be brought*) The apostles did not come ultroneously to the rulers, they were brought.—αὐτοῖς, *against them*) sc. the Jews, in contradistinction to the Gentiles mentioned immediately afterwards. —καὶ τοῖς ἔθνεσιν, *and the Gentiles*) This chapter therefore already contemplates matters more remote, and refers to the apostolate after our Lord's ascension.

19. Μὴ μεριμνήσητε, *Be not careful*) Your only care must be to be without care. We are not forbidden by this passage from all preparation; see 1 Tim. iv. 15, cf. Luke xxi. 14; 1 Cor. xiv. 26.

---

[1] It not seldom happens that one finds others, as it were, altogether the counterpart of one's self. But it is of use to remember, that many are worse than yourself, and some perhaps better.—V. g.

[2] In the original, "Declaratur τὸ *prudentes*: acceditque moniti extensio." —(I. B.)

[3] How strong are the reasons for being on our guard against men, is especially then made manifest, when one has to be conversant (to have intercourse) with them at a time of their being under the constraint of no external consideration.—V. g.

[4] See Append. on Epitasis. An emphatic addition to an enunciation already made.—ED.

But on a sudden emergency, even in these times, a faithful professor should not be anxious as to what he has to say.—ἢ, *or*) *Care* is elegantly mentioned; where, however, the "*what*" (*quid*, τί) is supplied, there the "*how*"[1] (*quomodo*, πῶς) is not wanting. The "*how or what*" includes whatever can fall under the idea of care; therefore, especially also the words, concerning which many, who have the matter ready, are wont to be over anxious. The Spirit does not speak without words; see ver. 20: and in Luke xxi. 15, we read, "I will give you a mouth and wisdom." Analogous combinations, under other circumstances, occur in John viii. 28, xii. 49, 50; Rom. viii. 26; 1 Pet. i. 11. The doctrine of verbal inspiration is not inferred from the difference of the words *how* and *what*, but from the promise itself.—ἐν ἐκείνῃ τῇ ὥρᾳ, *in that hour*) even though not before. Many feel most strongly their spiritual power when the hour arrives of imparting it to others.—τί, *what*) for ὅ, *that which*.—Cf. ch. xv. 32, and Luke xvii. 8.

20. Οἱ λαλοῦντες, *that speak*) A similar use of the article occurs in John vi. 63.—ἐν ὑμῖν, *in you*) As instruments.

21. Ἀδελφὸς, *the brother*) Those who are most near, are most easily divided.—θανατώσουσιν, *shall cause to be put to death*) By an atrocious death, even by the agency of the magistrates.

22. Διὰ τὸ ὄνομά Μου, *for My name's sake*) which the world hates.—οὗτος, κ.τ.λ., *this man*, etc.) truly. This is one of the apothegms which our Lord uttered more than once.—See ch. xxiv. 13.

23. Τὴν ἄλλην—κἂν ἐκ ταύτης διώκωσιν ὑμᾶς φεύγετε εἰς ἑτέραν, *the other*[2]—*and if they persecute you from this city, flee ye into another*) This is the most ancient Latin reading,[3] and also that of Origen[4] contra Celsum (p. 51, Ed. Hoesch.[5]), where, instead of "φεύγετε εἰς τὴν ἄλλην" [as in E.M.], we find "φεύγετε εἰς τὴν ἑτέραν· κἂν ἐν τῇ

---

[1] Referring to "HOW *or* WHAT ye shall speak."—(I. B.)

[2] E. V. *another.*—(I. B.)

[3] The words κἂν—ἑτέραν are not found in E. M.—(I. B.)

[4] ORIGEN was born at Alexandria, in Egypt, about A.D. 185; and died at Tyre, about A.D. 254.—(I. B.)

[5] DAVID HOESCHELIUS, born at Augsburgh 1556. He was a laborious and successful Editor. Among the authors he edited were Origen, Philo-Judæus, Basil, and Photius. He died 1617.—(I. B.)

ἑτέρᾳ διώκωσι, πάλιν φεύγετε εἰς τὴν ἄλλην." *Flee ye into the other;*[1] *and if they persecute you in that other, flee ye again into the other.*[2] Francis Lucas[3] of Bruges quotes old Latin Codices in favour of that reading. Thence, too, the Anglo-Saxon version has—"*and thonne hi on thære eowv ehtath, fleoth on tha thryddan;*" *i.e.* "*and when they persecute you in that* [city], *flee to the third.*" Ambrose[4] also, in his treatise, *De Fugâ Seculi* (ch. 4), says, "But if they shall persecute you in one, flee ye into another." And Juvencus[5] renders the passage thus:—

"Profugite e tectis quæ vos sectabitur urbis
    Inde aliam, mox INDE ALIAM, conquirite sedem."

"*Flee from the roofs of the city which persecutes you; thence seek another, and* THEN AGAIN ANOTHER *abode.*" Thus Augustine; thus the Armenian Version. The Codex Cantabrigiensis, the Codices Colbertini 2467 and 3947, Parisiensis 6, and the Codex Stephani η (to which some add the Codex Gonvillianus), contain this passage in various forms of words. The variety of the Greek words[6] suggests the suspicion that this verse has been

---

[1] τὴν ἑτέραν.—ἕτερος signifies originally, *other* in opposition to *one*, though it has also the force of *other* in opposition to *many*.—(I. B.)

[2] τὴν ἄλλην.—ἄλλος signifies originally, *other* in opposition to *many*, though it is used also to represent *other* in opposition to *one*. Here τὴν ἄλλην appears to have the force of *the former*.—(I. B.)

[3] FRANCIS LUCAS was born at Bruges in the sixteenth century. He studied under Arius Montanus, and became a Doctor of Louvain, and Dean of the Church of St Omer. He was profoundly skilled in the Greek, Hebrew, Syriac, and Chaldee languages, and is considered a judicious critic. He died in 1619.—(I. B.)

[4] Born at Treves A.D. 340; consecrated, in 374, Bishop of Milan, where he died in 397. He was an eloquent preacher, and an able and voluminous writer.—(I. B.)

[5] C. AQUILINUS VETTIUS (al. VECTIUS, or VESTIUS) JUVENCUS, a Spanish priest of good family, who flourished in the fourth century. He wrote, besides other works, a history of our Lord in good hexameter verse, considered both poetical and faithful, and published it about 330.—(I. B.)

[6] Lachm. reads ἑτέραν, with B*d* Orig. 1,295; 380; 3.473*c*; 709; cod. 4,398. But Tischend. ἄλλην, with D*abc* Vulg. Origen 3, 709, and Rec. Text. Lachm. adds in brackets, κἂν ἐν τῇ ἑτέρᾳ διώκωσιν ὑμᾶς, φεύγετε εἰς τὴν ἄλλην, with DL (ἐκ ταύτης, ἐκδιώξωσιν—τ. ἑτέραν) *ab* Orig. 1,295*b*; 380*a*; Hil. 656. But B*c* Vulg. and Rec. Text omit these words. Probably they come from a transcriber who fancied that φεύγετε εἰς τὴν ἑτέραν, so. "a second city," was incomplete without a clause, "And when they persecute you in

rendered from *Latin* into *Greek*: on the other hand, the antiquity and celebrity of the Latin text is proved by the very multitude and discrepancy of these Greek codices. The omission appears to have arisen from the carelessness so frequently manifested by transcribers, where similar words recur: the facility with which the mistake may occur, appears from the fact that Gelenius, in his Latin version of Origen, omits this very clause [which undoubtedly exists in the original]. Athanasius more than once substitutes ἑτέραν for ἄλλην, as is at present the case with the Codex Colbertinus, and from which you may conjecture, that another omission[1] might soon be made by other transcribers.

Οὐ μὴ τελέσητε, *ye shall not finish*[2]) cf. כָּלָה,[3] in 2 Chron. xxxi. 1. —τὰς πόλεις, *the cities*) not to say, *villages*, of Israel.—See ver. 6. Our Lord tells them that there was no fear of their not having where to preach, and that they were not to remain long in one place, as they would have the opportunity of remaining longer in other places.—ἕως ἂν ἔλθῃ ὁ Υἱὸς τοῦ ἀνθρώπου, *until the Son of Man be come*) Concerning this *coming*, see ver. 7, and xi. 1.[4]

25. Ὁ δοῦλος, κ.τ.λ., *the servant*, etc.) *i.e.* ἵνα ὁ δοῦλος γένηται ὡς ὁ κύριος αὐτοῦ, ἀρκετὸν αὐτῷ ἐστίν, *that the servant be as his lord, is sufficient for him*. An instance of *Zeugma*.—οἰκοδεσπότην, *master of the household*[5]) Jesus was indeed the Master of a household,

that *second* city, flee into *another, i.e.* a *third* city." To avoid the need for this, I believe the reading ἄλλην for ἑτέραν arose. The shorter is generally preferable to the longer reading, as it was the tendency of transcribers to insert all added matter, lest their copy should be incomplete.—ED.

[1] "hiatus," *hiatus, gap.* See Author's Preface viii. 14, and App. Crit. Part I. § xxii., obs. xxvii., etc.—(I. B.)

[2] E. V. *Ye shall not have gone over.*—(I. B.)

[3] כָּלָה—(1) To be completed, finished.—GESENIUS.—(I. B.)

[4] To wit, there is here meant that very advent, whereby, through His full presence, beneficence, and preaching, the preparatory announcement of His ambassadors in those days was, as it were, completed and fulfilled by Him, whom it behoved to come, to proclaim the Gospel, and to see that it was proclaimed by others, Matt. xi. 3, 5. In a similar manner, He commanded the Seventy disciples also to announce the approach of the divine kingdom, and followed up that announcement by His own very presence in those same places, Luke x. 1, 9.—*Harm.*, p. 293.

[5] In the original the word used is *pater-familias*, which is employed throughout the whole sentence.—(I. B.)

and brought up a large family of disciples (see Luke xxii. 35), affording the most perfect example of a domestic, as well as a solitary life; and He is also Master of the household of the whole Church.—Βεελζεβούλ, *Beelzebul*) Beelzebub was a god of Ekron; see 2 Kings i. 2. As the Greeks, however, seem to have been unable to pronounce the word *Beelzebub*, the LXX. rendered it Βααλμυῖαν (Baalmwian) : and the Evangelists also wrote it in Greek with a λ (*l*), instead of a β (*b*), as the final letter, on account, apparently, not of the derivation, but the pronunciation; just as the LXX. wrote Μελχόλ. (*Melchol*) for Michal. As this reason, however, did not hold good in other languages, translators have restored the original sound of the Hebrew word. The Jews, however, frequently employ the term זבל,[1] in contempt of idols; but the compound, בעל־זבל, is not found in Hebrew, although it is credible that the Hebrews who spoke Greek may have said Βεελζεβούλ for Βεελζεβούβ[2] the more willingly, on account of its resemblance to זבול.[2] Tertullian, when quoting Luke xi., in his work against Marcion, book iv., ch. 26, writes it, Beelzebul.—ἐκάλεσαν, κ.τ.λ., *have called*, etc.) See ch. ix. 34 and Mark iii. 22. They called Him Beelzebub, that is, the ally of Beelzebub.—πόσῳ μᾶλλον, *how much more*) The world hated Christ most and first; and it was the duty of His disciples to feel that they ought much more to endure that hatred, much less to refuse it.[3]—τοὺς οἰκιακοὺς αὐτοῦ, *his domestics*) *i.e.* they shall call them the domestics of Beelzebub.

26. Οὖν, *therefore*) although you will be hated.—οὐδὲν, *nothing*) Cf. Mark iv. 22; Luke xii. 2.—γάρ, κ.τ.λ., *for*, etc.) The world will not so quickly destroy you, by whom truth will be propagated far and wide.—κεκαλυμμένον, *covered*) *i.e.* removed from sight.—ἀποκαλυφθήσεται, *shall be uncovered*) especially in the time of the Messiah.—κρυπτόν, *hidden*) *i.e.* removed from hearing: cf. ver. 27.

---

[1] זבל,—(1) properly in my opinion, i.q. זבב *to be round, to make round*, whence the Talmudic זבל, זבל, round or globular dung, such as that of goats or camels.—GESENIUS.—(I. B.)

[2] זבו with the Kibbuts = זבול with the Shureq.—(I. B.)

[3] Those of Christ's household have less of the power which characterized their Master; and besides, they are not, as He was, without blemishes, and these last the world knows well how to upbraid them with.—V. g.

27. Οὕς, *ear*) sc. one, secretly.—ἐπὶ τῶν δωμάτων, *on the housetops*) A flat place, where men might converse, or even assemble as an audience: cf. 2 Sam. xvi. 22.[1]

28. Καὶ μὴ φοβηθῆτε, κ.τ.λ., *and be not afraid of*, etc.) The connection is as follows: He who publicly preaches hidden truth, him the world afflicts: he who fears God, ought to fear nothing except Him: he who does not fear God, fears everything except Him: see 1 Pet. iii. 14, 15.[2]—ἀπὸ, *of*) This preposition is not repeated. *I fear Him*, is a stronger phrase than *I am afraid of Him*.[3]—ἀποκτεινόντων,[4] *who kill*) From the root κτίω are derived κτένω, κτείνω, κτέννω. See Eustathius.—τὸν δυνάμενον, *Him who is able*[5]) and that too with the highest ability and authority (see Luke xii. 5), that is, GOD; see James iv. 12.—καὶ ψυχὴν καὶ σῶμα, *both soul and body*) the two essential parts of man.—ἀπολέσαι, *to destroy, to ruin*) It is not said *to kill*: the soul is immortal.—ἐν Γεέννῃ, *in hell*) It is not easy to preach the truth; and to none are severer precepts given than to the ministers of the Word, as is evident from the epistles to Timothy and Titus. The most efficacious stimulus is on this account employed. Many witnesses to the truth have been first excited, and afterwards led on, by the most fearful terrors from God.

29. Δύο στρουθία ἀσσαρίου, *two sparrows for a farthing*)[6] In Luke xii. 6, we read, *five sparrows for two farthings*. A reason why men are not to be feared.—ἓν, *one*) sc. one in preference

---

[1] He desires them to banish all fear from their minds.—V. g.

[2] The world admires the magnanimous spirit of those who fear nothing, and regards such a spirit worthy of heroes and great men. And yet the fear of GOD is the only heroism truly worthy of the name; and in the absence of it, all presence of mind, as it is called, is false, and only indicates reckless rashness.—V. g.

[3] i.e. Bengel would render the passage thus—"*Be not afraid of* them (μὴ φοβηθῆτε ἀπὸ τῶν) which kill the body, but are not able to kill the soul: but rather *fear* Him (φοβήθητε τὸν) which is able," etc.—(I. B.)

[4] E. M. ἀποκτεννόντων.—(I. B.)

[5] In the original there is a play on the words *potest* and *potestas*, which cannot be preserved in the translation. The passage runs thus—"*Eum qui potest*, et quidem cum summa *ἐξουσίᾳ, potestate*."—(I. B.)

[6] The ἀσσάριον, called λεπτὸν in Mark xii. 42, and rendered *mite* in that place and elsewhere by the E. V., was about $\frac{3}{330}$ of a farthing.—(I. B.)

to another.[1]—οὐ πεσεῖται, *shall not fall*) To fall on the ground is to die. The use of the future tense implies a condition: if it falls, it does not fall without your Father's permission.—ἄνευ τοῦ θελήματος τοῦ Πατρὸς ὑμῶν, *without the will of your Father*) This is the reading of Irenæus, Tertullian, Novatian, Cyprian, Hilary, Augustine, Cassiodorius; also of the Italic, Coptic, Arabic, Gothic, and Persic versions. It is therefore an ancient reading, and one too widely received to be accounted for on the hypothesis of its being a paraphrase, especially since the sense would be complete without the contested words " τοῦ θελήματος" (*the will of*), as the LXX. in Isa. xxxvi. 10[2] write ἄνευ Κυρίου, *without the Lord*, and the Hebrews say, מבלעדי שמיא, *without heaven*. The later Greeks omitted these words, τοῦ θελήματος, from the recurrence of the article τοῦ. The *numbered hairs* of the faithful, mentioned in the parallel passage of Luke xii. 7, correspond to this "*will*."[3]—ὑμῶν, *your*) not *their* Father.

30. Ὑμῶν, *your*) used antithetically.—αἱ τρίχες, *the hairs*) which you yourselves care little about. Who cares about the hairs once pulled out by the comb? A proverbial saying concerning a very small matter.

31. Πολλῶν, *many*) opposed to *one* in ver. 29.—ὑμεῖς, *you*) even each of you individually.

32. Ἐν, *in, on*) i.e., when the question is raised concerning Me. This "ἐν Ἐμοὶ," "*on Me*," differs from "Με," "*Me*," and "αὐτὸν," "*him*," in the next verse; cf. Luke xii. 8, 9.—ἀνθρώπων, *men*) Our Lord is speaking especially of persecutors.

33. Ἀρνήσομαι κἀγὼ αὐτὸ:,[4] *I also will deny him*) This order of the words, sc. "I-will-deny even-I-also him," which expresses more exactly the law of retribution, *jus talionis* (as in ver. 32), is supported by the Latin and Gothic versions,[5] by the Codex

---

[1] Bengel means, that this is a proof of God's individual providence even in matters relating to the brute creation.—(I. B.)

[2] In the Hebrew also, "without Jehovah."—(I. B.)

[3] BD Orig. (omitting ὑμῶν) Vulg. and Rec. Text, have ἄνευ τοῦ πατρὸς ὑμῶν. But "sine voluntate" is added by *abc* Hil. 657, 831 Iren. Cypr. 82, 121 (omitting 'vestri' before 'patris').—ED.

[4] E. M. ἀρνήσομαι αὐτὸν κἀγώ.—(I. B.)

[5] The Gothic version of the Bible was made from the Greek, both in the Old and in the New Testament, by Ulphilas, a celebrated bishop of the Mæso-Goths, who assisted at the Council of Constantinople in 359, and was

Byzantinus, and perhaps by other MSS. Such matters have been generally neglected by the collators of Codices. Others read ἀρνήσομαι αὐτὸν κἀγώ.[1]

34. Εἰρήνην, *peace*) sc. of the righteous with the wicked.—μάχαιραν, *a sword*) *i.e.*, violent division (called διαμερισμὸν in Luke xii. 51, xxii. 36), proceeding from the discord of families, mentioned in ver. 35, to wars and murders.

35. Διχάσαι, *to separate*) A necessary consequence of what precedes.—ἄνθρωπον, *a man*) sc. a son *who loves* Me; see ver. 37.—κατὰ, *against*) In this passage those are put in opposition, who are otherwise naturally most attached, to each other.

36. Ἐχθροὶ, *enemies*) A man shall have *them of his household*—his relations, servants, and acquaintances—for enemies, if he believes in Me; see Micah vii. 6.

37. Ὁ φιλῶν, κ.τ.λ., *he that loveth*, etc.) from aversion to the *sword* just mentioned. An ascending climax: to prefer Christ to parents, children, and, in the next verse, himself.

38. Τὸν σταυρὸν, *his cross*) The cross, which was unused by the Jews as a punishment, was not employed proverbially to denote

---

sent on an embassy to the Emperor Valens, about the year 378. He is said to have embraced Arianism, and to have propagated Arian tenets among his countrymen. Besides translating the *entire* Bible into the Gothic language, Ulphilas is said to have conferred on the Mæso-Goths the invention of the Gothic characters. The character, however, in which this version of the New Testament is written, is, in fact, the Latin character of that age; and the degree of perfection which the Gothic language had obtained during the time of Ulphilas, is a proof that it had then been written for some time. The translation of Ulphilas (who had been educated among the Greeks) was executed from the Greek; but, from its coincidence in many instances with the Latin, there is reason to suspect that it has been interpolated, though at a remote period, from the Vulgate. Its unquestionable antiquity, however, and its general fidelity, have concurred to give this version a high place in the estimation of biblical critics; but, unfortunately, it has not come down to us entire. The only parts extant in print are, a fragment of the book of Nehemiah, a considerable portion of the four Gospels, and some portions of the apostolic epistles. The most distinguished manuscript of the Gothic version of Ulphilas is the justly celebrated CODEX ARGENTEUS, now preserved in the Library of the University of Upsal, in Sweden."—*Hartwell Horne*, vol. ii. p. 240.—(I. B.)

[1] The order κἀγώ αὐτὸν is supported by BDΔ Vulg. *abc* Orig. 1, 298*d*, 3.543*b*, Hil. 985, Cypr. But Rec. Text αὐτὸν κἀγώ, with Orig. 1,296*b*. Orig. 3,543*b* puts the ἀρνήσομαι after αὐτόν.—ED.

extreme adversity: our Lord therefore, in this passage, alludes to His own Cross, which He was already bearing in secret.—λαμβάνει, *taketh*) sc. willingly.

39. Ψυχὴν, *soul*) *i.e.*, man with respect to his natural life, himself; cf. Luke ix. 24, 25.—ἕνεκεν Ἐμοῦ, *for My sake*) Many lose their soul for the sake of the world.

40. Ὑμᾶς, *you*) A descending gradation: sc. *you* (apostles), a *prophet*, a *righteous* man, a *little one*.—Ἐμὲ, *Me*) It is not only of the same avail as if he received Me, but he actually does receive Me.

41. Εἰς ὄνομα, κ.τ.λ., *in the name*, etc.) *i.e.*, on this ground, and on no other.[1]—προφήτην—δίκαιον, *a prophet—a righteous man*) A prophet is one who speaks, a righteous man one who acts, in the name of God, and is distinguished for his remarkable righteousness; see ch. xiii. 17, xxiii. 29; Heb. xi. 33.—μισθὸν, *hire, reward*) for he shows himself as obedient to God as if he were a prophet himself. It may be asked how he who is not righteous himself can receive a righteous man as a righteous man? The reply is easy: Such a man, by the very act, abandons his evil way, and ceases to be the enemy of righteousness.

42. Μικρῶν, *little ones*) (see ch. xi. 11, and Zech. xiii. 7). A sweet epithet for *disciples* (cf. ver. 41, for the double mention of *prophet*, etc.) The world cares not for such as these. From these *little ones* are made *prophets* and *righteous* men.—ψυχροῦ, *of cold water*) This is without expense, and may be done even on the road. A proverbial expression, and contrasted with *he that receiveth*.[2]—μὴ ἀπολέσῃ, *shall not lose*) A consolation which, arising from former good deeds, cheers the disciple even in the midst of subsequent dangers.[3]—αὐτοῦ, *his*) *i.e.*, *of the little one*, or rather *his own*. It is more to *receive* any one than to *give him to drink*, and therefore it has a greater reward.

---

[1] So the French Version, published in Geneva in 1744 A.D., "En qualitè de Prophete." The Latin expression, *Prophetæ nomine*, is similar.—E. B.

[2] *i.e.* to receive any one into the house as a guest—this is an act of *hospitality*, whereas to give a cup of cold water to a wayfarer is merely an act of *kindness*.—(I. B.)

[3] O the boundless riches of GOD, who both has it in His power and delights to pay in full such great rewards.—V. g.

CHAPTER XI.

1. Ἐτέλεσεν, *concluded*) Our Lord did nothing abruptly. See Gnomon on ch. xxvi. 1; and Luke vii. 1.—κηρύσσειν, *to preach*) sc. everywhere. Cf. John iii. 2, etc.¹—αὐτῶν, *of them*) the Israelites [the people, namely, who were deserving of His " compassion,' ch. ix. 36.—V. g.]

2. Τοῦ Χριστοῦ, *of Christ*) Those works which it was the part of *the Messiah* to perform.²—μαθητῶν αὐτοῦ, *of His disciples*) whom He wished to confirm and resign to Christ.³

3. Ὁ ἐρχόμενος, *he that should come*) cf. Ps. xl. 7; Heb. x. 37.—ἤ, κ.τ.λ., *or*, etc.) There was not at that time any other, for John excludes himself by this disjunctive particle.—ἕτερον, *another*) They recognise as a certain fact that there is *some one* who should come.—προσδοκῶμεν, *must we await*) sc. with longer delay.⁴

4. "Α ἀκούετε καὶ βλέπετε, *those things which ye do hear and see*) The testimonies of facts of seven kinds, enumerated in ver. 5, 6. The miracles which our Lord performed had been foretold; they were beneficent, many, and various.⁵

5.⁶ Εὐαγγελίζονται, *are evangelized*) The word is passive; cf. Luke xvi. 16. For the works of our Lord Himself, which the

---

¹ The verb διδάσκειν implies private instruction, as κηρύσσειν implies public instruction.—V. g.

² Jesus had done similar works before John was imprisoned; but now He did such works in much greater numbers.—V. g.

³ He does not seem to have entertained any doubt himself as to Christ. —V. g.

⁴ The time of waiting in expectation was now by this time coming to an end; for the Seventieth week of Daniel was close at hand.—V. g.

⁵ *Sight* in other cases is wont to precede *hearing;* but the word of Christ [*heard* by them] answered more closely, as it were, to the desires of faith than the works of Christ [*seen* by them], John xiv. 11. Even in this place, Jesus speaks humbly, as in ch. xii. 17, 41, 42. He does not say, *Those things which I speak and do.*—V. g.

⁶ Τυφλοὶ ἀναβλέπουσι) At that very moment (period of time) such miracles were being performed (Luke vii. 21), which were the very miracles reserved for the Christ. In ancient times, sinners used to be punished with blindness, leprosy, and death.—νεκροὶ ἐγείρονται) A miracle which had been very recently performed in the case of the young man of Nain, Luke vii. 14.—V. g.

disciples of John then saw and heard, are meant; cf. Luke iv. 18, concerning the prediction of this work.[1] Nor did all poor men as yet preach the Gospel, but only the apostles. See Matt. x. 7.

6. Μακάριος, *blessed*) A rare felicity. That very circumstance, that many should be offended in Him, was foretold as a sign of the Messiah.[2] He loaded others with benefits; He Himself was weak, poor, despised.—ὅς ἐάν, *whosoever*) especially of the disciples of John, who saw the difference between his mode of living and that of our Lord. See ver. 18, 19.

7. Πορευομένων, *as they departed*) Otherwise they might have become puffed up. The world praises to the face, reviles behind the back. Divine truth does the opposite.—ἤρξατο, *began*) The multitude would not have begun, had He not done so first. —περὶ Ἰωάννου, *concerning John*) The state of John is described in ver. 7, 8, 9, with reference to men, to himself, to God.— θεάσασθαι, *to see as a spectacle*) idly. See John v. 35.—κάλαμον, *a reed*) The ford of Jordan abounded with them. They would have wished John to be such in conduct as they liked to be themselves, and as they are described in this verse and the following. They sought a man of easy disposition, and one ready to second their desires, whom they would not themselves style a reed; but Jesus calls *a reed, a reed*. For often does truth attribute to man a speech, not such as he frames himself, but such as expresses the reality. See Jer. xviii. 12. The people themselves did not sufficiently know why they had gone forth. On the other hand, the character of John is described (cf. ver. 18), and at the same time the stumbling-block is taken away, which might have arisen from the imprisonment of our Lord's precursor.—ἀνέμου, *by the wind*) of favour (by his having been supposed to be the Messiah) or persecution.—σαλευόμενον, *agitated*) The word is here in the middle voice, and signifies *permitting himself to be agitated*. This opinion is not refuted like those which follow, because it refutes itself.

---

[1] Which was peculiarly a work of the Christ, who was anointed for that very purpose, Isa. lxi. 1.—V. g. Comp. Luke iv. 1.—ED.

[2] Isa. liii. 14. That very fact was an argument likely to be easily appreciated, especially by the disciples of John. See ver. 18, with which comp. ver. 19.—V. g.

8. Ἀλλά, *but*) The conjunction is employed to show that the preceding hypothesis has been dismissed.—ἐν μαλακοῖς ἱματίοις ἠμφιεσμένον, *clothed in soft raiment*) They would have wished the forerunner, and the Messiah Himself, to have been such.—τά, *the*) The article refers to the preceding μαλακοῖς.[1]—φοροῦντες, *who wear*) John, if he had wished it, might have been a courtier.—οἴκοις, *houses*) Not in the desert or the prison.—τῶν βασιλείων,[2] *of palaces*) See Esth. iv. 2. The LXX. have τὰ βασίλεια in Esth. i. 9, ii. 13.—οἶκοι τῶν βασιλείων = *the halls of the palace*.

9. Προφήτην, *a prophet*) For a long time they had had no prophets.[3]—ναί, *yea*) A prophet, I say unto you, and something greater than a prophet.—περισσότερον, *more*) Neuter, as in τί, *what*: sc. when ye went out ye saw something more, etc., although ye did not know it.—προφήτου, *than a prophet*) For a prophet announces only distant events.

10. Οὗτος γάρ ἐστι, κ.τ.λ., *for this is he*, etc.) This makes John much greater than that what is spoken of[4] in ver. 7, 8, could.—ἰδοὺ ἐγὼ ἀποστέλλω τὸν ἄγγελόν Μου πρὸ προσώπου Σου, ὃς κατασκευάσει τὴν ὁδόν Σου ἔμπροσθέν Σου, *behold I send my messenger before Thy face, which shall prepare Thy way before Thee*) In the S. V. of Mal. iii. 1, we read, ἰδοὺ ἐξαποστελῶ τὸν ἄγγελόν Μου, καὶ ἐπιβλέψεται ὁδὸν πρὸ προσώπου Μου, καὶ ἐξαίφνης ἥξει, κ.τ.λ., *behold I will send forth My messenger, and he shall survey the road before My face, and suddenly shall arrive*, etc.—Ἐγώ, *I*) The Father addressing the Son.—τὸν ἄγγελόν Μου, *My messenger*) John was sent by God as a messenger, after whom came the Messenger of the Covenant Himself.—πρὸ προσώπου Σου, *before Thy face*) Immedi-

---

[1] Thus identifying μαλακά with μαλακοῖς ἱματίοις, and showing that the μαλακά, "*soft* things," now spoken of are, as in E. V., "soft clothing."—(I. B.)

[2] E. M. has "τοῖς οἴκοις τῶν βασιλέων," which E. V. renders "Kings' Palaces."—(I. B.)

The reading τῶν βασιλείων is regarded as equal to the other in the margin of the larger Ed.: but the margin of Ed. 2, as well as the Germ. Vers., prefer βασιλέων.—E. B. All the primary authorities read βασιλέων. But Griesb. and Scholz, with some inferior Uncial MSS., read βασιλείων or βασιλειῶν.—ED.

[3] He cannot be accounted as such, unless he were one far removed from (reed-like) fickleness and (courtier-like) effeminacy.—V. g.

[4] viz. His being "a reed shaken by the wind," or "a man clothed in soft raiment."—See Gnomon in loc.—(I. B.)

ately before Thee. The LXX. have ἐξαίφνης (*immediately*) in the passage just quoted. John was not a prophet of distant events.—See Luke i. 76. The advent of the Father and of the Son are the same, and so is the language which applies to them. It is one of the strongest arguments for the divinity of Christ, that those things which are said of Christ in the New Testament are quoted from the Old Testament, where they are predicated as exclusively belonging to God.—See Gnomon on John xii. 41; Acts ii. 33; Rom. ix. 33, xiv. 11; 1 Cor. i. 31, x. 9; Eph. iv. 8; Heb. i. 6, 8, 10, 11; Rev. i. 8, 17.

11. Οὐκ ἐγήγερται, *there has not arisen*) or *there hath not been raised up* as yet. The verb ἐγείρεσθαι, denotes an office conferred.—ἐν γεννητοῖς γυναικῶν, *among them that are born of women*) An expression of universal extent. Thus, ἐν γυναιξίν, *among women*, of the blessedness of Mary, Luke i. 28.—μείζων, *a greater*, sc. *prophet*) See Luke vii. 28, and i. 15, even if he be compared with Enoch, Moses, and Elias.—τοῦ βαπτιστοῦ, *the Baptist*) He was already then distinguished by this surname, on account of the novelty and magnitude of the matter, not merely afterwards to distinguish him from John the apostle.—ὁ δὲ μικρότερος, *but the least*) The comparative with the article has the force of a superlative. As far as John excels every one, even the greatest of the ancient prophets, so far is John himself excelled by every one, even the least, in the kingdom of heaven, whether he be a preacher of Christ, or merely a citizen thereof. John himself was not yet in the kingdom of heaven, but he preceded it [as a herald].[1] Jesus is not the least IN the kingdom of heaven, but is the King Himself; and He Himself is implied by the kingdom of heaven, which John announced.—See ver. 10 and 3, and ch. iii. 11. And the less and the greater are here spoken of as they are, not in the opinion of men, but in reality, in the knowledge of the revealed Christ.—See 1 Pet. i. 12. The idea of external appearance, in ver. 6, does not come in here. Jesus was despised and unknown amongst men, but He was not the least, as far as the kingdom of heaven was concerned; all the citizens of the kingdom of heaven already acknowledged Him

---

[1] Even at that time the Apostles themselves already were superior to John in their baptizing and teaching, John iv. 2; Matth. x. 7, etc.—*Harm.*, p. 299, at the end.

as their King.—Cf. the phrase in ch. v. 19. He is never called less than John, nor least in the kingdom of heaven. The least in the kingdom of heaven, is the least of the citizens of the kingdom. In that THIRD point [1] in which John is greater than others, the least in the kingdom of heaven is less than the other citizens of the kingdom of heaven. John did not yet know all, which at present even catechumens know from the Apostles' Creed. A noble climax—prophet, John, apostle or Christian. It is greater, in this kind of comparison of the Old and New Testament, to know things present than things future, however brief be the interval which separates them from the present;[2] but in another point of view, the knowledge of futurity is an especial distinction conferred by GOD.

12. Δὲ, *but*) Used antithetically in this sense—viz., although John is less than the least in the kingdom of heaven, yet even from the beginning of the days of John the Baptist, the kingdom of heaven exercises force. The kingdom of heaven came not in John, but immediately after John.—βιάζεται, *pushes itself forward as it were by violence*) Consider attentively ch. xiii. 32, 33, and Luke xiv. 23. The LXX. frequently use βιάζομαι to signify, *to employ force*. John calls in a mournful, Jesus in a joyful strain.[3] And there is a metonymy of *kingdom* for *King*, *i.e.* the Messiah. See Gnomon on ch. iv. 17.—βιασταί, *they who employ force*) See Luke xiii. 24. There is no complaint here of hostile force, for the complaint begins at ver. 16. Βιάζεται and βιασταί are correlative.[4]—ἁρπάζουσιν, *seize*) in order that by seizing it with swift force, all obstacles having been

---

[1] Beng. seems to me to use *Tertium* here in the logical sense of the intermediate term, affording a point of comparison between the other two: as here John stands midway between the Old Test. covenant and its prophets, on the one hand, and the N. Test. kingdom, and its preachers and members, on the other.—ED.

[2] In the original, "scire præsentia quam futura, quamvis proxime futura;" lit. "*to know present than future* [things], *although most closely future*," *i.e.* "*to know the things that are, than those that are to be hereafter*, however *close* that hereafter may be to the present."—(I. B.)

[3] In the original, "Johannes lamentatur; Jesus canit,"—lit. "John laments; Jesus sings."—(I. B.)

[4] It is in this way that the work goes on briskly, and advances as successfully as one could wish.—V. g.

broken through, they may obtain the blessing which is offered them.¹ See Luke vii. 29.

13. Γὰρ, *for*) Now is fulfilled that which had been predicted up to the time of John.—προφῆται—νόμος—Ἰωάνου, *prophets—law —John*) Cf. Mal. i. 1, iii. 22, 23; and see Gnomon on Matt. iii. 12. There were prophets also before Moses; and the law being put in the second place, makes a regular gradation; for Moses was the greatest of the prophets of the Old Testament. The law also is mentioned in this passage on account of its prophetic office. Where the Old Testament concludes at the end of Malachi, there the New Testament commences at the beginning of Mark. This phrase, therefore, *even until John*, holds good of Scripture. Its application extends also beyond Malachi, even to the father of John. See Luke i. 67. *Even until*, without change. Here was the boundary of prophecy and of the Old Testament dispensation; thenceforward is the fulfilling.—προεφήτευσαν, *prophesied*) This was the whole of their office, to bear witness to future things. John was something more. See ver. 9.

14. Εἰ θέλετε, *if ye will*) It is your interest that is at stake. The expression, βιασταί (used in the last verse), is explained: it is the willing only who are compelled. All is prepared: it only remains that you should be willing.—Ἠλίας, *Elias*) The absence of the article shows that the word is used *antonomatically*.² John makes βιασταί of both *fathers and children*. Cf. δὲ, *but*, in v. 16.³ The prophecy of the Old Testament concludes with this Elijah at the end of Malachi. John is called Elias on account of the office of forerunner, which he had in common with the Tishbite.—ὁ μέλλων ἔρχεσθαι, *who is about to come*) The language is, as it were, that of one looking forward from the Old Testament into the New.⁴

15. Ὦτα ἀκούειν, *ears to hear*) Thus the LXX. in Deut. xxix.

¹ Just as happens in the case of wares exposed for sale in public. —V. g.

² See Append. Antonomasia here applies the name Elias to John, not literally, but analogously; as Elias was in the O. Test., so John in preparing for the coming N. Test. kingdom.—ED.

³ *i.e.* John I have likened to Elijah; *but* to whom shall I liken this generation?—ED.

⁴ Moreover John is not called absolutely ὁ μέλλων ἔρχεσθαι, but Ἠλίας ὁ μέλλων ἔρχεσθαι.—V. g.

ST MATTHEW XI. 16–19.   257

4; cf. Rom xi. 8. "*He that hath ears to hear, let him hear,*" was a form of commanding attention peculiar to our Lord, and indicates, that the other things which might be said more expressly, are contained in those which have just been uttered.

16. Τὴν γενεὰν ταύτην, *this generation*) the evil men of this best[1] time.—παιδαρίοις,[2] *children*) Jesus compared not only the Jews, but also Himself and John, in different ways, to children, with a condescension, in His own case, most wonderful.—ἀγοραῖς, *market-places*) A large city has often many market-places. The preaching of John and Jesus was public.

17. Ηὐλήσαμεν, *we have piped*) i.e., *played on the pipe.* See ver. 19.—ἐθρηνήσαμεν, *we have mourned*) See ver. 18. An instance of *Chiasmus*.[3]

18. Ἦλθε, *came*) A striking instance of *Anaphora* ;[4] cf. ver. 19. —μήτε ἐσθίων, *neither eating*) John did not eat with others, nor even in the presence of others. His mode of life agreed with the character of his teaching, and so did that of Christ [with the character of His teaching.] Therefore the one is, as it were, implied by the other.—μήτε πίνων, *nor drinking*) See Luke i. 15.—λέγουσι, *they say*) The world disparages virtue, representing it as the extreme; it advocates the cause of vice, representing it as the mean.—δαιμόνιον, *a devil*) in common parlance, *a familiar spirit.*—ἔχει, *He has*) A reproach common to the Jews, by which they denoted one who was mad, or silly, or proud. They who abstain from the society of men, easily incur this suspicion.

19. Ἄνθρωπος φάγος, κ.τ.λ., *a gluttonous man*, etc.) They distinguish Him, as one out of many, by a distinction opposed to that mentioned in the preceding verse.— τῶν τέκνων, *children*) We have shown, in the Apparatus,[5] that τῶν ἔργων—*works*—

---

[1] "Hujus optimi temporis"—so called because it was that of our Lord's Ministry.—(I. B.)

[2] The margin of both Editions, as also the Germ. Vers., seem to prefer παιδίοις.—E. B. So BCDZ. The παιδαρίοις of Rec. Text is not supported by the primary authorities.—ED.

[3] See Explanation of Technical Terms in Appendix.—(I. B.)

[4] See Append. The same word repeated in the beginnings of sentences or sections, in order to mark them.—ED.

[5] In the Apparatus. p. 117, he says—
"19) τέκνων) *operibus* notat *Hieronymus* in *Evangeliis quibusdam* legi,

VOL. I.   R

was anciently a widely received reading. Ambrose, on Luke vii. 35, says:—"Therefore wisdom is justified of all her children.¹ It is well said '*of all*,' because justice is observed towards all [*i.e.* in God's dealings with all], so that the faithful may be accepted, the unfaithful rejected. Very many of the Greeks adopt the reading, '*Wisdom is justified of all her works*,' because it is the work of justice to observe the due measure towards the merit of every single individual." He, however, appears to mean the codices of St Matthew, not those of St Luke, for he is in the habit of recurring to them from time to time, although he is commenting on St Luke.²—αὐτῆς³) Valla⁴ thinks that this refers to γενεᾶς; but see Luke vii. 35, where there are more remarks on the present passage. Cf. ver. 31. [No doubt Christ is the Wisdom meant. The children of Wisdom are those who suffer themselves to be gathered by her into her company. It is for this reason that Wisdom is blamed on the ground of too simple and ready indulgence

in Comm. ad h. l. sic vero etiam *Æth. Copt. Pers. Syr.* Videtur Græcus librarius antiquissimus pro τῶν τέκνων in maxima literarum similitudine, legisse τῶν ἔργων. Quæ strictura docere nos possit, ex Græco Matthæi Evangelio deductum esse *Evangelium Nazarenorum* [an apocryphal gospel so called], quippe quod hoc loco sine dubio respexit Hieronymus. Eundem varietatem, ex Hieronymo, ut apparet, notavit Hafenrefferus in edit. suâ N. T."—(I. B.)

¹ The first sentence is not quoted by Bengel, but, on referring to the original, I considered the meaning so much plainer with it than without it, that I took the liberty of inserting it. The passage in Ambrose stands thus:—
"*Justificata est ergo Sapientia ab omnibus filiis suis.* Bene ab omnibus, quia circa omnes justitia servatur: ut susceptio fiat fidelium rejectio perfidorum. Unde plerique Græci sic habent: *Justificata est Sapientia ab omnibus operibus suis;* quod opus justitiæ sit, circa unius cujuscunque meritum servare mensuram."—(I. B.)

² Luke, vii. 35, adds πάντων. B corrected later, reads, as the MSS. alluded to by Ambrose, τῶν ἔργων: so MSS. in Jerome, both Syriac and Memph. Versions. But *Dae* Vulg., Orig., Hil. and Rec. Text, read τέκνων. —ED.

³ Gen. fem. sing. of αὐτός. E. V. renders it *her*, sc. *Wisdom's*. Valla would render it *of it*, sc. *of this generation.*—(I. B.)

⁴ LAURENTIUS VALLA, one of the most distinguished Latin scholars of the fifteenth century. Born in Rome about 1406; became Professor of Eloquence, first at Pavia, and afterwards at Milan; went to Rome in 1443, and became canon of St John the Lateran. Died 1457. He published, besides many other works, annotations on the N. T.—(I. B.)

towards such persons, and she is therefore thus compelled at last to justify herself. Luke xv. 1, 2, etc.—V. g.]

20. Τότε ἤρξατο, *then He began*) He had not previously upbraided them. This upbraiding is the prelude to the Last Judgment. Every hearer of the New Testament is either much more blessed (v. 11) or much more miserable than them of old time.—δυνάμεις, *mighty works*) See ver. 5. [Repentance and the knowledge of Jesus Christ are always conjoined.—V. g.]

21. Οὐαί, *woe*) This interjection is not imprecatory, but enunciatory. See ch. xxiv. 17. Its opposite is *blessed*. This should be observed everywhere.

21, 23. 'Υμῖν—σοί, *you—thee*) Two cities in the neighbourhood are compared with two mentioned in the Old Testament history, and one more miserable than the former is compared to one more miserable than the latter.—πάλαι, *long ago*) In that ancient time, in which it was more difficult to repent. See Acts xvii. 30. We must not say, "What doest thou?" Cf. Ezek. iii. 6. —ἐν σάκκῳ, *in sackcloth*) understand *sitting*, or some such word.

22. Ἀνεκτότερον, *more tolerable*) Because they were less impenitent, and would have repented, and have already been punished.—κρίσεως, *judgment*) The Judge will be the very same in whom they were then offended.

23. Καπερναούμ, *Capernaum*) This city had been more highly blessed than Chorazin and Bethsaida, but from its sin became more miserable. It is therefore compared with Sodom, not with Tyre and Sidon.—ἕως τοῦ οὐρανοῦ, *even unto heaven*) For the Lord from heaven had come to dwell there, and in bringing Himself, had brought heaven thither.[1]—ὑψωθεῖσα, *exalted*) In the sight of God, of Christ, and of the angels.—ᾅδου, *hell*) Which is lowest in the nature of things.—ἔμειναν ἄν, *they would have remained*) Instead of having been destroyed. Great is the effect of the conditional form.[2] The same verb occurs in John xxi. 22.

---

[1] For specimens of this exaltation, see John ii. 12, iv. 47; Matt. iv. 13-xiii. 53; John vi. 24; Matt. xvii. 24.—*Harm.*, p. 301.

[2] For they, in that case, either would not have perpetrated the enormities which they did, or else would have repented of having committed them: in which case they would not have been destroyed, either then or subsequently. —V. g.

25. Ἀποκριθείς, *answering*) Sc. to those things which He was considering concerning His Father's design, His own thoughts, and the character of His disciples.[1]—ἐξομολογοῦμαι, *I praise*) Nothing can be predicated with *praise* of God, which is not so in fact: תּוֹדָה, *praise*,[3] is predication.[4] Jesus returned thanks to His Father afterwards in the same words, when the seventy disciples had well performed the work which He had appointed them.—Πάτερ, Κύριε τοῦ οὐρανοῦ καὶ τῆς γῆς, *Father, Lord of heaven and earth*) He is frequently called the Father of Jesus Christ, sometimes also His God; never *His* Lord, but *the Lord of heaven and earth*. Let us learn, from the example of Jesus Christ, to apply to God those titles which are suitable to the subject of our prayers. The Jews also forbid to cumulate divine titles in prayers. The address in this passage is indeed most magnificent.—ὅτι ἀπέκρυψας—καὶ ἀπεκάλυψας, κ.τ.λ., *because Thou hast hid—and revealed*, etc.) A double ground of

---

[1] He uttered the words which follow with an exulting spirit.—V. g.

[2] The word used by Bengel is "*Confiteor*," which occurs in the Vulgate, both here and in 1 Chron. xvi. 35 with the same sense. That such is his meaning, is clear from his employing in his German Version the phrase, *Ich preise Dich*, which, when applied to God, signifies "*I* PRAISE or MAGNIFY *Thee*." Bengel employs the word "*Confiteor*" in preference to any other, because, like the Greek ἐξομολογοῦμαι, it signifies both generically, with an accusative, *to confess, acknowledge, proclaim*, etc., and specifically, with a dative, to *laud, praise*, or *magnify* [GOD].— See *Riddle* and *Schleusner* in voce.—E. V. renders ἐξομολογοῦμαι, *I thank*.—(I. B.)

[3] The word used by Bengel is "*Confessio*," which he employs with direct reference to his previous "*Confiteor*," on which see preceding footnote. On the meaning of תּוֹדָה, Gesenius says:—(1.) *Confession*, Josh. vii. 19; Ezr. x. 11. (2.) *Thanksgiving*, Ps. xxvi. 7, xlii. 5. זָבַח תּוֹדָה to offer praise to God (for a sacrifice), Ps. l. 14, 23, cvii. 22, cxvi. 17 (where the phrase is not to be taken as though proper sacrifices were spoken of). זֶבַח תּוֹדָה, Lev. xxii. 29; זֶבַח תּוֹדַת שְׁלָמִים, Lev. vii. 13, 15, comp. 12, and ellipt. תּוֹדָה, a sacrifice of thanksgiving, Ps. lvi. 13. (3.) *A choir* of givers of thanks, praising God, Neh. xii. 31, 38, 40.—(I. B.)

[4] And conversely, therefore. *Predication* is *Praise*. They are the two sides of an eternal and immutable equation. Much to the same effect, Bengel says elsewhere (ch. vi. 9). "Deus est sanctus, *i.e.*, Deus sanctificatur ergo, quando ita, ut est, agnoscitur et colitur et celebratur." Consequently, in *confessing, acknowledging*, and *proclaiming*, or in any other mode PREDICATING the truth concerning GOD (and not otherwise), we PRAISE Him. —(I. B.)

praise. For ἀπέκρυψας, *Thou hast kept concealed*, cf. ver. 27; for ἀπεκάλυψας, *Thou hast revealed*, cf. again ver. 27, at the end.—ταῦτα, *these things*) Concerning the Father and the Son, concerning the kingdom of heaven.—σοφῶν, *the wise*) *i.e.* those who arrogate to themselves the character of wisdom.[1]—συνετῶν, *prudent*) *i.e.* those who arrogate to themselves the character of prudence.[1] Cf. 1 Cor. i. 19.—ἀπεκάλυψας, *Thou hast revealed*) See ch. xvi. 17.—νηπίοις, *to infants*) Such as the twelve apostles and seventy disciples were: See Luke x. 21; they were *very young*, for they bore witness for a long time afterwards. They were infants, as being ready to believe and simple-minded; see Matt. xviii. 3.

26. Ναί, *yea*) *Even so*. Jesus assents to the good pleasure of the Father. " Even so, oh Father!" is an epitome of filial confession.—ὁ πατήρ is in this passage more significant than πάτερ would have been.[2]—εὐδοκία ἔμπροσθέν Σου, *well-pleasing in Thy sight*[3]) The will and the intellect of God put forth His decrees. His good pleasure is the highest limit, beyond which we are not permitted to go, in examining the causes of the Divine decrees. Thus presently, concerning the Son, we find the expression, βούληται, *may will*, Lat. *voluerit*.

27. Πάντα, *all things*) Here our Lord changes the direction of His words, and accosts His human auditors. After His resurrection, He more expressly said that *all things in heaven and in earth* were delivered to Him; see ch. xxviii. 18; but in the present passage the same truth is implied; cf. ver. 25. *All things* are delivered unto Him; also the authority to reveal them. *All things* are delivered unto Him; and therefore *all men*. See John xiii. 3, xvii. 2; 1 Cor. xv. 25, 27.—παριδόθη,

---

[1] Beng. attributes to the σοφοί the " habitus noëticus;" to the συνετοί, the " habitus dianoëticus;" the same difference as between νοῦς and διάνοια, *mind* and *discriminative intelligence* or *discernment*.—Ed.

[2] The latter, a simple vocative; the former, in form, a nominative with the article prefixed, in effect, an emphatic vocative of a peculiar character, similar to the analogous ὁ Θεός.—(I. B.)

" Thou, who art *the Father*" (par excellence).—Ed.

[3] In the original, "*Beneplacitum coram Te*." It is difficult to render *Beneplacitum* in this place so as to show its intimate connection, or rather identity, with " *Beneplacitum*" a few lines below, where I have rendered it, as elsewhere, *good pleasure*.—(I. B.)

have been delivered) The Father reserved nothing for Himself which He did not give to the Son. Cf. John xiii. 3; Matt. xxviii. 18. The intimate relation of the Father and the Son is implied in ver. 25–27, John vi. 39, 40, and so throughout the Apocalypse. See my exposition of the Apocalypse, p. 65.—οὐδείς;—οὐδὲ, *no one—neither*) On the order of the words, cf. John viii. 19.—εἰ μὴ ὁ πατήρ, *except the Father*) He does not add, "*and he to whomsoever the Father chooses to reveal Him*," because He has said that in ver. 25, and here He is teaching us what the Father has delivered to Him. The Holy Spirit is not excluded; He is not, however, mentioned here, because His office was not as yet so well known to men.—βούληται, *may will*) *shall choose*. To whom, however, He wishes to do so, is clear from the following verse.

28. Δεῦτε, *come ye*) sc. immediately.—See Gnomon on ch. iv. 19. —πρός Με, *unto Me*) Since the Pharisees, and even John himself, cannot satisfy you.—πάντες, *all*) Let not the limitation in ver. 27 deter you.—οἱ κοπιῶντες, *that labour*) Refer to this ζυγὸν and ζυγός, *yoke*, in ver. 29, 30.—πεφορτισμένοι, *heavy laden*) To this should be referred μάθετε, *learn*, in ver. 29, and φορτίον, *burden*, in ver. 30. The Hebrew משׂא signifies *a burden*, i.e., doctrine, discipline.—κἀγὼ, *and I*) Though you have sought elsewhere in vain, you will find it with Me, ver. 29.—ἀναπαύσω, *I will make you rest*) This is explained in the next verse.—ὅτι, κ.τ.λ., *because*, etc.) "*I will make you rest*," and "*ye shall find rest*," are correlative.

29. Ἄρατε, *take ye*) To take the yoke of Christ upon us, is to give oneself up wholly to His discipline.—ὅτι, κ.τ.λ., *because*, etc.) Hence it appears why we should willingly learn from Jesus. Our meekness and lowliness are consequent upon our so doing. —πραΰς εἰμι καὶ ταπεινὸς, κ.τ.λ., *I am meek and lowly*, etc.) Although His language is fearful in ver. 20, 24. Meekness produces easiness of yoke; lowliness of heart, lightness of burden. The Pharisees were austere and proud. Condescension (*Demissio*) is a much to be admired virtue of God, which is described as fully as possible, although it is not named in Scripture, by one word; whose likeness, humility, is found in the saints; whose opposite, pride, in Satan and the wicked. For it is *condescension*, that that highest Majesty should have deigned

at all to make creatures, and especially men, however contemptible, however mean, and to look on them without disdain, and to unite them to Itself. And the Son of God in a most conspicuous manner manifested His humility in our flesh.—See Ps. xxxiv. 7, cxiii. 6; Luke i. 48, 52, 53, xii. 37, xxii. 27; John xii. 26, xiii. 14; Phil. ii. 8; Heb. xi. 16.—τῇ καρδίᾳ, *in heart*) *Lowly* does not by itself express a quality of the heart, which *meek* does; therefore *in heart* refers rather to *lowly* than to *meek*. The word καρδίᾳ completes the expression: see Rom. ii. 5.— καὶ, *and*) καὶ is introduced as in κἀγὼ, *and I*, in ver. 28. Thus the LXX. in Jer. vi. 16, καὶ εὑρήσετε ἁγνισμὸν ταῖς ψυχαῖς ὑμῶν, *and ye shall find purification*[1] *for your souls*. Rest flows from the heart of Christ into our *souls;* see ver. 29.—εὑρήσετε ἀνάπαυσιν, *ye shall find rest*) as yet unknown to you, but sought for and desired.

30. Ζυγός Μου, *My yoke*) In one point of view, Scripture speaks of *the cross*, in another of the *yoke* of the godly, see ch. x. 38.— χρηστός, *easy*) for I am *meek*.—ἐλαφρὸν, *light*) for I am *lowly*.

CHAPTER XII.

1. Ἐν ἐκείνῳ τῷ καιρῷ, *at that time*) The Pharisees interrupted Him even at that most unseasonable[2] time.—ἤρξαντο τίλλειν, *began to pluck*) The Pharisees interrupted Him immediately. It required some labour to shake out a sufficient number of grains from the ears to appease their hunger.

2. Ἰδοὺ, κ.τ.λ., *behold*, etc.) They mean to say, "The Master ought to be accountable for what the disciples do in His very presence." *Behold!* They wish Him to issue an immediate prohibition.—ὁ οὐκ ἔξεστι, *that which is not lawful*) They do not put the matter doubtfully, and they are therefore rebuked severely in ver. 3, 5, 7. The proposition [may be put either

---

[1] In E. V. it is, "And ye shall find rest unto your souls."—(I. B.)
[2] "Alienissimo," i.e. *most foreign* to the subject.—(I. B.)

affirmatively or negatively], "*It is lawful*," or "*It is not lawful.*" A false reproof was more common at that time, than a true one is now.—ποιεῖν, *to do*) referring not to the *eating*, but the *plucking*.—ἐν σαββάτῳ, *on a Sabbath*) The subject of the Sabbath occupies great part of the Evangelic history.

3. Οὐκ ἀνέγνωτε, *have ye not read*) They had read the letter, without perceiving the spirit. Our Lord convicts them of error by the authority of the Old Testament.—Δαυίδ, *David*) whose conduct, in this instance, you do not find fault with.—ὅτι ἐπείνασεν, *when he was hungry*) This is left, in 1 Sam. xxi. 3, to be understood by the reader.—μετ' αὐτοῦ, *with him*) See ibid. ver. 4.

4. Τὸν οἶκον τοῦ Θεοῦ, *the house of God*) That which might have been considered as a ground of hesitation is exhibited in full force by this expression; the tabernacle is meant, as the temple was built somewhat later.—τοὺς ἄρτους, *the loaves*) There is much of a ceremonial character in the Sabbath: otherwise no argument could have been derived from the *shew-bread*.—τῆς προθέσεως, *of the laying before*,¹ Lat. *propositionis*) = Hebrew םינפ.²— εἰ μή, *except*) i.e., for any except.

5. "Η, *or?* Lat. *an?*)—ἐν τῷ νόμῳ,³ *in the Law*) He proceeds step by step to a more stringent argument, from the example of the Prince, which the priest had approved, to the Law itself; from the prophets, even the earlier, parts of whom were read, to the Law, all of which was read; and from the sacred food to the sacred day, concerning which the dispute arose.—οἱ ἱερεῖς, *the priests*) who ought especially to maintain the law, yet in this matter are especially excepted. Thus also, the priests of Christ are less bound to the Sabbath than the remaining multitude. —ἐν τῷ ἱερῷ, *in the temple*) Whilst they are employed in sacred rites.—βεβηλοῦσι, *profane*) (verb); the adjective βέβηλον, *profane*,

---

¹ This is expressed in English by the descriptive syllable *Shew:* so that, instead of saying with the Greeks and Latins—The bread *of-the-laying-before*, we say the *Shew-Bread*. Both idioms represent the same idea, viz., the bread that was laid before, or exhibited to. God.—(I. B.)

² םינפ םחל, *shew-bread*, lit. *bread of faces*. PATRICK on Exod. xxv. 30, in voc. shew-bread, says, " In the *Hebrew*, bread *of the face* or *presence*, because it was set before the Ark of the Covenant, where God was present.—(I. B.)

³ At that very time of year Leviticus was being read on the Sabbaths, the book in which there occur so many precepts as to sacrifices, which were required to be performed even on the Sabbath.—V. g.

is opposed to ἅγιον, *sacred*, nor does it always imply impurity or guilt.—See Lev. x. 10, and 1 Sam. xxi. 4.

6. Λέγω, *I say*) This form of speech expresses great authority.—τοῦ ἱεροῦ, *the temple*) In which the priests minister. The Temple gives way to Christ, the Sabbath (ver. 5) to the Temple; therefore the Sabbath (ver. 8) to Christ.—ἔστιν ὧδε, *there is here*) He does not say, "I am greater." Jesus was lowly in heart. See ver. 41, 42, ch. xi. 4, 5. Thus too in Luke iv. 21, He says, *This day is this Scripture fulfilled in your ears*; and again, ch. xix. 9, *This day is salvation come to this house.* See also Matt. xiii. 17; John iv. 10, ix. 37.

7. Ἐγνώκειτε, *ye would have known*) The pluperfect tense.—ἔλεον, *mercy*) See ch. ix. 13. The disciples accorded mercy to themselves,[1] and the Pharisees had violated it by their rash judgment.—θυσίαν, *sacrifice*) More sacred than the Sabbath. See ver. 5.—οὐκ ἄν κατεδικάσατε, *ye would not have condemned*) Rashly, quickly, cruelly.[2] By this argument an answer would have been given, if any one had doubted whether it were lawful to pluck the ears before the Passover.

8. Κύριος, *Lord*) The innocence and liberty of the disciples is guaranteed by the majesty of Christ, and the authority[3] of the Son of Man manifests itself in mercy.—σαββάτου, *of the Sabbath*) The Lord of the Temple, and of all things else, is undoubtedly the Lord of the Sabbath; nor has He merely that right which David had.[4]

10. Ἄνθρωπος ἦν, κ.τ.λ., *there was a man*, etc.) He had either come thither of his own accord, that he might be healed, or else he had been brought by others with an insidious design.—ἵνα κατηγορήσωσιν αὐτοῦ, *that they might accuse Him*) As if He had

---

[1] Imitating David in this respect.—V. g.

[2] By indulgence in condemning thoughts, one often falls into sin himself unawares, whilst he is arraigning another as guilty of sin.—V. g.

[3] "Dominatio"—domination, *lordship*. There is a play on the words *dominus* (lord) and *dominatio*, which cannot be preserved in English. It might be expressed by *sovereign* and *sovereignty*.—(I. B.)

[4] Ver. 9. Καί) This was eight days after those things which have been just mentioned (V. g.), and eight days before the Passover. In this brief interval very many events happened of the greatest moment. The people were now getting ready for the feast. Hence a large (abundant) opportunity of doing good presented itself to the Saviour.—*Harm.*, p. 309.

broken the Sabbath, which was then greatly respected even by courts of law. See ver. 14.

11. Πρόβατον ἓν, *one sheep*) The loss of which was not great.—οὐχὶ κρατήσει, *will he not take hold of*) A verb also suited to the healing of the hand. In our Saviour's time this was permitted, since then it has been forbidden by the Jews.

12. Τοῖς σάββασι, *on the Sabbaths*) For a good deed is not to be procrastinated.—καλῶς ποιεῖν, *to do well*) sc. to either a man or a sheep, nay, to a man much more than to a sheep.[1] We must not on the Sabbath-day perform daily wonted tasks for hire, although we may do those things which time and place suggest to us for the good of our neighbour and all other living creatures, and especially for the honour of God.[2]

15. Ἀνεχώρησεν, *He departed*) This is especially referred to in ver. 19. Our Lord avoided noise.

16. Ἵνα μὴ, *that they should not*) Such was the authority of Jesus, even commanding silence to the multitude.[3]

18. Ἰδοὺ ὁ Παῖς Μου, ὃν ᾑρέτισα· ὁ ἀγαπητός Μου, εἰς ὃν εὐδόκησεν ἡ ψυχή Μου· θήσω τὸ πνεῦμά Μου ἐπ᾿ Αὐτόν, καὶ κρίσιν τοῖς ἔθνεσιν ἀπαγγελεῖ οὐκ ἐρίσει οὐδὲ κραυγάσει, οὐδὲ ἀκούσει τίς ἐν ταῖς πλατείαις τὴν φωνὴν Αὐτοῦ· κάλαμον συντετριμμένον οὐ κατεάξει, καὶ λίνον τυφόμενον οὐ σβέσει ἕως ἂν ἐκβάλῃ εἰς νῖκος τὴν κρίσιν· καὶ ἐν τῷ ὀνόματι Αὐτοῦ ἔθνη ἐλπιοῦσι,—*Behold My Servant, whom I have chosen; My Beloved, in whom My soul is well pleased; I will put My Spirit upon Him,*

---

[1] Some one may think that there was danger in delay as regards the sheep, but that a man affected with a bodily infirmity for such a length of time, might easily be put off for once from one day to another day. But the answer is, it was the fitting time that the relief should be given, when the patient met the physician. A larger crowd of men was assembled together on the Sabbath, who were thus enabled to be spectators of the miracle, and to be profited (won over) by it.—V. g.

[2] Ver. 14. οἱ δὲ Φαρισαῖοι) It was not with the same laborious exertion as is needed in order to pluck ears of corn, and to draw out a sheep from a pit. that Jesus had effected the cure, but by mere words spoken. It was a pure undiluted benefit conferred without difficulty (pains): and yet blind men, notwithstanding, were regarding His act as if the Sabbath were profaned by it.—V. g.

[3] Ver. 17. ὅπως πληρωθῇ) The calm (placid) and most salutary mode of action, which Jesus employed, is intimated by these words.—*Vers Germ.* How widely does this in truth differ from the ways and modes of action of His adversaries!—*Harm.*, p. 310.

and He shall announce judgment to the Gentiles. He shall not strive nor cry; neither shall any man hear His voice in the streets. A bruised reed shall He not break, and smoking flax shall He not quench, till He send forth judgment unto victory. And in His name shall the Gentiles trust. The LXX. thus render Is. xlii. 1—4,—Ἰακὼβ ὁ παῖς Μου, ἀντιλήψομαι αὐτοῦ· Ἰσραὴλ ὁ ἐκλεκτός Μου, προσεδέξατο αὐτὸν ἡ ψυχή Μου, ἔδωκα τὸ πνεῦμά Μου ἐπ᾽ αὐτὸν, κρίσιν τοῖς ἔθνεσιν ἐξοίσει· οὐ κράξεται, οὐδὲ ἀνήσει, οὐδὲ ἀκουσθήσεται ἔξω ἡ φωνὴ αὐτοῦ· κάλαμον συντεθλασμένον οὐ συντρίψει, καὶ λίνον καπνιζόμενον οὐ σβέσει, ἀλλὰ εἰς ἀλήθειαν ἐξοίσει κρίσιν, κ.τ.λ.[1] *Jacob is My servant; I will defend him. Israel is my chosen; My soul has accepted him: I have given my Spirit upon him; he shall bear forth judgment to the Gentiles. He shall not cry, nor lift up* [*his voice*]; *nor shall his voice be heard without. A bruised reed shall he not crush, and smoking flax shall he not quench; but he shall bear forth judgment unto truth.*—ὁ παῖς μου, *my servant* = the Hebrew עבדי,[2] in Is. xlii. 1. And the LXX. frequently express that Hebrew word[3] by παῖς,[4] *e.g.* where Moses, or even the Messiah, is spoken of. Cf. Acts iii. 13, 26, iv. 27, 30. For it is not again repeated in the New Testament concerning the Messiah, either because neither the Greek παῖς, or any other word, corresponds sufficiently to that Hebrew word, which the apostles also used in the beginning, or else because neither of them is suitable to our Lord's state of glorification. The words, *servant* and *beloved*,

---

[1] In E. V. it stands thus—" Behold my servant, whom I uphold; mine elect, in whom my soul delighteth: I have put my Spirit upon him; he shall bring forth judgment to the Gentiles. He shall not cry, nor lift up, nor cause his voice to be heard in the street. A bruised reed shall he not break, and the smoking flax shall he not quench: he shall bring forth judgment unto truth."—(I. B.)

[2] Sc. עבד *servant*, with the pronominal suffix י, *my*.—(I. B.)

[3] עבד, *i.e. a servant: the minister* or *ambassador* sent by God for accomplishing some service: also *a familiar servant chosen and beloved* of God on account of his piety and approved fidelity; also a term especially applied to the Messiah. See GESENIUS, etc.—(I. B.)

[4] παῖς. According to Schleusner, (1) a child in age; (2) a child in relation to its parents; (3) one pre-eminently beloved; (4) a servant; (5) the minister of a king, etc. According to Liddel and Scott, (1) a child in relation to its parents; (2) a child in age; (3) a servant. The passages, however, in these writers are too long for insertion, and cannot be adequately abridged.—(I. B.)

are parallel; and also, *I have chosen,* and *I am well pleased.*—ᾑρέτισα, *I have chosen*—αἱρετίζειν = αἱρετὸν ὁρίζειν, *to set apart as chosen.*—εἰς ὃν, *towards whom*) The preposition εἰς denotes the perpetual tendency of the Father's mind *towards* His Beloved [Son]. See 2 Pet. i. 17.—κρίσιν, *judgment*) salutary to men. See ver. 20, and John xvi. 11.—κρίσις, *judgment*, is the separation of sin and righteousness.—τοῖς ἔθνεσιν, *to the Gentiles*) when He shall have departed from the Jews.—ἀπαγγελεῖ, *He shall announce*) He both performed and announced it. The *future* tense is employed here; but the *past* afterwards by St Paul, Eph. ii. 17 [with reference to the same matter].

19. Φωνὴν αὐτοῦ, *His voice*) sc. from the house. This example of the lowliness and meekness of Jesus aptly precedes the manifestation of His severity in ver. 34; thus also He wept when about to enter Jerusalem, and then expelled them that bought and sold from the temple.

20. Κάλαμον, *a reed*) In Hebrew קנה.[1] Jerome ad. Algasiam,[2] quæst. 2, interprets *the bruised reed* of Israel; and the *smoking flax*, of the *people congregated from the Gentiles, who, the fire of the natural law being extinguished, were enveloped in the errors of a most bitter smoke, which is hurtful to the eyes, and of a thick darkness. Whom He not only forbore to extinguish and reduce to ashes, but also, on the contrary, from the spark, which was small and all but dying, aroused great flames, so that the whole world should burn with that fire of our Lord and Saviour which He came to send upon earth, and desires to kindle in the hearts of all.*—οὐ κατεάξει, οὐ σβέσει, *shall He not break, shall He not quench*) An instance of *Litotes* for "He shall especially cherish." Cf. ver. 7, ch. xi. 28; Isa. xlii. 3, lxi. 1–3. —ἐκβάλῃ, *send forth, extend*) In the Hebrew יוציא and ישים.

---

[1] קנה, a reed—evidently the original of the word *cane*, which has found its way, I believe, into every European language. Gr. κάννα, κάννη, or κάνη. Lat. *Canna*; Fr. *Cane*; Span. *Cuna*; Port. *Cana* or *Canna*. Cf. also the German *Kancie*.—(I. B.)

[2] An epistle written by St Jerome to an Eastern lady of the name of Algasia, who had propounded twelve questions to him. He begins by a quaint and courteous proemium, in which he fancifully compares her to the Queen of Sheba, and then proceeds to answer her questions in order. —(I. B.)

In the S. V. both verbs[1] are commonly rendered by ἐκβάλλειν, *to extend.*— εἰς νῖκος, *unto victory*) The LXX. frequently render לנצח (*for ever*) by εἰς νῖκος, which is the force of the phrase in this passage; *i.e.* so that nothing may resist them for ever.

20, 21. Κρίσιν καὶ τῷ, κ.τ.λ.) After κρίσιν the LXX. have ἀναλάμψει καὶ οὐ θραυσθήσεται ἕως ἂν θῇ ἐπὶ τῆς γῆς κρίσιν, καὶ ἐπὶ τῷ ὀνόματι αὐτοῦ ἔθνη ἐλπιοῦσιν, *He shall shine forth, and He shall not be broken, until He establish judgment on the earth: and in His name shall the Gentiles trust.* And on this verse of Isaiah (viz. xlii. 4) Jerome thus comments: "But that which follows, '*He shall shine, and shall not be consumed, until He establish judgment on the earth,*' Matthew the evangelist has not inserted. Or else the words between '*judgment*' and '*judgment*' have been lost by the error of a transcriber, for which we have given this interpretation, '*He shall not be sad nor turbulent, but shall always preserve an equability of aspect.*' Aquila and Theodotion have interpreted it, *He shall not darken, and He shall not flee, until He establish judgment on the earth.* And the meaning is, *He shall repel none by the sadness of His aspect, nor be hasty to punish, since He has reserved the reality of judgment* (veritatem judicii) *for the last time.*" The intervening passage in the Hebrew runs thus: לא יכהה ולא ירוץ עד ישים בארץ משפט, rendered in the E.V. *He shall not fail nor be discouraged* (margin, *be broken*). Jansen[2] rejects the suspicion of Jerome of the chasm admitted by the transcriber, but Drusius[3] adopts it, not undeservedly. More-

---

[1] Sc. הוֹצִיא the Hiphil of יצא, and שׂוּם. Bengel does not mean to say that the LXX. render them so in this passage (which is not the case with either of them), but that they do so elsewhere; and, consequently, that St Matthew is justified in doing so here.—(I. B.)

[2] CORNELIUS JANSENIUS (*major*), Bishop of Ghent, must not be confounded with his celebrated namesake, the Bishop of Ypres. He was born at Hulst, and became Professor of Divinity at Louvain. He attended the Council of Trent; became Bishop of Ghent in 1568; and died 1576. He published, besides other works "*Commentarii in suam concordiam ac totam historiam evangelicam.*" Folio, Louvain, 1572.—(I. B.)

[3] JOHN VAN DEN DRIESSCHE, commonly known as Johannes Drusius, was born at Oudenard, in Flanders, in 1550. He was educated at Ghent and Louvain, after which he studied Hebrew at Oxford, where he became Professor of Oriental Languages in 1572. In 1576 he returned to Louvain, and studied Law. He became Professor of Oriental Languages at Leyden in 1577, and of Hebrew at Francker in 1585, where he died in 1616. His critical labours

over, since the Evangelist, in the whole of this passage, differs widely from the words of the LXX., you will not easily discover by what Greek words the Hebrew hemistich of Isaiah has been expressed in St Matthew. The sentence itself, indeed, most becomingly expresses the placid and moderate action of the Messiah. See Apparatus, p. 474[1] [2d Edition, p. 118].

21. Καὶ, κ.τ.λ., *and*, etc.) Jerome ad. Algasium, in the passage cited above, refers to these words those of Isaiah. *He shall shine, and shall not be broken, until He establish judgment on the earth: so that*, says he, *the light of His preaching shall at length shine forth in the world, and* [11c] *be consumed and overcome by the devices of no one, until He establish judgment on the earth, and that be fulfilled which was written, Thy will be done, as in heaven so on earth.*—ὀνόματι, *name*) In the Hebrew the word is תורה, *law*. The whole Gospel is a discourse on the name of Christ.

22. Δαιμονιζόμενος, *one possessed with a devil*) extremely miserable.—καὶ λαλεῖν καὶ βλέπειν, *both spake and saw*) The order of the miracle appears to be thus expressed.

24. Ἀκούσαντες, *when they heard*) sc. what the people said.—οὗτος, *this*) man. A contemptuous mode of expression.[2] [E. V. are highly esteemed, and he was honoured by the approval of the great Scaliger.—(I. B.)

The margin of the larger Ed. holds the proposed insertion of the words (Jerome's) doubtful. The margin of the 2d Ed. and the Germ. Vers. altogether omit them.—E. B.

[1] In the Apparatus he says, "Ob recurrens *judicii* verbum [*i.e.* κρίσιν], colon Jesajæ hoc loco per errorem excidisse putat *Hieronymus*, dissentiente *Jansenio*, assentiente *Drusio*; et in Evang. Hebr. [the Gospel according to the Hebrews: an Apocryphal production so called] plena prophetæ periocha reponitur: quanquam hoc colo *Eusebius* caret. Certe hæc sententia magnopere congruit cum sensu Matthæi, sive ipse eam repetiit, sive ex Jesaja repetendam innuit: nec vero sine ea videtur repetiturus fuisse ulterius illud. Et in ejus nomine gentes sperabunt." Bengel has, however, omitted the clause in his own German Version.—(I. B.)

Grotius rightly opposes the insertion of the words. What Isaiah, xlii. 3, repeated *twice*, viz. "bring forth judgment unto truth," ver. 4, "set judgment on the earth;" Matthew omitting the poetic pleonasm, *condenses into one*, and takes the 'until' from ver. 4, and " bring forth judgment to victory" from ver. 3. He also expresses the *sense* of the last clause of verse 3 ("bring forth judgment unto truth") more fully.—ED.

[2] Of what great moment a very few words may be.—V. g.

This fellow].—*εἰ μή, except*) A vehement affirmation.—*ἐν τῷ Βεελζεβοὺλ ἄρχοντι τῶν δαιμονίων, by Beelzebub the prince of the devils*) They call Satan thus. In the Old Testament this was the name of an idol. Cf. 1 Cor. x. 20.

25. *Ἐνθυμήσεις, thoughts*) most bitter ones; cf. ver. 34, 35.—
— *βασιλεία, kingdom*) First the kingdom of Satan is treated of, then his house, and, in ver 26, Satan himself; whose kingdom contains wicked men, whose house, devils.—*οὐ σταθήσεται, shall not be established, shall not be made to stand*) sc. by its master or lord. Ammonius[1] says: *σταθῆναι μέν ἐστι τὸ ὑφ' ἑτέρου· στῆναι δὲ, τὸ κατ' ἰδίαν ῥώμην, καὶ προαίρεσιν, i.e. σταθῆναι* is to stand by means of another, but *στῆναι* is to stand by its own strength and will.

26. *Εἰ ὁ Σατανᾶς τὸν Σατανᾶν ἐκβάλλει, if Satan cast out Satan*) Satan or the devil is one. I, says our Lord, cast out Satan. In the kingdom of darkness there is none greater than Satan. If therefore your words are true, it must be Satan who casts out Satan. But this is clearly absurd: one kingdom, one city, one house, is not divided against itself; neither is one spirit divided against himself. The noun is used for the reciprocal pronoun (*ἑαυτόν*) as in Exod. xvi. 7; Lev. xiv. 15, 26; 1 Kings viii. 1, x. 13, xii. 21; 2 Kings xvii. 31. This does not however prevent the supposition, that the accusative *τὸν Σατανᾶν, Satan*, is put by synecdoche for his comrades. Thus, for example, you might say, "The Gaul destroyed himself," if at any time one Gallic cohort should put another to the sword. Thus Satan would cast himself out, *i.e.*, Satan, the prince, who is one, would cast out those whom he knew to be his own, his comrades.—*βασιλεία, kingdom*) which is however very stable. Satan is said to have a kingdom, and yet he is never called a king, for he is an usurper.

27, 28. *Εἰ—εἰ δὲ, if—but if*) A dilemma.

27. *Οἱ υἱοὶ ὑμῶν, your sons*) whom you cannot but accuse, says Jesus, if you calumniate Me. See also Mark ix. 38, and cf. Acts xix. 13.—*ὑμῶν, your*) whom you do not harass in this

---

[1] Not the author of the Ammonian Sections, but Ammonius, the son of Hermias, a Peripatetic philosopher, disciple of Proclus, who flourished in the sixth century. His work, *De differentia dictionum*, is to be found in a Greek dictionary, published in folio at Venice in 1497; and it is also printed in a collection of ancient Grammarians which appeared in quarto at Leyden in 1739.—(I. B.)

manner, since they are of your own race and discipline.—*ἐκβάλ-λουσι, cast out*) See ch. vii. 22, and Mark ix. 38.—*αὐτοὶ, they*) emphatically.

28. Εἰ, κ.τ.λ. *if*, etc.) The first portion of the dilemma having been dismissed, this particle has the force of *since*.—*ἐκβάλλω, I cast out*) Jesus in every way destroyed the kingdom of Satan.—*ἄρα, therefore*) The expulsion of Satan, together with his belongings, is the mark and token of the kingdom of God; for this was reserved for the Messiah.—*ἔφθασεν, has prevented*)[2] This word is used here in its strict and proper sense, and intimates something important; cf. *πρῶτον, first*, ver. 29.—*ἡ βασιλεία τοῦ Θεοῦ*, the kingdom *of God*) in contradistinction to that of Satan, mentioned in ver. 26.

29. ἤ, *or else?*) = Latin, *an?* A disjunctive interrogation.—*οἰκίαν, house*) The world was the house of Satan.—*τοῦ ἰσχυροῦ, of the strong*) sc. of any one who is strong; cf. Heb. ii. 14.—*πρῶτον, first*) Jesus bound Satan: then took his spoils.—*δήσῃ, shall have bound*) by superior strength.—*διαρπάσει, shall spoil*) See Gnomon on Mark iii. 27.

30. Ὁ μὴ ὢν, κ.τ.λ., *he that is not, etc.*) The latter part of the dilemma contained in ver. 27, 28, is confirmed by ver. 29; the former by ver. 30, with this meaning, *your sons are not against Me, nor do they scatter abroad; therefore they are with Me, and gather with Me.* There is no neutrality in the kingdom of God; that activity which is natural to man is exercised either in good or in evil, especially in the case of those who hear the word of God. The work and cause of Christ is, however, simple and pure; and though it has so many enemies and adversaries, it overpowers them all, nor does it enter into collusion with them: see Luke xii. 51. This verse forms a Divine axiom.—*συνάγων, that gathereth*) The work of Christ and of Christians is to gather; see ch. xxiii. 37, John xi. 52. This word corresponds with the Hebrew קֹהֶלֶת,[3] *one that gathereth*, or *a preacher*.

[1] In My name.—V. g.

[2] *Prævenit.* Wesley, who avowedly copied from Bengel, explains the passage, "*The Kingdom of God is come upon you*—unawares, before you expected: so the word implies." Bengel himself renders it, "*So ist je das Reich Gottes bereits über euch kommen.*"—(I. B.)

[3] קֹהֶלֶת, *Koheleth* is the appellation by which Solomon is designated in the

31. Βλασφημία, *blasphemy*) The most atrocious kind of sin. He who insults the majesty of an earthly king by injurious language, is much more severely punished than he who steals many thousands of gold pieces.—ἀφεθήσεται, *shall be forgiven*) so that the punishment may be remitted to the penitent.—ἡ τοῦ Πνεύματος βλασφημία, *the blasphemy against the Holy Ghost*) Sin against the Holy Spirit is one thing, blasphemy against the Holy Spirit is another. The word ἁμαρτία, *sin*, is not repeated here. The sinner injures himself by sin; the blasphemer affects many others with irreparable harm. And the Pharisees blasphemed the Holy Spirit, not in a mere ordinary holy man, but in the Messiah Himself.

32.[1] Τοῦ υἱοῦ τοῦ Ἀνθρώπου, *the Son of Man*) This expression is used in accordance with our Lord's condition as it appeared to men, inasmuch as He was then conversing with them on an equal footing, see Phil. ii. 7, as He is described in ch. xi. 19; cf. also Gnomon on ch. xvi. 13. It is not therefore easy, in these times, to say anything against the Son of Man: it is more easy to commit blasphemy against the Holy Spirit.[2]—οὔτε—οὔτε, κ.τ.λ.,

book which bears this name, viz. Ecclesiastes. On the signification and derivation, see *Gesenius* in voc.—(I. B.)

[1] Καὶ ὃς ἐάν, *and whosoever*) The words immediately preceding are hereby further explained and illustrated.—V. g.

[2] Therefore their words were directed against **the Son of man**, when they spake insultingly concerning Him on account of His connection with Nazareth, on account of His lowly bearing and conversation, etc.; but it was against the Holy Spirit that those words of theirs were directed, whereby they brought allegations against His miracles, which were performed by the instrumentality of the Holy Spirit, and ascribed them to the powers of darkness. It was at that time especially, when Christ was sojourning in the midst of them, that men were able to incur the guilt of both kinds of sinful speeches. But what is the present state of those who, in our time, bring criminations against the good operations of the Holy Spirit in His instruments? Christians, no doubt, for their part have the Spirit, and besides His presence, are not without their own blemishes. If, then, any one brings charges against some Christian, perhaps he in a great degree sees only the blemishes of that Christian, and so in a less degree observes the good that is in him; and, therefore, he does not blaspheme against the Spirit in others, however grievously he sins in other respects. Christ Jesus, being endued with the Spirit beyond all measure, had no foreign element at all intermixed: therefore the blasphemies with which He was assailed, were much more enormous sins.—V. g.

neither—neither, etc.) *i.e.*, he shall in both drain to the dregs the most sure and most grievous punishment. See Chrysostom on this passage.

33. Καί, *and*) Understand again ποιήσατε, *make*; resolving the imperative into the future.—καλόν, *good*) The Jews wished to be a good tree with bad fruit, though they plainly knew it to be contrary to the truth.

34. Τῆς καρδίας, τὸ στόμα, *of the heart, the mouth*) See ch. xv. 18; Rom. x. 9; 2 Cor. iv. 13.

35. Θησαυροῦ, *treasure*) There is truly treasure and hidden abundance in every man.[1]—τὰ ἀγαθά—πονηρά, *the good things, evil things*) The article has frequently a relative value: I have therefore sometimes thought that it was on that account added to ἀγαθά, *good things*, as being already mentioned in ver. 34, and not to πονηρά, which does not there occur. But many have either written or omitted the article too promiscuously.[2] The ancient Cambridge MS. has ἀγαθά without an article.[3]

36. Ῥῆμα, *word*) A nominative absolute, as in Luke xxi. 6; John xvii. 2; Acts vii. 40; Rev. iii. 12, 21, and in the S. V. of Ps. xvii. (xviii.) 31.—ἀργόν, *idle*) not only *evil*. Goodness of

---

[1] This word *treasure*, which plainly implies abundance, proves that also in the preceding ver. the word πλήρωμα is not to be too readily understood as *fulness* (Germ. *Ueberfluss*): although in its own proper place it may be understood, by a Hebraism, simply as a *thing contained*, אֵת. Luther himself does not translate it Was im Herzen ist, *what is in the heart*, but, Wess das Herz VOLL ist, *that with which the heart is* FULL. Comp. Luke vi. 45, where Θησαυρός is explained by περίσσευμα. See Ernesti Neueste Theol. Bibl. T. i., p. 809.—E. B.

[2] See f. n. on Maestricht's twenty-second Canon, quoted in Section ix. of the Author's Preface.—(I. B.)

[3] In his App. Crit. in loc. Bengel writes—

"τὰ ante πονηρά) *Er. Bas. α.β.γ.*, etc., τὰ *Comp. Aug.* 2. *Byz. Par.* 6, vel plures; *Chrys*. Articulus in priore colo lectus, in altero non lectus, medium: et articulus sæpe vim relativam habet: ideo ad τὰ ἀγαθά versu 34 laudata, non ad πονηρά, ibidem non memorata, adhiberi, aliquando mihi visus est, unde alii bis, alii ne semel quidem, alii posteriore tantum loco scribendum putarint. Sed nimis promiscue, etc.," as in Gnomon.—(I. B.)

In the margin of Ed. 2, and in Vers. Germ., the article τὰ is omitted.—E. B.

BD omits τὰ before ἀγαθά. Perhaps the τὰ of Rec. Text crept in from the τὸ ἀγαθόν of Luke vi. 35, through the Harmonies. LΔ read also τὰ πονηρά. But the primary authorities oppose this reading.—ED.

treasure does not produce even anything *idle*.[1]—*ἀποδώσουσι λόγον, they shall render account*) i.e., they shall pay the penalty of. A metonymy of the antecedent for the consequent.

37. *'Εκ, κ.τ.λ., by*, etc.) Words exhibit the righteousness or unrighteousness, which is in the heart.

38. *Ἀπεκρίθησαν, κ.τ.λ., answered*, etc.) As though they would not otherwise believe the words which they had just heard.—*θέλομεν, we wish*) Why do we wish? Because it so pleases us. They thus deny the signs which our Lord had already performed.—*ἀπὸ σοῦ, from Thee*) i.e. from Thee Thyself, as in ch. xvi. 1—*ἐκ τοῦ οὐρανοῦ, from heaven.*

39. *Γενεά, a generation*) A race of the same age and disposition.—*μοιχαλίς, adulterous*) i.e. strictly so speaking: see ch. v. 32; and also, by synecdoche, very guilty; see James iv. 4.—*σημεῖον, a sign*) and one too of a certain special kind. This word is thrice repeated here with great emphasis; cf. 2 Cor. xi. 12, where the meaning is, *They wish for an occasion, and no occasion is given them;* which resembles what is said here, *They seek for a sign, and no sign shall be given them.*—*ἐπιζητεῖ, seeketh in addition*) i.e. beyond those which it has already seen, it requires further signs, as if it had seen none yet.—*τὸ σημεῖον Ἰωνᾶ, the sign of Jonah*) that is such a one as was given in Jonah.

40. *Ἰωνᾶς, Jonas*) Jonas did not then die, but yet it was as much believed that he would not return from the fish, as it was that Jesus would not return from the heart of the earth; yet both of them did return.—*ἐν τῇ κοιλίᾳ τοῦ κήτους, in the belly of the whale*) We ought not to doubt that Jonah was in the belly of the whale, on account of the narrow throat of some animals

---

[1] I can hardly think that it can be proved by the *Arabic idiom*, that this precept of our Lord ought to be restricted to *lies*; for the words λέγω δὲ ὑμῖν not obscurely intimate that the language of Christ moves in a descending climax, and that from *evil* words, mentioned in ver. 35, He goes down also to *idle* words. Compare the similar Epitasis (successive increase in the force by the descending climax) in αἰσχρότης, μωρολογία, εὐτραπελία, Eph. v. 4. Let us weigh well the caution which is found in Matt. v. 19, and which can never be too much recommended to all Critics, Teachers, and Sacred Orators, when about to enter on the investigation of the force of expressions and phrases, especially in morals.—E. B.

[2] Ἐν ἡμέρᾳ κρίσεως, *in the day of judgment*) Oh! what a great day!—V. g.

of that kind. For there are various sorts of whales, and in these days, the bodies of men are found in their stomachs; and even if such were not the case, we must suppose that fish especially made for the occasion; see Jon. ii. 1.—ἔσται, *shall be*) A sign for the future, as in John ii. 19, vi. 62, 39.—γῆς, *of the earth*) From thence shall they have a sign, and not one from heaven before that, although they sought it thence; cf. Luke xi. 16. No signs, except such as were exhibited from the earth, and performed for the good of men, were suitable to the Messiah's state of humiliation. They did not know that the sign of that time was suitable to that time; see ch. xvi. 3. Afterwards signs were shown, and shall be shown from heaven: see Acts ii. 19; Matt. xxiv. 30.—τρεῖς ἡμέρας καὶ τρεῖς νύκτας, *three days and three nights*) No one doubts that Jesus was in the heart of the earth *three days.*—He remained there however only two nights, as far as night signifies the darkness interposed between day and day (cf. Mark xiv. 30); and yet the calculation of three days, and the same number of nights, holds good if you do not interpret it with astronomical exactness, but resolve it by synecdoche. For *three days and three nights* are the periphrasis of a single idea, and have the force of a single word and term, if such existed, by which the remaining of Jesus in the sepulchre is expressed, as if you should say *a-space-of-three-days-and-nights* (*triduinoctium*), or *three-nights-and-days* (*tria noctidua*). *Three days* might have been simply expressed, but this is the idiom of the sacred style, that in indicating *continuous* time the intervening nights are added; see ch. iv. 2; Gen. vii. 4; 1 Sam. xxx. 12, 13; Job ii. 13. And then it sounds better to say[1] *three days and three nights*, than *three days and two nights*, although the Lord was buried on the actual day of the preparation, not on the night preceding and joined to it, and the space of twenty-four hours is regarded simply as a natural day without the change of darkness and light; and in fact the first night-and-day, used synecdochically,[2] was from about the tenth hour of the Friday up to the night exclusively;[3] the second and

---

[1] In the original, "concinnius dicitur," *i.e.* it sounds more *systematic*, it sounds more *uniform*, to say.—(I. B.)

[2] See Appendix on the figure Synecdoche.—(I. B.)

[3] The night not being included.—ED.

fullest, from the beginning of that night up to the end of the Sabbath and beginning of the following night; the third, strictly speaking, from the beginning of the following night up to the resurrection of the Lord, and the rising of the sun on Sunday morning. Two nights, therefore, were certainly joined with two days; nor does one night taken from one day, *i.e.* the first, affect the truth of the language, which denominates the thing in question from its superior part (locutionis a potiori[1] rem denominantis). In fine, there were not two nights and days, nor four; therefore there were three. The Hebrew mode of expression is agreeable to this; concerning which, see Lightfoot and Wolfe on this passage, and Michaelis on Josh. ii. 16. Although what I have here said may satisfy a reader who is not unreasonable, I would also further observe, that the synecdoche does not belong so much to *the three-days-and-three-nights* as to the actual remaining in the heart of the earth. Scripture indeed frequently defines a certain time, and expresses not the whole matter which commensurately and exactly occupied that time, but a part of the matter longer in duration than the other parts; as, for example, the four hundred and thirty years of the sojourning in Egypt, Ex. xii. 40; and thus *passim* the whole book of Judges. In this passage, therefore, the remaining in the heart of the earth, *i.e.* in the sepulchre, is expressed, but at the same time the whole period of the Passion is implied, certainly from the agony in Gethsemane, when Jesus fell on the earth which He was the next day to enter, and from the capture by which the Jews commenced their undertaking to destroy that Temple (as Erasmus thinks, Annot. F. 134). Nay, the glorious beginning of the three days on Thursday is clearly intimated, in John xiii. 31 [comp. Harmon. Evang. p. 310, 366], as dating from the time when the Jews bargained for the Saviour, who was to be committed to the earth. The remaining in the earth, taken in a wider signification, includes all these things; see Ps. lxxi. 20.

---

[1] " A potiori" implies that the whole twenty-four-hour-day (the first of the three in question) is denominated, not only from a part, but also from *the superior* part, viz. the part *which had the daylight*, and which is regarded as superior to the part during which darkness prevailed, viz. the night preceding Friday, and attached to it, according to the Jewish mode of counting. —ED.

For the Son of Man was *a sign* to that generation, not only in His sepulchre, but most especially in His passion; see John viii. 28. In this manner, the *three days and three nights* are exactly completed from the dawn of Thursday to the dawn of Sunday. The time of the death of the two witnesses is exactly defined, Rev. xi., to be three and a half days; therefore we ought to consider that the three days and three nights of our Lord's remaining in the middle of the earth have been also exactly defined. The *middle*, or *heart*, of the earth should not be precisely sought for; but these phrases are opposed to the earth itself, on the surface of which Christ dwelt for more than thirty years.

41. "Ἄνδρες Νινευῖται, *men of Nineveh*) whose example was followed by their wives and children. In the following verse, the example of one *woman* is added, who heard a *wise man*, though it might seem more natural for the weaker sex to seek *prophecy* than wisdom.—ἀναστήσονται, *shall rise*) In the next verse, we find ἐγερθήσεται, *shall be raised up;* cf. in Luke xi. 32, 31; *shall rise* of their own accord, *shall be raised up* by the Divine volition. The force of each word is contained in the other.—μετὰ, *with*— κατακρινοῦσιν, *shall condemn*) Cf. Rom. ii. 27. Therefore, at the Last Judgment, those whose conduct is similar or opposite,[1] will be pitted in turn against each other.—εἰς, *at*) The faith of the Ninevites is hereby[2] asserted (proprie dicitur).—See Jonah iii. 5. Cf. the use of εἰς, in Rom. iv. 20.—κήρυγμα, *preaching*) without miracles.[3]—Ἰωνᾶ, *of Jonah*) who was mentioned also in ver. 39. The messengers of salvation are prophets, wise men, and scribes; see ch. xxiii. 34. It did not become the Lord to act the Scribe; see John vii. 15, and cf. Gnomon on Luke iv. 16: but He, the greatest Prophet, from the race of prophets selects him who best suited this occasion, namely Jonah; and, being wisdom itself, He, from the race of wise men, selects that distinguished wise man, Solomon; and declares that Something Greater than either of them was then present. Both of them had been believed

---

[1] " Quorum par aut opposita est ratio,"—who stand on a like, or a contrasted and opposite footing, in relation to the judgment.—ED.

[2] The εἰς implies the faith whereby they turned *to*, and believed *in*, the preaching of Jonah.—ED.

[3] As in the case of Solomon. ver. 42.—V. g.

without signs.—Πλεῖον, *Something Greater*) He who is rather to be heard.[1]—ὧδε, *here*) close at hand, cf. in the following verse.—ἐκ τῶν περάτων τῆς γῆς, *from the uttermost parts of the earth*.

42. Νότου, *of the south*) from Arabia-Felix.—Πλεῖον Σαλομῶνος, *Something Greater than Solomon*) Solomon was wise, but here is Wisdom itself.—See Luke xi. 49.

43. Ὅταν, κ.τ.λ., *when*, etc.) Having rebuked and dismissed the interruption of the Pharisees, Jesus pursues those matters which depend upon ver. 30; cf. Luke xi. 23, 24.—ἐξέλθῃ, *has gone out*) as had been said in ver. 29.—διέρχεται, *he goeth through*) one after another.—ἀνύδρων, *without water*) Where there is no water, men do not dwell; see Ps. cvii. 35, 36.—ἀνάπαυσιν, *rest*) Rest is wished for by every created being. The devils think that man is their proper resting-place.—οὐχ εὑρίσκει, *findeth none*) sc. except in man. It is miserable always to seek and never to find it.

44. Οἶκόν μου, *my house*) What the enemy had once occupied, he considers as a portion of his property.—ἐξῆλθον, *I came out*) He speaks as if he had not been cast forth See the pride of the unclean spirit, which shows itself not merely in this word, but from his whole speech, as though it had been at his option either to *come out* or to *return*. Our Lord uses the same word without any particular emphasis in ver. 43. The same word may either have emphasis, or be without emphasis, in different speeches, according to the different condition and mind of the speaker.—ἐλθὸν, *when he is come*) for the sake of reconnoitering.—εὑρίσκει, κ.τ.λ., *he finds*, etc.) Therefore, the house was not so before the enemy had been cast forth.—σχολάζοντα, *vacant*) Tranquillity, although in itself good, is not far distant from peril. The same verb σχολάζειν occurs in the S. V. of Ex. v. 8, 17, for נרפה, *to be idle*.—σεσαρωμένον, *swept*) i.e., cleared from evils.—κεκοσμημένον, *adorned*) sc. with good things; see ver. 28. The enemy seeks especially clean places to rest in, not that they may remain clean, but that he may render them also unclean

45. Τότε, *then*) sc. when he has reconnoitred it —ἑπτὰ, *seven*) Therefore, counting him, there are *eight*. The fathers have

---

[1] Who is Himself about to be the Judge.—V. g.

numbered also eight deadly sins: see Columbanus,[1] and Goldastus[2] on him; also Ephraem Syrus,[3] f. υκβ. The seven, however, differ from that one in wickedness, perhaps also among themselves. The greater number includes the lesser numbers also disjunctively; cf. Luke viii. 8, with Matt. xiii. 8. Therefore, six spirits may occupy one, five another, four another, etc.—πονηρότερα, *more evil*) i.e., operating with greater subtilty, not by violent paroxysms. There are, therefore, *unclean* spirits who are yet less evil than others; and there are other spirits exceedingly *malignant*.—κατοικεῖ, *inhabit*) make their habitation more perseveringly than before.—χείρονα, *worse*) Seven times worse and more.—καὶ, *also*) That which happened to the man in his body, shall be done to this generation spiritually.[4]

46. Μήτηρ, *mother*) It is clear that, on this occasion, the thoughts and feelings of Mary were not in unison with those of her Son.—[5]Αὐτῷ, *unto Him*) as if for His sake.[6]

48. Τίς ἐστιν, κ.τ.λ., *who is*, etc.) He does not scorn His mother, but He places His Father before her (see ver. 50): and, with reference to this principle, He does not acknowledge His mother and brethren; and uses this form of words to convey a reproof.

49. Καὶ, κ.τ.λ., *and*, etc.) The greatest gentleness and sobriety

---

[1] ST COLUMBANUS was a native of Ireland, who flourished towards the close of the sixth and commencement of the seventh century. He was celebrated for his writings, theological and poetical, as well as for the extent and success of his missionary labours.—(I. B.)

[2] MELCHIOR GOLDASTUS VON HAIMENSFELD, a Swiss by birth, edited the works of St Columbanus, and others, in 1604. He was a laborious antiquarian and philologist. Born in 1576 or 1578; died in 1635.—(I. B.)

[3] EPHRAEM SYRUS was an eminent father of the Church, who flourished in the fourth century. He was born at Nisibis, where he became a pupil of St James, the celebrated bishop of that place. He went to Edessa A.D. 363, and, embracing a monastic life, retired to a cavern in one of the adjacent mountains, where he is said to have composed most of his works, which are very numerous. Some, however, are attributed to him, of which he was not the author. He obtained a high character for sanctity, and died in 378 or 379.

[4] Inasmuch as this generation has had so great a deliverance vouchsafed (offered) to it by the power of Christ.—V. g.

[5] Οἱ ἀδελφοὶ αὐτοῦ) These were not sons whom Joseph had brought to Mary at their marriage: for Christ, as He was accounted the Son of Joseph, so was accounted as absolutely his first-begotten Son.—V. g.

[6] Their intention was to interrupt him; Mark iii. 21, 31.— V. g.

are here combined with the greatest severity.¹—*ἰδοὺ, behold*) corresponding to the same word in ver. 47.

50. Ποιήσῃ, *shall do*) He does not say *does*, but He speaks somewhat conditionally.—τὸ θέλημα, *the will*) by which we are born again.²—αὐτός, *he*) *This* man, and he only.—ἀδελφός, *brother*) This word is said for the third time with great force.—καὶ ἀδελφή, *and sister*) The plural appellation of *brethren* in ver. 46, 47, 48, 49, includes sisters also.—μήτηρ, *mother*) The climax.

CHAPTER XIII.

2. Τὸ πλοῖον, *the vessel*) The article indicates a particular vessel which was wont to be had there.—καὶ, κ.τ.λ., *and*, etc.) sc. when the people saw Him.—αἰγιαλὸν, *beach*) Hesychius renders αἰγιαλὸς by ὁ παραθαλάσσιος ἐν τόπῳ ψαμμώδει ἢ ψηφίδας ἔχων,—i.e. "the seaside in a sandy place, or abounding with pebbles."

3. Ἐν παραβολαῖς, *in parables*) The Evangelist here indicates a remarkable period of Christ's teaching to the people in Galilee, as to the chief priests and elders of the people in Jerusalem. See Mark xii. 1,—ἤρξατο αὐτοῖς ἐν παραβολαῖς λέγειν, *He* BEGAN *to speak to them in parables*.³ Parables are frequent in the East: but our Lord had previously taught much, in both places, without parables. The parables in the present passage are seven: four addressed to the people, in ver. 3, 24, 31, 33; and three to the disciples, in ver. 44, 45, 47.⁴

---

¹ The reason for this severity is to be found in the parallel passage, Mark iii. 21, as Michaelis shows in the Einleitung, etc., T. ii., p. m. 1162.—E. B.
² James i. 18.—E. B.
³ Compare Matt. xxi. 23. [Qy. 28].—E. B.
⁴ The parable concerning the four different kinds of soil the Saviour explained to His disciples, at their request, before that He returned to the house—all other *witnesses*, however, being *out of the way*—whether His explanation was given on the sea or on land, ver. 10; with which comp. Mark iv. 10. Then next He set forth the rest of the parables before the multitude, Mark iv. 33; and, returning to the *house*, He cleared up also the parable

The first four and the last three form severally two groups, which are, respectively, intimately connected together. The former are connected by the formula, "*another parable;*" the latter, by the formula, "*Again the kingdom of heaven is like.*" And since the seventh refers more than any of the others to the end of the world, which the first does not refer to at all, but applies the prophecy of Isaiah to the people at the time of our Lord's teaching,—these seven parables have a most recondite meaning (see ver. 35), applying especially to distinct periods of the Church's history and condition, besides the common and universal principles which they teach concerning the course and administration of the kingdom of heaven; and this in such a manner, that each begins successively to be fulfilled after that which preceded it, though no preceding one concludes before the beginning of that which follows. The first and second, and only these two, were explained to the apostles. In the first, before the explanation—in the second, after it—occurs the formula, "*He that hath ears to hear, let him hear.*" The first, indeed, was fulfilled, as we have already observed, in the first age—namely, that of our Lord's ministry; the second, in that of His apostles, and thenceforward, for then men began to sleep (see ver. 25); the third and fourth denote the propagation of the kingdom of God among princes and the whole human race; the fifth describes the darker condition of the Church; the sixth, the state of the kingdom of God when esteemed above all things; the seventh, the condition of the Church in the last days, greatly mixed. It may be asked, whether these seven parables extend through the whole period of the New Testament dispensation in such a manner that the three latter begin from the goal of the four former; or whether those four extend from the beginning to the end, and also these three? On the settlement of these questions depends a more accurate distribution, which I leave to be decided by the wise, [merely subjoining the following sketch]:—

of the tares for the disciples, who begged Him to do so, ver. 36; with which comp. Mark iv. 34. After the setting forth of these parables, of which several are derived from the tillage of land, within the lapse of a few days the *barley harvest* began. In like manner the parable of the net (ver. 47) cast into the *sea*, was put forth close by *the sea.—Harm.*, p. 322.

1. The time of the apostles, . . ver. 16
2. After the decease of the apostles, . 25
3. Constantine, . . . 32
4. Nine centuries under the trumpet of the seventh angel, ... 33
5. The kingdom of the Beast, and the Reformation, ... 44
6. The kingdom of God esteemed above all things, Satan being bound, . . 46
7. The last confusion, . . . 47

Ὁ σπείρων.—*He that soweth*) in the present tense; *i.e.* Christ.

4. Παρὰ τὴν ὁδόν, *by the wayside*) when the field and the road touch each other.

5. Πετρώδη, *rocky*) This expression does not indicate stones lying scattered over the field, but a continuous bed of rock under the ground, with only a slight covering of soil.—οὐκ εἶχε, *had not*) We must understand ἄλλα, *other*, in the nominative plural. πολλήν = the Hebrew רב, *much* : it sometimes signifies *too much*; here, *sufficiently much*.—ἐξανέτειλε, *grew up high*) not merely ἀνέτειλε, *sprang up*.

6. Ἐκαυματίσθη, *they were scorched*) sc. in a less degree from without.—ἐξηράνθη, *they were dried up*) sc. utterly from within.[1]

7. Ἀνέβησαν αἱ ἄκανθαι, *the thorns sprang up*) beyond the crop itself. They had not before then grown so high. Those who have heard the Word, yet do not grow in good, turn their strength to increase in evil.

8. Καλήν, *good*) sc. soft, deep, clean (purgatam, *i.e.* cleared of stones, thorns, and weeds).[2]—ὃ μὲν—ὃ δὲ—ὃ δὲ, *some—some—some*) referring to ἄλλα, *other*, at the commencement of the same verse.

9. Ὁ ἔχων, *he that hath*) Cf. ver. 11, 12, 13.[3] Let him that heareth, hear: to him that hath shall be given.

10. Διατί, κ.τ.λ., *why?* etc.) It seemed a new thing to the disciples; see ver. 3.

---

[1] A man, to whom any degree of good begins to adhere, is liable to the loss of it, even though he may not lose it all at once.—V. g.

[2] *Soft* or friable, *deep*, and *cleared* of weeds and thorns, are respectively opposed to the hard stiff soil of the wayside, the shallow soil spread over the underlying rock, and the thorny ground.—ED.

[3] E. B. adds 43.

11. Ὅτι, *because*) This may be referred to the preceding διατί, *why?* Cf. in ver. 13, διὰ τοῦτο, *therefore.*—ὑμῖν, *to you*) who have.—τὰ μυστήρια, *the mysteries*) This term is applied, not to all things which all ought to know from revelation, but to those things which they, to whom secret things are revealed, know beyond those who know only what is strictly necessary.—ἐκείνοις, *to them*) who are without, in contradistinction *to* ὑμῖν, *you,* who are within.[1] οὐ δέδοται, *it is not given*) sc. to comprehend mysteries fully and clearly.[2]

12. Ἔχει, *hath*) *to have,* signifies to be rich. He who hath rejoices in this as his distinguishing criterion, viz. that he is *one that hath,* and becomes day by day more sure of perseverance.— περισσευθήσεται, *he shall be rendered more abundant*[3]) and shall surpass his former self.[4]—ὅστις οὐκ ἔχει, *whosoever hath not*) The conjunction ὅτι (*because*), in ver. 13, refers to this, and μήποτε (*lest at any time*), in ver. 15, to ἀρθήσεται (*shall be taken away*).— καὶ ὃ ἔχει, *even that which he hath*) shall be taken away.—ἀρθήσεται, *shall be taken away*) Even though he hear, yet he shall not hear; and that which he hath heard shall at length (undoubtedly after the judgment) be so taken away from him, that he shall be as if he had never heard anything. The damned shall be tortured with ignorance, and the thirst for knowledge.

13. Ὅτι, κ.τ.λ., *because,* etc.) Our Lord, therefore, did not speak to the people in parables without a cause. And nevertheless He had often before spoken to them without parables, out of compassion (see ch. ix. 36, and Mark vi. 34), and they had not profited [by His teaching].—οὐδὲ συνιοῦσι) *neither do they understand.*

14. Καί, *and*) therefore.—ἀναπληροῦται, *is now being refulfilled*[5])

---

[1] In the original, "hoc vim habet removendi." I have paraphrased it, so as to express Bengel's meaning in a manner intelligible to the English reader.—(I. B.)

[2] In the original, "nosse mysteria nuda." Literally, *to know mysteries naked, i.e.* fully revealed, without concealment or obscurity.—(I. B.)

" Mysteria nuda," *mysteries without the clothing of the parabolic form* or *guise.*—ED.

[3] E. V. Shall have more abundance.—(I. B.)

[4] "This is the case in things temporal, and much more so in things spiritual."—B. G. V.

[5] E. V. "is fulfilled."—(I. B.)

" Is receiving its *complete* (*full measure* of) fulfilment."—ED.

This word differs from the simple verb πληροῦται (*is now being fulfilled*), which is employed elsewhere in citing prophecies. The saying of Isaiah (vi. 9) was being fulfilled in his own days, and in the ages which followed, and also clearly and especially in the days of the Messiah.—ἀκοῇ, κ.τ.λ., *by hearing*, etc.) *i.e.* by however little you come short, yet you shall come short [of *understanding*] what ye hear to the salvation of your souls].

15. Ἐπαχύνθη γὰρ ἡ καρδία τοῦ λαοῦ τούτου, FOR *this people's heart is waxed gross*) It stands thus in the S. V.; but in the Hebrew there is no word corresponding to the Greek γὰρ, *for*. The language, however, rapidly turns itself away from them.[1]— ἡ καρδία, *the heart*, τοῖς ὠσί—τοὺς ὀφθαλμοὺς, *with their ears, their eyes*) These three occur again immediately in the opposite order: "*with their eyes,*" "*with their ears,*" "*with their heart.*" The heart is the first in the beginning, the last in the end. From the *heart* corruption flows into the *ears* and *eyes*; through the *eyes* and *ears* health[2] reaches the *heart*.—ἐκάμμυσαν—μήποτε— ἰάσωμαι αὐτούς, *they have closed, lest at any time I should heal them*) God therefore had wished to *heal* them; and it is clear that *healing* was close to them, if they had only turned to it. In Mark iv. 12, we read " καὶ ἀφεθῇ αὐτοῖς τὰ ἁμαρτήματα;" *i.e.* "*and their sins be forgiven them.*" Cf. Ps. ciii. 3.—συνῶσι, *should understand*) The seat[3] of σύνεσις, *understanding*, and νόησις, *perception*, is the heart, not the brain: this is equally true of πώρωσις, *hardening* (see John xii. 40), and of σκοτασμός, *darkening* (see Rom. i. 21); as also of ἀπιστία, *unbelief*, and πίστις, *faith*, which is followed by ἐπιστροφή, *conversion*.[4]

[1] "Sermo autem celeriter se ab iis avertit." This is one of many instances where it is impossible to find an English equivalent to the Latin "*Sermo.*" Bengel's meaning is, that whereas, in ver. 9, God had commanded the prophet to go and speak to the Jews, saying, "Hear ye indeed, but understand not; and see ye indeed, but perceive not," in ver. 8, He suddenly changes the *Sermo, i.e.* the mode of speech, the *direction* of His words; and, instead of desiring Isaiah to address the people, turns from them, as it were, and gives an injunction to the prophet, *regarding* them, it is true, but not addressed *to* them : sc. "*Make the heart of this people fat,* etc."—(I. B.)

[2] "Sanitas," lit. *soundness*, an expression applied indifferently to mind or body, as in the well-known passage of Juvenal:—
   "Ut sit mens sana in corpore sano."—(I. B.)

[3] "Subjectum quo."—(I. B.)

[4] "The Hebrew accents undoubtedly connect the words καὶ ἐπιστρίψωσι

16. Ὀφθαλμοί—ὦτα, *eyes — ears*) i.e. those of your body, above the saints of the Old Testament; those of your soul, above the people now present. Their eyes and ears were the subject of which blessedness could be predicated.[1]

17. Προφῆται, *prophets*) See Gnomon on 1 Pet. i. 10, 12.—ἐπεθύμησαν, *have desired*) And that desire was pious and precious in the sight of God: see Gnomon on John viii. 56.—οὐκ εἶδον, *have not seen*) See Heb. xi. 13, 39.

18. Ὑμεῖς, *you*) in contradistinction to the people.—τοῦ σπείροντος, *of the Sower*) i.e. so called from the Sower.

19. Μὴ συνιέντος, *understandeth it not*) The verb συνιέναι signifies to understand.[2] The Evil One, or devil, who especially, rather than his angels, is meant by the fowls of the air, has less power over those things which have entered into the σύνεσις, or understanding.—ἁρπάζει, *catcheth away*) sc. with violence and quick cunning, like a bird of prey; see ver. 4.—ἐν τῇ καρδίᾳ, *in his heart.*—ὁ σπαρείς, *he that is sown*) i.e. as a farm is sown.

20. Ὁ δέ, κ.τ.λ., *but he*, etc.) In every individual soul one distinguishing characteristic is especially conspicuous.—εὐθύς, *immediately*) Too great haste and joyfulness is not always the best sign, when the whole strength pours itself forth in outward demonstrations, and consumes itself in them.—μετὰ χαρᾶς λαμβάνων, *with joy receiving*) see Gal. iv. 14, 15.

21. Ῥίζαν, *root*) which is plainly necessary, and springs from the word itself.—πρόσκαιρός ἐστι, *is temporary*)[3] He believes whilst the time inclines him; see Luke viii. 13. The adjective

---

(*and should be converted*) more closely with συνῶσι (*should understand*) than with ἰάσωμαι (*I should heal*). And in many passages of the Old Testament which are quoted in the New, the Hebrew accents agree more accurately with the force of the exact words of the Inspired original than the punctuation employed by the Greeks: *e.g.* Matt. iv. 15, xix. 5, xxi. 5; Luke iv. 18; Acts vii. 6, viii. 32; Heb. i. 12, iii. 9, xii. 26, xiii. 6. And yet these Greeks were Christians. We ought not, therefore, to think that the Hebrew accents have originated with the modern Jews left to their blindness. Their origin is far more ancient, far more sublime."—App. Crit., Ed. II., p. 120.

[1] "Subjectum quo beatitudinis."—(I. B.)
[2] That such is Bengel's meaning is clear from his own German Version, where he renders μὴ συνιέντος by "*und nicht vernimmt.*"—(I. B.)
[3] E V. "dureth for a while."—(I. B.)

πρόσκαιρος, taken alone, expresses somewhat good, but without perseverance; it is therefore followed here by the adversative particle δὲ, *but*, and in Mark iv. 17, by εἶτα, *afterwards*.— θλίψεως, *affliction*) generally.—διωγμοῦ, *persecution*) specifically.[1] —διὰ τὸν λόγον, *because of the word*) when it is propagated by the mouth and expressed by the life.—εὐθὺς, *immediately*) That which is quickly produced, perishes quickly.[2]

22. Ἡ ἀπάτη τοῦ πλούτου, *the deceitfulness of riches*)[3] Riches remove the soul from that tranquillity which is here opposed to *the care of this world*.[4]—ἄκαρπος γίνεται, *becometh unfruitful*) sc. the word in man becometh so (see Mark iv. 19); *i.e.*, the word in him who hears it does not arrive at good and perfect fruit fit for use: the man *bringeth no fruit to perfection*, οὐ τελεσφορεῖ, Luke viii. 14. Thomas Magister[5] says, εὔκαρπα δένδρα, ὧν ὁ καρπός ἐστι χρήσιμος ἀνθρώποις εἰς τροφήν· ἄκαρπα, τὸ ἐναντίον, ὧν τοῖς καρποῖς οὐ χρῶνται οἱ ἄνθρωποι· ἄκαρπον δέ, τὸ μὴ ποιοῦν καρπόν, παρ' οὐδενὶ τῶν παλαιῶν εὕρηται: *i.e.*, "Trees which are styled εὔκαρπα, are those, the fruit (καρπός) of which is serviceable for food to men: ἄκαρπα, on the other hand, are those, the fruit of which men do not use for food: but ἄκαρπον, in the sense of having no fruit, is not found in any of the ancients."

23. Ὅς, *who*) sc. the hearer; cf. Mark iv. 20: otherwise ὅς might also be referred to τὸν λόγον, *the word*.—καρποφορεῖ, *beareth fruit*) sc. perfect fruit.—ὃ μὲν—ὃ δὲ—ὃ δὲ, *some—some—some*) The pronoun ὅ is clearly here in the accusative neuter; for the

---

[1] Persecution can be brought to bear against one either by an unkind side look, or by a jesting speech added in the way of mockery.—V. g.

[2] Σκανδαλίζεται) He *is offended*, and therefore relapses into unbelief. —V. g.

[3] Which is manifold in its varieties of form, and which, though it deceives men in an awful manner, yet scarcely ever seems to them worth while being taken into consideration at all.—V. g.

[4] Συμπνίγει, *choke*) Many engage in the discussion (treating) of the Word of God in such a way as if the heart were not a field in which the seed is to remain and grow, but a granary which can contain at one time less stores, at another time more—at one time something, at another time nothing. —V. g.

[5] Thomas Magister, surnamed Theodulus (ΘΕΟΔΟΥΛΟΣ, *The Servant of God*), was a Monk and a Grammarian, who flourished at the beginning of the fourteenth century. Saxius describes him as "*vocum Atticarum magister.*"—(I. B.)

subject[1] ὅς, which occurs here in the singular number, cannot possibly be divided into three classes of good hearers of the word by ὁ μὲν—ὁ δὲ—ὁ δὲ (*one—another—a third*), which is the common reading.[2] Moreover the *protasis* has ὅ in ver. 8, and the parallel passage in Mark iv. 8, 20, has ἓν also twice over.[3] A single hearer's plentiful, moderate, and less plentiful progress from three several grains, so to speak, is signified by a *hundred, sixty,* and *thirty.*[4] As there are three degrees of hearing without fruit, so there are also three degrees of fruitfulness; which is not, however, restricted precisely to the proportions an hundred, sixty, and thirty fold: for another grain might also produce forty, fifty, seventy, eighty, ninety fold, etc.: since there is a greater distance between the numbers one hundred and sixty, than there is between sixty and thirty. To him that hath shall be given.

---

[1] The word "*Subject*" is used here in its *logical* sense, viz. the *Subject of the Proposition, i e.* the person or thing concerning which something else is predicated or asserted.—(I. B.)

[2] Such is the reading of E. M. In his App. Crit. Bengel writes: "ὁ ter) codd. nonulli vetusti apud *Stapulensem,* vel etiam alii apud *Rus* T. i., Harm. Evang. p. 1047; *Ephrem* Syrus f. σ.κ.δ. in vitâ Abrahamii; *Isidorus* Pelus. l. 2, ep. 144. *Lat. Neogræc.* vel plures nec non *Syr.* (ὁ ter) edd. *Aug.* 1, *Byz.,* etc., perinde ut versu 8, ὁ pro ὅ, et *Marc.* iv. 8, ἐν pro ἓν, non nulli habent codices."—(I. B.)

Beng. does not seem to me to speak of a different *reading,* but of the *common interpretation,* that there are here three classes of good hearers. He plainly understands there to be *the one and the same* good hearer, who bears fruit from the same seed *in different degrees at different times.* Hence Luke viii. 8 gives the *one* degree only, viz. the hundredfold, as the normal state of the believer's fruitfulness. However, in opposition to Beng., the transition from ὅς to ὁ μὲν, ὁ δὲ, neut. *nominative,* would not be unnatural (whether taken of one and the same good hearer, or of different classes of good hearers), as the *individual becomes in a manner identified with the seed* in process of time, just as the nutritive elements of the soil become identified with, and taken up into, the young germ: hence σπαρείς, *he who is sown* (applicable to the *seed,* but here also to the *person*), occurs in ver. 19, and ἄλλα, ver. 8, is nominative neuter, and plural, followed by ὁ μὲν, ὁ δὲ. There is no notable variety of *readings* in the case.—ED.

[3] *i.e.* the ἓν, which occurs three times in Mark iv. 8, is repeated as many times in ver. 20.—(I. B.)

[4] When such a hearer turns the one and the same doctrine, on the opportunity of hearing it being given him even a hundred times, to his own profit and that of others.—V. g.

ST MATTHEW XIII. 24, 25.

24. Παρέθηκεν αὐτοῖς, *He set before them*¹) as food is set before a guest.²—ἐν τῷ ἀγρῷ, *in the field*) sc. that in which He Himself is: for it is said "*In*," not "*into*" His field.

25. Τοὺς ἀνθρώπους, *the men*) sc. those whose business it was to watch the field. The Lord Himself does not sleep.—Αὐτοῦ, *His*) it is not said *their* enemy.—ζιζάνια, *zizans*³) This word does not occur in the LXX. nor in the more ancient Greek writers; it is therefore evidently formed from the Hebrew ציץ, *a flower*. Many flowers which are noxious to the husbandman grow among the corn.—ἀνά, κ.τ.λ., *throughout*, etc.) everywhere among the wheat.—ἀπῆλθεν, *departed*⁴) on which account the *zizans* ⁵ remained for some time unnoticed.

¹ E. V. "put He forth unto them."—(I. B.)
² Ἡ βασιλεία τῶν οὐρανῶν, *the kingdom of heaven*) As often soever as mention is made of this in the discourses and parables of our Lord, this very expression is to be regarded as a succinct recapitulation of the whole Gospel.—V. g.
³ E. V. "*Tares*."—" Apparently the *darnel* or *bastard wheat* (lolium album), so often seen in our fields and by our hedgerows; if so, what follows will be explained, that the '*tares*' appeared when the wheat came into ear, having been previously not noticeable. It appears to be an Eastern word, expressed in the Talmud by זונין. Our Lord was speaking of an act of malice practised in the East; persons of revengeful disposition watch the ground of a neighbour being ploughed, and in the night following sow destructive weeds." (Roberts' Oriental Illustrations, p. 541, cited by Trench on the Parables, p. 68.) (The practice is not unknown even in England at present. Since the publication of the first edition of this Commentary, a field at Gaddesby, in Leicestershire, was maliciously sown with charlock [sinapis arvensis] over the wheat. An action at law was brought, and heavy damages obtained against the offender.) " Jerome in loc. says:—'Inter triticum et zizania quod nos appellamus lolium, quamdiu herba est, et nondum culmus venit ad spicam, grandis similitudo est, et in discernendo nulla aut perdifficilis distantia.' Jerome, it must be remembered, resided in Palestine."—ALFORD in loc. Wordsworth says, that it was a degenerate wheat, and which may also be reclaimed into wheat. See also footnote 5.—(I. B.)
⁴ *He went his way*, in order that he might not be observed.—V. g.
⁵ Dr KITTO, in his Illustrated Commentary, says, "The Darnel, called *Zuwan* by the Arabs and Turks, and *Zizanion* by the Spaniards, is described by Dr Russell and Forskal as well known to the people of Aleppo, as often growing abundantly in their corn-fields. If its seeds remain mixed with the meal, it is found to occasion dizziness and other injurious effects upon those who eat of the bread: the reapers in that neighbourhood, however, do not separate the plant, but, after the threshing, reject the seeds by means of a

26. Τότε, *then*) Where the good grows, there the evil becomes at length more apparent.

27. Κύριε, *Lord*) The name of the Son of Man; see ver. 37.—πόθεν, κ.τ.λ., *whence?* etc.) The servants did not know who had done it, or when.—ζιζάνια, *zizans*) Zizans have a greater resemblance to wheat than thistles and thorns have; the toleration therefore of the former, does not involve as a consequence that of the latter. They often not only pass themselves off for wheat, but also attempt to root out the wheat as if it were zizans.

29. Οὔ, *no*) The zeal of the godly against the zizans is not blamed, but yet it is reduced to order.—ἅμα) *at the same time.*—τὸν σῖτον, *the wheat*) which you might mistake for zizans.

30. Συναυξάνεσθαι, *grow together*) Growth in good and evil takes place simultaneously, sometimes in the case of individuals, and generally in that of men taken collectively; and the further that ages proceed, the more conspicuous do they both become.—ἐν τῷ καιρῷ, κ.τ.λ., *in the time*) Then it will at length be the right time to do so.—πρῶτον, *first*) that the godly may behold the punishment of the ungodly; the ungodly not see the glory of the godly. Thus in ch. xxv., though the Judge addresses the righteous first, yet afterwards in the last verse the ungodly are banished into eternal fire before [the godly are admitted into heaven].—δέσμας, *bundles*) As from σταθμὸς (*a standing place, station*, etc.) comes στάθμη (*a carpenter's rule*, etc.), and from λῦμα (*physical or moral filth*, etc.) comes λύμη (*outrage*, etc.); so from δεσμὸς (*a band or bond*) are derived δέσμα (*a bond*), and δέσμη (*a bundle*); see Eustathius. They will have no choice: those of like kind will be joined together.—κατακαῦσαι, *to burn utterly*) They will be burned, and that utterly.—δὲ, *but*) Then the separation will have been effected.—συναγάγετε, *collect*) and bring.

• 31. Ἄνθρωπος, *a man*) The similitude is here taken from a man, as in ver. 33, from a woman; cf. Luke xv. 4, 8.

32. Ὅ, *which*) sc. *seed*: for κόκκος (*grain*) is masculine.—μικρότερον, *the least*) i.e. not absolutely, but in the proportion which the seed bears to the plant. It was a well-known kind of seed, used proverbially; see ch. xvii. 20.—σπερ-

van or sieve. We are also informed that, in other parts of Syria, the plant is drawn up by hand, in time of harvest, along with the wheat, and is then gathered out, and bound up in separate bundles."—(I. B.)

μάτων, *of seeds*) The world contains various seeds of wisdom, power, and virtue; the Christian faith has surpassed them all, having been propagated through the whole world. The kingdom of heaven is like a grain; and so is the whole of Christianity, faith, etc. These things may be variously expressed. The faith here intended is that of all those believers, who embrace it before others: the others are those who believe afterwards—nations, kings, etc.—μεῖζον—λαχάνων—δένδρον, *greater herbs—tree*) two classes of vegetables. Tremellius,[1] on this passage in the Syriac Version, adduces examples of such immense trees.—It became a tree, one may say, in the time of Constantine.[2] —τὰ πετεινὰ, *the birds*) see Ezek. xvii. 23.—κλάδοις, *branches*) sc. widely spreading.

33. Ἐνέκρυψεν, *concealed*) The LXX. in Ezek. iv. 12, render the Hebrew עוּג[3] (*to bake*) by ἐγκρύπτω (*to conceal*[4]), whence is derived ἐγκρυφίας, a cake.—σάτα[5] τρία, *three measures*) As much as was generally carried by a man, or taken for baking, at once; see Gen. xviii. 6.—ἐζυμώθη, *was leavened*) I would rather refer this to the propagation, than the corruption of the Church. The *leaven* is the *kingdom of heaven* itself, including both the gospel and the apostles.[6]—ὅλον, *the whole*) sc.

[1] EMMANUEL TREMELLIUS was born in the sixteenth century at Ferrara, of Jewish parents. He rendered himself master of the Hebrew language, and secretly embraced Protestantism. He became Professor of Hebrew at Heidelberg, from whence he went to Metz, and thence to Sedan. He made himself known by his *Latin Version of the Syriac New Testament*. He died in 1580.—(I. B.)

[2] The kingdom of Christ is being extended now throughout the whole world.—V. g.

[3] " עוּג, (1.) prop. *to go in a circle*. . . . Hence עֻגָה and גָּלִיל a round cake. . . .

(2.) denom. from עֻגָה *to bake bread* or *cake*, Ezra iv. 12."

" עֻגָה and עֻגָּה (1 Kings xix. 6; Ezek. iv. 12), fem. *a cake baked under hot cinders*," etc., GESENIUS.—(I. B.)

[4] *i.e.*, in the passage from Ezekiel, *to cover with*, sc. hot embers; E. V., *bake.*—(I. B.)

[5] ἐγκρυφίας, ου, ὁ, ἄρτος ἐγκ., *a loaf baked in the ashes*, Hipp. Luc. Dial. Mort. 20, 4, etc. LIDDELL and SCOTT.—(I. B.)

[6] " Cujus rationes et evangelium et apostolos complectuntur."—(I. B.)

No necessity, in fact, compels us to take the leaven in a bad sense: hence, as the word does not necessarily imply censure, bad leaven is termed the *old* leaven in 1 Cor. v. 7.—V. g

flour.¹ A strong expression. This appears to refer to the whole human race, which consists of three measures, having spread over the earth from the three sons of Noah.²

35. Τὸ ῥηθὲν, *which was spoken*) viz. Ps. lxxviii. 2—ἀνοίξω ἐν παραβολαῖς τὸ στόμα μου, φθέγξομαι προβλήματα ἀπ' ἀρχῆς, *I will open my mouth in parables, I will utter* [things which have been] *problems from the beginning.*—προφήτου, *prophet*) who was the author of that psalm. The Spirit of Christ was in the prophets; therefore the prophets could, after their manner, predicate of themselves those things which were afterwards most richly fulfilled in Christ.—ἀνοίξω, *I will open*) which before had not been done.—ἐρεύξομαι, *I will utter*) in Hebrew אביעה, *I will pour out*, which the LXX. elsewhere render ἐρεύγομαι in Ps. xix. 3, and ἐξερεύγομαι in Ps. cxix. 171, and cxlv. 7. Hesychius renders ἐρεύγεται by ἀναβάλλει, *throws up*, i.e. as a spring does water. He also renders ἐρεύγετο by ἐβρύχετο, *roared*, ἔβρυεν, *was overflowing with*; but βρύχειν is said of the noise of the floods, and the roaring of the lion. Therefore the verb ἐρεύγομαι denotes a gushing spring, which resounds by reason of the abundance and impetuosity of its waters; whence the LXX. put ἐρεύγεσθαι also for שאג, *to roar.*—καταβολῆς, *foundation*) It does not mean only the foundations, but also the building; see 2 Macc. ii. 29.

36. Φράσον, *explain*) The disciples, being teachable, ask for further instruction.

38. Οὗτοι, *these*) Of whom most account is taken; or especially the disciples then present.—τοῦ πονηροῦ, *of the wicked one*) The word is in the masculine gender.

39. Συντέλεια—ἄγγελοι, *consummation—angels*) They form the predicate here, the subject elsewhere.—συντέλεια in ver. 49, is the meeting or combination of the ends (τῶν τελῶν); see 1 Cor. x. 11.

41. Αὐτοῦ, *His*—Αὐτοῦ, *His*) Such is the majesty of the Son of Man. His are the *angels* (see the end of ver. 39); His is the

---

¹ A little leaven, as in evil, Gal. v. 9, so in good, leavens the whole mass.—V. g.

² This conjecture will not be thought ridiculous by him, who remembers that there may be not merely one reason for a particular circumstance or expression (as the reason already given in the note above on σάτα τρία, which see), but *several* reasons.—E. B.

kingdom of heaven; His is *the world*; cf. ver. 24, with ver. 38.
—βασιλείας, *the kingdom*) which is the kingdom of grace.—
σκάνδαλα, *stumbling-blocks*) obstacles, which had hindered the
good seed even in the case of others. The punishment of these
is peculiarly great.[1]

42. Καὶ βαλοῦσιν, *and they shall cast*) This is repeated in the
same words in ver. 50.

43. Τότε, *then*) After the ungodly have been removed.—
ἐκλάμψουσιν, *they shall shine forth*) They shall not burn as the
ungodly, but they shall shine forth, singly, and much more,
collectively.[2] The same word is employed by the LXX. in Dan.
xii. 3.—τοῦ Πατρὸς αὐτῶν, *of their Father*) who is righteous and
glorious. How great is the difference of the righteous from the
children of the wicked one! see ver. 38.—ὁ ἔχων ὦτα, κ.τ.λ., *he
that hath ears*, etc.) A formula suited, not only to the people, but
also to the disciples.

44. Θησαυρῷ, *treasure, store*) Not of corn,[3] but of gold, gems,
etc.—κεκρυμμένῳ—ἔκρυψε, *hidden—he hid*) It had escaped the
notice of him who found it; then, when he found it, he concealed it from others. He hid it in the same field in which he
found it. Such are the earnestness and prudence of the saints;
see Prov. vii. 1. They find the things which are hidden; they
hide them when found. The finding the treasure does not presuppose the *seeking* for it, as in the case of the pearls, which are
found by diligent search.—χαρᾶς, *for joy*) Spiritual joy is an
incentive to deny the world.—αὐτοῦ, *of it*) i.e. the treasure; or
else it is an adverb.[4]—ὑπάγει, *departeth*) In the present tense, as
πωλεῖ, *he sells*—ἀγοράζει, *he buys*. In ver. 46, the preterite is
put. The *state* follows the *act*.[5]

45. Οὐρανῶν—ἀνθρώπῳ, *of the heavens—to a man*) Comparisons
of heavenly from human things. See ver. 52; ch. xviii. 23, xx.

---

[1] Τὴν ἀνομίαν, *iniquity*) for their part—to the utmost of their ability, and as far as in them lies.—V. g.

[2] What can be sweeter, even to think of, than this?—V. g.

[3] Cf. Jer. xli. 8.—B. G. V.

[4] Meaning "THERE." In which case, instead of "*for joy* THEREOF," the passage would be rendered "*for the joy* which he has found or stored up THERE, sc. in the field."—(I. B.)

[5] Τὸν ἀγρὸν ἐκεῖνον, *that field*) with the treasure. If thou art influenced by the desire of true gain, follow this parable.—V g.

1, xxii. 2.—ἐμπόρῳ, *a merchant*) The word ἔμπορος denotes one who travels and voyages for the sake of merchandise.—μαργαρίτας, *pearls*) The plural passes to the singular in the following verse.

46. Ἕνα, *one*) An incomparable one; that is, the kingdom of heaven itself.[1]

47. Ἐκ παντὸς γένους, *of every kind*) See John xxi. 11, and Gnomon thereon.

48. Ἐπληρώθη, *was filled*) The number of the wicked and the righteous will be completed in the last days.—καὶ καθίσαντες, *and having sat down*) Deliberately, with the purpose of performing their task.—καλὰ—σαπρά, *good—putrid*) Individuals out of every kind of fishes.[2]—ἔξω, *without*) sc. the net.

49. Πονηροὺς, *the wicked*) and unrighteous.—ἐκ μέσου, *from the midst*) The wicked, although they are more in number, are not accounted of any value;[3] cf. ver. 30.—τῶν δικαίων, *of the righteous*) and good.[4]

51. Πάντα, *all things*) Our Lord was ready to explain the other parables also to His disciples; but they understood them, if not perfectly, yet truly.

52. Πᾶς γραμματεὺς, *every scribe*) Jesus Himself is neither γραμματεὺς, *a scribe*, nor μαθητευθεὶς, *discipled*, i.e. *instructed as or made a disciple (initiatus)*. He speaks therefore in the present instance of His disciples; and that which had previously been said to the disciples in plain words (ver. 12), is now (that they have made such advance in learning as to be styled even *scribes*) confirmed to them by a parable. A scribe is a man imbued with the doctrine, or even the letter, of the Old Testament; by παλαιά (*old*), therefore, are meant things known from Moses and the prophets. This is the genus: the species[5] is supplied by the clause μαθητευθεὶς, κ.τ.λ.—*i.e.* a man *instructed*

---

[1] Πέπρακε, *sold*) This is indeed to renounce all things whatsoever thou mayest possess.—V. g.

[2] How is it that the bad man does not loathe himself?—V. g.

[3] Cf. Gnomon on ch. iii. 12, in voc. ἄχυρον.—(I. B.)

[4] Ver. 50. Εἰς τὴν κάμινον τοῦ πυρός, *into the furnace of fire*) O what wretched beings are they who are tormented in that fire!—V. g.

[5] The words *genus* and *species* are here used in their logical sense. Bengel means to say that the character indicated is not only that of a "*scribe*," *generically* (or universally), but of one who is "*instructed* to *the kingdom of heaven*."—(I. B.)

also in the doctrine of the *New* Testament: such is the force of καινά, *new*—things then first revealed; see ver. 35. *New* things are here mentioned before *old*, as the latter receive light and savour from the former, and are at length tempered together most harmoniously. See 1 John ii. 7, 8.—μαθητευθείς, *instructed*) as βασιλεύω signifies both to make a king, and to act the king, so also μαθητεύω, to *make disciples* (expressed in John iv. 1 by μαθητὰς ποιεῖ), and *act* or *be a disciple*; see ch. xxvii. 57. The former meaning obtains in this passage.—τῇ βασιλείᾳ, *in the kingdom*) Others[1] read εἰς τὴν βασιλείαν, *unto the kingdom*. In either reading, by metonymy or prosopopœia, Christ Himself is intimated, as in ch. xi. 12. If you accept the latter reading, cf. 2 Cor. xi. 3; if the former,[2] ch. xxvii. 57.—ἀνθρώπῳ, *unto a man*) Almost all the parables are taken from human affairs, for the sake of perspicuity.—ἐκβάλλει, *bringeth forth*) plentifully.—θησαυροῦ, *treasure*) store, sc. of corn.—καινὰ καὶ παλαιά, *new and old*) a proverbial mode of speaking of a great plenty from the last and the present year; see Cant. vii. 13.—The *new* things, as from the treasures of the kingdom of heaven; the *old* things,

---

[1] Such is the reading of E. M. In his App. Crit. Bengel writes: "εἰς τὴν βασιλείαν) edd. Bas. a. β. Stap. etc. Ex μαθητευθείς, εἰς facile iteratum. (τῇ βασιλείᾳ) Bas. γ. Cypr. Par. 6, 8; *Vsser*, 2; *Origenes* constanter, sæpe; *Cyrillus, Procopius*. Placet Heinsio. Lectio media. unde ἐν τῇ βασιλείᾳ, *Med.* Chrysost. *Cyrillus* alibi, *Lat. Irenaeus*, latine certe, *Cant.*—(I. B.)

[2] The margin of both Editions, as well as the Germ. Vers., prefer the Dative.—E. B.

Tischend. with BC Syr. Orig. 3, 459 f, reads τῇ βασιλείᾳ. Lachm. with Dbc Vulg. Iren. 237, Hil., reads ἐν τῇ βασιλείᾳ. Lachm. claims C for ἐν τῇ βασ. in opposition to Tischend. Rec. Text, εἰς τ. βασιλείαν, is not supported by primary authorities. The shorter reading, τῇ βασιλείᾳ, is *cæteris paribus* preferable to the longer, as the shorter would be more likely to originate the other two, the longer ones, εἰς τ. βασ. and ἐν τ. βασ. (which look like glosses of the shorter), than either of them to originate it; ch. xxvii. 57 supports it. Besides, it is not simply *members of* the kingdom who are here spoken of, but those who, being *already in* it themselves, are qualified henceforth to be *teachers for* it. I prefer, with Olshausen and Storr, explaining it, "made a disciple for the kingdom," *i.e.*, for its benefit; one who, being *instructed himself*, is capable of *labouring for* the kingdom. But Beng. takes τῇ βασιλείᾳ as a Prosopopœia—*the Kingdom* meaning *Jesus Christ*, who is the *embodiment of the Kingdom*—"made a disciple *to the* Kingdom," *i.e.* to Jesus Christ.—ED.

as a scribe from the scriptures of the Old Testament; cf. ver. 35.[1]

53. Ἐτέλεσεν, *finished*) These parables form a regular and perfect whole, which He is therefore said to have *finished*; see ch. xi. 1.[2] Thus, in Luke vii. 1, we have ἐπλήρωσε, *He completed*. These parables contain, however, besides the general condition of the Church of the New Testament, a more special account of future events. Cf. Gnomon on ver. 3, and on John xvi. 13.—μετῆρεν, *He departed*, Lat. *migravit*)[3] He ended for the time His sojourn at Capernaum.[4] Thenceforward Jesus did not remain so long in one place, being harassed by Herod.

54.[5] Σοφία, *wisdom*—δυνάμεις, *mighty works*) supernatural powers: See 1 Cor. i. 24. We ought to be carried forward, by admiration of the teaching and works of our Lord, to a believing (fidelem) recognition of His person; otherwise admiration ends in stupor.

55. Τοῦ τέκτονος—ἡ μήτηρ, *of the carpenter—His mother*) Hence

---

[1] The new things already have the palm of superiority.—V. g.

[2] sc. ἐτέλεσεν διατάσσων τοῖς δώδεκα.—ED.

[3] The word implies *change of abode* as well as departure.—(I. B.)

[4] In the same manner, the same word, μετῆρεν, is used in ch. xix. 1 of the last journey of the Saviour from Galilee to Judea, which He took before the Passion.—Comp. Jer. xxxix. 9. Therefore that verb is opposed to the dwelling which, for a considerably long time, Jesus had had at Capernaum, ch. iv. 13. Not long after, the Saviour returned thither afresh; but after having made a survey [lustratione, *a purifying examination*: see John vi. 66–71] of His disciples, He presently departed again, John vi. 22–71 [see ver. 24, 59]. The same thing happened after the interval of nearly a year, Matt. xvii. 24: and this was the last of all His visits there. His address to the city of Capernaum, Luke x. 15, was delivered at a distance from it, when He had already finished no inconsiderable part of the journey which led to the Passion: comp. Luke ix. 51. He subsequently addressed Jerusalem in the same manner from a distance, Luke xiii. 34.—*Harm.*, p. 324.

[5] Εἰς τὴν πατρίδα αὐτοῦ) In the same way as He had gone forth into public, in a manner which was clearly "His custom," at Nazareth, Luke iv. 16: so, having left Capernaum, He returned afresh to Nazareth. It was then that the people of Nazareth said those things which He had foretold in Luke iv. 23 they would say. [See Gnomon there: where Beng. explains, "Ye will say," etc., thus: This feeling, owing to which ye say (ver. 22), Is not this Joseph's Son? will wax stronger, *when ye shall hear* of my future miracles, which, owing to your unbelief, shall be less numerous among you than others: You *will then say*, Physician, heal thyself.—ED.]—*Harm.*, l. cit.

it may be inferred that Joseph had long been dead, and that Mary had lived in obscurity.—Μαριὰμ—'Ιάκωβος, *Mary—James*) They speak of them thus as if they had nothing but a name, by which name they were well known.

56. 'Ἀδελφαί, *sisters*) These they do not condescend even to name.

57. 'Ἐσκανδαλίζοντο, *they were offended*) as it happens with those who observe one thing, but neglect to observe another, which ought rather to have been observed.—προφήτης, κ.τ.λ., *a prophet*, etc.) In a prophet there are two parts: the one which he possesses in common with others, ordinary, natural, domestic; the other, which is peculiar to his calling, heavenly, spiritual, public. Those who know the former do not observe the latter. Familiarity breeds contempt. Such is the case in our own country, much more so in our home.—ἄτιμος, *contemned*) The contempt which a prophet meets with elsewhere, is not contempt if it be compared with that which he meets with in his own country; elsewhere he certainly receives some honour.

58. 'Ἀπιστίαν, *unbelief*) The reason why many miracles are not performed at present, is not so much planted Christianity, as reigning infidelity.[1]

CHAPTER XIV.

1. 'Ἐν ἐκείνῳ τῷ καιρῷ, *at that time*) It was now about a year from the commencement of our Lord's public ministry.—ἤκουσεν, *heard*) The ears and courts of kings resound with news; but spiritual matters, however widely published, scarcely ever arrive there.[2]

---

[1] In the original, "non tam est *fides* plantata quam *infidelitas regnans; i.e.* it is not so much that Christianity, having been already planted, does not require the aid of miracles, as that the wide prevalence of unbelief prevents their being performed.—(I. B.)

[2] And if they do reach them at all, they appear in an imperfect form and blended with what is false; nor are they easily turned to good purpose. Nevertheless, at times, a joyful exception to this is to be met with.—V. g.

2. Παισίν, *servants*) The friends of princes are for the most part young.[1] In time of fear, the great speak promiscuously with the small.—οὗτος, *this*) Herod was tormented by his conscience.[2] It was not consistent with the character of such a king to arrive at an absolute decision. He concluded, but with doubt; see Luke ix. 7, 9. Herod was a Sadducee; but Sadduceeism wavers when anything strange occurs. Reason [mere human reason] prefers ascribing marvellous circumstances to ancient, or at least departed saints, rather than to those who are alive; and to those whom it has once begun to esteem highly rather than to others.[3]—Ἰωάννης, *John*) Herod had not heard of the works of Jesus before the death of John. John had not performed any miracles during his life; but because he had been a holy man, men now suppose that he must nevertheless have possessed miraculous power; cf. ch. xvi. 14. So great power has the reputation of holiness even with those who are themselves unholy. Moreover, as the actions of Christ were ascribed to John even when dead, it was necessary that he should decrease in order that Christ might increase. The Greeks speak much and often of the things which our Lord's forerunner, slain before Him, announced and preached to the dead; see Leo Allatius,[4] de libris ecclesiast. Gr. pp. 303, 304; and Wetstein[5] on the dialogue against the Marcionites, p. 33.

---

[1] Alluding to two of the meanings of παῖς, the one implying youth, the other attendance on a superior.—(I. B.)

[2] So far was he from speaking thus *in jest*.—E. B.

[3] John most speedily attained the consummation of his course; but those who had deprived him of life, subsequently atoned most dearly for it. —V. g.

[4] Leo Allatius (or Allacci). A laborious and indefatigable writer, of a vast memory, whose writings display great reading. Born in the Isle of Chios, of Greek parents, 1586. Having been admitted into the Greek College at Rome, he embraced the Roman Catholic religion, and was eventually appointed keeper of the Vatican library by Pope Alexander VII. Died 1669.—(I. B.)

[5] The author here intended is not J. J. Wetstein, Bengel's great critical rival, but John Rudolph Wetstein, son of the author of the same name. He was a native of Basle, and became a theologian and philologist of that Academy. He was born in 1647, and died in 1711. He published at Basle, in 1674, "*Origen against the Marcionites*," in Greek and Latin, with notes. —(I. B

So do the Latins also, quoted by Ittigius[1] in his dissertation on the gospel preached to the dead, § xi.; see also Ambrose on Luke i. 17, and Gerson's[2] second lecture on St Mark.—ὁ βαπτιστής, *the Baptist*) This surname is given to John even by Herod, even by the daughter of Herodias, even by Josephus, so celebrated was it.—αὐτός, *he*) himself.—αἱ δυνάμεις, *mighty works*) He speaks of them as objective realities.—ἐν αὐτῷ, *in Him*) sc. in Jesus.

3–12. Ὁ γὰρ Ἡρώδης, κ.τ.λ., *for Herod*, etc.) It was not necessary that the death of John should be foretold in the Old Testament, or be described professedly and in order; because he did not die for us. The mention of him, however, is gracefully resumed when our Lord was now in the zenith of His career.

3. Ἡρωδιάδα, *Herodias*) This princess was hostile to the latter Elias, as Jezebel to the former.—τοῦ ἀδελφοῦ αὐτοῦ, *his brother*) Most authorities[3] prefix Φιλίππου from St Mark, who is known not to have taken all things from St Matthew by his being the only one who names this brother of Herod. The shorter reading of St Matthew has been preserved intact by the Vulgate, 'fratris,' *of his brother*, alive, and not childless, as we learn from Josephus, xviii. 7; but it was sufficient for the Evangelist

---

[1] THOMAS ITTIGIUS, a native of Leipsic, of which Academy he became a theologian and historian; was born 1643, and died 1710. He was the author of many learned works.—(I. B.)

[2] JOHN GERSON; born at Gerson, in France, in 1363; educated at Paris, where he became Canon and Chancellor of the Church. He greatly distinguished himself, at the Council of Constance, by many speeches, especially by one, in which he enforced the superiority of the Council over the Pope. He was one of the most illustrious men of his time, and obtained the surname of *Doctor Christianissimus*. Cave says that no one can be conversant with his works without very great benefit. His writings are very numerous.—(I. B.)

[3] Such is the reading of E. M. In his App. Crit. Bengel writes,—"(Φιλίππου) *Lat.* plerique, et inde *Cant. Angl. Mag. Augustin.* sed habet *Sax.* Φιλίππου, præmittunt plerique ex Marco. Brevior," etc., as in Gnomon.—(I. B.)

Lachm. with BZ Orig. 3, 470*b*, reads Φιλίππου—αὐτοῦ. *b* has αὐτοῦ Φιλίππου. Tischend. omits Φιλίππου with D*a* (?) *c* Vulg. Φιλίππου looks like a gloss of the harmonies from Mark vi. 17. However, the *omission* might also come similarly from Luke iii. 19.—ED.

The marg. of both Editions agree with the Gnomon. But Vers. Germ. retains Φιλίππου in this passage.—E. B.

to say that he was his *brother*. Herodias[1] was also the niece of both, being the daughter of their brother Aristobulus.

4. Οὐκ ἔξεστι, *it is not lawful*) John did not break the force of bitter truth by arguments of a too conciliatory nature; neither his words were soft, nor his dress. John did not come into Galilee, but yet he was able to reprove Herod.—σοί, *to thee*) Sins even of kings should be rebuked in the second person.—ἔχειν, *to have*) Theologians must not give up questions concerning marriage (see ch. xix. 3, 4), since it is their duty to examine everything which is lawful or unlawful; cf. ch. xxii. 17.

5. Ἐφοβήθη, *feared*) They often fear who crush the witnesses of truth, whilst the witnesses themselves fear not their oppressors.[2]

6. Γενεσίων) Either *the day on which he was born*, as the LXX use the word in Gen. xl. 20, or *that on which he began to reign*. Remarkable days of high festival are accompanied with great danger of falling into sin.[3]—ὠρχήσατο, *she danced*) A light matter; the handle of a most weighty matter.—θυγάτηρ, *daughter*) Salome by name.—ἐν τῷ μέσῳ, *in the midst*) in the sight of all during the banquet.

7. Ὡμολόγησεν, *promised, agreed*) The girl had asked by dancing; and the king appears, even before this, to have been in the habit of giving her something on his birth-day.

8. Προβιβασθεῖσα, *being before instructed*) i.e. before she asked. —ὧδε, *here*) Before the king could repent.—πίνακι, *in a charger*) which perhaps she held in her hand. The ungodly know how to propose the most horrible things with elegance of language and sweetness of sound.

9. Ἐλυπήθη, *was grieved*) Conscience was not yet entirely banished from the monarch's breast. The sudden necessity of executing an evil purpose startles even the worst. The joys of this world are accompanied by sadness.—ὁ βασιλεύς, *the king*) strictly *tetrarch*; see ver. 1.—συνανακειμένους, *reclining at his table*) The king feared the guests, the guests the king. By not

---

[1] See Genealogical Table, p. 120.—(I. B.)

[2] An evil purpose, which has been scarcely begun, is afterwards, whenever a very slight opportunity may present itself, brought forth into action.—V. g.

[3] Of this kind are, for instance, dedication-festivals, market-days, etc.; for, when these are celebrated according to custom, often weariness and lamentations succeed to vain rejoicings. And yet the world does not allow itself to be advised to better things.—V. g.

interceding as they ought to have done for John, they became accomplices in his murder.

10. Ἀπεκεφάλισε, *he beheaded*) Even this kind of death was a proof that John was not the Messiah: cf. John xix. 36.[1]—Ἰωάννην, *John*) a sudden and violent death, even by decapitation, is not always miserable.

11. Τῇ μητρὶ αὐτῆς, *to her mother*) who without doubt treated it cruelly.

12. Τὸ σῶμα, *his body*) without the head.— ἐλθόντες, κ.τ.λ., *coming*, etc.) From that circumstance the death of John was advantageous to his disciples.[2]—ἀπήγγειλαν, *announced*) It is not said with what manifestation of feeling Jesus received this announcement; doubtless He received it as it befitted the Lord.

13. Ἀκούσας, *having heard*) sc. those things which are mentioned in ver. 1–12.[3]—ἀνεχώρησεν, *departed*) The murderer of the Baptist was unworthy to hear or see the Lord: see ch. xxi. 23–27. Afterwards, indeed, he did see Him; Luke xxiii. 8; not, however, coming of His own accord, but forced by the violence of His enemies; and therefore Herod's seeing Him, on that occasion, was not a sign of favour. Cf. the case of Samuel and Saul, 1 Sam. xv. 35 and xix. 24.—κατ' ἰδίαν, *apart*) no one being taken with Him, except His disciples.—πεζῇ, *on foot*) See Eustathius.[4]

14. Ἐξελθών, *having come forth*) sc. from His retreat into public.

15. Ὀψίας, *evening*) The evening has various degrees; see ver. 23.— ἡ ὥρα, *the hour*) sc. for dismissing the people, of taking food and rest, or of going to search for food.—ἑαυτοῖς,

---

[1] It was not fitting, to wit, that even a bone of Christ's body should be broken, much less His head taken off.—V. g.

[2] That is, the death of their master was the means of leading them to Jesus—the greatest of all blessings.—ED.

[3] Namely, that the fame of Himself had reached Herod. Comp. John iv. 13.—*Harm.*, p. 331.

[4] EUSTATHIUS, the grammarian, who flourished in the twelfth century, was Bishop of Thessalonica. He wrote commentaries on Homer, and on Dionysius the geographer. He must not be confounded with the amatory writer, *Eumathius the Macrembolite*, who wrote under this name in the fifteenth century, and was an obscure grammarian.—(I. B.)

for themselves) The disciples seem sometimes to have bought food for them.

16. Οὐ χρείαν, *no need*) We should not labour for that which is not necessary.—ὑμεῖς, *you*) significantly. The disciples already possessed the rudiments of miraculous faith.[1]

17. Ἄρτους, *loaves*) obtained for the present exigency one by one.

19. Ἀνακλιθῆναι, *to be seated*) The faith of the people is thus exercised.—τοὺς ἄρτους, *the loaves*) so, whatever was there.—ἀναβλέψας, *looking up*) Jesus referred everything to the Father (see John xi. 41, xvii. 1) with the most entire confidence: far different from the practice of sinners; see Luke xviii. 13.—οἱ δὲ μαθηταί, *but His disciples*) A prelude to their future administration.[2] See Acts iv. 35.

20. Πάντες, *all*) How much more can *all* partake of the *one* body of the Lord in the Holy Supper.—κλασμάτων, *of fragments*) of most excellent bread; cf. John ii. 10. A most substantial miracle. The people were not permitted to carry any away for the sake of curiosity.—δώδεκα, *twelve*) see Gnomon on ch. xvi. 9. There were remnants also of fishes; see Mark vi. 43. They were preserved for future eating, not, like manna, as a memorial.

21. Γυναικῶν καὶ παιδίων, *women and children*) of whom no doubt there was a large number.

22. Εὐθέως, *straightway*) Our consideration ought not to dwell on things which we have well done.—ἠνάγκασεν, *constrained, compelled*) as it is allowable to believe, for important reasons. They did not willingly sail alone.—τὸ πλοῖον, *the vessel*) mentioned in ver. 13.—ἕως, κ.τ.λ., *until*, etc.) He is not said to have told them that He should pray. He gave an example of praying in secret.

23. Τὸ ὄρος, *the mountain*) which was in that region. Mountains and elevated places (see Acts x. 9) are especially suited for prayer, on account of their solitude, and their being open to heaven.—κατ' ἰδίαν, *apart*) Not even the disciples being present. In such a retreat, matters of the greatest importance took place

---

[1] In the original, "Rudimenta fidei miraculorum apud discipulos"—*i.e.* that *special* faith which is required for the performance of miracles.—(I. B.)

[2] Sc. of the charities distributed to the needy brethren.—ED.

between God and the Mediator. It was no dramatic representation that interceded for us.[1] What passed between Christ and the Father may be inferred, for example, from Ps. xvi. and Luke xi. 2, 3. Cf. ver. 1 and John xvii.—προσεύξασθαι, *to pray*) beyond midnight; see ver. 25. The fruit may be seen in ver. 33, 34.

25. Τετάρτῃ, *fourth*) and last. The Jews also divided the night into four watches. The disciples were subjected to great straits for some time, till He brought them help.—ἀπῆλθε, *He departed*) His prayers, though they had lasted a long while, being as it were broken off, He departed to help His disciples.—περιπατῶν, κ.τ.λ., *walking*) though the wind blew strong.

26. Ἐταράχθησαν, *they were troubled*) We often take Christ for another rather than for Christ: cf. ver. 2. The disciples now feared not only the sea, but also the Lord.—φάντασμα, *an apparition*) φάντασμα and φάσμα are identical in meaning. See Wis. xvii. 15, 4. Nor does φαντασία greatly differ from them. Ibid. xviii. 17.

28. Κέλευσον, *command*) A remarkable exercise of faith. Peter, from desire for Jesus, leaves the vessel, whether he has to walk on the sea or to swim through it. Cf. John xxi. 7.

29. Ἐλθέ, *come*) More is required of him who offers himself spontaneously to Christ; he is more greatly tempted, more mightily preserved.

30. Βλέπων, *seeing*) Peter both *felt* the wind, and *saw* it on the waves.—τὸν ἄνεμον *the wind*) The wind had been strong before that, but had not been so much observed by Peter.—ἐφοβήθη, *he was afraid*) Although he was a fisherman, and a good swimmer; see John xxi. 7. They who have begun to depend on grace are less able to employ nature.—καταποντίζεσθαι, *to sink*) According to the measure of his faith, he was supported by the water; just as the Israelites prevailed according as the hands of Moses were held up.

31. Ὀλιγόπιστε, *O thou of little faith*) Even great faith is little in comparison of that which we ought to have. We should also possesss constancy.—εἰς τί, *wherefore? to what end?*) With what advantage? He is not blamed because he came out of the

---

[1] "Non intercessit actio scenica"—*i.e.* our Lord's intercession was real, genuine, substantial; not mythical, theatrical, or fictitious.—(I. B.)

vessel, but because he did not remain in the firmness of faith. He was right in exposing himself to trial; but he ought to have persevered.—*ἐδίστασας, didst thou doubt*) The nature of faith is perceived from its opposites, doubt and fear. See Mark v. 36; Rom. xiv. 23; James i. 6.[1]

36. Μόνον, κ.τ.λ., *only*, etc.) Such was their pious humility.[2]

CHAPTER XV.

1.[3] Οἱ ἀπὸ Ἱεροσολύμων, *which were of Jerusalem*) Who appeared to excel in authority and zeal, having come such a long way.[4]

2. Τῶν πρεσβυτέρων, *of the ancients*) The word πρεσβύτερος sometimes denotes a dignity or office; sometimes it is opposed to youth; sometimes, as in this place, to later generations.—ἄρτον, *bread*) The Jews eat other kinds of food without washing their hands more readily than bread. See Wall's[5] Critical Notes, p. 47.

---

[1] Ver. 33. Θεοῦ υἱός εἶ, *Thou art the Son of God*) Since they perceived that Jesus was such by reason of His miraculous walking on the sea, they ought not to have wondered at this very miracle to such a degree as to be lost in amazement. It is for this reason they are censured by Mark vi. 51, 52. For the mind, which faith has rendered intelligent and sober, unlearns excess of astonishment.—*Harm.*, p. 333.

Ver. 35. οἱ ἄνδρες, *the men*) who perhaps were engaged in labouring in the fields.—V. g.

[2] Ὅσοι ἥψαντο, *as many as touched Him*) Out of so great crowds of miserable men, not even one is found who met with a repulse in seeking help from Jesus. However, those who were ungrateful were subsequently reproved, and those who needed it were warned to avoid new acts of sin.—*Harm.*, p. 337.

[3] Τότε, *then*) By this particle, the narration of the events which had happened before and after the Passover is connected together: from which we may infer that Jesus, at that time, had not gone up to Jerusalem.—*Harm.*, p. 340. It was at a time most unseasonable that the hypocrites made an oblique attack on Him, starting a question, high sounding, no doubt, but after all ending in mere minutiæ.—V. g.

[4] After the feast of the Passover had been celebrated at Jerusalem.—*Harm.*, p. 340.

[5] WILLIAM WALL, D.D., sometime Vicar of Shoreham, a learned divine

3. Διατί, *why*) He replies by a question similar in form to that which they had proposed in ver. 2.[1]—καὶ ὑμεῖς, *ye also*) Whether My disciples transgress or not, you are the greatest transgressors.—διά, κ.τ.λ., *on account of*, etc.) Traditions, even where you could least expect it, detract from the commandments of God.[2]—ὑμῶν, *your*) They had said, *of the ancients*; Jesus is no respecter of persons.

4. Ὁ γὰρ Θεός, *for God*) In contrast with ὑμεῖς δέ, *but you*, in ver. 5.—τίμα, *honour*) Honour signifies benefits which are due (see Gnomon on 1 Tim. v. 3), the denial of which is the *greatest insult*. Thus, in the S.V. of Prov. iii. 9, τίμα τὸν Κύριον (*honour the Lord*) occurs with reference to sacrifices. An instance of metonymy of the antecedent for the consequent. In Exod. xx. 12, S.V., it stands thus:—τίμα τὸν πατέρα σου καὶ τὴν μητέρα σου: *honour thy father and thy mother*. The second σου (*thy*) is not expressed in the present passage.—ὁ κακολογῶν, *he that curseth*) In Exod. xxi. 16: ὁ κακολογῶν πατέρα αὐτοῦ ἢ μητέρα αὐτοῦ θανάτῳ τελευτάτω:[3] *he that curseth his father or his mother, let him die*[4] *the death*.—Life is assailed by curses, and children receive their life through their parents.—θανάτῳ, *death*) Observe this, O youth!

5. Ὑμεῖς δέ, *but you*) What God commands are the offices of love; human traditions lead into all other things.[5]—δῶρον, *a gift*) *i.e.* it is a gift. *Whatsoever*, etc., *is Corban*. The formula was קרבן שאני נהנה לך, *Let all that by which I might be serviceable to thee in any way whatsoever, be to me Corban; i.e.* Let it be as much forbidden to me to benefit thee in anything, as it is un-

---

of the English Church; born 1645 or 1646; died 1727-8. The work here alluded to is entitled—

"Brief Critical Notes, especially on the various readings of the New Testament Books; with a Preface concerning the Texts cited from the Old Testament, as also concerning the use of the Septuagint Translation. 8vo. London, 1730."—(I. B.)

[1] The truth is never at a loss for questions, which it may put in opposition to the questions of hypocrites.—V. g.

[2] And what an amount of injury, from time to time, has been the result of the accumulation of such traditions, however much particular ones may be not without their show of plausibility, can hardly be stated.—V. g.

[3] The Vatican MS. reads τελευτήσει θανάτῳ.—(I. B.)

[4] Lit. "Let him die by death."—(I. B.)

[5] In the original, "in alia omnia eunt," *i.e.* into all things which are of a different, nay, a contrary character.

lawful for me to touch the Corban. See L. Capellus[1] on the Corban. Or else, to avoid the appearance of avarice, they actually offered to the Corban what was due to their parents; as many persons give to the poor or to orphans those things which they grudge to others, which they extort from them, or deny them.—ὃ ἐάν, κ.τ.λ., *whatsoever thou mightest be profited by me*—ὠφεληθῇς, *thou mightest be profited*) The priests used to say, יְהִי לָךְ, It be useful to thee,[2] when the people offered anything. —καί, *and*) This particle denotes the commencement of the apodosis.[3]—οὐ μὴ τιμήσῃ, *shall not honour*) The decree of the Pharisees was, *such an one shall be free from all obligation towards father and mother*. Our Lord, however, expresses this in words which bring out more clearly the unrighteousness of the Pharisees in opposition to the commandment of God.

6. Καί, *and thus*) διά, *on account of*) The heart which is occupied with traditions, has no room for the commandments of God.

7. Προεφήτευσι, *prophesied*) i.e. foretold.

8. Ὁ λαὸς οὗτος, κ.τ.λ., *This people*, etc.) In the S. V. of Is. xxix. 13, it stands thus, ἐγγίζει Μοι ὁ λαὸς οὗτος ἐν τῷ στόματι αὐτοῦ καὶ ἐν τοῖς χείλεσιν αὐτῶν τιμῶσί Με, ἡ δὲ καρδία—διδάσκοντες ἐντάλματα ἀνθρώπων καὶ διδασκαλίας,—*This people draweth nigh unto Me with their mouth, and they honour Me with their lips: but their heart—teaching precepts and doctrines of men.*—οὗτος, *this*) The pronoun here implies contempt; see 1 Cor. xiv. 21.—Με, *Me*) sc. God, speaking by the mouth of Isaiah.—καρδία, *heart*) by the approach of which[4] (cujus accessu) God is truly and fully worshipped.[5]

9. Μάτην, *in vain*) How much vanity has there been in the

---

[1] LUDOVICUS CAPELLUS was born at Sedan in 1586. He became a theologian and philologist of Saumur, was a first-rate Hebrew scholar, and deeply versed in Rabbinical learning. His writings are very numerous. He died in 1658.—(I. B.)

[2] Sc. "It (*i.e.* the offering) be profitable to thee." A form of benediction.—(I. B.)

[3] By a Hebraism, which however is also found in Greek, ex. gr. Demosthenes de Cor., "Whosoever (when any one soever) shall say, etc.—*then* (καί) he shall not (need not) honour," etc.—ED.
Compare a similar construction occurring Rev. ii. 24.—E. B.

[4] *i.e.* by the drawing nigh of which, as well as with the lips.—ED.

[5] Most stress is indeed made to rest on the heart. See ver. 19.—V. g.

greatest part of religions throughout so many ages and climates! —σέβονται, *they worship*) They paid little regard to the commandments of God, and that little they defiled by observing the commandments of men.—διδάσκοντες διδασκαλίας, *teaching doctrines*) laboriously, constantly, in great numbers, cf. Mark vii. 13.— ἐντάλματα, *precepts*) In apposition with διδασκαλίας, *doctrines*: these ἐντάλματα, *precepts*, were unworthy to be called ἐντολαί, *commandments*. Precepts are adorned and seasoned by doctrines. —ἀνθρώπων, *of men*) although they be *ancients* (ver. 2); who have no authority in religion.

10. Προσκαλεσάμενος, *having called to Him*) All were not always attentive. The Pharisees were not worthy that this should be said to them; see ver. 14.—τὸν ὄχλον, *the multitude*) Lest they should be deceived by the speech of the Pharisees.

11. Οὐ, κ.τ.λ., *not*, etc.) Unless such were the case, the faithful could not, without the greatest disgust, inhabit a world subject to vanity.—τὸ ἐκπορευόμενον, *that which cometh out*) Original sin is evidently here implied.—τοῦτο, *this*) used demonstratively.

12. Οἶδας, *knowest thou*[1]. They perceived the omniscience of Jesus.—ἐσκανδαλίσθησαν, *were offended*[2]) Having taken, or rather laid in wait, for offence.

13. Φυτεία, *plant*) Doctrine, or rather man. The φυτὸν is so by nature, the φυτεία by care.—Πατήρ, κ.τ.λ., *Father*, etc.) See John xv. 1. 2.—ἐκριζωθήσεται, *shall be rooted up*) And this shall be the result of their being offended with Christ. Such a plant, however fair in appearance, is without Christ (*extra* Christum).

14. Ἄφετε αὐτούς, *let them alone*) Do not regard[3] them.—ὁδηγοί, *guides*) see Is. ix. 16.[4]

15. Ἀποκριθεὶς, *answering*) The candour of sacred historians in recording the errors of holy men is remarkable in all the books

---

[1] Rather *Thou knowest*: for the comment, which follows, shows that Beng. did not read these words with an interrogation.—ED.
 He does so, however, both in his Greek New Testament and German Version.—(I. B.)

[2] And regard Thee with aversion in consequence.—V. g.

[3] There is a *verbal* reference to ἄφετε αὐτούς in the original, "nolite eos morari," which cannot be preserved in the translation—q. d., Let them go: do not *detain* them, or trouble yourselves about them.—(I. B.)

[4] Ἀμφότεροι, *both*) In the case of senseless men, it is better that the one should withdraw from the other.—V. g.

of the Bible.—παραβολὴν ταύτην, *this parable*) Our Lord's language becomes parabolic in ver. 13, but was plain and literal in ver. 10, 11. Peter therefore, as a disciple, speaks incorrectly. Our Lord, however, does not expressly find fault with this. So that they held fast the matter, [He excuses the manner.]

16. Ὑμεῖς, *you*) corresponding with ἡμῖν, *to us*, in ver. 15. *You*, not only the Pharisees and the multitude.—ἀσύνετοι, *without understanding*) corresponding with συνίετε, *understand*, in ver. 10.

17. Οὔπω, *not yet*) Although you have been instructed in ver. 11, and elsewhere, in the whole system of divine morality, from which you might have inferred this matter also.—νοεῖτε) *perceive*.—εἰς, *into*) Into is repeated thrice without any mention of the heart, which is the true seat of real purity or impurity.

19. Διαλογισμοὶ πονηροί, *evil thoughts*) such as the Pharisees entertained. The article is added in Mark vii. 21.—φόνοι, μοιχεῖαι, κ.τ.λ., *murders, adulteries*, etc.) Sin against the sixth and following commandments. The plural number increases the force.—βλασφημίαι, *curses*) sc. against our neighbour, combined with *false witness*. In such enumerations, the absence of the copulative conjunction has often the force of etc., as if he who speaks wished to add more, or to leave more to the imagination.—Cf. Mark vii. 22.[1]

20. Οὐ κοινοῖ τὸν ἄνθρωπον, *do not defile the man*) In the very appellation of *man*, is contained (latet) an argument: for the spiritual nature, which is the superior part in man, is not reached by outward filth.

21. Τὰ μέρη, *parts*) i.e. not towards the whole region.

22. [2] Ἐξελθοῦσα, κ.τ.λ., *having come forth*, etc.) For Jesus did not enter the borders of the Canaanites.—ἐκραύγασεν, *cried out*)

---

[1] The filth of the draught is not so great as is that of a human heart not yet cleansed. Who is there that thoroughly weighs this consideration? who strives earnestly after true purity? But, as concerns the man who leaves this life destitute of such purity, whither is he rushing? Into the gulf of fire and brimstone. Alas! what a mass of filth that shall be, which is made up of so many impure beings! Be not offended, Reader. Offensiveness of language is profitable to be used in this case. See that thou dost conceive a loathing of the thing itself, and be moved to flee from impurity of heart. --V. g.

[2] Χαναναία) of the posterity of Canaan.—V. g.

from a distance, from behind; cf. ver. 23, 25.[1]—μὲ, *me*) The affectionate mother had made her daughter's misery her own; see ver. 25 and 28.—Υἱὲ Δαυίδ, *Son of David*) Therefore the woman had heard of the Promise either long ago or lately.

23. Δὲ, *but*) It was fitting that this declaration, and as it were protestation of the unworthiness of the heathen, should precede the declaration of individual worthiness for which it prepared the way: nor did our Lord grant help so much to the prayers of the Canaanitess alone, as to those of the Canaanitess and the disciples together.—οὐκ ἀπεκρίθη—λόγον, *answered not—a word*) Thus the LXX. in Is. xxxvi. 21; 1 Chron. xxi. 12.—ἀπόλυσον, *dismiss*) An instance of metonymy of the consequent for the antecedent: *i.e.* Help as you are wont, cf. ver. 24; for our Lord was not wont to dismiss those who called upon Him for aid without according it.—κράζει, *cries out*) We may suppose that the disciples feared the judgment of men, and made their petition to our Lord, both for their own sake, lest her crying out should produce annoyance, and for the sake of the woman herself.

24, 26. Εἰ μὴ—τοῖς κυναρίοις, *except—to little dogs*) Our Lord's language, in ver. 24, contains no repulse, as explained in ver. 26,[2] but rather suggests hope to constant faith. The twenty-fourth verse is to be understood, not with reference to the whole mediatorial office, but only our Lord's preaching and miracles.

24. Ἀπεστάλην, *I am sent*) Our Lord referred everything to His *Mission*.—πρόβατα, *sheep*) Israel is the Lord's flock (see Ps. xcv.), Jesus the Shepherd.—οἴκου Ἰσραήλ, *the house of Israel*) This appeared to restrict His grace.

25. Ἐλθοῦσα, *coming*) sc. in front of the Saviour from behind Him;[3] although He appeared to have given a repulse even to His disciples.

---

[1] That is, ver. 23, "She crieth *after* us," shows she was *in the rear, behind* Him; ver. 25, "Then *came* she," etc., shows she had previously been at a distance.—ED.

[2] Bengel's words are, "Sermo in thesi expressus, in hypothesi nullam habet repulsam: sed potius spem facit fidei constanti. Thesis autem accipienda est, non de officio toto mediatorio, sed de praedicatione et miraculis." I have endeavoured to render this so as to be intelligible to the general reader.—(I. B.)

[3] Thereby stopping up the way before Him [as if she would not let Him go farther without blessing her].—V. g.

26. Τῶν τέκνων, *the children's*) Our Lord spoke severely to the Jews themselves, but honourably of them [to those without]; see John iv. 22. Thus we, concerning the Evangelic Church. κυναρίοις, *to little dogs*[1]) who are not worthy to receive it. But yet κυνάριον, the word employed by our Lord, is a diminutive, and Jesus thereby gives a handle to the woman to take hold of Him. Midrasch Tillim.[2] says, "The nations of the world are like dogs."

27. Ναί, *yea*) The woman seizes upon the appellation κυνάρια, for she says immediately, καὶ γὰρ, which must be rendered, for even (etenim). The particle ναὶ partly assents, partly as it were places on our Lord's tongue the assent to her prayers, *i.e.* prays. The word is thus used in Philem. ver. 20, and Judith ix. 12.[3]—ἐσθίει, *eat*) since the children often waste their bread.—ἀπὸ τῶν ψιχίων, *of the crumbs*) She does not say the *morsels*, nor the *bread*.—τῶν πιπτόντων, *which fall*) in opposition to λαβεῖν καὶ βαλεῖν, *to take and cast*, in the last verse. She asks for it as a favour, essential to herself, injurious to no one.—ἀπὸ, *from*) She does not ask to be admitted to the table, but implies that she was not far distant from it. Her nation was contiguous to Israel.—τῶν κυρίων αὐτῶν, *of their masters*) This indicates the prerogative of the *children*, and yet a certain tie of connection (necessitudinem) with them on the part of the *little dogs*. The language of the Canaanitess corresponds with the curse addressed to Canaan, Gen. ix. 26: "*A servant of servants* shall he be," etc.

28. Ὦ γύναι, *O woman*) Now at length our Lord addresses her.[4]—μεγάλη, *great*) Modesty does not interfere with greatness of faith; see ch. viii. 8, 9.—ὡς, *as*) After the hard struggle, so

---

[1] Diminutives are used as terms of endearment. Therefore κυναρίοις probably here means *the household dogs—pet dogs*.—ED.
Even the third effort was seeming likely to be abortive. Yet she did not give over.—V. g.

[2] *i.e.* "Allegorical Commentary on the Psalms," a Rabbinical work of high repute among the Jews.—(I. B.)

[3] Such modes of pleading she could not have learned from books by anticipation. The Spirit of faith supplies the best forms of prayer.—V. g.

[4] Assigning to her no ordinary phrase, with which there was no danger of the woman being inflated on account of her extraordinary humility of mind.—V. g.

much the more is given.—θέλεις, *thou wishest*) There is faith even in wishing.—ἀπὸ, κ.τ.λ., *from that very hour*) The soundness which followed was lasting.

29. Ἐκάθητο, *sat*) He did not take the initiative and command the multitudes to approach, but He awaited them.

30. Ἑτέρους, *others*) sc. who were sick.—ἔῤῥιψαν, *cast*) since they pressed upon each other.[1]

32. Σπλαγχνίζομαι, *I have compassion*) Whilst the people forget hunger in admiration, Jesus pities them, and is not affected by their praise of His miracles. Glory and mercy elsewhere seldom meet.—προσμένουσί Μοι, *they remain with Me*[2]) It was the interest of the people to remain with Jesus; and yet He embraces that as a reason for conferring a fresh benefit upon them. The people were ready to remain longer.—τί, *what*) for ὁ, *that which*, see the LXX. in Gen. xxxviii. 25.—νήστεις, *fasting*) Our Lord never dismissed any one without relieving their necessities.

33. Πόθεν, *whence*) Cf. Num. xi. 21; 2 Kings iv. 43.—ἡμῖν, *to us*) The disciples already understood that they would have to take some part in the matter.

34. Ὀλίγα ἰχθύδια, *a few little fishes*) They speak disparagingly of their provision, for in ver. 36 the diminutive form is no longer employed.

36. Εὐχαριστήσας, *having given thanks*) It is right to give thanks even before food (see Acts xxvii. 35), and there it is the same as εὐλογία, or *benediction*, for it is an acknowledgment of the Divine blessing for the past and the future. Jesus referred everything to the Father, and here gave thanks for the loaves, and for the approaching satisfying of the people; cf. John xi. 41.— εὐχαριστεῖν is a verb found fault with by Phrynichus,[3] but used also by Diodorus Siculus.[4]

---

[1] Ver. 31. τὸν Θεὸν Ἰσραὴλ, *the God of Israel*) See ver. 24.—V. g.

[2] Fresh patients being ever and anon laid down in the midst, one after the other.—V. g.

[3] PHRYNICUS, a rhetorician and sophist of Bythinia, who flourished in the second century of the Christian æra.—(I. B.)

[4] DIODORUS SICULUS, an ancient Greek historian. Born at Agyrium in the first century after Christ.—(I. B.)

39. Ἀνέβη εἰς τὸ πλοῖον, *He again went on board the vessel*)[2] sc. that mentioned a little before in ch. xiv. 33. The word ἀνέβη occurs with the same force in Mark vi. 51.

CHAPTER XVI.

1. Οἱ Φαρισαῖοι καὶ Σαδδουκαῖοι, *the Pharisees and Sadducees*) The common people were mostly addicted to the Pharisees, men of rank to the Sadducees (see Acts v. 17, xxiii. 6); as at present the crowd is more inclined to superstition, the educated to atheism, the two opposite extremes. The Evangelists describe only two attempts of the Sadducees against our Lord (the first of which occurs in the present passage), for they cared less than the Pharisees about religion.—ἐκ τοῦ οὐρανοῦ, *from heaven*) Miracles had been performed from heaven in the times of Moses, Joshua, and Elijah. The reason why the Pharisees were unwilling to accept as Divine the miracles hitherto performed by our Lord, seems to have been this: that since He had not yet produced any sign from heaven, they thought that the others might proceed even from Satan (cf. ch. xii. 24, 38); and that they considered that a sign from heaven affecting the whole creation, would be greater than any signs performed on the microcosm of man. [Perhaps, also, they were relying on the prophecy of Joel; see Acts ii. 19.—V. g.] The Sadducees, who disbelieved the existence of any Spirit, and therefore of Satan himself, were of opinion that our Lord's power extended only to hunger, and the diseases of the body, not to all greater matters. Both were influenced also by

---

[1] Ver. 38. Τετρακισχίλιοι, *four thousand*) They were in truth mighty miracles, whereby five thousand (ch xiv. 21) and four thousand men were fully satisfied with food; and it was then that the abundance of Jesus' miracles had reached its highest point. How widely His glory ought to have been spread abroad by so many thousands of witnesses!—*Harm.*, p. 344.

[3] "Signa in microcosmo," signs performed in *the little world*, the limited horizon, of which man is the centre.—ED.

[2] E. V. "took ship." Bengel would give another force to the preposition ἀνά, and renders ἀνέβη, *iterum conscendit.*—(I. B.)

another motive, namely, the desire to witness a variety of miracles, considered merely as sights. Their lust[1] (libido) is indicated by the word θέλομεν, *we wish*, in ch. xii. 38.

2. 'Οψίας, πρωΐ, *evening—morning*) Two most common and most popular signs;[2] for when the sky is red in the evening, the coldness of the night astringes the thinner vapours, so that no storm occurs, even though there be wind; on the other hand, when in the morning the sky is red and dark, the thick vapours burst into a storm by the heat of the sun.

3. Ὑποκριταί,[3] *hypocrites*) The hypocrisy was their greater skill in natural than in spiritual things; for they who have the former have much less excuse than dull men for being wanting in the latter, although they are often wanting in it. For an example of both united, see ch. ii. 2.—πρόσωπον τοῦ οὐρανοῦ, *the countenance of the sky*) not *face*. A man's *countenance* varies, his *face* is always the same. An instance of Prosopopœia,[4] as just before in the word στυγνάζων, *lowering*.—τὰ σημεῖα τῶν καιρῶν, *the signs of the times*) *i.e.*, those which are suitable to (congruentia) each time. Our Lord indicates, that not only are times to be distinguished by their signs, but also signs by the character of the times, and signs and the kinds of them from each other. For the mode of God's dealing with man[5] is various—by various

---

[1] The word is, of course, not to be taken in the literal force of its ordinary signification, but rather in the wider sense which it has in English writers of the sixteenth and seventeenth centuries (cf. 1 John ii. 16, and Gal. v. 17), though there is a special allusion to the epithet *adulterous* in Matt. xii. 38, and infra ver. 5, and to the common source of the various manifestations of the Φρόνημα σαρκὸς.—(I. B.)

[2] Although, from the different relations of the powers of nature, they are not applicable to all climes.—App. Crit., Ed. ii., p. 124.

[3] The *larger Ed.* gave more weight to the reading of this word than the margin of the *second Edition*: however, the *Ver. Germ.* has not rejected it.—E. B.

Rec. Text has ὑποκριταί with b. But CDLΔ *ac* Vulg. omit it. It is plainly an interpolation through the harmonies from Luke xii. 56. Lachm. reads καὶ before τὸ μὲν with C. But Tischend. omits it, with DLΔ *ac* Vulg.—ED.

[4] *i.e.* Personification. See explanation of technical terms in Appendix.—(I. B.)

[5] "Influxus Dei in homines," the influx of the Deity into and among men.—ED.

doctrines, persons, signs, times—all of which correspond among themselves: wherefore different signs suit different times. Those signs, less splendid indeed, but such as were altogether beneficial to man on earth (see ch. ix. 6), were suitable to the Messiah then being on earth; see ch. viii. 17, Luke ix. 54. Wherefore it was incumbent upon them to obtain proofs, not from heaven, but from themselves: see Luke xii. 57. For the same reason, after His ascension our Lord did not exhibit signs on earth, as He had previously done.[1]—οὐ δύνασθε; *are ye not able?*) sc. to distinguish sign from sign:—said with astonishment. If you wished it, you could do so most fully: as it is, you are prevented from doing so by a voluntary blindness.

4. Γενεὰ, *nation*[2]) Itself the sign of its own time: for such it was to be in the time of the Messiah; see ch. xi. 6.—πονηρά, *wicked*) and perverse.—μοιχαλίς, *adulterous*) accustomed to break the marriage vow, which it ought to have preserved inviolate to God.—σημεῖον, καὶ σημεῖον, κ.τ.λ., *a sign, and* [no] *sign*, etc.) A weighty repetition. They prescribe the kind of miracles just as if there were no other kind; therefore[3] all kinds of miracles are denied to them. The miracles which our Lord performed afterwards, were done not for the sake of such as these, but for that of the poor[4] and the sick.[5]—τὸ σημεῖον Ἰωνᾶ, *the sign of Jonah*) that was not from heaven, but from the middle of the earth. Jonah returning from the whale proved his mission to the Ninevites; thus by the resurrection of Jesus, whom they had not before believed, a proof was given to the Jews, that He was the Messiah. He silently intimates, moreover, that after the three days spent in the middle of the earth, there should be plenty of signs from heaven, which were performed by His ascension into heaven, and shall be performed

---

[1] Nor will hereafter signs be wanting from heaven.—B. G. V.

[2] E. V. *generation*.—(I. B.)

[3] Being weary of those miracles, which in great numbers they had seen heretofore; and, therefore, once and again demanding signs from heaven.—*Harm.*, p. 345.

[4] "Popelli," "the lower classes," of conventional phraseology.—(I. B.)

[5] And of these miracles, Matthew mentions subsequently scarce one: Mark mentions only that upon the blind man of Bethsaida, ch. viii. 22. But as regards teaching, Jesus continued it without intermission.—*Harm.*, p. 346.

at the destruction of the heavens; cf. ch. xxiv. 30, Acts ii. 19. Nay more, not even then was it true that were there no signs from heaven; see ch. iii. 16.—*καὶ καταλιπὼν αὐτοὺς ἀπῆλθε, and He left them and departed*) Just severity; see Tit. iii. 10. Our Lord never left *the people* in this manner.

6. Ὁρᾶτε, *take heed*) It is necessary to be careful of the purity of doctrine.—ζύμης, *leaven*) The language is metaphorical, and therefore enigmatical; and by it our Lord tries the progress of the disciples, who had already been long His hearers. The metaphor, however, alludes to the thoughts with which the mind of the disciples was then overflowing; *q. d.*, " Do not care about the want of earthly bread, but about the perilous aliments which the hypocrites offer to your souls." It is probable that the disciples had forgotten the loaves, because the controversy raised by the Pharisees and Sadducees (ver. 1) had put them into a state of anxiety and temptation. The Pharisees and Sadducees were elsewhere strongly opposed to each other, but yet on this occasion they conspire together against Jesus (see ver. 1); therefore He included both of them under the one title of hypocrites (ver. 3), and guards His disciples at once against both in this passage. And their hypocrisy itself was this leaven (Luke xii. 1), induced by which, they did not acknowledge the very sufficient signs of the present time, but, on the contrary, demanded the signs of another time; whence the plural καιρῶν, *times*, is used in ver. 3.[1] The believer both believes and speaks; he who separates either of these from the other is an unbeliever, is a hypocrite; see Gnomon on ch. xxiv. 51. Neither therefore is he free from hypocrisy who has *little faith;* see ver. 8. The disciples are most opportunely admonished to beware of this leaven, as they did not yet understand it from the present signs; see ver. 11.[2]

[1] Nay more, every error of all sects is the one leaven, which the old man cherishes.—V. g.

[2] There is also in this a suitableness of words [His mode of address], inasmuch as the disciples, who had been present, and themselves taken a part in the proceedings, on the occasion of the divine miracles which had been twice performed in the case of bread a short time before, were feeling the need of bread, now that a sudden want of it had arisen. For that reason, they might have the more deeply been mindful of spiritual bread, and have seen clearly the need of sound doctrine.—V. g.

7. Ἄρτους, *loaves*) The mode of living in the family of Jesus was extremely simple and frugal. They thought that they should have to buy bread in the place to which they were now coming, and that there would not be a sufficiency of bread there, which could be ascertained not to have been subjected to the leaven of the Pharisees. Our Lord answers, that even if no other bread could be procured, yet that He would feed them even without the bread of the Pharisees or any of that whole region.

8. Τί διαλογίζεσθε, *why reason ye*)[1] Man imputes more grievously to himself a defect in the care of outward things, to which God most easily accords indulgence. Faith's mode of estimating is of a higher kind.—ὀλιγόπιστοι, *O ye of little faith*) It is easy to fall, from want of faith, not only into doubts and fears, but also into errors of interpretation and other mistakes, and even forgetfulness.[2]

9. Οὔπω, *not yet*) The fault of the slow learner is increased by his having heard long ago.—νοεῖτε—μνημονεύετε, *understand, remember*) The verb νοέω expresses something more voluntary than συνίημι; see ver. 12; Mark vii. 18; 2 Tim. ii. 7. Sin affects also the mind and the memory. They ought to have understood, even if those two miracles had not been performed. We ought to remember even the circumstances of Divine works, and from former to hope for further help.[3]

9, 10. Πόσους κοφίνους, πόσας σπυρίδας, *how many cophini—how many spyrides*)[4] In the first miracle, as the number of the loaves

---

[1] Men pass a considerable part of their time, day and night, in turbulent thoughts.—V. g.

[2] By the setting forth of the caution concerning the leaven, *the smallness of the faith* of the disciples, who were disquieted concerning bread, was betrayed: but that faith the Lord subsequently strengthened, by reminding them of His having twice fed to the full so many thousands.—*Harm.*, p. 347.

[3] It is not such forgetfulness as they upbraided themselves with, ver. 7, but one altogether distinct, arising from unbelief accompanied with stupidity, that is here attributed to them as a fault.—V. g.

[4] On the distinction between *Cophini* and *Spyrides*, both of which are rendered *baskets* in E. V., much has been said and written; some maintaining their identity, others their dissimilarity. Much difference of opinion also exists as to the derivation and original force of the words. The following observations of the able and indefatigable Kitto will be read with interest.

corresponds to that of the thousands, so does that of the *cophini* to that of the apostles; so that each of them had the cophinus

"These words, although the same in our version, are not so in the original. That is to say, the 'baskets' in which the fragments were deposited on these two occasions are denoted by different words, both here and in the regular narratives of the transactions to which our Saviour refers. The first (κόφινος), was proverbially a Jewish travelling-basket, and is mentioned as such by Juvenal (iii. 15; vi. 542), where the word rendered 'basket' is *cophinus*, the same as this:—

'Banish'd Jews, who their whole wealth can lay
In a small basket.'

"The other passage we are tempted to cite entire, as it applies to the condition of the Jews after the desolation of their city and temple, and the ruin of their nation; when it is well known that such numbers of them gained a wretched subsistence by pretending to tell fortunes, that 'Jew' and 'fortune-teller' became almost synonymous:—

'A gipsey Jewess whispers in your ear,
And begs an alms: a high-priest's daughter she,
Versed in the Talmud and divinity,
And prophesies beneath a shady tree.
Her goods, *a basket*, and old hay her bed,
She strolls, and, telling fortunes, gains her bread:
Farthings, and some small monies are her fees;
Yet she interprets all your dreams for these.'

"The other word, also rendered basket, in ver. 10, is σπυρίς: it appears, from the citations of Wetstein, to have been a kind of basket for *storing* grain, provisions, etc.; and therefore larger than the former, probably much larger. Campbell translates this by '*maund*,' and retains '*basket*' for the former; and observes, that although these words are not fit for answering entirely the same purposes as the original terms, which probably conveyed the idea of their respective sizes, and consequently of the quantity contained; still there is a propriety in marking, were it but by this single circumstance, that there was a difference."—*Kitto's Illustrated Commentary*, in loc. —(I. B.)

It is a remarkable instance of undesigned coincidence—one of the best indirect proofs of genuineness—that *all* the four Evangelists uniformly apply the term κόφινοι to the twelve baskets in the miracle of the five thousand fed; and the two Evangelists, who record the miracle of the four thousand, apply the term σπυρίδες to the seven hampers mentioned in that miracle. Matt. xiv. 20; Mark vi. 43; Luke ix. 17; John vi. 13 (so here also Matt. xvi. 9, 10): and Matt. xv. 37; Mark viii. 8. Clearly, the two miracles were distinctly impressed on the minds of the Evangelists as *distinct* and *real* events; the circumstantial particulars peculiar to each miracle being noted with the accuracy of an eye-witness, even to the shape and size of the baskets. A teller of the tale, at third or fourth hand, would have lost this

which they carried full; in the second, the number of *spyrides* corresponds to that of the loaves. If they had had more *cophini* in the one instance, or *spyrides* in the other, the loaves would without doubt have been increased in quantity (cf. 2 Kings iv. 6), that the baskets might be all filled; see Mark viii. 20. But the *spyris*, rendered in Latin *sporta*, was larger than the *cophinus*; an ancient gloss renders κόφινος, *corbis, corbula, i.e.,* a twig basket or pannier. Juvenal[1] speaks of needy Jews, whose household stuff consisted of a *cophinus* and some hay; from which it is evident that the *cophinus* was κουφότερον, *lighter;* so that it might be carried about by any one for daily use. The *spyris* seems to have held the proper burden for a porter; cf. Acts ix. 25.[2]

10. Τῶν τετρακισχιλίων, *of the four thousand*) That which any one enjoys and uses may be said to be his.—ἐλάβετε, *ye took*) sc. for future food, as a compensation for the five and seven loaves which ye spent.

11. Πῶς, *how*) A particle expressing astonishment.—Cf. Gnomon on ch. viii. 10.—οὐ περὶ ἄρτου, *not concerning bread*) The literal meaning is frequently more true and more sublime than the meaning of the letter; and where the latter treats of things natural, the former leads to things spiritual. In things spiritual, heavenly words ought to be taken more closely.

12. Συνῆκαν, *they understood*) Our Lord still left something to be understood by His disciples. He shows them what leaven did not mean in this passage; it was their part, when they heard what it was not, to gather what it must be. Thus also in ch. xvii. 13.—ἀπὸ τῆς διδαχῆς, *from that of the doctrine*)[3] sc.

delicate mark of truth. Accordingly, our translators, who were not witnesses, have lost the point, their attention not being turned to the distinction, by rendering both alike *baskets*.—See Blunt Script. Coinc., p. 285.—ED.

[1] See preceding footnote.—(I. B.)

" Quorum *cophinus* fœnumque supellex."—Juv. iii. 14.

[2] Where we read, "Then the disciples took him [Paul] by night, and let him down by the wall in a basket (ἐν σπυρίδι).—(I. B.)

[3] In E. V. the verse is rendered, "Then understood they how that He bade them not beware of the leaven of bread, but of the *doctrine* of the Pharisees and of the Sadducees."—(I. B.)

from the leaven of the doctrine.¹ The word doctrine, in opposition to bread, is taken in a wide signification, so as to mean even hypocrisy. The leaven was this hypocritical doctrine.

13. Ἐλθὼν ὁ Ἰησοῦς, κ.τ.λ., *But when Jesus had come*, etc.) A noticeable interval of time occurred between the things just narrated and those which are now declared.² The connection, therefore, of the passages is not close. The matters which follow took place a short time before our Lord's Passion; and the shortness of this interval³ assists the right interpretation of the promises made in ver. 18, 28, and of the prohibition uttered in ver. 20, ch. xvii. 9, etc.⁴—Καισαρίας, *of Cæsarea*) This very name, which had not heretofore been given to the towns of Palestine, might have warned all that the Jews were subject to Cæsar, that the sceptre had departed from Judah, and that the Messiah had therefore come. See, however, *James Alting*,⁵ *Schilo*, pp. 147, 153. In Scriptural exegesis, the reader ought to place himself, as it were, in the time and place where the words were spoken, or the thing was done, and to

---

¹ Of which a specimen occurs in ver. 1.—V. g.

² Mark and Luke, it seems, as well as Matthew, here begin a new section, wherein, with a common design, they show how He proceeded upon His last journey (tour of preaching), replete with salvation, in the northern coasts of the land of Israel. Near Cæserea Philippi, He asks the disciples, when He was alone with them, " Whom do men say that I am ?" and then He informs them of His Passion. Then He so arranges His departure (the course of His journey), as that He now imbues the whole land of Israel with the good seed. After having exhibited His glory on the mountain of Transfiguration, He returns to Capernaum, directing His course from thence through the midst of Samaria and Galilee ; then onward beyond Jordan, bending His course towards Judea, He bids farewell to Bethabara [John x. 40, comp. with i. 28], and, having crossed the Jordan afresh, He came finally to Jericho and Bethany, Matt. xvi. 13-xx. 34, etc.—*Harm.*, p. 367.

³ Consisting of about one month and a half.—V. g.

⁴ A few weeks later, all the details of the truth concerning Him were published on every side, the restraints (which He had imposed on them, ver. 20) being removed. The sum of all which the disciples heretofore learned was this, *Jesus is the Christ:* This is repeated and confirmed, ver. 16, and furthermore on it this additional thesis is built, *Christ shall suffer*, etc., which constitutes the sum and substance of the rest of the Gospel history.—V. g.

⁵ JAMES ALTING was born at Heidelberg in 1618: he studied at the Academy of Groningen, where he attained distinction as a divine, a Hebrew philologist, and a Syriac scholar. He died in 1679.—(I. B.)

consider the feelings[1] of the writer, the force of the words, and the context.—τῆς Φιλίππου, *Philippi*) Thus the inland Cæsarea is distinguished from that on the sea-shore.[2]—τίνα, *whom*) The disciples had profited by listening and inquiry; now their Master examines them by questioning, and gives an example of catechising.—τὸν υἱὸν τοῦ ’Ανθρώπου, *the Son of Man*) *i.e.* Me, whom I myself am wont to call the Son of Man. Peter gives the right antitheton [in his reply[3]], ver. 16: *Thou art the Son of the living God.*—Cf. John v. 19, 27. This title, the Son of Man, which frequently occurs in the Evangelists, should be carefully observed: no one was so called but Christ Himself, and no one, whilst He walked on earth, so called Him except Himself. He first applies this appellation to Himself in John i. 51, when they were first found who acknowledged Him as the Messiah and the Son of God (ibid. ver. 50), and thenceforth very frequently, both before and after His prediction of His Passion. For they who expressed their faith in Him, called Him the *Son of David*. The Jews rightly suspected (John xii. 34), that by this title He claimed to be the Messiah. For as the first Adam, with all his progeny, is called *Man*, so the second Adam (see 1 Cor. xv. 45) is called *Son of Man*, not with that notion with which בְּנֵי אָדָם (filii hominis), *i.e.* the weak, are opposed to בְּנֵי אִישׁ (filii viri), *i.e.* the powerful (in Ps. xlix. (xlviii.) 2); or that in which men are called generally, sons of men (*filii hominum*), as in Mark iii. 28; Eph. iii. 5; Ezek. ii. 1, etc.; but with the article, ὁ υἱὸς τοῦ ’Ανθρώπου. The article appears to refer to the prophecy of Daniel, vii. 13. This, in sooth, is that One Man whom Adam, after the fall, expected by promise for his whole race: ὁ δεύτερος, *the second* (1 Cor. xv. 47), to whom every pro-

---

[1] *Affectus.* See Author's Preface, Sect. xv., and Translator's foot-notes in loc.—(I. B.)

[2] Cæsarea Philippi, previously called Paneas, was enlarged and adorned by the Tetrarch Philip, who gave it the name of Cæsarea in honour of the Emperor Tiberias, adding the cognomen Philippi to distinguish it from the great Cæsarea, the Roman metropolis of Judea. For further particulars, see *Kitto's Scripture Lands*, and *Lewin's Life and Writings of St Paul.* —(I. B.)

[3] In the original, "Petrus antitheton tangit,"—literally, "Peter touches the antitheton," a metaphorical expression apparently derived from shooting at a target.—(I. B.)

phecy of the Old Testament pointed, who holds the rights and primogeniture of the whole human race (see Luke iii. 23, 38), and to whom alone we owe that we are not ashamed of the name of man: see Ps. xlix. (xlviii.) 20, and cf. Rom. v. 15. Moreover, our Lord, whilst walking amongst men, by this appellation, both expressed, and as suitable to the circumstances (pro economiâ) of that time, concealed amongst men (cf. ch. xxii. 45) and hid from Satan the fact that He was ὁ Υἱὸς, *the Son*, absolutely so called, *i.e.* the Son of God promised and given to man, Gen. iii. 15; Isa. ix. 6; and sprung from man, Heb. ii. 11; and at the same time, as it were, reminded Himself of His present condition, Matt. xx. 28; Phil. ii. 7, 8. In the same manner, He expressed both His crucifixion and His ascension by one word, ὑψωθῶ, *I be lifted up*, John xii. 32. Neither is this appellation suited only to the state of His humiliation, but the expression, the Son of man, is used for every conspicuous situation of His, either in humiliation or exaltation; see John xii. 34, and compare therewith, in the following verse, *the light is with you*. And it agrees with the very form of His body, as implying youth; see Dan. vii. 13. Consider the following passages:—ver. 27, 28; ch. xii. 32, xxiv. 27, 30, 37, 39, 44, xxv. 31; Luke xvii. 22; John xii. 23–36, v. 27; Acts vii. 56. Therefore also this appellation does not once occur in the whole of the twenty-one apostolic epistles, but instead of it, the appellation, *the Son of God;* for in Heb. ii. 6 the article is not added, and the words are those of David, not of St Paul, who yet frequently calls Christ both ἄνθρωπος (homo), and ἀνήρ (vir). See the Gnomon on Rom. v. 15. And even in the Apocalypse i. 13 and xiv. 14, as long before in Dan. vii. 13, that appellation is only alluded to, not actually applied to our Lord. The agreement of the apostles, even in the case of this single phrase, shows that they wrote by the same Divine inspiration.

14. Οἱ μὲν—ἄλλοι δὲ—ἕτεροι δὲ, *some—some—and others*) It is not sufficient that we should know the various opinions of others, we ought ourselves to have a fixed faith, which then may make progress, even by the opinions of others, though vain in themselves.—Ἰωάννην—ἢ ἕνα τῶν προφητῶν, *John—or one of the prophets*) There is no need to refer this to the notion of a metempsychosis believed by the Pharisees; for they expected the return of Elias

himself in person, who was not dead, or the resurrection of the others from the dead;[1] see ch. xiv. 2: Luke ix. 8, 19.—Ἰερεμίαν, *Jeremiah*) who was at that time expected by the Jews.—ἕνα, *one*) *i.e.* some one indefinitely. They did not think that anything greater could come than they had already had. They did not compare Jesus with Moses.

16. Ἀποκριθεὶς, *answering*) Peter everywhere, from the warmth of his disposition, took the lead among the apostles in speaking.—Σίμων Πέτρος, *Simon Peter*) On this solemn occasion his name and surname are joined. It is clear that Simon acknowledged the Son of God more quickly and fully, and outshone his fellow-disciples.—Σὺ εἶ, *Thou art*) He says firmly, *Thou art*, not *I say that Thou art*. It behoved that Peter should first believe this, and then hear it on the Mount of Transfiguration; see ch. xvii. 5. Peter had already uttered a similar confession; see John vi. 69; but this is mentioned with greater distinction, since he delivered it after so many temptations,[2] on being so solemnly interrogated.—ὁ Χριστὸς, ὁ Υἱὸς τοῦ Θεοῦ τοῦ ζῶντος, *the Christ, the Son of the living God*) These two appellations, therefore, are not exactly synonymous, as John Locke[3] pretended, though the one is implied in the other (see Acts ix. 20); and there is a gradation here; for the knowledge of Jesus as the Son of God is sublimer than that of Him as the Christ.

17. Μακάριος, *blessed*) This word signifies a condition not only blessed, but at the same time rare; see ch. xiii. 16. Jesus had not previously told His disciples explicitly that He was the Christ. He had done and said those things by which, through the revelation of the Father, they might recognise Him as the Christ.—Σίμων Βὰρ Ἰωνᾶ, *Simon Bar-jona*) This express naming signifies that the Lord knoweth them that are His, and recalls to Peter's remembrance that sample of omniscience which had been given to him in John i. 42; cf. ibid. xxi. 15.[4]—σὰρξ καὶ

---

[1] The suspicion they formed was not that the soul of Elijah or others had passed into the body of Jesus, according to the Pythagorean doctrine of metempsychosis, but an actual return of Elijah in person, or a resurrection of the others named.—ED.

[2] John vii.-x.—E. B.

[3] The Author of the Essay concerning "The human understanding:" born at Wrington in 1632, died in 1704.—(I. B.)

[4] Peter himself hardly thought that he was so acceptable [before God].

ἧμα, flesh and blood) *i.e.* any man whatsoever; flesh and blood are put by metonymy[1] for body and soul: see Eph. vi. 12; Gal. i. 16. No mortal at that time knew this truth before Peter; see ver. 14.—οὐκ ἀπεκάλυψε, *hath not revealed*) The knowledge of Christ is not obtained except by Divine revelation; see ch. xi. 27.—ὁ Πατήρ Μου, κ.τ.λ., *My Father*, etc.) By these words the sum and substance of Peter's confession is repeated and confirmed. The heavenly Father had revealed it to Peter by the teaching of Jesus Christ, and thus inscribed it on the apostle's heart.

18. Σὺ εἶ Πέτρος, *thou art Peter*) This corresponds with great beauty to the words, *Thou art the Christ*.[2]—Πέτρος, πέτρα, *Peter—rock*) πέτρος elsewhere signifies *a stone*; but in the case of Simon, *a rock*. It was not fitting that such a man should be called Πέτρα, with a feminine termination; on the other hand, St Matthew would gladly have written ἐπὶ τούτῳ τῷ πέτρῳ, if the idiom would have allowed it; wherefore these two, πέτρα and πέτρος, stand for one name and thing, as both words are expressed in Syriac by the one noun, *Kepha*. *Peter* is here used as a proper name; for it is not said, Thou shalt be, but, Thou art; and yet the appellative is at the same time openly declared to denote a *rock*. The Church of Christ is certainly[3] (Rev. xxi. 14) built on the apostles, inasmuch as they were the first believers, and the rest have been added through their labours; in which matter a certain especial prerogative was conspicuous in the case of Peter, without damage to the equality of apostolic authority; for he first converted many Jews (Acts ii.), he first admitted the Gentiles to the Gospel (Acts x.[4]) He moreover was especially commanded to *strengthen his brethren*, and to *feed the sheep and lambs* of the Lord. Nor can we imagine that this illustrious surname, elsewhere commonly attributed to Christ

Blessed is the man, not he who attributes aught to himself on his own authority, but whom the Lord pronounces to be blessed.—V. g.

[1] See explanation of technical terms in Appendix.—(I. B.)

[2] Christ addresses His own, and Christ's own address Him most becomingly throughout the whole of Scripture.—V. g.

[3] Eph. ii. 20.—E.B.

[4] And the same apostle, in this very passage, was superior to the rest of the disciples in the fact of his knowledge and his confession, seeing that it is probable that none of them would have answered at that time with so great alacrity as did Peter.—V. g.

Himself, who is also called the Rock, could without the most important meaning have been bestowed on Peter, who in the list of the apostles is called *first*, and always put in the first place; see Matt. x. 2; see also 1 Pet. ii. 4–7. All these things are said with safety, for what have they to do with Rome?[1] Let the Roman rock beware, lest it fall under the censure of ver. 23. —καὶ, κ.τ.λ., *and*, etc.) A most magnificent promise, including, in different ways, the gates of hell, the kingdom of heaven, and the earth.—οἰκοδομήσω, *I will build*) He does not say, *on this rock* I WILL FOUND; for Peter, nevertheless, is not the foundation. The wise build on a rock; see ch. vii. 24.— Μου τὴν ἐκκλησίαν, *My Church*) A magnificent expression concerning Jesus, not occurring elsewhere in the Gospels.—πύλαι ᾅδου, *the gates of hell*) The word πύλαι (*gates*) occurs here without the article. *Heaven* is in the next verse put in opposition to τῷ ᾅδῃ, *hell*, which occurs here, as in ch. xi. 23. *Hell* has no power against faith; faith has power with reference to heaven.[2] *The gates of hell* (as elsewhere, *the gates of death*) are named also in Isa. xxxviii. 10; Wis. xvi. 13. Hell, ᾅδης, is exceedingly strong (see Cant. viii. 6); how much more its gates? The metaphor in "*gates*" is of an architectural kind, as in the expressions, "*I will build,*" and "*the keys.*" The Christian Church is like a city without walls, and yet the gates of hell, which assail it, shall never prevail. The defences of hell, and the fortifications of the world, corresponding to them, are here intended; as, for instance, the Ottoman Porte, and Rome, where Erasmus Schmidt[3] thinks that the mouth of hell is; that it was opened in the time of Marcus

---

[1] Whether Peter was for any time at Rome, and that too not in imprisonment, is a matter full of doubt. Grant even that he was: he was so certainly in no other way save as an Apostle; and the Church planted there was blessed with its own ordinary ministers. It was, therefore, to the place of these latter, not to his place, that the Bishops of subsequent ages succeeded, who afterwards degenerated into Lords and Popes.—V. g.

[2] In the original, "Contra fidem nil potest *infernus:* fides potest in *cœlum :*" where the preposition "*in*" implies also *motion*, or *progress towards* heaven.—(I. B.)

" Even to heaven."—ED.

[3] ERASMUS SCHMIDT was a learned Philologist, born in Misnia in 1560. He became eminent for his skill in Greek and in Mathematics, of both or which he was Professor at Wittenberg, where he died in 1637.—(I. B.)

Curtius, and will be opened again hereafter, when the prophecy in Rev. xix. 20 is fulfilled. "Rome," he says, "is situated very near those parts of Italy where, before the foundation of Rome, Homer makes his Ulysses descend to hell, and where, after the foundation of Rome, without the intervention of any great distance, Virgil makes his Æneas do the same. But lest I should appear to wish to plead on poetical credit (although these poetical assertions may be regarded like the prediction of Caiaphas), attend to historical testimony:—In the middle of the Roman Forum, once upon a time, if we are to credit Livy and other Roman writers, the hell, which you (Papists) place in the bowels of the earth, opened its mouth, and that chasm could not be filled up with any amount of earth thrown in, until Marcus Curtius, armed, and on horseback, leapt in—in order, forsooth, that as the heaven received Enoch and Elijah alive, so hell might receive this Curtius alive, as the first fruits, by these *gates of hell* then opened in the middle of the Roman Forum, which will, without doubt, again be opened by Divine power, when the beast and the false prophet shall be cast alive into the lake of fire burning with sulphur, as is foretold in Rev. xix. 20."

19. Δώσω σοί,[1] *I will give thee*) The future tense. Christ Himself, after His glorification, received the keys economically.[2] See Rev. i. 18, and German exposition of the Apocalypse. Our Lord afterwards gave the keys, which He here promised, to Peter, not alone, but first in order of time (cf. Luke v. 10); since Peter was the first who, after the resurrection of Christ, exercised the apostolical office; see Acts i. 15, ii. 14. If the keys had been given exclusively to Peter, and the Bishop of Rome after him, and not to the other apostles also, even after the death of Peter, the Bishop of Rome should have acted as pastor to the other apostles.—τὰς κλεῖς, *the keys*) Keys denote

---

[1] The margin of Ed. 2 makes the reading σοὶ δώσω equal in authority to δώσω σοί.—E. B.

B*a*, Rec. Text, Origen 3,525*a*, 529*d*, 530*a*, support δώσω σοί. D*bc* Vulg. Cypr. support σοὶ δώσω.—ED.

[2] *i.e.* As Christ, without any derogation to His proper Divinity.—(I. B.) 'Œconomice,' in conformity with the Mediatorial economy, which appertains to Him.—ED.

authority. Tertullian, in his work on fasting, ch. 15, says, *Apostolus claves macelli tibi tradidit: the apostle[1] has given thee the keys of the meat market*, where he alludes to 1 Cor. x. 25. The keys are available for two purposes, to close and to open ; the keys themselves are not said to be *two*.[2] One and the same key closes and opens in Rev. iii. 7. The Jews declare that a thousand keys were given to Enoch. See James Alting's Hist. promot. acad. Hebr. p. 107.—τῆς βασιλείας τῶν οὐρανῶν, *of the kingdom of heaven*) He does not say *of the Church*, nor *of the kingdoms of the world*.—δήσης, λύσης, *thou shalt bind—thou shalt loose*) The keys denote the whole office of Peter. By the expressions, therefore, of binding and loosing,[3] are comprehended all those things which Peter performed in virtue of the name of Jesus Christ, and through faith in that name, by his apostolic authority, by teaching, convincing, exhorting, forbidding, permitting (see Tertullian, already quoted), consoling, remitting (see Matt. xviii. 18, 15; John xx. 23); by healing, as in Acts iii. 7, ix. 34 ; by raising from the dead, as in Acts ix. 41 (cf. ibid. ii. 24) ; by punishing, ibid. v. 5; cf. 1 Cor. v. 5 ; he himself records, in Acts xv. 8, an instance of a matter performed on earth and sanctioned in heaven. It is advisable to compare with this passage that in Matt. xviii. 18, and with both of them the third in John xx. 23. In this passage, to Peter alone, after uttering his confession concerning Jesus Christ, the authority is promised, first of binding, and secondly of loosing sins, and whatsoever is included under that authority ; and this is done as it were enigmatically, it not being expressed what things were to be bound and loosed, because the disciples were not yet capable of understanding so wonderful a matter; see Luke ix. 54. In chapter xviii., after our Lord's transfiguration, the disciples,

---

[1] Sc. St Paul.—(I. B.)

"The keys of the market," *i.e.* the *free use of authority* to buy and eat whatever meat is sold in it.—ED.

[2] More keys, in fact, may be accounted to have been delivered to Peter. Hence it was that with so great efficacy he opened the entrance into the kingdom of heaven to the Jews and Gentiles. Comp. the opposite case [of the Pharisees, who *shut up the kingdom of heaven against men*], ch. xxiii. 4, 13 ; Luke xi. 52.—V. g.

[3] These words as to *binding* and *loosing* do not properly apply to the keys, but yet have a close connection with the use of the keys.—V. g.

who had made some progress in faith, are invested in common with the authority, first of binding, and secondly of loosing, the offences of their brethren, but most especially of loosing them by prayers in the name of Christ. In John xx., after His resurrection, our Lord having *breathed upon* His disciples, gives them the authority, firstly of remitting, and secondly of retaining sins; for thus are the words and their order[1] changed after the opening of the gate of salvation. The greatest part of the apostolic authority regards sins (cf. Hosea xiii. 12). The remaining particulars are contained in this discourse by synecdoche. It is not foreign to our present purpose to compare a passage of Aristophanes as to the use of the verb λύειν—Frogs; Act ii. scene 6, Epirrhema[2] [Ed. Dindorf, 691],—αἰτίαν ἐκθεῖσι, ΛΥΣΑΙ τὰς πρότερον ἁμαρτίας (χρή)—*i.e.* "we ought to forgive (or *remit*) the faults of those who explain the cause of them."

20. Μηδενί, *to no one*) Jesus had not, even to His apostles, said that He was the Christ, but He left it that they might discover it themselves from the testimony of facts. It was not suitable, therefore, that that should be openly told by the apostles to others before His resurrection, which was to corroborate the whole testimony to the fact of His being the Christ.[3] For he who injudiciously propounds a mystery to those who do not comprehend it, injures both himself and others. Had they done so, those who believed in any way that Jesus was the Christ might have sought for an earthly kingdom with seditious uproar; whilst the rest, and by far the greater number, might have rejected such a Messiah at that time more vehemently, and have been guilty of greater sin in crucifying Him, so as to have had the door of repentance less open to them for the future. Afterwards,[4] the apostles openly bore witness to this truth.—ὁ Χριστός, *the Christ*) Soon after the disciples had acknowledged and confessed that Jesus was the Christ, He exhibited to them His

---

[1] The order before had been—1. *Binding* (answering to *retaining*); 2. *Loosing* (answering to *remitting*). The order is now reversed.—ED.

[2] In old comedy, a speech, usually of Trochaic tetrameters, spoken by the Coryphæus after the Parabasis. *Liddell and Scott*, q. v.—(I. B.)

[3] Inasmuch as even Peter himself could hardly have reconciled the doctrine concerning *the Son of* GOD with that of His *Passion*.—*Harm.*, p. 369.

[4] And that, too, after the lapse of but a few intervening weeks,—*Harm.*, p. 369.

transfiguration (ch. xvii. 1–5), and openly spoke of Himself among them as the Christ; see Mark ix. 41, and John xvii. 3.

21. Ἀπὸ τότε, *at that time and thenceforward*—ἤρξατο, κ.τ.λ., *began*, etc.) It is clear, therefore, that He had not shown it them before.[1] The Gospel may be divided into two parts, from which the Divine plan of Jesus shines forth. The first proposition is, *Jesus is the Christ;* the second, *Christ must suffer, die, and rise again* (cf. John xvi. 30, 31, 32), or more briefly, *Christ by death will enter into glory*. Jesus first convinced His disciples of the first proposition (de subjecto):[2] in consequence of which they were bound to believe Him concerning the second (de prædicato), even before His passion. After His ascension, the people first learnt the second proposition (prædicatum), and thence were convinced of the first (de subjecto); see Acts xvii. 3. As soon as Jesus had persuaded His disciples of the first proposition (ver. 16), He added the second.[3] Afterwards He led them to the mountain of Transfiguration.[4] The order of the evangelic harmony is of great importance with regard to the observing of these things. Men frequently teach all things at once: Divine wisdom acts far otherwise.—δεικνύειν, *to show*), *i.e.* openly.—ὅτι δεῖ Αὐτὸν ἀπελθεῖν, *that He must go*) and at the same time relinquish that mode of living to which the disciples had become habituated.—παθεῖν, *to suffer*) When aught of glory accrued to Jesus, as in this instance by the confession of Peter, then He was especially wont to make mention of His approaching passion. This first announcement mentions His passion and death generally; the second, in ch. xvii. 22, 23,

---

[1] Except in covert [enigmatical] words.—V. g.

[2] "De subjecto," "de prædicato," lit. "of the subject," "of the prædicate." I have ventured to render the passage in language more generally intelligible.—(I. B.)

[3] Viz., In ver. 21, etc., as to His suffering, death, and resurrection.—ED.

[4] Where the same voice sounded from heaven, as before His baptism, "This is my Beloved Son;" there being added the Epiphonema, or appended exhortation, "Hear Him." To wit, He was to be heard, or given heed to, especially in regard to those things which had constituted the main subject of the conversation very recently held on the mountain (between the Lord and Moses and Elias, Luke ix. 31), concerning his approaching "decease at Jerusalem"—concerning His *Passion*, I say, His *Death* and His *Resurrection*.—*Harm.*, p. 370.

adds His being betrayed into the hands of sinners; the third, in ch. xx. 17–19, at length expresses His stripes, cross, etc. The first was nearer in point of time to the second, than the second to the third.—πρεσβυτέρων, ἀρχιερέων, γραμματέων, *elders—chief priests—scribes*) Three classes of those who ought to have led the people to the Messiah; corresponding nearly to the Council of Justice, the Consistory, and the Theological Faculty of modern times.—ἐγερθῆναι, *to be raised*) He adds nothing yet of His ascension. By degrees, all further and later particulars are disclosed; see ver. 27.

22. Προσλαβόμενος, *taking hold of*) as if he had a right to do so. He acted with greater familiarity after his declaration of acknowledgment. Jesus however reduces him to his proper level; cf. Luke ix. 28, 48, 49, 54, 55.—ὁ Πέτρος, *Peter*) The same mentioned in ver. 16.[1] Reason endures more easily the general proposition concerning the person of Christ, than the word of the Cross. Sudden changes occur in Peter, in ver. 16, 22, and ch. xvii. 4. Thence he bears witness from experience to the truth, that we are preserved by the power of God (1 Pet. i. 5), not our own.—ἤρξατο, *he began*) He had received the other doctrines without making any objection.—ἵλεως Σοι, *propitious unto Thee*) sc. May God be. An abbreviated formulary. Thus in 1 Mac. ii. 21, we meet with ἵλεως ἡμῖν καταλιπεῖν νόμον, *God forbid that we should forsake the law.* And thus the LXX. sometimes express the Hebrew חלילה.[2]

23. Ὕπαγε, *depart*) It is not your place to take hold of and rebuke Me. By how much the more He had declared Peter blessed, by so much the more does He now reprove him who was previously prepared by faith to digest the reproof, in order that He may both correct him and preserve the other disciples; see ver. 24.—ὀπίσω Μου, *behind Me*[3]) out of My sight. He had commanded Satan to do the same; see ch. iv. 10.—Σατανᾶ, *Satan*)

---

[1] There being thus afforded a remarkable specimen of how easy it is for one to stumble [to be offended with the humbling truths as to Christ] the more grievously [in proportion as one had the more boldly avowed the truth before].—V. g.

[2] As in 2 Sam. xx. 20.—(I. B.)

[3] It becomes thee not to be My adviser, but My follower [ὀπίσω Μου]. —V. g.

an appellative. Cf. John vi. 70, where our Lord says, concerning Judas Iscariot, καὶ ἐξ ὑμῶν εἷς διάβολός ἐστιν, *and one of you is a devil*.—But cf. Gnomon on Rev. xii. 9.—Peter thought himself very kind when he said ἵλεως, κ.τ.λ., but yet he is called *Satan* for so doing. Cf. 2 Sam. xix. 22, where משׂטן signifies one who puts himself in the way as a hinderance.[1]—σκάνδαλόν Μου, *My stumbling-block*[2]) *i.e.* thou dost not only stumble or take offence at My words, but, if it were possible, thou wouldst furnish Me with a hurtful stumbling-block by thy words. This is said with the utmost force, and declares the reason of our Lord's swift severity towards Peter.[3] If anything could have been able to touch the soul of Jesus, the words of the disciple would have been more dangerous than the assaults of the tempter, mentioned in the fourth chapter of this Gospel. Cf. Gnomon on Heb. iv. 15.—*Rock* and *stumbling-block* (LAPIS *offensionis*, lit. *stumbling* STONE) are put antithetically. Our Lord sends away behind Him the stumbling-block placed before His feet.—τὰ τοῦ Θεοῦ, *the things of God*) sc. the precious word of the Cross. The perception of Jesus is always divine.[4]—τῶν ἀνθρώπων, *of men*) the same as flesh and blood in ver. 17.

24. Θέλει, κ.τ.λ., *wishes*, etc.) No one is compelled; but if he wishes to do so, he must submit to the conditions.—ὀπίσω Μου ἐλθεῖν, *to come after Me*) This denotes the state and profession, as ἀκολουθείτω (*let him follow*) does the duty, of a disciple.[5]—ἀπαρνησάσθω, *let him abnegate*, or *utterly deny*) Weigh well the force of

---

[1] Where David so calls the sons of Zeruiah.—(I. B.)

[2] E. V. "An offence unto Me."—(I. B.)

[3] In this way the Saviour repelled, at the very moment of their approach, all things whatever might have been *a stumbling-block* or offence, just as fire repels water which approaches very close to it, but which cannot possibly mix with it.—V. g.

[4] The Cross is a stumbling-block to the world: the things which are opposed to the Cross were a stumbling-block (offence) to Christ. This feeling and perception concerning the 'suffering' of Christ, and of those who belong to Christ, and concerning the 'glory' which follows thereupon [1 Pet. i. 11], Peter cherished at a subsequent time, as his own first Epistle abundantly testifies.—V. g.

[5] "Id denotat statum et professionem; *sequatur*, officium." For a person may go after or behind another without following in his steps. In the one case, he appears and professes to walk in his steps; in the other, he really does so: the one implies profession—the other involves practice.—(I. B.)

the word in ch. xxvi. 70. To abnegate is to renounce oneself. Thus, in Tit. ii. 12, we have the simple word ἀρνεῖσθαι, *to deny*; in Luke xiv. 33, ἀποτάσσεσθαι, *to set apart from himself—to bid farewell to*, or *forsake*. These expressions are contrasted with ὁμολογία, *confession*, or *accordant profession*; see Heb. x. 23.[1]— καὶ ἀκολουθείτω Μοι, *and follow Me*) that he may be where I am.

25. Θέλῃ—σῶσαι, *shall wish—to save*) It is not said, "*shall save.*"—ψυχήν, *soul*) The soul is the man in his animal and human capacity.—σῶσαι, *to save*) sc. naturally.—ἀπολέσει, *shall lose*) sc. spiritually, or even corporeally.—ἀπολέσῃ, *will lose*) sc. naturally, having cast away all *egoism*[2] by self-abnegation. It is not said, *shall wish to lose.*—ἕνεκεν Ἐμοῦ, *for My sake*) This is the object of self-abnegation: but many from other causes lose their lives, sc. *for their own sake*, or *that of the world.*—εὑρήσει, *shall find*) In St Mark and St Luke it is σώσει, *shall save*, *shall save* sc. spiritually, or even corporeally. The world is full of danger. The soul that is saved is something that has been *found*.

26. Τὸν κόσμον ὅλον, *the whole world*) No one has ever yet gained the whole world; yet, if he should gain it, what would it profit him?—ψυχήν, *soul*) True wisdom refers everything to the interest of the soul; false, to that of the body.—τί δώσει, *what shall he give?*) The world is not enough.[3]—ἀντάλλαγμα, *as an equivalent*, lat. *redhostimentum*) which ought not to be of less value than the soul for which it is given.

27. Μέλλει ἔρχεσθαι, *is about to come*) A stronger expression than ἐλεύσεται, *will come*. As the teaching concerning the person of Christ is immediately followed by that concerning His Cross, so is the latter by that concerning His glory.—τότε, *then*)

---

[1] Peter disowns himself, when he suffers himself to do that which he had done in the disowning of Christ. When the human feelings of Peter desire this or that thing, Peter retorts—I do not know Peter any longer; there is no relationship at all between me and him, nor is it evident to me what the man means or intends. Whoever has gained such power against himself, to him the Cross is anything but irksome, and there is nothing sweeter than the following of Christ.—V. g.

[2] "*Suitate.*"—(I. B.)

[3] The whole world is not enough as a ransom to redeem the one soul of even one man. But what a vast multitude, in truth, Christ redeemed by His own blood, namely, the whole world!—V. g.

All things are put off till then.—ἀποδώσει ἑκάστῳ, *He will render to each individual*) This is the attribute of Divine Majesty; see Rom. ii. 6.[1]—πρᾶξιν, *action, conduct, doing*) The word is put in the singular, for the whole life of man is one *doing*.[2]

28. Τινὲς, *some*) Our Lord does not mention them by name; and it was profitable for them not to know that they were the persons meant.[3] Peter then scarcely hoped that he would be one of them.—ὧδε, *here*) A strikingly demonstrative particle.— ἕως ἂν ἴδωσι, *until they see*) Something is indicated which was to happen, but not immediately (otherwise all, or nearly all, would have lived to that time), but yet something which would take place in that generation of men. This *term* (*terminus*) or period has various intervals: the *vision*, or *seeing*, various degrees *up to the death* of those who saw it, which followed at various times: cf. in Luke ii. 26, the expression πρὶν ἢ ἴδῃ, *before he had seen*, used with regard to Simeon. And the advent of the Son of Man advanced another step before the death of James (see Acts ii. 36, and passim till xii. 2, and cf. Heb. ii. 5, 6, 7); another before the death of Peter (see 2 Pet. i. 14, 19, and Luke xxi. 31); another, and that the highest, before the death of John, in the most magnificent revelation of His coming, which the beloved disciple has himself described (see Gnomon on John xxi. 22); a revelation to which the event foretold will correspond; see ver. 27, and ch. xxvi. 64. And a previous proof of this matter was given in a week[4] from this time on the Mount of Transfiguration; and, at the same time, out of all the disciples those were chosen who should most especially see it. It is beyond question, that those three[5] who witnessed our Lord's transfiguration were peculiarly favoured with reference to the subsequent manifestations of His glory. This saying of our Lord appears to have been referred to, but not rightly under-

---

[1] There is most frequent recurrence of this expression in Scripture.—V. g.

[2] From which, according as it is subject to Christ or to the belly, many *works* continually, and as a natural consequence, either good or else bad, come forth (result).—V. g.

[3] And He may have thereby also at the same time sharpened others. —V. g.

[4] "After six days," chap. xvii. 1.—ED.

[5] Of whom James, in the year 44, Peter in 67, John in 102, are generally said to have died.—*Harm.*, p. 372.

stood, by those who imagined that the last day was near at hand. —τὸν Υἱὸν τοῦ Ἀνθρώπου ἐρχόμενον, *the Son of Man coming*) His conspicuous coming to judgment (see Gnomon on ver. 13) is meant, which would begin to follow immediately after His ascension.

CHAPTER XVII.

1. Ἡμέρας ἕξ, *Six days*) St Luke says, ὡσεὶ ἡμέραι ὀκτώ, *as it were, about, eight days*; enumerating the days both of the word and the deed. This definition of time intimates some connection with what has just preceded. The teaching concerning the *Son of God*, and His *departure*, or *Passion*, was confirmed by the Transfiguration.—παραλαμβάνει, *taketh with Him*) Our Lord knew what was about to happen on the Mount.—ὁ Ἰησοῦς, *Jesus*) As the name of Jesus is introduced here to indicate the commencement of a new portion of the Gospel history, it is clear that the declaration in ch. xvi. 28 does not refer exclusively to the Transfiguration.—τὸν Πέτρον καὶ Ἰάκωβον καὶ Ἰωάννην, τὸν ἀδελφὸν αὐτοῦ, *Peter and James, and John his brother*) St Matthew candidly relates those circumstances also in which other apostles were preferred to himself. The writings of Peter and John, who were present on the occasion, are extant: the former mentions this event in his second epistle (2 Pet. i. 17, 18): the latter takes it for granted,[1] as a thing well known, and attested by sufficient evidence. Cf. on the choice of the three apostles here selected, ch. xxvi. 37.—ὄρος, *a mountain*) The name of the mountain is not mentioned, and thereby superstition is prevented. Several very remarkable divine manifestations have been made on mountains; see Acts vii. 30, 38. The opinion which regards Tabor as the scene of the transfiguration is specious. See Jer. xlvi. 18.

2. Μετεμορφώθη, *was transfigured*) This verb implies that our Lord had always possessed the glory within Himself. The force

---

[1] No doubt the transfiguration was included in the reference, John i. 14, "We beheld His *glory*, the glory as of the Only begotten of the Father, full of grace and truth."—ED.

of the verb μετασχηματίζεσθαι is different, as in Phil. iii. 21 and 2 Cor. xi. 14; cf. also the distinction between μορφή and σχῆμα, in Phil. ii. 6, 7, 8.[1]—φῶς, *light*) inferior to that of the sun;[2] for His garments diluted the splendour of His body.

3. Ὤφθησαν, *appeared*) sc. with their bodies.—Μωσῆς καὶ Ἠλίας, *Moses and Elias*) The departure of each of them from this world had been singular: each of them was remarkable for revelations vouchsafed to him on Mount Sinai and Horeb. Both of them are mentioned together in Mal. iv. 4, 5. It is probable that Moses was raised to life immediately on his death and burial, so that he was not dead whilst Elias was living in heaven: he certainly, after his decease, entered the land of promise, in which this holy mountain was situated. And yet Christ, not Moses, is the ἀπαρχή, the primitiæ, the *first-fruits*. The resuscitation of Moses does not confer life upon others; that of Christ does. This appearance, however, of Moses alive from the dead, is full of mystery. Who will venture to assert that he had already obtained immortality (ἀθανασία), and did not receive any advancement in bliss (βελτίωσις) after the resurrection of Christ?[3] Oh, how many things there are in the world of

---

[1] Sc. ἐν μορφῇ Θεοῦ ὑπάρχων—μορφὴν δούλου λαβών—καὶ σχήματι εὑρεθεὶς ὡς ἄνθρωπος.

Μορφή, *forma*, according to Beng. l. c., expresses something absolute. Σχῆμα, *habitus*, refers to the aspect and feeling (refertur ad aspectum et sensum). I think as *habitus* is from *habeo*, so σχῆμα from ἔχω, σχῶ; and therefore σχῆμα is *the whole external condition of man*, as seen in his *form* (μορφή), gesture, and gait,—*the bearing and state* of a man.—ED.

[2] Whereas His *face* shone as the *sun*, His *raiment* was only white as the *light*.—ED.

[3] On the first day of the month Adar, according to Josephus, B. IV. Ant., at the end, Moses died (comp. Deut. xxxiv. 8; Josh. i. 11, iv. 19). Beng. had mentioned this in Harm. Ev., Ed. i. on this passage, and had noticed that Christ's transfiguration had taken place at the same time of year, in the presence of Moses; subjoining a caution, that though this remark might not seem to have much weight, yet it was possible *it might be of use to some hereafter*. Shortly after, some one appealed to the transfiguration of Christ as having occurred in the month of *September*, as a ground of expecting the coming of Moses and Elias in the month of September A.D. 1737: an error which this observation of Beng., however minute and overstrained it may seem to some, might have served to refute. See Harm. Ev. Ed. ii., pp. 375, 376.
—E. B.

glory above our comprehension! If this appearance of Moses and Elias were not mentioned in the canonical Scriptures, although attested by other sufficient witnesses, who would not consider it as a fable?—μετ' Αὐτοῦ συλλαλοῦντες, *conversing with Him*) There is no pleonasm.[1] *Each* of them conversed with Jesus. A conversation of the highest importance (colloquium maximum). Moses stood at the end of the first dispensation,[2] Elias, in the middle of the middle dispensation; Jesus, on the threshold of the last. They bear witness to the true Messiah, and to Him only.—μετ' Αὐτοῦ, *with Him*) They conversed with Him only, not with the three apostles.

4. Καλὸν, *good*) the Hebrew טוב in the first chapter of Genesis.—ἶναι, *to be*) *i.e.* to remain. Nay, something very different—καλὸν ἦν, *was good* ["expedient for them"]; see John xvi. 7. There was no need of tabernacles for *standing* (see Luke ix. 32), nor for a single night (see ibid. 37.)[3]—εἰ θέλεις, *if Thou wilt*) A good and necessary condition.—τρεῖς, *three*) not six. The apostles wished to be with Jesus.—Μωσῆ, κ.τ.λ., *for Moses*, etc.) Peter knew Moses and Elias in that light.

5. Ἔτι, *yet*) with but little delay.—λαλοῦντος, *speaking*) His speech had clearly not been suitable.—ἰδοὺ—ἰδοὺ, *behold! behold!*) Matters of great moment, one of the greatest revelations.—νεφέλη, *a cloud*) Human nature cannot bear the glory of God without admixture or interposition. Strong medicine is diluted with fluid. Sleep must be added; see Luke ix. 32. Moses and Elias, however, were permitted to enter the cloud (ibid. 34): a great admission! The Divine majesty is frequently conspicuous in clouds.—αὐτοὺς, *them*) sc. the disciples; see Luke ix. 34.—φωνὴ, *a voice*) A voice came from heaven, firstly, ch. iii. 17; secondly, at this central period; thirdly, and lastly, a little

---

[1] See explanation of technical terms in Appendix.—(I. B.)

[2] At the end of the first dispensation, viz. the patriarchal; though Moses also stood at the beginning of the second, viz. that of the law. In this latter point of view, as Moses stands at the beginning of the law as its representative, so Elias at the beginning of the prophets, and the Lord Jesus at the beginning of the Gospel, at once its representative and embodiment.—ED.

[3] Peter no longer now has the wish that he had continued on that mountain. It is now his privilege, by means of the Cross, to pass from that which is *good* to those things which are *better*.—V. g.

before our Lord's Passion, John xii. 28. After each of these voices from heaven, fresh virtue shone forth in Jesus, fresh ardour and fresh sweetness in His discourses and actions, fresh progress.—οὗτός ἐστιν, κ.τ.λ., *This is*, etc.) This speech has three divisions, which regard the Psalms, the Prophets, and Moses, from which they are derived[1].—Αὐτοῦ, *Him*) In contradistinction to Moses and Elias. This command, *hear Him*, was not uttered at His baptism; see Matt. iii. 17.—ἀκούετε, *hear*) It is the business of wayfarers rather to hear and publish what they have heard, than to *see* as Peter wished to do. The Father sanctioned all things which the Son had said of Himself as the Son of God; and what He was about to say even more fully, especially concerning the Cross. For the Father on this occasion bore witness Himself expressly concerning Him as His *Son*: concerning the *Cross*, His Son was *to be heard* more and more.

7. Ἥψατο, *touched*) They were prostrated by what they saw and heard; they were raised again by His familiar and efficacious touch.—μὴ φοβεῖσθε) *cease to fear*.

8. Ἰησοῦν μόνον, *Jesus alone*) Hence it is evident that He is the Son, who is to be heard, not Moses, nor Elias.

9. Μηδενί, *to no one*) not even to their fellow-disciples.—ἕως οὗ, κ.τ.λ., *until*, etc.) After His resurrection they did mention it; see 2 Pet. i. 18. St Matthew also recorded it, although he had not been present.—ἀναστῇ, *have risen*) The glory of the resurrection rendered this previous manifestation more credible.

10. Τί οὖν, κ.τ.λ., *how then*, etc.) To the mention of His death they oppose the restitution of all things by Elias, whom (see ver. 31) they suppose to have come; and they think that this fact ought not to be concealed, but, on the contrary, published

---

[1] Viz., "I will declare the decree: the Lord hath said unto Me, *Thou art my Son;* this day have I begotten Thee," Ps. ii. 7. "Behold My Servant, whom I uphold; mine Elect, *in whom My soul delighteth:* I have put My Spirit upon Him; He shall bring forth judgment to the Gentiles," Isa. xlii. 1. "The LORD thy God will raise up unto thee a Prophet from the midst of thee, of thy brethren, like unto me; *unto Him ye shall hearken*," Deut. xviii. 15.—(I. B.)

And not long before his decease, Peter, in his Second Epistle, appealed to this very testimony which declared Jesus' glory.—V. g.

for the promotion of the faith, that the event may be recognised as already corresponding to the expectation of the Scribes. — πρῶτον, *first*) sc. before the Messiah's kingdom.

11. Ἔρχεται, *cometh*) The present tense, midway between prediction and fulfilment; and the ministry of John was efficacious also after his death.—ἀποκαταστήσει, *shall restore*) The same verb is used by the LXX. in Mal. iii. 24 [iv. 6]. And this office of restoring all things furnishes a proof that the prophecy concerning Elias did not refer to his brief appearance on the Mount of Transfiguration.—πάντα, *all things*) sc. regarding parents and children, *i.e.* seminally;[1] see John x. 40, 41, and Acts xix. 3.

12. Δὲ, *but*) He teaches that there is not only no inconsistency, but also an actual congruity, between the coming of Elias and the death of the Messiah.—οὐκ ἐπέγνωσαν αὐτὸν, *they knew him not*) although Jesus (xi. 14) had openly told it them.[2]—ὅσα ἠθέλησαν, *whatsoever they listed*[3]) The death of John is not ascribed to Herod alone; cf. Gnomon on ch. xiv. 9. Jesus asserts that Elias has come in the person of John the Baptist; John denies it; both truly, if you compare these apparently conflicting statements with the questions to which they were replies. The Jews asked John, whether he were Elias (cf. ch. xxvii. 49)— he, that is to say, who was to come before the second advent, or great and terrible day of the Lord. John therefore replies in the negative. The disciples, comparing the opinion of the Scribes with the discourses of Christ, and endeavouring to reconcile them together, fancied that Elijah the Tishbite would

---

[1] "Seminaliter," *i.e.*, he will sow the seed of these things: he will *initiate* them, as the *preparation* for what is to follow.—(I. B.)

[2] The world either altogether disbelieves the truth, or else, clinging to mere expectations, refuses to believe the actual fulfilment itself. —V. g.

[3] *Whatsoever they listed*, and that too owing to their evil and wanton *lust*. It is this very blind perversity of the world which causes the necessity that one must burst through so many obstacles to a good cause. It not seldom happens, that one who has effected some good, waits in expectation of most splendid recompences from the world on that account. But the man who knows God, the world, and himself, cannot long persist in such an expectation. The merits which receive remuneration of this kind are not spiritual, but worldly.—V. g.

come before the first advent; therefore Jesus replies, that *he*[1] has already come in the person of John the Baptist.[2]

14. Καὶ ἐλθόντων αὐτῶν, κ.τ.λ.., *and when they were come*, etc.) A very different scene is here opened to view from that which Peter had wished for in ver. 4.—Whilst Moses was on the mountain, the people transgressed; see Exod. xxxii. 1; whilst Jesus was on the mountain, matters did not proceed very well with the people.

15. Ἐλέησόν μου τὸν υἱόν, *have mercy on my son*) The lunatic might have said, in the words of David (see Ps. xxv. [xxiv.] 16), both in the Hebrew original and S.V.:[3] "*Have mercy upon me, for I am an only son.*" And this his father repeats.— τὸ πῦρ—τὸ ὕδωρ, THE *fire*—THE *water*) The article implies that the nature of these elements universally[4] is intended: because the lunatic is more liable to fall into the paroxysm when near fire or water: but in Mark ix. 22 (see Gnomon) fires and waters are mentioned, and that indefinitely, without the article.

16. Οὐκ ἠδυνήθησαν, *were not able*) It was a disgrace for the disciples to be accused from another quarter. Observe the candour of St Matthew's confession, implicating himself in this

---

[1] *i.e.*, *The* Elias, who was appointed to precede the first advent.—ED.

[2] Ver. 13. περὶ Ἰωάννου, *concerning John*) not concerning that Elias, or Elijah, whom they had seen, as recorded in ver. 3.—V. g.

[3] Ps. xxiv. 16, LXX. ἐπίβλεψον ἐπ' ἐμὲ καὶ ἐλέησόν με, ὅτι μονογενής εἰμι ἐγώ.—ED.

[4] Middleton remarks on this, "*Bengel* (in Gnom.) has here a note which I do not understand: he says, '*Articulus* UNIVERSE *innuit naturam horum elementorum, quod lunaticus apud ignem et aquam proclivior sit in paroxysmum.*'" Though it savours of presumption to attempt any explanation of that which Middleton did not understand, I would venture to suggest, that Bengel means to say, that *the article* shows that the element of fire is intended, in the abstract, and consequently every presence of it (universè), in the concrete.—(I. B.)

In Mark ix. 22, *fire* and *water* are not used in the *general* sense as here (Oft-times he falleth into a paroxysm, wherever fire is and wherever water is,"—this is the effect which these elements produce on him): but of *particular* fires and waters. Though the sing. τὸ πῦρ is used there, it stands for the plural, as the accompanying ὕδατα show: also the article τὸ gives the same force, as there is no plur. of πῦρ, else τὰ πῦρα would be found. However, BCD *abcd* reject the τὸ there; but Α supports it.—ED.

charge. It is wonderful that the devil did not injure the disciples; cf. Acts xix. 16.

17. Ἄπιστος, κ.τ.λ., *faithless,* etc.) By a severe rebuke the disciples are reckoned as a part of the multitude.—ἕως πότε, *how long*) After Jesus had received an accession of strength on the Mount, a more grievous instance of human unbelief and misery demanded and obtained His succour; cf. Ex. xxxii. 19.[1]—ἔσομαι, κ.τ.λ., *shall I be,* etc.) He was in haste to return to the Father; yet He knew that He could not effect His departure until He had conducted His disciples to a state of faith. Their slowness was painful to Him; see John xiv. 9, and xvi. 31.—μεθ' ὑμῶν, *with you*) Jesus was not of this world.—ἀνέξομαι, *shall I suffer*) An instance of *Metonymia Consequentis*.[2] The life of Jesus was a continued act of toleration.

18. Ἐπετίμησεν αὐτῷ, *He rebuked it*) as an enemy.—αὐτῷ, *it*) sc. the devil.—αὐτοῦ, *of him*) sc. the child.

19.[3] Καὶ εἶπον, κ.τ.λ., *and said,* etc.) A salutary submission, and enquiry as to the cause.—διατί—οὐκ ἠδυνήθημεν, *why—were we unable?*) They had been already in the habit of performing the miracle in question; see ch. x. 1.

20. Ἀπιστίαν, *unbelief*) in this case.—πίστιν ὡς κόκκον σινάπεως, *faith as a grain of mustard seed*) contrasted with a huge mountain. This faith is contrasted with a strong faith, and one stimulated by prayer and fasting [see ver. 21]. From this it is clear, that the transportation of a mountain is a less miracle than the ejection of a devil of the kind mentioned in the text; for the devil clings more closely to a man spiritually, than the mountain to its roots physically; and faith, even the smallest, is more powerful than the fixture of a mountain. You will say,

---

[1] The transfiguration may have probably been the most delightful, and the case of the lunatic the most painful, of the events which befell Jesus whilst sojourning on the earth.—V. g.

[2] See explanation of technical terms in Appendix.—(I. B.)
Here, the substitution of the consequent for the antecedent. Jesus puts His *toleration* of them (the consequent) instead of His *sojourning* with them (the antecedent of the former).—ED.

[3] Οἱ μαθηταί, *the disciples*) Not even Peter, James, and John being excluded (excepted). Otherwise, one would think that the expulsion of the demon should have been committed to them on their return from the mountain.—V. g.

"Why then is that miracle less frequent (than the other)?" *Answer.* It has nevertheless been performed sometimes; but it is not necessary that it should be performed frequently, although the opulence of faith reaches thus far. A mountain is naturally by creation in its proper place: a devil is not so when possessing a man: wherefore it is more beneficial that the latter should be cast out, than that the former should be removed; cf. on faith, Mark xi. 22, 23, 24, xvi. 17; John xiv. 12, 13.—ἐρεῖτε, *ye shall say*) i.e. ye are able to say—ye have the power of saying. This is said especially to the apostles; for all have not the gift of miracles.—τῷ ὄρει τούτῳ, *to this mountain*) sc. that mentioned in ver. 1; see also ch. xxi. 21. Examples of such miracles are not wanting in the history of the Church; see one of them in Note to the Panegyric on Gregory Thaumaturgus,[1] pp. 127, 128; see also Le Fevre's Commentary, f. 78.—ἐκεῖ, *there*) Ye shall be able also to assign a place to a mountain.—οὐδὲν, *nothing*) not even if the sun is to be staid in his course.

21. Τοῦτο δὲ τὸ γένος, κ.τ.λ., *but this kind*, etc.) Our Lord does not in this passage speak of the *whole* race of devils, but of this particular kind or class of them; from whence it appears that there are more than one kind of devils. The disciples had before this cast out devils even without prayer and fasting;[2] but this kind of devils has a disposition especially opposed to, and reducible by, prayer and fasting. The disciples were not accustomed to fasting (see ch. ix. 14); and they appear to have been somewhat self-indulgent (sobrietatem . . . minus servare) during their Lord's absence.

22.[3] Μέλλει—παραδίδοσθαι, *shall be betrayed*—εἰς χεῖρας ἀνθρώπων, *into the hands of men*) What a grievous condition! Thus was He delivered up who exhibited such great authority in ver. 18.

24. Καπερναούμ, *Capernaum*) where Jesus dwelt.[4]—τὰ δίδραχμα,

---

[1] See foot-note, p. 187.—(I. B.)

[2] Since by [prayers and] fastings faith is increased.—V. g.

[3] Ἐν τῇ Γαλιλαίᾳ, *in Galilee*) As yet abiding in a place separated by a long distance from the scene of His passion.—V. g.

[4] On a different footing, however, from what He had been on before: for He was now dwelling in obscurity with His disciples, to whom He gave the information as to His Passion, Luke ix. 18, etc., until He set out on the journey which was to end in His Passion; Luke ix. 51, xiii 32.—*Harm.*, p. 380.

the didrachms)[1] the Hebrew שקל, *shekel*, is frequently rendered δίδραχμον by the LXX.—οἱ λαμβάνοντες, *they that received*) sc. for the Temple.[2]

25. Ναί, *yes*) It is clear therefore that our Lord had paid it the previous year.[3]—ὅτε εἰσῆλθεν εἰς τὴν οἰκίαν, *when he was come*

[1] "In the original [*i.e.*, the Greek of St Matthew], the 'tribute-money' which was demanded, and the 'piece of money,' of twice its value, which Peter was to find in the mouth of the fish, are discriminated by their proper names. The former is called *didrachma*, or 'two drachmæ,' and the latter *stater*. The latter was of equivalent value to the Hebrew shekel, and was equal to four drachmæ; and, consequently, two drachmæ were equivalent to half the stater and shekel. Leaving the terms untranslated, Peter is asked if his Master paid the *didrachma?* and Peter is told that he should find a *stater* in the mouth of the fish. The stater was also called *tetradrachmon*, from its containing four drachmæ. It exhibited on one side the head of Minerva, and on the reverse an owl, together with a short inscription. After the destruction of the Temple, the Jews were obliged to pay this tribute to the Romans; and the passage in which the historian relates this, affords one of those minute incidental corroborations which have been so abundantly adduced in evidence of the verity of the evangelical narratives; for he states that the emperor imposed a tribute of two drachmæ (δύο δραχμάς) upon the Jews, wherever they were, to be paid every year into the Capitol, in the same manner as it had been previously paid into the Temple at Jerusalem—thus concurring with the Evangelist, that the half-shekel was usually paid in the form of two drachmæ, or of a single coin of that value. The tax continued to be paid to the Romans in the time of Origen. It is understood, however, that the Temple tribute, though collected in heathen coin, was to be exchanged for Hebrew money before it could be finally paid into the Temple—probably on account of the idolatrous symbols which the former so generally bore. Hence the vocation of the money-changers, whom our Saviour drove from the Temple. They were accustomed, on and after the fifteenth of the month Adar, to seat themselves in the Temple, in order to exchange for those who desired it, Greek and Roman coins for Jewish half-shekels."—*Kitto's Illustrated Commentary*, in loc.—See also Wordsworth, in loc.—(I. B.)

[2] The exaction of this Temple tribute usually took place on the 15th day of the month Adar. And, in accordance with this, the length (interval) of time admirably corresponds to the events and journeys, as frequently recorded, from the feast of dedication, John x. 22, up to this place, and further in continuation up to the Sabbath, of which we have the mention in John xii. 1. Both the Sabbaths noticed, Luke xiii. 10, xiv. 1, occupy the middle portion in that time; and the raising of Lazarus took place a few days before the solemn and triumphant entry of our Lord.—*Harm.*, p. 380.

[3] But, meanwhile, having been solemnly recognised as the *Son of God*. He most becomingly, at this time, enters this protest in presence of Peter in vindication of His own dignity.—*Harm.*, p. 380.

into the house) for that very purpose.—προέφθασεν, *prevented, anticipated*) Peter was wishing to ask [when Jesus anticipated him]. The whole of this circumstance wonderfully confirmed the faith of Peter. Our Lord's majesty shines forth in the very act of submission.—Σίμων, *Simon*) An address as it were domestic and familiar.[1]—τέλη ἢ κῆνσον, *custom or tribute*, lat. *vectigalia aut censum*) i.e. land-tax and poll-tax.—ἀλλοτρίων, *strangers*) subjects who are not sons.

26. Ἐλεύθεροι, *free*) The argument is as follows: Jesus is the Son of God (ver. 5), and the heir of all things; but the Temple, for the sake of which the didrachms are paid, is the house of God: it behoved Jesus, on paying the didrachm, to do so under protest. They who received the tribute were not capable of comprehending (non capiebant) the protest, therefore it is addressed to Peter. They who pertain to Jesus, possess also the right of Jesus.

27. Ἵνα δὲ μὴ σκανδαλίσωμεν αὐτούς, *But lest we should offend them*) Our Lord even performed a miracle to avoid giving offence; cf. ch. xviii. 6, 7.—αὐτούς, *them*) who were ignorant of our Lord's claims. Men who are occupied in worldly affairs, most easily take offence at the saints when money is in question.—τὸν ἀναβάντα πρῶτον, *that first cometh up*) A manifold miracle of omniscience and omnipotence: 1. That something should be caught; 2, and that quickly; 3, that there should be money in a fish; 4, and that in the first fish; 5, that the sum should be just so much as was needed; 6, that it should be in the fish's mouth. Therefore the fish was commanded to bring a stater, or four-drachm coin, that very moment from the bottom of the sea.—ἀντὶ Ἐμοῦ καὶ σοῦ, *for Me and thee*) A pair of great disparity; for what was Peter compared to the greatness of Jesus? Peter had a family of his own; the other disciples[2] were the family of Jesus (cf. Gnomon on Matt. viii. 14); therefore they said *your*, not *thy Master*, ver. 24.

---

[1] Οἱ βασιλεῖς τῆς γῆς, *the kings of the earth*) With these is compared the Lord Jehovah, for whose worship the tribute was paid.—V. g.

[2] The other disciples, as we may reasonably suppose, had not yet passed their twentieth year; and therefore were not yet bound to pay the sacred tribute.—V. g.

CHAPTER XVIII.

1. Ἐν ἐκείνῃ τῇ ὥρᾳ, *in that hour*) when they had heard of the freedom of the children, declared in ch. xvii. 26 (which accounts for the use of ἄρα, *then*, in this passage); and when they had seen that Peter, James, and John (ch. xvii. 1), had been all summoned to the Mount.—τίς ἄρα, κ.τ.λ., *who then*, etc.) They put the question indefinitely *in words*, but in their own hearts they think of themselves.[1]—ἐν τῇ βασιλείᾳ τῶν οὐρανῶν, *in the kingdom of heaven*) See that thou enter there: do not enquire beforehand what are the several portions allotted to each therein.

2. Παιδίον, *a little child*) A diminutive, to rebuke the disciples who sought *great* things. It is said to have been Ignatius— ὁ Θεοφόρος.[2] Without doubt it must have been a child of excellent disposition and sweetest appearance who was then present by Divine appointment.—ἐν μέσῳ αὐτῶν, *in the midst of them*) see Gnomon on Mark ix. 36.

3. Καὶ εἶπεν, *and said*) By asking *who is the greatest?* each of the disciples might offend himself, his fellow-disciples, and the child in question. The Saviour's words (ver. 3–20) meet all these offences, and declare His own and His Father's anxiety for the salvation of souls. We perceive hence the connection between the different portions of His speech.—ὡς τὰ παιδία, *as little children*) They must possess a wonderful degree of humility, simplicity, and faith to be proposed as an example to adults. Scripture exhibits everywhere favour towards little children.— οὐ μὴ εἰσέλθητε, *ye shall not enter*) So far from being the greatest,

---

[1] In Mark ix. 33, 34, and Luke ix. 46, 47, the fact is stated with some little change in the form in which the circumstances appear; namely, the disciples, after that they had disputed on the way, and were on that account set to rights by our loving Saviour, were at first silent: but then, all having been convened together by the Saviour, some finally proposed the question to Him. Harm., p. 381, 382. Comp. Michaelis in der Einleitung, etc., T. ii., p. m. 911, etc.—E. B.

[2] Considerable difference of opinion exists as to the meaning of this word: some rendering it "*one who was carried by* God," in allusion to the circumstance mentioned in the text; others explaining it to mean "*one who carried God always about with him*, sc. *in his heart*."—(I. B.)

ye shall not even enter therein. He does not say, "ye shall not remain," but, "ye shall not enter," so as to repress their arrogance the more.

4. Ὅστις, *whosoever*) No answer is given concerning the individual whom they inquired about.—οὗτος, *this man*) sc. he, I tell you.

5. Δέξηται, *shall receive*) sc. humbly, lovingly, to the profit of his soul, as appears from the contrast in the next verse.—τοιοῦτον, *such*) For little children also are sometimes corrupt.[1]— The same termination occurs in Acts xxi. 25.[2]—ἕν, *one*) God's providence is exercised also on individuals; see the next verse. *One* is frequently mentioned in this chapter.—ἐπὶ τῷ ὀνόματί Μου, *in My name*) Not from natural or political causes.—ὀνόματι, *name*) see ver. 20.—Ἐμὲ, *Me*) sc. who am in the little ones which believe on Me, as the Father is in Me. In like manner it may be said that, in Justification, when God receives a believer, He receives Christ.

6. Σκανδαλίσῃ, *shall offend*) sc. by putting a stumbling-block in the way of either his faith or practice, by provoking to pride or strife, by calling him away from the virtues of that early age. The greatest reverence is due to a child, if you are employed in anything which is wrong.[3] Children are more easily impressible; therefore they are more easily injured.—τῶν πιστευόντων, *who believe*) Jesus paid great attention to little children, and endued them with faith; see ch. xiv. 21, xix. 13, 14, and xxi. 15, 16.—συμφέρει αὐτῷ, *it is expedient for him*) i.e., it is his *interest*—*it were better for him*; for drowning is far less horrible than the fire spoken of in ver. 8, or the lake of fire mentioned in Rev. xix. 20.—μύλος ὀνικὸς, *a millstone*)[4] An appropriate phrase in a discourse concerning offence, for stumbling is produced by stones.—καταποντισθῇ, *be drowned*) A frequent and horrible punishment.[5]

---

[1] Therefore He marks out one endued with humbleness of heart.—V. g.

[2] τοιοῦτος, τοιαύτη, τοιοῦτο, Att. also τοιοῦτον, which however is also found in Od. vii. 309, and xiii. 330; and seems to prevail in Herodotus. *Liddell and Scott.*—(I. B.)

[3] See Juvenal xiv. 47, 48.—(I. B.)
"Maxima debetur puero reverentia, si quid
Turpe paras."—ED.

[4] Literally, an ass millstone—i.e. the millstone of a mill worked by an ass and therefore larger than a common hand-mill.—(I. B.)

[5] In opposition to the kingdom of heaven.—V. g.

—πελάγει, *the sea*) sc. the deep; see Gnomon on Acts xxvii. 5.—τῆς θαλάσσης, *of the sea*) which was near at hand; see ch. xvii. 27.

7. Τῷ κόσμῳ, *to the world*) offences spread far and wide,—τῶν σκανδάλων, *of* THE *offences*) τὰ σκάνδαλα, THE *offences.*—τὸ σκάνδαλον, THE *offence*) The article is emphatic.—ἀνάγκη[1] γάρ ἐστιν ἐλθεῖν τὰ σκάνδαλα, *for it must needs be that offences come*) especially in the age blessed by the presence of the Messiah; just as insects abound in summer. The disciples were near offence: how much nearer must others have been!—πλὴν, *but*) used emphatically.[2] Woe to the world which is injured by offences; *but* woe *indeed* to the man who injures it by offence.

8. Εἰ δὲ, κ.τ.λ., *but if*, etc.) He who is not careful to avoid offence to himself, will cause offence to others, and *vice versa.—*χείρ, πούς, *hand—foot*) In the impulse of sinning, acting ill, going where we ought not, the hands or other members are urged on by the animal spirits rushing together into them: and there is great propriety in the expressions employed by our Lord: for the imperative ἔκκοψον (*cut off*), holds good with regard to the hand, in as far as it is thus affected, and so on with the rest.—ζωὴν, *life*) opposed to eternal fire.—χωλὸν κ.τ.λ., *lame*, etc.) The godly, forsooth, in this world are lame, deaf, dumb, etc., both to themselves and others;[3] see Ps. xxxviii. 14. This must be taken of the time of mortification, not that of glorification; for those members which have been most mortified will shine the most in glory; see Gal. vi. 17. — αἰώνιον, *eternal*) The word, eternal, signifies sometimes in the Old Testament a finite eternity more clearly than it does in the New.

9. Ὀφθαλμός, *eye*) The eye offends by pride, as in this place; by envy, as in Mark vii. 22; by wantonness [as in Matt. v. 28, 29.] There is a gradation here; for the eye is dearer than the hand or foot. Frequently, when the offence of one member has been conquered, offence ensues from another.—μονόφθαλμον, *with one eye*) μονόφθαλμος has the same force in Matthew and Mark as ἑτερόφθαλμος has in Ammonius.—τὴν γέενναν, *hell*) eternal fire: see the preceding verses.

---

[1] Ἀνάγκη, *it is necessary*) On account of the frequency of unbelief.—V. g.

[2] Πλὴν being added to the previous enunciation, forms an 'Epitasis,' or emphatic addition. See Append.—ED.

[3] Comp. Rev. iii. 17; 1 Cor. iv. 8-13.—ED.

10. Μὴ καταφρονήσατε, *do not despise*) They appear to have done so from ver. 1, 2. The adult frequently exhibit pride towards " little ones," by whose appearance they are reminded of their origin : whence it comes to pass, that they hold them of no account, and pay them no reverence.[1] He despises them who corrupts or neglects to edify them.—οἱ ἄγγελοι, *the angels*) whom you ought not to offend, but imitate, in this very care for the " little ones."—αὐτῶν, *of them*) The angels take care of the " little ones," both in body and soul; and so much the more, the less that they are able to protect themselves. Grown-up men have also their guardian angels, but yet they are in some sort left more to themselves.—βλέπουσι, *see*) as attendants. And this concerns not only the dignity, but also the safety of the " little ones." Their function is twofold; see Heb. i. 14.—τὸ πρόσωπον, *the face*) See Ex. xxxiii. 14–20, and Num. vi. 25, 26.

11. Γὰρ, κ.τ.λ., *for*, etc.) Infants are objects of Divine care, not because they have not been under the curse like others, but because they have been rescued from it.—τὸ ἀπολωλός, *that which was lost*) The human race was one mass of perdition, in which infants, even those of better disposition, are also included, on account of original sin, but the whole of it has been redeemed. If a king were to say that he would rebuild a city which had been consumed by fire, he would not wish his words to be understood of a single street. The *loss* of a sinner is, in the sight of God, something as it were contingent. Therefore foreknowledge does not imply necessity.

12. Τί ὑμῖν δοκεῖ, κ.τ.λ., *what think ye?* etc.) A gracious instance of *Communicatio*.[2]—ἑκατὸν, *an hundred*) Otherwise the loss of one out of so great a number would be easier.[3]—ἕν, *one*) The roundness of the number would be broken, and the exact hundred diminished, by the loss even of one.—ἀφεὶς, *leaving*) It is the business of shepherds to give their first care to wandering sheep, as distinguished from those which are in the right way.—ἐπὶ τὰ ὄρη, *into the mountains*) even with great toil, into solitary

---

[1] See Gnomon on ver. 6, voc. σκανδαλίσῃ, and footnote.—(I. B.)

[2] " A figure in rhetoric, whereby the orator consults the audience what they would do in such a case."—*Ainsworth*. It is used in this sense by Cicero. See also explanation of technical terms in Appendix.—(I. B.)

[3] *i.e.* If it were not a round number.—(I. B.)

places. The discourse appears to have been delivered on the shore of the lake of Gennesareth.[1]

13. Ἐὰν γένηται εὑρεῖν, *if it happen that he find it*) The finding of the sinner, therefore, is, in the sight of God, a something as it were contingent—IF IT HAPPEN that *he find it*: cf. on the *loss of a sinner*, ver. 11, and Gnomon in loc. Therefore grace is not irresistible; cf. Luke xv. 6, 9, 24, and xvii. 18.—ἀμὴν λέγω ὑμῖν, *verily I say unto you*) This formula refers to the Apodosis,[2] as in Luke xi. 8, and John xii. 24; cf. the Divine adjuration in Ez. xxxiii. 11.

14. Οὐκ ἔστι θέλημα, *it is not a wish*)[3] or anything to be desired (cf. Ez. xviii. 23). The article is not added in the present passage; cf. θελήματα, *wishes*, in Acts xiii. 22.[4] We ought to subserve the Divine will in caring for the salvation of all.—ἔμπροσθεν,[5] *in the presence of*) [6]The Divine intellect is intimated as discerning what things please His will.[7]—ἵνα, κ.τ.λ., *that*, etc.) *i.e.* He wishes most earnestly that all should be saved.—εἷς, *one*) The disciples had asked in the comparative;[8] our Lord answers specially in the positive degree.

15. Ἐὰν δὲ, κ.τ.λ., *but if*, etc.) The sum of this chapter is as

---

[1] Which was surrounded by mountains —(I. B.)
[2] See explanation of technical terms in Appendix.—(I. B.)
[3] E. V. "It is not the will." Middleton renders it, "There is no wish."—(I. B.)
[4] Rendered in E. V. by, "Which shall fulfil all My *will*."—(I. B.)
[5] In his own German Version Bengel renders the passage thus:—"*Also ist es kein Wille* von *eurem Vater, dass*," etc.—(I. B.)
[6] E. V. renders the passage, "It is not *the will* of your Father," etc. Bengel would render it literally, "It is not a wish in the presence of your Father," etc., and explain it as representing the Divine Intellect as surveying all possible contingencies (rendered by the Divine power visible to the Divine perception), and distinguishing between those which are, and those which are not, agreeable to His Will.—(I. B.)
[7] Bengel has used the word *Voluntas* four times in this paragraph, and that in two different senses. In the first instance, I have rendered the singular by *Wish*; in the second, the plural by *Wishes*; in the third and fourth, the singular by *Will*.—(I. B.)
[8] *i.e.* The disciples had asked, "Which is the *greatest* in the kingdom of Heaven?"—their question therefore referred to the *comparative degrees* of glory. Our Lord's reply directs their attention to the simple notion, the *positive degree* of salvation; the universal requisites on man's part to attain —the universal desire on God's part to bestow it.—(I. B.)

follows: Every one is under an obligation, not to place obstacles before himself and others, but to aid both on the way of salvation. Also: we ought to respond to the Divine will, expressed in ver. 14. Also: do not offend thy brother; cure thy brother's offence.—ἁμαρτήσῃ εἰς σέ, *sin against thee*) sc. by giving offence; see 1 Cor. viii. 12.—ὕπαγε, *go*) (cf. πορευθείς, *having gone*, in ver. 12). That will be derogatory to no one. Even Christ came to us and sought us.—ἔλεγξον αὐτόν, *reprove him*)[1] Afterwards our Lord speaks of witnesses. In the present instance, the matter takes place in the presence of only two [sc. the parties themselves]; in the latter, of more.— αὐτόν, *him*) sc. *thy brother*. He is reproved and forgiven because he is a brother.—μόνου, *alone*) Solitary reproof is gracious.—ἐκέρδησας, *thou hast gained*) Therefore thy brother had previously been lost through his sin. A gain, and a blessed one. The body of the sick man does not become the property of the physician who cured it; the burning house does not become the property of him who extinguished the fire: that is, they are not *gained*. But the man whom I have *gained* becomes in some sort my own, as amongst the Romans a conquered people became bound, by the ties of clientship, to the general who had conquered them; cf. Luke xix. 24, 17; Philem. ver. 19, and Gnomon on 1 Cor. ix. 19.

16. "Ενα ἢ δύο, *one or two*) so that, reckoning thyself the complainant, there may be two or three witnesses. The evidence of the complainant is of greater weight.—ἵνα ἐπὶ στόματος, κ.τ.λ., *that in the mouth*, etc.) referring to Deut. xix. 15, the latter part of which the LXX. render: ἐπὶ στόματος δύο μαρτύρων καὶ ἐπὶ στόματος τριῶν μαρτύρων σταθήσεται πᾶν ῥῆμα—*at the mouth of two witnesses, or at the mouth of three witnesses, every word shall be established.*—σταθῇ πᾶν ῥῆμα, *every word may be established*) sc. both against the sinner and afterwards to the Church. This passage is one of those which prove that the principles and rules of the

---

[1] E. V. "Tell him his fault."—(I. B.)

The margin of both Editions observes that this verb is brought into prominence by the absence of the copula between it and ὕπαγε, "Go, tell him his fault." This has not been noticed in the Vers. Germ.—E. B.

Rec. Text has καί, with *abc* Vulg. Hilary, and Lucifer. But BD Orig. omit κα[1]—ED.

forensic law of Moses are not entirely excluded from the polity of the Church of Christ.

17. Παρακούσῃ, *do not obey*) disregarding the reproof.—τῇ ἐκκλησίᾳ, *the church*) i.e., which is in that place where thou and thy brother dwell. The church is opposed to two or three in about the same proportion as two or three are to one. Amongst the Jews, ten men are considered to constitute עדה, *a church*,[1] or public assembly for the decision of private disputes. See Rhenferd Opera philologica,[2] p. 729; Buxtorf,[3] Synagoga Judaica, ch. xxv., where the same things are prescribed to the offender which our Lord prescribes here to the injured party. —ἔστω, κ.τ.λ., *let him be*, etc.) Cf. Rom. xvi. 17; 1 Cor. v. 11; 2 Thess. iii. 14; 2 Tim. ii. 21; Tit. iii. 10; 2 John ver. 10.— σοί, *to thee*) Although, perhaps, not to the witnesses and the church. Therefore no one should be considered as a stranger before he has been reproved, and disregarded the reproof.— ὁ ἐθνικὸς, THE *heathen*) (sing.) We take this opportunity of making some observations on the Greek Article.[4] B. Stolberg rightly remarks, in his manuscript collection on the particles, that "there is scarcely an instance in the Scriptures where the article is redundant." It is nowhere clearly useless; it is never added without an object, although philologists frequently attribute to it a wrong force and meaning. It is equivalent to the German der (*the*), and denotes less than *hic* (*this*), more than *quidam* (*some, a certain one*, or *thing*). It has, therefore, a determinating value; and it determines either (1) the universality

---

[1] See *Bloomfield* and *Kitto* in loc., and *Trench's New Testament Synonyms* in voc.—(I. B.)

He is not here speaking of the Catholic or universal Church.—V. g.

[2] For RHENFERD, see p. 82, f.n. 2.—(I. B.)

[3] JOHN BUXTORF, the elder, one of the greatest Hebrew scholars of modern times. He was born at Camen in 1564, and died in 1629. He devoted himself to the study of Hebrew and Chaldee literature, and became Professor of those languages at Basle. The great Scaliger declared that he was the only person who understood Hebrew thoroughly. The work cited by Bengel is, "*Synagoga Judaica, de Judaeorum fide, ritibus, ceremoniis, tam publicis et sacris quam privatis;*" a third and enlarged edition of which was published by his no less celebrated son, at Basle, in 1661.—(I. B.)

[4] I have, in the disquisition which follows, inserted *in extenso* the passages referred to by Bengel. For a full consideration of this important subject, see that inestimably valuable work, *Middleton on the Greek Article*.—(I. B.)

and totality of the subject, as in Matt. vi. 22, Ὁ λύχνος, κ.τ.λ., THE *light*, etc., q.d. the body has no light except the eye; *or* (2) the whole species, as in Matt. xv. 11, ΤΟ εἰσερχόμενον, *that which entereth*—ΤΟ ἐκπορευόμενον, *that which cometh out*—and in Rom. i. 17, Ὁ δὲ δίκαιος, *but* THE *just, i.e.* he that is, or every one that is, just; or (3) the singularity and oneness [*i.e.* the definite and exclusive individuality] of the subject, as in Matt. i. 23, Ἡ παρθένος, THE *virgin*—in John i. 21, Ὁ Χριστός, THE *Christ,* Ὁ προφήτης, THE *prophet*—in John xiii. 13, Ὁ Διδάσκαλος, καὶ Ὁ Κύριος, THE *Teacher, and* THE *Lord;* or (4) the restriction of the whole genus to a particular species, as in Acts xix. 17, ΤΟΙΣ κατοικοῦσι, WHO *dwelt at*. In logic, however, universal and singular propositions are equivalent; whence (5) it has frequently a relative force, and that even in partition,[1] as in Luke xviii. 10, Ὁ εἷς φαρισαῖος καὶ Ὁ ἕτερος τελώνης, THE *one a Pharisee and* THE *other a publican*—and in Rev. xvii. 10, Ὁ εἷς ἐστιν, Ὁ ἄλλος οὔπω ἦλθε, THE *one is,* THE *other has not yet come;* or (6) it expresses a certain peculiar degree of a thing (rei exquisitam quandam rationem), as in Matt. viii. 12, Ὁ κλαυθμός, THE[2] *weeping,* sc. weeping, compared with which earthly weeping is *not* weeping. It is, in fact, a subject which deserves to be more carefully examined by Philologists.[3] In this passage, Ὁ ἐθνικὸς signifies the whole race of Heathens, and any one thereto belonging. Thus, in the S.V. of Deut. xxviii. 29, we have Ὁ τυφλός, THE *blind.*—καὶ ὁ τελώνης, *and the publican*) It was easy for the Jews to consider any one in the light of a heathen, therefore this clause is added to increase the force of the language; for the publicans dwelt amongst the Jews, but were shunned by them.

18. Ὅσα ἐὰν, *whatsoever*) *i.e.* all things with regard to which the power of binding and loosing holds good, especially of-

---

[1] *i.e.* In distinguishing between divisions of a whole, classes of a mass, species of a genus, or individuals of a certain description. The two men mentioned in the example both answered to the description of those that "went up into the temple to pray;"—here their similarity or affinity, as parts of a whole, or members of a class, ceased;—the article separates them from, and contrasts them with, each other.—(I. B.)

[2] Cf. Gnomon in loc.—(I. B.)

[3] Bengel saw the want: it has since been supplied by Middleton.—(I. B.)

fences.¹—δήσητε, *ye shall bind*) see the end of ver. 17.—λύσητε, *ye shall loose*) see the end of ver. 15. There is an intimate connection between the retention of a private² and that of a public offence, and so also in the case of remission. See ver. 15–35. Our Lord teaches that His disciples can bind and loose the sins of their neighbours in His name; see ver. 20. Neither is it totally void of effect when they, even for their own sake, through anger, bind and hold the offences of their brethren.

19. Πάλιν, *again*) The same thing is repeated in somewhat different language. The particle πάλιν is used *epitatically*,³ as in ch. xix. 24, and Gal. v. 3. In this place, our Lord speaks of His disciples as acting together; in ver. 18, in their individual capacity. Cf. ch. xvi. 19.—δύο, *two*) sc. two, if not more, contrasted with *all*; cf. ver. 18: *two*, *e.g.* husband and wife. Great is the virtue of united faith. That which may hinder the prayers of one man, from his own weakness, is made up by the fellowship (*societas*) of even one brother.—ἐπὶ τῆς γῆς—ἐν οὐρανοῖς, *on earth—in heaven*) The same antithesis occurs in ver. 18.—αἰτήσωνται, *shall ask*) sc. with regard to binding or loosing.

20. Οὗ γὰρ, κ.τ.λ., *for where*, etc.) The name of Jesus gives power to prayer.—δύο ἢ τρεῖς, *two or three*) see Eccles. iv. 12 and the preceding verses. Three is a number which can be procured even in a barren age of the Church: a greater number is not so easily obtained, and is accompanied by the danger that a hypocrite may be present; yet where *many* sincere professors are together, how great will be the power of their prayers.—εἰς τὸ Ἐμὸν ὄνομα, *in My name*, lit. *into My name*⁴) sc. with the

---

¹ Christ gave this power to His disciples then, and not till then, when, having had experience of the gracious will of our Heavenly Father (ver. 14), they had recognised Himself, *i.e.* Jesus, as the Son of God (ch. xvi. 16), and had received the Holy Spirit, John xx. 22.—V. g.

² Privatæ, *pricate, i.e.* not one privately committed, but one against the individual: communis *public, i.e.* not one committed in public, but one of a public character.—(I. B.)

³ See explanation of technical terms in Appendix, on the figure Epitasis. —(I. B.)

⁴ Εἰς—ὄνομα is not identical with ἐν—ὀνόματι, either here or in xxviii. 19 (Baptizing them—not *in* the name, but *into* the name, etc., *i.e. into the fellowship* of the Father, etc.—so that they may be members of the church

object of worshipping it. All prayers that are offered in the name of Jesus Christ are accepted by the Father; see ver. 19.—ἐκεῖ εἰμί, *there am I*) and all grace with Me; see ch. xxviii. 20; Acts xviii. 10; 2 Tim. iv. 17. Where the Son is, there is the Father: what the Son wishes, the Father wishes.

21. Ποσάκις, *how often?*) in one day, or my whole life. Cf. Luke xvii. 4. [*This question arose from some sense of super-abounding Divine grace, which had been so much dwelt upon and magnified in the preceding discourses.*—V. g.—ἁμαρτήσει, *shall my brother sin?*) *These words are to be understood, not of some slight offence, which excites a sudden burst of indignation, though this also is indeed sinful, yet ready to forgive of its own accord, but of some more heavy offence or injury.*—V. g.]

22. Ἑβδομηκοντάκις ἑπτά, *seventy-seven*[1]) The termination κις makes the whole number seventy-seven. Thus the LXX., in Gen. iv. 24, use the same phrase regarding Lamech.[2]

23. Διὰ τοῦτο, *therefore*) understand, "*I say.*"—ἠθέλησε, *willed, determined*) of His own free will, by His supreme authority.

24. Ἀρξαμένου, *when He had begun*) Before the servant knew what was the condition[3] of his fellow-servants.—εἷς προσηνέχθη Αὐτῷ, *there was brought unto Him*) though against his will.—εἷς, *one*) sc. a servant, *who owed*, etc. How great must be the debts of all, if that of one is so great! Every one ought to consider himself as that *one*; cf. ver. 35, 12, ch. xx. 13; for the condition[4] of all is equal.—μυρίων ταλάντων, *of ten thousand talents*[5]) The Greek language cannot express by two words, as a distinct

bearing the name of, etc.). The words probably mean "Gathered together *unto* my name;" the sense which Bengel seems to imply—εἰς, "Ut nomen meum colant."—ED.

[1] E. V. "Seventy times seven." Vulg., "Septuagies septies."—(I. B.)

"If Cain be avenged sevenfold, truly Lamech *seventy and sevenfold;*" not "seventy times seven;" LXX. ἑπτακοντάκις ἑπτά.—ED.

[2] One could hardly believe that so great dissension could arise even among those entertaining the worst feelings towards others. Therefore there is required a willingness to forgive, which cannot be wearied out by any provocations, however numerous.—V. g.

[3] "Ratio," lit. *reckoning*—i.e. what was the state of their balance or deficit in the debtor and creditor account with their Lord.—(I. B.)

[4] "Ratio." See preceding footnote.—(I. B.)

[5] The Jewish talent was about £342, 3s. 9d. The talent of gold was worth about £5475.—(I. B.)

and continuous quantity, a larger sum than this. If we ought to remit an hundred denarii to our brother, *i.e.* forgive him seventy-seven times, what a vast amount of sins does the Lord forgive us in remitting ten thousand talents! A talent contains about six thousand denarii; therefore a thousand talents contain sixty million denarii, of which how small a part are one hundred denarii! For six denarii make a florin, and nine denarii an imperial dollar, or not much more; one Hebrew talent, or two Attic ones, are two thousand two hundred and fifty florins.[1]

25. Ἐκέλευσεν, κ.τ.λ., *he commanded*, etc.) The Lord shows His right, but does not use it: the servant, however, abuses whatever right he possesses.—ὅσα εἶχε, *all that he had*) The peculium,[2] which, indeed, itself belonged to the Lord.

26. Μακροθύμησον, *have patience*) Do not act hastily towards me.—πάντα, *all*) The servant could not procure so large a sum in the whole period of the world's existence; he merely exhibits, therefore, his contrition.

27. [3] Ἀπέλυσεν, *loosed*) as the servant had besought him to do. ἀφῆκε, *forgave*) which the servant had not dared to ask. He had prayed for one kindness; and he obtained two.

28. Ἐξελθὼν, *having gone forth*) being now released from his difficulties. Before the accounts had been examined, he treated

---

[1] There thus results a sum of 15,000,000 thalers, or 22,500,000 florins. If even one servant can become liable for such a debt—and Peter, as also the other Apostles, ought to have considered that servant as a type, each one of himself—what will not the load amount to, which is made up of the accumulated debts remitted by the Lord to the whole collective body of those who obtain grace? And still more of those sins which must be atoned for in the place of torture by those who are the vast majority, whose debt is not remitted in any measure.—V. g.

[2] Amongst the Romans, slaves had a certain allowance granted them for their sustenance, commonly four or five pecks of grain a month, and five denarii. They likewise had a daily allowance. Whatever they saved of these, or procured by any other means, with their masters' consent, was called their PECULIUM. This money, with their masters' permission, they put out at interest, or sometimes purchased with it a slave for themselves, from whose labours they might make profit. Such a slave was called *servi vicarius*, and formed part of the PECULIUM, with which also slaves sometimes purchased their own freedom. See *Adams's Roman Antiquities* in voc.—(I. B.)

[3] Σπλαγχνισθεὶς) *To forgive* and *remit* constitute the highest work of compassion.—V. g.

his fellow-servant more tenderly; the very joy of recovered liberty, or restored health, etc., is accompanied by a greater danger of sin:[1] see John v. 14; 2 Kings xx. 13.[2]—ἑκατὸν δηνάρια, *a hundred denarii*)[3] The names of coins are neuter in Greek. This was a sufficiently large debt for a fellow-servant: but nothing in comparison with even a single talent, and ten thousand is a hundred times a hundred.—ἀπόδος, κ.τ.λ., *pay*, etc.) An importunate demand.—εἰ, *if*)[4] a particle of some force for *since*.

29. Παρεκάλει, *besought*) In ver. 26, the word used is προσεκύνει, *worshipped*.—λέγων, *saying*) sc. in the same words which are found in ver. 26.

30. Οὐκ ἤθελεν, *would not*) opposed to σπλαγχνισθείς, *being moved with compassion*, in ver. 27.[5]—ἀπελθὼν, *having departed*) sc. to the officer.—ἔβαλεν, κ.τ.λ., *cast*, etc.) By which act he invaded the right of his Lord.

31. Ἐλυπήθησαν σφόδρα, καὶ ἐλθόντες διεσάφησαν, κ.τ.λ., *they were very sorry, and came and told*, etc.) Their sorrow and their information were righteous.—λύπη, *sorrow*, frequently includes the idea of indignation.

32. Αὐτὸν, *him*) singly; for in ver. 24, he had been cited in company with the rest.—δοῦλε πονηρὲ, *thou wicked servant*) He had not been called thus on account of his debt. Woe to him whom the Lord upbraids; see ch. xxv. 26. Mercilessness is

---

[1] So that it is even then in particular, that one becomes liable to anger.—V. g.

[2] See Jer. xxxiv. 8-16.—(I. B.)

Εὗρεν, *he found*) After you have experienced the divine free favour, soon the opportunity will present itself to thee of adopting either a similar, or else a different mode of action.—V. g.

Ἕνα, *one*) It sometimes happens that one wishes well to all (other) men, and yet remains inimical and hostile at least to *one* particular person.—V. g.

[3] E. V. "An hundred pence." The denarius was about sevenpence three farthings.—(I. B.)

[4] Bengel reads εἴ τι ὀφείλεις, which he interprets, IF, *i.e.* SINCE *thou owest me something*. E. M. has ὅ τι ὀφείλεις—*that which*, or *whatsoever thou owest*.—(I. B.)

BCD Orig. 3,622a read εἴ τι. But *abc* Vulg. Lucifer support the ὅ τι of Rec. Text.—ED.

[5] Of how great consequence, frequently, is the presence or absence of *willingness* (Velle-Nolle) in cases which are not in themselves of the greatest weight.—V. g.

peculiarly wickedness.—ἐκείνην, *that* [*debt*]) This word refers with peculiar emphasis to the former occurrence.

33. Οὐκ ἔδει; *did it not behove?*) It did, indeed, by the highest rule of equity.[1]—τὸν σύνδουλόν σου, *thy fellow-servant*) whom thou oughtest to have pitied; My servant, by injuring whom thou hast injured Me.

34. Ὀργισθεὶς, *wroth*) He had not been wroth before, cf. Luke xiv. 21. Those who have experienced the mercy of God, ought to be very careful of exciting His anger.—τοῖς βασανισταῖς, *the tormentors*) not merely jailors (custodibus).—ἕως οὗ, *until*) Such is the enduring character of guilt, founded on the inexhaustible claim of God over His servants.[2]

35. Ἀπὸ τῶν καρδιῶν ὑμῶν, *from your hearts*) A wrong is recalled to the mind: it must be dismissed from the mind and from *the heart*. Things which are thus done, are done with unwearied frequency [*But if not, whenever the debtor unexpectedly meets us, our indignation is liable to revive.*—V. g.]; cf. σπλαγχνισθεὶς (*being moved with compassion*) in ver. 27.

CHAPTER XIX.

1. Ἐτέλεσεν, κ.τ.λ., *finished*, etc.) All the discourses addressed to the people in Galilee have a great connection with each other, and form a perfect course.[3]—μετῆρεν, *he departed*[4]) having concluded His perambulation through Galilee.[5]

[1] Πᾶσαν, *all*) Comp. the πᾶν in ver. 34. O how royal is as well His lenity, as also His severity !—V. g.

[2] "*Servos*." The word is used with special reference to the parable, and does not indicate "the servants of God," in the usual meaning of that phrase, but all those who were formed for the service of God, *i.e.* all His creatures.—(I. B.)

[3] He was wont to break off nothing abruptly, but to bring all things to a complete conclusion; ch. xxvi. 1.—V. g.

[4] "*Migravit*." Cf. Gnomon and footnotes on ch. xiii. 53, where the same word occurs.—(I. B.)

[5] We may reasonably infer, from this departure, that the events which are recorded, Luke xiii. 31—xviii. 14 (for Jesus was not wont to stay long in Samaria), occurred in the space of those three days, of which mention occurs in Luke xiii. 32.—*Harm.*, p 421.

2. Ἐκεῖ, *there*) In many places a number of cures were performed at once by our Lord.

3.[1] πᾶσαν, *every*) They wished to elicit from our Lord a universal negative, which they thought would be contrary to Moses.

4. Ὁ ποιήσας, *He who made*) sc. them; with this construction, *He who made them in the beginning, made them male and female.* ὁ ποιήσας, ἐποίησεν (*He who made, made*), is a striking example of Ploce.[2]—ἀπ᾽ ἀρχῆς, *at the beginning*) In every discussion or interpretation recourse should be had to the origin of a Divine institution; see ver. 8 and Acts xv. 7.

5. Εἶπεν, *said*) sc. GOD, by Adam.—ἕνεκεν τούτου, *for this cause.* In wedlock, the bond is natural and moral.—καταλείψει, κ.τ.λ., *shall leave*, etc.) Therefore already at that time the same woman could not be both wife and mother of the same man. Such is the commencement of the prohibited degrees. The conjugal relation, to which alone the paternal and maternal yield, is the closest of all ties.—πατέρα, *father*) Although neither Adam had yet become a father, nor Eve a mother.—τῇ γυναικὶ αὐτοῦ, *to his wife*) and thus also the wife to her husband. The husband is the head of the family.—ἔσονται, *shall be*) one flesh while they are in the flesh.—οἱ δύο, *the two*[3]) Thus also Mark x. 8; 1 Cor. vi. 16; Eph. v. 31; the Samaritan[4]

---

[1] Πειράζοντες αὐτὸν, *tempting Him*) At the beginning of His career, His adversaries questioned the Saviour concerning several of the acts committed either by Himself or His disciples. But when He had left nothing still remaining to be done for the defence of His own cause and that of His followers, they thenceforth refrained from objections and interrogatories of that kind, and the more for that very reason heaped upon Him general questions, unconnected with any immediate act of His, it being their purpose thereby to surprise Him when off His guard and unprepared.—*Harm.*, p. 422.

[2] See Explanation of Technical Terms in Appendix.—(I. B.)

[3] E. V. "They twain."—(I. B.)

[4] The Samaritans reject all the Sacred Books of the Jews, except the Pentateuch. Of this they preserve copies in the ancient Hebrew characters; which, as there has been no friendly intercourse between them and the Jews since the Babylonish captivity, must unquestionably be the same that were in use before that event, though subject to such variations as are always occasioned by frequent transcribing. Although the Samaritan Pentateuch was known to and cited by Eusebius, Cyril of Alexandria, Procopius of Gaza, Diodorus of Tarsus, Jerome, Syncellus, and other ancient Fathers, it

Pentateuch, the Septuagint, and the Syriac[1] version of Genesis.

6. Οὐκ ἔτι εἰσί, *they are no more*) They are now no longer two, as they were before.—δύο, *two*) We should not understand σάρκες, *fleshes* (carnes): for in ver. 5 we find οἱ δύο (*the two, they twain*).—ὅ, *that which* (quod), not ἅ, *those which* (quae): for they are now one flesh.—συνέζευξεν, *hath joined together*) hath made one.—ἄνθρωπος, *man*) see ver. 3.—μή, κ.τ.λ., *let not*, etc.) The principle here involved admits of a widely extended application: what GOD hath separated, commanded, conceded, prohibited, blessed, praised, loosed, bound, etc., let not Man join together, prohibit, forbid, command, curse, blame, bind, loose, etc., not even in his own case; see Acts x. 15; Num. xxiii. 8; Rom. xiv. 3, 20.—χωριζέτω, *put asunder*) In every case of sexual connection, either God hath joined the two, or He hath not joined them: if He hath not joined them, their connection is unlawful; if He hath joined them, why are they separated?

7. Δοῦναι, *to give*) St Mark (x. 4) has γράψαι, *to write*. Moses employs both expressions.—βιβλίον ἀποστασίου, *a writing of divorcement*) the LXX. use the same phrase.—καί, *and*) sc. thus.

8. Πρός, *for, because of*[2])—ἐπέτρεψεν, *permitted*) not ἐνετείλατο,

afterwards fell into oblivion for more than a thousand years, so that its very existence began to be questioned. Joseph Scaliger was the first who drew the attention of learned men to this valuable relic of antiquity; and M. Peiresc procured a copy from Egypt, which, together with the ship that brought it, was unfortunately captured by pirates. Archbishop Usher, however, procured six copies from the East; and Father Morinus printed the Samaritan Pentateuch, for the first time, in the Paris Polyglott (which was published in 1645, in ten volumes, large folio), from another copy, procured by the French Ambassador at Constantinople. For further particulars, see *Hartwell Horne* in voc.—(I. B.)

[1] Considerable doubt exists as to the origin and date of the PESCHITO SYRIAC (or literal Syrian) VERSION of the Old Testament. It was printed for the first time in the Paris Polyglott. For an account of the various opinions entertained regarding the date and authorship of this celebrated Version (ranging over a period of more than a thousand years), and of the arguments by which they are supported, see *Hartwell Horne* in voc.—(I. B.)

[2] Τὴν σκληροκαρδίαν, *the hardness of heart*) So great is the perversity of the human mind, that there are not a few things by which it ought to be put

enjoined, except in that sense in which St Mark (x. 3) employs the word.—ἀπ' ἀρχῆς, *in the beginning*) The origin of wedlock was recorded also by the same Moses, from whom our Lord demonstrates the matter.

9. Μὴ, *not*[1]) The word occurs with the same force in 1 John v. 16.—καὶ γαμήσῃ, *and shall marry*) The criminality of the divorce is especially aggravated by a second marriage.

10. Τοῦ ἀνθρώπου—μετὰ τῆς γυναικός, *of the man—with the woman*) The nouns are used generically.

11. Ὁ δὲ εἶπεν αὐτοῖς, κ.τ.λ., *But He said unto them*, etc.) To that universal, but less well-founded reason for not contracting matrimony, grounded on the inconvenience which the disciples inferred must arise from its indissolubility, our Lord opposes the legitimate, particular, and only good reason, viz. the being an eunuch,—*i.e.* the being exempted by any exceptional cause from the universal law of contracting matrimony.—οὐ πάντες, *not all*) Our Lord opposes these words to the universal proposition of His disciples (sc. οὐ συμφέρει γαμῆσαι, *i.e. it is not expedient to marry*), and they are equivalent to "*none*."—Cf. Rom. iii. 9, οὐ πάντως, *not at all* [English version, "No, in no wise."] The important exception is added.—ἀλλ' οἷς δέδοται, save those to whom it is given.—τοῦτον, *this*) This pronoun refers also to what follows. Cf. the *Epiphonema*,[2] in ver. 12, sc. ὁ δυνάμενος,

to the blush, as the Jews ought to have been in the case of the writing of divorcement, but which it abuses to a preposterous clearing (justification) of itself.—V. g.

[1] Lachm. reads παρεκτὸς λόγου πορνείας with BD Orig. 3,647c, 648ac, 649b; "exceptâ causâ fornicationis" in c. CZ read μὴ ἐπὶ πορνείᾳ, and so Tischend. Rec. Text reads the same, prefixing εἰ. Vulg. "nisi ob fornicationem," which favours Rec. Text. "Nisi ob causam fornicationis" in ab seems a blending of the two readings, εἰ μὴ and λόγου.—ED.

Bengel reads ὃς ἂν ἀπολύσῃ τὴν γυναῖκα αὐτοῦ. μὴ ἐπὶ πορνείᾳ, *whosoever shall put away his wife* NOT *for fornication;* E. M. has εἰ μὴ ἐπὶ πορνείᾳ, IF NOT (i e. *except*) *for fornication*. The meaning is the same. In his Apparatus Bengel writes, in loc—

"μὴ) *Comp. et al. edd. Aug.* 1, 4, *Bas.* 1, *Byz. Cypr. Gehl. Med. Mosc. Steph. omn. Wo.* 2, *et sedecim et viginti alii: nec obstat Cant. Colb.* 8, *L. Par.* 6, *Arab. Syr.* εἰ μὴ. *Er et al. edd. cum pauculis* MSS."—(I. B.)

[2] EPIPHONEMA is an exclamation subjoined to the narration, or demonstration of an important subject. See *Gnomon* on Rom. i. 15 in voc οὕτω.

κ.τ.λ., *He that is able*, etc.; and γὰρ, *for*, is added at the commencement of the same verse.[1]

12. Εἰσὶ, κ.τ.λ., *there are*, etc.) There are three kinds of eunuchs: the first and second of which are treated *indirectly*, the third *directly*, in this passage. For the two former are either produced thus by nature, or made thus by the hand of man: to the latter *it is given* from above, although they may have been endowed with a body capable of marriage. And these (the latter) *can receive* the saying concerning blessed eunuchism: whereas, of those (the former), it can only be said that they *cannot receive* the law concerning marriage; although they too may *accidentally* (per accidens) obtain blessed eunuchism.—ὑπὸ τῶν ἀνθρώπων, *by men*) by whose art they are castrated, that they may act as chamberlains, singers, etc., or that they may, on some other ground, be prevented from contracting marriage, of which they had been previously capable. For these, also, are included in a perfect enumeration.—εὐνούχισαν ἑαυτοὺς, *have made themselves eunuchs*) which they alone can do, to whom *it is given*. It is not in man's power *thus* to make another an eunuch; see 1 Cor. vii. 7.—ἑαυτοὺς, *themselves*) sc. by a voluntary abstinence from marriage; sometimes having even relinquished a wife for the name of Christ (see ver. 29), and adding exercises calculated to preserve chastity, and subdue the fires of nature.—διὰ, κ.τ.λ., *for the kingdom of heaven's sake*) Not because they can only be saved by remaining unmarried, but that they may be able to devote themselves more entirely to the contemplation and propagation of Divine Truth; see 1 Cor. vii. 32, ix. 12.—χωρείτω, *let him receive*) A precept not addressed to all, but only to those who are able to receive it. Not even all the Apostles seem to have been able to receive it; see 1 Cor. ix. 5.

13. Προσηνέχθη Αὐτῷ, *were brought unto Him*) sc. by the zeal

It is a rhetorical term employed by Quinctilian. See in Append., explanation of Technical terms.—(I. B.)

[1] As in Matt. i. 18, where Tischend. and Rec. Text have μνηστευθείσης γὰρ τῆς μητρός, etc. (Lachm. omits γὰρ with BZ Vulg., Iren., etc.): the γὰρ, as here, beginning the Discussion (Tractatio) which answers to the Statement of Subject (Propositio or Thesis) immediately preceding.—ED

of those who were older.[1] And the disciples blamed, not the little ones, but those who brought them.—*ἵνα, κ.τ.λ., that,* etc.) If they had asked for baptism, baptism would, without doubt, have also been given them.—*οἱ δὲ μαθηταί, but the disciples*) The greater part of whom appear to have been unmarried: and unmarried men, unless they are humble-minded, are not so kind (*minus comes*) to infants, inasmuch as they remind them of their own former littleness: and the disciples who had left all, do not appear always to have sufficiently favoured the admission of others; at any rate, they certainly thought that the care of little children was inconsistent with their Master's dignity. The humanity of Jesus, however, descends even to little children; cf. ch. xviii. 2, 3, etc.—*ἐπετίμων, rebuked*) We ought not to be deterred by those who enjoin an unseasonable timidity,[2] cf. ch. xx. 31.

14. Εἶπεν, κ.τ.λ., *said,* etc.) Previously He had defended the law of marriage; now he defends the rights of children.—*ἄφετε καὶ μὴ κωλύετε, permit—and do not prohibit*) A most ample permission. The verb ἀφίημι does not always mean *to dismiss,* but frequently, as here, *to permit;* see Mark xi. 16.—*τὰ παιδία, the little children*) Haffenreffer renders it *infantulos,* little infants. —*τοιούτων, of such*) *i.e.,* infants, sc. such infants, especially when they desire to come to Christ. τοιοῦτος denotes substance combined with quality; see Acts xxii. 22. Grant that such are intended as are like infants, it follows of necessity, that much rather the infants themselves, who are such, have the kingdom of God, and both can and ought to receive it by coming to Christ. Many of those who then were infants, afterwards believed in Christ Jesus, when they had grown up.—*ἡ βασιλεία τῶν οὐρανῶν, the kingdom of heaven*) He who seeks the kingdom of God must come to Jesus.

15. Ἐπιθεὶς αὐτοῖς τὰς χεῖρας, *having laid His hands upon them*) as He had been asked to do in ver. 13. The imposition of the

---

[1] They were therefore in such a state as not yet to be able either to seek earnestly after, or understand anything, of their own accord.—V. g.

[2] In the original, "intempestivam verecundiam," lit. *unseasonable bashfulness.*—(I. B.)

Nay, but the desire of the little ones was the more enkindled thereby. —V. g.

hand, and more particularly of the hands, was employed for conferring on, and propagating to, human beings, especially children and ministers of the Gospel, bodily blessings and spiritual gifts; see Acts ix. 12; Heb. vi. 2; 1 Tim. v. 22; 2 Tim. i. 6. Our Lord is not said to have prayed, as He had been asked to do in ver. 13, by those forsooth who were not fully aware of His oneness with the Father.

16. Ἰδοὺ, *behold*) sc. whilst Jesus is opening the kingdom of heaven, even to infants.—εἷς, *one*) From the rank to which he belonged, at length comes *one*.—Διδάσκαλε ἀγαθέ, *good Teacher*) He that is good teaches well concerning that which is good; see John vii. 12.—ποιήσω, *shall I do?*) the young man asks about *doing;* but belief goes before.—ζωὴν αἰώνιον, *eternal life*) Eternal life was known under the old dispensation, as we are assured in Heb. xi. 16; and it is explicitly called so in Dan. xii. 2.

17. Τί, κ.τ.λ., *why?* etc.) He who [alone] is Good,[1] should be asked concerning that which is good.[2] For the rest, see Gnomon on Mark x. 18.—εἰ δὲ θέλεις, *but if thou wishest*) as thou declarest. The expression εἰ θέλεις (*if thou wishest*) occurs again at ver. 21. —τήρησον τὰς ἐντολάς, *keep the commandments*) Jesus refers those

[1] In the original, "Qui Bonus est, *de bono* interrogandus est," where "Bonus" is used as a substantive (corresponding to the German "*der Gute*" employed by Bengel in rendering this verse), which has no equivalent in English; for though we speak of "the Evil One," we cannot say "the Good One." The passage might be paraphrased thus—"He who is personally and absolutely good, should be asked concerning that which is abstractly and relatively good."—(I. B.)

[2] The reading is here meant, which the margin of both Editions prefers to the reading λέγεις—Θεός, viz. ἐρωτᾷς περὶ τοῦ ἀγαθοῦ; εἷς ἐστιν ὁ ἀγαθός. Comp. the margin of the Vers. Germ. and Michaelis' Einleitung, etc., T. i., p. m. 224.—E. B.

BDL*abc*, Vulg. Memph. Orig. 3,664*bc*, read τί με ἐρωτᾷς περὶ τοῦ ἀγαθοῦ (D and Origen 3,664*c* omit τοῦ). Τί με λέγεις ἀγαθόν is the reading of Rec. Text with Iren. 92, Hil. 703, 994*ac* ('vocas' for λέγεις). Origen 3,664*cd*, writes, Ὁ μὲν Ματθαῖος, ὡς περὶ ἀγαθοῦ ἔργου ἐρωτηθέντος τοῦ Σωτῆρος ἐν τῷ τί ἀγαθὸν ποιήσω; ἀνέγραψεν· ὁ δὲ Μάρκος καὶ Λουκᾶς φασὶ τὸν Σωτῆρα εἰρηκέναι, τί με λέγεις ἀγαθόν; οὐδεὶς ἀγαθὸς εἰ μὴ εἷς ὁ Θεός. BD*abc* Vulg. Orig. Iren. 92 read εἷς ἐστιν ὁ ἀγαθός (D omits ὁ. *bc* Vulg. Memph. add ὁ Θεός; evidently, as I think, a gloss of the Harmonies from Mark x. 18 and Luke xviii. 19. Iren. adds "pater in coelis"). Rec. Text, with Hil. 994, reads οὐδεὶς ἀγαθὸς εἰ μὴ εἷς ὁ Θεός. This is still more palpably a reading copied from the parallels in Mark and Luke.—ED.

who feel secure to the law: He consoles the contrite with the Gospel.

18. Ποίας; *which?*) There was no need to ask *which*, as our Lord had said *the* [commandments] τάς.[1]

18, 19. Οὐ φονεύσεις—ἀγαπήσεις, κ.τ.λ.., *thou shalt not murder—thou shalt love*, etc.) Precepts negative and affirmative. The duties of the Second Table are more palpable than those of the First.

19. Τίμα, *honour*) Honour implies somewhat in addition to love.—τὸν πατέρα, *thy father*) It may be supposed that the young man in question had transgressed this more than the negative commandments; on which ground it is placed last.—τὸν πλησίον, *thy neighbour*) The Jews were peculiarly deficient in the love of their neighbour.—ὡς σεαυτὸν, *as thyself*) The love wherewith God loveth us, is the standard of the love wherewith we ought to love one another. God loves Titius as He does Caius: therefore Caius ought to love Titius as he does Caius, *i.e.*, as himself.[2] Yet the love of the godly, like that of God, is not without discrimination of the good and the bad.[3]

21. "Ἔφη αὐτῷ ὁ Ἰησοῦς, κ.τ.λ.., *Jesus said unto him*, etc.) As the young man asks more, and binds himself to more, more is proposed to him.—τέλειος, *perfect*) He is *perfect* to whom nothing is *wanting* that he may enter into life eternal. As he urgently asks it, our Lord proposes to him the most glorious condition, the nearest to that of an apostle.—ὕπαγε—καὶ δεῦρο, ἀκολούθει Μοι, *go—and come, follow Me*) sc. immediately. It is a command, not a counsel;[4] necessary, not optional (cf. ver. 24, 25): but particular, not universal, accommodated to the idiosyncrasy

---

[1] Thus indicating those pre-eminently so called, and implying the necessity of keeping *all* of them.—(I. B.)

[2] He who is endued with this love will evince it even to the child of beggars: he who is not endued with it will prefer himself to all men whatsoever, even to the elect of God.—V. g.

[3] Ver. 20. ἐκ νεότητός μου, *from my youth*) The reading which omits these words, however less probable it be declared by the margin of both Editions, has nevertheless been subsequently received into the Vers. Germ., the reasons on both sides being regarded by Bengel in a different light from what they had been.—E. B.

BL Vulg. Cypr. Iren. omit the words. But D*abc* Orig. 3,609*d*, Hilary 704, retain them (D omitting μου). The words are plainly, I think, interpolated through Harmonies from Mark x. 20, Luke xviii. 21.—ED.

[4] As opposed to the Romish doctrine of " counsels of perfection," on which

of his soul, to whom it was addressed. For many followed Jesus, to whom He did not give this command. He may be perfect, who still possesses wealth; he may give all to the poor, who is very far from perfection.[1] Our Lord's words laid an obligation on the man who offered himself ultroneously, and that so unreservedly; although to him, being as yet somewhat of a stranger, it was not expressly enjoined, but rather given in the form of advice to one seeking advice. In the case of others, who are not yet able to receive peculiar commands, a compensation is made by the leading of divine Providence.—πώλησον, κ.τ.λ., *sell*, etc.) If the Lord had said, Thou art rich, and art too fond of thy riches, the young man would have denied it: wherefore, instead of so doing, He demands immediately a direct proof[2] [of the contrary].—ἕξεις, κ.τ.λ., *thou shalt have*, etc.) A promise inserted in the command, and at once surely guaranteed: *q.d.* Thou shalt have, and thou shalt know that thou hast.[3] —θησαυρὸν, *treasure*) The inheritance is called treasure, in opposition to worldly goods. Dost thou wish to be rich? Seek this treasure.—ἀκολούθει Μοι, *follow Me*) Instruction in faith would not then be wanting.

22. Λυπούμενος, *grieved*) sc. because he could not at the same time both retain his wealth and follow Jesus. Obedience would have absorbed grief.—κτήματα, *possessions*) sc. immoveable goods; cf. *sell* in ver. 21. These are referred to in the *lands* spoken of in ver. 29.

23. Δυσκόλως, *with difficulty*) This young man, when he had his foot already on the threshold, withdrew it on account of his riches. It is difficult for a rich man to relinquish all things.[4]

---

they build the notion of works of 'supererogation': quoting this instance in support of their theory.—ED.

[1] Zaccheus, as recorded Luke xix. 8, when distributing one half of his goods to the poor, obtained the Lord's commendation. [He was not required to give *all* that he had to the poor: nay, what he did give was voluntarily, not by command.—ED.]—V. g.

[2] In the original the words are, "ipsum statim documentum postulat;" lit. "he demands *the very* proof."—(I. B.)

[3] For already now, in this life, those things which are needful are freely held out to believers from this treasure, ver. 29.—V. g.

[4] Nay, it is not even readily that he thinks of the subject of obtaining eternal life at all.—V. g.

24. Κάμηλον, *a camel*) *i.e.* the animal of that name; cf. ch. xxiii. 24. It is not a rope[1] that is compared to a thread, but the eye of a needle to a gate.

25. 'Ακούσαντες δὲ οἱ μαθηταὶ αὐτοῦ, κ.τ.λ., *but when His disciples heard it,* etc.) Scripture everywhere shows a middle path between excessive confidence and excessive timidity. See ver. 26, 28, 30; 1 Pet. v. 7, compared with 6, 8.—τίς ἄρα, κ.τ.λ., *who then,* etc.) The disciples were anxious, either for themselves, lest other obstacles should equally impede them, or because they entertained the hope of acquiring wealth (see ver. 27), or else for others: which fear is far more laudable. Cf. Rev. v. 4.

26. 'Εμβλέψας, *having looked upon*) in order to fix the thoughts of the terrified disciples. Jesus taught many things even by His look and by the expression of His countenance. This look first moved Matthew, once a publican.—εἶπεν, *said*) with the greatest sweetness.—ἀδύνατον, *impossible*) more even than morally impossible.—πάντα, *all things*) Therefore even this. The Divine omnipotence is seen, not only in the kingdom of nature, but in those also of grace and glory. That power is more than human by which the human heart is led away from earthly things. The cause of the rich may be pleaded with the greatest effect by the poor and the scrupulous.[2]—δυνατά, *possible*) as each of the elect will know.

---

[1] Bengel alludes to a reading which is evidently corrupt, and an interpretation which is manifestly erroneous. "Some ancient and modern commentators," says Bloomfield, "would read κάμιλον. *a cable, rope;* or take κάμηλον in that sense. But for the former there is little or no manuscript authority, and for the latter, no support from the *usus loquendi.*" For interesting illustrations of the subject, too long to insert, see *Kitto,* and *Wordsworth,* in loc. —(I. B.)

[2] In the original, "timoratos." In illustration and explanation of this barbarous word, the following extract will not be unwelcome:—

"TIMORATUS. Wippo de Vita Chunradi Salici, p. 428: *In Dei seruitio Timorata,* in orationibus et *eleemosynis assidua.* Gesta Innocentii iii. p. 77: *Deuotus et timoratus.* Ditmarus lib. 2: *Filiam bene Timoratam, etc. Humiliter et Timorate,* apud eumdem lib. 3. Fulbertus Carnot. Epist. 40: *Haerebam timorate suspensus et expectans,* etc. Occurrit non semel: Gallis *Timoré,* Dei timidus et a lenibus culpis auersus. *Timoratus et totus plenus Deo,* in Chronico Noualic. apud Murator, to. 2. part. 2, col. 735. Adde P. 2 de Imit. Christi, c. 10, n. 3, etc." GLOSSARIUM MANUALE AD SCRIPTORES MEDIÆ ET INFIMÆ LATINITATIS ex magnis Glossariis CAROLI DU FRESNE,

27. Εἶπεν, *said*) in all simplicity.—ἡμεῖς, *we*) not like that rich man.—πάντα, *all things*) His few things are as much *all* to the workman, as his many things to the satrap.—τί ἄρα ἔσται ἡμῖν; *what therefore shall there be for us?*) Our Lord replies by ἑκατονταπλασίονα λήψεται, *he shall receive an hundredfold*, in ver. 29, and δώσω, κ.τ.λ., *I will give*, etc., in ch. xx. 4, 2, 7, etc.—ἡμῖν, *for us*) sc. in the kingdom of God.

28. Ὁ δὲ Ἰησοῦς εἶπεν αὐτοῖς, κ.τ.λ., *but Jesus said unto them*, etc.) Peter had joined together *we have left all*, and *we have followed Thee*. Our Lord replies to these things separately; for the latter (ver. 28) was peculiar to the apostles; the former (ver. 29) common to them with others. See Ps. xlv. 10, 11.—ὑμεῖς —καὶ ὑμεῖς, *ye—ye also*) sc. you Twelve.—ἐν τῇ παλιγγενεσίᾳ, *in the regeneration*) This is to be construed with the following, not the preceding words: for the *following after Jesus* is usually mentioned alone, without this addition: by which the time of the *session*, which is immediately spoken of, is suitably marked. There will be a new creation, over which the second Adam will preside, when the whole microcosm of human nature, by means of the resurrection, and also the macrocosm of the universe, will be born again (genesin iteratam habebit). Cf. Acts iii. 21; Rev. xxi. 5; Matt. xxvi. 29.—Regeneration (παλιγγενεσία) and renovation (ἀνακαίνωσις) are joined together in Tit. iii. 5.—Then we shall be *sons;* see Luke xx. 36; Rom. viii. 23; 1 John iii. 2. —καθίσεσθε, *ye shall sit*) The middle voice is used in the case of the disciples, the active, καθίσῃ, in that of the Lord. At the beginning of the judgment the disciples will stand; see Luke xxi. 36; 2 Cor. v. 10; afterwards, having been absolved from all charges against them, they will sit with Him; see 1 Cor. vi. 2.—θρόνους, *thrones*) Another has taken the throne of Judas; see Acts i. 20. Concerning the thrones, cf. Rev. xx. 4.— κρίνοντες, *judging*) In the time of the Judges there was a theocracy, concerning which see my exposition of the Apocalypse, p. 553. Thus, in the first millennium, restored Israel, its enemies having been destroyed, will have judges again; see Is. i. 26. The promise, however, given to the apostles, refers to a still more distant period.—δώδεκα, *twelve*) The number of

Domini Du Cange, et Carpentarii in compendium redactum multisque verbis et dicendi formulis auctum.—Tom. vi., p. 563, b.—(I. B.)

princes in Num. viii. 2, etc., and of apostles in Rev. xxi. 12, 14, corresponds with that of the tribes of Israel.—φυλάς, κ.τ.λ., *tribes*, etc.) to which the apostles had, in the first instance, been sent.

29. Καὶ πᾶς, *and every one*) Not only apostles, to whom Peter's question ought not to have referred exclusively. See 2 Tim. iv. 8.—ἀφῆκεν, *hath relinquished*) If the Lord so command (as in iv. 19), or thus guide by various means.—οἰκίας, *houses*[1]) This is placed first; cf. concerning it, ver. 21, 27.— St Matthew, in the present instance, and St Mark, in x. 29, maintain the order of affection in the enumeration of relations, mentioning them by pairs in an ascending scale, *lands* being placed last; whereas St Luke, in xviii. 29, follows the order of time.—ἢ γυναῖκα, *or wife*) *i.e.* without breaking the law of Moses; see ver. 9. The singular number of this word (*i.e. wife*) should be remarked, as an argument against polygamy; for those things of which there can be more than one, *brothers*, etc., are put in the plural number in this passage. In like manner in Mark x. 29, οἰκία, *a house*, is also put in the singular number. A man may, indeed, have more than one house, though such is the case of few; but no one *dwells* in two at the same time, so as to be able to leave them both at once.—ἕνεκεν τοῦ ὀνόματός Μου, *on account of My name*) sc. on account of confessing and preaching the name of Christ.—ἑκατονταπλασίονα, *an hundredfold*) *i.e.* of the same things which are enumerated in this verse; cf. Mark x. 30. —λήψεται, *shall receive*) sc. in this life: for the future life is an hundredfold, nay, a thousandfold more productive in its returns;

---

[1] Beng., in his Appar. Crit. on this passage, p. 482, had considered the singular, οἰκίαν, had been derived from the parallel passages in the other Gospels. Hence also in the Gnomon (Ed. ii., p. 128) he preferred the plural number. But in the smaller Ed. of N. T. Gr., A.D. 1753, he changed his opinion, and gave the superiority to the singular, οἰκίαν, by appending the sign β, and with this the Germ. Vers. of the passage subsequently corresponds. In this view, the observation in the Gnomon which immediately follows, has the more force.—E. B.

Tischend. reads ἢ οἰκίας after ἢ ἀγρούς, with CL Memph., MSS. of Vulg. Origen 1, 283c ; 3,089a. Lachm., as Rec. Text, reads οἰκίας ἢ before ἀδελφούς with BD. The oldest MS. of Vulg. (Amiatinus) reads the sing. 'domum,' and puts it before "vel fratres aut sorores." *abcd* Hil. also read 'domum.' Irenaeus, "agros aut domos aut parentes (ἢ γονεῖς) aut fratres aut filios." The ἢ οἰκίαν first in the enumeration is probably drawn from Mark viii. 29 and Luke xviii. 29.—ED.

see Luke xix. 16, 17. He *shall receive* them, however, not as civil or personal possessions; yet he truly *shall receive* them, as far as the believer needs to do so, and he does so in the person of others, to whom, as a believer, he would especially wish them to belong; cf. Matt. v. 5; Acts iv. 35; 1 Cor. iii. 22.—The ungodly are usurpers; the right of possession belongs to God and His heirs; they receive as much as is expedient for them. The word λήψεται (*shall receive*) agrees rather with the notion of *hire* or *wages*: but κληρονομήσει (*shall inherit*) implies something far more abundant. Scripture speaks more expressly and copiously of temporal punishments than of temporal rewards, and of eternal rewards than of eternal punishments.—ζωὴν, *life*) see ver. 16, 17.

30. Πολλοὶ δὲ, *but many*) in opposition to πᾶς (*every one*), in ver. 29. Perhaps also it is hinted that the young man in question would return again, and from being one of the last, become one of the first.—πρῶτοι, *first*) In the first clause of the verse this word is the *subject*, as is clear from its attributive, πολλοί (*many*), which absorbs the article; in the latter clause it is the *predicate*: in ch. xx. 16 the opposite is the case. In the present instance, therefore (since the greatest emphasis is placed on the last clause), the apophthegm is propounded rather by way of encouragement, as in Mark x. 31; whereas in Matt. xx. 16 and Luke xiii. 30, by way of warning. In both cases the assertions are modified by the addition of the attributive πολλοὶ (*many*), which applies especially to the worse class; for the better contains but *few*. The "*first*" and "*last*" differ; either, (1), in kind, so that the former means those who are saved, the latter those who are lost; or, (2), (which is preferable) in degree, so that the "*last*" may mean those who are also saved, but who obtain a station far inferior to that of the "*first*." F. S. Loefler (p. 106), in his exposition of the following parable, supposes ὡς (*as*) to be understood here, so as to produce the following meaning: *The First shall be* AS *the Last; and the Last* AS *the First*. Nor is the idea of such an ellipsis in itself objectionable: but this interpretation is irreconcileable with the context in the parallel passages, of St Mark who does not give the subsequent parable, and of St Luke who records this saying when uttered on another occasion. Our Lord intimates parti-

cularly the change of relative condition which was to occur between the Jews and the Gentiles.—Cf. ch. viii. 10, 11, 12; Luke xiii. 28–30 (taken in connection with ib. ver. 23–27), and Rom. ix. 30, 31.

CHAPTER XX.

1. Γάρ, *for*) referring to the last verse of the preceding chapter. There is a similar connection of a parable with what immediately preceded it, in ch. xviii. 23. Peter is taught to be more diffident in asking questions (cf. ch. xix. 27), and in comparing himself with others; cf. Luke xvii. 5, 10, where we see that they think more rightly who consider themselves as unprofitable servants, than they who consider themselves better than others.

2. Συμφωνήσας, *when he had agreed*) He deals with the first labourers more by legal compact; with the latter, more by mere liberality, even in the hiring them, though He blames them for standing idle; see ver. 4, 6, 7. They make up for their previous idleness by their obedience, without stipulating for a fixed amount of wages. The day, divided into twelve hours, signifies *not* the whole duration of the world, *nor* that of the New Testament dispensation, which the life of a single labourer can never equal; neither, as it seems, does it represent the space of life given to each human being, in which one labours a longer and another a shorter time from his call to his death: although one who came before us might labour only one hour (*i.e.* the last), and another who comes after us may begin at the first; so that in this passage that saying should hold good, "*In any hour is any hour;*"[1]—But it represents the space of time from the first calling of the apostles to the ascension of Christ and the descent

---

[1] " Quâlibet horâ est quælibet hora." In every hour whatever, there is the hour of some one or other [some hour or other, whatsoever that hour be]. Any hour of labour whatsoever is counted to the labourer as such, whensoever it be, whether at an earlier or later date. This seems to me Bengel's meaning, though the words are rather ambiguous.—ED.

of the Paraclete. The denarius is that one amount of wages in the present and future life, equally offered to all, mentioned in ch. xix. 29, 21; the difference of which, though corresponding with the difference of labours, is not only not apparent in this life, but frequently appears inverted: therefore the middle term, equality, is here assumed.[1] The evening is that time when each one is, or appears to be, much nearer the close than the commencement of his labours; and therefore, in the case of the disciples, the time then close at hand, immediately before the departure of our Lord. They cast their own evening and that of others into the same balance, who compare themselves with others. The labourers are all who are called, not only the apostles. The feeling of the discontented labourers concerning the whole day, resembles that of Peter, when he alluded, without sufficient discretion, to the difference between himself and that rich man. And every one is tempted by such a feeling towards those whom he most knows, and who are his equals He who has a wider range of thought is liable to the same temptation with regard to those who are more remote.—μετὰ τῶν ἐργατῶν, *with the labourers*) The Householder makes an agreement with the labourers, and they (see ver. 13) with him. The one ensures the payment of the wages; the other shows what the labourer should be contented with.—ἐκ δηναρίου, *for a denarius*) This was a day's wages, as it is commonly at present. The ἐκ (*for*) is not repeated in ver. 13.

3. Ἄλλους, *others*) who had not been there at the first hour.

6. Τὴν ἐνδεκάτην, *the eleventh*) The article is emphatic, as it does not occur in the case of the ninth, sixth, or even third hour.—ὅλην τὴν ἡμέραν, *all the day*) They could not offer themselves for hire elsewhere.

7. Ἡμᾶς, *us*) This suits the Gentiles.

8. Ὀψίας δὲ γενομένης, *but when even was come*) A prophetic allusion is made to the Last Judgment. The evening of each individual's life resembles the evening of the world.—ἀπὸ τῶν ἐσχάτων ἕως τῶν πρώτων, *from the last unto the first*) They were all

---

[1] Here again there is some obscurity. "Ideo medium, paritas, sumitur." It seems to me to refer to His fixing on the denarius as a *mean*, merging the various diversities of reward answering to the diversities of labour, not *now* apparent, in the *one common sum alike and equal to all.*—ED.

divided into these two classes; for all are reckoned amongst the first, who came before the eleventh hour; see ver. 9, 10.

9. Ἀνὰ, *apiece*) See John ii. 6.

10. Οἱ πρῶτοι, *the first*) The intermediate labourers did not murmur; for they saw themselves also made equal to the first. He who is liable to be envied himself, is less likely to envy others.—πλείονα, *more*) sc. denarii, *i.e.* twelve denarii for twelve hours.

11. Ἐγόγγυζον, *murmured*) Cf. Luke xv. 28–30.

12. Οὗτοι, κ.τ.λ., *these*, etc.) Envy is frequently more anxious to take from another than to obtain for itself. They envy, not those of the ninth, sixth, and third, but only those of the eleventh hour.—οἱ ἔσχατοι, *the last*) The labourers use this expression from envy.—ἐποίησαν, *have spent*) See Acts xv. 33.[1]—ἡμῖν, *to us*) They speak also for those who had come at the intermediate hours, and who, though they had borne a less burthen than that of the whole day, had yet endured the midday heat.—βάρος, *burthen*) internally, of labour.—τῆς ἡμέρας, *of the day*) sc. the whole.—καύσωνα, *heat*) externally, of the sun.

13. Ἑνὶ, *to one*) who was a sample of the rest of the murmurers. Cf. concerning *one*, the Gnomon on ch. xxii. 11.—ἑταῖρε, *friend*) An expression used also to those with whom we are not on friendly or intimate terms.[2]

14. Τὸ σὸν, *that which is* THINE) There is an evident contrast intended between these words and ἐν τοῖς ἐμοῖς, *with* MY OWN, in the following verse.—ὕπαγε, *Depart*) This expression is not addressed to those who came at the eleventh hour.—θέλω, *I will*) The force of this word is very great.[3] See ver. 15, and cf.

---

[1] Ποιήσαντες—χρόνον, *Having tarried a space*: as ποιέω is here taken by Beng. and the margin of our Engl. Bible of *continuance of time*, "These last have *continued* one hour only."—ED.

[2] "ἑταῖρε, at first sight a friendly word merely, assumes a more solemn aspect when we recollect that it is used in ch. xxii. 12, to the guest who had not the wedding garment; and in ch. xxvi. 50, by our Lord to Judas." *Alford* in loc.—(I. B.)

Οὐκ ἀδικῶ σε, *I do thee no wrong*) To do wrong to GOD is bad; but it is even worse to suppose one's self wronged by GOD: and this happens more often than is generally supposed.—V. g.

[3] *i.e.* denoting the absolute freedom of GOD'S Grace, and the entire sovereignty of His Will.—(I. B.)

Gnomon on Mark xii. 38.—*τούτῳ τῷ ἐσχάτῳ, to this last*) The expression is repeated from the speech of the murmurer, but used in the singular number, and applied to *the last of the last*. Every one who is envious, envies some one individually.—*σοὶ, to thee*) The addition, "who hast borne the burden and heat of the day," is not repeated.

15. '*Οφθαλμὸς, eye*) The mind shines forth from the eyes.—*ἀγαθὸς, good*) He is *good*, who grants more than *justice* (see ver. 4, sc. *whatsoever is right*) requires. See Rom. v. 7.

16. Οὕτως, *in such a manner*) The conclusion enunciated in ch. xix. 30 is inferred again from the parable, though somewhat inverted, and at the same time limited by the οὕτως, as in Rev. iii. 16. Not all who are first shall fail, yet all require to be on the watch, lest they should fail; and all do fail who conduct themselves as the ἑταῖρος ('*friend*,' or *comrade*) mentioned in the parable. Many, also, from the intermediate ranks, may take up a higher or a lower position.—*ἔσονται, shall be*) With respect to the apostles, it is not a prediction, but a warning.—*οἱ, the*) The article is here the sign of the subject (as it is everywhere, except when that is still more definitely determined by a proper name or a pronoun, demonstrative or personal), and at the same time has reference to ch. xix. 30; thus showing that the proposition is not to be taken as of universal application.—*πρῶτοι, first*) See the end of ver. 8.—*πολλοὶ, many*) sc. of the first, who themselves are many (see ch. xix. 30); and moreover of οἱ ἔσχατοι, *the last*.—*κλητοί, called*) The term κεκλημένος is applied to a labourer who has been invited, even though he should not enter the vineyard: the term κλητὸς signifies one who has embraced the calling.[1]—*ἐκλεκτοί, chosen*) i.e. selected in preference to others. In this passage, the first where it occurs, the word seems to denote, not all who shall be saved, but, the most excellent of human beings. See Franck's Sermons for Sundays and Holidays, pp. 431, 432, and W. Wall's Critical Notes, p. 27.

17. '*Αναβαίνων, as He was going up*) A very memorable journey, in which great and various emotions were manifested.—

---

[1] '*Ολίγοι, few*) who, as clinging to mere [unmixed] faith, give [cause] more honour to God, than the most zealous workmen.—V. g.

παρέλαβε, κ.τ.λ., *He took*, etc.) He propounded the subject, not as in His daily conversation, but more solemnly.[1]

18, 19. Παραδοθήσεται—παραδώσουσι, *shall be delivered up, shall deliver up*) A momentous verb. See Luke xxiii. 25.

18. Ἀρχιερεῦσι, *to the chief priests*) This appellation seems to have been very common at that time.—γραμματεῦσι, *to the scribes*) whose duty it was to examine, as of the priests to decide.[2]

19. Τοῖς Ἔθνεσι, *to the Gentiles*) *i.e.* to the Roman nation, which was the chief of them all.—ἐμπαῖξαι, *to be mocked*) What ignominy! He had, on two previous occasions, foretold His passion less definitely: He now expressly mentions the *stripes*, the *cross*, etc., as in ch. xxvi. 2, He does the consummation, namely, His crucifixion.

20. Τότε, *then*) at a most inappropriate time.[3]—προσκυνοῦσα, *worshipping*) Him. From the adoration and discourse of this woman, it is evident that she entertained a high idea of our Lord's majesty, but possessed very little knowledge.—τὶ, *something*) She asked for *something*, indefinitely, as they do who knew that a refusal would not be unjust; see 1 Kings ii. 20.

21.[4] Ἵνα καθίσωσιν, *that they may sit*) She seems to refer to the promise of the twelve thrones mentioned in ch. xix. 28, and to have taken occasion to apply the promise more especially to her own sons from the appellation, *sons of thunder*, which our Lord

---

[1] Viz. in this His third announcement of His coming death, etc.—V. g. Of the preceding declarations as to His approaching Passion, the one had been made after the confession of the disciples, the other after the Transfiguration on the Mount (which was attended with an universal admiration of His works, Luke ix. 43, 44, 35; Mark ix. 15): a third is now added of His own accord, more solemn than the rest.—*Harm.*, p. 432.

[2] Bengel's very sentences have a rhythm, which brings out happily the antithesis intended: "*Scribis*) quorum erat scientia; uti *pontificum* sententia." The province of the former was *knowledge* of the written law; of the latter, to *decide* or *give sentence* in accordance with it.—ED.

[3] Ἡ μήτηρ) This thought seems to have entered the mind of the anxious *mother* altogether sooner than it did that of her sons: and even in her very supplication she acted the part of an intermediate agent or intercessor.—*Harm.*, p. 433.

[4] Τί θέλεις, *what wilt thou*) The Saviour does not act hastily in promising. —V. g.

had bestowed upon them; see Gnomon on Mark iii. 17.—[1]*υίοί μου, my sons*) Natural relationship had nothing to do with this. —ἐκ δεξιῶν σου, *on Thy right hand*) The words τὰ δεξιὰ signify, *passim*, the *right* hand, foot, and side. Before then, Jesus would have others on His right and left; see ch. xxvii. 38.[2]—εἷς, *one*) It may be supposed that the order of the disciples in their glory will correspond to the order in their office.

22. Εἶπεν, *said*) gravely, and with pity.—οὐκ οἴδατε, *ye do not know*) Ye do not know what My glory is, what it is to sit on My right hand and on My left, to whom it is given, and what is required beforehand.—τί αἰτεῖσθε, *what ye ask*) sc. what it is that ye ask.[3]—δύνασθε; *can ye?*) He replies to the sons, instead of the mother, Are you equal to this?—τὸ ποτήριον, *the cup*) In St Mark He speaks also of "*the baptism*;" see the Gnomon on Mark x. 38, 39. Some copies of Matthew have the clause concerning baptism, others are without it.[4]—ὃ ἐγώ, *which I*) Jesus already as it were then dwelt on His passion, and draws His discourse from it; and the speech of those two, whom He thus directs to follow Him, was, as it were, outstripping not only their ten fellow-disciples, but also the Lord Himself.[5]—δυνάμεθα, *we are*

---

[1] Οἱ δύο) She seemed to herself at the time to be speaking altogether seasonably.—V. g.

[2] Sc. The two thieves who were crucified with Him.—(I. B.)

[3] One ought to know this, who wishes to ask.—V. g.

[4] In his Apparatus Criticus, Bengel says on this passage—

22 ἤ) Comp. Aug. 1, 2; Colb. 5 et Colb. n. 4112; Cypr. Laud. 2, 4; M. 1, 2; Wo. 1, 2, et c Classe ii. *undecim* alii, pluresve, *Pers. Rus. Syr. καὶ Er.* et al. E. Marco. ¶ ἢ τὸ usq. βαπτισθῆναι) edd. MSS. *Arab. Hebr. Pers. Rus. Syr. Chrys.*, Opus imperf. *Basilius* Sel. *Theophyl.* (—) *Origenes, Epiphanius, Æth. Copt. Lat.* et inde *Cant. Colbert.* n. 2467, *Steph. v. Sax. Ambr. Hilar. Hieron.*, Tr. de Bapt. inter opera *Cypriani.*—(I. B.)

Rec. Text with C adds after τίνειν, ἤ (καὶ) τὸ βάπτισμα ὃ ἐγὼ βαπτίζομαι βαπτισθῆναι. But BDLZbc Vulg. Memph. Theb. Orig. 3,717c, 719b (ascribing the words to Mark), Hil. 709, omit the words.—ED.

However the margin of Ed. 2 reckons that clause concerning *the baptism* among the readings better established in the following verse than in this verse.—E. B.

Rec. Text adds in ver. 23, with C, καὶ τὸ βάπτισμα ὃ ἐγὼ βαπτίζομαι βαπτισθήσεσθε. But BDLZabc, and the others quoted in note, ver. 22, reject the words.—ED.

[5] What Beng. seems to mean is, The request of the two sons of Zebedee, as it were, went before even Himself, not to say the ten disciples, in proceed-

able) They did not even know sufficiently what they were answering; the Lord, however, bears with them, and accepts their confession;[1] cf. ch. xxvi. 39, 37.

23. Τὸ μὲν ποτήριόν, κ.τ.λ., *the cup indeed*, etc.) This, together with the parallel passages, has been treated with singular industry by Thomas Gataker in his *Adversaria Miscellanea*, B. i. ch. 3, of which we shall take the chief points.—καθίσαι, κ.τ.λ., *to sit*, etc.) There will, therefore, clearly be some who will sit on the right and left hand of Christ.—ἀλλ' οἷς, κ.τ.λ., *except to those for whom*) By this opposition or exception (for it comes to the same thing) Jesus does not deny that it is His to give (see Rev. iii. 21), but limits and declares to whom He will give it, as well as the time and the order, referring, as is His wont, all things to the Father. Jesus did not give it until, His passion having been suffered and concluded,[2] He had sat down Himself on the right hand of the Father. It is neither an earthly kingdom in which He gives it, nor does He give it to those who have not yet suffered. Under, therefore, the very appearance of a repulse, He gives a promise to James and John.

24. Οἱ δέκα, *the ten*) Amongst these was the candid Evangelist himself.—ἠγανάκτησαν, *were indignant*) They feared lest they should lose something[3] [*i.e.* lest James and John should gain something at their expense].

25. Προσκαλεσάμενος αὐτοὺς, *having called them to Him*) They had been moved, therefore, with indignation when their Master was not present. He avowedly corrects them.—οἴδατε, κ.τ.λ., *ye know*, etc.) Therefore ye think that it will be the same in the kingdom of the Messiah.—κατακυριεύουσιν [E. V. *exercise dominion over*]—κατεξουσιάζουσιν [E. V. *exercise authority upon*]—In both these compound verbs the κατὰ intensifies the signification (see S. V. of Gen. i. 28, and Ps. lxxii. 8), and in this passage distin-

ing to the *Kingdom* at once, whereas He was dwelling on the intermediate *Passion*: He therefore urges them to *follow after* Him, not to *take the lead* of Him, and to bear the *Cross* of His followers before receiving the *Crown*. —ED.

[1] Intending subsequently to perfect in them those things, which at that time were above their own comprehension.—V. g.

[2] 'Exantlatâ,' 'having been drained to the dregs.'—(I.B.)

[3] Luke records a similar dispute as having arisen at the Last Supper, ch. xxii. 24.—*Harm*, p. 433.

guishes between the legitimate use and frequent abuse of authority.—οἱ μεγάλοι, *they that are great*) sc. ministers of state, who are often more imperious than their lords.

26. Οὐχ οὕτως δὲ ἔσται ἐν ὑμῖν, *but it shall not be so among you*) " It appears to me not at all natural to suppose that all use and exercise of civil authority is in this passage utterly forbidden to those to whom these words apply, and much less so that our Lord meant to forbid, by these words, all precedence and inequality amongst His followers, since He Himself both expressly recognises degrees amongst them, by which some are preferred to others, as greater to less (see Luke xxii. 26), and also proposes Himself to them as an example (ὑπόδειγμα); see ibid. 27 ; Matt. xx. 28. Christ therefore, by this prohibition, did not derogate more from the authority of His followers over each other, than He did from His own over them."—GATAKER: hierarchically enough.—ἐν ὑμῖν, *amongst you*) These words " seem to apply to all Christians, whether princes or plebeians."—Ibid. " Christ teaches that His kingdom is carried on upon different principles from those of this world ; for that in those there were external dignities, princedoms, and satrapies, which the respective kings were in the habit of conferring, according to their caprice, upon those whom they wished to honour ; but that in His kingdom nothing of this sort was to be found ; not because those things were not to be met with, or might not be lawfully exercised in the Church of Christ or amongst the professors of the Christian name, but because they do not pertain to, or arise from, the spiritual kingdom of Christ, to which He invites His followers. Moreover, that there was no reason why any one, in following Him, should promise himself the possession of such dignities, since He neither promised such things to any one, nor took or exercised them Himself : that He professed Himself, by practice as well as precept, to be, not the dispenser of secular dignities, but the author and teacher of humility and spiritual modesty. He exhorts all His followers, therefore, that (utterly laying aside all ambition) they should conform themselves to these virtues, of which they have an example in Himself."—Ibid.—μέγας, *great*) the minister of a great king is himself great.

27. Πρῶτος, *chief.*

28. Ὥσπερ, κ.τ.λ., *even as*, etc.) The greatest example which could be adduced or imagined.—διακονῆσαι, *to minister, to serve*) See Rom. xv. 8.—καὶ, κ.τ.λ., *and*, etc.) An ascending climax.—τὴν ψυχὴν Αὐτοῦ, *His soul*) i.e. *Himself*; see Gal. i. 4, ii. 20.—λύτρον, *a ransom*.—ἀντὶ πολλῶν, *for many*) A great *ministry*, and one of vast condescension. That for which a price is given, is in some sort more an object of desire to him who gives the price than the price itself. And the Redeemer spends Himself for many, not only taken as a whole, but also as individuals.

29. Ὄχλος πολύς, *a great multitude*) which had been in that city.[1]

30. Δύο, *two*) St Mark (x. 46) mentions only one, Bartimaeus, the most distinguished;[2] as St Matthew in the next chapter mentions both the ass and the colt, St Mark only the colt which was actually employed by our Lord; as St Luke (xxiv. 4) the two angels who appeared, St Matthew and St Mark, the one who spoke.

31. Οἱ δὲ, κ.τ.λ., *but they*, etc.) We must not listen to those who inculcate perverted shame or noxious decorum.

32. Τί θέλετε; κ.τ.λ., *what will ye?* etc.) We ought sometimes in our prayers to make special petitions.

34. Σπλαγχνισθεὶς, *being moved with compassion*) The compassion of Jesus was aroused by every human misery.—ἠκολούθησαν Αὐτῷ, *they followed Him*) with the multitudes mentioned in ch. xxi. 8, and without any one to lead them.[3]

---

[1] And were subsequently present at His royal entry.—V. g.

[2] The same one is meant also in Luke xviii. 35, that Evangelist having had occasion to transpose the order of the narration, owing to the fact that one of the two blind men made acquaintance with the Divine Physician on the way, when Jesus was entering Jericho. In the meantime, whilst the Saviour was dining or rather passing the night with Zaccheus, the other of the two blind men, whom Matthew adds to the former one, joined Bartimaeus.—*Harm.*, pp. 434, 435.

[3] Sc. as formerly, when they were blind.—Ed.

CHAPTER XXI.

1. Καὶ ὅτε, κ.τ.λ., *and when*, etc.) From this point forward, the actions and contests of our Lord are described by the several Evangelists with great fulness and agreement.—εἰς Ἱεροσόλυμα, *to Jerusalem*) which they were about to enter.—τότε, κ.τ.λ., *then*, etc.) not before. It is clearly intimated, that the event[1] about to be described was full of mystery. Often had Jesus entered Jerusalem;[2] now, in this His last journey, and at the conclusion of it, He rides for the only time, solemnly taking possession of the Royal City (see ch. v. 35), not only for a few days, but on account of that kingdom (see Mark xi. 10) which He was just about to institute; see Luke xxiv. 47, i. 33, and the conclusion of Zech. ix. 10, with the whole context.

2. Τὴν ἀπέναντι ὑμῶν) *which is over against you.*—εὐθέως, *immediately*) The word is repeated in the next verse. All things are easy to the Lord.—δεδεμένην, *tied*) already as it were prepared.—πῶλον, *a colt*) The colt had never carried any one before. Jesus had never been carried before by any animal, except perhaps at a very tender age. He took the mother from the village for a short way.

3. Ὁ Κύριος, *the Lord*) The owners of the ass were devoted to Jesus.[3]—εὐθέως δὲ, *but immediately*) i.e. You will not need

---

[1] In the original, "Vectura (*a being carried or borne, a riding*) mysterii plena innuitur." See ver. 2–9.—(I. B.)

[2] "The Saviour had come to Jerusalem— (1), in infancy (Luke ii. 22, seqq.); (2), in childhood (Luke ii. 42, seqq.); (3), in His temptation (chap. iv. 5); (4), at the Passover (John ii. 23.); (5), at the Day of Pentecost (John v. 1); (6), during the Feast of Tabernacles (John vii. 10); and now, for the seventh time, to His Passion. After the entrance (*Einritte*) [described in the following verses], He went daily to and from Jerusalem, until, at the commencement of the Friday, [for the Jewish days began at six o'clock in the evening,] He was carried in bound, and taken forth in the morning to Golgotha."—B. H. E.

[3] χρείαν ἔχει, *hath need*) How great were the needs of so great a Lord!—V. g.

many words.—¹ ἀποστέλλει, *he sends*)² The present tense is used because the event was sure and speedy, as they were already prepared to send it : cf. Mark iv. 29, εὐθέως ἀποστέλλει τὸ δρέπανον, *immediately he sendeth the sickle.*—See ibid. xi. 6, καὶ ἀφῆκαν αὐτούς, *and they let them go.*

5. Εἴπατε, κ.τ.λ., *tell ye,* etc.) This passage is one of those which show that many things in the prophets ought to be received by us, not only as they were meant by them, but as they were destined to be meant by the apostles. This part occurs in Isa. lxii. 11 ; the rest in Zechariah, whom St Matthew quotes, beginning at the more important part ; for the word " *rejoice*" is thus supplied. At the time of its fulfilment *it is to be told :* joy then arises spontaneously.³ In Zech. ix. 9, the LXX. have Χαῖρε σφόδρα θύγατερ Σιών, κήρυσσε θύγατερ Ἱερουσαλήμ· ἰδοὺ, ὁ Βασιλεύς⁴ ἔρχεταί σοι, δίκαιος καὶ σώζων Αὐτός·⁵ πραῢς καὶ ἐμβεβηκὼς ἐπὶ ὑποζύγιον καὶ πῶλον νέον,—*Rejoice greatly, daughter of Sion ; shout,*⁵

---

¹ Such is the reading also of Griesbach and Scholz. E. M. reads ἀποστελεῖ (the future), rendered therefore in E. V. " he will send." In his App. Crit. Bengel writes—

"ἀποστέλλει) *Comp. Er.* ed. i. et seqq. ; *Stap. Aug.* i. 2 ; *Bodl.* 1, 2, 7 ; *Bu. Byz. Cov.* i. *Cypr. Gal.* ; *Gehl. Go. Laud.* 1, 2, 5 : *Lin. Lips. Mont.* manu prima, *M.* 1, *Mosc. N.* 1, *Par.* 1, 3, 4, 7, 8 ; *Per. Roe. Steph. omn. vss.* 1, 2, *Wh.* 1 *nonnulli* codd. apud Er. vel etiam *Barb. decem, et Cum.* item *Chrys. Theophyl. Cant.* latine, *Syr.* Accedunt Evangelistaria, *Aug.* 4 (in quo cum verbum hoc jam λ simplici scriptum fuisset, λ alterum est suppletum), *Bodl.* 4, 5, *Laud.* 4, *Wh.* 3. Itaque ἀποστέλλει Matthæi, et ἀποστελεῖ Marci se mutuo confirmant, nam librarii videntur lectionem ἀποστέλλει ex publica Matthæi recitatione ad Marcum traduxisse, et aliquando ἀποστελεῖ a Marco ad Matthæum retulisse. Vid. *Gnom.* (ἀποστελεῖ) *Lat.* et inde *Er.* vel etiam *Parisini et Seldiani* aliquot, cum *Bodl.* 6, *Cant.* græce, *Gon. Hunt.* 2 *Magd.* et perpaucis aliis."—(I. B.)

² Ἀποστελεῖ is the reading of BD*bc* Vulg. Orig. and Rec. Text, and so Lachm. and Tischend. Ἀποστέλλει is read by CLXZΔ*d*.—ED.

³ Beng. seems to mean, the introductory words in Zech. ix. 9, " *Rejoice greatly,*" etc., " Shout," etc., are omitted here, on the occasion of the passage being quoted by St Matthew, because, at the time of the fulfilment of the prophecy, all that was needed was the *telling* (and therefore " *Tell* ye" is substituted from Isa. lxii. 11, " *Say* ye") : the *joy* was sure to arise of its own accord.—ED.

⁴ The Codex Alexandrinus reads βασιλεύς σου.—(I. B.)

⁵ The Oxford Edition of 1848 has a comma after σώζων, and omits the colon after Αὐτός.—(I. B.)

⁶ The word denotes, in the orig., the voice of a herald or a preacher.—(I. B.)

daughter of Jerusalem: behold the King *cometh unto thee;* He is just and having salvation: [1] *meek, and riding on an ass, even a young colt.*—τῇ θυγατρὶ Σιών, *to the daughter of Sion*) put synecdochically for Jerusalem.—Βασιλεύς σου, *thy King*) and also Bridegroom.—σοί, *to,* or *for thee*) sc. for thy sake or advantage.—πραΰς καί, κ.τ.λ.., *meek and,* etc.[2]) The same thing is frequently expressed in the same passage by literal and metaphorical words. The horse is a warlike steed, which the King of Peace did not make use of; see Zech. ix. 10. He will make use of it hereafter; see Rev. xix. 11.—ὄνον, *an ass*) not a she ass. In Hebrew, חֲמוֹר.—υἱὸν ὑποζυγίου, *the male foal of an ass*[3]) who, though the offspring of one that had borne the yoke, had not himself yet borne it. Our Lord rode upon the foal, but employed also the mother as a companion to the foal.

6. Καὶ ποιήσαντες, *and when they had done.*

7. Ἐπεκάθισεν,[4] *He sat upon*) becomingly; His disciples attending on Him;[5] see Luke xix. 35. The Persian kings were rather placed by others, than themselves got on horseback. See Brisson.—ἐπάνω αὐτῶν, *on them*) though, strictly speaking, on the foal; see Mark xi. 2, 3; John xii. 14, 15.

8. Ὁ δὲ πλεῖστος ὄχλος, *but the people, who were in great numbers.*—ἐν τῇ ὁδῷ, *in the way*) [*i.e* in the midst of the *way* or *road*]; not only κατὰ τὴν ὁδόν, *by the side of the way;* for St Luke (xix. 36) uses the expression ὑπεστρώννυον, *they spread them under,* [*i.e.* so that He should ride over them].—κλάδους, *branches*) It was customary with the Jews and other ancient nations to manifest their public joy by cutting down branches from trees.

---

[1] Lit. "*Himself saving.*"—(I. B.)

[2] It is this very virtue that renders both her King, and the tidings as to the approach of her King, so delightful to the daughter of Sion.—V. g.

[3] Literally, *the son of one who bears the yoke;* rendered accurately by the Vulgate, which Bengel has followed here, *filium subjugalis.* He has not been equally exact in his German Version.—(I. B.)

[4] BC Origen read, as Beng., ἐπεκάθισεν, *He sat :* abcd also have ' sedebat :' D has ἐκάθητο. Vulg. has *imposuerunt;* and so Rec. Text ἐπεκάθισαν, *they set* Him thereon. This last plainly comes through Harmonists from Luke xix. 35, ἐπεβίβασαν, *they set* Jesus thereon.—ED.

[5] That is, His disciples *helped Him to mount,* which harmonises the statements, that *He sat* upon the colt, in Matt., and that *His disciples set Him on,* in Luke.—ED.

9.[1] *Ὡσαννά, Hosanna*) i.e. הרשיעה נא, *Save, I pray.* The LXX. render Psalm cxviii. (cxvii.) 25—ὦ Κύριε σῶσον δή· ὦ Κύριε εὐόδωσον δή,—*O Lord, do save: O Lord, do give prosperity.* The words, Ἰησοῦς (*Jesus*) in ver. 11, נושע (*having salvation*) in Zechariah ix. 9, and ὡσαννά in the present verse, are all cognate terms.—τῷ, κ.τ.λ., *to the,* etc.) We sing Hosanna, say they (as was foretold by the prophets), to the Son of David. Agreeable to the account given by the Evangelists of our Lord's entry, is that which Isidore Clarius says that he heard from a certain Jew, viz., that these words, "*Hosanna! Blessed is He that cometh,*" etc., were customarily said by the priests, when victims were offered for sacrifice. And the formula, Hosanna, was so frequently uttered, that they even gave that name to the branches which were carried about on the Feast of Tabernacles.[2] —εὐλογημένος, κ.τ.λ., *blessed,* etc.) Thus the LXX. in Psalm cxviii. (cxvii.) 26, which psalm formed part of the *Hallel,* or Paschal hymn, which they would have to recite in a few days' time.—ἐν ὀνόματι, *in the name*) These words should be construed with εὐλογημένος (*blessed*), according to the Hebrew accents.[3]—

---

[1] οἱ προάγοντες—ἀκολουθοῦντες, *that went before—and that followed*) Of whom *the former* had gone from the city to meet Him; *the latter* had gathered themselves together to Jesus, either at Jericho or elsewhere, as He was passing along.—V. g.

[2] Hartwell Horne says on this subject: "During the continuance of this feast, they carried in their hands branches of palm trees, olives, citrons, myrtles, and willows (Lev. xxiii. 40; Neh. viii. 15; 2 Macc. x. 7); singing, *Hosanna, save I beseech thee* (Ps. cxviii. 25); in which words they prayed for the coming of the Messiah. These branches also bore the name of Hosanna, as well as all the days of the Feast. In the same manner was Jesus Christ conducted into Jerusalem by the believing Jews, who, considering Him to be the promised Messiah, expressed their boundless joy at finding in Him the accomplishment of those petitions which they had so often offered to God for His coming, at the Feast of Tabernacles. (Matt. xxi. 8, 9.) During its continuance, they walked in procession round the altar with the above-mentioned branches in their hands, amid the sound of trumpets, singing Hosanna; and on the last, or seventh day of the Feast, they compassed the altar seven times. This was called the Great Hosanna. To this last ceremony St John probably alludes in Rev. vii. 9, 10, where he describes the saints as standing before the Throne, "*clothed with white robes, and palms in their hands; and saying, Salvation to our God, which sitteth upon the throne, and unto the Lamb.*"—(I. B.)

[3] *i.e.* Bengel would render it, "*Blessed in the name of the Lord,* etc." In

ἐν τοῖς ὑψίστοις, *in the highest*) Succour [us], O Thou who art in the highest.

10. Λέγουσα, *saying*) sc. *from amazement.*—τίς, κ.τ.λ.., *who?* etc.) The chief personage is not immediately seen in a large concourse; nor had the Jews been accustomed to see Jesus journeying except on foot.

11. Ὁ προφήτης, *the Prophet*) Jesus was first acknowledged as a Prophet, then as Priest and King.—ὁ ἀπὸ Ναζαρέτ, *of Nazareth*) This was a customary appellation [for Him].

12. Ἐξέβαλε, *cast out*)[1] though He was meek, and had been just called so in ver. 5. In the early part of His ministry, our Lord had purified the temple; see John ii. 14. Those who profaned it had, however, returned; and now, when near the end of His course, He purifies it once more, though it was soon to be destroyed; see ch. xxiii. 38.—πάντας, *all*) A great miracle. Even a large body of soldiers would not have ventured to attempt it. —τοὺς πωλοῦντας, κ.τ.λ., *those who sold*, etc.) They had wished to offer every accommodation for public worship, especially at the time of the Passover; but by degrees they appear to have pushed their licence further.—ἐν τῷ ἱερῷ,[2] *in the temple*) and indeed in its uttermost part, the court of the Gentiles; where the Gentiles [or *nations*] were wont *to pray*. See Mark xi. 17.

a note to his German Version, he says, "That is, *Let him, who cometh here, be in the name of the* LORD *blessed*." For some account of the Hebrew Accents, see p. 132, f.n. 5.—(I. B.)

But Engl. Ver., "Cometh in the name of the Lord:" joining ἐν ὀνόματι with ἐρχόμενος.—ED.

[1] This *casting out* did not occur on that very day, a day so full of grace and joy; but when men refused to obey the *intimation* conveyed by His eyes and *look* (of which Mark, ch. xi. 11, makes mention: [in the 'eventide' of the same day "Jesus entered the temple, and *looked* round about upon all things," and not until the morrow He "began to cast out them that sold." —ED.]), the Lord on the following day exhibited more severe specimens of His most just indignation. Comp. with this, Mark xi. 15.—*Harm.*, p. 447.

[2] The fuller reading, ἐν τῷ ἱερῷ τοῦ Θεοῦ, which the larger Ed. had pronounced to be an inferior reading, is regarded as almost equal in authority to that of the text by the margin of the Ed. 2 and the Germ. Vers.—E. B.

There is no primary authority for the fuller reading here. Εἰς τὸ ἱερόν, omitting Θεοῦ *in the beginning of the sentence*, is read by Lachm., with BL*b* Orig. Hilar. 713, Memph. and Theb. Versions. *Dac* Vulg. and Rec. Text add τοῦ Θεοῦ.—ED.

13. Ὁ οἶκός Μου οἶκος προσευχῆς κληθήσεται· ὑμεῖς δὲ αὐτὸν ἐποιήσατε σπήλαιον λῃστῶν, *My house shall be called (a or the) house of prayer; but ye have made it a den of thieves.*—The LXX., in Isaiah lvi. 7, have—ὁ γὰρ οἶκός Μου, οἶκος προσευχῆς κληθήσεται πᾶσι τοῖς Ἔθνεσιν, *My house shall be called (a or the) house of prayer for all nations;* and in Jeremiah vii. 11, μὴ σπήλαιον λῃστῶν ὁ οἶκός Μου; *is My house become a den of thieves?*—προσευχῆς, *of prayer*) Prayer is the principal part of public worship; see 1 Kings viii.; therefore prayer is put before the apostolic ministry of the Word in Acts vi. 4. The synagogues also were places for teaching and houses of prayer as well. In the temple there was more *prayer*, in the synagogues more *teaching*.—σπήλαιον λῃστῶν, *a den of thieves*) A severe and proverbial expression, used of a place which admits all infamous characters and all profane things. He does not say, A *market-place*. In a den, thieves do not so much attack others, as house themselves.

14. Ἐν τῷ ἱερῷ, *in the temple*) The right use of the temple; which was found fault with by His adversaries, who tolerated the abuse of the temple. No one else ever performed miracles in the temple; this was peculiar to the Messiah.

15. Τὰ θαυμάσια, *the wonderful things*) see ver. 12, 14.

16. Ἀκούεις, κ.τ.λ., *dost Thou hear?* etc.) Every thing which is not commonplace and traditional, is too much for hypocrites.¹—θηλαζόντων, *sucklings*) who might be as much as three years old.² See 2 Maccabees vii. 27.

---

¹ νηπίων) They who to the world seem still infants, may notwithstanding have their mouths opened to utterance by Divine power. We may suppose that the little children in this instance caught up the words of those of riper age (with which view, comp. ver. 9): and yet that circumstance was not without being valued in the sight of God. Only let one not be wanting to his fellow in setting a good example: the Lord will take care of the rest, nay, indeed He will take care of all things.—V. g.

² The passage in Maccabees runs thus:—" O my son, have pity upon me that bare thee nine months in my womb, and *gave thee suck three years*, and nourished thee, and brought thee up unto this age." The same practice still prevails in the East. In Persia, male children are often kept at the breast till three years of age, and are never taken from it till two years and two months. In India the period is precisely three years. In 2 Chron. xxxi. 16, no provision is assigned for the children of Priests and Levites until after three years of age, which gives additional weight to the supposition that

17. Αὐτοὺς, *them*) Whose perversity has just been mentioned.
18. Ἐπείνασε, *He hungered*) though He was the King of Glory, see ver. 5. Wondrous humiliation!
19. Συκῆν μίαν, *a certain fig-tree*) the only one in that place.—ἦλθεν, *He came*) sc. as the road led by it. The fig-tree appears to have stood in a place of public resort. Our Lord's partaking of refreshment in public is illustrated also by John iv. 6, 7. [*i.e.* at Jacob's Well. See Gnomon in loc.]—ἐπ᾽ αὐτὴν, *near to it*[1])—λέγει, κ.τ.λ., *says*, etc.) By that very act He meets the difficulty which some might have otherwise experienced from astonishment at the Lord's being hungry, and coming to a tree without fruit.[2] He was wont to display at the same time the greatest proofs of both His manhood and His Godhead; see John xi. 35, 40.[3]—μηκέτι ἐκ σοῦ καρπὸς γένηται εἰς

they were not weaned till that time. Amongst the ancient Greeks, also, it appears that mothers suckled their children till a comparatively late period. —(I. B.)

[1] εἰ μὴ φύλλα μόνον) It is better to exhibit and produce nothing at all, than merely *leaves*. Reflect, O man, what kind of a tree thou art.—V. g.

[2] Viz. That as God He should be hungry at all, or if hungry, that He should not create fruit.—ED.

[3] Such instances, for example, were:—The humble condition of His nativity, on the one hand; the testimony of the angels, on the other:

His circumcision, and yet His receiving the name Jesus (expressive of Godhead and salvation):

His purification, and yet at the same time the Hymns of Simeon and Anna:

His dwelling at despised Nazareth, and yet His thereby fulfilling the prophecy:

His obedience to His parents, and yet the specimen of noble gravity exhibited in a boy twelve years old:

His baptism; and, on the other hand, the protest of John, the very becoming reply of Jesus, the Voice from heaven, the Spirit of GOD descending on Him:

The Hunger and Temptation; and, on the other hand, the ministry of angels:

His informing them of His approaching Passion, followed however by His Transfiguration on the Mount:

His paying the tribute-money at Capernaum, and yet His declaration as to the Son's being free, His miracle in the case of the fish and the coin:

His washing the feet, yet declaring Himself Master and Lord:

His being taken prisoner, yet declaring I am He!

His Cross, yet the royal inscription over it:

His death and burial, yet the miracles, accompanied with the testimony of the centurion.—*Harm. Gosp.*, p. 455.

τὸν αἰῶνα, *let no fruit grow on thee henceforward for ever*) The Old Testament contains many miracles of vengeance: the evangelical history, at its close, this almost alone; cf. Gnomon on ch. viii. 32.—καρπὸς, *fruit*) And therefore it was not to receive any more sap in vain. Such was the punishment of the Jews; see Luke xiii. 6. This is an example of what *malediction* is.— ἐξηράνθη, *was dried up*) Its outward appearance was changed; its leaves shrivelled, or even fell off.

21. Ἀποκριθεὶς δὲ ὁ Ἰησοῦς εἶπεν, κ.τ.λ., *but Jesus answering, said*, etc.) Our Lord frequently led the disciples from admiration of miracles to things more profitable for salvation; see Luke x. 20.—πίστιν, *faith*) The nature of Faith is declared by its opposite, which is *Doubt*.—τῷ ὄρει τούτῳ, *to this mountain*) sc. that mentioned in ver. 1 [*i.e.*, the Mount of Olives]. A proverbial expression.—τὴν θάλασσαν, *the sea*) which was far from Jerusalem. Though such things have not hitherto been fulfilled; they may nevertheless be fulfilled hereafter.

22. Αἰτήσητε ἐν τῇ προσευχῇ, *ye shall ask in prayer*[1]) see Mark xi. 24. Miracles are performed by *the prayers* of the faithful.—λήψεσθε, *ye shall receive*, etc.) sc. as a gift. Thus, in Mark xi. 23, 24, ἔσται αὐτῷ, κ.τ.λ., *he shall have*, etc.

23. Προσῆλθον Αὐτῷ, κ.τ.λ., *came unto Him*, etc.) This was the solemn[2] question, which occasioned the final trial.—οἱ ἀρχιερεῖς, *the chief priests*) who considered their right to be invaded.— λέγοντες, κ.τ.λ., *saying*, etc.) The morose scepticism of His adversaries now at length demands credentials for the Son and Heir's caring for His vineyard; see ver. 37, 38. They thought that Jesus had no call to teach, since He was neither a Priest nor a Levite.—ποίᾳ ἐξουσίᾳ; *by what authority?*) divine or human.— ταῦτα, *these things*) sc. teaching; cf. διδάσκοντι, *as He was teaching*, and Mark xi. 27.[3]

24. Ἀποκριθεὶς δὲ ὁ Ἰησοῦς, *but Jesus answered*, etc.) A suitable mode of answering those who tempted Him.—ἐρωτήσω ὑμᾶς κἀγὼ, κ.τ.λ., *I will also ask you*, etc.) Thus also in ch. xxii. 41.

---

[1] The relation of faith to prayer is the same as that of fire to flame. —V. g.

[2] Solennis quæstio, "Their *customary* question." Acts iv. 7, and vii. 27. —ED.

[3] τίς, *who*) viz. of the order of the chief priests, or other rulers?—V. g.

Mosheim rightly observes, "Those expositors are mistaken, who imagine that Christ had no other object in this question than to silence His adversaries."—*Oration on Christ the only model for the imitation of Theologians*, p. 17.—ἵνα, *one*) and that too connected with your own question; *one*, after you have asked Me so many things, both now and heretofore. John the Baptist, though without a human call, could be and was a prophet; therefore also Jesus. If they had acknowledged the baptism of His forerunner, they would have acknowledged the authority of Christ; but since they did not acknowledge John (see ver. 32), they could not believe in Jesus. Nor did they deserve that any further communications should be thrown away by Him on their pride and unbelief. To him that hath is given; from him that hath not is taken away.

25. Τὸ βάπτισμα, *the baptism*) *i.e.* the whole mission: cf. further on in the verse, "οὐκ ἐπιστεύσατε;" "*did ye not believe?*"—ἐξ οὐρανοῦ, *from heaven*) *i.e.* from God. An instance of Metonomy of a reverential character.—διελογίζοντο, *they reasoned with themselves*) That is an evil mind which, instead of looking at the truth in a divine matter, assumes that which suits its purpose.—αὐτῷ, *him*) sc. bearing witness in My favour.

26. Φοβούμεθα, *we fear*) They were unwilling to confess their fear.—τὸν ὄχλον, *the multitude*) The multitude was scarcely likely to proceed at once to the extremity which the chief priests dreaded, yet it burned with ardent zeal in favour of John. And the Jewish population was wont, under sudden impulses, to assail, with the utmost violence, those who uttered, or were supposed to utter, impious things.—προφήτην, *a prophet*) sent from heaven, which had not happened for a long while.

27. Οὐκ οἴδαμεν, *we do not know*) A forced confession of most disgraceful ignorance.[1]—οὐδὲ, κ.τ.λ., *neither*, etc.) A repulse rare and just, by which itself Jesus proves His divine *authority*.[2]— ὑμῖν, *to you*) you unbelievers, who do not ask for the sake of learning. He gave them a clue by which to ascertain

---

[1] In which, however, the proud at times prefer seeking a refuge, rather than yield themselves up to the truth. The Wicked is caught in (his own) snare.—V. g.

[2] It would not have been becoming that more should be given to one who hath not.—V. g.

that authority; see ch. xxii. 43. He had often *told* them before.

28.[1] Τέκνα δύο, *two sons*) A specimen of two classes.[2]—προσελθὼν, *having come to*) sc. kindly.—τῷ πρώτῳ, *the first*) who went before the other; see ver. 31 ["*Go into* the kingdom of God *before* you].

30. Τῷ ἑτέρῳ, *the other*) Who, in a different point of view, is called the *eldest* in Luke xv. 25.—ὡσαύτως, *in like manner*) with undoubtedly the same spirit. Their calling was equal.—ἐγώ, *I*) sc. ὑπάγω, *go*; cf. in Acts ix. 10, the reply of Ananias, ἰδοὺ, ἐγώ, *Behold, I*, sc. am here; and in S. V. of Judges xiii. 11, that of the angel to Manoah, ἐγώ, *I*, sc. am.—Κύριε, *Lord*) cf. ch. vii. 22.

31.[3] Εἰς, *into*, or *as regards*) the kingdom of heaven.

32. Ἐν ὁδῷ δικαιοσύνης, *in the way of righteousness*) "The way of righteousness" expresses more than "A righteous way."—

---

[1] τί δὲ ὑμῖν δοκεῖ, *But what think ye?*) After that the Jews had declined to commit themselves, by expressing an opinion concerning the baptism of John, the Saviour defends Himself along with John, thereby reproving the unbelief of the chief priests.—*Harm.*, p. 460.

[2] In the dialogue which Athanasius is said to have had at Nicæa with Arius, the First Son is referred to the Jews, the Second, to the Gentiles.—See *App. Crit.*, ed. ii., p. 131.—E. B.

In ver. 31, Lachm. reads ὁ ὕστερος with B. Ὁ ἔσχατος is read by D*abd*, MSS. Amiat. (the oldest existing), and Fuld. and Forojuliensis of the Vulg. However Jerome, though editing, as appears from his commentary, 'novissimus,' yet states that good copies have 'primus' (ὁ πρῶτος): *c* also, and some less ancient copies of the Vulg., agree with Rec. Text, ὁ πρῶτος. But Hil. 717 has 'junior.' The ὁ ὕστερος or ἔσχατος, as being the *more difficult* reading, would be more likely to be changed by a corrector into ὁ πρῶτος, than *vice versa*. Jerome vii. 168e explains the former reading, 'novissimus,' thus:—"The Jews understood the truth, but shrunk back, and would not say what they thought; just as, though knowing the baptism of John to be from heaven, they would not acknowledge in words that it was so." They did not like, I think, to repeat again the same reply as before in ver. 27, οὐκ οἴδαμεν, therefore they doggedly, in spite of convictions, replied, ὁ ὕστερος. However, the words, Λέγουσιν ὁ ὕστερος: λέγει αὐτοῖς ὁ Ἰησοῦς, seem to be an interpolation: for Origen, who seldom passes over difficult passages, takes no notice of these words; and besides, ὕστερος, as an adjective, is found nowhere in the New Testament except in 1 Tim. iv. 1.—ED.

[3] ὁ πρῶτος, *the first*) Work without words is better than splendid words unaccompanied with work; and also it is better to adopt a praiseworthy course subsequently, rather than not at all.—V. g.

τελῶναι, *publicans*) who were unjust.—αἱ πόρναι, *the harlots*) who were unchaste.—It may be asked whether these, and consequently women in general, and also infants, were baptized by John: cf. Acts xvi. 15.—οὐ μετεμελήθητε, *did not alter your way of thinking.*¹—ὕστερον, *afterwards*) when you had seen their example.

33. Οἰκοδεσπότης, *a householder*) who had a large family [sc. of servants, labourers, etc.]—ἀμπελῶνα, *a vineyard*) i.e. the Jewish Church.—φραγμὸν, *a hedge*) i.e. the law.²—ληνὸν, *a winepress*) i.e. Jerusalem.—πύργον, *a tower*) i.e. the temple; see ver. 23.³—ἀπεδήμησεν, *went into a far country*) The time of Divine silence is meant, when men act according to their own will and pleasure [pro arbitrio]: cf. ch. xxv. 14, and Mark xiii. 34.

34. Ὅτε δὲ ἤγγισεν ὁ καιρὸς τῶν καρπῶν, *But when the season of the fruit drew near*) Comp. John iv. 35. Here also lurks the reason why the Messiah had not come sooner.—τοὺς δούλους, *His servants*) Servants here represent the extraordinary and greater ministers of God; labourers, the ordinary.⁴—τοὺς καρποὺς, *the*

---

¹ Bengel's words are, *non mutastis sententiam.* In his German Version he renders it, "*habt euch hernach nicht anders bedacht,*" "*have not after that changed your mind.*"
In his Harmony, however, he renders it, "*thatet ihr dennoch nicht busse,*" "*notwithstanding did not repent.*" E. V. has "*repented not afterward.*"—(I. B.)

² In the note in the Germ. Vers., Bengel interprets the *Hedge*, with a slight change of the figure, of the separation of the people of Israel from all the nations of the earth, including at the same time the idea of the divine protection afforded to the former against the latter: *the Winepress*, the order of the priesthood: the *Tower*, the Kingdom (Theocracy). We should not, however, on account of this difference between his former and his latter views in this instance, conclude that such details in *Parables* are mere *empty flowers of ornament.* The parts of an enigma, however abstruse, are not idle. Comp. what is said below in Gnomon on ch. xxii. 11.—E. B.

³ ἐξέδοτο αὐτὸν, *let it out*) This is the ground on which rests *the power of the Church.* The vineyard was *let out* to husbandmen. They who preside in either political or ecclesiastical offices, can indeed act according to their own pleasure, and, like the holders of the vineyard, consult only their own private interests: they can maltreat the servants of the Lord: they can wantonly wrest aside the laws of the Church according to their caprice: and can in this way, though not now as then kill the Heir Himself, yet thrust Him out for some time from His own proper place. But—the time of Visitation is coming at last.—V. g.

⁴ Of whom the *former* are for the most part received badly by the *latter*,

fruits) understand, of *the householder*, or rather, *of the vineyard*.

35. Ἔδειραν, *they beat*) The LXX. generally put ἐκδέρω, *to skin off*, only once δέρω, *to skin*, for the Hebrew פשט in the sense of *to flay*. They never use the verb otherwise. The Old Vocabulary renders the Latin "*excorio*" (*to skin*) by the Greek, ἀποδέρω. But δαίρω signifies *to beat* in Arrian, B. iii., and Epictetus, ch. xix. and xxii. Whence Suidas and Favorinus draw a clear distinction between the two verbs, δέρω and δαίρω. Hesychius also renders δείραντες by ἐκδείραντες, and ἔδειραν by ἐξέδειραν, which he further explains by ἐξεδερμάτησαν, *they flayed*. Old glosses, however, render δέρω by τύπτω, *to beat*: and Aristophanes, in the Wasps (ed. Dindorf, 485), says, "Η δέδοκταί μοι δέρεσθαι καὶ δέρειν δι' ἡμέρας, "I have indeed determined to be beaten, and to beat all the day long,"—where the Scholiast says, "δέρεσθαι and δέρειν" are for τύπτεσθαι (*to be beaten*). In fact, the verbs, κεφαλαιόω (*to capitate*), τραχηλίζω (*to jugulate*), γαστρίζω (*to stomachize*), and thus also δέρω (*to skin* or *hide*), have a wide signification, implying the infliction of injury on the *head, throat, stomach*, or *skin* respectively, either by removing them altogether, or else by striking them. The desire to avoid ambiguity induced the later Greeks to write either δέρω or δαίρω, and thence, in this passage, ἔδηραν.[1]

Ἔδειραν—ἀπέκτειναν—ἐλιθοβόλησαν, *beat—slew—stoned*) An ascending climax, in which the third degree is an atrocious species of the second; cf. Mark xii. 3, 4, and Luke xx. 10, 11, 12, where a greater number of intermediate degrees occurs.

36.[2] Πλείονας, *more*) sc. superior (*potiores*), like the Hebrew רבים (*great* or *numerous*): superior, certainly in number, and without doubt also in virtue, dignity, etc. The increase of calling[3] is no sign of a more faithful people.

inasmuch as these take it ill that they should be disturbed in their quiet holding of the vineyard.—V. g.

[1] So the uncial Cod. U, etc.—ED.

[2] πάλιν ἀπέστειλεν ἄλλους) We may regard the servants *first sent* as meaning the Prophets of the middle period, which is called that of the Kings, the servants *subsequently sent*, as meaning those who flourished about the time of the Captivity in Babylon.—V. g.

[3] *i.e.* An increase in the number of those who are sent to call men to repentance.—(I B.)

37. Ὕστερον, *last of all*) Cf. Hebrews i. 1.—ἐντραπήσονται, *they will reverence*) *i.e.* they were in duty bound to do so.

38. Οὗτός ἐστιν ὁ Κληρονόμος, *this is the Heir*) They might have known Him to be the Heir, and yet they opposed His right.— δεῦτε, ἀποκτείνωμεν Αὐτὸν, *come, let us kill Him*) Thus the LXX. in Gen. xxxvii. 20.—κατασχῶμεν, *let us seize upon*) They thought to have done so after Christ was slain: see ch. xxvii. 63, 64.

39. Ἐξέβαλον—καὶ ἀπέκτειναν, *they cast* Him *out—and slew* Him) St Mark reverses the order of these verbs. They rejected the Lord Jesus both *before* His death, by denying His right (ver. 23), and even more so, by delivering Him up to a Gentile tribunal; and also *after* His death, by a hostile interference with His sepulture; see ch. xxvii. 63, 64, etc.[1]

41. Κακοὺς κακῶς ἀπολέσει αὐτοὺς, *He will miserably destroy those wicked men*[2]) An act of retaliation.[3] He will do so *miserably* with reference to the miserable and wicked husbandmen; cf. in Hebrews x. 29, χείρονος—τιμωρίας SORER *punishment*.— ἐκδώσεται, *will let out*) In the Church gathered from the Gentiles, the ministers and overseers enjoy great liberty.[4] The same verb occurs in ver. 33.—καιροῖς, *seasons*) sc. different seasons.— αὐτῶν, *their, of them*) referring to καρποὺς, *the fruits*, in ver. 34.

42. Ἐν ταῖς γραφαῖς, *in the Scriptures, Writings*). There is one volume which deserves the name of "Writing"[5] (*Scripture*), and "Book." The rest deserve to be valued only so far as they aid mankind in understanding and obeying this One Book, and are conformed to that Archetype.—λίθον—ἐν ὀφθαλμοῖς, ἡμῶν, *the stone—in our eyes*) This is an exact quotation from Ps. cxviii.[6] 22, 23, as rendered by the LXX. This Psalm was

---

[1] Ver. 40. ὅταν οὖν ἔλθῃ) This *coming* was accomplished in the destruction of Jerusalem.—V. g.

[2] In the original the words are, "κακοὺς κακῶς—*male malos*," which cannot be rendered in English so as to give the full force of the words: perhaps "*ill* (adverb) them *ill* (adjective)" is about the nearest approach that can be made—or, He will *wretchedly* destroy those *wretches*.—(I. B.)

[3] *Talio*—*i.e.* doing *ill* to *ill* doers.—(I. B.)

[4] Such as the Jewish Church did not enjoy, as being but local and elementary.—ED.

[5] In Greek and Latin the same word signifies both *Writings* and *Scriptures*.—(I. B.)

[6] Numbered cxvii. in S. V.—(I. B.)

particularly well known. See Gnomon on ver. 9 (comp. ch. xxvi. 30).—ἀπεδοκίμασαν, *rejected*) They did not consider Him as even a fit stone or worthy member of the Church at all.—παρὰ Κυρίου ἐγένετο, *is the Lord's doing*) This is known to be the case, from the importance of the matter, and the disagreement of the builders.—αὕτη, *this* [Lat. *hæc*, Fr. *cette*]) The feminine for the neuter: a Hebraism. *This*, sc. thing. In Psalm cii. 19[1] the LXX. render זאת (*this*, fem.) by αὕτη, thus preserving the gender of the original: as also in the analogous phrases in Ps. cxix.[2] 50, 56; Judg. xv. 7 and xxi. 3, where ἐγενήθη αὕτη (*is* THIS *come to pass*) occurs. Cf. 1 (in S. V. 3) Kings iii. 18.—καὶ ἔστι, *and is*) sc. היא, *it* (fem.), *i.e.* אבן, the *stone*, itself is wonderful.—θαυμαστή, *wonderful*[3]) sc. on account of the great glory which it has obtained. The Evangelist uses the feminine, because he was unwilling to depart from the LXX.—ἐν ὀφθαλμοῖς ἡμῶν, *in our eyes*) sc. of us believers [1 Pet. ii. 7].

43. Αὐτῆς, *thereof*) sc. the kingdom.[4]

44. Ὁ πεσὼν ἐπὶ, κ.τ.λ., *whosoever shall fall on*, etc.) He falleth on this Stone (sc. Christ in His humiliation) who stumbles (offendit) by not believing, whilst the Gospel is being preached; but this Stone (sc. Christ in His glory) falleth on him, who is crushed by His sudden coming to judgment. Both happen especially to the Jews, and also to the Gentiles. See 2 Thess. i. 8, and Dan. ii. 34, 45.—λικμήσει, *shall scatter, dissolve, dissipate, reduce to dust*) The verb λικμᾶν signifies to *scatter*, as when chaff is given to the winds. See the LXX., who employ this verb in Job xxvii. 21 for the Hebrew שער, *to sweep away in a storm*; in Dan. ii. 44, for אסף, *to destroy*; and repeatedly elsewhere for זרה, *to scatter* or *disperse*.

45.[5] Λέγει, *He is speaking*) They perceived that Jesus had not yet concluded what He had to say. See ch. xxii. 1.

---

[1] These are the Hebrew numbers. In S. V. it is ci. 18; in E. V. cii. 18.—(I. B.)

[2] Numbered cxviii. in S. V.—(I. B.)

[3] Bengel in both instances uses the word *mirabilis*, which implies in this place *admiration* as well as wonder.—(I. B.)

[4] Even though thou mayest be a good tree, yet thy fruit is not thine own, but that of the vineyard. Rom. xi. 17.—V. g.

[5] περὶ αὐτῶν) as being the 'husbandmen' and the 'builders.'—V. g.

CHAPTER XXII.

1. Ἀποκριθείς, *answering*) Not only he who has been questioned, but he also to whom a reason for speaking has been given, may rightly be said to answer.—πάλιν, *again*) construe this word with ἐν παραβολαῖς, *in parables, i.e.* with the design of putting forth more.

3. Καλέσαι τοὺς κεκλημένους, *to call those that had been called*) The first call was before the wedding; the second, on the day of its celebration.

4. Ἄριστον, *dinner*) sc. with regard to the Jews in the early time of the New Testament dispensation, but *supper* with regard to the saints at the actual consummation of the spiritual marriage: see Rev. xix. 9.[1] This parable embraces the history of the Church from the one time to the other.—ἡτοίμασα, *I have prepared*) Our salvation is effected, not by our power, but by that of God.—σιτιστὰ, *fatlings*) a general word.—πάντα, *all things*) For there are many things besides oxen and fatlings.—δεῦτε, *come*) sc. forthwith.

5. Ἀμελήσαντες, *making light of, neglecting*) This is a greater offence than the previous, *They would not come*. They ought

---

[1] For although we freely grant that by the term γάμος at times is meant, according to the Scripture style, any *solemn feast* whatever; yet that this more general meaning holds good in this passage, is by some concluded, from the fact that mention of the *Bride* is wanting here, with more confidence than is warranted. For instance, in ch. xxv. 1, etc., where the *Bridegroom* is once or twice mentioned, the mention of the *Bride* also is not introduced even by the smallest word. Moreover, I feel fully persuaded that *the analogy of the texts*, Matt. xxii. 2, 13, when compared with Rev. xix. 9, 20, requires the more strict signification in this place. Nor can I think that no weight is to be rested on the fact, that the word γάμος in that one parable is repeated *eight times*, and only once it is called ἄριστον. Finally, ἀγαθαὶ ἡμέραι γάμων καὶ εὐφροσύνης (Esth. ix. 22), lead to the meaning, *the* so-called *nuptial* (joyous) *life*, in general, more readily even than the expression here, ἐποίησε γάμους τῷ υἱῷ αὐτοῦ; not to mention that the very Feast of *Purim*, mentioned in the passage of Esther, plainly involves a remembrance of the *nuptials* (in the strict sense) celebrated *between the King and Esther*. Comp. ch. ii. 17, 18.—E. B.

to have *understood* (see Acts vii. 25), and to have watched.—ἀπῆλθον, *they departed*) leaving even the city, which was therefore burnt; see ver. 7. He who does not answer the call, loses even those advantages which he previously had possessed.—τὸν ἴδιον—αὐτοῦ, *his own—his*) Egoism.¹—ἀγρὸν—ἐμπορίαν, *field—merchandise*) The one busied with immoveable, the other with moveable goods; the one detained by a false contentment (αὐτάρκεια²), the other by the desire of acquiring more.

6. Οἱ δὲ λοιποί, *and the remnant*) Who did not wish to appear to have *made light of it*.³—ὕβρισαν, *treated* them *with insult and injury*) see 2 Chron. xxx. 10 ; 1 Tim. i. 13 ; Heb. x. 29.

7. Ἀκούσας δὲ ὁ βασιλεύς, *but when the king heard thereof*) The transgression of the disobedient was a *crying* sin.—τὴν πόλιν αὐτῶν, *their city*) sc. that of the murderers.—στρατεύματα, *armies*) sc. the Roman forces.⁴—φονεῖς, *murderers*) The chief crime provokes the whole punishment; see Amos ii.—αὐτῶν, *of them*) viz. of those murderers and despisers.

8. Τότε, κ.τ.λ.., *then*, etc.) see Acts xiii. 46.—λέγει, κ.τ.λ.., *saith He*, etc.) The Lord frequently reveals the principles of His counsel to His servants.—ἕτοιμός ἐστιν, *is ready*) and will not be dispensed with on account of the ingratitude of them which were bidden.⁵—οὐκ ἦσαν ἄξιοι, *were not worthy*) cf. Acts xiii. 46. No one is considered unworthy until the offer has been made to

---

¹ In the original, "ἴδιον αὐτοῦ, *proprium : suum*) *Suitas*." This is one of those passages which it is far more easy to understand than to translate. There is a connection between the expression "*Suitas*" (a word, I believe, coined by Bengel for the occasion) and *suum* immediately preceding. The meaning is, that the words, ἴδιον αὐτοῦ, both refer to *Self*, and imply a recognition of *Self* as the object of thought and consideration, apart from, independent of, in contradistinction, nay in preference to, GOD—in fact, a state or feeling the very opposite to that involved in the Apostle's words (1 Cor. vi. 19, 20), *Ye are* NOT YOUR OWN: *ye are bought with a price. Therefore glorify* GOD *in your body, and in your spirit*, WHICH ARE GOD's.—(I. B.)

² See p. 150, f. n. 3, and on Matt. x. 9.—(I. B.)

³ And who did not attend either to *farming* or *merchandise*. To wit, those who have less of hinderances in their way not rarely sin the more grievously for that very reason, when they thrust themselves into sacred things, by their perverse mode of behaving with respect to them.—V. g.

⁴ Who were let loose upon Jerusalem forty years from this time.—V. g.

⁵ The Wedding *is* truly even still ready for the guests who are willing to come.—V. g.

and refused by him: by doing which he betrays himself. The past tense, *were* not *worthy*, is used to show that the opportunity of the unworthy has passed away.

9. Τὰς διεξόδους, *the cross ways*) It would be pleasant to see a map of the journeys of all the apostles through the world, like that of St Paul's Voyages and Travels.—ὁδὸς signifies *the whole road*,—διέξοδοι, *the parts*, and as it were, *branches of it*.

10. Συνήγαγον, *brought together*) partly by *calling* them as they had been commanded, and partly by employing unjustifiable compulsion.—πονηροὺς τε καὶ ἀγαθοὺς, *both bad and good*) A proverbial mode, as it were, of expression.[1]

11. Ἄνθρωπον, *a man*) Some remarkable one amongst the many bad who were called, and yet not chosen; who is individually a sample of all such, one whom you would especially suppose to be chosen, and from whose not being chosen, the small number of the chosen is perceived. The singular number is emphatic; for the passage would otherwise have equally admitted of the plural.—ἔνδυμα γάμου, *a wedding garment*)[2] sc. the righteousness of Christ; see Gnomon on ch. vi. 33.

12. Ἑταῖρε, *comrade*) A word of ambiguous meaning, which is also applied to those with whom we are not on terms of intimacy or friendship.—πῶς, κ.τ.λ., *how*, etc.) by what culpable indulgence of the servants? by what audacity on thine own part? —[ἐφιμώθη, *he was speechless*) By this speechlessness [implying, as it does, that the lost perish altogether through their own fault] all objections whatever that are directed against Christianity are dissipated.—V. g.]

13. Διακόνοις, *attendants*) Servants, δοῦλοι, are sent forth; attendants, διάκονοι, wait at table; see John ii. 5.—ἐκβάλετε εἰς, κ.τ.λ., *cast him into*, etc.) This will take place a little before the nuptial evening; see Rev. xix. 20.

14.[3] Πολλοὶ γάρ, κ.τ.λ., *for many*, etc.) Our Lord adds this

---

[1] This is the aspect of the Church in the present day. It was not exactly such instructions as these that the King had given to His servants, ver. 9. No one is good before his call: but when the call has been duly accepted, all things are well.—V. g.

[2] Beng. states, in the note of the *Germ. Vers.* on this passage, that the persons themselves who were celebrating the marriage feast, distributed such garments to the guests.—E. B.

[3] ἐκεῖ ἔσται—πολλοὶ γάρ εἰσι κλητοί) Two expressions somewhat frequently

remark in His own person to the conclusion of the king's speech. Cf ὅτι, κ.τ.λ., *for*, etc., in Luke xvi. 8.—γὰρ, κ.τ.λ., *for*, etc.) This general sentiment is a proof, that this man without a wedding garment, and all who are like him, will be cast forth.

15. Τότε πορευθέντες οἱ Φαρισαῖοι, κ.τ.λ., *then went the Pharisees*, etc.) On the malignant spirit of our Lord's adversaries, see Mark xii. 12, 13; Luke xx. 20.

16. Μαθητὰς, *disciples*) With whom they thought that our Lord would deal less cautiously, and whose overthrow they thought would be attended with less disgrace to themselves.— Ἡρωδιανῶν, *of the Herodians*) who were especially attached to the party of Herod, and consequently to that of Cæsar, which the Pharisees viewed with aversion; see Josephus Antiq. xvii. 3; and see Mark iii. 6 and xii. 13. There might be, moreover, a variety of opinion amongst the Herodians themselves concerning holy things, Herod, etc.—ἀληθής—ἐν ἀληθείᾳ, *true—in truth*) Truth should be known and spoken. Truth is the agreement of things with the faculties of knowing, willing, speaking, and acting.—τὴν ὁδὸν τοῦ Θεοῦ, *the way of God*) A part of which way is the doctrine concerning what ought to be given to God. There is a striking antithesis here between Θεοῦ, *of God*—and ἀνθρώπων, *of men*.—οὐ γὰρ βλέπεις εἰς πρόσωπον, *for Thou regardest not the person*) They wished Jesus to deny that tribute ought to be given to Cæsar.[1] Truth truly estimates both things and persons; but he who regards persons easily betrays truth.

17. Ἔξεστι, *is it lawful?*) They do not merely say, is it *incumbent?* but, is it *lawful?* [not *must we?* but *may we?*] *i.e.* on account of what was due to God.—ἢ οὔ, *or not*) They demand a categorical answer.

18. Γνοὺς, *knowing*) sc. without delay, or instruction from any one.—ὑποκριταί! *hypocrites!*) Our Lord shows Himself to them *true*, as they had said; ver. 16.

20. Εἰκών, *image, likeness*) ἐπιγραφή, *letters inscribed*.

repeated by the Saviour, and therefore most worthy of consideration.— *Harm.*, p. 463, 464.

[1] Which tribute, either a short while before (comp. ch. xvii. 24) or at that very time, namely in the month Nisan, was being paid according to custom.—*Harm.*, p. 465.

21. 'Απόδοτε, *render*) sc. as it is just.—οὖν, *therefore*) In these days the coins of one country are used promiscuously in others, as happens with French money in Germany; but none except Roman money appears to have been current at that time in Judea But if the Jews had not been subject to Cæsar, they were not of such a disposition as to have employed foreign coin, especially when stamped with heathen likenesses (imaginibus).—καὶ, κ.τ.λ., *and,* etc.) The one duty is not, as you suppose, destroyed by the other. The things which are God's, those which have been set apart and dedicated to Him are not Cæsar's; but the things which are Cæsar's are, in some sort, also God's.[1]—τὰ τοῦ Θεοῦ, *the things that are God's*) whose cause you wish to appear to plead; see ver. 16.

22. 'Εθαύμασαν, *they marvelled*) And showed their astonishment at His safe and true answer.

23. Σαδδουκαῖοι, *Sadducees*) Towards the close of His earthly career all rise together against Jesus. The Sadducees are seldom mentioned by the Evangelists; on *that day* not even the Sadducees remained quiescent.—ἀνάστασιν, *resurrection*) It is clear that this article of faith was well known at that time, from the Evangelist not having added the words, " of the dead." And the adversaries of this article contravene it in various degrees, some by denying[2] altogether the immortality of the soul, others, its being joined again to its former body. And there may also have been a variety of error among the Sadducees themselves.

24. Τέκνα, *children*) sc. a son or a daughter, or more, see Deut. xxv. 5.

25. Παρ' ἡμῖν, *with us*) The Sadducees raise this doubt on a

---

[1] Very frequently human sagacity fastens only upon one side, whichever side it be, of Duties [having a twofold side or aspect]: true wisdom weighs all things at the same time and together. These hypocrites were thinking thus: tribute ought to be given *either* to God for the use of the Temple, *or else* to Cæsar. Jesus saith, It is right, according to divine law, that *both* be done. So also the Sadducees were thinking thus: If the resurrection be admitted, the wife must be given back *either* to the first brother, *or* to the second, etc. But Truth subjoins the reply, She is to be given back *not even to any one* out of them all.—V. g.

[2] The Wisdom of the world, like the barren figtree, fruitless and most beggarly, is in fact for the most part occupied in negations.—V. g.

circumstance, rare, and perhaps long since canvassed,[1] which might have been nearly as well raised from the case of any woman who had married more than one husband. The maintainers of errors frequently seek for a colour for them from things which are little or nothing to the point.

28. Τίνος, *whose*) She will, say they, be the wife either of all or of one: but none of them has a superior claim to the rest. Jesus answers (ver. 30) she will be the wife of none. The Pharisees also had divided and opposed those things which are Cæsar's, and those which are God's: He who is the Truth, affirms both in His reply to them: to the Sadducees He denies both. Earthly wisdom frequently precipitates itself into absurdity from an imperfect enumeration, even in an easy matter, of parts, not one of which escapes heavenly wisdom.—μὴ εἰδότες, κ.τ.λ., *not knowing*, etc.) This twofold ignorance is the mother of almost all errors. The resurrection of the dead rests on the power of God: and the belief in the resurrection rests on the Scriptures. Jesus refutes their *first* and fundamental error (πρῶτον ψεῦδος): which they did not suppose themselves to labour under at all. He first answers the argument by which they opposed the truth: then He proves the truth itself.—τὰς γραφὰς, *the Scriptures*) which clearly look to a future life; see ver. 31, 32. The Sadducees did not understand Moses: they did not receive the prophets who explain Moses.—τὴν δύναμιν τοῦ Θεοῦ, *the power of God*) The power of God will make man *equal to the angels*; see ver. 30. To be ignorant of God and His perfections is the fountain of error; see 1 Cor. xv. 34 [Rom. iv. 17, E. B.]

30. Οὔτε γαμοῦσιν, *neither marry*) sc. men —οὔτε ἐκγαμίζονται, *nor are given in marriage*) sc. women; cf. ver. 25.—ὡς ἄγγελοι τοῦ Θεοῦ, *as the angels of God*) The absurdity which the Sadducees supposed would apply to the righteous rather than the unrighteous, as no one could imagine that the unrighteous would enjoy the blessing of marriage. Our Lord therefore replies only concerning the righteous. The righteous will then be in the same condition as the angels of God,[2] without wedlock,

---

[1] But which had not heretofore been sufficiently and decidedly cleared up.—V. g.

[2] The unrighteous will be in the same condition as the sinful and fallen angels.—V. g.

meat and drink, etc. Elsewhere it is said that those who obtain the life to come, will be *like God:* but, since God has one Son and many sons, in this passage, where there is question concerning begetting, it is said that they will be as angels; and simultaneously the existence of angels also is defended against the Sadducees who ignored it.—εἰσί, *are*) sc. both men and women.

31.[1] Ὑμῖν, *unto you*) To *you* He says, not to *us.* They were not written for Christ.[2] To *you* the descendants of Abraham.

32. Ὁ Θεός, *the God*) see Ex. iii. 6. These words are not put only once, but three times, because Jacob did not hear the promise of God merely from Isaac, or Isaac merely from Abraham, but each of them separately also from God Himself; and Abraham's name was Divinely changed, Isaac's Divinely given, that of Israel Divinely added to Jacob: see Gen. xvii. 5, 19, xxxii. 28.—οὐκ ἔστι Θεὸς νεκρῶν,[3] *He is not God of the dead*) i.e., God *is not God of the dead.* There is an ellipsis as in Rom. iii. 29. The value of inferential[4] reasoning is seen by this example,—" *God is thine.*" This phrase expresses both a Divine gift and a human duty. The Divine gift (for that is considered in this passage) thus expressed, is infinite, everlasting, and one which could never be fully realized to us by an earthly life, however long or happy (see Ps. cxliv. 15, and Luke xvi. 25), much less by a pilgrimage of a few and evil days, such as were the lives of Abraham, Isaac, and above all, Jacob, compared with those of their ancestors,[5] who, nevertheless, had not ob-

---

[1] περὶ δὲ τῆς ἀναστάσεως) Jesus not merely refuted the objection of those in error, but also demonstrates the truth to them.—V. g.

[2] Nor were they written even for Abraham, Isaac, and Jacob, who had lived before that the Vision was vouchsafed to Moses, which was subsequently committed to writing.—V. g.

[3] The reading of E. M. is " οὐκ ἔστιν ὁ Θεὸς Θεὸς νεκρῶν," rendered in E. V. "God is not the God of the dead."—(I. B.) BL*Δbc* Vulg. omit the second Θεός: so Iren. Hil. 77, 484, 500, 722. But Orig. 3,828*b*; 829*b* support it, with the Rec. Text.—ED.

[4] Bengel means to say, that we are bound to receive not only what is actually written *totidem verbis* in Scripture, but also what may be logically inferred from the words of Holy Writ—not merely what "is contained therein," but also what "may be proved thereby."—(I. B.)

[5] Comp. Gen. xlvii. 9.—ED.

tained that promise. For it is not said wealth, long life, security, or, in short, the world is thine, but, *God is thine:* nor is it said God is thine for fifty, an hundred, or seven hundred years, but simply *God is thine.* When, therefore, God first declared Himself to Abraham to be his God, He conferred, and was acknowledged to have conferred, upon him the everlasting communion of Himself everlasting. And though the death of the body has intervened in the case of the patriarchs, it cannot last for ever, nor produce a long delay, long in comparison with everlasting life. For Abraham himself, the whole man, and all that is included under the name Abraham, that is, not only his soul but also his body, which also received the seal of the promise, *possesses* God. God, however, is not the God of that which is not: He is the Living God; they therefore who possess God must themselves also be living, and as to any portion of them in which life has been suspended, must revive for ever. The force of the formula is shown also in Gnomon on Heb. xi. 16, which passage is chiefly to this effect, " He hath prepared for them a city," and that principally in eternity; and therefore He is called *their God.* And this reasoning of Christ is sound, evident, and then heard for the first time : and most effectually proves both the immortality of the soul, and the resurrection of the body, against the Sadducees, who denied altogether the existence of spirits. The force, however, of the argument does not consist in the verb εἰμὶ, *I am,* nor in the use of its present tense at the time of Moses (for though it is expressed by St Matthew, it is not found in the parallel passages of St Mark or St Luke, or the original of Moses), but in the formula itself.[1] And these phrases, *My, Thy, His,* etc., God, are by far the most frequent. This passage, however, here cited against the Sadducees is furthermore the most striking of all of them, on the following grounds: (1) In it God speaks Himself, an irrefragable proof of its truth; (2) He speaks on the occasion of a most solemn and visible manifestation of Himself; (3) He speaks of Abraham, Isaac, and Jacob conjointly; (4) And indeed after their death, and that a long while after, at the very time of perform-

---

[1] For the possession of that which is everlasting implies everlasting possession, and everlasting possession involves everlasting duration.—(I. B.)

ing the promise to them, even in the persons of their descendants, which was a proof that these patriarchs had not in their own lifetime themselves obtained the promises. And thus, as we are told in Luke xx. 37, ΕΥΕΝ, ΚΑΙ, *Moses showed* the resurrection of the dead, *even Moses*, not only the prophets, in preference to whom, Moses was read publicly before the time of Antiochus.[1] At the same time, our Lord reduces to its proper shape the proverb of the Jews, who said, "God is not the God of the living but of the dead." See Axiom ix. of Alexander Morus, and the Dissertation of E. F. Cobius, on the force of this passage.

35. Εἷς ἐξ αὐτῶν, *one of them*) This man is less blamed by our Lord; wherefore he seems to have been led on by others.— νομικὸς, *a lawyer*) How great soever he was, and proud of that abundance of knowledge which he was now about to exhibit.—

---

[1] Hartwell Horne says, "The third part of the synagogue service was the *Reading of the Scriptures*, which included the reading of the whole law of Moses, and portions of the Prophets, and the Hagiographa or holy writings. (1.) The *Law* was divided into fifty-three, according to the Masorets, or, according to others, fifty-four *Paraschioth* or sections: for the Jewish year consisted of twelve lunar months, alternately of twenty-nine or thirty days, that is of fifty weeks and four days. The Jews, therefore, in their division of the law into *Paraschioth* or sections, had a respect to their intercalary year, which was every second or third, and consisted of thirteen months; so that the whole law was read over this year, allotting one *Parascha* or section to every Sabbath; and in common years they reduced the fifty-three or fifty-four sections to the number of the fifty Sabbaths, by reading two shorter ones together, as often as there was occasion. They began the course of reading on the first Sabbath after the Feast of Tabernacles; or rather, indeed, on the Sabbath-day before that, when they finished the last course of reading, they also made a beginning of the new course; that so, as the rabbies say, the devil might not accuse them to God of being weary of reading His law. (2.) The portions selected out of the Prophetical writings are termed *Haphtoroth.* When Antiochus Epiphanes conquered the Jews, about the year 163 before the Christian æra, he prohibited the public reading of the Law in the synagogues on pain of death. The Jews, in order that they might not be wholly deprived of the Word of God, selected from other parts of the Sacred Writings *fifty-four* portions, which were termed HAPHTORAS הפטרות (HaPHTORoTH), from פטר (PaTaR), he *dismissed, let loose, opened* —for though the Law was *dismissed* from their synagogues, and was *closed* to them by the edict of this persecuting king, yet the *prophetic writings,* not being under the *interdict*, were left *open;* and therefore they used them in place of the others."—(I. B.)

νομικός = γραμματεύς, *a scribe*, in Luke xi. 45, 44, 53; and νομοδιδάσκαλος, *a doctor of the law*, in Luke v. 17, 21.

37. Ἀγαπήσεις, κ.τ.λ., *thou shalt love*, etc.) Moses repeats this in Deut. vi. 8, from the Decalogue in Ib. v. 10; and it is frequently repeated in the same book, of which it is the sum, the last time with a most solemn adjuration; Ib. xxx. 19, 20.—ἐν ὅλῃ καρδίᾳ σου καὶ ἐν ὅλῃ ψυχῇ σου, καὶ ἐν ὅλῃ τῇ διανοίᾳ σου,[1] *with all thy heart, and with all thy soul, and with all thy mind*. Those who have copied or collated MSS., have for the most part treated the article with indifference; but as far as can be gathered from MSS. lately collated, St Matthew introduced the article only in the last clause. In the Hebrew it is ובכל מאדך, *q. d.*, *and with all thy strength* (*et in omni validitate tuâ*). The LXX. render it καὶ ἐξ ὅλης τῆς δυνάμεώς σου, *and with all thy might*. In St Mark it is, καὶ ἐξ ὅλης τῆς διανοίας σου, καὶ ἐξ ὅλης τῆς ἰσχύος σου, *and with all thy mind and with all thy strength*. In St Luke x. 27, it is καὶ ἐξ ὅλης τῆς ἰσχύος σου καὶ ἐξ ὅλης τῆς διανοίας σου, one Hebrew word, מאד,[2] being expressed by two Greek ones. [sc. ἰσχύος, *strength*, and διανοίας, *mind*, or *understanding*.] Even the Hebrew accents[3] distinguish this third clause from the two previous ones, which are closely united. They all form an *epitasis*,[4] with which St Matthew's introduction of the article only in the third clause agrees. John James Syrbius, Philos. primæ, Part I., ch. i., § 1, thus expresses himself,—" Of ALL those things which are ever found in man, there are three fundamental principles, idea, desire, and emotion." ALL ought to be animated and governed by the love of God.

38. Πρώτη, *first*) This commandment is not only the *greatest* in necessity, extent, and duration, but it is also the *first* in nature, order, time, and evidence.

---

[1] E. M. has ἐν ὅλῃ τῇ καρδίᾳ σου, καὶ ἐν ὅλῃ τῇ ψυχῇ σου, καὶ ἐν ὅλῃ τῇ διανοίᾳ σου.—(I. B.)

DZ. support the articles before καρδιά, and before διανοίᾳ: the reading of B. is doubtful. Only inferior uncial MSS. Δ., etc., omit the articles.—ED.

[2] מְאֹד—(1) subst. m. *strength, force*, from the root אוד. No. 3, Deut. vi. 5, "And thou shalt love Jehovah thy God with all thy heart, with all thy mind, וּבְכָל־מְאֹדֶךָ, and with all thy strength," *i.e.* in the highest degree. Gesenius.—(I. B.)

[3] For some account of the Hebrew accents, see p. 132, f. n. 5.—(I. B.)

[4] See explanation of technical terms in Appendix — (I. B.)

39. Δευτέρα, *second*) Corresponding with πρώτη, *first.*— ὁμοία, *like*) sc. of that same character as contrasted with sacrifice; see Mark xii. 33. The love of our neighbour resembles the love of God more than all the other duties, just as the moon resembles the sun more than the stars do: see Gen. i. The lawyer might easily omit the latter, whilst anxious about the former. Our Lord guards him from that danger, and answers more than he had asked.—ὡς, *as*) sc. as thou lovest thyself. Self-love needs not to be enjoined separately. He who loves God will love himself in a proper degree without selfishness. God loves me as He does thee; and thee as He does me: therefore I ought to love thee, my neighbour, as myself; and thou me as thyself: for our love to each other ought to correspond to God's love towards us both.

40. Κρίμαται—καὶ οἱ προφῆται,[1] *hangs*[2]—*and the prophets*. The Latin Codices have *pendet, et prophetæ*—*hangs, and the prophets:* whence the Canterbury MS. has the reading κρέμαται καὶ οἱ προφῆται. The question was concerning the law: the reply concerns the law especially: see ver. 36, 40. The Anglo-Saxon version has not καὶ οἱ προφῆται; and it might seem a gloss from ch. vii. 12, because the verb κρέμαται is in the singular number, and the disputed clause follows afterwards. The fathers, however, have it, including even Tertullian, if the copies of him are not corrupt. And again, the Anglo-Saxon version frequently omits something which is found in the Latin. The matter requires further consideration. κρέμαται is an elegant verb. He who takes away either of these commandments, takes away the law.[3]

41. Συνηγμένων δὲ τῶν Φαρισαίων, *but while the Pharisees were gathered together*) sc. solemnly; see ver. 34.

42. Τί, κ.τ.λ.., *what?* etc.) You Pharisees, says our Lord, are always putting questions concerning commandments; now I will propose to you something else, concerning which also *it is writ-*

---

[1] E. M. reads καὶ οἱ προφῆται κρέμανται.—(I. B.)
[2] E. V. has "*hang*," which agrees with the reading of E. M., q. v. supra. —(I. B.)
BDLZ*abc* Vulg. Syr. and Hil. read κρέμαται. Orig. 3, 981*b* supports Rec. text, κρέμανται after προφῆται—ED.
[3] Which comprises so many commandments.—V. g.

ten (*scriptum est*), as of an important matter; that you may see that the Gospel is as much to be sought for *in the Scriptures* (*Scripturis*) as the Law is.[1]—ὑμῖν δοκεῖ, *seems to you*) [*i.e. is your opinion*]. Jesus employs the word δοκεῖ[2] (*seems*) with greater right towards the Pharisees than they had done to Him, in ver. 17. Even *opinion* might become the beginning of faith.—τίνος υἱός, *whose son?*) Jesus thus gave them an opportunity of acknowledging Him as the Messiah. The doctrine of the Divine Unity (ver. 37), is illustrated by that of the Trinity.—τοῦ Δαυίδ, *of David*) Human reason more easily accepts moderate views concerning Christ, than those which are either more humble or more glorious.

43. Ἐν Πνεύματι, *in Spirit*) and therefore truly: see 1 Cor. xii. 3.—Κύριον Αὐτὸν καλεῖ, *calleth Him Lord*) a sign of subjection: see Phil. ii. 11; cf. 1 Pet. iii. 6. It was a higher honour to have Christ for his Son, than to be a king; and yet David does not say that Christ is his son, but rejoices that Christ is his Lord, and he Christ's servant. But this joy has also been procured for us: see Luke i. 43; John xx. 28; Phil. iii. [3], 8. They who regard the Messiah only as the son of David, regard the lesser part of the conception of Him. A dominion to which David himself is subject, shows the heavenly majesty of the King, and the heavenly character of His kingdom.

44. Εἶπεν ὁ Κύριος, κ.τ.λ., *the Lord said*, etc.) The whole of this verse agrees verbatim with the S. V. of Ps. cx. 1.—τῷ Κυρίῳ μου, *to my Lord*) Therefore He was David's Lord, before the Lord said to Him, "Sit Thou on My right hand," etc.—κάθου, *sit*) in token of command; see 1 Cor. xv. 25.—ἐκ δεξιῶν μου, *on My right hand*) in token of power.—ἕως ἄν, *until*) The eternity of the session is not denied; but it is denied that the assault of the enemies will interfere with it. The warlike kingdom will come to an end (as in earthly wars the heir of a kingdom commonly

---

[1] The sum of both law and Gospel is set forth, in this concluding passage, by the greatest of the prophets. The first discourse of Jesus was in the temple, in which He professed that GOD was His Father: Luke ii. 49; John ii. 16. And now this last question, put forth in the temple by the same Jesus, points out the truth, that He is Himself the Lord of David.—*Harm.*, p. 469.

[2] Τί ὑμῖν δοκεῖ, E. V. *What think ye?*—(I. B.)

resigns the command which he held during the war, when the enemy has been conquered); the peaceful kingdom, however, will have no end. Cf. 1 Cor. xv. 25, etc. Even before that, the Son was subordinate to the Father, but did not then appear so, on account of the glory of His kingdom: even after that, He will reign, but as the Son, subordinate to the Father.—θῶ, κ.τ.λ., *I place*, etc.) The enemies will lie prostrate.—ἐχθρούς, *enemies*) and amongst them the Pharisees.—Σου, *Thy*) *i.e.* of *Thee.* The hatred of the enemies is directed especially against the First-born.—ὑποπόδιον, *footstool*) The enemies will themselves be the footstool of Christ by right of conquest. Cf. Josh. x. 24; Ps. xlvii. 4.

45. Εἰ οὖν Δαυίδ, *if David therefore*) It was the duty of the Jews to study that point with the utmost earnestness, especially at that time. It is considerably more evident of Christ that He is the Lord, than that He is the Son of David.[1]

46. Λόγον, *a word*) On that question or any other.—Ἐπερω-τῆσαι, *to question*) sc. with the object of tempting Him; the disciples questioned Him with the object of learning.—οὐκέτι, *no more*) A new scene, as it were, opens from this point.

CHAPTER XXIII.

1. Τότε, *then*) Having left His adversaries to themselves.

2. Ἐκάθισαν, κ.τ.λ., *sit*, etc.) Representing Moses, reading and interpreting his law, and even urging more than he enjoined.— οἱ Γραμματεῖς καὶ οἱ Φαρισαῖοι, *the Scribes and the Pharisees*) The sins which are here enumerated, did not belong all equally to both of these classes; but they had many in common, and participated in many; see Luke xi. 45.[2]

3. Οὖν, *therefore*) This particle limits the expression "*what-*

---

[1] So great is the glory of the Son of God! David as well as Abraham alike, John viii. 56, saw the day of Christ, the last great day we may suppose, when all His adversaries shall become the Lord's footstool.—V. g.

[2] And of those sins of the Scribes and Pharisees specified in the discourses of Christ, which are described more fully by Matthew, Mark and Luke,

soever they bid you observe," so that the people should not think that they were bound to observe the traditions of the Pharisees equally with the law of Moses;[1] see ver. 4.—τηρεῖτε, *observe*) sc. mentally.[2]—ποιεῖτε, *do*) sc. actually. An imperative corresponded with by the other which follows.—λέγουσι, *they say*) Mosaic commands, which ought to be "*observed*" and "*done*."

4. Δεσμεύουσι γάρ, *for they bind*) This explains the words, *They say and do not*.—βαρία καὶ δυσβάστακτα, *heavy and grievous to be borne*) epithets suitable to the doctrines of men.[3]—ὤμους—δακτύλῳ, *shoulders—with the finger*) There is an evident contrast intended between these words.—κινῆσαι, *to move*) much less to bear. Scripture has an incomparable felicity in describing the inner characters of minds, of which the whole of this chapter affords a striking instance; see also Luke xii. 16, 17.

5. Δὲ, *but*) sc. although they appear to do many good things.—φυλακτήρια, *phylacteries*) see Ex. xiii. 9, 16; Deut. vi. 8, xi. 18.—κράσπεδα, *fringes*) see Numb. xv. 38.

6. Φιλοῦσι, κ.τ.λ., *they love*, etc.) Both individually and for their order.

6, 7. Ἐν τοῖς δείπνοις—συναγωγαῖς—ἀγοραῖς, *in banquets—synagogues—market-places*) public places.

8. Μὴ κληθῆτε, *be ye not called*) i.e. do not ye be thus treated, nor seek to be thus treated.—εἷς γάρ ἐστιν ὑμῶν ὁ Διδάσκαλος, *for one is your Teacher*[4]) Others read, εἷς γάρ ἐστιν ὑμῶν ὁ Καθηγητής, ὁ Χριστός,[5] *for one is your Guide, even Christ*. And this is indeed

---

have selected those sins which would most clearly show to the untutored populace why they should *beware of the Scribes*—viz., their haughtiness, their avarice, and their hypocrisy.—*Harm.*, p. 472.

[1] *i.e.*, because it implies that their claim to obedience rested on their sitting in Moses' seat.—(I. B.)—*i.e.*, so far, and only so far, as they really *sat in Moses' seat*—viz., taught only what Moses in the written law commands.—Ed.

[2] τὰ ἔργα αὐτῶν) Verse 5–7.
  μὴ ποιεῖτε) Verse 8–12. } V. g.

[3] Which both are not contained in the law, and are contrary to the law.—V. g.

[4] E. V. "one is your Master."—(I. B.)

[5] Such is the reading of E. M.

In his App. Crit. Bengel writes thus:—"καθηγητής) *codd. Bas.* α. β. γ. etc. Ex. v. 10 (διδάσκαλος). *Aug.* 1 4, in duabus pericopis, *Bodl.* 7, *Colb* 3, *Gal.* Go. *Lin. Mont. N.* 1, *Par.* 1. 4, *Roe. Sild.* 1, *Steph.* ε, *Vsser.*

found in ver. 10; in the present instance, however, it is our Heavenly Father who is spoken of; cf. ch. xvi. 17; John vi. 45; Acts x. 28; Gal. i. 1, 15; Eph. i. 9; Ps. xxv. 12, xxxii. 8. Therefore our Lord adds, *but all ye are brethren*, which principle applies also to the ninth verse, that we should neither ourselves *be called masters*, nor *call* any one on earth *father*. Christ is treated of in verse 10, and verse 11 is appropriately subjoined. Cf. concerning the Father as Teacher, and Christ as Guide, ch. xi. 25, 27.—ἐστέ, *ye are*) The indicative mood.¹

9. Πατέρα, *father*) This also was the grand title given by the Jews to their teachers, especially in old age.—μὴ καλέσητε, κ.τ.λ., *do not call*, etc.) Let not either your tongue or your mind ascribe infallibility to any man.

10. Καθηγηταί, *guides*)² i.e leaders, authorities. There is a gradation in these phrases: Rabbi, Father, Guide. They were titles of spiritual eminence amongst the Jews. The same principle is enforced in 1 Cor. iii. 5, 6.³

11. Ὁ δὲ μείζων, *but he that is greatest*) i.e. he who wishes to

2, *Wheel.* 1, et alii apud *Erasmum* et *Bezam*; *Orig. Chrysost.* ad h. l. et *Homil.* 77 in Ioh., *Arab. Syr.* Probat Beza, Grotius, Seldenus, nec non L. de Dieu, Rus.

"¶ ὁ Χριστός) edd. etc. Ex. v. 10 (\ ) [*i.e.* for the omission], *Bas.* unus, γ. opinor. *Eph. Med. Vss.* 1, duo apud Bezam, *Aeth. Arab. Armen. Copt. Lat.* (et inde *Cant.* quem tamen Beza videtur innuere, *Colb.* 8), *Pers. Syr. Orig. Chrysostomus* clare. *Theophyl.* in comm. Vid. Gnom."

Tischendorf, Lachmann, and Wordsworth read διδάσκαλος, but they do not omit ὁ Χριστός.—(I. B.)

Ὑμῶν ὁ διδάσκαλος is the reading of B; "vester doctor," *d*; "vobis magister," Cypr.; "magister vester," *abc* and Vulg. But ὑμῶν ὁ καθηγητής, D; to which Rec. Text adds ὁ Χριστός.—Ed.

Some one of the learned has supposed it more probable that the term καθηγητής, as being one of less common occurrence, has been changed by transcribers into διδάσκαλος, rather than that διδάσκαλος has been substituted instead of καθηγητής. But the arguments drawn from solid criticism have more weight than such mere *conjectures*; not to mention that the other *conjecture*, by which καθηγητής is supposed to be transferred from ver. 10 (as to which there is no dispute), has at least as much show of probability. Cf. *App. Crit. Ed.* ii., p. 133.—E. B.

¹ i.e. not the imperative, "*Be ye*," as it might be rendered.—(I. B.)
² E. V. "Masters."—(I. B.)
³ In the original, "quæ destruitur etiam 1 Cor. iii. 5, s.:" lit., "which [sc. spiritual eminence] is demolished also in 1 Cor. iii. 5, 6."—(I. B.)

be the greatest (corresponding with the Hebrew רַב[1]); cf. ch. xx. 26.

12. Ὅστις δὲ ὑψώσει ἑαυτὸν, κ.τ.λ., *but whosoever shall exalt himself*, etc.) In the S. V. of Ezek. xxi. 26, we read ἐταπείνωσας τὸ ὑψηλὸν, καὶ ὕψωσας τὸ ταπεινόν, *Thou hast humbled that which is exalted, and exalted that which is humble*.—ὑψώσει ἑαυτὸν, *shall exalt himself*.) As the Scribes and Pharisees did.

13, 14. Οὐαὶ, *woe*) *Woe* is uttered eight times in this passage:[2] *blessed* is uttered eight times and more in Matt. v. from ver. 3, where see Gnomon.—οὐαὶ ὑμῖν—κλείετε τὴν βασιλείαν—κατεσθίετε τὰς οἰκίας τῶν χηρῶν, κ.τ.λ., *woe unto you—ye shut up the kingdom—ye devour widows' houses*, etc.) In many MSS. these words are transposed;[3] but that must come first in which the

---

[1] "רַב . . 2. *great* . . specially (a) i.q. *powerful*, Psa. xlviii. 3; Isa. lxiii. 1. Pl. רַבִּים the mighty, Job xxxv. 9; Isa. liii. 12.—(b) *elder*, Gen. xxv. 23. Pl. רַבִּים the old, Job xxxii. 9.—(c) subst. *a great man, leader*, i.q. שַׂר, especially in the later Hebrew. . . —(d) *a master*, one who is skilled in any art, *skilful*, Prov. xxvi. 10. Compare Talmud. רַב doctor, excellent teacher."—*Gesenius*. Bengel evidently intends to refer the reader to *Rabbi* in verse 7, on which *Wordsworth* says:—"ῥαββί] רַבִּי, *My Master. Rabbi*, from root רַב, *rab* = great; as *Magister* from *magnus*, μέγας."—(I. B.)

[2] Our Saviour had used various degrees of argument against His opponents all along from ch. ix. 4; but now, at the last, moved by a holy fervour, He brings forth most plainly the whole fact as it really was.—*Harm.*, p. 472.

[3] Such is the reading of E. M.; but E. V. supports the order approved by Bengel. In his Apparatus Criticus, Bengel says of the reading:—" κλείετε—κατεσθίετε "—" Sic Erasmus, Beza, Bodl. 1. 2. Cypr. Laud. 1. 2, Roe et sex et octo alii, vel etiam Cam. Item Hilar. Euthym. Copt. Lat., etiam apud Hieron." Of the order " κατεσθίετε—κλείετε," he says:—" Comp. Stap. Steph. edd. Aug. 1, 2, 4, Byz. Gehl. Mosc. Wo. 1, 2, etc., Chrysost. Theophyl., opus imperf. Arab. Lat. pauculi, Syr. Quinque Colbertinos pro illâ lectione citat Millius, a silentio amicorum, qui Bezam adhibuerant argumentatus; pro hâc Simonius in notis ad h. l. Vide Gnomon: quanquam is prior videtur esse versus, quem seorsum referunt Marcus et Lucas."—(I. B.)

BDLZ a Vulg. (Amiat. MS.) omit all the words of ver. 14, οὐαὶ—κατεσθίετε τ. οἰκίας τ. χηρῶν (Rec. Text adding καὶ) προφάσει—προσευχόμενοι διὰ τοῦτο—κρίμα. The Canons of Euseb. seem to omit the words: also Origen, who speaks of " the *second* woe in Matthew " being οὐαὶ—ὅτι περιάγετε τὴν θάλασσαν, etc. 4, 352a. Therefore Lachm. and Tischend. rightly omit them. The words seem to me to have crept in from Mark xii. 40 and Luke xx. 47. However bc and Hilary 725d and 89 supports the words here.—ED. The margin of Bengel's Ed. ii. holds the omission of ver. 14 as all but equal to the Rec. Text.—E. B.

kingdom of heaven is mentioned; cf. ch. iv. 17, v. 3, etc.[1]—ὑποκριταί, *hypocrites*) The characteristics of hypocrites may be ascertained from this indictment, as Thomasius has done in his Cautions. Woes were denounced against them, not because they were Scribes and Pharisees, but because they were hypocrites.—κλείετε, *ye shut up*) i.e. with a key : ye shut up as being ignorant and blind.—ἔμπροσθεν τῶν ἀνθρώπων, *before men*[2]) sc. before their eyes, when they were just close.—οὐκ εἰσέρχεσθε, *ye do not enter*) a great woe, and the first; cf. Matt. v. 3, on the first degree of blessedness.—τοὺς εἰσερχομένους, *them that are entering*) sc. either in will or in deed.

14. Κατεσθίετε, κ.τ.λ., *ye devour*, etc.) The extreme of avarice. To devour widows' houses[3] is the most atrocious species, which is put for the whole class of rapacious actions.—καὶ, *even*)—μακρὰ, *long*) The word has here the force of an adverb.[4] Some MSS. also read suitably enough, μακρᾷ, in which case it must be construed with προφάσει, sc. with a long, or great pretence—i.e. they made of their prayers a great pretence, pretext, or plea for devouring widows' houses. Herodian uses the expressions, πρόφασις ὀλίγη, εὐτελής, μικρά, sc. a *small, useful, little pretext or plea.*—λήψεσθε, κ.τ.λ., *ye shall receive*, etc.) sc. as the reward of such prayers.—περισσότερον κρίμα, *more abundant damnation*) He who acts ill is condemned ; he who abuses that which is good, to adorn that which is bad, is condemned to sorer punishment.

15. Περιάγετε, κ.τ.λ., *ye compass*, etc.) A proverbial expression. Ye compass, or *go about*, as Rabbis; see ver. 7.—ἵνα προσήλυτον, *one proselyte*) with great zeal, but little efficacy; so that you hardly obtain one.—υἱὸν Γεέννης, *a child of hell*) i.e. *worthy of hell*. Thus in Deut. xxv. 2, בן הכות[5] is rendered by the LXX. ἄξιος

---

[1] Although that verse seems likely to come first, which Mark and Luke represent as spoken separately.—App. Crit. Ed. ii. p. 134.

[2] E. V. "*against men.*"—(I. B.)

[3] Who of all persons ought especially to be spared, but who, as being liable to be easily acted on by persuasion, are most open to oppression.—V. g.

[4] According to this reading, which is that of EM, it must be construed with προσευχόμενοι, *praying;* and the words must be rendered, "*who pray long*"—i.e. "*who spend a long time in prayer.*"—(I. B.)

[5] Literally, "*a son to be beaten.*"—(I. B.)

πληγῶν, *worthy of stripes.*[1]—διπλότερον, *twofold more*) on account of his greater hypocrisy,[2] though he might have attained to a high rank among the people of God.

16. Ὁδηγοὶ τυφλοί, *blind guides*) Previously they were styled hypocrites, and that again and again; now the appellation is changed according to the subject in hand. The two appellations are combined in ver. 23, 24, and ver. 25, 26. The denunciation reaches its climax in ver. 33.—οὐδέν ἐστιν, *he is nothing*)[3] sc. ὠφείλων, *owing*, i.e. *he owes nothing.*—ἐν τῷ χρυσῷ, *by the gold*) with which the temple was adorned.

17. Μωροὶ καὶ τυφλοί, *fools and blind*) They sinned even against common sense; according to the judgment of which that thing, on account of which another thing is of a certain character, must be much more so, than that which merely derives its character inferentially therefrom.

18. Ἐν τῷ δώρῳ, *by the gift*) The error originated in the mistaken views entertained by the offerers with regard to their own righteousness. They esteemed their own gifts more highly than the Divine institution.—ἐπάνω αὐτοῦ, *upon it*) sc. the altar.

20. Ἐν πᾶσι τοῖς ἐπάνω αὐτοῦ, *by all things thereon*) As in ver. 21 the gold of the temple is not again mentioned, but He is mentioned who dwelleth therein; so in this verse the expression, all things which are upon the altar, signifies something much greater than the gift on the altar, nay, something in contrast with that gift, sc. the sacred fire and the whole divinely appointed ministry of the priests, who stood and walked, not only beside, but upon the altar.

23. Ἀποδεκατοῦτε, κ.τ.λ., *ye tythe*, etc.) And command others to tythe; cf. in ver. 24 the expression *"guides."*—ἡδύοσμον,[4] *mint*) not only grain but *herbs.*—κύμινον, *cummin*) which is proverbially a small thing.—ἀφήκατε, κ.τ.λ., *have omitted*, etc.) sc. long since; or also, ye have remitted to others, by your silence.—βαρύτερα,

---

[1] E. V. "*Worthy to be beaten.*"—(I. B.)

[2] Which he adopts from his teachers, independently of and exceeding his heathen corruptions, which he has not laid aside.—V. g.

[3] E. V. "*It is nothing.*"—(I. B)

[4] On this word Bengel, in his Apparatus Criticus, has the remark:— 'נענע *Hebr.* ex Lat.," sc. *mentha;* from which also our English word, *mint* —(I. B.)

weightier) These questions belong to comparative theology. Three weightier matters are enumerated in contrast with three smaller matters. Concerning these weightier matters, see Ecclus. iv. He, and he alone, who does not neglect these, may judge rightly in smaller matters.—τὴν κρίσιν, *judgment*) by which men distinguish between good and evil, and in either of them between weightier and smaller matters; see the Gnomon on ch. xii. 18, and xvi. 3; Luke xii. 57; 1 Cor. xi. 31; Micah vi. 8.—τὸν ἔλεον, *mercy*) See ch. ix. 13.—τὴν πίστιν, *faith*) sc. *sincerity*, which is opposed to *hypocrisy*: for those who, in ch. xxiv. 51, are called hypocrites, are called *unbelievers* (*infideles*) in Luke xii. 46. Cf. 1 Tim. iv. 2, 3. There are clearly these three principal heads, *Judgment, Mercy, Faith*: and divisions of theological topics ought to have been arranged under such heads as those which Scripture itself lays down, as in John xvi. 8; Romans iii. 27; 1 Cor. xiii. 13; 1 Thess. iv. 9, v. 1;[1] Heb. vi. 1, 2.—μὴ ἀφιέναι, *not to omit*) corresponding with ἀφήκατε, *ye have omitted*; and therefore ταῦτα, *these*, refers to mint, etc.—ἐκεῖνα, *those*, to *judgment*, etc.; and the words, ταῦτα ἔδει ποιῆσαι, *these ought ye to have done*, express approbation of their conduct in this matter;[2] whilst the words κἀκεῖνα μὴ ἀφιέναι, *and not to leave the other undone*, belong to the indictment. In Greek οὗτος and ἐκεῖνος, in Latin *hic* and *ille* (*this* and *that*), are frequently employed with reference, not to the order of the words, but to the nature of the things. See my note to Chrysostom on the Priesthood, pp. 509, 510.

24. Τὸν κώνωπα, *the gnat*) They who object to *swallowing a camel* should not be found fault with for merely *straining a gnat*,[3]

---

[1] There is evidently some mistake in the references to Romans and Thessalonians—a mistake which I have bestowed much labour to correct, but in vain. For the reference to 1 Thess. v. 1, I would suggest 1 Thess. v. 8.—(I. B.)

[2] Truly, even in the smallest things remarkable and pre-eminent grace may exhibit itself, Mark xii. 42.—V. g.

[3] The clause rendered by E. V., "who strain at a gnat," is interpreted more correctly by Bengel, "who strain a gnat," on which Alford observes in loc., "*The straining the gnat* is not a mere proverbial saying. The Jews (as do now the Buddists in Ceylon and Hindostan) strained their wine, etc., carefully, that they might not violate Levit. xi. 20, 23, 41, 42 (and it might be added, Levit. xvii. 10–14). The camel is not only opposed as of *immense size*, but is also *unclean*."—(I. B.)

such being far from our Lord's intention: for no one can safely swallow a gnat, which may choke him. A beam is the worse of the two, and yet a chip[1] is not disregarded, even in the hand, much more in the eye. See ch. vii. 5. The noun κώνωψ is a word of common gender, and signifies *a gnat*, properly one belonging to wine, which easily falls into a strainer.[2]

25. Τὸ ἔξωθεν, *that which is without*) sc. the external surface.—ἔσωθεν δὲ, *but within*) where the meat and drink are.—γέμουσιν, *they are full*) sc. *the cup and dish.*—ἁρπαγῆς, *of rapacity, extortion*) see ver. 14.—καὶ ἀκρασίας, *and excess*) *Excess*, ἀκρασία, is opposed to *abstinence*, not only in meat and drink, but also in money and gain. With this idea, Aristotle (Eth. Nicom. vii. 6) says that the particular thing should be mentioned in regard to which any one is remarkable for excess or the opposite; as gain, honour, anger, etc. And this is evident in the present passage, from the use of the synonymous term, ἁρπαγή. Gregory Nazianzen says, ἀκρασία ἐμοὶ πᾶν τὸ περιττὸν καὶ ὑπὲρ τὴν χρείαν, *everything which is superfluous and more than necessary, is, in my opinion,* ἀκρασία.

26. Καθάρισον, *cleanse*) sc. by removing *rapacity* by almsgiving. See Luke xi. 41.—πρῶτον, κ.τ.λ., *first*, etc.) This may also be applied to the matter of decorum.—ἵνα, κ.τ.λ., *in order that*, etc.) for otherwise that outward cleanliness is not cleanliness.

27. Ὅτι, κ.τ.λ., *for*, etc.) In this verse the especially distinctive characteristic of hypocrites is described: for hypocrisy is named in ver. 28. Cf. Luke xi. 44 with the context.—κεκονια-

---

[1] In the original, "*Festuca*," corresponding to the English word, *Mote*; the meaning of which, in Matt. vii. 3 (which is here referred to), is not a *mote* such as we see in sunbeams, but a small particle of straw. I know of no English word that *now* corresponds to this idea: it is something between a *chip* and a *speck*.—(I. B.)

[2] The wine-gnat, according to Rosenmüller, is found in wine when turning acid. The Jews used to strain out their wines through a napkin or strainer, to prevent this wine-gnat being swallowed unawares. See Buxtorf on the root יבק. Beng. wishes to guard us against the abuse of this passage, whereby it is often said to those who are careful in the greater duties, when particular also on minor points, "Oh! you are straining at a gnat." They forget that Jesus does not object to tenderness of conscience as to moral *gnats*, but to those who, whilst scrupulous as to gnats, are unscrupulous as to moral *camels*, Eccles. x. 1.—ED.

μένοις, *whited*) The Jews used to whiten their sepulchres with chalk.

28. Ἀνομίας, *unrighteousness*) This is strictly opposed to righteousness.

29.[1] Ὅτι οἰκοδομεῖτε—τῶν προφητῶν—κοσμεῖτε—τῶν δικαίων, *because ye build—of the prophets—and garnish—of the righteous*) (see ver 35). This was all that they did in memorial of the ancient prophets and righteous men, without observing their words or imitating their deeds; with a resemblance to their fathers in their dispositions; with a contempt of the Messiah, to whom those prophets had borne witness. Understand, therefore, *only*, as in ch. xxiv. 38. Scripture is wont to call those who have died in the Lord *righteous*, rather than *saints*;[2] see Luke xiv. 14, and Heb. xii. 23.

30. Λέγετε, *ye say*) By your public protestation.—οὐκ ἂν ἦμεν, κ.τ.λ., *we would not have been*, etc.) Such was their self-confidence.

31. Μαρτυρεῖτε, *ye bear witness*) sc. by your deeds, ver. 29, by your words, ver. 30.

32. Καὶ ὑμεῖς πληρώσατε, *fill ye up then*) The pronoun ὑμεῖς, *you*, is not only introduced in contrast to *your fathers*, but also shows that there is an indicative force in the imperative πληρώσατε, *fill ye up*; q.d. *ye will fill up, fill ye up* therefore; cf. John xiii. 27. *Fill ye up* whenever ye will, be ye no longer hindered; be ye left to yourselves: perform then with the hand that which you cherish in the heart.—τὸ μέτρον, *the measure*) As there is a measure of life and of suffering, so is there also of sin, when, for example, to three transgressions is added a fourth; see Amos i. 3, etc.

33. Ἐχιδνῶν, *of vipers*) Which are mentioned in ver. 30, 31, 32.—πῶς φύγητε, *how can ye escape*) The subjunctive.

34. Διὰ τοῦτο, κ.τ.λ., *wherefore*, etc.) A corollary of the eighth woe.—Ἐγὼ, *I*) In the parallel passage of St Luke, xi. 49, we read, διὰ τοῦτο καὶ ἡ σοφία τοῦ Θεοῦ εἶπεν, Ἀποστελῶ, κ.τ.λ., *wherefore also said the wisdom of God, I will send*, etc. The first chapter of the second book of Esdras[3] and this passage have a wonder-

---

[1] ὅτι οἰκοδομεῖτε) A hypocrite brings guilt on himself, even in respect to those things which are not unrighteous or wrong in themselves.—V. g.

[2] In Latin, "*saint*" and "*holy*" are both expressed by the same word, "*sanctus*."—(I. B.)

[3] In the original, "Liber iv. Esrae, cap. i."—(I. B.)

ful resemblance. In 2 Es. i. 30, we read, "*I gathered you together as a hen gathereth her chickens under her wings:*" in ver. 32, "*I sent unto you My servants the prophets, whom ye have taken and slain, and torn their bodies in pieces, whose blood I will require of your hands,* saith the Lord:" in ver. 33, "Thus saith the Almighty Lord, *your house is desolate.*" That book of Esdras is greatly esteemed by many, amongst whom of ourselves are found Schickardus *on Tarich*,[1] p. 135, and Hainlin, *in his Sol*[2] *Temporum;* and this quotation in the Gospel gives very great weight to it. J. C. Scaliger says (Exerc. 308), "I possess an admirable and divine compendium of the books of Esdras, composed in the Syrian language; they contain far more valuable sentiments than the harangues of their base calumniator." That Syrian composition, which Scaliger calls a compendium, may have been a translation of the original Hebrew work, the longer Latin paraphrase of which may have many apocryphal additions. Such appears to be the case of the books of Wisdom and Ecclesiasticus, which at one time show evident signs of a Hebrew origin, and at another have a purely Greek character.—ἀποστέλλω, *I send*) The present tense. God's messengers were sent when wickedness was most widely prevalent among His people.—προφήτας, *prophets*) Who are taught by special revelation, as David. These alone are mentioned with reference to the past; see ver. 30. Now *wise men* and *scribes* are added.—σοφοὺς, *wise men*) who have an habitual sense[3] of the true and the good, corresponding with the Hebrew חכם, *wise*, derived from חך, the *palate,* or *sense of taste;* such as was Solomon. These are midway between prophets and scribes.—γραμματεῖς, *scribes*) who edit and illustrate the remains of the pro

---

[1] The title of the work in full, as edited by Schickardus, is, "Tarich; *h. e. series regum Persiae ab Ardschir—Babekan usque ad Jasdigerdem a chaliphis expulsam, ex fide MS. vol. authentici; restita comm., etc., authore W. S.* 4°. Tubingen, 1632."—(I. B.)

[2] A chronological work, the full title of which is, "*Sol Temporum seu chronologia mystica et elenchus chronologicus per totam S. Scripturam deductus.*" It was published in folio at Tubingen, A. D. 1646. The author is described as "Ecclesiæ Derendingensis Pastor, et Vicinarum Superintendens."—(I. B.)

[3] The word used by Bengel is *gustum,* the original and literal sense of which is, *taste.*—(I. B.)

phets and wise men, as Ezra did. In these last the character is for the most part acquired; in wise men, innate; in prophets, inspired.[1] Therefore the world hates and despises prophets most, wise men much, scribes less, yet not little.—*ἀποκτενεῖτε, ye shall kill*) as James [the son of Zebedee].—*σταυρώσετε, ye shall crucify*) as Peter and Andrew, although Peter suffered martyrdom elsewhere.

35. *Ἔλθῃ, may come*) This is repeated in ver. 36, sc. *ἥξει, shall come*. Cf. Luke xi. 50, etc.—*πᾶν, all*) especially that of the Messiah Himself. Cf. Luke xiii. 33.—*αἷμα, blood*) This word occurs thrice in this one verse with great force.—*ἐκχυνόμενον, which is being shed*) The present tense is used to show that the blood-shedding was not yet concluded.—*ἐπὶ τῆς γῆς, on the whole earth*) Cf. Gen. iv. 11.—*Ζαχαρίου υἱοῦ Βαραχίου, Zacharias the son of Barachias*) whose prophecy and death are mentioned in 2 Chron. xxiv. 20–22.[2] The Jews say a great deal about him. See Lightfoot.[3]—*τοῦ Ναοῦ, the Temple*) Jesus spake these words

---

[1] In the original, *infusus;* literally, *infused.*—(I. B.)

[2] And who, as Michaelis, in der Einl., etc., T. ii., p. m. 1078, 1079, shows at large, is called in the *Gospel of the Nazarenes*, according to Jerome's statement, not the Son of *Barachias* (as it is found in our Greek copies), but the Son of *Jehoiada*. Indeed it would not be amiss to compare this with what S. R. D. Crusius, Hypomn., p. i. p. 301, suggests, viz., that Jehoiada [= *the knowledge of the Lord*] received the surname from the *Blessed Jehovah*, because that he had preserved the house of David, by having stealthily saved Joash from being murdered, and by having subsequently placed him on his father's throne, after having slain Athaliah, owing to which meritorious deed he was ever after commonly called by this honourable title. —E. B.

[3] To understand these words of a certain *Zacharias, the son of Baruch,* a person of proved excellence, who was killed in the midst of the temple (as *Josephus* records) a short while *before its destruction*, as Kornmann and others think, we are not bound to the end that the glory of Christ's Omniscience may be maintained inviolate: for, in fact, this prophecy concerning vengeance impending over *that generation*, as well as many other prophecies, was proved by its fulfilment. Luke, in the passage in question, is speaking only of *Prophets:* but the Zacharias of Josephus was not a prophet. Indeed Christ had many reasons for making mention of *the former Zacharias* above others. It is such personages in this passage (as in Ezek. xiv. 14) that are especially referred to and quoted, who have their names recorded *in Scripture:* and that ancient Zacharias, as in the similar instance of Abel, was accounted by the Jews without dispute as a Saint and Prophet; nay, indeed

in the Temple: in the Temple especial vengeance was to be executed hereafter.

36. Λέγω, *I say*) sc. again. Cf. Gen. xli. 32.—ἥξει, *shall come*) *i.e.* as far as the beginnings of vengeance are concerned; for its consummation extends far further; see ver. 39.—πάντα, κ.τ.λ., *all*, etc.) He who commits a sin becomes a partner in crime with all who have committed the same sin.—γενεάν, *generation*) see Gnomon on ch. xxiv. 34.

37. Ἱερουσαλήμ, Ἱερουσαλήμ, *Jerusalem, Jerusalem!*) A most solemn repetition.[1]—ἡ ἀποκτένουσα, *thou that killest*) The participle has the force of a noun.[2]—λιθοβολοῦσα, *that stonest*) Such was the fate of Christ's protomartyr, Stephen, recorded in Acts vii. 58, 59.—τοὺς ἀπεσταλμένους, *them that are sent*) Although ambassadors are considered inviolable by the law of nations.—πρὸς αὐτήν, *to her*) *i.e.* πρός σε, *to thee*. Cf. Luke i. 45; Isa. xlvii. 10.—ποσάκις, κ.τ.λ., *how often*, etc.) As often especially as Jesus entered Judea, Jerusalem, or the Temple. See my Harmony of the Four Evangelists, and Gnomon on ch. xxi. 1.—καὶ οὐκ ἠθελήσατε, *and ye would not*) although *I was willing*. Cf. Isa. xxx. 15.

38. Ἰδού, ἀφίεται, *Behold* [your house] *is left*) The present tense twice expressed.[3] He uttered these words as He was going out of the Temple. See ch. xxiv. 1, and cf. John xii. 36.—ὁ οἶκος ὑμῶν, *your house*) which is otherwise called the *house of the Lord*. Thus, in Ex. xxxii. 7, God says to Moses, *thy people*.[4]—ἔρημος, *desolate*, or *desert*) sc. as being left by the Messiah.[5] Even after His ascension, Christ employed the Temple in a remarkable manner with His disciples. But with regard to Judaism, the Temple now ceased to be what it had been, and for this reason was at length destroyed; see ver. 36. The word ἔρημος is often

---

the guilt incurred in his case was not altogether obliterated from the memory of the Jews.—*Harm.*, p. 472.

[1] "Epizeuxis." See Appendix.—ED.
Full of compassion and horror alike.—V. g.
[2] *i.e.* "Thou that art the *Murderess* of."—(I. B.)
[3] This refers to ἀποστέλλω in ver. 34.—(I. B.)
[4] Though on other occasions God said of them, "*My* people."—ED.
[5] For when the Messiah is absent, there is nothing that is not desolate and deserted.—V. g.

employed with a particular reference.[1] Thus the Forum is said to be ἔρημον, when no judicial proceedings are being carried on in it.

39. Λέγω, *I say*) See Gnomon on Luke xiii. 35.—Ἴδητε, *ye shall see*) sc. you, inhabitants of Jerusalem. Cf. Luke xiii. 35.—ἀπ᾿ ἄρτι, *from the present time*[2]) The short interval preceding our Lord's death (and that spent without the Temple[3]) is included in the present time [the ἄρτι of the text].—ἕως, *until*) sc. after a long interval.—εἴπητε, κ.τ.λ., *ye shall say*, etc.) They would say so when reciting the Hallel[4] at the Passover, but without applying the words to Jesus. That which is here foretold will actually come to pass at the appointed time, as in ch. xxi. 9 was performed that which had been predicted in Luke xiii. 35. Our Lord, however, does not add " *again*," although the people had shouted those words on the occasion recorded in Matt. xxi. 9. For neither had all joined in this acclamation to Him, nor had they who did so understood what they were saying, as Israel shall understand hereafter : and soon after they, as it were, retracted their acclamation. The first utterance of these words was less complete, the second will be worthy of the name.[5] Cf. Gnomon on the omission of " *again*," in Acts i. 11.—εὐλογημένος, κ.τ.λ., *Blessed*, etc.) With this verse concludes our Lord's public discourse to the Jews : with this verse will begin their repentance.

---

[1] *i.e.* To denote the absence of that which constituted the characteristic or excellence of the object under consideration.—(I. B.)

[2] E. V. Henceforth.—(I. B.)

[3] Within which, and in reference to which, these words, ver. 38, were spoken.—Ed.

[4] "Lastly," says Hartwell Horne, in describing the Jewish Passover, " a fourth cup of wine was filled, called the cup of the Hallel : over it they completed, either by singing or recitation, the great Hallel, or hymn of praise, consisting of Psalms cxv. to cxviii. inclusive, with a prayer, and so concluded."—(I. B.)

[5] Sc. of an utterance or saying, *dictio*, referring to the words, " Ye shall say." Cf. in 1 Cor. xiv. 15, " I will sing with the spirit, and I will sing *with the understanding also*."—(I. B.)

CHAPTER XXIV.

1. Καὶ ἐξελθὼν ὁ Ἰησοῦς ἀπὸ τοῦ ἱεροῦ, ἐπορεύετο, *and Jesus having come forth from the temple, went His way*) Such is the reading of the Colinæan editions, and of the following MSS., viz.: Bunkleanus, Cantabrigiensis, Paris, 5, 6, Stephanus η or more; also of Chrysostom, and the Æthiopic,[1] Arabic, Latin, Persian, and Syriac versions: according to which ἐπορεύετο (*went His way*) has greater force, being contrasted with, and in antithesis to, καθημένου δὲ Αὐτοῦ, *and as He was sitting*.[2] Modern transcribers have, as though it mattered nothing, written ἐπορεύετο ἀπὸ τοῦ ἱεροῦ, *He went His way from the temple*.[3] A discourse, which embraced even the end of the world, was appropriately held in the open air.—οἱ μαθηταί, *the disciples*) one especially, as we learn from Mark xiii. 1.—ἐπιδεῖξαι, *to show*) It is possible that Jesus had never looked at the outside of the temple, for He was not curious; cf. Gnomon on Mark xii. 15. He had looked, and that deservedly, at the inside of the temple; Ibid. xi. 11.— τὰς οἰκοδομάς, *the buildings*) The separate parts were in themselves great buildings: even at that time the building was being carried on, which is mentioned in John ii. 20. And perhaps it was being the more zealously done, on account of the proximity of the Passover.—τοῦ ἱεροῦ, *of the temple*) which was doomed to destruction; see ch. xxiii. 38; and in that very age, too, only a few years after its completion.

2. Πάντα ταῦτα, *all these things*) as they are standing.—οὐ μὴ

---

[1] That portion of the Æthiopic or Abyssinian Version which contains the New Testament, is supposed to have been executed in the fourth century by Frumentius, who, about the year 330, preached Christianity in Æthiopia. —(I. B.)

[2] The verb πορεύομαι, signifying *progressive motion*, corresponds with the Latin *progredior*, or the French *marcher*.—(I. B.)

He had now been in the temple for the last time.—V. g.

[3] Such is the reading of the E. M., and of Bengel's own Edition of the Greek Testament.—(I. B.)

BD*abc* Vulg. place the ἐπορεύετο last: and so Hil. 728. Rec. Text puts ἐπορεύετο, without good authority.—ED.

ἀφεθῇ, κ.τ.λ., *there shall not be left*, etc.) Jesus makes the curious thoughts of His disciples give place to more serious considerations.—λίθος, κ.τ.λ., *a stone*, etc.) A proverbial expression implying the utmost devastation. Even the very soil on which it stood was ploughed up.

3. Ἐπὶ τοῦ ὄρους, *on the mountain*) Whence the temple could be seen, and where the siege operations were destined to commence.—τὸ σημεῖον, *the sign*) Signs have frequently been added to predictions of important events; hence arose the question of the disciples regarding the sign of that time.—τῆς σῆς παρουσίας, *of thy coming*) The disciples appear to refer to ch. xxiii. 39.

4. Καὶ ἀποκριθεὶς ὁ Ἰησοῦς εἶπεν αὐτοῖς, κ.τ.λ., *and Jesus answered and said unto them*, etc.) The disciples had asked without distinguishing their questions—(1) Concerning *the time* of the destruction of the temple; (2) Concerning *the sign* of the coming of the Lord and the end of the world, as if both events would occur simultaneously, and consequently have a common time and a common sign. Our Lord answers them distinctly [and separately]—(1) Concerning the destruction of *the temple* and the city, and the signs of this event, in ver. 4, 5, 15, 16; (2) Concerning His *coming* and the end of the world, and the signs of that event, in ver. 29–31; (3) Concerning the *time* when the temple was to be destroyed, in ver. 32, 33; (4) Concerning *the time* of the end of the world, in ver. 36. Thus is it also in St Mark, and St Luke, who in ch. xxi. 11, 25, distinguishes the signs of each event.—βλέπετε, *see*) i.e. take heed. We ought to inquire concerning future events, especially those of the last days, not for the sake of gratifying our curiosity, but from a desire to fortify ourselves. All things in this discourse must be referred to firmness in acknowledging and confessing Jesus Christ; for the drift and object of the prophecy is to enforce this duty: other matters, which we might make use of for mere knowledge, are mentioned abruptly and obscurely. A thesis on the perspicuity and perfection of Scripture might be suitably illustrated from this discourse of our Lord.—ὑμᾶς, *you*) This is said not so much to the apostles, who were shortly to receive the Holy Ghost, as to the whole flock of believers whom they then represented, lest they should be seduced by the greater perils to which they would be exposed. The beginning is *Prudence*; the end, *Patience*.

5. Πολλοὶ γὰρ, κ.τ.λ., *for many*, etc.) In the beginning will come false Christs; in the middle, false prophets, ver. 11; in the end, both (22, 24). A twofold climax.[1]—ἐπὶ τῷ ὀνόματί Μου, *in My name*) They will not only say that they have been sent by Me, but that they are He who I am.—λέγοντες, ἐγώ εἰμι ὁ Χριστός, *saying, I am Christ*) Joachim Camerarius says, "Theophylact has recorded that a certain Samaritan, Dositheus by name, gave out that he was the prophet foretold by Moses; that Simon the Samaritan also (mentioned in the apostolic history of St Luke) called himself *the Great Power of God*, i.e. ἡ Δύναμις Μεγαλή: the prediction seems also applicable to Theudas,[2] and "the certain Egyptian,"[3] and another pretender mentioned by Josephus (who records those matters in the eighteenth book of his Antiquities, and the second of his Conquest of Judea), all claiming the character of prophet, though being in reality seditious impostors. And, in later times, Manes even dared to call himself Christ and, in imitation of Him, appoint twelve apostles.

6. Μελλήσετε δὲ ἀκούειν, *but ye shall be about to hear*) A compound future. The writings of the Evangelists having been published before the fulfilment of this prediction, were greatly confirmed when it took place. *About to hear*: Christians rather *hear of* than wage wars.—πολέμους, *wars*) sc. close at hand.—ἀκοὰς πολέμων, *rumours of wars*) sc. at a distance.—μὴ θροεῖσθε, *be ye not troubled*) A case of metonymy of the antecedent; i.e. do not immediately take to flight. The verb θροέομαι (to be troubled) is peculiarly appropriate in this place, for θρόος[4] is from θρέω,[5] which signifies σὺν θορύβῳ βοῶ ἢ λαλῶ, i.e. *to cry, or speak with tumult*.—δεῖ γὰρ πάντα γενέσθαι, *for all these things must come to pass*) This is the ground of the believer's tranquility.—οὔπω, *not yet*) The godly are always prone to think that evils have reached their utmost limit: therefore they are warned.—τὸ τέλος, *the end*) mentioned in ver. 2, 14, is not yet; nor is it yet time to fly;

---

[1] i.e. The presence of the two classes together will be a greater evil than that of either of them alone.—(I. B.)
[2] See Acts v. 36.—(I. B.)
[3] Acts xxi. 38.—(I. B.)
[4] *A noise* as of many voices, ... a *murmuring* of discontented people, ... a *report*. Lat., Rumor.—*Liddell and Scott*.—(I. B.)
[5] Whence comes θρῆνος, a *dirge*.—ED.

see ver. 15 and 18; Luke xxi. 20, 21. The beginning is only mentioned in ver. 8.

7. Ἐγερθήσεται, *shall be roused*) sc. after a period of greater peace.—ἔθνος, κ.τ.λ., *nation*, etc.) even beyond the limits of Judea.—λιμοὶ, καὶ λοιμοὶ, καὶ σεισμοὶ, *famines, and pestilences, and earthquakes*) Almost all matters treated of in the Novellæ, may be referred to one or the other of these classes, though historians frequently regard such things less than the deeds of men.—κατὰ τόπους, *in divers places*) There always have been pestilences, etc., but not of such frequent occurrence.

8. Ἀρχὴ, *the beginning*) sc. with regard to the Jews; contrasted with *the end* spoken of in ver. 6, 14.—ὠδίνων, *of pangs*) which precede the *regeneration* [or new birth of the world]: see ch. xix. 28, and Rom. viii. 22. A metaphor taken from childbirth.

9. Ἀποκτενοῦσιν ὑμᾶς, *they shall kill you*) sc. some of you; see Luke xxi. 16. The Lord does not point these out, in order that all may watch. Before the destruction of Jerusalem, James the Greater was slain by Herod, as St Luke mentions; Peter, by Nero, as ecclesiastical history hands down. *You*: as if you were in fault, and were the authors of the misery of the human race. This is the last consolation of the world. "Judgment begins with the house of God."—μισούμενοι, *hated*) The Christian religion has something peculiar, hateful to the corrupt world, which tolerates all other denominations.

10. Σκανδαλισθήσονται, *shall be offended*) sc. shall make shipwreck of their faith.[1]—ἀλλήλους, *one another*) This is the saddest of all.

11.–13. Καὶ πολλοὶ, κ.τ.λ., *and many*, etc.) Faith, love, and hope must be anxiously preserved.

12. Τὴν ἀνομίαν, *unrighteousness*) *Unrighteousness* and *love* are opposites; for *love is the fulfilling of the law. Unrighteousness* involves compulsion, *love*, as it were, something natural.—ψυγήσεται, *shall wax cold*) It is the character of love to burn.—ἡ ἀγάπη, *love*) sc. towards God, mankind, our neighbour, and ourself; of a spiritual and also natural kind; love, which is the sum of the *law*.—στοργὴ (*natural affection*) makes parents rejoice in the birth of their offspring: when iniquity has made times

---

[1] As of love, v. 12.—V. g.

hard, they rejoice in losing their offspring or having none. *Love* is the ornament and very life of Christians, and of their whole condition and conduct, Phil. i. 9; 2 Pet. i. 7; Rev. ii. 4. It is also the foundation of that ὑπομονὴ, *patience* or *endurance*, mentioned in the next verse.—τῶν πολλῶν, *of the many*) i.e. of *the majority*, sc. of those who do not excel in *love*. Unrighteousness is especially practised by those who are exceedingly powerful or excessively poor : whence also the *love of the rest* waxes cold.[1] That justice which is called particular, being violated, that which is called universal, languishes.[2]

13. Ὁ δὲ ὑπομείνας, *but he that endureth*) By constancy, we preserve faith, love, and hope.—εἰς τέλος, *unto the end*) sc. of the temptation.—οὗτος, *this man*) i.e., *he, I say*, being as it were exempted from the general lot; see ver. 22.—σωθήσεται, *shall be saved*) When the city was destroyed, the Christians were saved; see Luke xxi. 28, 31.

14.[3] Τοῦτο τὸ Εὐαγγέλιον τῆς Βασιλείας, THIS *Gospel of the Kingdom*) sc. which Jesus preached.—ἥξει, *shall come*) The verb ἥκειν does not signify merely *to approach*, but *to arrive*, nay, actually *to be present*.[4]—τὸ τέλος, *the end*) spoken of in the following verses, on which account we find οὖν, *therefore*, in the next verse. Before that *end*, Peter, Paul, and others alluded to in ver. 9, had concluded their apostolate.

15. Τὸ βδέλυγμα τῆς ἐρημώσεως, *the abomination of desolation*) The abomination of profanation was followed by the abomination of desolation. Such was the name given by the Jews to the Roman army, composed of all nations, the standards of which they held in abomination as idols, since the Romans attributed divinity to them. See Spizelii Collatio de vaticin. ang., p. 135.—Δανιὴλ τοῦ προφήτου, *Daniel the prophet*) Cf. Heb.

[1] Since their power and means of doing good are taken violently from them by *unrighteousness* or *injustice*.—V. g.

[2] Universal justice comprehends the whole of our duty to our neighbour; particular justice is that strictly so called. See Aristotle's Nicomachæan Ethics, Book V. passim.—(I. B.)

[3] κηρυχθήσεται) This was accomplished before the destruction of Jerusalem. Col. i. 23.—V. g.

[4] ἔρχομαι denotes progress to, or arrival at, a place; ἥκω, that the progress has been effected, and the arrival taken place; so that ἥκω must be rendered, not *I come*, but *I am come*.—(I. B.)

xi. 32–34 [1] with reference to Daniel's being a prophet, although by many of the Jews he was not considered as one of the prophets. A slight cause may frequently produce an important error. In the Latin Bibles, the apocryphal writings were long ago mixed with the canonical books according to the connection of their subjects, and were distinguished from them in the index of books by certain marks, as one may see in MSS.; in process of time, this caution, feeble at best, having been neglected, they came to be considered canonical. On the other hand, since they who first collected the books of the Old Testament into one volume, did not possess the book of Daniel, that book, which was written both at a later period and also out of Palestine, was added to the Hagiographa; not inappropriately indeed, since the weeks predicted by Daniel began to be fulfilled in Ezra iv. 24; yet from this circumstance, some persons thought that Daniel was not a prophet at all, as he was not placed with the prophets, and as they furthermore disliked the occupation of examining his prophetical periods. The Great Prophet, however, confirms his claim to the prophetical character.—ἑστώς, *standing*) It should be written thus (not ἑστός),[2] even in the neuter: for ἑστώς is contracted from ἑσταώς, whence also we find ἑστῶτα in Luke v. 2—ἐνεστῶτα in Rom. viii. 38, etc. It must be referred to βδέλυγμα, *the abomination—already firmly standing, and destined long to stand*. An instance of Prosopopœia.—ἐν τόπῳ ἁγίῳ, *on* (or *in*) *a* (or *the*) *holy place*) In Dan. ix. 27, the LXX. have ἐπὶ τὸ ἱερόν, *on the holy place* (or *the temple*). The time of flight is joined in Luke xxi. 20 with the actual moment of the approach of the army; and Eusebius mentions (H. E. iii. 5), that at that very time the Divine warning to fly had been repeated. The *holy place*, therefore, does not here signify the temple, or the holy of holies, for it would have been too late to flee after that had been profaned, but a definite place without and near

---

[1] "*The Prophets*, who—stopped the mouths of lions:" with which compare Dan. vi. 22.—ED.

[2] Lachm. and Tisch. read ἑστός, with B corrected later (and D corrected?) LΔ. The rough Alexandrine forms have been retained in the best editions of the LXX., edited from the Vatican MS. They ought to have been also retained in the New Testament: and they would have been, had the latter been edited from the oldest MSS. instead of from those inferior ones used by the originators of the Textus Receptus.—ED.

the Holy City; in short, that very place which our Lord (as He had often done) regarded as made holy by His presence, whilst He was uttering these words: cf. Acts vii. 33. We learn certainly from Josephus, that the principal strength of the besieging army was upon *the Mount of Olives*: "They were commanded," says he, "to encamp on the mount which is called the Mount of Olives, which lies over against the city on the east."—Wars of the Jews, vi. 3. And that mount was considered holy also by the Jews, because the neighbouring temple could be looked into therefrom; and they had also a tradition that the Shechinah had stood there for three years and a half. They called it also הר המישיחה, *the Mount of Unction*. Very pertinent to this is Zech. xiv. 4, where the very mention of the eastern quarter (plaga) appears to denote holiness. And therefore that *place* which St Matthew designates as "*holy*," is described by St Mark as "*where it ought not*." Both of which passages refer to that in Dan. ix. 27; where the region of that mount is said to be בנף שקיצים,[1] *a quarter* (plaga) otherwise holy, but then, on account of the idolatrous besiegers, *abominable*: because there the שקוץ שמם, *the abomination that maketh desolate*, Dan. xii. 11, and xi. 31, was to stand. For בנף signifies also a quarter of the world, even without mention of the wind, as in Is. xi.-12. Punishment generally begins in the more holy places, and thence spreads to other parts.—ὁ ἀναγινώσκων νοείτω, *let him that readeth understand*) St Mark has the same parenthesis in ch. xiii. 14, although in many copies that clause from Daniel is not to be found there. Both Evangelists, writing before the siege of the city, warned their readers to observe the accurate advice of the Lord concerning the place and the rapidity of flight. In Dan. xii. 10, the LXX. have οἱ νοήμονες συνήσουσι, *the wise will understand*: and the Hebrew has המשכלים יבינו, *the wise will understand*.—ὁ ἀναγινώσκων, *he that readeth*) does not mean the public reader of Daniel (for at the commencement of the siege, the public lessons in the Law were taken from Leviticus, and none from Daniel were associated with them or with any others), but any *reader* either of Daniel

---

[1] E. V. "*The overspreading of abominations.*" Otherwise, *pinnacle of.*—(I. B.)

or of the Evangelist, especially when the siege was approaching. All ought to *understand*: and, since they were commanded to pray that their flight might not take place on the *Sabbath* day, why should the *Sabbath* reader be warned more than others?

16. Τότε, *then*) This answers to πότε, *when*, in ver. 3. The word "*then*" often occurs in this discourse.—οἱ ἐν τῇ 'Ιουδαίᾳ, *those that are in Judea*) not all the Jews, nor Christians dwelling elsewhere; but those who, believing the word of Jesus, should be in Judea.—φευγέτωσαν, *let them flee*) without hope that the siege might be raised.—ἐπὶ τὰ ὄρη, *into the mountains*) Safety was here promised in the mountains: and it was afterwards found there at Pella. See Eusebius H. E. iii. 5. Jesus warns His followers not to think that they would be safe within the city, in opposition to the persuasion pertinaciously maintained during the actual siege by the carnal prudence of the Jews.

17. Μὴ καταβαινέτω, *let him not come down*) sc. let him come down, not by the inner, but by the outer stairs.[1]—ἆραί τι, *to take anything*) *e.g.* victuals; corresponding with *garments* in the next verse.

18. 'Εν τῷ ἀγρῷ, *in the field*) Husbandmen go lightly clad into the field.

19. Οὐαί, *woe!*) This is not put by way of imprecation, but of indication. Neither is it an interdiction against the generating of children, but only a prediction of misery.—ταῖς ἐν γαστρὶ ἐχούσαις, κ.τ.λ., *to them that are with child*, etc.) Because they will not be able to flee quickly. Godly women will share the common calamity; see Luke xxiii. 29.

20. Προσεύχεσθε, *pray ye*) Many things are rendered less grievous in answer to the prayers of the righteous. They *did* pray, and their flight did not take place in the winter.—χειμῶνος, *winter*, or *cold and tempestuous weather*) Not merely the time of the year, but the state of the weather, seems to be intended by this word; see ch. xvi. 3.[2] The event certainly occurred in

---

[1] The roofs of Jewish houses could be reached either by the inner staircase, which communicated with the interior, or by the outer steps, which led directly to the ground without.—(I. B.)

[2] Where the word χειμών is rendered in E. V. *foul weather*. This signification is frequent in classical authors.

The Portuguese word *inverno* has the same double force.—(I. B.)

spring; cf. ver. 18 concerning *the field.*—Σαββάτῳ, *on the Sabbath day*) Not because it would have been unlawful to flee or carry burdens on the Sabbath day, especially for Christians, but because it is peculiarly miserable on that day, which is given to joy, to break off the rites of religious worship and flee, and because, being less prepared for flight, each hinders the other in attempting it by crowding the doors of synagogues or the gates of cities much more than when they are in the country or in private houses. Ptolemy Lagus, according to Josephus, took Jerusalem by surprise on the Sabbath day: Ant. xii. 1. In fine, punishments which happened to the Jews on the Sabbath day were more grievous than others: see Hainlin Chronol. Explan. fol. 19, 20. Their enemies also were more truculent on that day than on any other, from hatred of the Sabbath. At the time when sin is at its height, punishment arrives; cf. Hos. iv. 7. The observance of the Sabbath did not wholly expire before the destruction of the temple.

21. Ἀπ' ἀρχῆς κόσμου, *from the beginning of the world*) in the time of the Deluge, etc.

22. Οὐκ ἂν ἐσώθη, *would not be saved*) They would be excluded by premature death from the *salvation* of the soul which is ascribed to *the elect*. They who have already *attained salvation* will utter the words which resound in Rev. vii. 10.—πᾶσα σάρξ, *all flesh*[1]) in itself weak.—τοὺς ἐκλεκτούς, *the elect*) The elect, whether already converted or hereafter to become so, or as yet unborn, are mingled with the rest of mankind. Where the force of temptations exceeds the ordinary strength of the faithful, election is mentioned—see ver. 24, 31, and Luke xviii. 7—and the faithfulness and power of God; see 1 Cor. x. 13; 1 Pet. i. 5; Rev. xiii. 8.—κολοβωθήσονται, *shall be shortened*) An appropriate verb, since that which is shortened loses the entireness of its parts, yet so that it may nevertheless be considered as the whole.

23. Τοτέ, *then*) sc. at the time of the fall of Jerusalem.—μὴ

---

[1] In E. V. the words are rendered, "*no flesh should be saved.*" The difference is one of idiom, not of sense. E. V. applies the negative universally to the subject; Bengel, translating the Greek words literally, applies the negative to the predicate: sc. *all flesh would not be saved*—*i.e.* all flesh would come under the category of *not being saved;* in other words, *would perish.*—(I. B.)

πιστεύσητε, *do not believe*) For from that time forth the Son of Man will not be seen until His Advent. His coming to judgment, therefore, is mentioned incidentally in ver. 27, and professedly in ver. 29,[1] 30.—ὧδε, *here*) sc. where any one is who calls himself the Messiah.

24. Σημεῖα καὶ τέρατα, *signs and prodigies*) Signs affect the intellect; prodigies, one class of which is *fearful sights* (see Luke xxi. 11, and cf. Acts ii. 19), trouble the mind.—εἰ δυνατόν, *if* [it were] *possible*) This clause denotes the utmost endeavour, yet made in vain; cf. Acts xxvii. 39.[2]

26. Ἐν τῇ ἐρήμῳ, *in the desert*) This might be said speciously (cf. ch. iii. 3), and is applicable to those who drew crowds and bands tumultuously after them; see Acts xxi. 38. Therefore our Lord adds, " *Go not forth*."—ἐν τοῖς ταμείοις, *in the secret chambers*) This applies to those who pretended to possess hidden treasures, therefore our Lord adds, " *Believe it not*."

27. Ἀστραπή, *lightning*) It is not all lightning that is meant, but that which sometimes suddenly fills the whole horizon without previous warning.—ἀπὸ ἀνατολῶν, *from the east*) The lightning comes also from the other quarters; but in this passage it is said to come from the east. It may be supposed that Christ's Advent will take place from the east. The interval which is to elapse between the *appearance* of the Lord's Advent (see Gnomon on 2 Thess. ii. 8) and the Advent *itself*, enables the actual Advent to be sudden.—τοῦ Υἱοῦ Ἀνθρώπου, *of the Son of Man*) From this place to ver. 44, especially, He is frequently called *The Son of Man*; cf. ch. xxv. 31.

28. Ὅπου γὰρ κ.τ.λ., *for where*, etc.) This adage is combined here with the mention of the false teachers which occurs in ver. 23; but in Luke xvi. 37, 31, 32, with that of sufferings caused

---

[1] Bengel means, that until His final Advent, which *all* must recognise when it takes place, Christ shall not be visible; and that, therefore, any who says he is Christ before then, is *ipso facto* an impostor. The coming, accordingly, in ver. 27, is not a *personal* one, but a *virtual* coming in *the judgments inflicted on Jerusalem and Judea*: therefore it is only incidentally dwelt on as His coming. But the coming, in ver. 29, is the *personal, visible*, and final coming; and therefore it is described professedly as such: "Then shall *appear* the sign of the Son of man—they shall *see* the Son of man."—ED.

[2] προσήκει) Exercising peculiar faithfulness and divine affection towards you.—V. g.

by war. The *carcase*, therefore, must be carnal Judaism, devoid of that life by which the body of Christ is sustained, and yet boasting some appearance of a body, upon which, as upon a carcase left to them, the eagles will pounce greedily and in great numbers.—(συναχθήσονται, *will be gathered together*—the future tense.) Christ, however, who comes as the lightning, is not to be sought for at that carcase; ver. 23, 27. All kinds of eagles are not carnivorous, but only some species;[1] cf. Job xxxix. 30. These eagles are partly the false Christs and false prophets, partly the Roman forces. The Romans bore an eagle on their standards, and were not the first nation who did so; and some are of opinion that the eagle in this passage, and the boar in Ps. lxxx. 14 (13) allude to their military standards; cf. Hos. viii. 1.

29. Εὐθέως δὲ μετὰ τὴν θλίψιν τῶν ἡμερῶν ἐκείνων, κ.τ.λ., *but immediately after the affliction of those days*, etc.) There are four things to be observed in this passage. (1) Our Lord speaks of the sun being literally darkened, etc. And this phrase frequently occurs in the prophets, concerning the destruction of a nation, and in such cases has a much more literal force than is generally supposed, for where there is a great destruction of men, the beholders of the sun are reduced to a small number; but much more in the present passage has it a literal force, for the whole of our Lord's language on this occasion is strictly literal; therefore this verse must be also understood literally. (2) The tribulation indicated will be that of the Jewish people, and that for one generation. (3) It is not said, *after that tribulation*, nor *after those days*, but *after the tribulation of those days*, as in Mark xiii. 24.—ἐν ἐκείναις ταῖς ἡμέραις μετὰ τὴν θλίψιν ἐκείνην, *in those days, after that tribulation*. The term, "*those days*," refers to ver. 22 and 19; and it is indicated that the tribulation will not be long, but brief in duration; ver. 21, 22, 34. (4) The expression, εὐθέως, *quickly* (*cito*), implies a very short delay, since οὔπω, *not yet* (ver. 6) *i.e.*, οὐκ εὐθέως, *not quickly* (Luke xxi. 9), is said of the short delay which must precede that tribulation; nay, the passage already cited from St Mark excludes delay altogether.

[1] Bengel would seem to mean, they do not all feed on carrion, as vultures do. The Greek word comprehends both tribes, the latter of which are probably meant in the text.—(I. B.)

The Engl. Vers. has "*immediately.*" You will say, it is a great leap from the destruction of Jerusalem to the end of the world, which is represented as coming *quickly* after it. I reply—A prophecy resembles a landscape painting, which marks distinctly the houses, paths, and bridges in the foreground, but brings together, into a narrow space, the distant valleys and mountains, though they are really far apart. Thus should they who study a prophecy look on the future to which the prophecy refers. And the eyes of the disciples, who had combined in their question the end of the temple and of the world, are left somewhat veiled (for it was not yet the time for knowing; see ver. 36), from which cause, imitating our Lord's language, they with universal consent declared that the end was near at hand. In their progress, however, both prophecy and contemplation (*prospectus*)[1] more and more explain things further distant. In which manner also we ought to interpret what is obscure by what is clear, not what is clear by what is obscure, and to venerate in its dark sayings that Divine wisdom which always sees all things, but does not reveal all things at once. Afterwards it was revealed that Antichrist should come before the end of the world; and again Paul joined these two rather nearly together, until the Apocalypse also placed an interval of a thousand years between them. The advent of our Lord, however, actually took place (as far as its commencement was concerned; see Gnomon on John xxi. 22) after the destruction of Jerusalem, and presently, too, inasmuch as no intermediate event was to be mentioned in the present passage; cf. Gnomon on ch. iii. 1. The particle εὐθέως; (*quickly* or *immediately*) refers to this advent, not absolutely to the darkening of the sun and moon, for that accords with the extent of our Lord's meaning; so that the meaning is "*soon after the tribulation of those days,* it will come to pass that the *sun shall be darkened,*" etc. A similar connection of an adverb[2] with a verb

---

[1] *Looking further forward*, as in the landscape already alluded to, wherein at first sight all the parts might seem projected into the one plane. But the eye, which has gradually come to discern perspective, and to substitute, by the judgment, causes for the visible effects, learns to *look further*, and to separate by wide distances the foreground and background of the picture.—ED.

[2] Sc. ביום *on the day that.*—(I. B.)

occurs in Gen. ii. 17 ; *in the day on which thou shalt eat thereof,* it will come to pass that *thou shalt die the death;* see also Gnomon on ch. xxvi. 64, and Luke i. 48. The expression may also be referred to the mode of speech, so as to mean *after that affliction* (which the plan of this discourse, and the point of view from which this time is regarded, permit to be subjoined *immediately,* provided it be indicated that the other things will intervene) *the sun shall be darkened,* etc. It frequently occurs that adverbs, as in this passage, εὐθέως, *immediately,* do not qualify the thing itself, but the language in which it is expressed. Thus, in Mark vii. 9, the adverb καλῶς, *well,* and the verb ἀθετεῖτε, *ye abolish* [Engl. Vers., *ye reject*], are joined with [a part of] the verb *to say* [viz. *it may be said that*], understood : thus, too, in Heb. i. 6, the adverb πάλιν, *again,* is joined with the verb λέγει, *He saith.* In fine, St Luke (xxi. 24, 25) separates the *signs* in the sun, etc. [from *that tribulation*] by a greater interval. Some explain εὐθέως as denoting, not the shortness of the interval, but the suddenness of the event after long intervening periods. We must, however, keep to our first interpretation, so indeed that the particle εὐθέως be understood to comprehend the whole space between the destruction of Jerusalem by Titus and the end of the world. On such passages there rests, as St Antony used to term it, a *prophetical cloudlet.* It was not yet the fit time for revealing the whole series of events from the destruction of Jerusalem down to the end of the world. The following is a paraphrase of our Lord's words, "Concerning those things which will happen *after the tribulation of those days* of the destruction of Jerusalem, THE NEAREST EVENT which at present it suits My condition to mention, and your capacity to expect, is this, *that the sun will be darkened,*" etc. Furthermore, it does not follow from this that the expression, μετὰ ταῦτα, *after these things,* should be understood loosely in Rev. iv. 1. Where quickness is presupposed from Rev. i. 1. Such formulæ are to be understood according to the analogy of the passages where they occur.—ὁ ἥλιος σκοτισθήσεται, *the sun shall be darkened*) This must be taken literally, of a calamity different from those which have been described before. In the Old Testament, such expressions are used metaphorically, the figure being derived from that which will literally happen at the end of the world.—ἡ σελήνη οὐ δώσει τὸ φέγγος αὐτῆς, *the moon shall not give her light*) sc. as she is wont to do both when filling and waning. According to the course of nature, the sun and moon are eclipsed at different times: then, however, they will both be eclipsed at once.—ἀπὸ τοῦ οὐρανοῦ, *from heaven*) It is not said *upon the earth*; cf. in Mark xiii. 25.—ἐκπίπτοντες, *falling out*. They shall be as though they were not, sc. without light.—δυνάμεις, *powers*) sc. those firm interchained and subtle powers of heaven[1] (distinct from the *stars*) which are accustomed to influence the earth. They are thus denominated by Matthew, Mark, and Luke.—σαλευθήσονται, *shall be shaken*) an appropriate metaphor from the waves of the sea.[2]

30. Τὸ σημεῖον τοῦ Υἱοῦ τοῦ ἀνθρώπου, *the sign of the Son of Man*[a]) This is a more special *sign;* those which are mentioned in Luke xxi. 25 precede it, and are more general. The very appellation, "the Son of Man," agrees with these things (cf. Gnomon on ch. xvi. 13): for the mourning of the tribes of the earth is joined in Rev. i. 7, with their seeing Him *in person.* Our Lord means therefore to say, " Do not seek for any previous *sign ;*" see ver. 27. He Himself will be His own *sign,* as in Luke ii. 12; and so much the more so, because conjointly with His actual appearance, or a little before it mankind will behold a triumphal procession (*pompam*) in the clouds: unless indeed a thick darkness, a dazzling glory, the form of the cross, or some star, also appear. Cf. ch. ii. 2. Before this He had been *a sign which was spoken against* (see Luke ii. 34) : then He will be a *sign* manifest to all. A *Sign* denotes something very remarkable and striking to the eyes, whether it contain the *signification* of something else, or of itself; see Rev. xii. 1. The sun, moon, and stars, having been extinguished, that sign will be visible in the brightness of the Lord, and thence in that of a cloud, and of the clouds.[4] In short, the *sign* (cf. Mark xiii. 26, 4) is the

---

[1] Prov. viii. 27.—E. B.
[2] Rev. vi. 14.—E. B.
[3] Herein is contained a reply to the question proposed at ver. 3.—V. g.
[4] Bengel's expression, "nubis ac nubium," "of a cloud and of the clouds," evidently refers to Luke xxi. 27, " *Then shall they see the Son of Man coming* IN A CLOUD, *with power and great glory*," and to the words which occur in the present verse, " *they shall see the Son of Man coming* IN THE CLOUDS *of Heaven with power and great glory.*"—(I. B.)

triumphal train of the Son of man coming in His glory, who is Himself to be beheld presently after, as this passage tells us.—αἱ φυλαί, *the tribes*) especially of Israel.—ὄψονται, *shall see*) Cf. Numb. xxiv. 17.—ἐπὶ τῶν νεφελῶν, *on the clouds*) St Luke says, ἐν νεφέλῃ, *on a cloud*) He will be attended by many chariots;[1] He will be borne on a very magnificent one.

31. Τοὺς ἀγγέλους Αὐτοῦ, *His angels*) It is likely enough that a certain number of angels may be called peculiarly the angels of Christ, although all are subject to Him.—σάλπιγγος, *of a trumpet*) Trumpets are employed to call multitudes together; that *trumpet* will have a *loud voice* [Eng. Vers. *great sound*].—ἐπισυνάξουσι, *they shall gather together*) Cf. 2 Thess. ii. 1.—ἀπ' ἄκρων οὐρανῶν, *from the extremities of the heavens*) In Mark xiii. 27, we have ἀπ' ἄκρου γῆς, *from the uttermost part of the earth.*—ἄκρον signifies any extremity. Where the earth ends, there the heaven begins: whence it happens, that the mountains and the heavens also sometimes represent each other in parallel passages. Cf. 2 Sam xxii. 8 with Ps. xviii. 8 (7). It corresponds with the Hebrew קצה (extremity). In Deut. xxx. 4, the LXX. have "ἀπ' ἄκρου τοῦ οὐρανοῦ ἕως ἄκρου τοῦ οὐρανοῦ," "*from* [the one] *extremity of the heaven* to [the other] *extremity of the heaven;*" and thus also in Deut. iv. 32.

32. Ἀπὸ δὲ τῆς συκῆς, *but from the fig-tree*) An obvious matter. —τὴν, *the*) sc. following.—παραβολήν, *parable*) a most beautiful one.

33. Ταῦτα πάντα, *these things all*) The order of words ought not to be always overlooked: the emphasis, and, in speaking, the accent, frequently falls upon the first of two words. The present is the first passage which has required this to be demonstrated; we will therefore do so [by the following examples]:—(1.) Luke xi. 36, εἰ οὖν τὸ σῶμά σου ΟΛΟΝ φωτεινὸν, μὴ ἔχον τι ΜΕΡΟΣ σκοτεινὸν, ἔσται ΦΩΤΕΙΝΟΝ ὅλον, ὡς ὅταν ὁ λύχνος τῇ ἀστραπῇ ΦΩΤΙΖΗ σὲ, *if then thy body* [be] ALL *light, not having any* PART *dark, it shall be* LIGHT *all over, as when the candle by its shining* LIGHTETH *thee*. In this passage ὅλον (*all, the whole,* Lat. *totum,* Fr *tout*) is emphatic before φωτεινὸν (*light,* Lat. *lucidum*), in opposition to μέρος (*part*): and φωτεινὸν is emphatic before ὅλον,

---

[1] As is usual in a royal procession.—V. g.

its emphasis being declared by the verb φωτίζῃ (*lighteth*, Lat. *illuminet*. (2.) John xiv. 2. 3, πορεύομαι ἑτοιμάσαι ΤΟΠΟΝ ὑμῖν. καὶ ἐὰν πορευθῶ καὶ ἑτοιμάσω ΎΜΙΝ τόπον, κ.τ.λ. *I go to prepare* A PLACE *for you, and if I go and prepare* FOR YOU *a place*, etc. Here the apparent contradiction is removed by the order of the words, "A PLACE *is not to be prepared for you, since it is already prepared*,"[1] is the negative proposition. "FOR YOU *is to be prepared a place, i.e.* the entrance into that place is to be rendered sure," is the affirmative proposition. Both are equally true. (3.) Eph. ii. 1, 5, ὙΜΑΣ ὄντας νεκρούς—ὌΝΤΑΣ ἡμᾶς νεκρούς, YOU *being dead*—BEING *us dead* [Fr. VOUS *etant morts*, ETANT *nous morts*]. Here ὑμᾶς (*you*) is put antithetically to ἡμᾶς (*us*), in Eph. i. 19: and then ὄντας (*being*), denotes the past *state* of death, opposed to vivification. (4.) James ii. 18, δεῖξόν μοι τὴν ΠΙΣΤΙΝ σου ἐκ (others read χωρὶς[2]) τῶν ἔργων σου, κἀγὼ δείξω σοι ἐκ τῶν ἜΡΓΩΝ μου τὴν πίστιν μου, *Show me thy* FAITH *by* (others read *without*) *thy* WORKS, *and I will show thee by my* WORKS *my faith*. Here the first πίστιν (faith) refers to the words σὺ πίστιν ἔχεις (thou hast faith), and the second, ἔργων (*works*), to the words κἀγὼ ἔργα ἔχω (*and I have works*). These instances, extracted from four different writers of the New Testament, will suffice for the present. Now let us return to St Matthew. As the best MSS. have ΤΑΥΤΑ πάντα, THESE *things all*, in ver. 33, and ΠΑΝΤΑ ταῦτα, ALL *these things*, in ver. 34 (although others confound the two modes of expression);[3] the first ταῦτα placed before πάντα is emphatic, so as to express things about to happen next (for which reason in the parallel passage, Mark xiii. 29; the πάντα is omitted); and this emphasis being granted, the second πάντα expresses *all*, including *these*, things which were to come to pass next, in that generation. The pronoun ταῦτα (*these*) does not refer to the whole preceding discourse (for the previous signs, and the events which were to

---

[1] See ch. xxv. 34, "Inherit the kingdom *prepared* (ἡτοιμασμένην) *for you from the foundation of the world.*"—ED.

[2] Such is the reading of E. M.—(I. B.)

[3] Dabc Vulg. Syr. Memph. with Bengel, read ταῦτα πάντα in ver. 33. But B and Rec. Text, πάντα ταῦτα, and so Lachm. Bc and Amiat. MS. of Vulg. read πάντα ταῦτα, with Lachm., Tisch., Beng., and Rec. Text, in ver. 34. But DLa read ταῦτα πάντα.—ED.

follow them indicated by the signs, are distinct from each other), but to the beginnings, which are compared with the fig-tree, in contradistinction to the summer itself, *i.e.* the approaching kingdom of God. Those things having been fulfilled which are described from ver. 4 to ver. 28, room was made for the kingdom of God, which would grow stronger and stronger, in one continuous progress. The beginnings, after all hindrances had been removed, were equivalent to the whole.[1] Furthermore, in St Matthew and St Mark, ταῦτα (*these*) is in each case contrasted with ἐκείνης (*that*) in ver. 36, with the following sense: THESE *all which concern Jerusalem shall come to pass before this generation passes away; but of* THAT (remoter and last) *day* (of judgment) *knoweth no one*, etc. This observation facilitates the interpretation of the whole of this discourse. St Luke also contrasts with each other ταῦτα, *these*, and ἐκείνη, *that*. See Gnomon on Luke xxi. 36.—γινώσκετε, *ye know*, Indicative): Cf. ver. 32, or *know ye*, Imperative.—ἐγγύς, *near*) sc. the thing itself is.—ἐπὶ θύραις, *at the doors*) i.e. extremely near.

34. Γενεά, *generation*) sc. an age of men. This notion, which agrees with the event, corresponds most properly with the question, *when?* etc., proposed in ver, 3; cf. ver. 15, 20, ch. xxiii. 36; Luke xxiii. 38. From the date of this prediction to the destruction of Jerusalem was a space of forty years, and from the true year of our Lord's nativity to that event was a space of about seventy-five years. The Jews, however (as, for example, in Seder Olam), reckon seventy-five years as one generation, and the words, οὐ μὴ παρέλθῃ, "*shall not pass away*," intimate that the greater part of that generation, but not the whole of it, should have passed away before all the events indicated should have come to pass. The prediction is true with respect to either the forty or the seventy-five years.[2] So accurately did the Evangelist describe it many years before the event took place.

[1] Sc. Were tantamount to a pledge that the whole would be accomplished.—ED.

[2] Various things [agreeing with our Lord's prophecy] can be brought forward from the writers of the Talmud, which are reported by them to have happened in the forty years before the destruction of the temple and the city, and which thus, with sufficient accuracy, harmonise with the history of the Passion.—*Harm.*, p. 481.

ST MATTHEW XXIV. 35–39.

35. Ὁ οὐρανὸς, *heaven*) The motion of which is otherwise regulated by the most unerring laws.—ἡ γῆ, *the earth*) which is otherwise most firmly founded.—λόγοι Μου, *My words*) The plural number is employed; cf. πάντα, *all*, ver. 34, which is likewise plural.—οὐ μὴ παρέλθωσι, *shall not pass away*) q.d. My words shall correspond exactly with the event; although it does not appear so to men immediately. Heaven and earth will give place to the new heaven and new earth, which are described *by My words*. The firmness of the *law* is illustrated in a similar manner in ch. v. 18.

36. Περὶ δὲ τῆς ἡμέρας ἐκείνης, *but of that day*) The Lord shows the time of the temple and the city in ver. 32–34; He denies in this verse that the day and hour of the world are known. The particle δὲ, *but*, implies a contrast: the pronouns ταῦτα, *these*, αὕτη, *this*, refer to events close at hand; the pronoun ἐκείνης, *that*, to that which is distant. If, however, the former time is defined with some latitude, THAT DAY and hour is much less definitely indicated here: and yet He does not speak of *the day and hour* without cause. A *day* is a whole; an *hour* is a part. The day is not necessarily unknown because the hour is: the time taken with somewhat greater latitude is not necessarily unknown because the day is. And that which was unknown when this discourse was delivered, might be revealed after the Ascension of the Lord and the Apocalypse given to St John; and as the sand by degrees glides away in the hour-glass of time,[1] it may be known more nearly. Otherwise, the last day and the last hour would not even then be known when it actually arrives. Our Lord goes on to speak of the *day* in ver. 37, 38, of the *hour* in ver. 42, 43, and of *both* in ver. 50.—ἄγγελοι, *angels*) whose knowledge is otherwise great.—τῶν οὐρανῶν, *of the heavens*) The plural number.

38. Τρώγοντες, *eating*) This includes the arts of cookery, confectionary, and other matters connected with luxury. They were employed in this, and in nothing else.

39. Οὐκ ἔγνωσαν, *knew not*) Their ignorance was voluntary.

---

[1] In the original, "*clepsydra sensim elabente.*" The ancients measured time in the hour-glass, not by sand, but by *water*. I have given the corresponding idiom.—(I. B.)

40,[1] 41. Παραλαμβάνεται, *is taken*[2]) sc. into safety, under protection; see ver. 31.—ἀφίεται, *is left*) sc. in the midst of the dangers, whatever may occur.[3] The present tense is used with reference to the time of the τότε, *then;* and the matter was already present to the Saviour's eyes.

41. Ἀλήθουσαι, *grinding*) Grinding was an occupation of women.

42. Γρηγορεῖτε, *watch*[4]) This was the reason, no doubt, that the names *Gregory* and *Vigilantius* were so common in the ancient Church. You may ask why those who were so far distant from the last day were exhorted to watchfulness on that ground? I answer—(1.) The remoteness of the event had not been indicated to them. (2.) Those who are alive at any particular time represent those who will be alive at the end of the world; see Gnomon on 1 Thess. iv. 15. (3.) The principle of the Divine judgments, and of the uncertainty of the hour of death, resembles in every age that of the last day; and the hour of death is equivalent to the hour of resurrection and judgment, as though no time had been interposed. (4.) The feeling of the godly, which stretches forward to meet the Lord, is the same, whether with the longest or the shortest expectation. (5.) If every one had had to watch, from the time of the Apostles to the Lord's coming, it would have been well worth the trouble of so doing.—ὁ κύριος ὑμῶν, *your Lord*) called in ver. 44 the Son of Man.

43.[5] Γινώσκετε, *ye know.*[6]—εἰ ᾔδει, *if he had known*) He would have watched; and that care on his part would not have been much to be wondered at.—ποίᾳ φυλακῇ, *in what* (Lat. *quali*) *watch*)

---

[1] τότε, *then*) at the actual time of the Advent, ver. 39. Comp. ch. xxv. 1.—V. g.

[2] In the original, *assumitur.*—(I. B.)

[3] As was the case with the men at the time of the Deluge.—V. g.

[4] Latin, "*vigilate,*" from which verb (*vigilo*) the name Vigilantius is derived; as Gregorius from the Greek verb employed in this passage.—(I. B.)

[5] Three parables in Matthew refer to watchfulness, or else careless security; a fourth refers to faithfulness, or else the want of it.—*Harm.*, p. 484.

[6] The word in the original of St Matthew may be either Indicative or Imperative. Bengel renders it as the former in the Gnomon, by "*scitis,*" and in his German Version by "*das ist euch aber bekannt.*" E. V. in the latter, by "*know ye;*" in which it is supported by the Vulgate, which has "*scitote.*" —(I. B.)

It is supposed that the *goodman* of the house has been warned of the coming of the thief. In carnal concerns we are vigilant, even though we know not in what portion of the night our goods will be endangered, if we know only that the danger will occur either on this, or on one of the next few nights.—φυλακῇ, *watch*) although a watch is longer than an hour.—ὁ κλέπτης, *the thief*) The last temptation, arising from the concealment of that hour, accompanied by other circumstances of difficulty, is the most severe. For the nearer that the actual accomplishment of anything approaches, so much the more keen become both hope and fear; and, generally speaking, so much the more impatient of any, even the least, delay. And thus will it be with those who live during the last small portion of time, when the other events which precede it in Rev. xx. shall have come to pass.—οὐκ ἂν εἴασι, κ.τ.λ., *he would not have allowed*, etc.) by yielding to sleepiness.—διορυγῆναι, *to be dug through*[1]) which would take some time to accomplish.

44. Ἔρχεται, *cometh*) The present tense.

45. Τίς ἄρα ἐστίν, κ.τ.λ., *who then is*, etc.) Who is there who would wish to be such? The ἄρα (*then*) in Luke xii. 42, refers to the question in the preceding verse; but here it expresses the magnitude and rarity of the matter.—πιστὸς καὶ φρόνιμος, *faithful and prudent*) Two cardinal virtues of a good servant, of which faithfulness (fides) is more frequently praised, because it is seated in the will, and has as its associate, prudence,[2] given from above.—δοῦλος, *servant*) i.e. pastor. The *article*[3] is emphatic.—θεραπείας,[4] *household*) i.e. flock.—τοῦ διδόναι, *to give*) This refers to the epithet *faithful*.[5] The opposite is exhibited in ver. 49.—τὴν τροφήν, *their food*) in just quality and measure; corresponding with the expression τὸ σιτομέτριον (*their portion of meat*) in Luke

---

[1] E. V. "*broken up*."—(I. B.)

[2] *Prudence* is the characteristic of those who do not live from day to day (*i.e.* making no preparation for the morrow), but who so behave themselves as they would wish that they had behaved themselves when, sooner or later, their Lord shall come.—V. g.

[3] The Greek is "ὁ πιστὸς δοῦλος καὶ φρόνιμος;" lit. "THE *faithful servant and prudent:*" rendered in E. V. "A *faithful and wise servant.*"—(I. B.)

[4] So D and Rec. Text. But BLΔ, οἰκετείας. *abcd* Vulg. Hil., 'familiam.'—ED.

[5] *i.e.* Faithful in respect of giving.—ED.

xii. 42.—ἐν καιρῷ, *in due season*) This refers to the epithet *prudent*.

46. Εὑρήσει, *shall find*) Therefore we are not under compulsion.

48. Ὁ κακὸς δοῦλος ἐκεῖνος, THAT *evil servant*) whom the Lord knoweth.—χρονίζει, *delayeth*) See xxv. 5 [cf. Eccles. viii. 11].

49. Συνδούλους, *fellow-servants*) They are called *fellow-servants*, to bring out in strong relief the injurious character of that *evil servant's* conduct towards them: they were, however, subject to him, though he with them was subject to their common Lord.—δὲ, *but*) His injurious conduct towards his fellow-servants, and his own self-indulgence, are put in strong contrast with each other.—μετὰ τῶν μεθυόντων, *with the drunken*) There will, therefore, at that time be many whose whole condition and character will consist in vicious self-indulgence. See 1 Thess. v. 7. A similar mode of speaking occurs in Genesis xlii. 5., where the LXX. have ἦλθον δὲ οἱ υἱοὶ Ἰσραὴλ μετὰ τῶν ἐρχομένων, *i.e. But the sons of Israel came with them that came*.

50. Ἐν ἡμέρᾳ ᾗ οὐ προσδοκᾷ, *on a day on which he doth not expect*) sc. Him to come. Cf. ver. 44.

51. Διχοτομήσει, *shall cut him in twain*[1]) A punishment frequent in ancient times, and an appropriate one for those who were δίψυχοι, *i.e. double-minded*. The Hebrew נתח [*to divide* or *cut in pieces*] is thus rendered by the LXX. The hypocrite divides his soul and body in the worship of God; wherefore his soul and body shall be divided in eternal perdition. Eternal perdition is called death: all death, however, has this characteristic, that it deprives the body of its soul. Then neither the soul shall rejoice in the companionship of the body, nor the body in that of the soul, but it shall rather increase its death. Then will each of the damned be able to say with truth, "*I am torn asunder*" (*disrumpor*): cf. Heb. iv. 12, as to the force of the word with reference to the wicked. The twofold punishment corresponds to the twofold offence; viz., the cutting in twain to his smiting the men-servants and maid-servants, the portion with the hypocrites to his gluttony and drunkenness.—ὑποκριτῶν, *hypocrites*) Hypocrisy is a moral evil: the punishment of hypo-

---

[1] E. V. "*Shall cut him asunder*."—(I. B.)

crites is a specimen of punishment. In the parallel passage, Luke xii. 46, we find ἀπίστων, *unbelievers* or *faithless*, *i.e.* those who are not *faithful*; cf. ver. 45.—θήσει, *shall appoint*) by a judgment, just, severe, and irreversible.

CHAPTER XXV.

1. [Τότε, *then*) sc. when the last day is close at hand.—B. G. V.] —δέκα, *ten*) There is a mystery in this number, employed also in Luke xix. 13, and in its division here into two equal parts.[1] The bride in ancient times had always ten virgins, at least, as bridesmaids.[2] We do not possess many remains by which to illustrate this parable from Jewish antiquities. It is better to compare it with Ps. xlv. and the Book of Canticles.—λαμπάδας, *lamps*) i.e. burning.—ἐξῆλθον, *went forth*) i.e. engaged to go forth; see ver. 6.—τοῦ Νυμφίου, *the Bridegroom*) See Luke xii. 36.

2. Φρόνιμοι—μωραί, *prudent—foolish*) See ch. vii. 24, 26.—καὶ αἱ πέντε μωραί, *and the five other foolish*) Their condition becomes better understood from the description given of the prudent.[3]

3. Ἔλαιον, *oil*) i.e. except that with which the lamps were then burning: see latter part of ver. 8. The lamp burning is faith; the lamp with oil beside is abundant faith.[4]

---

[1] Either because the number on both sides will be equal, or because the inequality will not be evident.—V. g.

[2] In general, at least among the Jews, *ten* constitute a society or company.—V. g.

[3] Both characters are clearly described in 2 Pet. i. 5–8, 9, 10, 11.—B. G. V. They aimed at what was right, but not consistently and steadily.—V. g.

[4] Elsewhere he suggests another interpretation, viz.: "In a Burning Lamp there is Fire and Oil. By the Fire is here signified the supernatural, heavenly, fiery Spirit-power (*Geisteskraft*) which is bestowed upon the soul without its co-operation (*ohne ihr Zuthun*): see 2 Pet. i. 3, 4; and by the Oil, holy Assiduity (*Fleiss*) on the part of man: see 2 Pet. i. 5. And of this, man should have not only enough for the exigencies of the present time, but also an *abundant* supply, see 2 Pet. i. 8 [sc. "if these things be in you

4. Ἀγγείοις, *vessels*) These represent the recesses of the heart.

5. Ἐνύσταξαν, *dozed*) The Hebrew verb נום, to *slumber* or *doze*, is rendered by the LXX., νυστάζειν. Dozing takes place, either after sleep, as in Prov. vi. 10, or before it, as in Isa. v. 27, which is the case in the present passage.—[πᾶσαι, *all*) The prudent also fell asleep, and that not without peril; but when they awoke, they had still oil enough. During the sleep of those, who have not previously enough thereof, their oil comes to an end.— B. G. V.]

6. Μέσης δὲ νυκτὸς, *but at midnight*) i.e. during the deep sleep of even these virgins.—κραυγὴ, *a cry*) sc. to arouse them, accompanied by the blast of a trumpet.[1]

7. Ἠγέρθησαν, *were aroused*) sc. from sleep.—πᾶσαι, *all*) Then will the evil and the careless also[2] awake. All things will be awakened. By how very little the foolish missed of entering in, and yet they are shut out.[3]

8. Σβέννυνται, *are being extinguished*[4]) this very moment, miserably.

9. Λέγουσαι, κ.τ.λ., *saying*, etc.) In this, as in everything else, they showed themselves prudent.—μήποτε, κ.τ.λ., *lest*, etc.) A broken[5] sentence, suitable to the hurry of that event.—οὐκ ἀρκέσῃ, *there be not sufficient*) sc. for both you and us: i.e. we cannot share with you: a metonomy of the consequent [for the antecedent]. Every one must live by his own faith.—ἡμῖν, *for us*) The prudent now have hardly[6] enough for their own use,

and *abound*"], for all future circumstances: so does the entrance to the Wedding-House become sure to him, and *abundant* besides, see 2 Pet. i. 11 [sc. "an entrance shall be ministered to you *abundantly*"]. The foolish virgins did not even remain resting only on their own unassisted nature: they too had something of grace and of the Spirit. Nowhere is it more clearly (*deutlicher*) written than here how far a soul can advance in good, and yet fall through (*durchfallen*): see ver. 8."—B. G. V. in loc.

[1] Far louder than earth's loudest artillery: see 1 Thess. iv. 16.— B. G. V.

[2] Sc. As well as the good and the prudent.—(I. B.)

[3] In the original, "et tamen exciderunt," corresponding with the "*durchfallen*" above.—(I. B.)

[4] E. V. "*are gone out.*"—(I. B.)

[5] "Not so," is not expressed in the original, which abruptly begins with "μήποτε," "lest haply."—Ed.

[6] "*Ægre.*" There is here an allusion to 1 Peter iv. 18, where Bengel

ST MATTHEW XXV. 10–15.   439

You ought previously to have followed the example of the prudent.—πορεύεσθε, κ.τ.λ., *go ye*, etc.) Let us do in time what will then prove to have been wise.—πρὸς τοὺς πωλοῦντας, *to them that sell*) although they are not traders [*i.e.* do not make salvation a matter of traffic].—ἀγοράσατε, *buy*) See Rev. iii. 18.

10. Ἀπερχομένων δὲ αὐτῶν, *but whilst they were going*) Their danger arose from the circumstance on which they asked advice.[1]—αἱ ἕτοιμαι, *they that were ready*) The prudent were ready.[2]

11. Αἱ λοιπαὶ παρθένοι, *the other virgins*) To whom the name of virgins was now of no avail.

13. Γρηγορεῖτε, *watch ye*) He who watches will have not only his lamp burning, but also oil in his vessel: he who has oil in his vessel is not greatly held, even by sleep; see ver. 5.

14.—Ὑπάρχοντα, *goods*) For the distribution of them, see the next verse.[3]

15. Ἔδωκε, κ.τ.λ., *gave*, etc.) He left them free to choose their method of trafficking without saying, "Give to the bankers."—πέντε—δύο—ἕν, *five—two—one*) A parable nearly resembling this occurs in Luke xix. 13, where one pound is given to each servant, and the pound of the first produced ten, of the second five, of the third none. The goods which God gives are distributed equitably: and who knows whether, in all their inequality, the most scantily provided is surpassed by the richest more than renders μόλις (E. V. *scarcely*, Vulg. *vix*) by *ægre*. See Gnomon in loc.— (I. B.)

[1] They came short of entering by but a little, yet they did come short.—V. g.

[2] Ἐκλείσθη, *was shut*) Hardly any one, whilst the door is still open, can realise by thought, how great will be the lamentation of those who shall stand outside when the doors are once shut. How often a mere trifle, as we should think, forms the boundary between wisdom and folly · and yet the decision we come to is of the utmost importance to us. There are—1) those who enjoy an abundant entrance into the eternal kingdom of joy: 2) those who, as it were rescued from shipwreck, are brought to shore: 3) those who are openly hurried along on the broad way to destruction: 4) those who, though having been very close to the obtaining of salvation, yet suffer themselves to lose it. The condition of these last is lamentable above that of all others.—V. g.

[3] There are intimated by these, spiritual gifts, temporal resources, time itself, and finally opportunities of every kind.—V. g.

by five parts? We may compare with this the circumstance, that Plato, in his book on Laws, has not permitted any citizen to possess an income more than five times that of the poorest. See Arist. Polit. ii. 5. A. Ruimer, the Flemish preacher, was of opinion that the Reformed Church had five talents, the Lutheran two, the Roman one. What has the Greek? What have other churches, ancient and modern? What has posterity?—δύναμιν, *ability*) sc. for trafficking. No one is required to do more than he is able; therefore he is rightfully compelled to render an account. —εὐθέως, *immediately, straightway*) See the two following chapters.

18. Ἀπέκρυψε, *hid*) sc. in the earth; see ver. 25.

19. Μετὰ δὲ χρόνον πολὺν, *but after a long time*) So that there had been time enough to double the capital entrusted. The quickness of the Lord's Advent is not absolute.

20. Προσελθὼν, *coming up to* Him) sc. with confidence. The bad servant did so with diffidence; ver. 24.—ὁ τὰ πέντε τάλαντα λαβὼν, *he that had received the five talents*) The righteous receive sentence before the wicked: cf. ver. 34.—ἴδε, *See!*) The freedom of speech of a good servant.—ἐπ᾿ αὐτοῖς, *on them*) The servant does not attribute the gain to himself, but to his Lord's goods.

21. Εὖ, *well-done*) A formula of praising. This praise is mentioned in 1 Cor. iv. 5.—ἀγαθὲ, *good*) opposed to πονηρὲ, *bad*, in ver. 26.—πιστὲ, *faithful*) opposed to ὀκνηρὲ, *slothful*, in ver. 26. Faith drives away sloth.—ὀλίγα, *few*) If five talents are *few*, how great will be the amount of the πολλὰ, *many!*—καταστήσω, *I will appoint*) Thou art fit for more, thou art trusty (*frugi*), opposed to ἀχρεῖον, *unprofitable*, in ver. 30.—εἴσελθε, *enter thou!*) opposed to ἐκβάλετε, *cast ye forth*, in ver. 30.—χαρὰν, *joy*) sc. the banquet, the feast:[1] light, laughter, applause. Cf. ver. 30.

24. Ἔγνων σε, κ.τ.λ., *I knew thee*, etc.) He does not know the Lord who thinks Him *hard*. God is LOVE.[2] Righteousness appears unrighteousness to the ungodly. The justice of God

---

[1] In the original the passage stands thus:—
"Convivium, *festin:* lusum, risum, plausum;" where the introduction of the *French* word FESTIN strikes one as strange.—(I. B.)

[2] And indeed it is not without appearance of good for one to dwell rather much in thought upon the Divine severity; but such thoughts are not void of all danger.—V. g.

transcends the comprehension of the creature.—σκληρὸς, *hard*) In Luke xix. 21, we find αὐστηρὸς, *austere*.—This Lord was not such; but let those earthly lords who really are so, consider what servant they will resemble on the judgment day.—οὐ διεσκόρπισας, *thou hast not strawed*) Though, in reality, God bestows all things liberally.

25. Φοβηθεὶς, *being frightened*) Without love, without confidence; *q.d.* " fearing that I should not satisfy Thee, that I might be compelled to spend somewhat from my own stock, that I might vainly endeavour to bring aught from the field *where* the crop did not seem worthy of Thee, into the barn *whence* nothing of Thine appeared to have been strawed." The wicked and slothful servant, whilst he imagined his Master to be one who would require excessive gain, beyond the strength of His servant, did not even obtain that legitimate profit which he might have obtained. Do what thou canst, and what thou art commanded; await success, and thou shalt be astonished at it.—ἔκρυψα, *I hid*) Contrast with this Ps. xl. 10, 11.[1]

27. Οὖν, κ.τ.λ., *therefore*, etc.) The goodness of the Lord remains unknown to the wicked servant, by whom it had been denied.—βαλεῖν, *to have put out*) The labour of digging was greater than this would have been; see ver. 18.—τὸ ’Εμὸν, *Mine*) corresponding with τὸ Σὸν, *Thine*, in ver. 25; but in this instance the words σὺν τόκῳ, *with interest*, are added.[2]

29. Τῷ γὰρ ἔχοντι παντί, κ.τ.λ., *for to every one that hath*, etc.) So that the more he has, the more will be given to him.—ὁ ἔχει, *that which he hath*) The servant actually *had had* the talent; see ver. 24.

---

[1] Ver. 26. Καὶ ὀκνηρὲ, *and slothful*) Slothfulness overpowers the mind at times more than it does the body. It would certainly have cost this servant no more trouble to have gone to the money-exchangers or bankers, than that which he expended uselessly in digging, ver. 18. Had the servants been ordered, in the first instance, to go to the bankers, without doubt he also would have obeyed the order. But in that case the servants would not have obtained so much praise. See, therefore, that you strenuously employ your powers.—V. g.

[2] Ver. 28. ἔχοντι τὰ δέκα, *who hath the ten*) Who was not even bound to share with him, who had the five talents. See herein how great distinctions in retributive rewards and punishments shall hereafter be made manifest.—V. g.

30. Ἀχρεῖον, *unprofitable*) sc. now and hereafter;[1] cf. Gnomon on ver. 21, and Luke xvi. 11.—ἀχρεῖος is in Attic Greek written ἄχρειος, according to Eustathius.—ἐκβάλετε, κ.τ.λ., *cast forth*, etc.) There is a contrast between this and ver. 21. The Lord Himself commands [the good servants] to enter; He desires His attendants to cast out [the unprofitable one], as in ch. xxii. 13.[2]

31. Ἐν τῇ δόξῃ Αὐτοῦ, *in His glory*) concerning which so many things have been foretold.—καὶ πάντες οἱ ἅγιοι ἄγγελοι μετ' Αὐτοῦ, *and all the holy angels with Him*) We must not here suppose ἔλθωσι, *shall come*, to be understood; but the nominative must be taken absolutely according to the Hebrew idiom, and rendered, *all the angels accompanying Him*.—πάντες, *all*) Add *all nations* from ver. 32. All angels; all nations. How vast an assembly! —τότε, *then*) As has been foretold. The disciples thought that this would take place immediately.

32. Ἀφοριεῖ, *he shall separate*) The separation will not be complete before then.

33. Ἐρίφια, *kidlings*) A diminutive. Although giants, they will be kidlings. They will not then be אלים, *mighty*, and עתודים, *he-goats*.[3]

---

[1] Even though he had caused no loss to his master.—V. g.

Ἀχρεῖος, though translated by Bengel, *unprofitable, useless*, is not to be confounded with ἄχρηστος, which more strictly expresses that meaning. A slave that has done all that his master commands is ἀχρεῖος, not in the sense that he is *worthless, useless*, which could not be said of such a servant, but he is one οὗ οὐκ ἔστι χρεία, a person to whom the master owes nothing, with whom he could dispense, Acts xvii. 25. God receives no benefit from man for which He owes a return, Luke xvii. 10. Here, in Matt. xxv. 30, though the servant had been also ἄχρηστος, *unprofitable, useless*, and slothful, yet the idea conveyed by the ἀχρεῖος is not this, but its consequence: for he who is *useless by doing no work* is *not wanted* (the latter expressing the true force of ἀχρεῖος). The ἄχρηστος, besides being *useless*, causes also *loss* to his master. See Tittm. Syn. Gr. Test.—ED.

[2] Cf. Gnomon on ch. vii. 24.—(I. B.)

[3] This play upon words, on such a solemn subject, appears rather extraordinary in a man of Bengel's piety. The Hebrew עתוד is used of the leader of a flock, and, metaphorically, of the leader of a people.—(I. B.)

Perhaps Bengel's language will not appear so inappropriate when compared with that of Scripture, to which he evidently alludes. Isa. xiv. 11, "Hell from beneath stirreth up the dead for thee, even all the chief ones

34. Τότε, κ.τ.λ., *then*, etc.) cf. this address with that to the kids [Eng. Vers., goats] in ver. 41.

Here, *Come*:	There, *Depart from me*:
ye blessed of my Father:	*ye cursed*:
inherit the kingdom:	*into the fire*:
prepared for you:	*prepared for the devil and his angels*:
from the foundation of the world.	*eternal*. (so called in ver. 46).

—ὁ Βασιλεύς, *the King*) an appellation full of majesty, and joyful only to the godly; see ver. 40.—τοῦ Πατρός Μου, *of My Father*) We have been chosen in Christ.—κληρονομήσατε, *inherit*) Therefore the γὰρ, *for*, in the next verse ought not to be pressed too much.—ἡτοιμασμένην, *prepared*) There is an intimate relation between this verb and the noun καταβολή, *foundation*. —ὑμῖν, *for you*) Therefore elect men have not supplied the place of the angels who sinned.—ἀπὸ καταβολῆς κόσμου, *from the foundation of the world*) The preposition ἀπὸ, *from*, corresponds with the Hebrew מ, which signifies *before*; cf. Eph. i. 4. When good and bad are compared together, good is frequently described by eternity, so to speak, antecedent; bad, by its hereafter: thus it is in this verse; cf. ver. 41, and 1 Cor. ii. 7, 6.

35. Ἐδώκατέ, κ.τ.λ., *ye have given*, etc.[1]) Of all good and bad actions, those will be especially mentioned which have been performed to the saints, which presuppose faith and love towards Jesus Christ and His brethren, and involve confession of His name, which are most frequent, and remarkable, and conspicuous; and then, from the manifest glory of the Lord, the dignity of His brethren, and the character of good and evil actions towards them, will be manifest; cf. ch. x. 40, 41. This discourse exhibits simultaneously the former misery and excellence of the saints, the former ability and wickedness of the ungodly, and the most righteous recompense of both. Of the works of mercy, however,

---

[Hebr. *leaders*; lit. *great goats*] of the earth." Comp. Ezek. xxxiv. 17; Zech. x. 3.—ED.

[1] Oh what a vast recompense (*Vergeltung*)! An eternal kingdom in return for such insignificant acts of kindness (*gegen solche Wohltaten*)!— B. G. V.

those only which have been done to the body are mentioned, which are both more despised in the world, and will then be a more evident specimen of faith, inasmuch as a man in them expends somewhat of his material resources and trouble (whereas those which concern the spirit are without expense), and will come more sensibly under the observation of the wicked. Nor was it suitable to the Judge to say: "I have erred, I have sinned, and you have recalled me,"[1] etc.—Μοι, *to Me*) This presupposes faith, for the faithful perform acts of kindness on this ground.—ἐδίψησα, κ.τ.λ., *I was thirsty*, etc.) Such is the condition of the faithful in this life: hunger, thirst, nakedness, captivity, etc.—συνηγάγετε, *ye took* (Me) *in*) The LXX. use the same verb in Judges xix. 15, 18.

37. Πότε Σὲ εἴδομεν, κ.τ.λ., *when saw we Thee*, etc.[2]) The faithful do not estimate their good deeds, nor the wicked their bad (ver. 44), in the same manner as the Judge.

40. Ἐφ' ὅσον, *inasmuch as, in as far as*) An intensifying particle. Without doubt, even individual acts will be brought forward.—ἑνί, *unto one*) All things are accurately reckoned up; nothing is omitted. Even a solitary occasion is frequently of great importance in either direction; see ver. 45.—τούτων, *of these*) used demonstratively.—τῶν ἀδελφῶν Μου, *My brethren*) It is better to do good to the good than to the wicked; yet these are not excluded from the operation of Christian love (see Matt. v. 44), provided that a due precedence be preserved in the character of the men and works. Men, the more that they are honoured, treat so much the more proudly those with whom they are connected (*suos*): not so Jesus: at the commencement of His ministry He frequently called His followers *disciples;* then, when speaking of His cross (John xiii. 33), He once called them *little sons*,[3] and (John xv. 15) *friends;* after His

---

[1] That is to say, The judge decides by the love, or absence of love, which existed towards *Him*. He could not speak of *spiritual* benefits done to Him, inasmuch as He was holy and sinless: He therefore mentions *temporal* and *corporeal* benefits.—ED.

[2] In like manner, many of the righteous, who have conferred benefits on each other in this world, remain mutually unknown.—B. G. V.

[3] *Filiolos.* The word in the original is τέκνια, plural of τέκνιον, which is the diminutive of τέκνον—*child or offspring*—derived from τίκτω, *to bring forth.*—(I. B.)

resurrection (John xxi. 5), παιδία, *children*,[1] and *brethren* (cf. ch. xxviii. 10; John xx. 17; and cf. therewith Ib. xiii. 1); and this appellation He will repeat at the judgment-day. How great is the glory of the faithful! see Heb. ii. 10, 11, 12, etc. During the time of His humiliation (exinanitionis) the honour of Jesus was guarded, lest from such an appellation He might appear to be of merely common rank; but in His state of exaltation no such danger exists. Observe, however—(1) that Christ addresses no one as *brother* in the vocative; the case is different in ch. xii. 48, 49, and Heb ii. 11, 12; (2) that Scripture does not call Christ our brother; and (3) that it would not have been suitable in Peter, for example, to have said, *Brother*, instead of *Lord*, in John xxi. 15, 20, 7 (see Ibid. xiii. 13). Even James, called by others the *Lord's brother*, calls himself *the servant of God and of the Lord Jesus Christ*, James i. 1. Jude also, in the first verse of his epistle, calls himself the *servant of Jesus Christ and brother of James;* see also Matt. xxiii. 8; Luke xxii. 32. Amongst mortals, unequal *fraternity* is so maintained, that the superior friend honours the inferior by the title of *brother;* whilst the inferior addresses the superior by his title of honour. Thus also the heavenly court has its own *etiquette*, without any conflict between humility and confidence. Thus, also, the appellation of *friend* appears one-sided, so that the Lord calls His own, "*friends*," but is not so called by them: see John xv. 15. We must except the faith whose freedom of speech attains to that of the Canticles.—τῶν ἐλαχίστων, *of the least*) sc. outwardly, or even inwardly. A certain species is pointed out in the whole genus of saints: there are some who have received, others who have conferred favours.—Ἐμοὶ ἐποιήσατε, *ye have done it unto Me*) not merely *to Me also*, but TO ME absolutely; cf. οὐδὲ Ἐμοὶ ἐποιήσατε, *neither have ye done it unto Me*, ver. 45.

41. Τότε, κ.τ.λ., *then*, etc.) And then the righteous shall immediately, by virtue of the word "*come*," sit *on kingly thrones* (*regaliter*) as assessors in the judgment on the cursed.—τὸ ἡτοιμασμένον, *which is prepared*) Thus is Is. xxx. 33. At the time of this judgment the devil will be already in hell; see Rev. xx. 10–13; cf. 2 Pet. iii. 7, fin.

[1] *Puerulos*—παιδία being the plural of παιδίον, which is the diminutive of παῖς.—(I. B.)

42. Οὐκ, κ.τ.λ., *not*, etc.) Sins of omission.

44. Καὶ αὐτοί, κ.τ.λ., *they also*, etc.) The process is distinctly described: they will answer either altogether or one by one.—πότε, κ.τ.λ., *when*, etc.) The ignorance of the wicked, and their endeavour to justify themselves, will remain up to that time.

45. Τούτων τῶν ἐλαχίστων, *of the least of these*) Our Lord does not add, *My brethren*, as in ver. 40. The wicked are ignorant of the relation which the righteous stand in to Christ, and will remain so.

46. Ἀπελεύσονται, *shall depart*) The place of judgment is distinct from the places into which the two classes will severally depart.—κόλασιν, *punishment*[1]) There is a difference between τιμωρία, *vengeance*, and κόλασις, *punishment*; for *punishment* is inflicted for the sake of him who suffers: *vengeance* for the satisfaction of him who inflicts it; see Arist. Rhet. i. 10, n. 31.[2]—αἰώνιον, *eternal*) *Eternal*[3] signifies that which reaches and passes the limits of earthly *time*: cf. Gnomon on Rom. xvi. 25.—οἱ δὲ, κ.τ.λ., *but the*, etc.) Christ the King shall first address the righteous, in the hearing of the unrighteous; but the unrighteous shall first depart, in the sight of the righteous; see ch. xiii. 49, 50. Thus the damned will see nothing of eternal life, though the righteous will see the vengeance inflicted on the damned.—δίκαιοι, *righteous*) declared to be so by this very judgment.

---

[1] "Of fire, see ver. 41. Righteous King, grant that I may hereafter find myself standing on the right hand."—B. G. V.

[2] In the Oxford edition of 1833, I. 10, § 17.—I. B.

[3] The Bible has no metaphysical distinctions, therefore it has no *one* word to express eternity; this it expresses by long periods joined with one another indefinitely. Αἰῶνες = עוֹלָמִים, *æva:* very long periods, which, multiplied indefinitely, give the only notion we can form of eternity. Ὥρα (Th. ὅρος, *terminus*), a *definite* space of time: καιρός, *the* time, the *fit* time: χρόνος, time, in its actuality, marking *succession*: αἰών, an *indefinite course of time*, without the notion of an end. See Tittm. Syn. Gr. Test. Ἀπ᾽ αἰώνων = from all eternity, *a parte ante*. Εἰς τοὺς αἰῶνας = to all eternity, for ages, for ever, *a parte post*. As these phrases are applied to the eternity of God Himself, and as, moreover, αἰώνιος is applied to ζωή, which none deny to mean *everlasting life*, no objections (such as have been lately raised), from the meaning of αἰών, will hold good against the everlasting duration of punishment.—Ed.

CHAPTER XXVI.

1. Ἐτέλεσε πάντας, *ended all*) He had said all that He had to say. He did not enter on his Passion sooner, or defer it later than this point. A regular systematic plan of our Lord's Discourses may be produced from the Harmony of the Gospels.

2. Μετὰ δύο ἡμέρας, *after two days*) Our Lord foretold His death by various measures of time.[1] καὶ, *and*) sc. *and* therefore, as this time is suitable for the transaction.—παραδίδοται, *is betrayed*) The present tense. Our Lord was preparing Himself entirely[2] for suffering, and His enemies were labouring to effect the same object: see Mark xiv. 1.

3. Συνήχθησαν, *were gathered together*) Thus also in ver. 57, and ch. xxvii. 1, 17, 27, 62; cf. Luke xxii. 66; Matt. xxviii. 12; Acts iv. 5, 26, 27.—οἱ ἀρχιερεῖς, *the chief priests*) They took the principal part in that matter; they were supported, however, by the *scribes*, the lawyers, and the *elders of the people*, who formed the remainder of the Jewish council.—τοῦ λεγομένου, *who was called*) St Matthew wrote for readers of times and places, in which the names of Caiaphas and Judas (see ver. 14) would not be known from any other source.[3]

---

[1] Just as there is said to be a *space of three days* from the evening of Friday to the dawn of light on the Lord's day: so here a *space of two days* is said to intervene between Wednesday and Thursday, which latter was the day of the *Passover* and of *unleavened bread*, Mark viii. 31, xiv. 11, 12. So among the Romans sometimes the expression ante diem Secundum Kalendas means the same as *pridie Kal.* Matthew narrates, in an abbreviated and condensed form, the *delivering up of Jesus to be crucified.* His being delivered up was accomplished step by step: through the instrumentality of Judas on the night of Thursday; through Caiaphas on the following morning; and through Pilate, after about two hours having intervened. Thus we come from the betrayal to the crucifixion.—*Harm.*, p. 487. The day (Thursday) which intervened between this speech of our Lord and the crucifixion is mentioned in ver. 17.—V. g.

[2] In the original, " Totum se comparabat Jesus ad patiendum.—(I. B.)

[3] This remark holds good rather of the present Greek translation, subsequently written for more general circulation, than of the original Hebrew

4. Δόλῳ, *by craft*) An unworthy consultation.

5. 'Εν τῇ ἑορτῇ, *in the feast*[1]) Even then! They wished to delay the matter until the people, who were then collected in great numbers on account of the Passover, should have departed, after the conclusion of the festival. But as the traitor offered his services, they cast delay aside. Thus the Divine counsel was fulfilled.—τῷ λαῷ, *the people*) who acknowledged Jesus as a Prophet, and were then assembled in great numbers.

7. 'Αλάβαστρον, *alabaster*) Rather of thin stone than glass, otherwise it could not have been (see Mark xiv. 3) broken without inflicting wounds.—ἔχουσα, *having*) She had one alabaster-box, and did not know how to employ it better.—ἀνακειμένου, *as He reclined*) at table.[2]—Others were anointed after death; it

---

Gosp. of St Matthew, written especially for the Jews, to whom the names Caiaphas and Judas would be familiar.—ED.

[1] Ver. 6. ἐν Βηθανίᾳ, *in Bethany*) No doubt the banquet or supper, with its attendant circumstances, and the anointing, were one and the same, which are specified by John in the regular order of time, ch. xii. 1, etc., but by Matthew and Mark merely incidentally in passing. The anointing excited the indignation of Judas; and, after he had cherished it in his bosom for several days, Satan suggested to him the act of betrayal, and in person took possession of the wretched man. It cannot readily be supposed, 1) that it was some other woman rather than Mary, the one so pre-eminently beloved by the Saviour, who obtained the promise of *her deed*, nay, even *her own self*, being had in *remembrance* [ver. 13]: for, in fact, of no other woman whatsoever, save Mary, is *the name* recorded in connection with this event. Also, it is rather hard to credit, 2) that the pious disciples would have employed *afresh* [ver. 8], within a few days after, the *pretext* [John xii. 5, 6] concerning the 300 pence which might have been given to the poor by the sale of the ointment,—a pretext which, when employed by Judas, our Lord had confuted with such force. Finally, 3) Jesus declared the very day of the anointing, as marked by John, to be the one and only day of *His being made ready* thereby *for His burial:* there cannot, therefore, be any second day, in Matthew and Mark, of His being in that same condition [viz. of being made *ready for burial*]. Nor, besides, is there anything to forbid the supposition, that all things which John records happened in the house of Simon the leper, and that Mary anointed with the precious ointment, first the head, then also the feet of the Saviour; which facts John states in an abbreviated form, as intending to record the wiping of His feet with the hairs of her head.—*Harm.*, p. 493, etc.

[2] E. V. *As He sat at meat.*—(I. B.)

Καὶ κατέχεεν, *and poured it down*) The mode of anointing in such a case is more readily understood, when it is taken into consideration that the an-

behoved Christ rather to be anointed whilst living: after His death it was needless.

8. Ἀπώλεια, *waste*) or *perdition*.—Nay, thou, Judas, art [the son] of Perdition;[1] see John xvii. 12.

9. Ἠδύνατο, *might*) The disciples exhibit in this instance great ignorance of comparative theology.—τοῖς πτωχοῖς, *to the poor*) Which is, generally speaking, a right employment of our means;[2] see ch. xix. 21, and Luke xix. 8.

10. Τί κόπους παρέχετε τῇ γυναικί, *Why trouble ye the woman?*) For it is a trouble to be doubtful in one's conscience, not only concerning a thing to be done hereafter (see Rom. xiv. 15), but also concerning a thing already done.—τῇ γυναικί, *the woman*) The disciples acted with incivility towards the Lord Himself; but this He finds less fault with than the annoyance given to the woman.—καλὸν, *good*) Although she was not herself aware that she had done so well. The simplicity of an action does not detract from its goodness.[3] It was not waste with regard to the poor (ver. 11) nor the disciples (Mark xiv. 7, middle of the verse), nor the woman (ver. 13), nor the Lord Himself (ver. 12).

12. Βαλοῦσα, *in that she hath poured*) The word implies profusion.—πρὸς τὸ ἐνταφιάσαι Με, *for My burial*) These words intimate that His death was certain and near at hand. The verb ἐνταφιάζειν does not mean "*to place in the sepulchre*," but "*to prepare for the sepulchre*." The ἐνταφιασμὸς of Jacob (Gen. l. 2, S. V.) took place in Egypt, his sepulture afterwards [in Canaan].

13. Τὸ εὐαγγέλιον τοῦτο, *this Gospel*) i.e. which Christ preached.[4]—λαληθήσεται, *shall be spoken of*) And so it is. This saying of our Lord was both heard and afterwards committed to writing by St Matthew. Its fulfilment furnishes a proof of the truth of

cients rather lay reclined at table than sat at it. They had couches furnished with cushions, and they lay in such a posture as that their feet rested backwards.—V. g.

[1] In the original, both Greek and Latin, the same word is used to express *Waste* and *Perdition*.—(I. B.)

[2] And that such was the practice of the disciples is evident from this very passage.—V. g.

[3] For often an action is either worse or better than the agent himself had supposed; ch. xxv. 38, 44; Heb. xiii. 2.—V. g.

[4] He speaks humbly and modestly.—V. g.

Christianity. No earthly monarch can bestow immortality on any action, even though he employ all his wealth and power to do so.—μνημόσυνον, *a memorial*) The memory of the godly may flourish, even though their names be unknown.[1]

14. Πορευθείς, *departing*[2]) The disciples were not under restraint. The wicked could depart when he would.

15. Ἔστησαν, *they weighed out*[3]) The LXX. frequently render the Hebrew שׁקל (to *weigh out*, or *pay*) by ἵστημι, and in Zech. xi. 12, where the prediction occurs concerning these thirty pieces of silver, the very word ἔστησαν is found.— τριάκοντα ἀργύρια, *thirty pieces of silver*) Such was the value of a slave, in Exod. xxi. 32 ; that of a freeman was double.

17. Τῇ δὲ πρώτῃ τῶν ἀζύμων, *now on the first day of unleavened bread*) It was now Thursday, the fourteenth day of the first month ;[4] cf. Exod. xii. 6, 15.—ποῦ, *where?*) They ask not *whether*, but *where*, they should prepare the Passover.[5] Jesus

---

[1] Comp., however, John xii. 3 [from which it seems the name of the woman *is* known, viz. Mary], and footnote on ver. 6 above, extracted from the *Harm. Ev.*: and again, the Gnomon on Luke xxiv. 18.—E. B.

[2] Judas *departed*, doubtless, about the nightfall of Wednesday. On that very night, being possessed by Satan, he seems, as we have reason to think, to have had an interview with our Lord's adversaries, but on the following day to have fixed with them on the further proceedings.—*Harm.*, p. 496.

[3] In the original Gnomon no rendering is given for ἔστησαν. In his Harmony, Bengel renders it *bieten—they tendered*, or *proffered ;* in his German Version *schiessen*—which seems to mean " *they threw, counting it as they threw it.*" Engl. Vers. has, " *they covenanted* with him *for.*"—(I. B.)

Beng. seems to take ἔστησαν in the sense " *they weighed out* to him." So ἵστημι is found used in Homer's Iliad xix. 247, xxii. 350) more than once ; lit., *I place in the balance, I poise.*—ED.

[4] Nisan 14, April 4. *Greswell.*—(I. B.)

On which they were bound to put away all leaven ; and so the consumption of the paschal lamb could not be put off beyond 24 hours, to the evening of the Friday.—*Harm.*, p. 499.

[5] Nor even do they say, *When?* all that they were concerned about was the supper-room *where*. Moreover, we may reasonably infer that the *Jews* also, and not Jesus alone, *celebrated the paschal feast* on the evening of *Thursday*, from the fact—1) That otherwise the disciples would undoubtedly have been censured by the Jews at the close of the Friday, for omitting to keep the Passover, which they were not ; and 2) Because, on the year on which Christ suffered, the conjunction of the Moon and Sun, before the Passover, fell on Wednesday, and therefore the new moon and Passover itself

was wont to perform all things which were enjoined by the law. —Σοὶ, *for Thee*) Jesus was as the father of a family, surrounded by the family of His disciples.

18. Τὸν δεῖνα, *a certain man*) This word is put instead of a proper name.[1]—ὁ Διδάσκαλος, *the Master*) Therefore the host in question was a disciple, but not one of the Twelve.—ὁ καιρός μου, *My time*) which I have long foreseen and foretold, when I shall suffer.—ποιῶ τὸ πάσχα, κ.τ.λ., *I celebrate the Passover*, etc.) A courteous mode of announcing the fact to that ready disciple at whose house the Master was about to *celebrate the Passover*. It is astonishing that some learned men should have called in question, or denied the fact, of our Lord's having then celebrated the Passover; see ver. 17–19, the commencement of ver. 30, and Luke xxii. 7, 8, 12, 14, 15.

23.[2] Ὁ ἐμβάψας, *he that dippeth*) The use of the same small dish, of which there were several on the table, and the dipping of the sop in it at the same moment with our Lord, was to be the distinctive mark of the traitor; see ver. 25. St Mark uses ἐμβαπτόμενος (present part. middle) to denote the same idea which St Matthew expresses by ἐμβάψας (1st Aor. part. act.); The former therefore employs the present in an indefinite sense.

24. Ὑπάγει, *goeth*) Through Passion to Glory.—καθὼς γέγραπται, *as it is written*) And therefore the woe does not affect the

could not be thrust forward to *the Sabbath-day*. There is to be added. 3) the consideration that the supper, which is recorded even by John, ch. xiii. 1, 2, was celebrated on Thursday, immediately before the feast of the Passover.—*Harm.*, p. 501, 502.

[1] *i.e.* Our Lord mentioned the man's name, though St Matthew has omitted it.—(I. B.)

[2] Ver. 21. ἀμὴν λέγω ὑμῖν, *Verily I say unto you*) Our Lord inserted His complaint as to the approaching treachery and uncleanness [John xiii. 10] of Judas in His discourses connected with the washing of the disciples' feet, and with the Lord's Supper, on the following day; but on both days the inquiry of the disciples as to the traitor, follows immediately after that complaint which He uttered. Both the complaint and inquiry of the second day are placed in Matthew and Mark, before the Lord's Supper : in Luke they are placed after it. They are, therefore, to be regarded as *simultaneous* with it—that is to say, the institution of the Supper held a middle place between the beginning and continuation (progress) of the complaint and inquiry.—*Harm.*, p. 510, 511.

Son of Man. A consolatory consideration.—οὐαὶ δὲ, *but woe!*) The Divine foreknowledge of the traitor's sin does not diminish its heinousness.—ἐκείνῳ, *to that man*); concerning which very man also *it has been written.*—παραδίδοται, *is betrayed*) By this word something further is added to ὑπάγει, *goeth.*—εἰ οὐκ ἐγεννήθη, *if he had not been born*) sc. if he either had not been conceived, or had died before his birth; see Job iii. 2, 10, 11. This phrase does not necessarily imply the interminable eternity of perdition: for it is a proverbial expression; cf. Luke xxiii. 29; Ecclus. xxiii. 19 (Gr. ver. 14).[1] Judas obtains a situation of exclusively pre-eminent misery amongst the souls of the damned. For so long a time he accompanied our Lord, not without sharing the sorrows connected therewith; a little before the joyful Pentecost he died.—ὁ ἄνθρωπος ἐκεῖνος, "THAT" *man*) The words, "*that man*," might seem a predicate. THAT is the designation of one who is considered already far off.

25.[2] 'Ραββί, *Master*) It is not recorded in Scripture that Judas ever called Jesus, Lord.—σὺ εἶπας, *thou hast said*) A formula of replying affirmatively, first to those who affirm, thence also to those who enquire, when the interrogation is taken away (as though it were a mode) and the sentence is left categorical.[3] The question is asked, "JUDAS *is the traitor?*" the interrogation is taken away, and the categorical reply remains: "*Judas* IS *the traitor.*" A similar form of expression is found in Ex. x. 29, כן דברת, So *it is as thou hast said;*[4] cf. 1 Kings xx. 40, and Gnomon on ver. 64.

26. 'Εσθιόντων δὲ αὐτῶν, *And as they were eating*) As in ver. 21.

---

[1] In the LXX. and Eng. Vers. it stands as the 14th. in the Vulgate as the 19th verse.—(I. B.)

A degree of misery is here awarded to him greater than that which is set forth in ch. xviii. 6.—V. g.

[2] μήτι ἐγώ εἰμι, *Is it I?* [Surely it is not I?] Hypocrites counterfeit by imitation that which the sincere-hearted speak under the influence of genuine love.—V. g.

[3] *i.e.* a simple and absolute affirmation.—(I. B.)

Categorical, naked, and absolute, as opposed to a sentence in which there is a "modus," *i.e.* some accompanying expression of *feeling, thanksgiving*, a *prayer*, or such like. See Append. on Sermo Modalis.—ED.

[4] S. V. Εἴρηκας; *thou hast said.*—E. V. *Thou hast spoken well.*—(I. B.)

Judas[1] therefore was present;[2] cf. the πάντες, κ.τ.λ. (*all*, etc.) in Mark xiv. 23, and πλὴν, κ.τ.λ. (*but*, etc.) in Luke xxii. 21.—

---

[1] *i.e.* In ver. 21 it is said, "AND AS THEY WERE EATING, *He said,* *Verily, I say unto you that one of you* (sc. of those who were then at table) *shall betray Me.*" The repetition of the expression, *And as they were eating*, implies, in Bengel's opinion, that the act was continuous, and that those spoken of in ver. 21, concerning whom it was said that one of them should betray our Lord, were all, including the traitor, still present.—(I. B.)

[2] I will state, in a summary form, the arguments, independent of the one given above, on which this proposition which I maintain, rests:—

1. If Judas had departed before the singing of the hymn, he would have been doing the same as if one in the present day were to depart before the offering of the grace and prayers at the close of a banquet, and would have thereby the more disclosed his atrocious design.

2. During the continuance of our Lord's supplications on the Mount of Olives, Judas had no lack of time sufficient for bringing the cohort to effect his purpose.

3. Luke, ch. xxii. 21, immediately subjoins after the words of the Institution, these words, BUT, NEVERTHELESS (πλὴν), *behold the hand of him that betrayeth Me is with Me on the table*; and as this very complaint is placed before the Lord's Supper by Matthew and Mark, these speeches [that as to Judas, and that in which the Institution took place] cannot be severed from one another.

4. To explain our Lord's words (Luke xxii. 21) of the *table*, in the sense, the counting-board [of the chief priests] on which Judas' hand was laid, with Jesus as the merchandize which he offered for sale, is out of place; for (1) It is not the seller that is said to be with the merchandize, but the merchandize with the seller [whereas Jesus says that Judas is with Him]; (2) Thirty pieces of silver was not so large a sum as to suggest the idea of a counting-board or banking-table; (3) The money had been already reckoned out to Judas, Matt. xxvi. 15; (4) The ἰδοὺ, *Behold*, Luke xxii. 21, implies, in fact, the presence of the traitor, as reclining *at the* same *banqueting table* with Jesus (comp. Luke xxii. 30, xvi. 21), and dipping his *hand* in the dish.

5. The words πλὴν ἰδοὺ, *But, nevertheless, behold*, being taken in their usual sense, are we to say that the traitor was driven away from the bread and the cup after these had been blessed? But Mark, after having made mention of the twelve, ch. xiv. 17, immediately subjoins the statement, that *they* ALL *drank of the cup*, ver. 23, with which comp. Matt. xxvi. 27.

6. If you say, the traitor was known to John or even to Peter already, on the preceding day, how, then, is it that they, not till now, one by one, are represented as having said, *Is it I?* For, in fact, when John, in a covert way, made enquiry, it was in a secret manner that the traitor was disclosed to him; and as to his having informed Peter of the fact, it is easier to suspect than to affirm this. The remaining nine disciples did not even observe

λαβὼν, *taking*) sc. in His hand. This implies the supreme dignity of the holy supper; cf. John iv. 2.[1]—τὸν ἄρτον, *the bread*) which was at hand.—εὐλογήσας, *having blessed*) In the next verse we find εὐχαριστήσας, *having given thanks* (corresponding to the Hebrew ברך). Each verb explains the other. He *gave thanks* to the Father, and at the same time *blessed* the bread and also the wine by the act of giving of thanks and by prayer; cf. Luke ix. 16; John vi. 11; 1 Cor. xiv. 16, 17.—ἔκλασε, *brake*) after blessing it (post benedictionem): which is inconsistent with the notion of transubstantiation. For an *accident*, as the Romanists declare the bread to be after it has been blessed (post benedictionem), cannot be broken.—καὶ ἐδίδου, *and gave*) Our Lord is not said Himself to have eaten and drunk on this occasion: since not for Himself was His body being given, nor His blood being shed.—Λάβετε, *Take*) Who could have taken (" *received*") if the Lord had not instituted it? Cf. John iii. 27.—τοῦτο, *This*) sc. in opposition to the shadows of the Old Dispensation; as much as to say, you have Me, My actual self; *This*, sc. which I command you to take: for it is immediately followed by *My blood*, which is of the New Testament.—Σῶμα, *Body*, must be taken as literally as Αἷμα, *blood*. The separate distribution, however, of His body and blood represents the actual death[2] of our Lord, in which His blood was drawn forth from His body. The benediction preceded and precedes the utter-

the nod of Peter [beckoning to John to ask the Lord]: therefore both the question of John and the reply of the Lord escaped their notice, John xiii. 28.

7. That the traitor should have been vouchsafed the washing of feet, is a circumstance almost as astonishing as his being admitted to the Lord's Supper: nor does even the permission of the kiss, given for the purposes of treachery, move us to less astonishment. As to the rest, we are here treating only of a question of *historical truth:* nor is it our intention ever to uphold the cause of unfair adapters of facts to their own aims (perfidorum œconomorum.)—*Harm.*, p. 511, etc.

[1] It is there said, "Jesus *Himself baptized* not." It is here said, "Jesus took bread," etc.—(I. B.)

[2] The memory of which ought to be perpetuated till His coming again.—B. G. V., ver. 29.

In the very moment of death Christ approached that state which is different from the life that He lived before His death and after His resurrection, and thenceforward for ever —*Harm.*, p. 510.

ance of the words, *This is My body*. We readily allow that there is an allusion to the formula of the Jews, who, in celebrating the Passover, when asked by their children, *What is this?* replied, זה נוף של פסח וגו, *This is the body of the Lamb which our fathers ate in Egypt*.—τὸ σῶμά Μου, *My body*) understand here "τὸ ὑπὲρ ὑμῶν διδόμενον," *which is given for you*, words implied in ver. 28, and expressed in Luke xxii. 19.—The Evangelist describes the matter briefly, as being well known by the practice of those for whom he writes. The expression, "*This do in remembrance of Me*" (which is recorded by St Luke), is implied in ver. 29.

27. Τὸ ποτήριον, *the cup*) The same which was there already, from which they had all drunk.—πάντες, *all*) Hence it is clear that even if one species[1] were sufficient, it must rather be the *wine* than the *bread*. Thus also in 1 Cor. xi. 25, the expression ὁσάκις, *as often as*, is employed in the mention of the *cup* [as well as of the *bread*].[2] Scripture expressed itself thus, foreseeing (Gal. iii. 8) what Rome would do.[3] The disciples then represented the "*many*" (πολλῶν) who are mentioned in ver. 28, where the reason of the injunction is given. Thus "many" and "all" are used together in 1 Cor. x. 17. The Holy Supper ought not to be a matter of indifference to Christians.

28. Τοῦτο, *this*) The true blood of Christ is shown to be actually present, just as the blood of the victims was in the Mosaic formula cited in Heb. ix. 20; for that formula is here referred to.—τῆς καινῆς, *of the New*) in contradistinction to the *Old*: see Ex. xxiv. 8, sc. "And Moses took the blood, and sprinkled it on the people, and said "*Behold the blood of the covenant*," etc.—διαθήκης, *testament, disposition, dispensation*) Many theologians of the Reformed Church, and some even of the Evangelical communion,[4] endeavoured in the last generation to reduce the whole scheme of Christian doctrine to the form of a *covenant*: a method pre-eminently suited to the

---

[1] The word is here used in the technical sense in which Theologians employ it to denote separately the bread and wine, in contradistinction to each other.—(I. B.)

[2] After eating the bread, the drinking of the cup is not left as a matter of our own option to do or not do as we think fit.—V. g.

[3] Sc. refuse the cup to the Laity, etc.—(I. B.)

[4] In Bengel, *Reformed* = Calvinistic : *Evangelical* = Lutheran.—(I. B.)

Jewish theology; but Scripture expresses the New divine economy in this case, as it is wont in other cases, by a word belonging to the Old scheme, although employed in a sense not exactly coinciding with its original meaning: nor can we easily speak of the NEW, διαθήκη, or *Dispensation* (*Dispositio*), except in contrast to the *Old*, either expressed or implied. In short, the very words ברית and διαθήκη [by which the Old and New Dispensation are severally indicated] differ from each other, and their difference corresponds wonderfully with the actual state of the case. For the word ברית accords more with the Old economy, which had the form of a *covenant*, whereas διαθήκη accords more with the New economy, which has the form of a *testament;* on which account the Talmudists employ the Greek word דייתיקי [διαθήκη, written in Hebrew characters] as not having a Hebrew word whereby to express it. But the idea of a *covenant* does not so well agree with that entire sonship which exists under the New Testament dispensation. Even the very notion of a *testament*, will at last, as it were, come to an end, on account of our intimate union with God: see John xvii. 21, 22, and 1 Cor. xv. 28.—πολλῶν, *many*) even beyond the limits of Israel.—ἐκχυνόμενον, *which is being shed*) The present tense. There is the same potency in the Holy Supper, as if in that self-same moment the body of Christ was always being given, and His blood being shed.—ἄφεσιν ἁμαρτιῶν, *remission of sins*) the especial blessing of the New Testament dispensation. [Eph. i. 7, E. B.]

29. Λέγω, *I say*) Concerning the order of these words, and those that immediately precede them: cf. Luke xxii. 15, 16, 17, etc.[1]—ἀπ' ἄρτι, *from henceforth*) A phrase suitable to taking leave.—γεννήματος τῆς ἀμπέλου, *of the produce of the vine*) A periphrasis for *wine*, somewhat different from the common lan-

---

[1] If you compare the order of the events narrated, as contained in Luke, with that which we have in Matthew and Mark, our Lord seems to have combined the promise of *eating* in the kingdom of God (Luke xxii. 16) with the lamb of the Passover supper; and the promise of the *drinking anew* in the kingdom of God with the cup of His (the Lord's) Supper (Matt. xxvi. 29; Luke xxii. 18), and, therefore, to have closely joined to one another these mysteries [*i e.* the symbolical institutions, the Passover and the Lord's Supper].—*Harm.*, p. 509.

guage of the inhabitants of earth, and therefore the more suitable to the meaning of the Saviour who was about to leave the earth.—γέννημα and γένημα occur in the LXX., also promiscuously, when wine and the vine are spoken of.—ἕως τῆς ἡμέρας ἐκείνης κ.τ.λ., *until that day*, etc.) Which had been foretold: see Luke xxii. 16, 18, 30. Hence St Paul (1 Cor. xi. 26) draws the inference that " as often as ye eat this bread and drink this cup, ye show forth the Lord's death till He come."—αὐτὸ, *it*) referring to *the produce of the vine, i.e. wine*, evidently of heaven.—καινὸν, *new*) sc. in the full consummation of the *New Testament*. This *new* is placed above the *new* spoken of in ver. 28. See the Prelude to this in John xxi. 12.[1] The Jewish Passover was superseded by the Lord's Supper, this will be again succeeded by further things of a heavenly nature. Elsewhere, in ch. ix. 17, instead of " καινὸς," we find " νέος," οἶνος, *new wine* [where νέος denotes newness of vintage, not novelty of kind]; but καινὸν in this passage evidently implies a *newness* in nature, not in age.[2]—ἐν τῇ βασιλείᾳ τοῦ Πατρὸς Μου, *in My Father's kingdom*) see 1 Cor. xv. 24; Luke xxii. 16, 30. Thomas Gataker considers *new* (καινὸν) wine to be the same as ἕτερον, *different* (cf. Mark xvi. 17, with Acts ii. 4),[3] so as to denote wine of a kind entirely different from that which the Lord was then taking with His disciples.

30. Ὑμνήσαντες, *having sung a hymn* or *hymns*) sc. they either sang or recited[4] Ps. cxiii., cxiv., cxv., cxviii., cxxxvi., in which the

[1] Our Lord's *dining* with them after the resurrection is a prelude to their hereafter *eating and drinking at His table in His kingdom*, Luke xxii. 30.—ED.

[2] Καινὸς, *new*, is opposed to that which has existed long and been in use, ex. Gr. ἱμάτιον παλαιόν, Matt. ix. 16. But νέος, *recent*, is opposed to that which was originated some time back, as οἶνος παλαιός, Luke v. 39. Καινὸν is in Matt. xxvi. 29, applied to γέννημα τῆς ἀμπέλου, because He refers to *another* wine than that then poured out—a wine not *recent* but *different*. See Tittm. Syn.—ED.

[3] For the γλώσσαις λαλήσουσιν καιναῖς of Mark answers to the λαλεῖν ἑτέραις γλώσσαις of Acts.—ED.

[4] After the recital of the hymn, and not previously, followed those things which John records in his chapters xv., xvi., xvii.; for the hymn is closely connected with the Passover supper; and such is the formula of connection, John xviii. 1, that the prayers of Jesus, John xvii., cannot be separated from His departure out of the city by the hymn. We may, not without good

mystery of Redemption is notably expressed. The *hymn* also contained the words which are quoted in ch. xxi. 9, 42. Our Lord is frequently said to have prayed while on earth; never to have sung.

31. Πάντες ὑμεῖς, *all ye*) Our Lord had before foretold the crime of a single traitor.—σκανδαλισθήσεσθε, *shall be offended*) So that your faith in Me shall totter exceedingly. The same word occurs in Rom. xiv. 21.—γέγραπται, *it is written*) The disciples might conclude that the prediction was about to be fulfilled that night, from the conjunction of the smiting of the shepherd, and the scattering of the sheep. —πατάξω, *I will smite*) sc. *with the sword*, put by metonymy for the Cross, concerning which it was not the part of the prophets to write more expressly. In Zec. xiii. 7, the LXX.[1] have πάταξον τὸν ποιμένα, καὶ διασκορπισθήσεται τὰ πρόβατα, *smite the Shepherd, and the sheep shall be scattered.* God smote Jesus, since He delivered Him to be smitten.— διασκορπισθήσεται, *shall be scattered*) The whole protection of the disciples, before the advent of the Paraclete, consisted in the presence of Jesus; who being smitten, they were dispersed.— τὰ πρόβατα, *the sheep*) The disciples were representatives of the whole flock which they were afterwards to collect.

32. Προάξω, *I will go before*) As a *shepherd*. A pastoral expression.—Γαλιλαίαν, *Galilee*) Where His appearance was to be exceedingly solemn to His sheep again collected together. Our Lord says to those who had come up with Him from Galilee, "Before you return home from the feast I will rise from the dead."

33.[2] Εἰ καὶ πάντες, κ.τ.λ., *Even though all*, etc.) He might rather

---

reason, suppose that the hymn was recited whilst they were yet in the supper room; but that the words of Jesus, in chapters xv. and xvi. of John, and also the prayers, ch. xvii., were spoken in the open air (ver. 1, "Jesus lifted up His eyes *to heaven*"), in the court of the house where He had supped, and within the city.—*Harm.*, p. 522.

[1] So the Ed. of Grabe and Breitinger from the Cod. Alexandr. The text of Reineccius has πατάξατε τοὺς ποιμένας, καὶ ἐκσπάσατε τὰ πρόβατα. —E. B.

[2] The word καί is pronounced by the margin of both Ed. spurious: but the Germ. Vers. answers to the Gnomon.—E. B.

ABCD*abc* omit καί, reading only εἰ. Vulg., however, has "etsi:" and Orig. 4, 412*c*; 437*a*, Hil. 742*d* read εἰ καί.—ED.

have said—"Even though no one else should deny Thee, yet I will do so."—οὐδέποτε, *never*) Not merely, not this night.

34. Ἐν ταύτῃ τῇ νυκτί *in this very night*) It was already night; and it was more wonderful that this should happen by night than by day.—πρὶν, *before that*) A considerable portion of the night remains after cock-crow. Peter's *never*, therefore, is utterly refuted.—ἀλέκτορα, *the cock*) The bird here intended is that strictly so called, cf. Mark xiii. 35; see 3 Macc. v. 23. There were some of them in Jerusalem, though, as Lightfoot says, they were few in number, at least with the Jews. They could not, however, prevent the Romans from having them; and so much the more wonderful, therefore, was our Lord's prediction.—φωνῆσαι, *crow*) St Mark adds δίς, *twice*. The sense in St Matthew is, Before the cock crow once thou shalt deny Me, and thou shalt deny Me thrice.—τρὶς, *thrice*) The Saviour knows us much better than we know ourselves.—ἀπαρνήσῃ, *thou shalt deny*) The sin of the mouth shall be added to the offence of the heart.[1]

35. Λέγει, *says*) With a sufficiently determined mind.—οὐ μή, *by no means*[2]) Peter therefore acknowledges denial to be sin.[3]—εἶπον, *they said*) The Saviour's lenity makes no further reply.

36. Αὐτοῦ, *here*) (an adverb). Thus the LXX. in Numb. ix. 8, xxxii. 6.—στῆτε αὐτοῦ, κ.τ.λ., "*stand ye* HERE," etc.; and Ib. xxxii. 6.—καὶ ὑμεῖς καθήσεσθε αὐτοῦ; "and shall ye sit HERE?"—ἕως οὐ ἀπελθὼν προσεύξωμαι, *whilst I go and pray*) Our Lord expresses only that which is less distressing; He maintains a reserve with regard to that which is more painful; cf. Gen. xxii. 5. In ver. 38 He says—γρηγορεῖτε μετ' Ἐμοῦ, *Watch with Me*; in ver. 41.—γρηγορεῖτε καὶ προσεύχεσθε, *watch and pray*: but He nowhere says, *Pray with Me*. The disciples could not join (on an equality) with Him in prayer. There is *One* Son: *one* Mediator.

37. Παραλαβὼν, *taking with Him*) As witnesses the three whom He had employed in the same capacity in ch. xvii. 1.—τοὺς δύο, *the two*) who had offered themselves, ch. xx. 20, 21.—ἤρξατο, *He began*) immediately.—λυπεῖσθαι καὶ ἀδημονεῖν, *to be sorrowful and*

---

[1] The sin of the mouth is hurtful to faith.—V. g.

[2] *Ne quaquam*. E. V. *not*.—(I. B.)

[3] καὶ πάντες, *also all*) Being freed and acquitted of risk of betraying their Lord, they do not suspect themselves capable of being offended at Him.—V. g.

very heavy) St Mark says, ἐκθαμβεῖσθαι καὶ ἀδημονεῖν, "*to be sore amazed and to be very heavy.*" Both λυπεῖσθαι and ἐκθαμβεῖσθαι denote the presence and effect of an object of horror,—ἀδημονεῖν, the loss of all power of deriving enjoyment from other sources. The same word occurs in Phil. ii. 26, where see Gnomon. Hesychius explains ἀδημεῖν by θαυμάζειν (*to be astonished*) ἀπορεῖν (*to be at a loss, to be in trouble, to be at one's wit's end*) and ἀδημονεῖν, the word which occurs in the text, Eustathius says, ἀδήμων signifies one who is overwhelmed with ἄδος, *irksomeness*, that is to say, by satiety or grief.—ἀδημονεῖν signifies, ἀλύειν καὶ ἀμηχανεῖν, i.e. *to be in great distress, and to be almost beside oneself for trouble.*

38.[1] "Ἕως θανάτου, *even unto death*) Such sorrow as might have led an ordinary mortal to commit suicide.—μείνατε ὧδε, *tarry ye here*) You must not go with Me.—μετ' Ἐμοῦ, *with Me*) In great trials solitude is pleasing, yet so that friends be near at hand. Jesus commands His disciples to watch with Him, though He knew that they would not afford Him any assistance.

39. Ἐπὶ πρόσωπον, *on His face*) not only *on His knees*[2]—the deepest humiliation.[3]—Πάτερ Μου, *My Father*) Jesus prays as a Son.—εἰ δυνατόν ἐστι, *if it is possible*) cf. ver. 53, from which verse it also appears how promptly and perfectly Jesus sur-

---

[1] ἡ ψυχή μου, *my soul*) How great must have been the emotions and thoughts in the most holy *soul* of the Saviour in reference to the work committed to Him by the Father, as also in reference to His passion and His glory, especially during the last months, days, and hours before His death, throughout the very precious alternations which befell Him; for instance when, as He said. "He must be about His Father's business;" when He received baptism; when He overcame the Tempter; when He put forth His zeal for His Father's House; when He rejoiced in the "revelation made to infants of things hidden from the wise and prudent;" when He was transfigured on the Mount; when He set His face stedfastly toward Jerusalem; when He solemnly entered the city; when He said, "Now is My soul troubled," etc.; when He washed the feet of the disciples; when He spake the words, "Now is the Son of Man glorified;" when He celebrated the last supper before His Passion with His disciples. And also in this very place, where He testifies that His "soul is sorrowful even unto death." Add the several divine sentences which He uttered on the Cross.—*Harm.*, p. 526, 527.

[2] Which Luke records.—V. g.

[3] Such as occurs in His history, nowhere else.—V. g.

rendered Himself to the will of the Father.—τὸ ποτήριον, *the cup*) offered by the Father, brimful with the whole draught of suffering.—θέλω, *I will*) This Will of Jesus that the cup might pass away from Him, was not absolute without reference to His Father's Will. Cf. the latter part of John xxi. 18.[1]

40. Εὑρίσκει καθεύδοντας, *findeth them asleep*) The disciples should have been differently prepared. In this sleep they forgot the promise which they had made in the thirty-fifth verse.—τῷ Πέτρῳ, *to Peter*) referring to ver. 35. Although Peter had heard that he was about to fall, he is nevertheless commanded to watch and pray.—οὕτως οὐκ ἰσχύσατε, *have you proved so utterly incapable?*[2]) You who promised such great things! This is too great weakness; see ver. 41.—μίαν, *one*) Jesus therefore frequently watched alone for a long time together.—γρηγορῆσαι, *to watch*) Prayers would gush forth spontaneously, if they watched; see the following verse.

41. Ἵνα μὴ εἰσέλθητε, κ.τ.λ., *that ye enter not*, etc.) This was to be the subject of their prayer; see Luke xxii. 40; cf. ἵνα μὴ in ch. xxiv. 20.—εἰς πειρασμόν, *into temptation*) which is close at hand, nay, which is already here.—τὸ μὲν πνεῦμα,[3] κ.τ.λ., *the spirit indeed*, etc.) This statement, sin only excepted, was true also of Jesus at that time; see Heb. v. 7. Therefore He also both watched and prayed, ver. 39, 40.—πνεῦμα, *spirit*) Thence it is that the Apostles mention frequently *flesh* and *spirit*.—σάρξ, *flesh*) We ought to take this, not as an excuse for torpor, but as an incentive to watchfulness.—ἀσθενής, *weak*) for the right performance of the matter in hand.

42. Ἐὰν μὴ, κ.τ.λ., *except*, etc.) Whilst Jesus drank the cup it passed away.—πίω, *I drink*) And now by this very utterance of that word He brings Himself nearer to the act of drinking.—γενηθήτω, *be done*) The prayer of Jesus approached now nearer to suffering; cf. ver. 39. Behold His obedience.

---

[1] Where Peter's flesh is represented as *not willing* (ὅπου οὐ θέλεις) that which his spirit would be willing to bear. The *not-willingness* is not absolute without reference to God's will and glory. His flesh would wish to escape, only if so were God's will.—ED.

[2] E. V. *What? could ye not?*—(I. B.)

[3] πρόθυμον—ἀσθενής, *willing—weak* See ver. 33, 35, and cf. ver. 40.—B. G. V.

43. Γὰρ, κ.τ.λ., *for*, etc.) The cause of their sleeping a second time ['Actiologia;' see Appendix].—βεβαρημένοι, *weighed down.* Such slothfulness frequently overpowers the godly when it is least becoming.

44. 'Εκ τρίτου, *the third time*) The third and last time.—τὸν αὐτὸν, *the same*) as suitable to sorrow. The repetition of the same words is frequently congenial to the soul.

45. Καθεύδετε τὸ λοιπὸν, *sleep on now*) An imperative, leaving the disciples, as it were to themselves, wholly given up as they were to sleep, and thus exciting them so much the more urgently by tenderness joined with severity. It is not an instance of irony, but metonymy, q.d. "You do not listen to Me when attempting to rouse you, others soon will come and rouse you. In the meanwhile sleep, if you have leisure for so doing." In St Luke (xxii. 46) we find τί καθεύδετε "*why sleep ye?*" with an interrogation, which some have introduced into St Matthew and St Mark.—ἀναπαύεσθε, *take your rest*), as *Sleep* is opposed to *Watching*, so *Rest* to the labour of prayer.—ἡ ὥρα, *the hour*) often foretold. In ver. 18 He had said less definitely "*My time*."

46. Ὁ παραδιδούς Με, *he that betrayeth Me*) Of whom I have already spoken: "that betrayeth *Me*," He says, not "*you*."

47. ξύλων, *staves*) as in a sudden tumult; see ver. 55.

[48. Κρατήσατε Αὐτὸν, *seize hold of Him*) Judas feared lest Jesus should escape on the present, as He had done on a former occasion.—καὶ ἐκράτησαν Αὐτὸν, *and they seized hold of Him*) First the *multitude seized upon* Jesus; in the meantime occurred the blow and the miracle on Malchus, whose ear the Saviour touched and healed;[1] then they surrounded and apprehended Him as an actual prisoner. The former is expressed in Matthew and Mark by the verb κρατεῖν, *to seize hold of*, the latter in Luke [xxii. 54] and John [xviii. 12], by συλλαμβάνειν, *to apprehend*. Then they moreover bound Him.—B. H. E., p. 530.]

49. Κατεφίλησε, *kissed Him repeatedly*, Lat. *deosculatus est*) He kissed Him more than once in opposition to what He had said

---

[1] In the German this is beautifully expressed by the words, "*dessen Ohr der* HEYLAND *angerühret und* GEHEILET."—(I. B.)

in the preceding verse, and did so as if from kindly feeling. He violated the inviolable countenance of Jesus with the utmost temerity.

50. Ἑταῖρε, *comrade*[1]) Ammonious says, "ἑταῖρος does not correspond exactly with φίλος" (a friend) " and ἑταῖροι" (in the plural number) " are those who have associated together for a long time in conversation and employment." In Luke xxii. 48 we have Ἰούδα, *Judas*; see Ps. lv. 14, and Eccles. xxxvii. 5, with ibid. ver. 1–4.—ἐφ ᾧ πάρει, *for which thou are come*[2]) An eliptical mode of expression for, Is this the object *for which thou art come?* Hesychius renders the words, " With what aim art thou present, and hast come here?"

51. Εἷς, *one*) St Matthew does not mention Peter by name. He might have had more reasons than one for his silence. Danger might possibly threaten Peter from the unbelieving Jews.—τὸν δοῦλον, *the slave*) He perhaps acted more violently than the rest by his master's desire.—τὸ ὠτίον, *his ear*) with a most dangerous stroke, He had aimed at the shoulder of the principal aggressor.

52. Σοῦ τὴν μάχαιραν, THY *sword*) most foreign to MY cause.—τόπον, *place*) The sword, when out of the scabbard, is not in its place, except when it ministers to the wrath of God.—λαβόντες, *they who take*) When God does not give it them.—ἐν μαχαίρᾳ, *by the sword*) Thus the LXX. use ἐν μαχαίρᾳ ἀποθνήσκειν (*to die by the sword*); 2 Chron. xxiii. 14, and Jer. xxi. 9.—ἀποθανοῦνται, *shall die*) This word implies a punishment in kind.

53. Ἄρτι, *now*) Even *now*.—τὸν Πατέρα Μου, *My Father*) Jesus even, when He is just about to drink the cup, retains that filial disposition which He had previously and always towards the Father; see ver. 42.—πλείους ἢ δώδεκα λεγεῶνας, *more than twelve legions*) A legion consisted of six thousand; twelve legions therefore of seventy-two thousand. A legion is contrasted with each of the twelve apostles; a thousand angels with each of the seventy disciples. The angels are divided into their numbers and ranks.

54. Πῶς οὖν, κ.τ.λ., *how then*, etc.) The Saviour altogether voluntarily undertakes His Passion.—ὅτι, κ.τ.λ., *that thus it*

---

[1] Engl. Vers. "*Friend.*"—(I. B.)
[2] Engl. Vers. "*Wherefore art thou come?*"—(I. B.)

must be) The Scriptures had said that thus it must be; see ver. 56.¹

55. Τοῖς ὄχλοις, *the multitudes*) Our Lord calmed their violence, so that, even though now under the influence of the chief men they did not return to sanity, they might do so more easily at a future period.—ὡς ἐπὶ λῃστήν, *as against a thief*) against whom, in a sudden tumult, all staves are used for arms.—καθ' ἡμέραν, *daily*) Especially from the Feast of Tabernacles, to that of the Dedication in the same year.—ἐν τῷ ἱερῷ, *in the Temple*) where you might easily have laid hold of Me.—οὐκ ἐκρατήσατέ Με, *ye laid not hold on Me*) An instance of Metonymia Consequentis; *q. d.* "You were not able to take Me before:" cf. Luke xxii. 53.²

56. Τοῦτο δὲ ὅλον γέγονεν, *but all this was done*) St Matthew appears to have interwoven this periphrasis with our Lord's words concerning the fulfilment of the Scriptures: cf. Mark xiv. 49.—αἱ γραφαί, *the Scriptures*) in the plural number. His Passion was the confluence of their fulfilments.³

58. Ἀπὸ μακρόθεν, *afar off*) With doubtful mind and the sense of danger midway between the spirit, displayed in ver. 51, and the fear evinced in ver. 70.—ἐκάθητο, κ.τ.λ., *sat*, etc.) An unseasonable fellowship.⁴

59. Ἐζήτουν, *sought*) Upon this arose that host of false witnesses. No greater act of injustice was ever committed than that against our Lord: in respect of God, however, it was the highest exercise of justice.⁵

---

¹ Jesus ever carried with Him "the law of God within His heart."—V. g. [Ps. xl. 8].

² You took me not, *i.e.*, rebuking their *insincerity*, "Ye were *afraid* of the people to take me openly." So Olshausen. Beng. seems to make the idea implied this—Ye were not then *able* to take me, for "your hour and the power of darkness" were not then, but are now. Luke xxii. 53.—ED.

John, for a considerable time before his being beheaded, was kept in prison. But the world was obliged to permit Christ to walk at large, and discourse unrestrictedly, up to these His last moments.—*Harm.*, p. 532.

³ Luke xxii. 53, mentions another cause of so sudden a change on the part of the Jews, viz. *the power of darkness*.—*Harm.*, p. 532.

⁴ In the original, "*communitas* non opportuna." There is an allusion in the word *communitas* to 1 Cor. xv. 33.—(I. B.)

⁵ Inasmuch as the holiness of God demanded such an awful sacrifice for

61. Δύναμαι καταλῦσαι, κ.τ.λ., *I am able to destroy*, etc.) He had not said so. False evidence seizes upon some true particulars; and a great calumny may frequently be produced by no great change of words. They distort the expression used by our Lord three years before, and now unconsciously subserve to its fulfilment.

62. Τί, κ.τ.λ., *what* etc.?) A separate interrogation.

63. Ὁ Υἱὸς τοῦ Θεοῦ, *the Son of God*) Caiaphas, in common with the rest of his nation, did not entertain a merely political idea of the promised Messiah.

64. Σὺ εἶπας, *Thou hast said*) "With regard to the question of Caiaphas, our Lord declares that He is the Christ, as though it were affirmed in the words of the interrogator. Nor is this form of speech uncommon in ordinary Greek discourse. In the Hyppolytus of Euripides, we find, σοῦ τάδ' οὐκ ἐμοῦ κλύεις,[1] *Thou hearest those things from thyself, not from me*. And in the third book of Xenophon's Memorabilia, αὐτὸς, ἔφη, τοῦτο λέγεις, ὦ Σώκρατες, *Thou thyself, said he, sayest this, O Socrates*."—CAMERARIUS.—πλὴν, *nevertheless*) although ye do not believe it.—πλὴν as well as ἀλλὰ is frequently used epitatically.[2]—ἀπ' ἄρτι, κ.τ.λ., *From this time forward*, etc.[3]) From this time forward, it shall come to pass that ye shall see and know, by visible proofs, that I am HE who shall sit on the right hand of power, and come in the clouds of heaven. A pregnant mode of expression (*sermo complexus*). *Henceforward* YE SHALL SEE *Me sitting* and COMING.[4] The return to judgment is combined with the sitting on the right hand: and after the Lord's Passion they believed (see John viii. 28), that which hereafter they shall see. They did not believe in the past; therefore Jesus (as He frequently did) appeals to the future. In the glory of

the sins, such a precious ransom for the souls of men.—(I. B.) Rom. iii. 26.—ED.

[1] Ed. Dindorf, line 352.—(I. B.)

[2] See explanation of technical terms in voc. *Epitasis*.—(I. B.)

[3] In the original *a modo*, which is found in the Vulgate. In his German Version Bengel renders it, *Von nun an*, i.e. *from this moment, henceforth*. E. V. renders it, *hereafter*.—(I. B.)

[4] Ye shall soon after this present time believe in my being the Son of God, and in this sense, *by faith shall see me sitting*; and thereby shall perceive also that I am *coming* as Judge.—ED.

Jesus this is the *first* thing, that He is the Son of God: that He will come to judgment is the *last*. The former is the foundation of the latter; the latter the most glorious proof of the former. In the most adverse circumstances, it always especially consoles the sons of God to contemplate the consummation of all things: cf. Gnomon on 2 Cor. xi. 15.—τὸν Υἱὸν τοῦ Ἀνθρώπου, *the Son of Man*) He speaks in the third person, modestly but openly.—καθήμενον, *sitting*) Jesus was then *standing*. On His ascension, He sat down at the right hand of God.—ἐκ δεξιῶν, κ.τ.λ., *on the right hand*, etc.) A manifestation of the deity of Christ.—δεξιῶν, *the right hand*) The neuter plural, τὰ δεξιὰ, is used in this sense.—τῆς δυνάμεως, *of power*) that is of God. The Hebrews often call God הגבורה [*Power*]. Power is manifested most widely and openly in all the works of God.

65. Διέρρηξε, *rent*) as if his garments were too tight for the intensity of his feelings. That old custom had some suitableness to the emotions which it indicated.—χρείαν, *need*) They had the greatest need, because the innocence of Jesus was undisproved.

66. Τί ὑμῖν δοκεῖ, *what think ye?*) He treats the matter as already finished. Moses says, "*Let the blasphemer die;*" Caiaphas says, "*Jesus is a blasphemer;*" his assessors, from these premises, draw the conclusion, "*Let Jesus die.*" St Mark has (ch. xiv. 64) τί ὑμῖν φαίνεται, *how does it seem to you?*—θανάτου, *of death*) Such is also their declaration to Pilate. See John xix. 7.

67. Τότε, κ.τ.λ., *then*, etc.) As if no outrage would now be unjust towards Him. The elders insult Him with greater subtlety, the multitude more grossly. He who assails the honour of God, deserves every contumely. Such an one they considered Jesus to be.—ἐκολάφισαν, *they struck Him*) with the fist, with the hand.—ἐρράπισαν, *they smote Him*) with rods, for the attendants carried these. See Mark xiv. 65. Chrysostom observes, οὐδὲν ταύτης τῆς πληγῆς ἀτιμότερον, *nothing is more disgraceful than this blow*.

68. Λέγοντες, *saying*) most insolently.—τίς, κ.τ.λ., *who*, etc.?) You will hereafter each of you see *Whom* you have smitten.

69. Μία παιδίσκη, *one maid-servant*) The temptation was not great, if you consider only the interrogatrix; far greater, if you

consider all who were present. [She feared lest it might bring her into trouble, if she were to admit any one of our Lord's followers, and on this ground she took Peter to task; the others took up the matter after her. None of them appear to have intended to bring Peter into danger. Careless worldlings frequently produce greater harm or advantage to the saints than they suppose or intend.—B. G. V.]—ἦσθα, for the ordinary ἦς, *thou wast*. Thus also the LXX. in Ps. ix. 14.

70. Λέγων, *saying*) In how few words how great a sin may be committed! See ch. xii. 24, and the close of Acts v. 8.

71. Ἐξελθόντα, *as he was going forth*) The flying from temptation, when it is too late, involves fresh danger.—ἄλλη, *another*) sc. maid-servant; and simultaneously the former, who instigated this other, and also a male attendant. See Mark xiv. 69, and Luke xxii. 58. The denial, made under one impulse, to the questions of more than one interrogator, is considered as one: and yet he is said to have denied thrice:[1] [how often, therefore, must he have uttered the denial!]—Ἰησοῦ τοῦ Ναζωραίου, *Jesus the Nazarene*) the surname *Nazarene* is added to distinguish Him from the many others who bore the name at that time. The Son of God bore a name common amongst men.

72. Μεθ᾽ ὅρκου, *with an oath*) Oaths do not seem to have been inconsistent with Peter's former habits.—τὸν ἄνθρωπον, *the man*) as if Peter did not even know the name of Jesus.

73. Εἶ, *thou art*) The present tense. The temptation increases. Previously they had said ἦσθα, *thou wast*, ver. 69, in the imperfect.—λαλιά, *speech*) *i.e., manner of speaking, dialect*. If Peter had remained silent, he would have been in less danger of discovery: by denying, which involved speaking, he increased the danger. Those men had, however, stronger proofs by which to convict Peter (see ver. 47 and 51); but the world generally employs 'the weakest arguments of all against the

---

[1] The threefold denial of Peter is not to be reckoned by the distinctness of the persons, who interrogated him indiscriminately, nor with reference to the variety of expressions, several of which were comprised in one denial; but in relation to the diversity of place, time, and degree, characterizing each denial respectively. His first simple denial was succeeded by an oath, and this was succeeded thirdly by curses and imprecations added to the former protestations: ver. 70, 72, 74.—*Harm.*, p. 535.

godly, especially in cases of misdirected zeal. Even as far back as the days of the Judges, tribes had peculiar dialects.[1]

74. "Ἤρξατο, κ.τ.λ., *he began*, etc.) Hitherto he had not gone so far: now he altogether lost command of himself.—καταθεματίζειν,[2] *to curse*) others read καταναθεματίζειν:[3] that double compound, however, is nowhere to be met with: whereas Irenaeus (Book I., ch. 13, § 2) has καταθεματίσαντες [the participle first aorist active of καταθεματίζω]. Justin Martyr also says, " κατάθεμα τὸ συνθέσθαι τοῖς ἀναθεματίζουσι," "*it is a cursed thing to be joined with them that curse.*" And again he joins together ἀναθεματισμός [an universally recognised word] and καταθεματισμός [a derivative of καταθεματίζω]. Œcumenius, on Acts xxiii. 12, says, " κατ᾽ ἐπίτασιν εἴρηται τὸ ἀνάθεμα ὡς καὶ τὸ κατάθεμα· συγκατατίθεται γὰρ τῷ ὄντι τῷ ἐναντίῳ καὶ συγκαταδικάζεται," i.e., "The word ἀνάθεμα is used with an intensive force, as also the word κατάθεμα [from which καταθεματίζω is derived]: for it is placed together with that which is opposed, and is condemned together with it." The word κατάθεμα is always taken in an evil sense, as in Rev. xxii. 3; whereas ἀνάθεμα is also used in a good sense.—τὸν ἄνθρωπον, *the man*) compare however ch. xvi. 16.—εὐθέως, *immediately*) An important circumstance (magna circumstantia).—ἐφώνησε, *crowed*) Sins committed in the early morning are heinous.

75. Καὶ, *and*) *then* at last. Unbelief, fear, sorrow, bind even the natural faculties, which the joy of faith revives. See Luke xxiv. 7, 8.[4]—εἰρηκότος, *which said*) A participle of mighty force.

---

[1] See Judges xii. 6, where the Ephraimites are discerned by the test of Shibboleth.—(I. B.)

[2] In his App. Crit., Bengel says in loc., καταθεματίζειν. *Comp. Al. Aug.* 1, 2, 4; *Byz. Cant. Gehl. Mosc. Steph. omn. Wo.* 1, 2: *et quindecim et viginti quinque alii, Orig.* ut videtur (καταναθεματίζειν) *Er.* et Al. vid. *Gnom.*—(I. B.)

[3] Such is the reading of E. M.—(I. B.)
Καταθεματίζειν is supported by the oldest uncial MSS. ABCD Vulg. has 'detestari ;' *abc*, " devotare se ;" which latter probably is the rendering of καταναθεματίζειν of the Rec. Text, as this word expresses more strongly than καταθεματίζειν, *extremis diris aliquem devovere*; "to make himself anathema."—ED.

[4] ἐμνήσθη, *remembered*) Forgetfulness is not unattended with loss and injury. But, nevertheless, if Peter had not ceased to remember the words of

—πικρῶς, *bitterly*) Tears are bitter or sweet, according to the emotion from which they spring. Even if Peter's weeping was not of long duration, his grief was so undoubtedly: see Mark xvi. 7. [*All his former presumption ceased then and for ever.*— B. G. V.] The tears of the godly, even of men, who do not easily weep from any other cause, furnish a great proof of the power, and consequently the truth, of Christianity.

CHAPTER XXVII.

1. Πάντες, *all*) This council was more fully attended than that of the preceding night; see ch. xxvi. 57.—ὥστε θανατῶσαι Αὐτὸν, *to put Him to death*) In execution of the sentence which had been passed on the preceding night.

2. Ἀπήγαγον καὶ παρέδωκαν Αὐτὸν, *they led Him away and delivered Him*) cf. ver. 9, and Gnomon on the latter part.—τῷ ἡγεμόνι, *to the Procurator*).

3. Ὅτι κατεκρίθη, *that He was condemned*) sc. Jesus, by the Priests.—μεταμεληθεὶς, *repenting himself*)[1] Judas had not anticipated this catastrophe: he would now wish, if he could, to render that, which was done, undone.[2]—ἀπέστρεψε, *brought again*) sc. in the morning.

4. Ἥμαρτον, *I have sinned*) Thus also the damned will feel in hell.[3]—αἷμα ἀθῷον, *innocent blood*) Miserably involved in his own darkness, he no longer acknowledges Jesus as the Messiah.—τί πρὸς ἡμᾶς, *what is that to us?*) See how they dismiss, without

Jesus in the very act of his denying Him, his sin would have been even still more heinous.—V. g.

[1] B. G. V. "*Reute es ihn.*" B. H. E. "*Gereute es ihn.*"—(I. B.)
[2] Cf. Gnomon on ch. iii. 8, voc. μετανοίας.—(I. B.)
[3] And O that the friends of Christ, moved by faith, love, and hope, would confess the truth as openly as men in despair are wont at times to do, when they feel that they have now no longer any opportunity of earning merit in the eyes of the world!—*Harm.*, p. 542.

remark, the question as to the *innocence* of their Victim.[1]—σὺ ὄψει, *see thou to that*) The ungodly, though associating in the commission of a crime, desert their associates when it has been accomplished:[2] the godly, though not taking part in the crime, endeavour, after its commission, to save the sinner's soul. Comp. ver. 24.

5. 'Ρίψας, *casting down*) in the disquietude of his mind.[3]—ἐν τῷ Ναῷ, *in the Temple*) Judas was therefore in the Temple, with the chief priests and elders; and, in order to soothe his troubled conscience any how, attempted to give his money to the Sacred Treasury. The part of the Temple where this took place is unknown. The word ναὸς, which, strictly speaking, signifies a *shrine*, is employed here in a wider signification, for ἱερὸν, *temple*. —ἀπήγξατο, *strangled himself with a noose*) which is usually done by hanging. The same expression is used by the LXX. in 2 Sam. xvii. 23, concerning Ahitophel, whom some, however, suppose to have died of the quinsey as well as Iscariot. Raphelius has diligently established the interpretation of hanging from Polybius, etc.; see also Gnomon on Acts i. 18.

7. Τὸν ἀγρὸν τοῦ κεραμέως, *the Potter's Field*) The article denotes that it was well known as such. A potter may have used it to obtain clay from.—εἰς ταφὴν τοῖς ξένοις, *to bury strangers in*) Thus, even then already did strangers gain more of a footing in Jerusalem: thus also the first possession of Abraham had been a burying-place.

8. Ἐκλήθη, κ.τ.λ., *was called*, etc.) A public testimony to the fact. The appellation of the field, though originating with the common people, was not fortuitous.—αἵματος, *of blood*) See ver. 6.—ἕως τῆς σήμερον, *unto this day*) St Matthew wrote some time after [the events which he recorded]; cf. ch. xxviii. 15.

Adrichomius says—" This soil (namely, that of the Field of Blood) possesseth a wonderful virtue, and one almost passing

---

[1] In the original, " Vide, quam transiliant τὸ *innocentem;*" literally, " See how they leap over the '*innocent;*'" referring to the words of Judas, " INNOCENT *blood.*"—(I. B.)

[2] But still punishment at last awaits all severally, according to the part which each took in the deed.—V. g.

[3] "That very thing which had previously proved a bait to the sinner, subsequently causes him the deepest sorrow."—B. G. V.

belief, viz., that within four and twenty hours it reduces the bodies of the dead to dust, which virtue, even when carried into other regions, it still preserves; for when, by command of the Empress Helena, as much earth, they say, as 270 vessels could hold, was taken from this field to Rome, and unloaded close by the Vatican Mount, on to that which the inhabitants call CAMPO SANTO, although it has changed its country, yet daily experience shows that it retains its power: for, rejecting Romans, it admits to sepulture only the bodies of strangers, the whole substance of whose flesh it here also entirely consumes within four and twenty hours, leaving only the bones." This statement is partly confirmed, partly denied, by recent travellers.

9. Τοῦ προφήτου, κ.τ.λ., *the prophet*, etc.) These words are clearly found in Zechariah, whose writings were well known to St Matthew; see ch. xxi. 4, 5; cf. App. Crit.[1] p. 493 (Ed. ii. pp. 141, 142).—καὶ ἔλαβον, κ.τ.λ., *and they took*, etc.) In Zech. xi. 12, 13, the LXX. have καὶ ἐρῶ πρὸς αὐτούς, εἰ καλὸν ἐνώπιον ὑμῶν ἐστι, δότε στήσαντες,[2] τὸν μισθόν μου, ἢ ἀπείπασθε· καὶ ἔστησαν τὸν μισθόν μου τριάκοντα ἀργυροῦς, καὶ εἶπε Κύριος πρός με· κάθες αὐτοὺς εἰς τὸ χωνευτήριον, καὶ σκέψομαι αὐτὸ, εἰ δοκιμόν ἐστιν, ὃν τρόπον ἐδοκιμάσθην ὑπὲρ αὐτῶν· καὶ ἔλαβον τοὺς τριάκοντα ἀργυροῦς, καὶ ἐνέβαλον αὐτοὺς εἰς οἶκον Κυρίου εἰς τὸ χωνευτήριον—*And I will say unto them, if it is good in your sight, weigh and give me my price, or else refuse it; and they weighed my price, thirty silver pieces. And the Lord said unto me, Cast them into the melting furnace, and I will assay it*

---

[1] E. M. has Ἱερεμίου.
Beng. shows, in his Apparatus, Ed. ii., p. 141, 142, 493, that the word Ἱερεμίου is a gloss, and that many modern writers wish to expunge it.—*Not. Crit.*

But the oldest authorities are against the omission. B reads Ἱερεμίου. A and C corrected, Ἱηρεμίου. Hil. 747, Vulg. and c, and MSS. quoted in Origen, Euseb., and Jerome, read *Jeremiah*. It is only the later Syr. in the margin, and other recent authorities, read Ζαχαρίου. ab, however, support the omission of *Jeremiah* or *Zechariah*, as Beng. would read. Comp. Jer. xviii. 2. The quotation is not *literatim* from Zech.: *Jerem.* xviii. 1, 2, and xxxii. 6–12, may have also been in the mind of Matthew. This may account for the presence of the name Ἱερεμίου. Lightfoot thinks that the 3d division of Scripture, *the Prophets*, began with Jeremiah; and that the whole body of the prophets is thus quoted by the name *Jeremiah*, he refers to *B. Bathra* and D. Kimchi.—ED.

[2] The Vatican MS. omits the word στήσαντες.—(I. B.)

(*whether it be good*) *in the same manner that I was assayed by them. And I took the thirty silver pieces, and cast them into the house of the Lord, into the melting furnace.* The Evangelist regards the scope of the matter, and adds a paraphrase.—τὴν τιμὴν τοῦ τετιμημένου, ὃν ἐτιμήσαντο, *the value of Him that was valued, whom they valued*) The force of the words is great.—ὁ τετιμημένος = הַיְקָר, *precious*, although in the Hebrew Bible it is הַיְקָר, *a price*; see Louis de Dieu.—ἀπὸ υἱῶν Ἰσραήλ, *from the children of Israel, or of the children of Israel*) cf. Zech. xi. 13—מֵעֲלֵיהֶם, *of them*. The preposition ἀπὸ, *from*, may be construed either with ἔλαβον, *they received*—or rather with ἐτιμήσαντο, *they valued*. The Chief Priests, as much as in them lay, alienated Christ from the children of Israel.

10. Ἔδωκαν, *they gave*) In Zechariah it is ἔδωκα, *I gave*; and some[1] have introduced it from the Prophet into the Evangelist, and Gebhardi clearly approves it on Zech. xi. 13. In this passage, however, it is written ἔδωκαν; and the force of ἔδωκα, and therefore the whole difference of the words of St Matthew from those of Zechariah, is supplied by the clause, "*As the Lord enjoined me.*"[2] The LXX. have the same formula in Exod. ix. 12—καθὰ συνέταξε Κύριος τῷ Μωυσῇ, *as the Lord enjoined Moses*.[3]—συνέταξε, *enjoined*) sc. to write or to say.

11. Ὁ βασιλεὺς τῶν Ἰουδαίων, *the King of the Jews*) Jesus before Caiaphas confesses Himself to be Christ, before Pilate, King.— σὺ λέγεις, *thou sayest*) An open and holy confession.[4] Jesus shows that His subsequent silence would not be from want of freedom of speech, and immediately answers Pilate, after having previously informed the Jews when adjured by Caiaphas. St Mark and St Luke also record the expression, "*Thou sayest;*"

---

[1] In his Apparatus Criticus, Bengel says, "ἔδωκαν) ἔδωκα, *Aug.* 4, duobus locis, *Syr.* Ex Zacharia. Probat Amama Antibarb., p. 573, et versu 9 construit, ἔλαβον ἀπὸ, κ.τ.λ. Sic quoque *Io. Kaiserus* et alii, quos notat *Rus.* T. 3, Harm. Ev., p. 1073, *accepi a filiis Israel*. ἔβαλον L. Ambigue. Vid. *Gnom.*"—(I. B.)

Tisch. says that 3 MSS. and both Syr. Versions read ἔδωκα. But the mass of authority is for ἔδωκαν.—ED.

[2] E. V. "As the Lord commanded me."—(I. B.)

[3] This is the reading of the Codex Alexandrinus: the Vatican MS omits the two last words.—(I. B.)

[4] Cf. 1 Tim. iv. 13.—E. B.

and this is clearly the sum of all that St John records to have been said by our Lord to Pilate in ch. xviii. 34, 36, 37.[1]

13. Τότε, *then*) Pilate conducted himself moderately at first in the judgment of the cause.—Πιλᾶτος,[2] *Pilatus, Pilate*) Nonnus shortens the middle syllable; and passim, the Greeks sharpen[3] the long vowel of the Latins in πρῖμος, Τουρκουᾶτος Δεντᾶτος, etc. (*primus, Torquátus, Dentatus*, etc.)—οὐκ ἀκούεις, *Dost thou not hear?*) A separate question;[4] cf. Mark xv. 4.

14. Πρὸς οὐδὲ ἓν ῥῆμα, *not to one word even*) i.e. as far as concerned answering the Jews concerning *the kingdom*. He afterwards once answered Pilate concerning another matter, John xix. 11.—ὥστε θαυμάζειν τὸν ἡγεμόνα λίαν, *so that the Procurator marvelled greatly*) For no one is wont to remain silent when his life is at stake, especially after he has once begun to speak.

15. Κατὰ δὲ ἑορτὴν, κ.τ.λ., *But at the feast*, etc.) This [custom of releasing a prisoner at the Feast] accorded with the deliverance from Egypt.—ἑορτὴν, *feast*) St John calls it expressly the Passover.—εἰώθει, *had been wont*) Even political customs subserve Divine Providence.—ἕνα, *one*) i.e., one, and not more than one.

16. Ἐπίσημον, *notorious*) A well-known robber, notorious for the gravest crime.[5] And yet he was preferred to Jesus. How great contempt! Soon after, in the ignominy of punishment, He was preferred to two other robbers.—λεγόμενον Βαραββᾶν, *called Barabbas*) who was much talked about. It is probable that Barabbas survived long as a monument of the history of Jesus. *Barabbas* signifies "*son of his parent;*" he had been longed for, loved, spoiled, by his parent.

17. Λεγόμενον Χριστόν, *called Christ*) Therefore Jesus had been already very frequently called Christ.

---

[1] Ver. 12. οὐδὲν ἀπεκρίνατο, *answered nothing*) As the accusers brought forward nothing new, the silence of Jesus was a subsequent confirmation of those things which He had already said.—*Harm.*, p. 547.

[2] Lachm. and Tisch. write it Πιλᾶτος.—ED.

[3] *i.e.* They distinguish it with the acute accent.—(I. B.)

[4] Although joined in the V. G. with the following words.—E. B.

[5] One who was, moreover, guilty of that very crime (treason) of which Jesus was accused; nay, even guilty of a worse crime. However, it was by the death of Him who was the Just One that those very persons, who had deserved death, are set free.—*Harm.*, p. 550.

18. Διὰ φθόνον, *for envy*) They envied Jesus because the people had adhered to Him.

19. Καθημένου δὲ αὐτοῦ, κ.τ.λ., *but when he was set down*, etc.) In the very moment of urgent business and impending decision. Warnings of a strange and marvellous character ought not to be neglected in times of noisy excitement.—ἐπὶ τοῦ βήματος, *on the judgment-seat*) Great was the influence of the dream, the purport of which, however, the woman understood better after the matter had begun to come to pass. Perhaps she had the dream when Pilate was already engaged in the business.—λέγουσα, κ.τ.λ., *saying*, etc.) A great benefit was offered by this warning to the governor, in contradistinction to the Jews, who had been sufficiently warned from other sources.[1]—τῷ δικαίῳ ἐκείνῳ, *to that righteous man*) Thus Pilate also calls Him in ver. 24, with a feeble reference to these words of his wife.

20. Ἔπεισαν, *persuaded*) by words fair in appearance.—Ἰησοῦν ἀπολέσωσιν, *they should destroy Jesus*) i.e. they should demand Jesus to be killed.

22. Τί οὖν ποιήσω, κ.τ.λ., *what shall I do then?* etc.) Pilate did not suppose that the Jews would demand any very severe punishment to be inflicted. He ought not to have asked. It would have been safer to have simply dismissed the prisoner; cf. Acts xviii. 14, 15, 16.—σταυρωθήτω, *let Him be crucified*) Barabbas had deserved the cross: hence they demand that Jesus should be crucified.

24. Οὐδὲν ὠφελεῖ, *he availeth nothing*[2]) Why not Pilate? This practical prejudging is desperate, when men say, "We do nothing."[3]—οὐδὲν, *nothing*, is in the nominative, or the accusative; cf. John xii. 19.—μᾶλλον, *rather*) not *greater*. He feared a sedition.—λέγων, κ.τ.λ., *saying*, etc.) A protestation contrary to fact.—δικαίου, *righteous*) Pilate adopted this word from his wife's warning; ver. 19.—ὑμεῖς ὄψεσθε, *see ye to it*) As the

---

[1] μηδὲν, *nothing*) saith she, in one word. So Pilate, in the business itself, ought to have taken the conscientious course without delay.—V. g. [Vacillation and hesitancy between conscience and love of popularity were his temptation in this case.—ED.]

[2] E. V. He prevailed nothing.—(I. B.)

[3] Sc. We make no progress, we are effecting nothing; and therefore it is useless to persist in the endeavour.—(I. B.)

Jews said to Judas, so Pilate says to the Jews. A formula of rejection; see Acts xviii. 15.

25. Πᾶς ὁ λαός, κ.τ.λ., *all the people*, etc.) An argument against the Jews why they are at present in exile, although that exile is somewhat less severe than formerly.—ἐφ' ἡμᾶς, κ.τ.λ.., *upon us*, etc.) cf. Deut. xxviii. 18; Ps. lxix. 24, cix. 17. They mean, "We will be accountable for it."[1]

26. Φραγελλώσας, *having scourged*) after passing sentence.[2]

27. Ὅλην τὴν σπεῖραν, *the whole band*) sc. even those soldiers who ought not then to have been present, and had not been so previously.[3]—σπεῖραν, *band*, Lat. *spiram*) Elsewhere the Greeks are wont to put a simple *ι* for the Latin *i* before a consonant, as in Πιλᾶτος, not Πειλᾶτος, etc.; they wrote, however, σπεῖρα, because it is thus nearest to πεῖρα, *an attempt*; σπείρω, *to sow*, etc.; to the sound of which they were accustomed.

28. Χλαμύδα κοκκίνην, *a crimson robe*) They make sport of His kingdom, as the Jews had done of His prophetical dignity; ch. xxvi. 68. It is called πορφύραν, *purple*, in Mark xv. 17, and ἱμάτιον πορφυροῦν, *a purple garment*, in John xix. 2. Sometimes these words are used promiscuously; sometimes they differ, as in Rev. xvii. 4. The one colour also used formerly to be superinduced upon the other.

29. Ὁ βασιλεὺς τῶν Ἰουδαίων, *the King of the Jews*) They treated Jesus as a madman who fancied Himself a King.

---

[1] They bind themselves with the bonds of guilt, but yet do not thereby set Pilate free from it. You may possibly, in a single moment, commit an act which you must pay the penalty of throughout your whole life, nay, even throughout eternity. Nor are there wanting persons who have much less hesitation in incurring guilt than Pilate had.—V. g.

[2] The delivering up of Jesus to the will of the Jews was immediately connected with the setting of Barabbas free, and both were followed by the scourging, accompanied with the mocking of our Lord. In the presence of Caiaphas, it was not till after the capital sentence, that the mocking followed; and, on the same principle, the soldiers could not at pleasure vent their wanton ribaldry on Jesus, before that Pilate delivered Him up to the will and pleasure of the Jews.—*Harm.*, p. 553.

[3] Hereby the delivery of the Saviour into the hands of the sinful heathen was consummated.—B. H. E., p. 220.

Bengel here alludes to our Lord's words in Matt. xx. 19, and xxvi. 45. —(I. B.)

31. Καὶ ὅτε, κ.τ.λ., *and when*, etc.) When the mockery was concluded, they removed also the crown of thorns.[1]

32. Κυρηναῖον, *a Cyrenian*) There was neither Jew nor Roman who was willing to bear the burden of the cross. Men were present at that time from Europe, Asia, and Africa. Even in the remotest regions Christ has since found those who would bear His cross.—ἵνα ἄρῃ, *to bear*) Simon is not said to have borne it unwillingly. Well has Athanasius (Book i. fol. 10, 11) said, in his sermon on the Passion, " Simon, a mere man, bore the cross, that all might know that the Lord underwent, not His own death, but that of men."

33. Κρανίου, *of a skull*) The hill was called so from its shape.[2]

34. Ὄξος, *vinegar*) St Mark (xv. 23) calls it, ἐσμυρνισμένον οἶνον, *myrrhed wine*: the liquor was of a taste between sweet wine and vinegar (cf. the Gnomon on ver. 48), seasoned with myrrh from custom, adulterated with gall from malice.—οὐκ ἤθελε πιεῖν, *He would not drink*) for that behoved to be deferred to the end of His sufferings; see John xix. 30. And Jesus wished to retain His senses fully undisturbed, even up to His death.[3]

36. Ἐτήρουν, *they watched*) cf. ver. 65.[4]

---

[1] Which ought to be therefore omitted in pictures representing Him crucified.—V. g.

[2] Not, as I am inclined to think, from the skulls of malefactors punished with death, which lay about there; for Golgotha, in the singular, means *a skull*, sc. the place of a skull.—B. H. E.

From all quarters in the circuit of the cross the whole world might behold the Son of God suspended thereon.—*Harm.*, p. 562.

[3] Ver. 35. σταυρώσαντες, *having crucified*) Christ, in order to be a blessing to us, was made *a curse*. Who is there would have dared to assert this, had not the Apostle declared it? Gal. iii. 13. Let the passages also, Gen. iii. 6, John iii. 14, 1 Pet. ii. 24, be well weighed.—*Harm.*, p. 563.—διεμερίσαντο τὰ ἱμάτια αὐτοῦ, *they parted His garments*) When the very poorest man dies, he has at least some covering on his body: Jesus had none. Not even are His garments given up to His friends and relatives, but to the soldiers.—*Harm.*, p. 564.

[4] The crucifixion and the parting of the garments took place about the *third* hour; the tumult, therefore, having for the most part passed away, they who acted as guards to our Saviour had sufficient time to consider what was the real nature of the matter. Prodigies, however, at length occurred, by which those men were brought to other [and better] thoughts. See verse 54.—B. H. E., p. 565.

37. Ἔστι, *is*) Yes; He truly *is* so! The inscription, perhaps, remained longer on the cross than the body of Jesus.[1]

39. Οἱ δὲ παραπορευόμενοι, *but they that were passing by*) Many did not even condescend to stand still.—κινοῦντες τὰς κεφαλὰς, *shaking their heads*) The gesture of one who refuses to acknowledge something.

40. Λέγοντες, κ.τ.λ., *saying*, etc.) Seven scoffs of His enemies may be counted.[2]—ἐν τρισὶν ἡμέραις, *in three days*) Yea, it was already now the first of them.—σῶσον, *save*) They use in mockery the name of *Jesus*; then that of "The Son of God," and that of King, ver. 42, 43, and His own words, ver. 40.—εἰ Υἱὸς εἶ τοῦ Θεοῦ, *if thou art the Son of God*) cf. ch. iv. 3.

41. Ὁμοίως, κ.τ.λ., *in like manner*, etc.) Now the chief men imitate the populace: a great confusion! but they surpass them in bitterness.[3]

42. Πιστεύσομεν Αὐτῷ, *we will believe Him*) We [Christians] believe on Him for that very reason, that He did not immediately descend from the Cross, but on the contrary consummated His work.

43. Πέποιθεν, *He trusted*) cf. the end of the verse.—εἶπε γὰρ, κ.τ.λ., *for He said*, etc.) We may consider that this was either uttered by those who were passing by, or added by the Evangelist for the sake of explanation. The LXX. in Psalm xxii. (xxi.) 8, have ἤλπισεν ἐπὶ Κύριον, ῥυσάσθω Αὐτόν· σωσάτω Αὐτὸν, ὅτι θέλει Αὐτόν, *He trusted in the Lord, let Him deliver Him: let Him save Him, since He delighteth in Him*.

44. Οἱ λῃσταί, *the robbers*) Some conceive that the plural is put here synecdochically for the singular, and thus except the converted robber: in such a horrible matter, however, there

---

[1] δύο λῃσταί, *two robbers*) Matthew and Mark mention their crucifixion at a later point of time than the other two Evangelists; from which we may infer that the crucifixion of *Jesus* was regarded by Pilate and his subordinates as the principal and most important case.—*Harm.*, p. 567.

[2] The most heinous robber, when visited with capital punishment, is scarcely ever reviled besides; but the Son of GOD, when hanging on the cross, is most bitingly insulted by word of mouth and by writing, on the part of the rulers and the common people—the Jews, as well as also the Gentiles.—*Harm.*, p. 568.

[3] Such persons scarcely at any other time betray in public what is the secret feeling which they cherish inwardly.—V. g.

seems to be no place for *Synecdoche*; nor are there wanting instances of men who, in the course of dreadful and lingering punishment, have at first blasphemed, and afterwards been converted.

45. Πᾶσαν, *all*) The whole of our planet is meant; for the sun itself was darkened.¹—ἕως ὥρας ἐννάτης, *until the ninth hour*) A three hours full of mystery. Psalm viii., in the third verse of which the omission of mention of the sun agrees with the darkness here spoken of, may be aptly compared with this period of dereliction and darkness.

46. Περὶ δὲ, κ.τ.λ., *but about*, etc.) From this connection, it may be inferred that the darkening of the sun (at the full moon²) represented, not so much the malice of the Jews, as the dereliction of Jesus; which lasted, as it may be supposed, the whole of that three hours, at the conclusion of which He uttered this exclamation. St Luke (xxiii. 45) joins the darkening of the sun with the rending of the veil without mentioning the dereliction. As soon as the dereliction was ended, the Holy of Holies became immediately open to the Mediator.³—ἀνεβόησεν, *cried out*) Both this cry (repeated in ver. 50), and the silence which preceded it, are of the utmost importance.—σαβαχθανί, *sabachthani*) i.e. שבקתני, *hast Thou forsaken Me?* The ק is rendered in Greek by χ, *ch*, when ט, *th*, follows.—Θεέ Μου, *My God*) On other occasions He was accustomed to say, "*Father*": now He says, "*My God*,"

¹ There are some who think that this was the same Eclipse as that which was noted by *Phlegon* [Trallianus] and others of the ancients, or even as that one, the traces of which are now found among the [traditions of the] *Chinese*. Whatever degree of plausibility there may be in this, they are convicted of error by far stronger arguments, since, in fact, they must thus thrust forward the passion of Christ beyond the thirtieth year of the Dionys. era.—*Harm.*, p. 571.

² This *could not* have been an eclipse of the sun, for the passover was celebrated at the time of full moon, when the moon is opposite to the sun. Luke xxiii. 45 says, "The sun was darkened."—ED.

³ ἐννάτην ὥραν, *the ninth hour*) Some one has thrown out the surmise that it was at mid-day the definitive sentence was pronounced by Pilate, and that His being led forth was delayed up to that point of time, so that the crucifixion would thus take place on the third hour from mid-day (3 o'clock), at the time of the evening sacrifice. Nay, rather His *death* occurred at that time, after that the gracious Saviour had hung for six whole hours on the cross.—*Harm.*, p. 571.

as being now in a degree estranged;[1] yet He does so twice, and adds "MY" with confidence, patience, and self-resignation. Christ was עֶבֶד, *the servant* of the Lord:[2] and yet He calls Him God, not Master (δεσπότην). In Ps. xxii. (xxi.) 1, the LXX. have ὁ Θεὸς ὁ Θεός μου, πρόσχες μοι, ἱνατί ἐγκατέλιπές με; "*My God, My God, protect Me! Why hast Thou forsaken Me?*" where the meaning is evident from the remainder of that and the following verse. He does not only say that He has been delivered by God into the hands of men, but also that He has suffered something, to us ineffable, at the hand of God.—ἱνατί, *why?*) Jesus knew the cause, and had prepared Himself for all things: but yet the *why* expresses that the Son would not have had to endure the dereliction on His own account, but that it happened to Him for a *new* cause, and would last but for a short time; after which His yearning desire[3] towards the Father would be again gratified.—ἐγκατέλιπες, *hast Thou forsaken*) The past tense.[4] At that very instant the dereliction came to an end, and shortly afterwards the whole Passion. In the midst and deepest moment of dereliction He was silent. He complains of the dereliction alone.[5]

47. Ἠλίαν, *Elias*) It is impious to distort sacred words, formularies, and prayers.

---

[1] In the original, "quasi jam alienior."—(I. B.)
[2] Isaiah xlii. 1.—ED.
[3] In the original, "*desiderium*," a word which is said by some to have no equivalent in any other language. It implies here *longing* and *love* in the highest and fullest degree, accompanied by sorrow for, and privation of, the object desired; and corresponds very nearly with the Portuguese word *saudade*, which I believe to be utterly untranslatable.—(I. B.)
The Greek πόθος.—ED.
[4] Some recent interpreters render it, *Why (How) can it (ever) come to pass, that thou shouldest forsake Me?* And yet that interpretation, however soothing it be to natural weakness (softness), does not satisfy the demands of divine rigorous strictness in this most momentous transaction. We may term it, as it were, a filial *expostulation*, wherein, if we may be permitted to express the sense with some little change of the words, the beloved Son speaks thus to His beloved Father, *What is this that thou hast done unto Me?* In truth, the best of deeds! Most excellently endured! A brief time so extraordinary, that, on account of it, He is to have [or else *feel*] everlasting thanks.—*Harm.*, p. 573.
[5] Not of His sufferings.—ED.

48. "Ὄξους, *with vinegar*) The soldiers were accustomed to drink vinegar[1] themselves, as Gataker remarks, Posthumous Miscellanies, ch. vi.

49. Οἱ δὲ λοιποί, *but the rest*) i.e. of those present, opposed to those whose speech and conduct is related in ver. 47, 48.[2]—ἔλεγον, κ.τ.λ., *said*, etc.) After the fearful darkness, they return to their scoffs.—ἄφες, *let be*) They mean, that the aid of their companion [who offered the vinegar] is unnecessary, as Elias has been summoned.

50. Κράξας, κ.τ.λ., *having cried*, etc.) A free laying down of life. He was not deprived of life by the power of the cross employed by men; see Mark xv. 44; but yet they are rightly said to have killed Him, because they did so, as far as lay in their power.—ἀφῆκε τὸ πνεῦμα, *He gave up the ghost*) The Divine history records the death of Jesus Christ in few words; the homilies and epistles of the Apostles preach the fruit of that death in many: thus the Gospel furnishes the wool, the Apostle makes the dress; which similitude is used by Macarius in his Treatise, de Elevatione mentis, cap. 19. The word κοιμᾶσθαι, *to sleep*, is never employed concerning the death of the Saviour (cf. ver. 52), but ἀποθνήσκειν, *to die*, which verb expresses the truth, the gravity, the brevity, and the virtue of Christ's death.[3]

51. Ἐσχίσθη, κ.τ.λ., *was rent*, etc.) Therefore the approach to the Holy Places was now free.[4]—ἡ γῆ, *the earth*) i.e. the globe

---

[1] Vinegar, mixed with water, and drunk by the soldiers, was called *posca* (*pusea*, Veg. Vet. ii. 48). Pl. Mil. iii. 2. 23 : Plin. xxvii. 4, 12, Th. PO- of potus ; comp. *esca*.—ED.

[2] Not, however, excluding the man who presented to Jesus, on a hyssop stick, the spunge filled with vinegar. We may readily suppose that this man was a Jew enlisted among the Roman soldiery. Comp. with this view Mark xv. 36.—*Harm*., p. 574.

[3] By it God was reconciled. Truly, a most precious moment!—V. g.

[4] Matthew and Mark place this rending of the veil after the death of Christ. Luke places it before the words, *Father, into thy hands I commend my spirit*. Both events occurred at this same incomparable moment. Luke, inasmuch as combining the darkness of the three hours with the rending of the veil, indicates, (1) that after the darkness was ended, all the remaining events, up to the death of the Saviour, mutually succeeded one another in most rapid succession ; and (2) that the rending of the veil, which occurred at the very moment of His death, has no less close connection with the supernatural darkness than with the subsequent miracles. To be left by

(see ver. 45), but especially the Land of Israel and the vicinity of Jerusalem.¹—αἱ πέτραι, κ.τ.λ.., *the rocks*, etc.) Travellers relate that rents in the rocks, the opposite sides of which correspond to each other, are still to be seen.

52. Τῶν κεκοιμημένων ἁγίων, *of the saints that had slept*) The name *saints* belongs equally to the living and the dead; yea, in the mention of the dead, the determining clause is added, "who had slept." And these saints are reckoned such, not by human, but Divine Canon. *Of the Saints*, who had died either a long while before the birth of Christ, or not much after (see Gnomon on John xi. 25), from all tribes no doubt. The ancients appear to have considered Job to have been one of these; for, at the end of his book, the LXX. and Theodotion add γέγραπται δὲ αὐτὸν πάλιν ἀναστήσεσθαι μεθ' ὧν ὁ κύριος ἀνίστησιν, *but it is written that he shall rise again with those whom the Lord raises*.

53. Ἐξελθόντες, *having come out*) i.e. the saints whose bodies had been resuscitated, in stately procession.—μετὰ τὴν ἔγερσιν Αὐτοῦ, *after His resurrection*) This clause refers to the verb ἠγέρθη, *were raised*, to which the verbal noun ἔγερσις (*the act of being raised*), which does not occur elsewhere in the New Testament, is fitted in this passage; and yet this same clause is placed between the egress of the saints from the tombs, and their ingress into the city. This intermingling of the words admirably corresponds with the facts. Immediately on our Lord's death, the veil was rent in twain, the earth shook, the rocks were rent; and St Matthew has woven together the other circumstances with these prodigies. From which we are able to gather that there was one continual earthquake from the death to the resurrection of our Lord, which first aroused the living (ver. 54), and afterwards the dead. There cannot be assigned any noticeable interval between the resurrection of the bodies of the saints, and

God was the same to the *soul* of Jesus, as to die was to His *body*: the former was signified by the darkness, the latter by the rending of the veil. His quickening in the Spirit followed immediately after He had drunk the cup of death to the uttermost (1 Pet. iii. 18), and that quickening produced the greatest effects upon things visible and invisible alike.—*Harm.*, p. 576.

¹ Those great commotions in created things went on, in continuous succession, from the moment of Christ's death to His resurrection, exerting their influence especially in the kingdom of things invisible.—*Harm., l. c.*

their coming forth from the tomb. The first who rose from the dead to die no more was Christ; he had however companions. After His resurrection, that of the saints also took place; but it is recorded that their egress from the tombs, and their ingress into the Holy City, occurred after His resurrection; because those many persons, to whom the saints appeared, knew the time of their ingress and appearance, but had not seen their actual resurrection. The silence of St Paul, in 1 Cor. xv. 23, does not prove, as Artemonius has inferred, *ad Init. Ev. Joh.* p. 571, that the bodies of the saints came forth from the tombs without their souls, and that their souls afterwards ascended to heaven without their bodies. — ἐνεφανίσθησαν, *appeared*) singly to individuals, or several at once, to more than one. An instance of real apparition.

54. Τηροῦντες, *watching*) In their turn.—ἀληθῶς, *truly*) This refers antithetically to ver. 40, 43.—Θεοῦ Υἱὸς, *Son of God*) He had said that He was so, and they acknowledge the truth of His assertion from the signs.[1]

56. Ἡ τοῦ Ἰακώβου καὶ Ἰωσῆ μήτηρ, *the mother of James and Joses*) When St Matthew wrote, the sons were better known than their mother; wherefore she was denominated from them.

57. Ὃς καὶ αὐτὸς, κ.τ.λ., *who also himself*, etc.) As well as those pious women.—ἐμαθήτευσι, *was a disciple*) and was anxious to make disciples.[2]

58. Ἠτήσατο, *begged*) Then the power of the Prætor was great over the bodies of those who had been executed; cf. in Mark xv. 45, ἐδωρήσατο, *he gave as a gift*. Buxtorf in his Lexic. Talm. fol. xix. 62, says, "For this cause, perchance, did Joseph of Arimathea beg that the body of Christ might be given to him, lest it should be committed to the public sepulchre of cri-

---

[1] Ver. 55. ἀπὸ τῆς Γαλιλαίας, *from Galilee*) The journey (of Jesus and His followers) *from Galilee* towards Jerusalem [His last journey], recorded in Luke ix. 51, is the one here meant. What great things these women, equally with the apostles, saw and heard in so short a space of time! These women already make up for His being deserted by the apostles.—*Harm.*, p. 578. They were the steady attendants of Jesus in His life and death. Therefore no part of the Gospel history is destitute of eye-witnesses.—V. g.

[2] Beng. takes ἐμαθήτευσι here not only in the intransitive sense, *He was a disciple*, but in the transitive sense, *He made, or wished to make disciples*, as in ch. xxviii. 19; Acts xiv. 21.—ED.

minals."—τὸ σῶμα, *the body*) All the Evangelists use this word for our Lord's frame when dead, since it would not have been becoming to designate it by the expression *corpse* (*cadaver*). Such is the Divine propriety of style, which has indeed been abandoned by human commentators.—ἀποδοθῆναι, *to be restored*[1]) The Jews had alienated it; Joseph, a member of the Sanhedrim, as it were in the public name received it from the Gentiles, and together with Nicodemus restored it to the Jews; cf. the conclusion of John xix. 40.

59. Σινδόνι, *a very fine linen or muslin cloth*) Such as had not hitherto been worn by our Lord. The beginnings of honour[2] already appear. Joseph is called in Mark xv. 43, εὐσχήμων βουλευτής, *an honourable senator*) It was not allowable to wrap the dead in anything more costly.

60. Καινῷ, *new*) Which had not been polluted by any corruption; and also lest any of the ancient saints should be said to have risen instead of Him, or to have given Him the power of rising.—αὐτοῦ, *his own*) Jesus Christ, the leader and guide of life, was placed in the tomb of another.[3]—τῇ θύρᾳ, *the door*) The sepulchre was not a narrow trench, but a crypt.—ἀπῆλθεν, *he departed*) Not hoping those things which soon were to come to pass.

61. Καθήμεναι, *sitting*) A holy and salutary delay.[4]

62. Τῇ δὲ ἐπαύριον, *but on the morrow*) A periphrasis for the Sabbath (cf. ch. xxviii. 1), which St Matthew employed for an important reason; perhaps because he did not choose to call the Jewish Sabbath any longer *The Sabbath*.—καὶ οἱ Φαρισαῖοι, *and the Pharisees*) They had taken no part in the actual trial; see ch. xxvi. 3, 57, yet they had not been altogether inactive; see John xviii. 3. Perhaps there were also Pharisees among the Scribes and the Elders. Perhaps the Pharisees, from their extreme zeal, did many things which did not exactly belong to their office.

---

[1] Engl. Vers. *To be delivered.*—(I. B.)

[2] Cf. 1 Cor. xv. 4.—E. B.

[3] Implying that the tomb was something *alien and strange* for Him, the Lord of Life, to be associated with. Therefore He had no tomb *of His own*. —ED.

[4] καὶ ἡ ἄλλη, *and the other*) of whom ver. 56 speaks.—V. g.

63. Λέγοντες, κύριε, *saying, my Lord*) They cringe to Pilate: they had not addressed him so before.—ἐκεῖνος, *that*) They already desired Jesus to be obliterated from the memory of all.—ἐγείρομαι, *I am raised*) The present tense.

64. Ἀσφαλισθῆναι, *to be made sure, to be secured*) They ignorantly minister to the confirmation of the truth. No human ἀσφάλεια (*making sure*) hinders God; see Acts v. 23, xvi. 23–26.—τῷ λαῷ, *unto the people*) The Pharisees supposed that they should not believe it themselves. They wish (as they persuade themselves) to take precautions for the people.—καὶ ἔσται ἡ ἐσχάτη πλάνη, κ.τ.λ., *and the last error shall be*, etc.) The latter victory of truth, however, spread more widely than the first.—ἡ ἐσχάτη, *the last*) A similar mode of expression occurs in 2 Sam. xiii. 16.

65. Ἔχετε, κ.τ.λ., *ye have*, etc.) Pilate gives the guards quickly; and yet, as it were with indignation (cf. ch. xxviii. 11, 12), dismisses the calumniators quickly also.

66. Ἠσφαλίσαντο, *they secured*) This is the whole: the parts were the *seal*, and the *watch*.

CHAPTER XXVIII.

1. Ὀψέ, *after*) *i.e.* after the Sabbath; cf. Mark xvi. 1. E. Schmidius compares with this expression that of Plutarch, ὀψὲ τῶν βασιλέως χρόνων, *after the times of the king;* and that of Philostratus, ὀψὲ τῶν Τρωϊκῶν, *after the Trojan war*.[1] Now with the new week very different matters arise.—σαββάτων—σαββάτων,[2] genitive plural of σάββατον, *the Sabbath*) The Vulgate has *Sabbati—Sabbati*, genitive singular, in both places, and it does not stand alone.—σαββάτου—σαββάτων, the first in the genitive singular, the second genitive plural, is the middle reading be-

---

[1] We may translate the Greek words thus:—"On that day which commences from the evening after the Sabbath, and on the following morning dawns upon the first day of the week." This was Sunday, very early in the morning.—*Harm.*, p. 584, etc.

[2] This too is the reading of E. M.—(I. B.)

tween these two.[1]—τῇ [sc. ἡμέρᾳ] ἐπιφωσκούσῃ, *as it began to dawn*) When the period of death had elapsed, our Lord rose as quickly as possible.—εἰς μίαν [sc. ἡμέραν] *on the first day, i.e. the whole day,* the *first* of the week. The first day of the week had already begun on the preceding evening; now the day, as opposed to the night, was dawning on that first day. The first remarkable mention of the Lord's day is combined with the resurrection of our Lord. It is generally called ἡ μία (*the first*) with the article: see Mark xvi. 2; Luke xxiv. 1; John xx. 1, 19; Acts xx. 7, and on the other hand 1 Cor. xvi. 2.[2]—σαββάτων, *of the days of the week*) ἦλθε, κ.τ.λ., came, etc.) Such offices were performed by those who were not connected by the closest relationship; so that it is not wonderful that our Lord's mother was not there with them.[3]

[1] In the original the passage runs thus:—" σαββάτων—σαββάτων, *sabbati —sabbati*) habet *Lat.* nec solus. σαββάτου—σαββάτων, lectio media.

In his own Greek New Testament (4to 1734) Bengel has σαββάτων— σαββάτων, and does not indicate the existence of any various reading. In his App. Crit., however, he writes in loc.:—" σαββάτων utrumque) *sabbathi* habet Lat. (passim) et alii.—(I. B.)

Besides Vulg. *sabbati, sabbati* is read by *abc.* L Δ and Syr. read σαββάτῳ. But ABD Orig. 1,440c read σαββάτων—σαββάτων with Rec. Text.—ED.

[2] In the last instance the omission of the article may be accounted for by the presence of the preposition κατὰ, which, as is frequently the case in similar instances, renders μίαν σαββάτων anarthrous. See Middleton on the article, who observes also, that if two nouns be in regimen, and if one be anarthrous, the other will be so too; so that σαββάτων, being without the article, causes μίαν to drop the article, which it otherwise should have.— (I. B.)

[3] It seems to be desirable to give the reader here a succinct history of this first Lord's day, framed from a comparison of the Evangelists as instituted by Bengel, in such a way, however, as that the *arguments* are left in their own places to be investigated by the reader. The summary of events which the *Harm. Ev.,* p. 584, etc., exhibits, amounts to this:—

The preparations for anointing Jesus, which had been begun before the Sabbath, having been continued and completed by the women after the end of the Sabbath, Mary Magdalene came to the sepulchre much sooner than the rest of the women; (for too long a space of time intervenes between *the time preceding day-break* [John xx. 1] and *the rising of the sun* [Mark xvi. 2] to admit of our supposing that all the women at one time left home before day, and only reached the tomb at sunrise. Meanwhile the angel sent down from heaven rolled away the stone from the door of the sepulchre, whilst an earthquake accompanied his action, very much to the terror of the

2. Ἀπὸ τῆς θύρας, *from the door*) sc. of the sepulchre. It did not behove that the sepulchre should remain closed.—ἐκάθητο, *sat*) Afterwards the angel *arose* with his companion. See Luke xxiv. 4 [where it is said, "Behold two men *stood* by them in shining garments.]—ἐπάνω αὐτοῦ, *upon it*) sc. the stone: so that no one could roll it back again to the sepulchre.

3. Ἰδέα, *appearance*)[1] sc. of his face.—λευκὸν, *white*) Heavenly messengers are not before this occurrence said to have appeared in this dress: they have done so however since: see Acts i. 10, x. 30.[2]

4. Ὡσεὶ νεκροί, *as dead men*) Not even military daring endures the power of the inhabitants of heaven.

5. Μὴ φοβεῖσθε, *fear not*) An expression used at the commencement of visions, which tempers fear, arising from the glorious sight overpowering the hearts of mortals, which promises soldiers on watch. Mary Magdalene is the first of all who perceived the stone rolled away, and, without having entered the sepulchre, she goes to tell tidings of the fact to Peter and John. Whilst these things are being carried on, the rest of the women, having entered the sepulchre, are thrown into a state of anxiety by not discovering the body of the Lord, and upon receiving the angel's announcement concerning the resurrection, they depart quickly [ver. 8]. Then Peter and John, coming to the sepulchre, and having seen the state of things there, believe that the body of the Lord has been carried away, and return home. But Mary, having now taken her stand at the sepulchre [John xx. 11]; (for she had followed the Apostles hither anew after her first visit to it), gives vent to her tears, and after having beheld the two angels, to whom she scarcely pays attention, *she sees Jesus Himself*, who presently after appears to the rest of the women also, as they were preparing to carry on the tidings of the angels to the disciples also. (Whilst these were going away, the soldiers in watch of the sepulchre, having brought to the priests tidings of what had happened, are bribed with money.) By this time Mary, attended by the rest of the women, has come to the disciples; but not even on the part of Peter does she find faith in the good tidings which she announces. Our Lord, meantime, appears to Cleophas and his companion (and elsewhere to Peter also). But not even to these announcements do the disciples give faith, before that, upon the intervention of the apparition, which had, in addition, been vouchsafed to Simon, the reports were confirmed by reports. In fine, on that very evening, when the disciples were congregated together, and were conversing with one another on these subjects, the risen Lord presents Himself to their view.—E. B.

[1] Engl. Vers. "*countenance.*"—(I. B.)
[2] The dress corresponded to the message they delivered.—*Harm.*, p. 589.

security, and conciliates attention.—ὑμεῖς, *ye*) Although the soldiers are left to their fear.—οἶδα, *I know*) Thus the angel impresses his words on their heart.

6. Οὐκ ἔστιν, κ.τ.λ., *He is not*, etc.) This verse contains short clauses which are exceedingly appropriate to the subject matter.—ὁ Κύριος, *the Lord*) A designation of honour.

7. Εἴπατε τοῖς μαθηταῖς αὐτοῦ, κ.τ.λ., *say to His disciples*, etc.) The apostles were especially bound to have believed before they saw; therefore the fact is announced to them through the women, and their faith is thereby tried.[1]—ἠγέρθη, *has been raised*) The message to the disciples extends as far as " αὐτὸν ὄψεσθε, *i.e. ye shall see Him;*" cf. ver. 10.—ἐκεῖ, *there*) And yet the kind Saviour showed Himself to them before then. The appearance in Galilee was very solemn and public (see ver. 10, 16), and had been promised before the Lord's death.

8. Φόβου καὶ χαρᾶς μεγάλης, *with fear and great joy*) These emotions can coexist in spiritual matters.

9.[2] Καὶ ἰδοὺ, *and behold*) An elegant expression, denoting something sudden and unforeseen.—ὁ Ἰησοῦς, κ.τ.λ., *Jesus*, etc.) The obedient receive a further revelation.—χαίρετε, *all hail*) A formula of frequent occurrence, which is employed by our Lord in a high and peculiar sense.—προσεκύνησαν Αὐτῷ, *they worshipped Him*) Before His passion, Jesus had been worshipped by strangers, rather than by His disciples.

10. Τοῖς ἀδελφοῖς Μου, *to My brethren*) See Gnomon on John xx. 17.

11. Τινές, *some*) The rest went elsewhere, or at any rate not to the priests.—ἅπαντα, *all things*) From all these things they gathered that Jesus had risen.

12. Ἀργύρια ἱκανὰ, *money sufficient*) i.e., to corrupt the

---

[1] However, it was a pre-eminent honour conferred on these women, that our Lord appeared to them the first after His resurrection.—V. g.

[2] The words immediately preceding, ὡς—μαθηταῖς αὐτοῦ, are no doubt expressed in the *Germ. Vers.*, but the margin of *both* the Greek *Editions* prefers their omission.—E. B.

A supports the Rec. Text, in reading at the beginning of ver. 4, ὡς δὲ ἐπορεύοντο ἀπαγγεῖλαι τοῖς μαθηταῖς αὐτοῦ. But BD Vulg. abc Memph. Syr. reject the words, which seem to me to have originated from a transcriber's accidental error in repeating the closing words of ver. 8—a class of errors of frequent occurrence.—ED.

Roman soldiers, and induce them to lie contrary to the truth, at their own great peril.[1]

13. Εἴπατε, κ.τ.λ., *say*, etc.) The priests were a great stumbling-block to the soldiers, and sinned most heinously against God.—ὅτι, κ.τ.λ., *that*, etc.) A specimen of Jewish perfidy and calumny.—νυκτὸς, *by night*) They instruct them how to lie speciously.

14. Ἐὰν, κ.τ.λ., *if*, etc.) How laborious is the warfare of falsehood against truth.—ἐπὶ, *officially before*).

15. Διεφημίσθη, *has been commonly reported*) There are many things of this kind by which the wretched Jews keep themselves in error.[2]

17. Οἱ δὲ, *others*, or, *some*) sc. of the Twelve. The day of Pentecost, however, removed all doubt from these, if any remained. The slower they were at first to believe, the greater credit is due to them afterwards as witnesses. Leo, in his first sermon on the Ascension, says, "They doubted, in order that we should not doubt."

18. Προσελθὼν, *having come unto*) And by that very circumstance, producing faith even in those who doubted.—αὐτοῖς, *to them*) i.e. addressing them.—ἐδόθη Μοι, *has been to Me*) especially to Me, risen and ascending. This passage contains the sum of those things which the Lord declared afterwards more fully in the Apocalypse, concerning His possession of all authority, and His presence with His own; see Rev. i. 18, 13.—πᾶσα, κ.τ.λ., *all*, etc.) This is the reason why Jesus sends His disciples into all the world, and why the whole world ought to worship Him, and

---

[1] The greed of gold has more power with them than their fear spoken of in ver. 4.—V. g.

[2] And how signal are the injuries which are subsequently given birth to by even a single false representation!—V. g.

Ver. 16. εἰς τὴν Γαλιλαίαν, *into Galilee*) This very appearance was the most solemn of all, being the one which the Lord had promised before His passion. And it is not without good reason that it is held to be the same one as that at which "more than 500 brethren" were present "at once," 1 Cor. xv. 6. For the Lord appeared to Paul after His ascension: but the rest of the Apostles (1 Cor. xv. 7) had not at that time need any more, as Paul had, of such a vision. No doubt at Jerusalem, after the ascension, only 120 disciples are reckoned (Acts i. 15). But Galilee contained far more disciples than that number.—*Harm.*, p. 611.

why He institutes baptism;[1] see Ephesians cited below.—ἐν οὐρανῷ καὶ ἐπὶ γῆς, *in heaven and on earth*) see ch. ix. 6, xvi. 1. Hitherto He had been on earth, now He ascends to heaven: He fills all things; see Eph. iv. 10, with the preceding and following verses.

19. [2]Πορευθέντες οὖν, κτλ., *go ye therefore*, etc.) This injunction, to go forth, presupposes the waiting for the Paraclete mentioned in Luke xxiv. 49. It is the sum of the Acts, which may with that view be profitably compared with the Gospels, the sum of which is " *all things whatsoever I have commanded.*"—μαθητεύσατε —βαπτίζοντες, *discipulize—baptizing*) The verb, μαθητεύειν, signifies *to make disciples;* it includes *baptism* and *teaching*; cf. John iv. 1, with the present passage.—αὐτούς, *them*) sc. τὰ ἔθνη, *the nations,* a synthesis[3] of frequent occurrence; see ch. xxv. 32, etc. The Jews who had been already brought into covenant with *God* by circumcision, were to be baptised in the name of *Jesus Christ*, and to receive the gift of the *Holy Ghost;* see Acts ii. 38. It is plainly commanded by these words of Institution, that the Gentiles should be baptized " *In the name of the Father, and of the Son, and of the Holy Ghost;*" they had been altogether aliens from God; see Gnomon on Eph. iii. 6, and cf. Gnomon on Acts xi. 21. The Gentiles, mentioned in Acts x. were not altogether ignorant of the God of Israel, nor altogether aliens from Him. The Jews, who had once acknowledged Jesus Christ to be the Son of God, could not but by that very

---

[1] For the salvation of men, to be converted on earth, and conducted to heaven.—B. G. V.

[2] The Saviour, when brought back from the dead, very frequently enjoined upon His Apostles the office of preaching the Gospel (John xx. 21, xxi. 15). The Evangelists, therefore, might present a summary of such injunctions, according as this or that opportunity presented itself. Matthew connects this summary with His appearance in Galilee; Luke records it after that appearing, ch. xxiv. 49, nay, at Jerusalem, up to and upon the day of His ascension. Comp. Acts i. 2, etc. And we may conjecture the same as to Mark, from ch. xvi. 15, 19.—*Harm.*, p. 612.

[3] The word *synthesis* is not used here in its logical or mathematical sense, but as a technico-grammatical term, representing the figure otherwise called *synesis*; *i.e.* a joining together of words with respect to the idea conveyed, and not to the word by which it is expressed: see *Riddle* in voce. In the present passage τὰ ἔθνη, *the nations*, are neuter and aggregate; αὐτούς, *them* masculine and individual. This is Bengel's meaning.—(I. B.)

act acknowledge the Father of our Lord Jesus Christ, and the Spirit of the Son.—εἰς τὸ ὄνομα, κ.τ.λ., *into the name*, etc.[1]) This formula of Baptism is most solemn and important; in fact it embraces the sum of all piety.[2] After our Lord's resurrection, the mystery of the Holy Trinity was most clearly revealed, together with the relations of the Divine Persons to each other and to us (see Gnomon on Rom. viii. 9); and since the confession of the Holy Trinity was so closely interwoven with Baptism, it is not to be wondered at, that it is not frequently put thus expressly in the Scriptures of the New Testament.

20. Αὐτοὺς, *them*) The disciples had been instructed in order that they might instruct others.—τηρεῖν, *to observe, to keep*) as it becomes the baptized to do by virtue of faith, not merely as a legal performance. John often speaks thus. This verb deserves especial attention, from its occurrence in this solemn place.—ἐνετειλάμην, *I have commanded*) These commandments are to be found in Matt. v.; John xv. etc.—μεθ' ὑμῶν, *with you*) even when you shall be scattered apart through the whole world. This promise belongs also to the whole Church, for our Lord adds, "*even to the end of the world.*"—πάσας τὰς ἡμέρας, *always*) literally, *all the days*, i.e., *every single day*. A continual presence, and one most actually present; see Mark xvi. 17, 19, 20.[3] —ἕως τῆς συντελείας τοῦ αἰῶνος, *unto the end of the world*) For then we shall be *with the Lord* [as He is even now with us]. [To Him, therefore, Reader, commit thyself, and remain in Him; so will it be best for thee in time and in eternity.—B. G. V.]

---

[1] Engl. Vers. "*In the name.*—(I. B.)

[2] At the baptism of Christ Jesus Himself, the Father, the Son, and the Holy Ghost manifested themselves [cf. Gnomon on ch. iii. 16, 17]. The entire Sum of Saving knowledge and doctrine is bound up with Baptism: and all the Ancient Creeds and Confessions of Faith are, in fact, a Periphrasis and Working-out [*Ausführung*, rendered by E. B. ἐξεργασία] of this incomparably momentous Formula of Baptism.—B. G. V.

[3] Therefore the Christian Church will never entirely expire.—B. G. V.

COMMENTARY

ON THE

GOSPEL ACCORDING TO ST MARK.

CHAPTER I.

1. Αρχὴ τοῦ εὐαγγελίου Ἰησοῦ Χριστοῦ Υἱοῦ τοῦ Θεοῦ, *the beginning of the Gospel of Jesus Christ the Son of God*) There is a considerable correspondence of Mark, in part with Matthew, in part with Luke. There is described by Mark,

I. THE BEGINNING OF THE GOSPEL.
    1. John prepares the way, . . Ch. i. 1—8
    2. He baptizes Jesus, who is thereat proclaimed the SON OF GOD, . 9—11
    3. Satan tempts Jesus: angels minister to Him, ... 12, 13

II. THE GOSPEL ITSELF,
    1. In Galilee. Here three periods are to be noted:
      A. John having been committed to prison: 14
        a. Summarily and Generally:
          α. The place and subject-matter of His preaching, . . 14, 15
          β. The call of His principal apostles, 16—20
        b. Specially:
          a. His actions, which were not found fault with by adversaries.
            1. He teaches with power, . 21, 22
            2. He casts out the demon from one possessed, . . 23—28

a b c d

3. He cures the mother-in-law of Peter, as also many other sick persons, . . . Ch. i. 29–34
4. He prays, . . . 35
5. He teaches everywhere, . 36–39
6. He cleanses the leper, . 40–45

β. Actions of His, found fault with by adversaries, and gradually more severely so. In this class are to be reckoned,

1. The man sick of the palsy, ii. 1–12
2. The call of Levi, and His eating with publicans and sinners, 13–17
3. The question as to fasting answered, . . . 18–22
4. The plucking of the ears of corn, 23–28
5. The withered hand restored, and the lying-in-wait for Him of His adversaries, . . iii. 1–6

γ. The Lord withdraws Himself; and His acts,

1. At the sea, . . . 7–12
2. On the mountain, where the twelve apostles were called, 13–19
3. In the house; where, after having refuted the most atrocious blasphemy of the Scribes, He corrects the question of His own friends,
20, 21 ; 22, 23 ; 31–35
4. From the ship, to the people; and apart to His disciples,
iv. 1, 2 ; 10, 11 ; 26, 27
5. On the sea, and beyond the sea, 35–41, v. 1–20
6. On the hither side of the sea again: where Jairus and the woman with the issue of blood, . . 21–43

ST. MARK I. 1.

    d 7. The Nazarites offended at Him, Ch. vi. 1–6
      8. The sending forth of the
       apostles, . . . 7–13
  B. John killed: . . . 14
    1. Herod hearing of Jesus, and his
     opinion of John, whom he had
     killed, being revived, . . 14–29
    2. The withdrawal of our Lord with
     His apostles on their return, . 30, 31
    3. The eagerness of the people: the
     compassion of the Lord: five
     thousand fed abundantly, 31, 32; 33–44
    4. The journey by sea, . . 45–52
    5. In the land of Gennesareth He
     heals many, . . . 53–56
     and shows what it is that defiles
     or does not defile a man, vii. 1, 2; 14, 15; 17, 18
    6. On the borders of Tyre and
     Sidon a demon is cast out, . 24–30
    7. At the sea of Galilee He cures
     one deaf and dumb: He feeds
     four thousand, . 31–37, viii. 1–9
    8. He comes to Dalmanutha, and
     answers as to the sign from heaven, 10–13
    9. In the ship, He warns them as
     to the leaven of doctrine, . 14–21
    10. At Bethsaida He gives sight to
     the blind man, . . 22–26
 C. Jesus acknowledged as the Son of God.
    1. On Peter confessing Him as the
     CHIRST, He enjoins silence on
     the disciples, and foretells His
     passion: reproves Peter: re-
     quires of His disciples that they
     must follow Him, . . 27, ix. 1
    2. On six days after, He is glorified
     at the transfiguration; explains
     the reasons for silence; cures a

      lunatic; again foretells His Pas-
      sion, . . . Ch. ix. 2–32
     3. Teaches the disciples moderation,
      leniency [æquitatem], and concord, 33, 34; 38–50
  2. In Judea:
   α. In the borders, . . . x. 1
    1. He treats of divorce, . . 2, 3; 10, 11
    2. Of little children, . . 13–16
    3. Of obtaining eternal life, and
     of the hinderance caused by
     riches, . 17, 18; 23, 24; 28, 29
   β. On the way to the city:
    1. He predicts His passion a third time, 32–34
    2. He answers James and John,
     and corrects the remaining ten, 35, 36; 41–45
   γ. To Jericho; on the way He gives
    Bartimeus his sight, . . 46–52
   δ. At Jerusalem: . . . xi. 1
    a. His royal entry, . 2–11
    b. On the following day, curses to
     barrenness the fig-tree, . 12–14
    The temple cleansed, . . 15–19
    c. On the following day,
     1. Near the withered fig-tree, He
      commends the power of faith, 20–26
     2. In the temple,
      1. The authority of Jesus is
       vindicated, . . 27–33
      2. The parable of the vineyard
       is set forth, . . xii. 1–12
      3. The question as to the law-
       fulness of the tribute, . 13–17
      4. As to the resurrection, . 18–27
      5. As to the greatest commandment, 28–34
      6. As to the Lord of David, 35–37
      7. The people are warned to
       beware of the Scribes, . 38–40
      8. The widow's mites are praised, 41–44

   d c 3. At the temple, on the Mount
of Olives, He predicts the end
of the temple, and of the city,
and of the world, Ch. xiii. 1, 2; 3, 4; 14, 15;
                          24, 25; 28, 29; 33–37

 d. TWO DAYS BEFORE THE PASS-
OVER: the compact between
His adversaries and the traitor,   xiv. 1–11

 e. THE FIRST DAY OF UNLEAVENED
BREAD.
  1. The two disciples get ready
    the passover, .   .   .   12–16
  2. At evening time, the supper,   17, 18; 22, 23
  3. After the hymn, He foretells
    that the disciples would be of-
    fended at Him, and Peter deny
    Him,   .   .   .   26–31
  4. In Gethsemane,
    α. Jesus prays; rouses the
       sleeping disciples, .   .   32–42
    β. Is betrayed; taken; deserted
       by His disciples, .   .   43–52
  5. In the hall of the high-priest,
    α. Is condemned to death, .   53–65
    β. Is denied by Peter,   .   66–72

 f. The sixth day of the week. His acts,
    α. In the Pretorium of the
       Governor,   xv. 1, 2; 6, 7; 16–20
    β. On the way to crucifixion,   21
    γ. In Golgotha,   .   22
      1. His drink,   .   23
      2. The cross itself, and part-
         ing of His garments,   24, 25
      3. The inscription,   26
      4. The two malefactors,   27, 28
      5. The railings,   .   29–32
      6. The darkness for three
         hours; the loud cry of
d   Jesus; the scoff of the by-

standers; the drink; the death; the rending of the veil, . . Ch. xv. 33–38

7. The centurion's remark; the women looking on, . 39–41

δ. The evening time, the burial, 42–47

g. After the Sabbath, the resurrection of our Lord, announced,

α. By the angel, . . xvi. 1–8
β. By Himself,
  1. To Mary Magdalene, . 9–11
  2. To two men going into the country, . . . 12, 13
  3. To the eleven as they sat at meat, . . . 14

III. THE GOSPEL,
  1. Committed by our Lord, after His resurrection, to the apostles, . 15–18
  2. And confirmed after His ascension, 19, 20

First, in the very term *the beginning*, the new economy is opened out, ver. 15. On this account the time specified in Luke iii. 1, is marked as an epoch of by far the greatest importance. The title, as we may see in the opening of Malachi, is משׂא, "The *burden;*" but now in the present case it is, *The beginning of the Gospel*. Moreover, this title has in it somewhat of an abbreviated mode of expression: for the *beginning of the Gospel* applies to [is in] John the Baptist; *the Gospel*, to the whole book. However, Mark terms it *the beginning*, not of his own book, but of the Gospel facts themselves, as appears by comparing ver. 2, as Hosea ch. i. 2 [*The beginning of the word of the Lord* by Hosea]. The commencement of this book of Mark is in elegant accordance with that commencement; and at the same time answers to the prophetical clause, quoted from the close of the Old Testament, written by Malachi [Mark i. 2]: just as the close of the second book of Chronicles answers to the beginning of Ezra. The proper scope of this *Evangelist*, as he himself professes in such a title as he employs, is to describe the originating sources [commencements], history, principles of action, course, and consummation of the *Gospel*, concerning *Jesus Christ the Son of God* (ver. 11, God's declaration at His baptism, "Thou art my beloved *Son*," etc.):[1] ch. i. 1, 14, etc., viii. 35, x. 29, xiii. 10, xiv. 9, xvi. 15. Hence it is that he so often employs the term, *the Gospel*: hence too it is evident that the last portion of Mark[2] is genuine: ch. xvi. 15, 20.[3] Hence he is wont to make such particular mention of Peter, a pre-eminent preacher of the Gospel.

2. 'Ως, *as*) Mark shows, from the prophets, that the beginning of the Gospel ought to have been such as it actually was; and having proved that point, all the rest is proved. The Apodosis is at verse 4.[4]—ἐν Ἡσαΐᾳ τῷ προφήτῃ, *in Isaiah the Prophet*) Mark brings forward a testimony first [ver. 2] from Malachi, next [ver. 3] from Isaiah. Therefore some have written thus, ἐν τοῖς προφήταις, *in the prophets*. But yet, in the same way as Matthew in ch. xxi. 4, 5, quotes Zechariah under the title of one *prophet* [That it might be fulfilled which was spoken by *the prophet*, Tell ye the daughter of Zion, Behold thy King cometh unto thee, meek, etc.], and at the same time blends with Zechariah's words something out of Isaiah lxii. 11 [*Say ye to the daughter of Zion, Behold thy salvation cometh*, etc.]; and as Paul also, in Romans ix. 27, quotes Isaiah by name, and yet has interwoven with Isaiah's words something out of Hosea ii. 1 : so Mark quotes two prophets, and yet mentions by name only the one,

---

[1] And he so constructs the order of this description, as that, moving forward in a twofold division (*dichotomia*), he relates, in an accumulated series,—I. Those acts of the Saviour, which happened, it is true, at different times, yet in one place (that is, at Capernaum), and from these facts, which none impugned, gathers the inference, that Jesus is the true Messiah, the Holy One of GOD, ch. i. 16–45. II. He at the same time likewise sets forth those questions and objections stated by his adversaries, which similarly were brought forward at different times, though for the most part in the same places, until their actual plotting against Him followed, ch. ii. 1—iii. 6.—*Harm.*, p. 203, 204.

[2] From ver. 9 to end of ch. xvi. Not found in many of the oldest authorities.—ED.

[3] It is quite in accordance with Mark's style of frequent and emphatic reference to the preaching of *the Gospel*.—ED.

[4] *As it is written*, etc., *Behold I send my messenger*, so "John did baptize," being that messenger.—ED.

the prophet Isaiah (as I have long since been of opinion) :[1] however it is not without show of probability, that Beza conjectures that the passage of Malachi crept from the blank space in the margin [*ex albo*] into the context of Mark. Isaiah is more copious and better known, and his testimony, which has been quoted by Mark, used to be read in public on the Sabbath: and Mark here produces the testimony of Malachi in a kind of parenthetic way, equivalent to a supplement, intending, as he did below, to omit *that* section of the Gospel history in which Malachi is *properly* [in the peculiarly appropriate place] quoted in Matt. xi. 10, and Luke vii. 27 : whereas the quotation of Isaiah, as in Matthew, Luke, and John, so also here in Mark, is peculiarly appropriate to this place. John the Baptist himself quoted Isaiah, not Malachi, concerning himself.

3. φωνή, *the voice*) see Luke iii. 4, notes.—ἐν τῇ ἐρήμῳ, *in the wilderness*) This is repeated in the following verse, where presently after also that expression, *preaching* (κηρύσσων), answers to, *the voice of one crying*, in this ver.

4. Ἐγένετο, *came forth* [not the same as ἦν]) The event is pointed out as answering to the prophecy.—κηρύσσων βάπτισμα, *preaching the baptism*) An abbreviated expression for, *preaching the preaching of repentance, and baptizing the baptism of repentance*; Luke iii. 3.—εἰς, *unto* [*for*]) Construe with *the baptism of repentance*; Acts ii. 38.—ἄφεσιν, *remission*) without [the need of] Levitical sacrifices.

5. Ἰουδαία χώρα, *the land of Judea*) So, τὴν Ἰουδαίαν γῆν, John

---

[1] Porphyry, an infidel of the third century, in charging Mark, on the ground that he has ascribed to Isaiah the words ἰδοὺ—πρόσωπόν σου, by the very fact of this charge establishes the fact, that the reading at that early date in the Greek or Syriac copies was ἐν Ἡσαΐᾳ τῷ προφήτῃ, and therefore that it was not a reading spuriously reproduced from the Latin copies, as may be seen at greater length in J. D. Michaelis' Enleitung, etc., T. i., p. m. 162, 586, 587.—E. B.

Ἐν τῷ Ἡσαΐᾳ τῷ προφήτῃ is the reading of BD (omitting the second τῷ) LΔ Vulg. *bc*, Syr. Memph. Origen, Iren. 191 : " in Esciam (Esaiam) prophetam" in *ad*. But Rec. Text ἐν τοῖς προφήταις, with A P, and Iren. 187, 205, expressly. Lachm. from Orig. 4,15*c*, which represents Mark, in accordance with his wonted style, abruptly to pass from " the beginning of the Gospel," etc., ver. 1, to ' John,' ver. 4, is of opinion ver. 2 and 3 were inserted by pious readers See Lachm. Gr. Test., vol. ii. p. 6.—ED. and TRANSL.

ST MARK I. 7–13.

iii. 22.[1]—οἱ Ἱεροσολυμῖται, *they of Jerusalem*) At other times, capital cities are not readily wont to follow a new institution [a new mode of life preached for the first time].

7. Ἔρχεται, *there cometh*) immediately, and even now present.—ὁ ἰσχυρότερος) *that One, who is mightier.* The One Christ is greater than John, yea, infinitely greater.—λῦσαι τὸν ἱμάντα, *to unloose the latchet*) We usually make fast our shoes with buckles, the ancients with thongs or strings. John seems by this proverbial saying, perhaps unconsciously, to make allusion to the baptism of Jesus, so as to express this meaning: I am not worthy to unloose His shoe-strings, much less to impart baptism to Him. For the shoes also, as well as the garments, used to be taken off, when a person was to be baptized.

9. Εἰς τὸν) *in* the river.

10. Εἶδε, *He saw*) i.e. Jesus saw: although John also saw it, John i. 32.—σχιζομένους, *rent open*) σχίζεται, *is rent open*, is said of that, which had not previously been open. Christ was the first who opened heaven.—ἀνοίγειν, *to open*, Matt. iii. 16, is used in the general sense; whereas in the special sense it is used in antithesis to [as distinguished from] *to rend*, Acts vii. 56. See on the difference of these words, Matt. xxvii. 51, 52.[2]—τὸ Πνεῦμα, *the Spirit*) with which Jesus was about to baptize.

12. Εὐθέως, *immediately*) So, in the case of the *sons* of God, temptation is wont speedily to follow after great and striking testimonies as to their state [their standing as accepted of God].—ἐκβάλλει, *driveth out*) The present.

13. Μετὰ τῶν θηρίων, *with the wild beasts*) An important fact; comp. Gen. i. 26. This was a state more trying than the mere solitude of the desert. [*Here the Saviour was removed apart from angels and men; and yet, however, not liable to the attacks of wild beasts. He even now, in the very height of His humiliation* (self-emptying), *exercised over the beasts the dominion which Adam had so soon suffered himself to lose; how much more so, when exalted!* Ps. viii. 8.—V. g.] Mark not only exhibits in a more compendious compass the history described by Matthew, but

---

[1] Two Substantives coming together in apposition, so that one acts as an Adjective.—ED.

[2] ἐσχίσθη is said of the *rending in two* of the veil: whereas ἀνεῴχθησαν is said of the *opening* of the tombs.—ED.

also, as it were in the manner of a supplement, some particulars of considerable value, which had not been previously recorded by Matthew, but which were calculated to afford profitable instruction to believers, who by this time had become proficients in the truth.[1]

14. Παραδοθῆναι, *was imprisoned*) Mark writes as of a fact known to the reader, either from Matthew or from some other source of information. [*Previously, more than once Jesus had visited the city of Jerusalem, as John relates. But His public walk in Galilee, and that a continued one* (uninterrupted in its continuity) *did not commence until after John was imprisoned.*—V. g.]

15. Πεπλήρωται ὁ καιρός, *the proper time is fulfilled*) the time, of which Daniel wrote, viz., that of His kingdom coming: the time which ye have been expecting. Those who acknowledged that the time was fulfilled, had, as the next step to take, either to embrace the true Messiah as set forth here, or else false Messiahs: comp. Luke xxi. 8. It was not John, but our Lord Himself, who openly declared the fulfilment of the time.—μετανοεῖτε καὶ πιστεύετε, *repent and believe*) then you will be partakers in the Gospel.

16. Σίμωνα, *Simon*) Mark writes of Peter in such a style, and with such fulness, that he might easily seem as if he wrote by dictation from the mouth of that apostle [comp. ver. 1, last note].—αὐτοῦ τοῦ Σίμωνος) Either we should read thus,[2] or only τοῦ Σίμωνος; others, only αὐτοῦ, in agreement with the parallel passages in the other Evangelists.[3] Mark sometimes repeats names, ch.

---

[1] *Michaelis*, in the *Einleitung*, etc., T. ii., p. 1154, etc., has tried to prove, by induction of particulars, that those things which Mark has either *omitted* or *supplied*, most especially accord with the tradition of the ancients, which represented Mark's aim in writing to have been with a view to the conversion and edification of *the Romans*.—E. B.

[2] This is preferred in the margin of *both Editions of Bengel*, to the omission of the reading τοῦ Σίμωνος, and is therefore marked with the sign ε; with which also the *Germ. Vers.* agrees on this passage.—E. B.

ABLa have Σίμωνος (and Λ prefixes τοῦ). Dbc Vulg. and Rec. Text read αὐτοῦ. Only later Uncial MSS. and later Syr. Version read αὐτοῦ τοῦ Σίμωνος.—ED.

[3] See Matt. iv. 18, *the Greek*. This makes αὐτοῦ look like a harmonist's reading here.—ED.

iii. 17, v. 37; sometimes he adds a relative pronoun to them, ch. ii. 20, iii. 24, etc., xvi. 14; and decidedly, ch. vi. 22, αὐτῆς τῆς Ἡρωδιάδος.—ἀμφιβάλλοντας ἀμφίβληστρον) So LXX., Hab. i. 17: ἀμφιβαλεῖ ἀμφίβληστρον in the best MSS. Whence Isa. xix. 8, οἱ ἀμφιβολεῖς, *the fishermen*.

18. Εὐθέως, *immediately*) Happy they, who quickly follow.

20. Μισθωτῶν, *the hired servants*) It is probable from this that Zebedee was not a poor man.

21.[1] Εὐθέως, *immediately* [straightway]) Mark delights in this adverb. It has the effect of beautifully characterizing, especially in the first and second chapters, the rapid career of Christ, who was ever tending towards the goal, and the opportunities rapidly presented to Him, and His rapid successes. The Saviour did not in His acts proceed tardily. The particle πάλιν, *again*, which is frequently found in Mark, has a similar force.

22. Ἐξουσίαν, *authority*) comp. ver. 27. [*Matthew observes the same fact in his ch. vii. 28. General truths of this kind are related by one Evangelist in one place and connection, and by another in another and different connection. So the people are compared to "sheep left without a shepherd," in Matt. ix. 36, but at a subsequent time in Mark vi. 34. Mark, however, in this passage, refers to the sermon on the mount; whence it is evident that the healing of the mother-in-law of Peter, which Mark transposes, followed the sermon on the mount, as we find the order of events in Matthew.*—Harm., p. 235.]

23. Καί, *and*) Mark, in the beginning of his history, records in what point of view both men and demons regarded Jesus. [*It may be taken for granted that neither Mark nor Luke* (ch. iv. 33) *in this narrative insist on the historic order of events.*—Harm., p. 256].—ἀνέκραξε, *cried out*) Most persons seem not to have previously known that the man was possessed. The power

---

[1] Καὶ εἰσπορεύονται, *and they enter*) Luke, in the parallel passage, ch. iv. 31, has καὶ κατῆλθεν, *and He came down to*. Nazareth no doubt was in a rather elevated position; Capernaum more in a hollow, towards the sea. Those particulars which Mark, in this passage, and Matthew, ch. iv. 13, record as to the city of Capernaum, Luke combines together in the passage quoted from him [viz. the coming to Capernaum *on the sea-coast*, peculiar to *Matthew*, iv. 13—and the *teaching in the synagogue on the Sabbath*, peculiar to *Mark*.—ED.]—*Harm*., p. 235.

of possession must have been great, inasmuch as the same predicate is often assigned both to the man possessed and to the demon possessing him: ch. iii. 11, ix. 20; Acts viii. 7.

24. Ἔα, *permit*) that is, *permit us to speak*, [but Engl. Vers., *Let us alone*]: Luke iv. 34, 41.—τί, *what*) A most miserable state; that he should desire not to have anything to do with Jesus [comp. Rev. vi. 15].—Ναζαρηνέ, *of Nazareth*) It is probable that the great Enemy had very closely observed what Jesus did at Nazareth during His youth.—ἀπολέσαι, *to destroy*) well said! comp. 1 John iii. 8.—ἡμᾶς, *us*)[1] The demons have a common cause among them [one common interest].—οἶδα, *I know*) He does not say, *we know*. He speaks of himself, not of the rest. The demons who were in those possessed, seem to have perceived sooner than the rest who Jesus was [*yea, sooner even than most of the men with whom He walked at that time.*— Harm., p. 256].

25. Ἐπετίμησεν, *He rebuked*) So ch. iii. 12. Hence it is evident that the hidden excellency of Jesus is far greater than Socinians suppose. It belongs to THE LORD as His prerogative to 'rebuke,' Jude ver. 9.—φιμώθητι, *be silenced*) This prohibition did not prevent the cry of the unclean spirit when going out of the man, but merely the utterance of articulate words, such as are mentioned at ver. 24.

26. Σπαράξαν, *having torn*) Our enemies, when they have possessed the inmost recesses of the soul, withdraw unwillingly; in fact, they are driven out.

27. Διδαχή, *doctrine*) with which these miracles were connected and accompanied.—καί, *even*).

29. Εὐθέως, *forthwith*) Jesus avoided the din of a crowd.—ἦλθον, *they came*) Jesus, and Simon, and Andrew.—μετά, *with*) Already, after having left one home, James and John had several homes [viz., those of their fellow-disciples].

32. Ὀψίας, *at even*) Implying the assiduity of Jesus. Comp. ver. 35, *in the morning*.—καί, *and*) specially.

33. Ὅλη, *the whole*) the sick, the bearers of them, and the spectators.

34. Οὐκ ἤφιε, *He suffered not*) So ch. xi. 16. The second

---

[1] The mark of interrogation after this word ought to be removed.—*Not. Crit.* Both Lachm. and Tischend. retain it.—ED.

aorist of the verb ἀρνέω, as Sylberg shows in his Not. ad Clenard., p. 468.—ὅτι, *because*) They were attempting to speak.

35. Ἔννυχον, *in the depth of night* [a great while before day]) Day and night He was on the watch for our salvation. Hence also is evinced the eagerness of the apostles and the people: see the following verses.—προσηύχετο, *He was in prayer*) specially for the apostles: see following verse.

36. Ὁ Σίμων καὶ οἱ μετ' αὐτοῦ, *Simon and they that were with him*) Already Simon is eminent among them. So Luke viii. 45, ix. 32. It is not said, for instance, "*Thomas* and they that were with him." [Comp. note 1 on ver. 16].

37. Εὑρόντες, *when they had found Him*) He therefore had not told them whither He was going. [*When He had passed the greatest part of His years in solitude, He at length presented Himself to be beheld in public; yet still His manifestation was subject to this condition, that even then He most prudently blended secret communion with His heavenly Father along with His public intercourse with men.*—Harm., p. 259].—πάντες, *all*) Why should not we also? saith Peter.

38. Ἐχόμενας, *which come next in our way*) According as things external, whether place or time, present themselves, so the kingdom of God introduces [insinuates] itself.—ἐλήλυθα, *I have come*) The first and earliest words of Jesus contain something of an enigmatical character: but by degrees He speaks more openly of Himself. He was afterwards about to speak in this way, *I went out* ["came forth"] *from the Father*.[1]

39. Κηρύσσων—ἐκβάλλων, *preaching—casting out*) Two kinds of benefits.

43.[2] Εὐθέως, *forthwith*) lest Jesus should seem to countenance anything derogatory to the law.—ἐξέβαλεν, *made him go away*) The man, when healed, was ready to remain with Jesus, and to stay away from his relatives. Adversities have the effect of transferring our affections from natural objects of affection to Christ.

---

[1] John xvi. 28. But *here*, in beginning His ministry, he does not add, *from the Father*.—ED.

[2] Ver. 41. σπλαγχνισθείς, *moved with compassion*) Mark exercises especial assiduity in observing the holy movements of feeling, and so the gestures also of Jesus. Whoever will pay marked attention to this characteristic of Mark in reading his Gospel, will derive from it no little delight.—V. g.

45.[1] Μηκέτι, *no longer*) Christ therefore was ready to teach rather in the cities, than in the place to which the men were going out.

CHAPTER II.

1. Πάλιν, *again*) Comp. ch. i. 21, 29.—δι' ἡμερῶν) After some days had intervened. [*It is one and the same return into the city of Capernaum, of which Mark makes mention in this place after the healing of the leper; Matthew, after the return from the region of the Gergesenes, in his ch. ix. 1 : it is also the same man sick of the palsy, whom Mark and Luke, after Matthew, treat of.* —Harm., p. 276].

2. Μηδὲ, *not even*) Not only the house within, but not even the hall, could contain them.

3. Ὑπὸ τεσσάρων, *by four*) He was then full grown, though not far advanced in years : comp. ver. 5, Son [implying he was not old].

4. Ἀπεστέγασαν, *they took off the roof*) out of love, without doing injury. [*So faith penetrates through all obstacles* (ver. 5) *to reach Christ.*—V. g.] It is probable that it was a cottage [*tugurium*, hut], not a large house.—ἐξορύξαντες, *digging out*) the ceiling, beneath the tiles of the roof, so as to make a large aperture. The people crowding in numbers, had caused great delay in reaching Christ.

5. Πίστιν, *their faith*) So painstaking.

8. Τῷ πνεύματι αὐτοῦ, *in His Spirit*) The prophets became cognisant of things through the Spirit of God, but not with their own spirit : Christ, with His own Spirit, which is omniscient and Divine ; comp ch. viii. 12. Moreover, the Holy Spirit is not called the Spirit of Christ before that great Pentecost recorded in Acts ii. The conclusion therefore remains, that we

---

[1] κηρύσσειν, *to publish*) This public and spontaneous proclaiming of facts served to give speedy publicity to facts worthy of remembrance : see ch. v. 20. Yet, in this place, it would have been better for the man to have obeyed Christ's inhibition.—V. g.

are to understand the Spirit of Jesus as applying to His Divine nature, which had its dwelling in His human nature.—τί, *why*) An allusion to their *Why?* in ver. 7.

14.[1] Τελώνιον, *the receipt of custom*) At the sea; ver. 13.

15.[2] Ἦσαν γὰρ, *for they were*) The Evangelist hereby explains why he had just written, *with Jesus and His disciples*; *for* they were many.

16.[3] Τί ὅτι) So the LXX.; Judg. xi. 7, etc.

18. Νηστεύοντες, *fasting*) This seems here to imply both their custom and their actual fasting at that present time; comp. note on Matt. ix. 14.

20.[4] Ἐλεύσονται, *shall come*) This is the first intimation of His Passion.—ἐν ἐκείνῃ τῇ ἡμέρᾳ) So also the Gothic version reads. Moreover, the plural, which is substituted by some, comes evidently from Luke.[5] There is but one day of the Bridegroom being taken away; many days, of His continuing absent after having been so taken away. *But the days will come, when the Bridegroom shall be taken away; and then shall they fast in that day* (In some one of those days, to wit, especially on the first of them). So in Luke xvii. 22 the plural number is used, *the days shall come*; and in ver. 31, *on that day*, in the singular number, with a force having relation to that plural.

21. Αἴρει τὸ πλήρωμα τὸ καινὸν τοῦ παλαιοῦ) This reading is a mean between extremes, brief, and likely to be genuine.[6] The

---

[1] Comp. on this history, note on Matt. ix. 9.—E. B.

[2] Λευΐν, *Levi*) called also Matthew.—V. g.

[3] Ver. 15. Καὶ ἠκολούθησαν, *and they were following*) Therefore even then already with reformed minds they were holding to [entering upon] the right way.—V. g.

[4] Ver. 19. Τοῦ νυμφῶνος, the *Bridegroom*) This means Jesus, in whose absence, they, to whom He is known, cannot feel the day joyful, and in whose presence they cannot feel the day sad.—V. g.

[5] Through Harmonists.—ED.

The Gnomon and margin of Ed. 2 and *Vers. Germ.* prefer the Sing. The Ed. Maj. has at it the mark ὅ.—E. B. ABCD and Amiat. Vulg. support the Sing.: *abc* later Vulg. and Rec. Text, the Plural.—ED.

[6] ΛΔ, later Syr., whom Tischend. follows, read αἴρει ἀπ᾽ αὐτοῦ τὸ πλήρωμα. B reads τὸ πλήρ. ἀφ᾽ ἑαυτοῦ. L, whom Lachm. follows, has τὸ πλήρ. ἀπ᾽ αὐτοῦ. D*ab* Vulg. and Rec. Text have τὸ πλήρωμα (to which Rec. Text adds αὐτοῦ) τὸ καινὸν ἀπὸ (omitted in Rec. Text) τοῦ παλαιοῦ. —ED.

meaning is: *the new piece put in* to patch up the rent, *takes away with it some of the old* cloth.

26. Ἐπὶ Ἀβιάθαρ, under Abiathar) Ahimelech was the priest who gave loaves of bread to David; but on his being put to death for that very act, his son Abiathar presently after succeeded to him; and afterwards the priesthood of Abiathar and the reign of David were contemporary. The series of the priests was very well known among the Hebrews, and so the denomination of [the mode of marking] the age of David is taken from the priest of that day; and indeed the Evangelist mentions Abiathar, in whose time the actions of David seem to have been entered in the sacred records, in preference to Ahimelech; comp. the use of ἐπί, Matt. i. 11. Not unlike is the phraseology, Gen. ii. 2, *on the seventh day* [God ended His work; we should have said, *at the close of the sixth day*], and ch. x. 25, *in the days of Peleg* (who was born a short while after) *the earth was divided*.

27. Ἔλεγεν, *He was saying*) Again beginning to address them; comp. ch. iv. 21, 24, 26, 30, vii. 20, ix. 1; Luke iv. 24, v. 36, vi. 5, xv. 11; John i. 52.—διὰ, *for the sake of*) An axiom. So almost similarly 2 Macc. v. 19: οὐ διὰ τὸν τόπον τὸ ἔθνος, ἀλλὰ διὰ τὸ ἔθνος τὸν τόπον ὁ Κύριος ἐξελέξατο—ἐγένετο, *was made*) The origin and end of things is to be kept in view. The blessing of the Sabbath, Gen. ii. 3, has regard to man.

28. Ὥστε, *therefore*) The more obvious sense of this remarkable enigmatical aphorism is, Whatever right as regards the Sabbath any man hath, I also have. The more august sense, though one kept hidden [recondite] then, as suited to the relations in which that time stood to the whole divine scheme, is this, The end of the institution of the Sabbath is the salvation [welfare] of man as to his soul and body. The Son of Man is bound to ensure this salvation; and, in order to bring about this end, He the same has also authority over all things, and expressly over the Sabbath, inasmuch as it was made for man; and with a view to [in accordance with] obtaining this end, He regulates aright the whole use of the Sabbath.

CHAPTER III.

1. Πάλιν, *again*) On another Sabbath [*which preceded the feast of the Passover by eight days.*—Harm. p. 309]. Luke vi. 6).[1]—ἐξηραμμένην, *withered*) not from the womb, but through disease or a wound. This is the force of the participle.[2]

2. Παρετήρουν, *they were watching*) Obliquely and secretly. On the immediately preceding Sabbath they had heard His doctrine concerning the Sabbath.

3. Λέγει, *He saith*) In order that the misery of the sick man might so much the more move the compassion of all.—ἔγειραι εἰς) An abbreviated expression for, *arise, and go forth into* the midst.

4. Ἤ, *or*) Not to save is to destroy. The opposition between the two words is immediate and direct. *To save life* refers to the whole man; *to do good*, to a part; and so in the respectively antithetic words—ψυχήν, *life*) of man; and therefore also a man's hand.—ἐσιώπων, *they were silent*); Luke xiv. 3.—ἡσύχασαν, They had nothing to say.

5. Περιβλεψάμενος, *looking round*) The expressions of Christ's countenance teach us many lessons, ver. 34 [comp. ch. x. 21, 27].—συλλυπούμενος, *being grieved*) In the case of the Pharisees, their *grief* was malignant; Jesus *grieves* with holy affection, individually for individuals. Along with His just grief was combined just anger; see note ver. 2.—πωρώσει, *the hardness*) The habitual disposition of the heart renders the perception of the truth, and of its conclusions, either difficult or easy. —πώρωσις, *hardness*, which destroys the use of the senses, for instance, the sight and the touch. It is *blindness*, not to see; *hardness*, not to perceive; John xii. 40.

[1] εἰς τὴν συναγωγήν, *into the synagogue*) What an amount of wickedness is there not introduced into holy assemblages, and perpetrated in them! —V. g.

[2] As distinguished from the adjective ξηράν, had it been used.—Ed. Mark groups together, in ch. i., those acts to which Jesus' adversaries made no opposition: he then also joins together those which they assailed, in ch. ii.; until, goaded on by hatred, they began laying plots for our Lord. The method of Luke is the same.—V. g.

6. Εὐθέως, *straightway*) Their hatred increased; comp v. 2 at the end of the v.—Ἡρωδιανῶν, *the Herodians*) although they perhaps had no great care for the Sabbath. Either by the order or permission of Herod, they were wishing to kill Jesus.

7. Ἀνεχώρησε, *He withdrew*) He avoided plots against Him, and yet He did not flee to a distance, nor in a fearful spirit, for He went to the sea [The particulars which Mark in this passage, ver. 7–19, records, he sets forth in the regular order of the narrative, and they are to be combined with Matt. iv. 24, etc. But the events which go before and follow in Mark, are parallel to the xiith. ch. of Matthew. Mark takes occasion [a handle] from the plots laid by His enemies, to record the withdrawal of the Saviour, ver. 7; and by that very fact, he returns in the meantime into the regular path from his digression, etc. —*Harm.*, p. 238. The *sea* is mentioned in this verse; the *house* in ver. 19; and again the *sea* in ch. iv. 1. In this fashion Mark combines the histories of different times.—V. g.].

7. 8. Πλῆθος, *the multitude*) There were two multitudes; the one was following Him out of Galilee, the other, from most diverse quarters, was then, for the first time, coming to Jesus. The former is called a *great multitude*, the latter, *a multitude that was great*, the epitasis (increase of force, in repeating the words, see Append.) being indicated by the transposition of the noun [before the adjective, instead of as in the first instance *after* it: πολὺ πλῆθος—πλῆθος πολύ.]

8. Ἰδυμαίας, *Idumea*) Therefore Esau was not altogether 'hated' [Mal. i. 3; Rom. ix. 13].—οἱ περί) These were Israelites *living near* Tyre and Sidon.

9. Πλοιάριον, *a small ship*) Nominative.—προσκαρτερῇ, *should wait on*) Not merely at that time alone.—ἵνα μή, *that not*) Having thus a regard to His due convenience.

10. Ἐπιπίπτειν, *pressed upon*) Illustrating the admirable patience and benignity of our Lord.

11. Ὅταν) ὅτ᾽ ἄν is here joined with a past tense of the Indicative, as ὅπου ἄν, ch. vi. 56.

12. Ἵνα μὴ φανερόν, *that not manifest*) It was not yet the time, nor were they the proper heralds.

13. Εἰς τὸ ὄρος, *into a mountain*) Apart.—οὓς ἤθελεν αὐτός, *whom He Himself would*) He had unlimited authority, and that the

highest. His will was in accordance with the will of the Father [*among these partly the Twelve, just mentioned, were included; partly others, for instance, Joseph and Matthias,* Acts i. 23.— V. g.]—ἀπῆλθον, *they came away*) leaving all things.

14. Δώδεκα, *twelve*) The characteristic notes of an apostle were, an immediate and direct call, a continuous intercourse with Christ, the being an eye-witness, the right of preaching universally [and not merely restricted to one locality], the gift of miracles.

16. Ἐπέθηκε, *He put upon*) It is a mark of Lordship to give a surname; this He gave also to James and John jointly, ver. 17; but to Peter first of all before them. So in the catalogue of the twelve spies of the land of Canaan, mention is made of Joshua receiving that name instead of Hosea; Numb. xiii. 4–16.

17. Ἰάκωβον, *James*) *He calls* to Him.—ὀνόματα, *names*) The plural intimates that this name applied even to each of the two separately [*Vers. Germ.* maintains, on the contrary, that it was only *conjointly* they seem to have been honoured with this surname. This is the only passage in which the surname of James and John is mentioned, whereas that of Peter occurs frequently].—Βοανεργές, *Boanerges*) "Without doubt Christ by this name alludes (בני רגשא) to the two Scribes, who, in the Sanhedrim, were wont to sit, one on the right hand, the other on the left of the high priest, of whom the former used to collect the votes of acquittal, the latter those of condemnation, and Christ applies this judicial custom of the Sanhedrim to His spiritual kingdom;" Mellant, Sac., p. 36, 37. The etymology of the surname is somewhat differently traced out by Hiller; *Onom.*, p. 117, 699.—υἱοὶ βροντῆς, *sons of thunder*) A magnificent appellation. Thunder in Scripture is something both terrible and joyous. So also the Gospel strikes terror into the world, and brings joy and gain to the godly. John in his mildness has, notwithstanding the hidden force of thunder, especially in his testimony as to the Godhead of Jesus Christ; comp. John xii. 29, 28; and in the Revelation he has written out the account of very many thunders; and he himself heard utterances of thunders, which he was forbidden to write out; Rev. x. 3, 4. Hiller, in the passage quoted from him, says, "The thunder-bolt (lightning)

is the son of thunder, inasmuch as it accompanies the crashing sound which proceeds from the rent clouds."

20. [Eng. Vers. 19] Ἔρχονται, *they come*) Jesus with His new family [This relation of Mark follows, not the order of *time*, but the change of *places*; comp. ver. 7, 13; Harm. p. 311].—εἰς οἶκον "*to the house*," rather than *into* the house; comp. ver. 21, 31.

21. Οἱ παρ' αὐτοῦ, *those belonging to Him*) See App. Crit. Ed. ii., p. 150. The Gothic Version *fram* answers to περί and παρά.[1] Who these were, *who belonged to Him*, is clear from ver. 31, where the particle οὖν,[2] *therefore*, refers to this 21st verse, after the intervening parenthesis 22–30 has been as it were cleared out of the way.—ἐξῆλθον, *they went out*) Their *coming* in ver. 31 followed their going out here. A table seems to have been laid at the house; see end of ver. 20.—Κρατῆσαι, *to lay hold*) to put a restraint on him.—ἔλεγον, *they were saying*) the messengers [not the relatives] from whom his relatives *heard* of His earnestness.—ὅτι ἐξέστη, *He is beside Himself*) By this word they were attributing to Him excess of ardour, overwhelming His intellect, but it was falsely that they attributed this to Him, as Festus did to Paul; Acts xxvi. 24, *Thou art mad.* Comp. by all means 2 Cor. v. 13; comp. ἱερεὺς καὶ προφήτης ἐξέστησαν διὰ τὸ σίκερα, Heb. שׁגו; Isa. xxviii. 7; so ὁ προφήτης παρεξεστηκώς, Heb. משֻׁגָּע; Hosea ix. 7. The singular number does not admit of this being understood of the people; for although ὄχλος, *a multitude*, ver. 20 is singular, yet after an interval [between ὄχλος and the verb, if the latter were to be understood of the former], there always follow the pronoun and the verb in the plural.

23. [3]Προσκαλεσάμενος, *having called them to Him*) By that very

---

[1] AB Vulg. Rec. Text read καὶ ἀκούσαντες οἱ παρ' αὐτοῦ; but Dabc read καὶ ὅτε ἤκουσαν περὶ αὐτοῦ οἱ γραμματεῖς καὶ οἱ λοιποί (c has Pharisæi.)—ED.

[2] But the oldest authorities BCDG Vulg. abc omit οὖν. A, however, supports it.—ED.

[3] Ver. 22. οἱ ἀπὸ Ἱεροσολύμων καταβάντες, *who came down from Jerusalem*) on the days immediately before the Passover, when by this time all other men were going up. Jesus had been away from Jerusalem for a considerably long interval of time: therefore at this particular time now they were trying to restrain [check] Him in Galilee, where a great multitude of people

act He led them on to some degree of attention.—Σατανᾶν, *Satan*) see Matt. xii. 26, note.

26. Ἀνέστη) A very suitable word; *rose up*, that is to say, it would be a strange thing!

27. Ἐὰν μὴ—δήσῃ, καὶ τότε—διαρπάσει) A most similar construction occurs; Deut. xx. 5, etc.—μὴ ἀποθάνῃ καὶ ἕτερος, ἐγκαινιᾷ; also Gen. xxvii. 12; Matt. v. 25, xxvi. 53, xxvii. 64; Rom. xi. 25, 26, 35; also Mark v. 23 at the end of the verse; Luke xiii. 25, xviii. 7; John xii. 35.

28. Τοῖς υἱοῖς τῶν ἀνθρώπων, *to the sons of men*) Ordinary sins are the sins of man; but blasphemy against the Holy Spirit is the sin of Satan.—καὶ αἱ βλασφημίαι) The omission of the article in some editions gives great force to the language.[1]

29. Αἰωνίου ἁμαρτίας, *everlasting guilt*) *Sin* in this place denotes *guilt*; and *everlasting sin* or *guilt* is opposed with great propriety of language to *forgiveness* [*It therefore carries with it the punishment consisting as well of* (in) *the feeling as also of* (in) *the penalty itself* (damnation). V. g.—Αἰωνίου κρίσεως [the reading of the Rec. Text] is a gloss.[2]

31.[3] Οἱ ἀδελφοὶ καὶ ἡ μήτηρ αὐτοῦ) See App. Crit. Ed. ii. on this passage.[4] Mark has placed the brothers first in order, implying that the brothers had made the first move in seeking Him, and the mother followed them. [*She is not, however, on that account, to be held free from all blame in the case.*—V. g.] There is a similar account to be given for the order of the words in Numb. xii. 1, 10, where *Miriam*, being the more prominent of the two in opposing Moses, is placed before *Aaron*. So *Rachel* and *Leah*, in inverse order, Gen. xxxi. 14; *Gad* and *Reuben*, Numb. xxxii. 6. She who was "blessed among women," suffered less

was flocking around Him, that multitude being free from other concerns at the time, and preparing to go up to celebrate the Feast.—*Harm.*, p. 314.

[1] D and Rec. Text, which Griesbach and Scholz follow, omit the αἱ. But ABC are against the omission.—ED.

[2] A, however, supports it. But BL Vulg. and Memph., and *bcd* ('delicti') support ἁμαρτήματος. D reads ἁμαρτίας; and so *a* and Cypr. have 'peccati.'—ED.

[3] ἔρχονται οὖν, *There come then*) This expression refers us back to the ἐξῆλθον, ver. 21.—V. g.

[4] A supports Rec. Text in this order of the words. But CDGLΔ*abc* Vulg. read them thus—ἡ μήτηρ αὐτοῦ καὶ οἱ ἀδελφοὶ αὐτοῦ.—ED.

from the taint of human infirmity than others, yet she was not entirely exempt from it.—ἔξω, *without*) outside of that circle ["the multitude about Him"], ver. 32; or even outside of the house, where He was teaching.—φωνοῦντες, *calling Him*) with a loud voice.

32. Εἶπον, *they said*) He Himself was well aware of it, without their telling Him.

34. Κύκλῳ, *in a circle round about*) With the utmost sweetness.

CHAPTER IV.

1. Ἤρξατο, *He began*) After the interruption.—παρὰ, *near* [by the sea side]) The words in antithesis are, *near the sea*, and *in the sea*.

3. Ἀκούετε, *Hearken*) A word pronounced in a loud voice, in order to still the noise among the people, lest the beginning itself of His discourse should be lost [*Mark especially commends the hearing of the word*, ver. 24, 25, 33.—V. g.]

8 Ἐδίδου, *yielded*: ἔφερεν, *brought forth*) The subject is ἄλλο, *some*:[1] comp. ver. 4–7.—ἀναβαίνοντα, *springing up*) above all obstacles.

9. Ἔλεγεν, *He said*) Frequent pauses are interposed in the case of the weightiest discourses like this: ver. 13, 21, 24, 26, 30.

10. Οἱ περὶ αὐτὸν, *they that were about Him*) Who enjoyed the privilege of the first admission to His presence: ch. iii. 34.

11. Ἔλεγεν, *He said*) With hearty good-will [with real pleasure].—ἔξω, *without*) outside of the circle of genuine discipleship. [*In antithesis to* ver. 10 (They that were about Him with the twelve).—V. g.]—γίνεται) *Fall to* [*are done* as concerns] them as parables.

12. Ἵνα, *that*) They already before saw not, Matt. xiii. 13. Now there is added [to their voluntary blindness] divinely—

---

[1] So AD*ab* Vulg. and Lachm. But ἄλλα BCL Memph. Tischend.—ED

sent judicial blindness.—ἵνα, *so that:* LXX. Gen. xxii. 14.—καὶ ἀφεθήσεται αὐτοῖς τὰ ἁμαρτήματα, *and their sins should be forgiven them*) This is the true *healing*, spoken of Matt. xiii. 15; Ps. ciii. 3.

13. Οὐκ οἴδατε, *do ye not know*) Jesus marks with reproof the question of the disciples.—καὶ πῶς, *and how then*) The parable concerning the seed is the primary and fundamental one [the foundation of all the others].—πάσας, *all*) constituting and comprising the perfect doctrine of Christ.

14. Ὁ σπείρων, *the sower*) Christ is the *sower*. Peter, Paul, and others, sow the seed of Christ, and are servants of Christ.

15. Ὅπου σπείρεται ὁ λόγος, *where the word is sown*) This clause is rather to be connected with what follows.—εὐθέως, *immediately*) Satan's most favourite time for lying in wait.—ἐν ταῖς καρδίαις, *in their hearts*) This means more than *into their hearts*.

16, 17. Εὐθέως, *immediately*) Great changes can take place in the soul very speedily.

19. Αἱ περὶ τὰ λοιπὰ ἐπιθυμίαι, *the lusts of other things*) the *pleasures of life*, in Luke viii. 14: in one's mode of living, loves, tastes for literature, etc.—εἰσπορευόμεναι, *entering in*) He who hath received the word of God, ought to see, lest the cares of the world wax strong upon him, and take more violent hold, than even before, of his new-born expansion of soul and his mental affections, which have been rendered more enlarged by means of the word of God.—γίνεται, *it becometh*) viz. the word.

20. Ἕν, *the one*) Accusative.

21. Καί, *and*) Ver. 24 is closely connected with ver. 20, and those that go before: therefore also this comes in between parenthetically; comp. Luke viii. 16. In this sense, the earth covers for a considerably long time the seed committed to it; whereas you, on the contrary, ought to put forth into action the power of the word, which you have heard, immediately upon hearing it.—ὁ λύχνος, *a candle* [*torch-light*]) So also Christ comes, together with His Gospel, as the true light. And a man himself ought to be, not the bushel, but the candlestick; comp. Luke viii. 16–18.—κλίνην, *a couch* [not us Engl). Vers., *a bed*]) where food is taken.

---

[1] Lachm. reads, with Rec. Text, ἐν, and so Vulg. But Tischend., with all the uncials which have accents, being of later date, ἐν.—ED.

ST MARK IV. 22–24.

22. Οὐ γάρ ἐστί τι κρυπτὸν—οὐδὲ ἐγένετο ἀπόκρυφον, *for there is nothing hidden—nor has anything become concealed*) There is a difference both in the verbs *is*, implying that it was so naturally, and *has become*, implying intentional concealment, and also in the nouns [adjectives] used; comp. κρυπτά, 1 Cor. iv. 5, and ἀπόκρυφον, Col. ii. 3;[1] to which corresponds the difference which is made in the corresponding antithesis, between φανερωθῇ, *be manifested*, and ἔλθῃ εἰς φανερὸν, *come to be manifested;* the former referring to manifestation by constraint, the latter to manifestation of its own accord, when it is ripe for manifestation. Therefore the former sentence can be understood of what is bad, the second sentence of what is good. This axiom holds good of the things in nature, of the feelings and actions of men, whether good or bad, in a natural condition or in a spiritual condition; as also of the divine mysteries.—ἐγένετο, *has become* ["was kept," Engl. Vers.]) The subject is τι, *anything*, to be repeated from the previous sentence: the predicate is, *hidden out of sight*, ἀπόκρυφον.—ἔλθῃ, *come*) of its own accord; comp. John iii. 21. This is done in successive stages in this present order of things; and it shall be done fully, when the light shall make manifest all secrets on the last day; 1 Cor. iv. 5.

23. Εἴ τις, *if any man*) Therefore it is not every one that hath them.

24. Βλέπετε τί ἀκούετε, *See* [*take heed*], *what ye hear*) The seeing organ, which is the more noble sense, directs and modifies the impressions of the hearing: it is the eye, not the ear, that can move itself.—τί, *what*) We are hearing the word, which is the word of God; account that as a high privilege: Or else the *what* is to be resolved into the *how* of Luke: see to it, what kind of a hearing you render to the word.—ἐν ᾧ μέτρῳ, *with what measure*) The *measure* alluded to is the heart, with its capabilities, desires, anxiety to impart blessings received to others, and obedience.—προστεθήσεται, *it shall be added* [more shall be given]) That ye may be not only hearers, but partakers.—τοῖς) *as concerns the hearers;*[2] comp. on Rom. ii. 8, as

---

[1] So Latin *conditus*, 'hidden,' whether undesignedly or otherwise: *absconditus*, "hidden out of sight," by design.—ED.

[2] The margin of both editions had left the reader to decide as to the

respects such datives. [Engl. Vers. makes the dat. follow προστεθ., "more shall be given to you that fear."]

26. Ἄνθρωπος, *a man*) With this man God and Christ are compared, with a view to describe the several ages and grades [stages of progress] of the whole Christian Church; comp. ver. 29.

27. Καθεύδῃ καὶ ἐγείρηται, *should sleep and rise*) With these two verbs are connected by Chiasmus [See Append.] the nouns *night* and *day* [*sleep* referring to *night*; *rise*, to *day*]. Moreover, sometimes night is wont to be put before day, as in Gen. i. [The evening and the morning were the first day, ver. 5].—οὐκ οἶδεν αὐτὸς, *he knoweth not himself*) After the safeguards of grace have been conferred on men, God leaves them in some measure to themselves. Yet this clause may be made to refer to the believing man himself; and then, *of its own accord*, in ver. 28, is opposed to man's care, not to the cultivation of the earth.

28. Αὐτομάτη, *of its own accord*) This is not to the exclusion of cultivation of the land, the rain from heaven, and the sun's beams. [*But there is also intimated a freedom of increasing and growing, either in good or evil, granted by the Lord of the land to the man.*—V. g.]—χόρτον, *the blade*) the grass-like young shoot; so in the commencement spiritual virtues [graces] are scarcely to be distinguished from natural ones.—εἶτα, *then next*) Marvellous is the process of the successive increase: this shall hereafter be made manifest.

29. Παραδῷ, *shall have yielded*) this also *of its own accord* [ver. 28]. Supply *itself*.—εὐθέως, *immediately*) As before he did not put in the sickle too soon, so now he does not put it in too late.—ἀποστέλλει, *He sendeth*) An abbreviated expression for, *He sendeth*, viz. men furnished with a sickle: for ἀποστέλλεσθαι is properly applied to a living person [agent].

30. Τίνι ὁμοιώσωμεν, *whereunto shall we liken*) The plural; comp. John iii. 11.

omission of this clause, τοῖς ἀκούουσιν. The Gnomon and Vers. Germ. retain it.—E. B.

BCDGLΔc Vulg. omit it. However A, with Rec. Text, supports it. —ED.

31. Ὡς κόκκον, *as a grain*) viz. let us *compare* [ver. 30] it.[1]—μικρότερος) *less*.

31, 32. Ὅταν σπαρῇ, *when it has been sown*) This clause, being placed twice, exactly defines that time when the grain ceases to be small, and begins to become great in size. In ver. 31, the emphasis in pronunciation is to be laid on the *when*, and in ver. 32, on the words, *it has been sown*.

33. Καθὼς ἠδύναντο ἀκούειν, *according as they were able to hear*) They did not admit in their then state to have the truth more openly spoken to them.

35. Ἐν ἐκείνῃ τῇ ἡμέρᾳ, *on that day*) See App. Crit. Ed. ii. on this passage. The pronoun ἐκείνῃ, *that*, does not denote precisely that day on which the Saviour put forth the parables of the sower and the rest of the parables, as Grotius, besides other commentators, acknowledge; but, with less definiteness, is to be referred to a day marked in the former course of this gospel, namely, ch. ii. 1. So Judg. xiii. 10, ביום, LXX. ἐν ἡμέρᾳ, or, as it is better read in the Cod. Alex. τῇ ἡμέρᾳ ἐκείνῃ. So Matt. xxiv. 48, ὁ κακὸς δοῦλος ἐκεῖνος.[2] And indeed Mark applies ἐκεῖνος in various senses; see notes ch. ii. 20, xiii. 24. As to the time of this voyage, comp. Harmon. Evang. § 49.

36. Παραλαμβάνουσιν, *they take Him with them*) i.e. they to whom the ship belonged took Him with them to cross the lake. —ὡς ἦν, *as He was*) Without any sumptuous preparation [or equipment]; Matt. viii. 20. So the LXX., ὥς ἐστιν, and ὡς ἦσαν, 2 Kings vii. 7.—πλοιάρια, *little ships*) and in them men.—μετ' Αὐτοῦ, *with Him*) with Jesus.

37. Λαῖλαψ) i.e. κίνησις νεφῶν καὶ ταραχὴ μετὰ εὐδίαν, κ.τ.λ., *An agitation and commotion of the clouds after a calm* [fair weather]. —Eustathius.—ἐπέβαλεν, *dashed into*) viz. dashed *themselves* into.

38. Πρύμνῃ, *the stern*) where the helm is.—τὸ προσκεφάλαιον, *the pillow*) This was a part of the ship, as one may infer from the article; it was of wood, as Theophylactus observes. See

---

[1] BDΔ read κόκκῳ, and so Tischend. But AC Vulg. *bc*, κόκκον; and so Lachm.—ED.

[2] Where the more *immediate* antecedent to ἐκεῖνος is *the faithful and wise servant*, and the antecedent *intended* must be supplied from the course of the previous discourse, ver. 38, 39, etc —ED.

Heupel. on this passage.—οὐ μέλει σοι, *it is not the case, is it? that thou hast no care*) The Lord is not moved to anger at their praying in a rather unseasonable [importunate] manner.

39. Σιώπα, *be silent*) cease from roaring.—πεφίμωσο, *be still*) cease from violence [*i.e.*, the σιώπα refers to the *noise*; πεφίμωσο, to the furious violence of the waves].—γαλήνη, *a calm*) of the sea; which, under other circumstances, would have continued in a troubled state even after the wind had lulled.

40. Οὐκ, *not*) His expression subsequently was, *not yet* [Do ye *not yet* understand?] Matth. xvi. 9. The *not* simply implies negation; the *not yet* implies that they already before had had good grounds afforded them for believing.

CHAPTER V.

1. Τῶν Γαδαρηνῶν, *of the Gadarenes*) Gadara, a city of Grecian origin [or *Greek-like*], subject to the Jews; wherein it may be inferred that many Jews dwelt, from the fact that our Lord came to them. [*Doubtless it had the same port in common with Gerasa or Gergesa.*—V. g.]

2. Εὐθέως, *immediately*) However, the man was preserved from casting himself into the sea as the swine did.—ἐν, *in*) The particle contains the emphasis of the clause.

3. Κατοίκησιν, *dwelling*) The dwellers among the tombs were of various descriptions. See ver. 5.

5. Ὄρεσιν, *in the mountains*) in solitary places. Mountains were in the locality, as we find in ver. 11.—ἑαυτὸν, *himself*) In the case of the possessed, even the natural and proper love of self [law of self-preservation] is in abeyance.

6. Ἔδραμε, *ran*) A specimen and foretaste of the Lordship of Christ. The man possessed ran in spite of the demons, as may readily be supposed.

7. Μή με βασανίσῃς, *do not torment me*) Whilst the demon is being tormented, the man possessed is tormented, and yet he

[the latter] is set free. The demon deprecates either the expulsion itself, or a second tormenting added to the expulsion.

8. Τὸ) The language is so framed, as if it were of only one demon; and ver. 13, 9, imply there were many demons, who rendered obedience to one superior, as a legion does to its commander. That one alone, and pre-eminently, seems to maintain a continual and uninterrupted connection with his own legion, inasmuch as they are comprehended under his own name.

9. Λεγιὼν, *Legion*) An appellation by Synecdoche [see Append., the genus for the species]. There was one principal leader among them, and the rest were conjoined with him, constituting thus the legion: and this, whether he had previously borne this Latin name, before that he entered this man, or then first assumed it.—πολλοί ἐσμεν, *we are many*) Luke affirms this in his own words [not in the man's or the demon's], ch viii. 30. If in one nest [dwelling] there can be so many, how many there must be in the whole aggregate throughout the world! [*Mere number in itself does not produce protection* (patronage).—V. g.]

10. Παρεκάλει, *he besought*) The singular number; the plural occurs in ver. 12.—χώρας, *the country*) which they loved, and were then dwelling in. [*And so, therefore, being acquainted with the men of that country, they were meditating to inflict the more injury by means of their acquaintance with them.*—V. g.] But it is marvellous that they did not avoid the locality in which the Messiah, the destroyer of their power, was sojourning.

12. Πάντες, *all*) with one consent.

13. Εὐθέως, *forthwith*) He did not require to deliberate in any case.—ὡς δισχίλιοι, *about two thousand*) The name legion implied a number exceeding this.

14. Ἀνήγγειλαν, *announced it*) to those to whom the swine had belonged, in the city and in the fields [the country].

15. Καθήμενον, ἱματισμένον, σωφρονοῦντα, *sitting, clothed, in his sound mind*) whereas previously he had been without rest, clothes, and the use of his reason. Those who had witnessed the miracle may have given him the *clothes*. He put forth and showed his possession of reason in his actions.—τὸν λεγεῶνα, *the legion*) This name seems to have been known in that locality, and to have kept the inhabitants in a state of fright. For there

is not any other apparent cause why this appellation, which describes the fact as they found it, should be repeated.[1]

18. Μετ᾽ αὐτοῦ, *with Him*) The cross had allured the man by its sweetness from his own relatives. The powerful influence of Jesus had possession of him. [*And so now on that account he had it in his power to be of the greater use to his relatives.*—V. g.]

19. Τοὺς σοὺς, *thine own* people) implying the obligation by which we are bound towards relatives.—ἀνάγγειλον, *announced*) There is a time for speaking; see ver. 30 and following verses; and also a time for being silent, ver. 43.—ὁ Κύριος, *the Lord*) Jesus; comp. ver. 20 ['Jesus.']

20. Κηρύσσειν, *to publish*) So they [the people of that country] were not without a testimony among them to the glory of God; although Jesus, by their own request [ver. 17], went away quickly.—ἐν τῇ) not merely in his own home, which had been all that Jesus had desired him to do; ver. 19.

22.[2] Ἰάειρος, *Jairus*) At the time that Mark wrote this, Jairus and his daughter might still have been found in Palestine. It is a strong proof of the truth of the Gospel, that the very proper names are given in the Evangelist's narrative.[3]—ἰδὼν, *when he saw*) having beheld the majesty of Christ.

23. Ἐσχάτως ἔχει, *is at the point of death*) It was great faith which impelled Jairus to leave her when just breathing her last.—ἵνα, *that*) This being put in recitative style, shows *what was the mental feeling* [intention] which led Jairus to mention the sickness of his daughter. [Eng. Ver. loses the beauty of the abrupt ἵνα, by inserting, *I pray thee*.]

29. Ἐξηράνθη ἡ πηγὴ, *the fountain was dried up*) It not merely decreased. There was the highest degree of instantaneous soundness and health.

---

[1] The larger Ed. is not so much in favour of this repetition as Ed. 2, the Gnomon, and Vers. Germ. ABLΔ read τὸν ἐσχ. τ. λεγεῶνα (BLΔ, λεγιωνα). But D*bc* Vulg. Memph. Versions omit the words.—ED.

[2] τῶν ἀρχισυναγώγων, *the rulers of the Synagogue*) Who were overseers of the doctors and teachers.—V. g.

[3] And, in the case of Jairus and others, in the vicinity of the very localities where the name was a prevalent one. Comp. Num. xxxii. 41; Deut. iii. 14; Judg. x. 3, 5; 1 Chron. ii. 22.—ED

30. Ἐπιγνοὺς, *perceiving*) Faith even acts.—ἐξελθοῦσαν, *had gone out*) A magnetic power.

33. Φοβηθεῖσα, *fearing*) Sometimes fear follows close upon a good action, which very fear subsequently the goodness of the Lord removes; Matt. xxvi. 10.—εἶπεν, *told*) publicly; Luke viii. 47; after having laid aside all unseasonable shame because of her disease.—πᾶσαν, *all*) Rightly done!

34. Ὕπαγε εἰς εἰρήνην, *go in peace* [lit. *into peace*]) comp. Luke vii. 50, note.—ἴσθι, *be*) permanently so. After her long continued misery, the benefit conferred is a lasting one.

35. Ἀπὸ, *from*) The house of the ruler of the synagogue.—τί ἔτι, *why any further*) This is a strong affirmation of the fact of the daughter being dead. They suppose the ruler's efforts to be vain and out of place.—σκύλλεις, *thou troublest*) This verb is properly used of the trouble attending a journey; Luke vii. 6, viii. 49. Herodian employs it of the difficult [severe] conveyance of captives, and of the setting out of an army. The walkings about of Jesus were then a perpetual σκυλμὸς, *trouble* [harass].—τὸν διδάσκαλον, *the Master*) There were therefore disciples of Jesus in the family of Jairus, and Jesus was the Teacher of the ruler of the synagogue.

36. Λαλούμενον, *that was spoken*) as it were privately.

37. Τὸν ἀδελφὸν, *the brother*) Mark wrote his Gospel not long after the Ascension, at the time when the memory of James, who had been beheaded, was still fresh in the disciples' minds, so that he was better known than even John himself.

38. Ἀλαλάζοντας, *them that chanted the funeral dirge*) in order to diminish and soothe the sorrowful thoughts of the mourners.

40. Κατεγέλων, *they began to laugh Him down*) with sorrowful laughter, free from insolence.—ἐκβαλὼν, *having put out*) Marvellous authority in a house, as one would have thought, judging externally, with which He had no connection. In reality there was in the house its true Lord.—τὸν) Therefore there were present three disciples, and three of the family, not more; comp. ver. 43.

41. Ταλιθὰ κοῦμι, *Talitha Cumi*) Peter had remembered the precise words used by the Saviour; and it was from his mouth [dictation] that Mark is said to have written. *Talitha* was used but once; for Jesus, in raising the dead, did not employ Epi-

zeuxis [repetition of the same word; see Append.], Luke vii. 14; John xi. 43. For His power was always instantaneous in its effect; comp. Num. xx. 11.—σοὶ λέγω, *I say unto thee*) This is not contained in *Talitha Cumi*, and yet it is with truth added.

42. Εὐθέως, *straightway*) It was not by degrees that at last she regained her consciousness.—γὰρ, *for*) She returned to the state consonant to her age.—δώδεκα, *twelve*) comp. ver. 25. It was at one and the same time the woman was healed [of the issue of twelve years' standing] and the girl [of twelve years] was raised to life; the one having begun life at the same time that the other had begun her misery.

43. Διεστείλατο, *He prohibited strictly*) [The crowd, no doubt, who were not unacquainted with the fact of the girl's death, might have both known the miracle, and published it for the glory of GOD.—V. g.—φαγεῖν, *to eat*) She was by this time alive and well, and not needing any medicine.—V. g.]

CHAPTER VI.

1.[1] Ἀκολουθοῦσιν, *follow*) Although they were not all admitted to see the raising of Jairus' daughter.

2. Γενομένου, *having come*) When the arrival of Jesus had taken place not very long before.—πόθεν—δοθεῖσα, *whence—given*) But indeed He is Wisdom itself.—καὶ δυνάμεις;) Understand τί, *what* [are also these mighty works]? *how* [has He been enabled to do them]?

3. Ὁ τέκτων) Son of the carpenter, or even Himself a *carpenter*; for they add, *the Son* of Mary, in antithesis to *the Son of the carpenter*. [*He Himself therefore toiled at that kind of labour, which was corresponding to His spiritual work;* Zech. vi. 12.—V. g.]

---

[1] ἐκεῖθεν) *from thence*: this term has a wider sense in this passage of Mark than in Matthew xiii. 53, and has respect to the whole sojourn of the Saviour at Capernaum and the adjacent district. Jairus dwelt in Capernaum; and, not long after the resurrection of his daughter, the parables recorded in Matt. xiii., etc., were put forth near Capernaum.—*Harm.*, p. 325.

4. Πατρίδι, *country*) in which there are many *ties of relationship*.—συγγενέσι, *relatives*) having many *houses* [each one having his own house or family].

5. Οὐκ ἠδύνατο, *He could not*) That is, *mighty works* could not be done, because the men were incapacitated [for the benefit through unbelief].—ὀλίγοις, *a few*) implying the quantity.—ἀῤῥώστοις, *infirm*) implying the quality.

6. Κύκλῳ, *in a circle round*) Yet Jesus conferred a benefit on His own country.

7. Ἤρξατο, *began*) After that they had made some progress.—δύο δύο, *by two and two*) six pairs; Matt. x. 2, 3.—καὶ, *and*) The rest of His instructions are evident from ver. 12, 13.

8, 9. Παρήγγειλεν) Mark uses this verb with a threefold construction in this passage; παρήγγειλεν—ἵνα μηδὲν αἴρωσιν—ἀλλ᾽ ὑποδεδεμένους (viz. εἶναι)—καὶ μὴ ἐνδύσησθε. So also the construction is varied in ch. xii. 38, θελόντων περιπατεῖν καὶ ἀσπασμούς; where the infinitive and the accusative are joined.

8. Ἵνα, *that*) That they might be unencumbered, unrestrained, and free [comp. note on Matt. x. 10].

13.[1] Ἐξέβαλλον, *they began casting out*) The demons, without doubt, bore their expulsion by the disciples with more vexation than that by the Lord Himself.—ἤλειφον ἐλαίῳ, *anointed with oil*) This anointing differed widely from that anointing which is called *extreme unction*. They did not carry oil about with themselves, as ver. 8 proves; but found and used it at the houses of the sick. The miracle was on that account the more unequivocal.

14. Φανερὸν, *manifested* [spread abroad]) Jesus had not come to be known by many before that John's death became known, otherwise they would not have supposed Him to be John. This observation is to be marked in opposition to those who extend the length of the times after the baptism of John too much.—γὰρ, *for*) Except for the public rumour, Herod would not have known of Him. A palace is generally late in hearing of spiritual news.—ἔλεγεν, *he said*) The plural is given in Luke ix. 7, and the circumstances of the case even in Mark require that number; for there are enumerated the opinions of men con-

---

[1] Ver. 10. ἐκεῖθεν, *from thence*) out of the city.

cerning Him, one of which in particular above the rest is indicated in fine in ver. 16, as having seemed probable to Herod. Therefore the parenthesis, if it be desirable to mark one before φανερὸν, ought to close, not at αὐτοῦ, but at προφητῶν, ver. 15, so that the ἤκουσεν of ver. 14 should be evidently resumed in the ἀκούσας of ver. 16. Nor should Mark thus be said to ascribe to Herod twice, although to others not even once, the opinion which Herod received from others, especially inasmuch as Herod was more in doubt than the others. Therefore either ἔλεγον,[1] *they were saying*, ought to be read; or else ἔλεγεν, *he said*, does not refer to Herod; but the participle [one] *saying* is to be supplied in an indefinite sense to that verb, as φησὶ, said one, is often used, viz. ὁ εἰπὼν, one saying [the sayer] being understood. See on Chrysost. de Sacerd., p. 477; Glass. Can. 23, de Verbo; and Hiller, Syntagm., p. 325.

15. Ἄλλοι, *others*) The variety of human opinions on Divine subjects is astonishing. It is of some benefit to the disciples to know it, ch. viii. 28; but it rather agitates than benefits Herod. However great be that variety, yet often the truth lies outside of it.

16. Ἀκούσας δὲ, *but having heard*) This is repeated from ver. 14.

19. Ἐνεῖχεν) *had an inward grudge towards him*.

20. Ἐφοβεῖτο, *feared*) Holiness makes a man an object of reverential awe. John did not fear Herod.—εἰδὼς, *knowing*) This affords an argument for the truth of religion: the fear of the bad, and their reverence towards piety. [*He did not, however, recognise him as a prophet. The estimate formed by men of the world does not reach to the main turning point of the truth. Judas himself, when now overwhelmed by the mists of despair, did not call Jesus the* Christ, *but the* innocent blood.—V. g.]—συνετήρει, *was guarding* him [but Eng. Vers. *observed* him]) against Herodias.—πολλὰ—ἤκουε, *many things—heard*) And yet Herod was not a pious man.

21. Γενεσίοις) Γενέσια, This is the genus: γενέθλια, the species. The latter denotes properly a birth-day feast [or celebration];

---

[1] Tisch. reads ἔλεγεν with ACGLΔ Vulg. *c*. Lachm. ἔλεγον with B and D (ἐλέγοσαν) *ab*.—ED. and TRANSL.

The Germ. Vers. does not follow the observation of the Gnomon in this place, but the margin of both editions, preferring the reading ἔλεγεν.—E. B.

the former, any anniversary feast-day whatever; for instance, the anniversary of entering on a kingdom.—μεγιστᾶσιν, *the great men*) of the palace and of the court.—χιλιάρχοις, *chief captains*) of his soldiery.—τοῖς πρώτοις, *the nobles*) in provincial posts.

22. Ὁ βασιλεὺς τῷ κορασίῳ, *the king unto the damsel*) An antithesis.

25. Μετὰ σπουδῆς) promptly.—Θέλω [I will] *I wish*) Boldness of speech.

27. Σπεκουλάτωρα, *an executioner*) This word is derived from "specula," *a look-out, a watch-tower.* The *Speculatores* executed capital punishments: Sen. l. 1, de ira, c. 16.

29. Πτῶμα) So נְבֵלָה of the prophet [Urijah], Jer. xxvi. 23, Lat. *cadaver.* The body of the Saviour is not so termed.—ἐν μνημείῳ, *in a tomb*) perhaps that of his father, in which it was natural for him to be laid, as *his own.* Jesus Christ, the Prince of Life, was laid in the sepulchre of another.

30. Συνάγονται, *gather themselves*) together.—οἱ ἀπόστολοι, *the apostles*) an appropriate appellation in this place.—πάντα, *all things*) The distribution of the *all things* follows, viz. *both what —and what* (ὅσα—καὶ ὅσα). A most noble narration.

31. Ὑμεῖς αὐτοί, *ye yourselves*) also. Often the Saviour betook Himself alone to solitude: now He says, Do ye also seek solitude [a desert place].—ὀλίγον, *a little while*) Solitude and intercourse with others should be blended together by the godly.—ἦσαν, *they were*) They did not always come and go together.

33. Προῆλθον, *outwent* [got before]) by various ways.—συνῆλθον, *came together*) in one place.

34. Ἤρξατο, *He began*) afresh, as if He had not taught them previously. There is need of real compassion, to enable one to teach; and compassion is the virtue of a good teacher.

35. Πολλῆς, *far spent*) Matth. xx. 1, etc.

36. Κύκλῳ, *in a circle round about*) For there was not a sufficiency of food for them in merely one or two of the adjoining districts and villages.

37. Ἀγοράσωμεν, *are we to buy*) The disciples intimate, by this question, that there is on their part no want of the will, both to give their exertion in going away, and their money, as much as they had, in buying what was needed; but what is wanting is the ability to satisfy such a multitude. Therefore, in their

question, they fix on the sum *two hundred denarii*,[1] not so much according to the supply which was in their purse at the time, as according to the number of the multitude. See what can be elicited from the data furnished to us : 5000 men is to 200 denarii, as one man is to $\frac{1}{25}$th of a denarius, *i.e.* about half of a German kreuzer (halfpenny). We have, besides the argument of changing the old money [mintage] into new, that expression of John vi. 7, "that every one of them may take a *little*," especially at that time of year, about the Passover, John vi. 4, when the price of provisions is usually higher; we have also the rational computation of the disciples, whereby in contrast on the opposite side is illustrated the omnipotence of our Lord. The sum of 200 zuzœi, or denarii, was among the Hebrews very frequent in the case of a dowry or fine : but this does not oppose the analogy of the 200 denarii and 5000 men.

40. Ἀνέπεσον, *they sat down*) A proof of faith on the part of the people.

41. Πᾶσι, *all*) All partook even of the accompaniment, the fish : even of it also remnants were left, ver. 43 ; [*which, as a fish consists of very different parts, is therefore less intelligible to mere reason, than the multiplication of the bread.*—V. g.]

45. Πρὸς Βηθσαϊδάν, *to Bethsaida*) This was the terminus, not of their whole voyage, but in part, until Jesus was about to come to them.

48. Εἶδεν, *He saw*) And yet He did not come to them, before that it was the full [proper] time.—ἤθελε, *was wishing* [would have]) Comp. Luke xxiv. 28.

52. Γὰρ, *for*) They ought to have inferred from the miracle of the loaves as to [His power also over] the sea. The more exercised that faith is, the more it becomes accustomed to the spectacle of [to seeing and discerning] the marvellous works of God. [Comp. Matth. xiv. 33.]—ἦν γὰρ, *for was*) Not only is that particular time denoted, but the habitual state of their heart during their then pupillage [early training].

53. Προσωρμίσθησαν, *they drew to the shore*) promptly.

55. Ἐπὶ τοῖς) The dative : *in beds*, as they had been lying.

---

[1] *Pence:* though the denarius, originally so called from being = 10 asses, is really somewhat more than 7½ pence; or, according to its earlier value, 8½ pence.—ED. and TRANSL.

56. [Ἐν ταῖς ἀγοραῖς, *in the streets* [or the *fora*]) where they would have the greater certainty of meeting Him, and where the greatest number might obtain relief at once.—V. g.]—Κἄν) This particle is compounded here, not of καί and ἐάν, as it is usually, but of καί and ἄν, as in 2 Cor. xi. 16. Comp. note on Chrys. de Sacerd., p. 459.—ἄψωνται, *they might touch*) after the example of the woman with the issue of blood: ch. v. 27.—αὐτοῦ) τοῦ κρασπέδου.

CHAPTER VII.

1–5. Οἱ Φαρισαῖοι—ἰδόντες τινὰς τῶν μαθητῶν αὐτοῦ κοιναῖς χερσὶ—ἐσθίοντας ἄρτους (οἱ γὰρ—κλινῶν) ἔπειτα ἐπερωτῶσιν αὐτὸν οἱ Φαρισαῖοι, κ.τ.λ.) The construction of the language is pendent: from not observing which, some inserted ἐμέμψαντο after ἄρτους. But the whole period, extended by the parenthesis, is sustained by the verb ἐπερωτῶσιν. For the verb is either repeated at the end of the parenthesis, Acts ii. 8, 11; 1 Cor. viii. 1–4; Judg. ix. 16, 19; 2 Sam. xxi. 2, 3, 4; 1 Kings viii. 41, 42; or it is then in fine [and not till then] set down, as in this passage, and Eph. iii. 1, 14, and the connection is marked by the particles καί, δέ, οὖν, and in this passage by ἔπειτα.[1] Very similar is the section of Gregory Thaumaturgus, which we shall give in a more contracted form than the original: κατορθοῦται ἡ ψυχή, ἵν᾽ ὥσπερ ἐν κατόπτρῳ ἑαυτὴν θεωρήσασα (τὸ ἄλογον, καὶ πάλιν τὸ λογικὸν, κ.τ.λ.) ΕΙΤΑ ταῦτα ἐν αὐτῇ κατανοήσασα, τὰ μὲν χείρονα ΕΚΒΑΛΛΟΙ, τὰ δὲ ἀγαθὰ ΕΚΤΡΕΦΟΙ. See Paneg. on Orig., p. 70, etc., ed. Stutgard.—[ἀπὸ Ἱεροσολύμων, *from Jerusalem*) The Passover had been celebrated there.—V. g.]

2. Τοῦτ᾽ ἔστι, *that is to say*) The Evangelist adds an interpretation, as in ver. 11, ch. v. 41, etc.; himself not regarding unwashed hands as defiled.

3. Πυγμῇ) Πυγμή, *the fist*.—פוגמה, עד הפרק, up to the wrist.

---

[1] BDL Vulg. *abc* Syr. Memph. read in ver. 5. καί instead of ἔπειτα. A supports the ἔπειτα, with Rec. Text.—ED. and TRANSL.

See Lightf.—παράδοσιν, *the tradition*) Its correlative is παρέλαβον, *they have received*, ver. 4.

4. Ξεστῶν, *pitchers* [larger vessels]) Whence the contents are emptied into *the cups*.—κλινῶν, [*tables*, Engl. Vers.] *couches*) which were used by persons in reclining to eat at table.

5. Ἐπερωτῶσιν, *ask* Him) The Pharisees were always giving their whole zeal to mere *questionings*.—περιπατοῦσιν, *walk*) הלך is often found in this sense among the Hebrews.

6. Ὑποκριτῶν, *hypocrites*) Indeed, we may derive from this passage a definition of *hypocrisy*. These Pharisees were a sample of hypocrites in general.

8. Ἀφέντες, *laying aside*) The antithetic word to *hold*. The terms akin are, to *reject*, ver. 9, and to *make of none effect*, ver. 13.—τὴν ἐντολὴν, *the commandment*) The commandment is one, even as virtue is one and uncompounded; as opposed to the multiplicity of traditions.—τοῦ Θεοῦ—τῶν ἀνθρώπων, *of God—of men*) An evident antithesis.—βαπτισμοὺς ξεστῶν, *the washings of pitchers*) worthless petty observances.

9. Καλῶς ἀθετεῖτε, *full well ye reject*) היטיב, for which the LXX. have καλῶς, i.e. it is well said, when it is so said [It is a true saying that ye, etc.] Just as a true picture of a conflagration is *well done*. And also they had supposed they were doing *well* in doing so.—ἵνα, *in order that*) This is a true accusation against them, although the hypocrites did not think that this was their own intention.

10. Μωσῆς, *Moses*) by Divine direction.

13. Ἧ παρεδώκατε, *which ye have delivered*) Ye have made into a tradition what was a mere custom among the ancients.

14. Ἀκούετε, *hearken*) An admonition salutary to *all*, in opposition to the prejudice which is most hostile to true Divine worship.

16. Εἴ τις ἔχει, *if any man have*) Few of them comprehended what He had said. See verses following.

18. Ἔξωθεν, *from without*) This is added for the sake of explanation.

19. Καθαρίζον) not polluting, but *purging*, whilst the wholesome nutriment remains, and the mere refuse so *purged* away goes out.

22. Πλεονεξίαι) Πλεονεξία, πλεονέκτης, πλεονεκτέω, as involving

the comparative by implication, denote a kind of mean between
theft and rapine, viz., when you aim by various artifices to
effect, that your neighbour of himself, but with injury to himself, may unwittingly or unwillingly offer, concede, and assign
to you some possession which it is not right you should receive.
Yet it approaches nearer to theft, and is more opposed to rapine or
open violence; and it is a sin chiefly characteristic of the rich, as
the two former are sins of the poor; 1 Cor. vi. 10, v. 10.—
ἀσέλγεια) a diffuse *wantonness* [lasciviousness] of mind. Comp.
the Syr. Version. This and *an evil eye* are contrary to the
ninth and tenth commandments.—ὀφθαλμὸς πονηρός, *an evil eye*)
envy and joy at the misfortunes of others.—ἀφροσύνη, *foolishness*)
under which they were labouring, who are refuted in this
passage: with this comp. *Ye fools*, Luke xi. 40. This is the
reason why *foolishness* is placed last of all, inasmuch as being
that which renders even all the rest incurable. Human corruption has its seat not merely in the will [but in the understanding also. Comp. ver. 18.]

23. Πάντα, *all things*) O how impure is the fountain of our
heart!

24. Μεθόρια) *the common boundaries.*—οὐδένα, *no man*) For
He was still within the borders of the land of Israel.¹

25. Ἀκούσασα, *having heard*) If faith could thus be originated
by a mere rumour, how much more ought it to be by a text of
Scripture, even though but a short one!—γὰρ, *for*) Referring to
the words, *He could not be hid*, ver. 24. Jesus put Himself in
her way, along with the help He meant to give her: but He
so controlled the affair, that He seemed to have acted as He
did towards this Grecian woman, as it were fortuitously, whereas
He had undertaken this whole journey for her sake. Comp.
Matth. xviii. 12.—τὸ θυγάτριον, *young daughter*) Boys also are
capable of being the subjects of demoniacal possession, ch. ix.
21, 24: as also heathens.

26. Ἑλληνίς, *a Greek*) The term being taken in a wide sense.
—Συροφοίνισσα τῷ γένει) Clemens Al., in Protrept., makes mention

---

¹ οὐκ ἠδυνήθη λαθεῖν, *He could not remain hid*) Things were so disposed
by the direction of God, that the benefit seemed to have been as if at random, and by fortuitous coincidence, conferred on her as being a heathen
woman.—V. g.

of τῶν τὴν Φοινίκην Σύρων κατοικούντων. Tertullian mentions *Syrophœnice*: see *ad Marcion*: also Justin M. against Trypho. Juvenal speaks of *Syrophœnix udus*. The feminine Φοίνισσα, which Herodian has, is formed on the same analogy as Κρῆσσα, Λίβυσσα, Θρᾷσσα, Κίλισσα.—[τὸ δαιμόνιον, *the demon*) that unclean spirit which had taken possession of the girl.—V. g.]

27. Ἄφες πρῶτον, *let first*) He does not give her a decided denial; He seems to mark to her the fact, that she is unseasonably importunate.—χορτασθῆναι, *be filled*) It would have been to derogate from the rights [privileges] of the Jews, had Jesus bestowed more time on the Gentiles.—[οὐ γὰρ καλόν ἐστι, *for it is not becoming*) That which is not in itself becoming, is altogether so in the case of those who duly pray.—V. g.]

28. Ὑποκάτω τῆς τραπέζης, *under the table*) Arguing great submission on the part of the woman. Yet she alleges as an argument the nearness [of her country to Israel; as of the dogs to their master's table].—τῶν παιδίων, *of the boys* [Engl. Vers., losing the distinction between this and τέκνων, *of the children*]) who often lavish bread wastely.—Παιδία[1] differ from τέκνα, *children*, ver. 27, a word whereby *right* to the father's bread is denoted.

29. Διὰ τοῦτον τὸν λόγον, *on account of this word* [*saying*]) This word, and the faith exhibited in it. There may be understood, *I say to thee*. [*Often, as well in evil as also in good, the whole power of the soul puts itself forth in one word.*—V. g.]—ἐξελήλυθε, *is gone out*) It was thus that Jesus immediately exhilarated her with the joyous information. [*For He knew what had been done, even at a distance, by His power.*—V. g.]

30. Ἀπελθοῦσα, *departing*) in faith.—εὗρε τὴν θυγατέρα βεβλημένην ἐπὶ τῆς κλίνης, καὶ τὸ δαιμόνιον ἐξεληλυθός) see App. Crit. Ed. ii. on this passage.[2] The position of the daughter *lying* on the bed was showing the great power of the demon, which had taken possession of the girl; and also the greater power of Jesus, who had expelled it. The daughter had previously been deprived of all rest. The mother, however, did not of course find

---

[1] *Boys*, not necessarily sons, and often used as *servants*.—ED. and TRANSL.

[2] τὸ παιδίον βεβλημένον ἐπὶ τὴν κλίνην καὶ τὸ δαιμ. ἐξελ. is the reading of BLΔ. Τὴν θυγατέρα βεβλ. is substituted by D Vulg. *bc*. Aa support Rec. Text, τὸ δαιμόνιον ἐξεληλυθός, καὶ τὴν θυγατέρα βεβλημένην ἐπὶ τῆς κλίνης.—ED. and TRANSL.

the demon itself, which had gone out; but she found that the demon had gone out, *i.e.* that such was the state of affairs. The force of the verb, *found*, rests rather on the participle, ἐξεληλυθός, than on the noun, τὸ δαιμόνιον.

31. Τῶν ὁρίων, *the boundaries*) That is, through the midst of Decapolis. [The region comprising Decapolis was situated, for the most part, outside of Galilee (Matt. iv. 25), beyond Jordan, and some portion of it, if this view be accepted, on the southern side of Galilee, and was accordingly chiefly inhabited by Syrians and heathens. To this region appertain Gadara (Mark v. 20) and Cæsarea Philippi. There is frequent mention in the Evangelists, about this time, of the heathen borders; whence it is evident that the Saviour traversed the whole land of Israel.— Harm. p. 343.] [Ver. 32. κωφόν, *deaf*) The narrative of this deaf man, as also of the blind man, concerning whom ch. viii. 22 treats, is recorded in Mark alone.—V. g.]

33. Ἀπολαβόμενος, *taking him aside*) The many outward acts [circumstances] which Jesus employed in this place, and the looks of others, who were healed, stood in the place of words [a sermon] to this deaf man, until he began to hear, inasmuch as Jesus was thereby healing his soul also. [*He imparted to the deaf man His healing power first through the avenue of the eyes, then next of the ears.*—Harm. p. 343.] Comp. ch. viii. 23 concerning *the blind man.*—πτύσας, *spitting*) The saliva is clean and salutary in its uses.

34. Ἐστέναξεν, *He groaned*) The power of sighs is great when the heart is *straitened*, στενῷ [whence στενάζω]. He who groans, γέμει,[1] This is a πάθος [not a feeling which we can command at will; see Append.]; for which reason we never find it said in the Psalms, *I will sigh*, as we find, *I will pray, I will cry aloud, I will lament* (flebo). Even sudden tears are not under our control. But *I will lament*, in the Psalms, is an act of deliberate purpose. [*That groan moved the wretched sufferer, and awakened in him the desire of relief.*—V. g.]—ἐφφαθά, *Ephphatha*) The first word heard by the deaf man.

35. Ἀκοαί) that is to say, *his powers of hearing*. Not merely the one passage for sound in the ear.

---

[1] Γέμω, *to be full* of a thing; Latin, *gemo*. Comp. στένω, to *straiten* by *over-fulness*; hence to *groan*. This shows the connection of γέμω and *gemo*. —ED. and TRANSL.

36. Αὐτοῖς, *them*) Those who had borne the dumb man. It was rather the part of the spectators to publish it abroad. And yet the former [the bearers] also published the fame of it, ver. 37. Silence was wont especially to be enjoined on those who had been cured of the diseases.—μᾶλλον περισσότερον, *the more exceeding abundantly*) The comparative contained in the μᾶλλον, *more*, stands in antithesis to His prohibition: that in the περισσότεροι, *exceeding abundantly*, stands in antithesis to the publishing of it, which they would have made, had there been no prohibition; comp. Phil. i. 23, note.

37. Καλῶς πεποίηκε, *he hath done well*) A formula, ἀποδοχῆς, *of satisfaction*; Acts x. 33; Phil. iv. 14. So in the present, 2 Pet. i. 19; in the future, 3 John ver. 6. So LXX., 1 Kings viii. 18. A similar formula of assenting occurs, Mark xii. 32, *Thou hast well said*—τοὺς) this deaf man and others [Matt. xv. 30].

CHAPTER VIII.

2. Ἡμέραι, *days*) The nominative of time, *there is*, or *there are*, being understood, forms an absolute mode of expression, Luke ix. 28.

3. Τινὲς, *some* of them) Those who had come a greater distance were more in want; and it is on account of these that even the rest are supplied with food. [*This clause is also a portion of Jesus' words.*—V. g.] [μακρόθεν, *from far*) impelled by a remarkable zeal.—V. g.]—ἥκουσι, *they are come*) The verb ἥκω signifies, in the present time [tense], *I am already come*, and *I am here*, rather than *I am coming*. They who have substituted ἥκασι in this passage, do not seem to have considered this force of the verb; see on Rev. ii. 25.[1]

6, 7. Εὐχαριστήσας—εὐλογήσας, *giving thanks—blessing*) Synonyms. They do right in taking food, who pray over the several courses.—καὶ αὐτὰ, *them also*) Implying the liberal bountifulness of the feast.

---

[1] Tisch. reads εἰσὶν instead of ἥκουσιν, with BLΔ Memph.; but Lachm. ἥκασι with AD; 'venerunt,' *abc* Vulg.—ED. and TRANSL.

11. *Ἤρξαντο, they began*) after a temporary cessation. [πειρα-ζοντες αὐτὸν, *tempting Him*) to try whether He could, after having exhibited so many signs on the earth, perform similar signs from heaven also.—V. g.]

12. 'Ἀναστενάξας) When *He has betaken Himself* to [having commenced] *sighing*. The word is inchoative or inceptive, as ἀναβοάω, etc. And yet *to begin to groan* or *sigh* remains a πάθος, or mental emotion.[1]

15. Τῶν Φαρισαίων καὶ 'Ἡρώδου, *of the Pharisees and Herod*) Two opposite extremes of religious sects. In Matt. xvi. 6, where see note, the words are, " the Pharisees and *Sadducees*." Therefore, instead of what Matthew has, viz. *the Sadducees*, Mark has, *Herod*. The leaven common to them all, at least in demanding signs on various pretexts at different occasions, was hypocrisy (Herod is called " the fox," Luke xiii. 31, where see note). As to Herod, Luke does not mention that indeed (viz. his demanding a sign), at ch. xii. 1, but he does at ch. xxiii. 8, as it were in the way of supplement. For although Herod approached nearer to the Pharisees in the article of the resurrection, ch. vi. 16, yet the licentiousness admitted by the doctrine of the Sadducees, was in other respects more suited to his palace and court, which bent religion into a mere species of political expediency.

17. [Τί διαλογίζεσθε, κ.τ.λ..) The sense of the discourse moves forward by distinct interrogations, as far as to the verb μνημονεύετε, ver. 18, inclusive.—*Not. Crit.*]—πεπωρωμένην, *hardened*) *Hardening* flows on from the heart to the sight, the hearing, and the memory; ver. 18.[2]

22. Φέρουσιν, *they bring*) The blind man himself does not seem then as yet to have had knowledge of Jesus.

23. 'Ἐπιλαβόμενος, *taking to Him*) Himself was leading the way, illustrating His great humility.—κώμης) Bethsaida is called

---

[1] Not a premeditated act of the mind: though *to begin* to groan might seem to imply it was the latter.—ED. and TRANSL.

[2] Ver. 21. πῶς οὐ συνίετε; *how is it that ye do not understand?*) viz. that there cannot possibly be with Me any want of bread for you, and that, therefore, it is against a different kind of leaven I am warning you.—V. g. Lachm. reads πῶς οὔπω with ADac Vulg. Tisch. reads οὔπω without πῶς with C*.*. Bbd read as Rec. Text οὐ.—ED. and TRANSL.

πόλις, *a city*, John i. 44. It was a κωμόπολις, *a village-town*. To the blind man, on recovering sight, the aspect of heaven and of the Divine works in nature was more joyous than that of man's works in the village.

24. '*Ως δένδρα, περιπατοῦντας*,'¹ *as trees, walking*) The blind man says, that it is by this alone [their walking] that he knows they are men, not trees, viz. because they walk.

25. '*Αναβλέψαι, lift up his eyes*) and try them.

26. Εἰς τὸν οἶκον—μηδὲ εἰς τὴν κώμην, *into the house—nor into the village*) His house therefore was in the remote extremity of the village.—μηδὲ εἴπῃς, *nor tell*) Jesus avoided celebrity, especially at that time. [*For this miracle is the last in the Evangelists before the Feast of Tabernacles (and before the discourses recorded in John ch. vii.–x.—V. g.); and He forbade this miracle to be published abroad, just as He did the healing of the deaf and dumb man, ch. vii. 36. The people, after having celebrated the Passover, repaired to their country employments: His adversaries were thenceforth honoured with no further sign; and whatever effects were needful to be produced in the case of the disciples by miracles of this kind, had now already reached their highest point. Behold the year of grace now completed in Galilee!*—Harm., p. 348.]—τινί, *to any one*) who is *in the town*.

27. Ἐν τῇ ὁδῷ, *on the way*) He held pious discourse whilst on the way.

31. Τὸν Υἱὸν τοῦ ἀνθρώπου, *the Son of Man*) He calls Himself by an humble title: after the resurrection, He says, *Christ ought to have suffered;* Luke xxiv. 26.—ἀποδοκιμασθῆναι, *to be rejected*) For they [the elders, etc.] denied that which Peter, ver. 29, had confessed; ch. xiv. 63, 64.

32. Παρρησίᾳ, *freely* [openly]) Heretofore He had only in an indirect manner indicated it, Luke iv. 23.—τὸν) τοῦτον.

32, 33. Ἐπιτιμᾶν—ἐπετίμησε, *to rebuke—rebuked*) Peter, whilst he *rebukes*, earns a *rebuke* himself. The same verb occurs, ver. 30, ἐπετίμησεν.

---

¹ The fuller reading, ὅτι ὡς δένδρα ὁρῶ περιπατοῦντας, was preferred by the margin of the Ed. Maj., but the Ed. 2 and Vers. Germ. agree with the Gnomon.—E. B. ABC corrected later GLXΔ, have ὅτι and ὁρῶ. But D*abc* omit both. Vulg., "homines *velut* arbores." The Elzevir Rec. Text omit both.—ED. and TRANSL.

[33. Τοὺς μαθητὰς αὑτοῦ, *His disciples*) who might have been very quickly carried away by Peter's objection, so as to embrace views merely human.—V. g.]

34. Τὸν ὄχλον σὺν τοῖς μαθηταῖς, *the multitude with His disciples*) The doctrine here taught was true catholic doctrine [*which is even inculcated upon the crowd, who were not yet quite distinctly instructed as to Jesus being the Messiah.*—V. g.].—ἀκολουθείτω, *let him follow*) in the death *of the cross*.

35. Καὶ τοῦ εὐαγγελίου, *and of the Gospel*) So, *and of My words*, ver. 38. [*Especially those concerning the cross.*—V. g.]

38. Ἐπαισχυνθῇ, *shall be ashamed*) in words and deeds. [*It is by the undaunted confession of Christ itself that His own life is brought into danger.*—V. g.]—Με—ὁ Υἱὸς τοῦ ἀνθρώπου, *Me—the Son of Man*) concerning the present time, He speaks in the first person [*Me*]; concerning the future, in the third [*the Son of Man*].—λόγους, *words*) of the cross [which carry with them the need of taking up a cross). The plural implies, that one may confess Christ in general, and yet be ashamed of this or that word, this or that saying of His; for instance, Matt. v. This kind of shame must also be overcome.—ἐν τῇ γενεᾷ ταύτῃ, *in this generation*) To this there stands in antithesis the general assembly of the last day, which is spoken of presently after.—τῇ μοιχαλίδι καὶ ἁμαρτωλῷ, *this adulterous and sinful*) which, as *an adulteress*, despises *Christ*:[1] as *sinful*, despises *His words:* and in consequence throws out in the way of those who confess Him all kinds of threats and promises. Such a crowd ought to be altogether despised. Who need fear them?—who regard them?—ὁ Υἱὸς ἀνθρώπου, *the Son of Man*) He had just now said, *Me and My words*, not *the Son of Man and His words;* but now He does not say, *I*, but the *Son of Man*, which appellation has a peculiar connection with His glorious and visible Advent. Luke ix. 26.—ἐπαισχυνθήσεται, *shall regard as an object of shame*) with good reason: and so shall not acknowledge as His, but shall put away from Him.—τοῦ Πατρὸς, *the Father*) Therefore His glory is, as of the Only-begotten of the Father, John i. 14.— μετὰ τῶν ἀγγέλων τῶν ἁγίων) This is the *Greek* reading, and that of the *Goth.* Version, etc. See App. Crit. Ed. ii. on this pas-

---

[1] The true Husband and Bridegroom of the Church.—ED. and TRANSL.

sage. O what shame! To be regarded as an object of shame in the presence of God the Father, of Christ, and of angels!

CHAPTER IX.

1. Ἐν δυνάμει, *with power*) Rom. i. 4; 2 Cor. xiii. 4.

2. Κατ' ἰδίαν, *apart*) In antithesis to *the people* [viii. 34].—μόνους, *alone*) In antithesis to the nine remaining *disciples*.

3. Χιών, *snow*) The production of nature.—λευκᾶναι, *make white*) the effect of art.

4. Σὺν, *with*) The appearance of Moses had been less anticipated by the disciples than that of Elias, ver. 11.

5. Καὶ ποιήσωμεν, *and let us make*) So also, *and let us make*, Luke ix. 33. Καὶ, *and so therefore*, represents the alacrity of mind on the part of Peter: or else the particle is that of the Evangelists, who join together two short speeches of Peter; comp. καὶ, ch. iii. 22; Luke vii. 16, or even Matt. viii. 13; John xiii. 13.

6. Τί λαλήσαι) So the LXX., γινώσκοντες τί ποιῆσαι Ἰσραήλ, 1 Chron. xii. 32, where also some have made a subjunctive of the optative.—ἔκφοβοι) *stricken with fear*, and that a mild kind of fear; for otherwise Peter would not have wished to remain there.

[7. Αὐτοῦ ἀκούετε) *Hear ye Him*: viz. Jesus. For Moses and Elias had by this time disappeared.—V. g.]

8. Ἐξάπινα) This is an adverb often found in the LXX.—μεθ' ἑαυτῶν, *with themselves*) because He was still about to suffer.

10. Ἐκράτησαν, *they laid hold of*) They received with attention, and did not treat with neglect.—τί ἐστι, *what is*) They did not so much feel difficulty respecting the thesis [the position or conclusion], as they did respecting the hypothesis [the foundation or assumption on which the conclusion was made to rest]. [*In fact, to those who had no idea that Christ must die, any discourse concerning His resurrection seemed out of place.*—V. g.]

11. Ὅτι λέγουσιν, *they say*) An interrogation by implication.[1] [πρῶτον, *first*) before that the great and terrible day of the Lord shall come, Mal. iv. 5. The disciples appear to have supposed,

---

[1] Ὅτι, for τί ὅτι, is often found in LXX. See Mark ii. 16.—ED. and TRANSL.

that it was to be on that day that the resurrection, even as of all the dead of every class, so also of Christ, since even He must die, would take place; and that it is for that reason the exceedingly long silence is imposed on them.—V. g.]

12. Εἶπεν, *told*) In this discourse, Jesus acts as a president would in a discussion, allowing its just weight to the argument of the opponent, and then meeting it fully in His reply.—πρῶτον, *first*) This is construed with *coming*, ἐλθών, and with *restoreth*, ἀποκαθιστάνει, although in the preceding verse it is joined with *come*, ἐλθεῖν, only. For so also *forty years* is construed in a double connection, Heb. iii. 9 [*Tempted* and *Saw* My works forty years], 17 [was He *grieved* forty years].—ἀποκαθιστᾷ, *restoreth*) The present indefinite, as in Matt. ii. 4.—καὶ πῶς, *and how*[1]) That is, the expectation of Elias as a restorer of all things, and the Scripture concerning the death of the Messiah, seems to you as not capable of standing together [seem irreconcileable]: but yet, for all that, they do stand together.—ἵνα, *in order that*) Because it was written, therefore He was bound to suffer.—ἐξουδενωθῇ, *be set at nought*) Isa. liii. 3. To reason, *the restoration of all things* seems not possibly compatible with this *setting at nought*.

13. Ὅτι καὶ) καὶ, *even*.—αὐτῷ, *to him*) to Elias. See by all means Matt. xvii. 12.—καθὼς, *even as*) Refer this to *is come*. He intimates, that the coming of Elias rests, not upon the opinion of the Scribes, but on a prophecy of Scripture, which was less known to the disciples. Nor, however, is this not also to be referred to, *they have done unto Him whatsoever*, etc. For our Lord quickly followed after the forerunner; therefore the forerunner made room for Him, being quickly taken out of the way.

14. Περὶ αὐτοὺς, *about them*) They were still labouring, though alone.

15. Ἐξεθαμβήθη, *were greatly amazed*) They were affected by the glory, even though they knew not what had taken place on the mountain; comp. ch. x. 32; Luke xix. 11; also Exod. iv.

---

[1] Engl. Ver. has no interrogation at ver. 12, but seems to mean (*Ye should know*) *how it is written of the Son of Man, that He must suffer*, etc. Lachm. puts an interrogation at ἀνθρώπου; and so in Vulg.: *and (yet) how is it written concerning the Son of Man? (It is written) that He must suffer*, etc. Tisch. puts the interrogation at ἐξουδενωθῇ; *and (yet) how is it written concerning the Son of Man, that He must suffer*, etc.?—ED. and TRANSL.

14, xxxiv. 29, 30. [*You may readily perceive that there follows upon secret communion with God a greater leaning on the part of men towards you.*—V. g.]—προστρέχοντες, *running up to*) eagerly.—ἠσπάζοντο, *began saluting*) with joy.

16. Αὐτοὺς, *them*) This is not reciprocal in the present instance, but is to be referred to the disciples, ver. 14.

17. Εἶς, *one*) Neither the Scribes nor the disciples were venturing to speak.

18. Καταλάβῃ, *he taketh* him) The term [demoniacal] possession, seems too narrow to express the idea here.

20. Ἰδὼν) Others read ἰδόν, which is to be referred to πνεῦμα. Comp. Heupelii annot. on Mark, p. 230. Ἰδὼν remains the established reading, *i.e.* the boy *seeing Him*, viz. Jesus: and the construction is conveniently analysed and explained by Hyperbaton,[1] *and seeing Him and falling*, etc.; wherein the *straightway*, etc., interrupts the construction the less violently, inasmuch as it is all the same as if he were to say, *forthwith he was torn by the spirit*. A similar figure of speech occurs, ch. iii. 17.

21. Καὶ, *and*) Jesus acted wisely, in interposing a delay.

22. Τὸ πῦρ) This noun is without a plural: otherwise, as ὕδατα, so πῦρα might have been said in this passage: but the place of the plural is supplied by the article.—ἵνα ἀπολέσῃ, *that it might destroy*) either because it was promising itself power even over the dead body of the possessed, or else lest it should be cast out by Jesus: for otherwise it would gladly have remained in a human body. It had not the power of itself to destroy a man without water or fire.

23. Τὸ, εἰ δύνασαι πιστεῦσαι, *this* (the), *if thou canst believe*) The expression of the man, *if Thou canst do anything*, ver. 22, is given back in reply to him. The father seems to have been offended at the disciples; ver. 18, at the end. Τὸ is nominative, and stands in apposition with, *If thou canst believe*. The predicate is the verb *is*, to be understood, as in Phil. i. 22. This, *if thou canst believe, is* the thing [the point at issue]: this is the question.—πάντα, *all things*) in antithesis to *anything*, in *if Thou*

---

[1] Words transposed contrary to the ordinary and natural construction: ἤνεγκαν αὐτὸν (the boy) πρὸς αὐτὸν (Jesus); καὶ ἰδὼν (the boy) αὐτὸν (Jesus), εὐθέως τὸ πνεῦμα ἐσπάραξεν αὐτὸν (the boy); καὶ πεσὼν (the boy), etc.—ED. and TRANSL.

canst do anything, ver. 22.—Τῷ πιστεύοντι, *to him that believeth*) Faith on the part of man, as an instrument, adapts itself to the Divine omnipotence, so as to receive, or even to act. [This is the dative of advantage.—V. g.]

24. Βοήθει μου τῇ ἀπιστίᾳ, *help Thou mine unbelief*) by removing mine *unbelief*: or else by healing my son, even though I have not sufficient faith. Comp. the *help*, βοήθησον, ver. 22.

25. Δέ, *but*) Jesus everywhere avoided a din.—ἀκαθάρτῳ —ἄλαλον—κωφόν, *unclean—dumb—deaf*) The *spirit* made the wretched boy be so, or else even the spirit itself was so [unclean, dumb, and deaf].—ἐγὼ σοὶ ἐπιτάσσω, *I charge thee*) *I*, in antithesis to the disciples, who had not been able to cast out the demon: the disciples themselves say, *we*, ver. 28 [*Why could not we cast him out?*]. This illustrates the great *power* of the Lord. The spirit was only the more exasperated to fury by the *inability* of the disciples.—μηκέτι, *no more any longer*) Those who in the beginning of life have undergone continued adversities, sometimes receive, as it were, a greater privilege as to the rest of their life. —εἰσέλθῃς, *enter into*) The *spirit* would have wished to enter again into him.

26. Κράξαν, *having cried*) although it would have preferred, in the present case, to have been altogether dumb.—σπαράξαν, *having rent*) In the vouchsafing of the Divine aid, the body of man is not always handled softly. A violent going out was the sign of a more permanent deliverance.

27. Ἤγειρεν, *raised him up*) A new part of the miracle.

28. Ὅτι) מה LXX. render ὅτι, Isa. lviii. 3; 1 Chron. xvii. 6.

29. Δύναται, *can*) That is, by no means can you cast out this class of enemies, save with the accompaniment of prayer and fasting.

30. Παρεπορεύοντο, *they were passing by*) not through the cities, but going *past [passing by]* them.—οὐκ ἤθελεν, ἵνα τις γνῷ, *He would not that any should know*) Hence may be inferred the reason, why the Saviour sometimes forbade Himself to be spoken of abroad, whilst at other times He did not forbid it: ver. 31.[1]

31. Ἐδίδασκεν, *He was teaching*) Not merely in a few words,

---

[1] Implies that His reason in the former case was, that He did not wish to hurry forward His crucifixion before the due time.—ED. and TRANSL.

which would be soon spoken, whilst they and He were retired apart; but according to a determined plan.—γὰρ, *for*) It was not the time, in which others [besides the disciples] could hear His words as to the passion of the Messiah.—παραδίδοται, *is delivered up*) The present: it is already being plotted [meditated] that He be delivered up. Comp. John vi. 70, 71.—ἀποκτανθείς, *after having been killed*) This word is emphatic: so [dependent on the event], if He shall be killed, He shall rise again.

32. Ἐφοβοῦντο. *They were afraid*) They ask questions of Jesus more readily concerning anything whatever, ver. 28, than concerning Himself. So it generally happens, even among intimates.

33. Ἐν τῇ οἰκίᾳ, *in the house*) A change having in some degree, simultaneously with the change of place, taken place in their state of feeling, which had been rather excited whilst in "the way." [Comp. Matt. xviii. 1, note].—τί, *what*) We must render an account of all things.

34. Ἐσιώπων, *they were silent*) A circumstance, which did not seem bad in itself at the time, appears in its true character such as it really is, when it is referred to the judgment of God and the knowledge of Jesus Christ.—μείζων, *the greater*) in virtue [or power] now; and therefore about to be the greater in dignity.

35. Καθίσας, ἐφώνησε, τοὺς δώδεκα, *sitting down, He called, the Twelve*) solemnly.—ἔσχατος—διάκονος, *the last—servant*) These two words differ. He who is the *last* is not by that very fact proved to be *a servant*. Therefore the ἔσται has rather this force, *he ought to be*, than, *he shall be*, by way of punishment. For *a servant* [*minister*] implies something of a voluntary character.

36. Ἐν μέσῳ αὐτῶν, *in the midst between Himself*) and His disciples: as appears by comparing Luke ix. 47, *by Himself* [He set the child by Him].—ἐναγκαλισάμενος, *having embraced him in His arms*) Symbolical of the intimate union between Him and such children. Comp. ver. 37; ch. x. 16. By that very act He conferred *grace* on *the little one* [*and how great was the sweetness, with which the child was thereby bedewed, is not hard to understand.*—V. g.]. So dear to Him, doth He teach us, that the lowly are.

37. Τῶν τοιούτων, *of such*) Little children; also those who are

such in heart.—ἐμὲ, *Me*) Who " am lowly in heart."—οὐκ ἐμὲ, *not Me*) That is, his act of reception does not terminate with this. [*What a difference there is between a little child and the Supreme* GOD! *Yet they are joined together through Christ*.—V. g.]

38. Ἀπεκρίθη, *answered*) The connection of the words of John with the preceding words of Jesus is manifold. The power of *the name* of Christ is asserted in the words of both, ver. 37, 38, 41. The disciples had previously discussed with one another, which among them should be the greater: now they are made to perceive, by the teaching of our Lord's words, that they are not even to despise others. If Christ, and faith in Him, has place in little children [*of whom not even the one, of whom mention is made in* ver. 36, *was following Jesus*.—V. g.], it might also have place in that person, whom they had forbidden. Hence there is manifested the moderation of John and his candour: he seems to have carried this doubt for some time in his breast, until he could, at a suitable opportunity, bring it forward.—ἡμῶν—ἡμῖν, *us*) The apostles, in subordination to Thee.

39. Μὴ κωλύετε, *forbid him not*) Let them give heed to these words, who tie down spiritual gifts to a canonical succession. *Forbid not*, if there should meet you again either that same person, or another like him.—ταχύ, *hastily*) For the soul is secured against doing so by the sense of [His] miraculous power. [*After the lapse of some* interval of time, *it may be possible to happen*.—V. g.]

40. Ὑμῶν—ὑμῶν, *you*—on *your* part) Comp. ver. foll., Matt. xii. 27. Jesus spake in the first person plural as to external things; Luke xxii. 8; xviii. 31: but not so as to the internal principles of His kingdom [John xx. 17]. He thus gently corrects the *we*—*us* of ver. 38.[1]—ἔστιν, *is*) He is speaking of those who undertake something for Christ's sake.

41. Ὅς, *who*) Jesus, after that He has satisfied the reverently-proposed difficulty felt on the part of John, returns to the former subject.—γάρ, *for*) All things are accepted, whereby help is ministered to you, even the smallest things.

[Ver. 42. καί, *and*) After the reply has been given to John,

---

[1] Lachm. agrees with Beng. in reading ὑμῶν—ὑμῶν here, ver. 40, with ADGabc Vulg. But Tisch. ἡμῶν—ἡμῶν with BCΔ Memph.—ED. and TRANSL.

the former discourse is continued. So ver. 42 coheres with ver. 37.—V. g.]—περίκειται, *is hanged about*) The present of the indicative has here an emphasis.

43, 45, 47. Εἰσελθεῖν, *to enter*) Thrice put; to which there stands in antithesis, once, ἀπελθεῖν, *to go away* into hell, ver. 43; and twice, βληθῆναι, *to be cast*, ver. 45, 47.—εἰς τὸ πῦρ τὸ ἄσβεστον, *the fire that cannot be quenched*) So ver. 45; and with a little variation, ver. 47.

44, 46, 48. Ὅπου, *where*) A most weighty repetition. The allusion is to the carcases, which are the food either of worms, or of the funeral pile. *The worm* expresses corruption; but this corruption is eternal, 2 Thess i. 9.—σκώληξ, *the worm*) Of the soul.—αὐτῶν, *their*) It is not expressed in Mark to what this word is to be referred. Therefore it is a quotation from Isaiah.[1]—οὐ τελευτᾷ, *dieth not*) The present.—πῦρ, *the fire*) of the body. Here we are to supply αὐτῶν, *their*.—οὐ σβέννυται, *is not quenched*) Either because it surely [certo] blazes [is kindled]; comp. 2 Kings xxii. 17: or because it blazes [burns] *without rest day and night*, Rev. xiv. 11, xx. 10, and for ever; see the same passage. An alternation of torments, with respect to the degrees of torment, may be inferred from Isa. lxvi. 23, 24: but yet the torments shall be unceasing.[2]

47. Βασιλείαν τοῦ Θεοῦ, *the kingdom of God*) Previously He had twice said instead, *life:* but the mention of *the kingdom of God*, and of *life*, is especially appropriate in connection with *the eyes*. John iii. 3 [*see the kingdom of God*], 36 [everlasting *life*—not *see life*]: comp. the parallel, Matt. xviii. 9 [enter *life* with one *eye*].

49. Πᾶς, *every, all*) *Every* [*all*] is here put without the noun being added. Some have supplied ἄρτος, *bread;* others, ἄνθρωπος, *man*. They seem to have felt, that it is hardly in accordance with usage, that πᾶς, *all* or *every*, should be put thus absolutely in the masculine. For where it seems to be put absolutely, the determining of the subject is left to be sought [gathered] from the predicate. Matt. xiii. 19, παντὸς ἀκούοντος τὸν λόγον, *when any*

---

[1] Ch. lxvi. 24, which furnishes the reference of the αὐτῶν here in Mark: "the men that have transgressed against me."—ED and TRANSL.

[2] Tischend. omits this whole ver. 44, with BCLΔ Memph. Lachm. retains it, with AD *abcd* Vulg. Iren. 165 [*abcd* Iren., however, read the future for the present, τελευτᾷ, σβέννυται].—ED. and TRANSL.

(hearer) *heareth the word*, etc. ; Luke vi. 40, κατηρτισμένος δὲ πᾶς, κ.τ.λ., every (disciple) *if he shall be perfected, shall be as his teacher* ; [Luke] xvi. 16, πᾶς εἰς αὐτὴν βιάζεται, *every one*, who employs violence, *by the employment of violence enters into the kingdom of heaven*: John ii. 10, *Every man* (who hath a marriage-feast, and sets forth wine) *sets forth first the good wine*. Phrases of this kind are to be met everywhere. So in this passage, *Every one*, who shall be salted at all, shall surely *be salted with fire*. But we will explain the idea of the passage a little more fully. It stands in position midway between the words concerning *the fire which is not quenched*, and the words concerning *salt and its goodness*. There are therefore three degrees: *to be salted with salt*; *to be salted with fire*; *to be cast into the fire that never shall be quenched*. The first degree is the most desirable: the third is the most bitter of the three: the second is intermediate, corresponding with the third in the mention of the *fire* (which in this passage is more often spoken of by *Homonymy, i.e.*, the calling of things that differ in nature by the same name by analogy [Append.], as in Matt. iii. 10, 11, 12), whilst it has a closer correspondence with the first in the mention of *the salting*. Salting, which is a process most natural and suitable, is effected by means of salt: this salt implies the Divine discipline, gently training us to the denial of self, and to the cultivation of peace and harmony with others. They who are thus salted become thereby *a sacrifice* pleasing to God, the type of which [spiritual sacrifice] existed in the Levitical sacrifices; Lev. ii. 13. They who shrink from and evade the salting by salt, are salted by fire (for even salt has in it the power of burning, Deut. xxix. 23; and again, in turn, that there is in natural fire the power also of salting, is shown even by flesh that is roasted; and in Plutarch, fire is said to be τῶν ἡδυσμάτων ἄριστον καὶ ἥδιστον, *the best and sweetest of modes of sweetening or seasoning*); *i.e.* according to what approaches most closely in analogy, they are salted by a Divine discipline of a severer kind, lest through the stumblingblock, occasioned by the hand, the foot, or the eye waxing stronger, they should go on to the fire that cannot be quenched. Therefore the connection and the idea of the passage stand thus: Without a moment's delay, and casting aside all self-indulgence, meet and counteract the stumbling-block occasioned by the hand, the foot, or the eye; for otherwise it will thrust you on into hell, and hell's eternal fire. For every one, who is about to be salted in any way, and who is by that salting to be snatched from the eternal fire, shall be salted, if not by salt, the milder remedy, but by fire, the more severe cure, yet still in this life [shall be so salted, not in the life to come] · and every sacrifice shall be salted with salt, which is a most lenient and excellent kind of salting. Therefore submit to [admit within you] and have this salt, so that, every stumbling-block [occasion of offence] having been laid aside, peace may flourish among you. You are certainly about [you are sure] to have to experience the salt and the fire: see that ye require to undergo [defungamini, *perform*] as lenient a salting as possible.—ἁλισθήσεται, *shall be salted*) The future: by which there is intimated the commandment as to the sacrifices of the Old Test. [which was couched in the future, Lev. ii. 13], as also their typical bearing in reference to the sacrifices of the New Test.— καὶ πᾶσα θυσία ἁλὶ ἁλισθήσεται) This is extant in Lev. ii. 13, καὶ πᾶν δῶρον θυσίας ὑμῶν ἁλὶ ἁλισθήσεται. Hence the sentiment in the former clause of the verse is inferred, πᾶς γὰρ πυρὶ ἁλισθ., which is more universal, inasmuch as the *being salted with salt* is now in fine added as if in the way of exception [qualification] to θυσίας, with the limitation standing in apposition [*i.e. shall be salted with salt*, in apposition to and qualifying the more universal, *shall be salted with fire*].

50. Καλὸν, *good*) Salt. For all other foods are seasoned by it. —ἐὰν δὲ τὸ ἅλας, *but if the salt*) In this passage the disciples themselves are called "the salt," inasmuch as being imbued [endued] with the salt themselves, and salting the world.— ἄναλον, *saltless* [insipid]) so as to have no pungency. *Pride* [referring to ver. 33 34, the dispute about who should be greatest] most especially makes men *saltless* [savourless].—αὐτὸ, *itself* [the very salt]) having lost its primary quality.—ἔχετε, *have ye*) To have 'fire,' is not within human ability: therefore it is not said, *have fire*. But he who is imbued with the fire is desired to have salt.—ἐν ἑαυτοῖς, *in yourselves*) In antithesis to, *among one another*, ἐν ἀλλήλοις. The former duty is in regard to ourselves; the second, towards others.—ἅλας) The singular, or else the plural from ἅλς. The *salt* is that of self-mortification,

whereby pride is destroyed.—*καὶ εἰρηνεύετε, and have peace*) or else, ye shall have: comp. ver. 34: viz. by removing a puffed up spirit, which is the source of quarrels [ver. 33, 34].

CHAPTER X.

1. Καὶ ἐκεῖθεν ἀναστάς, *and having arisen from thence*) The antithesis is not so much to Capernaum, where He had taught sitting, ch. ix. 33, 35, as to Galilee, ix. 30.—διὰ τοῦ) See App. Crit. Ed. ii. on this passage.[1]—ὡς εἰώθει, *as He had been wont*) The habitual acts of Jesus are well worthy of observation: Luke iv. 16.

5. Ἔγραψεν, *wrote*) viz. Moses, the writer of the Pentateuch: ch. xii. 19.

6. Ἀρχῆς κτίσεως, *from the beginning of creation*) Therefore there was not any *creation* anterior to the *creation* described in the beginning of Genesis.

[9. Ὁ Θεὸς—ἄνθρωπος, *God—man*) Whatsoever God doeth and ordaineth, it is man's part to regard as an established principle. It is an impiety to accept as authoritative what God rejects; or to approve of what God censures.—V. g.]

[10. Πάλιν, *again*) The Saviour had given the reply which follows to the *Pharisees*, Matt. xix. 9; but the *disciples*, by repeating the question, called forth a repetition of the same reply. —V. g.]

11. Ἐπ' αὐτήν, *against her*).

13. Ἄψηται, *should touch*) A modest request.

14. Ἠγανάκτησε, *was much displeased*) on account of the obstruction thrown in the way of His love by the disciples.—τοιούτων ἐστίν, *of such is*) Of such as these, it is [to such belongs] the privilege to receive the kingdom of God, ver. 15.

15. Ὃς ἐὰν, *whosoever*) This He did to mark His disapproval of that very feeling, by which the disciples were moved to put

---

[1] Καὶ πέραν is the reading of BC corrected later, L, Memph. But DGΔ bc Vulg. omit the καὶ. Rec. Text with A reads, διὰ τοῦ πέραν.—ED. and TRANSL.

away the infants from Him.—δέξηται, *shall receive*) for it is offered [to all].—ὡς παιδίον, *as a little child*) receives: for it receives the kingdom in very deed

16. Καὶ, *and*) He did more than He was asked, ver. 13. [εὐλόγει αὐτά, *He blessed them*) By that very act conferring on them the blessings, which He afforded to adults by the mediation of the word.—V. g.]

17. Ἐκπορευομένου αὐτοῦ, *as He was going forth*) from the house, ver. 10.—προσδραμών) The Vulg. has *procurrens*, as if it had the reading προδραμών.[1] This man was at all events impelled by a remarkable degree of earnestness. He seems to have been eagerly waiting for the Saviour's coming. [*Sudden impulses of this kind oftentimes by and by grow languid.*—V. g.]—γονυπετήσας, *falling at His knees*) He must therefore have felt great ardour.— ποιήσω, *shall I do*) Those who are in spirit little children, receive not the kingdom of heaven by *doing*: ver. 15.

18. Εἶπεν, *He said*) The Lord replies, I. To the remarkable title which the young man had addressed to Him: II. To the question which he proposed.—τί Με λέγεις ἀγαθόν; *why callest thou Me good?*) There were many things in Jesus, viewing Him merely externally, by reason of which the ignorant would not form the best opinion concerning Him: John i. 47; Matt. xi. 6, 19; Isa. liii. 2, etc. Moreover also He did not rest on Himself, but ever referred Himself wholly to the Father. He acted the part of a traveller and a pilgrim in the world; and in that condition, in which the Psalms describe Him as *wretched and needy*, He was ever aiming towards the eternal good and the eternal joy, concerning which this youth was enquiring. Ps. xvi. 2, 5, etc.: *My goodness* [*extendeth not to thee*, Engl. V.] *is not independent of thee*. Comp. John xiv. 28, xvii. 5; Heb. v. 8, 9, ix. 12. He did not " know Himself according to the flesh ;" as Augustine preaches [distinctly states], l. i. de Doctr. Christ., c. 34. For *good*, ἀγαθός, properly applies to one blessed.[2] The young man was seeking with [by application to] Jesus happi-

---

[1] So also *a*: 'præcurrens' in *b*: 'adcurrit,' *d*. A has ἰδού τις πλούσιος προσδραμών.—ED. and TRANSL.

[2] Beatum, a term appropriate in the full sense only to God.—ED. and TRANSL.

ness, in a too pure [unalloyed] sense. Jesus informs Him that he will not find this with Him: Comp. Luke ix. 57, etc. Nevertheless He does not say, *I am not good*: but, *Why dost thou call Me good?* Just as in Matt. xxii..43, He does not deny, that He, the Son of David, is at one and the same time also the Lord of David. God is good: there is no goodness without Godhead. The young man perceived in Jesus the presence of goodness in some degree; otherwise he would not have applied to Him: but he did not perceive it in its full extent; otherwise he would not have gone back from Him. Much less did he perceive [recognise] His Godhead. Wherefore Jesus does not accept from Him the title of goodness without the title of Godhead (Comp. the "*Why* call ye me, Lord, Lord," Luke vi. 46): and thereby vindicates the honour of the Father, with whom He is one. See John v. 19. At the same time He darts [causes to enter] a ray of His omniscience into the heart of this young man, and shows that the young man has not as yet the knowledge concerning Himself, Jesus Christ, worthy of so exalted a title, which otherwise is altogether appropriate to Him. Wherefore He does not say, *There is none good save one, that is, My Father*; but, *There is none good save one, that is, God*. Often our Lord proportioned [qualified] His words to the capacity of those who questioned Him, John iv. 22. So a warlike commander, of noble birth, might answer to a person, who knew not his noble birth, though knowing the fact of his being a commander, *Why do you call me, a gracious lord?* Jesus manifested His goodness to the disciples, Luke x. 23; Rom. xiv. 16.

19. Οἶδας, *thou knowest*) Why dost thou ask, *What shall I do?*—μὴ ἀποστερήσῃς, *defraud not*) by covetousness, Exod. xx. 17.[1] The same verb occurs, 1 Cor. vi. 8: see note.

20. Διδάσκαλε, *Master*) The young man now repeats the noun [title of address] without the epithet [*good*]. And yet Jesus loves him.

21. Ἐμβλέψας αὐτῷ ἠγάπησεν αὐτόν, *looking earnestly on him, loved him*) He expressed love with the earnest look, and as it

---

[1] Otherwise this command would not differ from the previous, "Do not steal."—ED. and TRANSL.

were smiling expression, of His eyes.—A ἐν διὰ δυοῖν, *He lovingly beheld*,[1] in order that He might thereby give him a token of His love for the time to come, if he would follow Jesus: and that He might counteract his 'sadness.' The antithetic word is στυγνάσας, *with saddened look* [countenance], ver. 22. It is for this reason mention is made in Christ's life of tears, rather than of laughter, because He had come to bear our sins. Yet benignity and joy sometimes shone forth from His countenance, as was the case in this passage, with the view of alluring the youth, who now was standing on the threshold of following Christ. Comp. ver. 16; Luke x. 20-24, xii. 32. A similar use of this verb occurs in Ps. lxxviii. 36, ἠγάπησαν αὐτὸν ἐν τῷ στόματι αὐτῶν and 2 Chron. xviii. 2, ἠγάπα αὐτὸν τοῦ συναναβῆναι: so also the use of the verb ἐλεῖν (οὓς δὲ ἐλεᾶτε [ἐλεεῖτε] ἐν φόβῳ), Jude ver. 22.— ἓν, *one thing*) In antithesis to ταῦτα πάντα, *all these*, ver. 20. [*The faithful Master wished to render the business* (his obtaining eternal life) *more easy and delightful to the man.*—V. g.] This *one thing* is a heart freed from the [idolatry of] creatures: the selling of his goods was intended to be the proof of his freedom. Generally speaking, to men, severally and individually, there is wanting some one thing, this or that; and by the want of that one thing they are kept back from Christ.—σταυρὸν, *cross*) Viz. that of poverty, etc. So the words, *with persecutions*, ver. 30, express the same sentiment.

[22. Ὁ δὲ, *but he*) How quickly do men refuse the happiest of all conditions!—V. g.]

23. Περιβλεψάμενος, *having looked round about*) We have often the look [countenance] of Christ described, corresponding as it did to His inward feeling, and adapted to the inward feelings of His hearers: Comp. v. 21, 27.—πῶς, *how*) The proposition stated is, A rich man is with difficulty saved: the subject of the proposition is limited in ver. 24 [*They that trust in riches* being substituted for, *they that have riches*]: the predicate is enlarged [amplified: ver. 25 being the amplification of the simple predicate, *enter into the kingdom of God*]. They [the subject and predicate of the proposition, A rich man is with difficulty saved]

---

[1] Comp. with these remarks what *D. Ernesti* has written against *Gerh. de Haas*, in *der Theol. Bibl.*, T. I., p. 130, etc.—E. B.

differ in the abstract; they for the most part agree in the concrete.[1]—οἱ τὰ χρήματα ἔχοντες, *they that have riches*) The few have most of the wealth of the world.

24. Τέκνα, *Children*) This term of address shows, that Jesus speaks with pity, but at the same time with truth: and that He freely declares the fact to His disciples.—τοὺς πεποιθότας, *those that trust*) puffed up thereby, so as not to obey the word of God: ch. iv. 19; Ps. lxii. 10; 1 Tim. vi. 17. [*The number of those who have riches is not much greater than that of those who trust in them.*—V. g.]

26. Καί, *and* [*i.e.* "who then?"]) This particle here expresses astonishment.

27. Πάντα, *all things*) Ps. lxii. 12. Comp. in that passage and here the preceding context.

28. Ἤρξατο, *began*) as having been led to entertain hope from the words of the Saviour.

29. Ἢ ἀδελφούς, *or brethren*) The goods which are left (for Christ's sake) are enumerated disjunctively ["house *or* brethren *or* sisters," etc.]: the goods, which are granted in reward, are enumerated copulatively ["houses *and* brethren *and* sisters," etc., ver. 30]: See following verse. Observe the rich plentifulness of the reward, illustrating the goodness of the Lord.—ἕνεκεν ἐμοῦ, *for My sake*) whilst I am in the world.—ἕνεκεν τοῦ εὐαγγελίου, *for the sake of the Gospel*) In order that he may preach My *name* after My ascension. For the sake of the world, many leave many things.[2]

30. Ἐὰν μή) *but he shall* [quin].—καὶ πατέρας καὶ μητέρας, *both fathers and mothers*) See App. Crit. Ed. ii. on this passage.[3] Each one has by nature but one *father* and one *mother* [favouring the Sing. reading of Lachm.]: but by means of [having regard to] benefits received, he is blessed with many, who follows Christ:[4] Comp. Rom. xvi. 13. There is not added,

---

[1] As a matter of fact, and not reasoning *a priori*, rich men are with difficulty saved.—ED. and TRANSL.

[2] How much more ought they for Christ's sake!—ED. and TRANSL.

[3] Tischend. reads only καὶ μητέρας with B and Vulg. Lachm. also omits πατέρας, but reads καὶ μητέρα with ACD *ab*. Only more modern uncial MSS., as X, etc., have καὶ πατέρα, and some καὶ πατέρας.—ED. and TRANSL.

[4] This favours the plur. reading of Tisch.—ED. and TRANSL.

wives:[1] for *that would* sound somewhat inconsistent with propriety.—τ ἴκνα, *children*) 1 Cor. iv. 14–17.—μετὰ διωγμῶν, *with persecutions*) This is added lest the disciples should look for [expect] external prosperity. Persecutions shall not be wanting: but these not only shall not prove prejudicial, but shall even be advantageous towards his receiving an hundred-fold, preventing him in the interim from being unduly elated by that 'hundred-fold.'—αἰῶνι, in the *world*) not καιρῷ, in this *time*.—τῷ ἐρχομένῳ, *coming*) Already that *world* is in the act of coming.

31. Ἔσονται πρῶτοι, *first shall be*) *First* (πρῶτοι), is the subject; see Matt. xix. 30, note.

32. Ἐθαμβοῦντο, *they were amazed* [fear-struck]) They knew not themselves the reason why. Often something, which does not fall under the vision [the ken] of the mind or of the eye, affects another sense; Dan. x. 7. They were fear-struck [shuddered with amazement] on account of Jesus, who *went before:* they were afraid, on account of their own selves, who *were following* Him. By this shuddering amazement and fear, they were divested of their opinion and hope of earthly things, if not completely, as, for instance, in the case of James and John [ver. 35, etc.], yet in part.—ἤρξατο, *He began*) Already He had *begun* before, ch. viii. 31; but now He *began* to speak more fully and at large. And this even as yet was but *the beginning*.

35. Προσπορεύονται) *go together* to Him.—θέλομεν, ποιήσῃς, *we would that thou shouldst do*) So in the following ver., What would ye that I should do?—ποιήσῃς· ποιῆσαι· δός, *that thou shouldst do; that I should do? Grant*) They use art in their request; for petitions are often more readily asked and obtained, which consist in *doing*, than those which consist in *granting* or *giving*.

38. Τὸ ποτήριον—τὸ βάπτισμα, *the cup—the baptism*) To drink this *cup* was difficult (as often death itself is taken in the act of drinking). *Baptism* also, among the Jews, was a thing to be shuddered at, inasmuch as the whole body was dipped in a stream, however cold. Accordingly, by both words the passion of Christ is denoted: by *the cup*, His inward passion; the cup is therefore placed first: by the *baptism*, chiefly His external passion. He was *distended* inwardly with His passion [referring

---

[1] γυναῖκας. Two later MSS. add καὶ γυναῖκα.—ED. and TRANSL.

to *the cup;* He was *filled with the cup of anguish*]: He was *covered over* [as a person baptized is with water] with His passion. Moreover, both are appropriately employed; for they who take the sacraments, are partakers of the baptism and the cup of Christ; 1 Cor. xii. 13: and the baptism of Christ and our baptism, as also the Holy Supper, have a close connection with Christ's passion and death, and with ours also.—πίεσθε—βαπτισθήσεσθε, *ye shall drink—ye shall be baptized*) James, when slain with the sword, drank the cup [Acts xii. 2]; afterwards John was baptized in boiling oil, as Ecclesiastical History represents. Boiling oil is in consonance with the term, *baptism.* Our Lord Himself, in Gethsemane, also calls His suffering of death *a cup.* It is in consonance with this, that the *cup* is placed before the baptism.¹

[41. Οἱ δέκα, *the ten*) When one of two persons seeks some special privilege, the other takes it ill, who would have been contented of himself.—V. g.]

42. Δοκοῦντες) *they who think* [*which are accounted*, Engl. Vers.] *that they rule.* A Metonymy of the antecedent for the consequent; that is, they who strenuously exercise rule. [*Worldly princes have but little greatness in the eyes of the Divine Majesty.*—V. g.]

44. Πάντων, *of all*) ver. 43, *of you* [your]. Thus there is an Epitasis in this verse.²

[45. Διακονῆσαι, *in order to minister*) Who is there, whom the Saviour's incomparable example ought not to put to the blush, and sweetly gain over to Him?—V. g.]

46. Βαρτίμαιος, *Bartimæus*) A proparoxyton [accented on the antepenult] as the simple name Τίμαιος. Timæus seems to have been a man at that time known at Jericho; and Bartimæus seems to have been made a beggar only by reason of his blindness [and not previously].—ὁ τυφλός, *blind*) This epithet had become an equivalent to a surname. Bartimæus was very well known in the time of the apostles. [*As to the other blind man*

¹ Just as Jesus' and James' cup of suffering was before John's baptism in sufferings.—ED. and TRANSL.

² *i.e.*, An emphatic augmentation of force added to a previous enunciation: as πάντων is here, when compared with the previous ὑμῶν. See Append.—ED. and TRANSL.

associated with him, see the note Matt. xx. 30.]—ὁδὸν, *the way*) On the highway to Jerusalem there was the greater opportunity of begging.

47. Ὁ Υἱὸς Δαυίδ, Ἰησοῦ, *Thou Son of David, Jesus*) See App. Crit. Ed. ii. on this passage.[1] It was a great instance of faith that the blind man calls Him Son of David, whereas the people announced Jesus to him as Jesus of Nazareth.—[ἐλέησόν με, *have mercy on me*) This is the very marrow of all real prayers.—V. g.]

49. Θάρσει, *Be of good comfort*) in mind.—ἔγειραι, *rise*) with the body. An elegant asyndeton [omission of the copula]. They had no doubt but that He was both willing and able to help.

50. Ἀποβαλών, *casting away*) through eagerness and joy.

52. Ἐν τῇ ὁδῷ, *in the way*) towards Jerusalem.

CHAPTER XI.

1. Εἰς Βηθφαγὴ καὶ Βηθανίαν, *unto Bethphage and Bethany*) See App. Crit. Ed. ii. on this passage.[2] *Bethany* was already, by the time that the Lord commenced these things [His directions as to preparing for His triumphal entry], in His rear: Bethphage was before His eyes; therefore the latter is placed first, not according to the geographical order, but as being of superior consideration; and at Jerusalem, as it appears, they

---

[1] Lachm. reads Υἱὲ with BCLΔ. Tisch. ὁ Υἱὸς with AD, Orig. 3,734 (except that the two last authorities omit ὁ). L and Orig. omit Ἰησοῦ.—ED. and TRANSL.

[2] Lachm. reads καὶ εἰς Βηθανίαν, omitting Βηθφαγὴ, with D abc Vulg., Origen 3,743a expressly (ἴδωμεν δὲ περὶ τῆς Βηθφαγὴ μὲν κατὰ Ματθαῖον, Βηθανίας δὲ κατὰ τὸν Μάρκον, Βηθφαγὴ δὲ καὶ Βηθανίας κατὰ τὸν Λουκᾶν), making it likely the Βηθφαγὴ was interpolated in Mark from Luke by Harmonists of the Ev. But Tisch. reads Βηθφαγὴ, on the weighty authority of AB Orig. 4,181d.—ED. and TRANSL. In the Vers. Germ. Beng. altogether omits Bethphage, in accordance with his Appar. on this passage.—E. B.

were wont thus to name the two places, which were most closely joined, *Bethphage* and *Bethany*.

2. Κώμην, *village*) Bethphage.—ἐφ' ὃν οὐδείς,[1] *upon which no man*) Not readily would there be found such a colt at one and the same time and place; this one, therefore, was reserved for the Lord. Those creatures or things which are to serve Christ, must be free from all pollutions of sinful bodies; see Matt. xxvii. 60. This colt, though untamed, yet bare Him as a sitter.

4. Ἀμφόδου) Ἄμφοδον, *a way, a broad street* [Eng. Vers. *where two ways meet*].

10. Τοῦ πατρὸς ἡμῶν Δαυΐδ, *of our father David*) Construe with *the kingdom* [*For many acknowledge that the words* ἐν ὀνόματι Κυρίου *have been repeated from the preceding verse.*—Not. Crit.[2] *They call David their father, as being the king, the father of their nation. Yet, however, we may suppose that the posterity also of David were mixed up with them. The throne of David has been assigned to the Messiah*, Luke i. 32.—V. g.]

11. Περιβλεψάμενος, *having looked round about*) His visitation. [*Which, on the following day, He followed up with a most weighty reproof. For if His expulsion of the money-changers had been repeated on each of the two days, Mark would use the verb* ἤρξατο *with less propriety in ver.* 15. *In like manner, Luke assigns the plucking of the ears of corn and the healing of the withered hand to two distinct Sabbaths, though in Matthew and Mark that distinctness of the Sabbaths is less plainly marked. So Matthew sets forth at the same time, and together, all that happened in the case of the fig-tree; Mark divides the incidents respecting it between two days: so Matthew and Mark join the transfiguration with the account of the lunatic boy; Luke* (ch. ix. 37) *represents the lunatic as healed on the following day after the Saviour's transfiguration.*—Harm., p. 447, 448.]—πάντα, *all things*) What holy

---

[1] The reading οὔπω οὐδείς, which had been deemed not worthy of approval in the marg. of *the larger Ed.*, is judged equal to that of the text in *Ed.* 2, and is even approved by *Vers. Germ.*—E. B. Lachm. also so reads with BLΔ, Orig., and after ἀνθρώπων C, πώποτε A, *b* Vulg. "nemo ad huc." Tisch. omits οὔπω with Dac. πωποτε evidently is an interpolation of Harmonists from Luke xix. 30.—Ed. and Transl.

[2] A supports the ἐν ὀνόματι Κυρίου of the Rec. Text. But BCD *alc* Vulg., Orig. 3,744, 4,182*a*, omit these words.—Ed. and Transl.

meditations He had respecting the sacrifices, and the types about to be so soon fulfilled in Himself.

13. Ἔχουσαν φύλλα, *having leaves*) And on this account promising fruit.—*εἰ ἄρα, whether accordingly* [if haply] The whole question as to the kinds of fig-trees may be set aside [dispensed with]. The leaves, which were on it, gave promise ostensibly of an abundance of fruit: *accordingly* the Lord approached to see, whether He would find anything more than leaves; but He found *nothing but* leaves, and not also figs: for it was not the time of figs. A nearer view of the tree showed that the tree was not such, as the leaves peculiarly [extraordinarily] promised it would be; but just such as was to be expected from the ordinary season, which was not the time of figs (comp. Matt. xxiv. 32); that time either refers to the part of the year, a very few days after the vernal equinox, ch. xiii. 28, or, independently of the time of year, it is denoted that trees of that kind were not then fruit-bearing. Therefore every fig-tree ought either to have not even leaves; or else, having leaves, to have had fruit also. Other fig-trees, which were clad neither with leaves nor fruits, were exempted from blame: this fig-tree, laden as it was with leaves, though promising, yet in fact refused the fruit which it promised. Therefore it was made to suffer the penalty.—γὰρ, *for*) This particle intimates the reason for which, both on a tree, though laden with leaves, yet the Lord *sought* fruit *in particular*, namely, because it was not the time of fruits: and why He found on it nothing save leaves. [It had seemed likely that at least unripe fruits would be found on it: what use these would have been made to serve by our Lord, it is needless to inquire. He may have been impelled, by the promptings of hunger, to seek for fruits, even though not wishing to eat such food. Nay, even unripe eatables relieve at times, when hunger is pressing. And He who had turned the water into wine, and a very few loaves into a banquet, sufficient for thousands of men,—with what ease may we suppose that HE would have been likely to impart instantaneous ripeness to the fruit.—*Harm.*, p. 453]. This clause [*for the time of figs was not yet*] applies [is intended] for the explanation of the whole period, as the γὰρ, *for*, ch. xvi. 4, where see note.

14. Ἀποκριθεὶς, *answering*) To the tree which refused food.—

μηδείς, *no man*) Whatever does not serve Jesus Christ, is unworthy to serve any one of mortals. [*Therefore the tree was doomed to the curse for the honour of the Son of* GOD. —V. g.]

15. "Ἤρξατο, *began*) Men ought to have been wise [*the day before*], whilst the Lord was still sparing and warning by mere gestures [In the temple, " He *looked round about* upon all things,"] ver. 11.

16. Διὰ τοῦ ἱεροῦ, *through the temple*) As if through a street.

17. Ἐδίδασκε, *He taught*) The addition of *teaching* makes punishment salutary in its effect.—πᾶσι τοῖς ἔθνεσι, *to all nations*) Construe with *the house of prayer*. Comp. the accents, Isa. lvi. 7 [My house shall be called an *house of prayer for all people*.]

18. Καὶ, *and*) They either had approved of that traffic as lawful, or as a source of gain : or else they thought that it ought to have been done away with rather by their agency than by His.—ἐφοβοῦντο, *they feared*) Therefore they sought for artifices.

[19. Ὅτε ὀψὲ ἐγίνετο, *when evening was come*) Mark has given with peculiar and extraordinary distinctness, the description of these last walks of the Saviour.—*Harm.*, p. 457.]

22. Ἔχετε, *have*) Hold fast.—πίστιν Θεοῦ, *faith*) Such as it is right that they should have, who have *God* [as their God] : faith great and sincere, which believes in God, and believes in there being no foundation save God in all the things of the natural world. So ἐν τῇ προσευχῇ τοῦ Θεοῦ *in prayer of God, i.e.* to God in solitude, Luke vi. 12. So *the kindness of God* is used of the kindness, which is bestowed on the *orphan* [of Jonathan] from a regard to God alone, 2 Sam. ix. 3, with which comp. ver. 1. So the *cedars of God* are trees not planted by human hands. The *mountains* [hills] *of God*, those which human culture does not reach.

25. Καὶ ὅταν, *and when*) The connection is, We must pray " without doubting and wrath," 1 Tim. ii. 8.—στήκητε, *stand*) When in respect to the very attitude of your body you have laid yourselves out for prayer: com. Jer. xviii. 20. *To stand* is the attitude of one praying with confidence [Luke xviii. 11, 13]: to lie prostrate is that of one praying so as to deprecate vengeance. στήκω, from ἕστηκα, signifies *I am he* [one] *who have betaken myself to standing;* a signification which admirably suits the other passages also, where στήκω is read. When standing we touch the earth with as small a part of us as possible; for which

reason it is an apt posture for those who pray; in which the ascetics forbid '*appodiare*.'[1]—ἀφίετε, *forgive*) [Thus an especial hinderance (ver. 26) to believing (faithful) prayer is removed. Sin not yet forgiven hinders all things else.—V. g.] Jesus cursed the fig-tree: the believer ought not to curse his brother.

[26. Ἀφήσει, *neither will forgive*) And so will also refuse to give ear to.—V. g.]

27. Περιπατοῦντος, *walking about*) As in his own house.—ἔρχονται, *come*) A weighty and solemn interrogation this was, made by men of different ranks.

CHAPTER XII.

2. Τῷ καιρῷ, *at the season*) *Of fruits*, Matt. xxi. 34 ["the time of the fruit"].—ἀπὸ, [a portion *of*) A portion of the fruits was allowed to the husbandmen. This particle is appropriate to the first-sent servants, who were expected to bring a *specimen* of the fruits.

4. Ἐκεφαλαίωσαν, *wounded him in the head*) So γναθοῦν, γυιοῦν, similarly constructed forms of verb, occur in Hesychius.

6. Ἔτι, *as yet*) Construe with *having*.—ἵνα ἀγαπητὸν, *one—His well-beloved*) These two words do not altogether signify the same thing.

10. Οὐδὲ, Have ye *not even*) The adverb gives Epitasis. [See Append., Increase of force.]

12. [Ἔγνωσαν γὰρ, *for they knew*) Their conscience supplying the testimony to its being so.—V. g.]—πρὸς, [Engl. Ver., *against*] *in reference to*) So πρὸς is used, Heb. i. 7, xi. 18.

14. Ἀλλ', *but*) The truth is not consistent with having respect to persons.

15. Ἵνα ἴδω, *that I may see*) The Saviour seems [judging by the ἵνα ἴδω, as if He had not looked at one before] then for the first time to have handled and looked at a denarius [penny].

[17. Τὰ τοῦ θεοῦ, *the things that are God's*) All things are GOD'S,

---

[1] Lit. *ad podium stare, podioque inniti*, "to lean upon some prop."—ED. and TRANSL.

heaven and earth, all men, and therefore Cæsar himself. Yet nevertheless He hath made a wise distribution as regards His goods. On that account the less ought He to be defrauded of those things which He hath peculiarly reserved to Himself.—V. g.]

19. "Ἔγραψεν, *wrote*) The Sadducees, though sceptics, acknowledged Moses to be the writer of the law.—ὅτι—ἵνα) A rare phraseology; comp. ch. v. 23.

22. Ἑπτὰ, *seven*) The fact of there being no seed left, even by the seventh, increases the plausibility of the question.

23. Ὅταν ἀναστῶσι, *when they shall rise again*) viz. the brothers and the wife.

24. Διὰ τοῦτο, *on this account*) The particle strengthens the refutation: your very words betray your error, Lat. *atqui*. Ps. lxvi (lxv.) 19.

25. Ἐκ νεκρῶν, *out from the dead*) The ἐκ, *out from among*, implies the new condition of the saints when they rise again out of the state of the dead, at the same time that it does not set aside the universality of the resurrection.

26. Βίβλῳ, *the book*) The volume of Moses is mentioned in this passage; that of Isaiah in Luke iii. 4; that of the Prophets, Acts vii. 42; that of the Psalms, Acts i. 20.—Μωσέως, *of Moses*) concerning whom you have spoken, ver. 19.—ἐπὶ τοῦ βάτου, *in the bush*) A formula of quoting a section or division of Scripture, frequent with the Rabbins [Comp. *Michaëlis* in der *Einleitung*, etc., T. i. p. m. 87.—E. B.] So Pliny, "Molybdænam *in plumbo* dicendam," *i.e.* in the chapter concerning lead [plumbus]. Furthermore, ὁ βάτος is the measure, *bath*; ὁ or ἡ βάτος (as ὁ or ἡ θάμνος) not an unproductive bramble, but a valuable shrubbery [place of bushes], at least in Exodus. A noble image is derived from this, Deut. xxxiii. 16 [the goodwill of Him, that dwelt *in the bush*].

27. Οὐκ ἔστιν ὁ Θεὸς νεκρῶν, ἀλλὰ ζώντων) This is a reading midway between the extremes.[1] Starting from it, some have re-

---

[1] The margin of Ed. 2 supports this reading, as also the *Germ. Vers.*, although the *larger Ed.* does not approve of it.—E. B.

BDLΔ omit the ὁ before Θεὸς. A supports it, as does the Rec. Text. Orig. in different passages gives it differently. ABCDabe Vulg. Orig. 3, 829; 4, 69; 341 omit the Θεὸς, inserted in Rec. Text before ζώντων without any adequate authority.—ED. and TRANSL.

peated Θεός before νεκρῶν, others after ἀλλά.—[ὑμεῖς οὖν, *ye therefore*) viz. *ye* Sadducees, the doctrine of the resurrection is the primary one.—V. g.]—πολύ *greatly*) An antithesis to this follows at ver. 34, *not far* [from the kingdom of God].

28. Καλῶς, *well*) Admirably. The admirable character of Christ's teaching is often conspicuous, even to those who do not comprehend it wholly [in all its parts]. To this we are to refer ver. 32, καλῶς, *well*.

29. Πρώτη πασῶν ἐντολή) This is a reading midway between extremes, and answers to ver. 28. The editions read πρώτη πασῶν τῶν ἐντολῶν, and so the Syr. Vers., as also Greek MSS.: however, for πασῶν, *Al. Byz. Gehl. Mosc. Wo.* 1, 2, and many others, have πάντων, though some of them retain πασῶν at ver. 28. πάντων has originated by an alliteration to [an assimilation of letters to those of] πρώτη, and ἐντολή, as in the same *Al.* ἀπὸ πάντων τῶν ἐντολῶν in Lev. iv. 13, 27 [instead of the genuine reading, πασῶν]. Furthermore ἐντολή, not τῶν ἐντολῶν, is the reading of *Al. Gehl.*, along with many MSS., and the same Nomin. case is defended by the *Goth.* and *Lat.* versions.[1]—[ἄκουε, *hear*) Even this word is a portion belonging to the first commandment.—V. g.]—Κύριος, *the Lord*) This is the foundation of the first commandment, nay, rather of all the commandments. The Subject of the proposition is, THE LORD our God: the Lord, I say (the God of all); the Predicate, = "is One (God)" [not as Engl. Vers., "The Lord our God is one Lord"]; comp. ver. 32, in order that the proper name employed *twice* [Κύριος—Κύριος] may signify the *two* great revelations of Jehovah, of which the one embraced the Jewish people, the other the Gentiles also; comp. Ps. lxxii. 18, where the proper name is put once, the appellative twice, "Jehovah God, the God of Israel" [Engl. Vers., *The Lord God, the God of Israel*], the position of the accents being the same as occurs also in 1 Chron. xii. 18, *Peace, peace be unto thee!* From this unity of God it flows as a consequence, that we owe the whole of our love to Him alone.

---

[1] Tisch. omits παντ. or πας. τῶν ἐντολῶν, and reads only ὅτι πρώτη ἐστίν, with BLΔ Memph. Lachm., ὅτι πρώτη πάντων [ἐντολή ἐστίν] with ACc Vulg. (save that *c* omits πάντων; A omits ἐστίν; C reads ἐστιν αὐτή. Therefore he brackets ἐντολή ἐστίν). D*abc* omit ὅτι, which is supported by AB Vulg. D*ab* also read πάντων πρώτη.—ED. and TRANSL.

30. Καρδίας, *with all thy heart*) Which lives and loves.—ψυχῆς, *with all thy soul*) which enjoys and relishes.—διανοίας, *with all thy mind*) which is that ever-continuing power which engages itself in thoughts. σύνεσις is employed in ver. 33; in Luke x. 27, ἰσχύος—διανοίας.[1]—ἰσχύος, *with all thy strength*) the ability which carries into effect the volition throughout the whole body.

32. Καλῶς, *excellently* [*well*]) Construe with, *Thou hast said:* for His " saying well" is made to rest *on the truth*, ἐπ' ἀληθείας, as in Luke iv. 25 [ἐπ' ἀληθείας λέγω, *I say, resting on the truth,* " I say of a truth"], εἷς ἐστι καὶ οὐκ ἔστιν ἄλλος πλὴν αὐτοῦ, *there is One, and there is none other but He*) *There is One* [or rather *He is One*], an absolute phraseology, is repeated from ver. 29, that is, from Moses' writings; comp. Zech. xiv. 9. The subject, Θεός, *God*, is left to be supplied, by a striking εὐλάβεια of language [reverent caution is needlessly repeating God's name], although many have inserted this very word, Θεός, after ἐστί. See App. Crit. Ed. ii. on this passage.[2]

33. Ὁλοκαυτωμάτων, *whole burnt-offerings*) The most noble species of sacrifices.—Θυσιῶν, *victims in sacrifice*) of which very many commandments treat.

34. Οὐ μακρὰν εἶ, *thou art not far*) They therefore are *far* from the kingdom who *have not* νοῦς, *intelligent perception*.[3] [*Such, for instance, were they who were still clinging to* sacrifices.—V. g.] Seeing that thou art not far from it, enter into the kingdom: otherwise it would have been better for thee to have been far off.

36. Ἀυτός,) *Himself.*

37. Πολύς) The people, who were *many* [But Engl. Vers., " The *common* people."]

38. Αὐτοῖς, *unto them*) Especially to the disciples, Luke xx. 45. [βλέπετε, *beware*) lest ye incur the same condemnation, ver. 40.—V. g.]—γραμματέων, *the Scribes*) An open accusation.

---

[1] Tsch. omits διανοίας here in Mark, as perhaps interpolated by harmonists from Luke, with Dc, Cypr. 199, 213, 264. But AB Vulg. support it.—ED. and TRANSL.

[2] AB Vulg. omit Θεός. Dabc and Rec. Text (which prefixes ὁ) insert Θεός.—ED. and TRANSL.

[3] Referring to νουνεχῶς, *having intelligence*, Th. νοῦν ἔχειν, *to have intelligence*.—ED. and TRANSL.

—θελόντων, *who wish*) The *wish* or *intention* often make an act, which is in itself indifferent [neither good nor bad], a bad one: but the verb θέλω, *I will*, or *wish*, often includes the act in it, whether good, Matt. xx. 14, or bad, Gal. iv. 9. And it is a characteristic, even in the present day, of false theologians, to be captivated with splendour of robes, with sustaining the leading parts as to celebrity, with a display of offices and honours, as also of their intercessory prayers before others.

40. Οἱ κατεσθίοντες, *who devour*) Construe with the following words.

41. Ἐθεώρει, *beheld*) Christ, in our worship at even the present day, beholds all.—πολλοί, πλούσιοι, *many rich men*) The state was then flourishing.

42. Ἐλθοῦσα, *having come*) Jesus had His eye chiefly on her.—δύο, *two*) one of which the widow might have retained. [*This had been enacted by no commandment: but the intention in her mind, by which she was moved was good.*—V. g.]

43. Προσκαλεσάμενος, *having called unto Him*) As being about to speak of a momentous subject. He thus gives us a specimen of the judgment which He will hereafter exercise, according to the state of hearts.—τοὺς μαθητάς, *the disciples*) who had not estimated the widow's gift so highly. [*It is for this reason the* καρδιογνώστης, *Knower of hearts, prefaces His words with* Amen, *verily.*—V. g.]—πλεῖον, *more*) not in mere geometrical proportion, but in mind [intention, motive], to which the Lord had regard. If any rich man had contributed all his resources, the act, viewed extrinsically, would have been greater, in so far as two pieces of money are more readily acquired again, than many: but yet he would not thereby have surpassed the mind [influencing motive] of this poor woman. [*That praise, wherewith Jesus honoured the poor widow, altogether exceeds (to what an amazing degree!) all the acclamations of the world.*—V. g.]

CHAPTER XIII.

[1. Λίθοι—οἰκοδομαί, *stones—buildings*) The very work of building was at that time going forward briskly: therefore many stones were lying scattered apart on this, and on that side.—V. g.]

3. Εἰς, *upon*) The mountain. The wall of the temple was rather sunk towards the Mount of Olives: in consequence of which the interior of the temple could be conveniently seen.—Πέτρος, κ.τ.λ., *Peter, etc.*) James and Peter were about to die sooner than the rest: and yet the subject of inquiry appertains even to them: yet still more to John.

4. Ταῦτα, *these things*) viz. as concerns the temple.—πάντα ταῦτα, *all these things*) viz. as concerns not only the temple, but also all other things, that is, the whole world.

5. Ἤρξατο, *He began*) Previously He had not spoken much concerning these things.

6. Ἐγώ εἰμι, *I am*) The Predicate is to be supplied, viz. *the Christ;* Matt. xxiv. 5. Hebrew אני הוא, Isa. xliii. 10.

8. Ταραχαί, *troubles*) in the great and lesser world [macrocosmo et microcosmo].

9. Δὲ, *but*) Do not concern yourselves about other matters, ver. 11: only take heed to *yourselves.*—παραδώσουσι, *they shall deliver you up*) From this verse to ver. 13, the words are parallel to Matt. x. 17, 18. Therefore Mark is not an epitomizer of Matthew.—εἰς) An abbreviated mode of expression: ye shall be brought *into* the synagogues, amidst stripes. See Glass. canon 2 de verbo. Or rather εἰς is for ἐν, as in ver. 16. At all events the mention of stripes is consonant with the synagogues. Matt. x. 17, xxiii. 34.—αὐτοῖς, *to them* [against them]) viz. the Jews.

10. Καὶ εἰς, *and among*) The preaching of the Gospel was helped forward by the very persecutions, ver. 9; 2 Tim. iv. 17. —πρῶτον, *previously*) before that the end shall come, ver. 7. [*When Jerusalem was being destroyed, already a church was collected from among the Gentiles.*—V. g.]

ST MARK XIII. 11–30.

11. Μηδὲ μελετᾶτε, *neither do ye meditate*) Not merely you have need of no anxiety, but not even of premeditation.—τοῦτο, *this very thing*) the whole of it, and without fear. [*For it is with that aim it is supplied to you.*—V. g.]

14. Ὅπου οὐ δεῖ, *where it ought not*) Language adapted to His hearers' modes of thought. The Jews' mode of thinking was, that it ought not. And indeed it ought not, in so much as the place was *the holy place;* so, "speaking things *which they ought not*," 1 Tim. v. 13. Comp. also Jer. xlix. 12. [*It was from that place that the Romans invaded the city.*—V. g.]

20. Οὓς ἐξελέξατο, *whom He hath chosen*) Herein is illustrated the power of prayer.—ἐκολόβωσε, *He hath shortened*) by His decree.

22. Ἀποπλανᾶν, *to seduce*) by error [πλάνη, *wandering*] from the right path.

24. Ἐν ἐκείναις ταῖς ἡμέραις μετὰ τὴν θλίψιν ἐκείνην, *in those days after that tribulation*) *After that* tribulation shall come *those* days. Therefore the ἐκείνην, *that*, refers to a different thing from ἐκείναις, *those*. *That* refers back to the whole preceding discourse; but *those*, looks forward to the last events of all, as in ver. 32. For the question of the disciples, to which the Lord replies, in Mark also, ver. 4 [as in Matthew], had reference by implication, to the end of the world.

25. Ἔσονται ἐκπίπτοντες, *shall be falling*) A metaphor from a flower, James i. 11. [The flower thereof falleth.]

26. Μετὰ δυνάμεως πολλῆς καὶ δόξης, *with great power and glory*) The adjective in the middle, applying to both nouns. Mark frequently employs a Zeugma of this kind, so as to put some word in the middle, which is intended to be connected with the preceding, and also with the subsequent word or words. See ch. iii. 26, iv. 21, v. 40, 42, vi. 13, vii. 2, 21, x. 7.

27. Ἀπ᾽ ἄκρου) This is an abbreviated mode of expression, in this sense, *from the uttermost part of* the heaven (sky) and *earth* in the east, *even to the uttermost part of the heaven* and earth in the west. [*O blessed general assembly, of which who would not desire to form a member?*—V. g.]

[30. Ἡ γενεά, *generation*) These words were spoken in the 30th year of the Dion. Era, and it was in A.D. 70 that they came to pass. Comp. on Matt. xxiv. 34.—*Not. Crit.*]

VOL I.   N N

32. Οὐδὲ ὁ υἱὸς, *neither the Son*) This, which had been omitted in Matthew, has been recorded by Mark, inasmuch as believers being by this time confirmed in the faith, could now more readily bear it [than they could have borne it in Matthew's early time]. [It is also omitted by Luke, who seems to have softened down several passages of Mark, with which Theophilus, an excellent person, but a νεόφυτος, *novice*, might have been readily offended.—*Harm.*, p. 481.] Moreover, both in the twelfth year of His age and subsequently, " Jesus increased in wisdom," [Luke ii. 52]: and the accessions of wisdom which He then gained, He had not had before. Since this was not unworthy of Him, it was also not even necessary for Him in teaching to know already at that time the one secret reserved to the Father. Moreover the assertion is not to be taken absolutely (comp. John xvi. 15), but in reference to the human nature of Christ, independently of [as separated from] which, however, He is not denominated, even in this passage, where there is a climax, which sets Him even as man above the angels: it is also to be taken with reference to His state of humiliation, whence the language which He employs subsequently, after the resurrection, is different, see notes, Acts i. 7: in fine, both the human nature and the state of humiliation in respect to the office of the Christ being supposed, His words may be understood to mean, without mental reservation, that He knows not, because He had it not among His instructions, to declare that day; as also in order to deter His disciples from requiring to know it. An apostle was able both to know and not to know one and the same thing, according to the different point of view, see note, Phil. i. 25: how much more Christ? There is an admirable variety in the motions of the soul of Christ. Sometimes He had an elevated feeling, so as hardly to seem to remember that He was a man walking on the earth: sometimes He had a lowly feeling, so that He might almost have seemed to forget that He was the Lord from heaven. And He was wont always to express Himself according to His mental feeling for the time being: at one time as He who was one with the Father: at another time again in such a manner, as if He were only of that condition, in which are all ordinary and human saints. Often these two are blended together in wonderful variety. He speaks most humbly in this passage, and thereby qualifies [modifies] the feeling of His glory, which His discourse concerning the judgment was carrying with it. You may say, Why is He in this passage called *the Son*, a denomination which is not taken from His human nature? The answer is: In enunciations concerning the Saviour, He is wont to join a lowly Subject with a glorious Predicate: Matt. xvi. 28; John i. 51, iii. 13; and *vice versa*, a glorious Subject (as here) with a lowly Predicate: Matt. xxi. 3; 1 Cor. ii. 8; moreover, in this passage, *the Son* is in antithesis to *the Father.*—εἰ μὴ ὁ Πατὴρ, *but the Father*) Illustrating the great glory of His omniscience. Comp. Acts i. 7.

[34. Ὡς ἄνθρωπος) D. Hauber has ably proved that this passage is parallel, not to Matt. xxv. 14, but to ch. xxiv. 45.—*Harm.*, p. 484].—τὴν ἐξουσίαν, *authority*) This He gave to His servants conjointly, as is evident from the antithesis, *and to every man*) καὶ ἑκάστῳ. The authority so assigned was a great authority: Matt. xxi. 33.—καὶ) *also* [even].—τῷ θυρωρῷ, *to the porter*) [He gave charge], inasmuch as the porter is one who keeps watch even for others, and whose duty it is to rouse them up.

35. Γρηγορεῖτε, *watch*) Watchfulness, the foundation of all duties, is enjoined not only on the porter, but on all the servants. —μεσονυκτίου, *at midnight*) Matt. xxv. 6.

37. Πᾶσι, *unto all*) Even to those of after ages. [ὑμῖν, *unto you*) In antithesis to πᾶσι, viz., the Apostles, and their contemporaries.—V. g.]

CHAPTER XIV.

1. Τὸ πάσχα, *the passover*) This is said in a strict sense, as in ver. 12; for τὰ ἄζυμα, "the feast of *unleavened* bread," is added. —μετὰ δύο ἡμέρας) That is to say *on the following day*.[1]

3. Πιστικῆς, *genuine*) French *veritable* [So marg. of Eng.

---

[1] Two days before the Passover.—ED. and TRANSL.

Vers., *pure*, or else *liquid;* but its text, *ointment of spikenard*"].
Pliny, on the contrary, mentions *Pseudo-nardum.* Nonnus
lengthens the middle syllable in πιστικῆς; viz. as if formed from
Pista, a city of the Indians in the region of Cabul; a region
from which most of the aromatic perfumes even already at that
time used to be derived; see Lud. de Dieu, in Act, p. 133.
But πιστᾶιος would rather be the form, if derived from the
proper name. [συντρίψασα, *having broken*) That none of the
ointment might remain in the vessel, which, had it been of
glass, would have burst asunder into a number of fragments.
—V. g.]

5. Ἐπάνω τριακοσίων, *above three hundred*) It may be doubted
whether they could have accurately estimated its value. It is
a phrase, resembling an adage [*At all events almost 5000 men
might have been fed for two hundred denarii; therefore one may
judge that that sum was to be estimated as of much higher value.*
—V. g.]

7. Τοὺς πτωχοὺς, *the poor*) Whom ye speak of.—ὅταν, *if* [when-
soever]) ye will, as ye here show [by your very remark as to
the poor].—δύνασθε, *ye can*) Never is there any one so needy, as
to be able to give nothing.—ἔχετε, *ye have*) thus present with
you as now. It is not always that such an honour can be conferred on me.

8. Ὅ, *What*) An abbreviated mode of expression; *i.e. What
she had,* she has freely bestowed; *and what she could, she hath
done;* or else, what she had [it in her power] to do, she hath
done.—αὕτη, *she,* emphatically coheres with ἔσχεν, *she had.*
Hardly any one else of those, who were in attendance on Jesus,
had so costly ointment. It was divinely designed and appointed
for the purpose of this being done.—προέλαβε, *she has anticipated*
[she is come aforehand] *to*) It would not have been becoming
for the body of Christ, which knew not corruption, to have been
anointed after death; on this account it was anointed beforehand.

9. Εἰς ὅλον, *throughout the whole*) In all its wide extent.—
αὕτη, *she*) Demonstratively.

11. Ἐχάρησαν, *they were glad*) They felt joy, and they testi-
fied it.

12. Τὸ πάσχα ἔθυον, *they killed* [sacrificed] *the passover*) viz.

The Jews, according to the commandment of the law, and therefore so also the disciples, were killing it.—V. g.]

13. Ἀπαντήσει, *there shall meet*) A wonderful sign: 1) that a person is about to meet them: 2) that person a man: 3) that man alone: 4) that too, immediately: 5) he should be bearing a vessel: 6) and that vessel, one of earthenware [κεράμιον]: 7) and containing water: 8) and that, too, going to the house which the disciples were looking for [*It was in deep humiliation, even like as an ordinary Israelite, that Christ ate the Passover Lamb; wherefore He put forth His glory into exercise in the preparation for it.*—V. g.]

14. Ποῦ ἐστι, *where is*) It is taken for granted in this question, that there is some guest chamber already prepared through the providence of the Lord.

15. Ἀνάγαιον μέγα, *a large supper-room* [upper room]) It is probable, that Jesus had before this kept the passover in the houses of other inhabitants of the city; but this Passover Himself celebrated [marking it] with greater solemnity.—ἐστρωμένον, *laid out*) with carpets. This householder had been guided by Divine Providence. This circumstance illustrates the omniscience of Jesus, more than if it had been laid out (paved) with precious stones.—ἑτοιμάσατε, *make ready*). The verb is neuter: Luke ix. 52.

16. Εὗρον, *they found*) Attended with [having the effect of] the confirmation of their faith, their admiring wonder and joy.

19. Εἷς καθεῖς) So John viii. 9, and ὁ δὲ καθεῖς; Rom. xii. 5. —ὁ καθεὶς δὲ τῶν φίλων; 3 Macc. v. 31. From κατὰ (not καὶ εἶτα) and εἷς comes καθεῖς, of similar formation to οὐδείς, μηδείς, unless you prefer accenting it καθεῖς, in order to distinguish it from the participle καθείς; κατὰ is used adverbially, as ἀνὰ μετά.

20. Ἐμβαπτόμενος, *that was dipping* [but Eng. Vers., *that dippeth in*]) With his own hand; this is the force of the middle voice. The participle is in the imperfect tense, as ὤν is used in John ix. 25, and ἐρχόμενος in 2 John v. 7.

22. Ἄρτον, *bread*) Mark does not add the article.—μου, *my*) Understand, *which is given for you*, to be supplied by implication from ver. 24 [*My blood, which is shed for many*].

23. Καὶ ἔπιον ἐξ αὐτοῦ πάντες, *and they all drank of it*) This

clause interposed between the words of the Lord is an argument, that the words, *This is My body, this is My blood*, were said, during the time whilst they were eating, and whilst they were drinking. Whence the evangelists either prefix or else subjoin those words; comp. note, Matt. iii. 7. All drank, even Judas; for who is there that will say that Judas might have stolen away from the company in the midst of the supper? [Comp. ver. 17, 18, 22] [Nay, even in ver. 31, we may suppose that, under the word *all*, Judas is even still included. It is not unlikely that he crossed the brook Kedron along with the Saviour and the disciples, and after that acted as conductor to the armed band which was waiting for Him in the neighbourhood.—*Harm.* p. 528.]

27. Γέγραπται, *it is written*) Comp. Matt. xxvi. 31, note.

30. Σὺ, *thou*) In antithesis to "yet will *not I*," ver. 29.—ἢ δίς, before *that twice*) A very striking circumstance, that Peter would not collect [recover] himself at the first cock-crowing. [Comp. note on Matt. xxvi. 34.]

31. Ἐκ περισσοῦ μᾶλλον, *the rather, the more exceedingly*). Comp. ch. vii. 36, note. Peter, in this passage, *rather* (μᾶλλον) spake of his own stedfastness, than trusted [believed] in the words of Jesus.

33. Ἐκθαμβεῖσθαι, Hesychius writes, ἔκθαμβος, ἔκπληκτος. Eustathius, θαμβεῖν, τὸ ἐπὶ θέᾳ τινὸς ἐκπλήττεσθαι.[1]

[35. Παρέλθῃ ἀπ' αὐτοῦ ἡ ὥρα, *the hour might pass from Him*) *The hour*, He saith. Jesus knew that the cup would *speedily* be drained, and His passion *speedily* be terminated; and as heretofore He had been sure of the issue being good, so not even now had He any room for doubting it. This certainty of the issue does not in any degree detract from the love either of the Son delivering Himself up, or even of the Father delivering His Son up for us. Yet the cup and the hour struck Jesus with anguish; for which reason He prayed for their passing from Him, subject to the condition of the Father's will, and the possibility of the case.—*Harm.* p. 527.]

36. Ἀββᾶ ὁ πατήρ, *Abba Father*) Mark seems to have added

---

[1] θάμβος is akin to θήπω θέαομαι, *wonder at some amazing sight* being the connecting idea; as in Lat. *suspicio*.—ED. and TRANSL.

Father, by way of interpretation: For Matthew, ch. xxvi. 39, 42, says that what was said by Jesus was simply, "My Father:" Luke, 'Father,' ch. xxii. 42. On the cross, He said *Eli, Eli.*—τί, *what*) The question in the case, saith He, is not *what* I will, but *what* Thou wilt.

41. Καὶ ἔρχεται, *and He cometh*) The third departure [ver. 39, "*He went away*"] is taken for granted, as well as the third offering of the same prayer.—καθεύδετε, *sleep on*) Matt. xxvi. 45, note.—ἀπέχει, *it is enough*) Sleep has its turn [the office which it sustains] by this time fully served: now there is another business before us [*And though ye do not regard my efforts to awaken and rouse you, yet your rest is being* (must now be) *broken.*—V. g.]

44. Ἀσφαλῶς, *with due precaution* [safety]) The traitor was afraid, lest Jesus should slip from their hands [*Therefore the wretched man was now no longer anxious merely about gaining the thirty pieces of silver, but was hurried along by a deadly hatred against Jesus.*—V. g.]

51. Σινδόνα, *a linen cloth*) He was therefore rich, Matt. xi. 8.—ἐπὶ γυμνοῦ, *upon his naked*) viz. body. He had perhaps by this time gone to bed.—κρατοῦσιν, *lay hold*) He had not been desired to follow. No one tried to apprehend the disciples: this young man was apprehended by either the armed men or others.[1]

52. Γυμνὸς ἔφυγεν, *fled naked*) He fled, the night not being without the light of the moon: fear overcame shame, in the case of such great danger.

53. Συνέρχονται αὐτῷ, *are assembled with him*) By his edict.

54. Μετὰ τῶν ὑπηρετῶν, *with the attendants*) Often a fall is incurred more easily in the presence of such as servants, who are less feared, than among their masters, [the great].—θερμαινόμενος, *warming himself*) Often under care for the body the soul is neglected.—φῶς, *the light*) Appropriately *light* is the expression used instead of *fire:* Peter was recognised by the *light*,

---

[1] The *Germ. Vers.* approves of the omission of the subject οἱ νεανίσκοι, though that omission has been less approved of by the margin of the *larger Ed.* and of *Ed.* 2.—E. B. It is omitted in BC corrected later, DLΔαο Memph. Syr. Vulg. However AP supports the words with Rec. Text.—ED and TRANSL.

when under other circumstances he might have been safer: comp. ver. 67.

60. Οὐκ; τί; answerest thou *not*? *What is it that, etc.*?) Two distinct interrogations.[1]

61. Εὐλογητοῦ, *of the Blessed*) ברוך, the Blessed God.

[62. Ἐγώ εἰμι, *I am*) Jesus, when His enemies spake false witness against Him, and when His disciples withdrew themselves from the confession of the truth, Himself made an open profession of the truth.—V. g.]

65. Ἤρξαντο, *began*) A new step in their dealings with Him. —ὑπηρέται, the *servants*) who used to have in their hands ῥάβδοι, *rods*.[2]

66. Κάτω, *beneath*) There seem to have been a flight of steps there.

69. Ἡ παιδίσκη, the maid [not as Engl. Ver. *a* maid]) That same maid: or else a second one, so that the πάλιν, *again*, may be connected with the participle alone, ἰδοῦσα, *having seen him*.[3]— τοῖς παρεστηκόσιν, *to them that stood by*) She said it then in the spirit of joking, not with intent to hurt him [Comp. note on Matt. xxvi. 69].—ἐξ αὐτῶν, *of them*) The expression, *of them*, shows, that speaking against Jesus and His disciples was most common and frequent.

72. Ἐπιβαλὼν ἔκλαιε, *he betook himself*) To weeping, or, as Stapulensis interprets it, *He broke forth into weeping*. The French happily express it, *il se mit à pleurer* Theophr. charact., περὶ λογοποιίας· εὐθὺς ἐρωτῆσαι—καὶ ἐπιβαλὼν ἐρωτᾶν: as to which see Casaubon [Engl. Ver., *When he thought thereon*.]

---

[1] But Tischend. has but one interrogation at the end of καταμαρτυροῦσιν; Lachm. says in his Preface that to introduce an interrogation after οὐδὲν (;) here, where the τί is used for the relative, is subversive of the sense. B reads ὅ τι. But ADP*d*, τι. Vulg. "non respondes *quicquam ad ea quæ* tibi objiciuntur."—ED. and TRANSL.

[2] So marg. of Engl. Ver. translates Matt. xxvi. 67, ἐρράπισαν, they smote Him with *rods*, instead of " with the *palms* of their hands."—ED. and TRANSL.

[3] Tischend. omits πάλιν, with B, Memph. and Theb. But Lachm. reads it with ADac Vulg.—ED. and TRANSL.

CHAPTER XV.

7. 'Εν τῇ στάσει, *in the insurrection*) A charge most offensive in the eyes of Herod, who would therefore be likely to punish Barabbas with hearty good-will.

8. 'Αναβοήσας) *having raised a cry*. It is to this the reference is, ver. 13, *They cried out again*. Formerly the Vulg. read ἀναβὰς; or even other paraphrasers: and that reading is consonant with Matt. xxvii. 17, *therefore when they were gathered together*. Certainly both the people gathered themselves together to the chief priests, who were accusing Jesus in an invidious manner, for the purpose of praying that some prisoner should be given up to them: and an *ascent* to the Pretorium [Governor's Hall], and some *cry*, were begun by the people. Whoever will compare ἀναβοήσας with the words following, and ἀναβὰς with the words preceding, will perceive that either reading might have been formed from the other by alliteration.[1]—αἰτεῖσθαι, *to desire*) Understand from the context, ποιεῖν, *that he should do*. Often the verb is omitted, it being intended that it should be repeated from the following clause. John v. 21, vi. 32, 35, xii. 25, 35; Rom. v. 16; Phil. ii. 1, 2; Tit. ii. 2, note. So LXX., 2 Kings ix. 27, καίγε αὐτόν (viz. πατάξατε·) καὶ ἐπάταξεν αὐτόν. Comp. Glass., B. iv., Tract. 2, Observ. 5 and 12 all through: and, if you have a mind, the remarks which we formerly made on Cic. Ep., p. 143.

9. Τὸν βασιλέα τῶν Ἰουδαίων, *the King of the Jews*) A Mimesis [*i.e.* a using of the words of an opponent in irony, or in order to refute him. See Append.]

15. Τὸ ἱκανὸν ποιῆσαι) *to content*, or *satisfy*.

16. Αὐλῆς, *the hall*) The Greek word is put before its Latin synonym, *Prætorium*.

[20. Καὶ ἐξάγουσιν αὐτὸν, *and lead Him out*) What is the mystery which lies hid under the fact, that our gracious Saviour was

---

[1] ἀναβὰς is the reading of BD*cd* Vulg. Memph. Theb. *a* has *accensa*. A supports Rec. reading, ἀναβοήσας.—ED. and TRANSL.

led out of the city, no mortal man, we may suppose, would have been likely to have discovered, not to say, would have been able to have persuaded others, had not the wisdom of the apostle instructed us on the subject, Heb. xiii. 11–14.—*Harm.*, p. 559.]

21. Ἐρχόμενον, *coming*) either in order to be present at the Passover, or in order to see what would be done to Jesus.— ἀπ' ἀγροῦ) Where perhaps he had his home. Happy man, in that he was not present, and had no part in the accusation: but in consequence of that very fact he was the less agreeable to the Jews.—Ἀλεξάνδρου καὶ Ῥούφου, *of Alexander and Rufus*) These two, at the time when Mark wrote, were better known than their father, inasmuch as he is denominated from them [instead of *vice versâ*]: They were distinguished persons among the disciples (see Rom. xvi. 13 as to Rufus, who also is set down in that passage as one better known than his mother, though Paul seems to have regarded her as his mother at Jerusalem): which is an evidence whereby the truth of the whole fact, as it happened, may be perceived.

22. Φέρουσιν, they bring [*bear* or *take*]) not merely *lead*.— Γολγοθᾶ) The genitive.

23. Οὐκ ἔλαβε, *He took it not*) He tasted, but did not drink it. Matt. xxvii. 34: comp. ch. xxvi. 29.

24. Σταυρώσαντες) *having crucified*.—τίς τί, *what*, and *who* [*what every man* should *take*]) See *Bud.* Comm. 1349, 27.

25. Τρίτη, *third*) which the *sixth* and *ninth* hour follows, ver. 33. Therefore it is Jewish hours that are here marked. However the case stands in Mark and John as to both the kind of hour and the mode of enumeration respectively employed by them, both mean the one and the same portion of the day, viz. in the forenoon. Nor is there any reason why we should desire to diminish the number of hours of His remaining on the cross. Jesus hung upon it more than six hours: for even *six hours*, from the third to the ninth hour, were in themselves a longer time than ordinary hours of equal length, inasmuch as the equinox was now past: for they were wont to divide the day, whether it were shorter or longer, into twelve hours: and between the close of the supernatural darkness and the death of Jesus many events intervened. There are some who explain this verse thus: *It was the third hour from the time that they*

had crucified Him. But if this had been his meaning, Mark would have said, *There were three hours;* and in that case, passing by the hour of the crucifixion itself, he would say, what occurred three hours afterwards [which is not likely]: for, both the casting of lots, and the superscription written, were acts more speedily done [than the act of crucifixion].—καί) *Καί* either is used in its strict meaning, *and;* in order that Mark may intimate, that first of all the soldiers nailed Jesus to the cross, next, that they divided His garments, and then erected the cross: or else, rather, the καί has a relative force, so that the hour should be precisely denoted, to which the mention of the crucifixion is both prefixed and subjoined.[1] Comp. John xix. 14; comp. καί, ch. ii. 15, at the end of verse.—ἐσταύρωσαν) elevating the *cross*.

28. Καὶ μετὰ ἀνόμων ἐλογίσθη) Isa. liii. 12, LXX., καὶ ἐν τοῖς ἀνόμοις ἐλογίσθη. The μετὰ has a stronger force than ἐν: *He suffered Himself to be reckoned with the transgressors.*

29. Οὐά, *Ah!*) An interjection and exclamation, having the force of expressing astonishment, as Franc. Bernardinus Ferrarius, L. 3. de Acclam. Vet. c. 15, shows at large. In this passage, it has the force of expressing wonder along with irony.

32. Ὁ Χριστὸς ὁ βασιλεύς, *Christ the King*) A Mimesis [an allusion to the words of an opponent, with the intention of refuting them.—See Append.] The expression, *Christ*, refers to the proceedings before Caiaphas; the expression, *King*, refers to those before Pilate.

34. Ἐλωΐ) Hebr. אֱלֹהַי, as בָּרוּךְ־יָהּ Βερζελλί, בְּנֵי βαβί, אֲבִישַׁי Ἀβεσσά, etc.: Hiller, Onom. p. 707. For not even שָׂרַי in Greek is Σαραί, Gen. xvii. 15. Matthew has ἠλί, ἠλί· and so the Hebrew Psaltery [Ps. xxii. 1]: Mark has ἐλωΐ, ἐλωΐ, and so the Syriac Psaltery, as John Gregorius observes.—εἰς τί, *for what* [why]) See Matt. xxvii. 46, note.

37. Ἐξέπνευσι, *He expired*) *To breathe*, is conducive to the good of the body: *to cease to breathe* [expire], is conducive to the good of the spirit.

[39. Οὕτω κράξας, *having thus cried out*) Christ was not ex-

---

[1] "It was the third hour *when* they crucified Him."—ED. and TRANSL.

hausted to death by faintness, but most voluntarily laid down His life.—V. g.]

41. Γαλιλαίᾳ, *Galilee*) Here it was that He had sojourned for a great part of His time: He had come to Jerusalem, especially at the times of the festivals.

42. Προσάββατον, *the day before the Sabbath*) When there was the beginning made of resting.

43. Ὁ ἀπὸ Ἀριμαθαίας, *who was from Arimathea*) The article shows, that this had become a surname of Joseph. Matthew does not employ the article, because he wrote before Mark.— εὐσχήμων, *honourable*) Distinguished by both honour and dignity. —βουλευτής, *senator*) of the Jerusalem Sanhedrim.—τολμήσας, *having boldly ventured*) A praiseworthy boldness. [*Not unattended with personal risk.*—V. g.] John xix. 38. An elegant and effective Asyndeton.[1] [*It very frequently happens in the case of those making such bold ventures, that their efforts succeed better than you would have supposed.*—V. g.]

44. Ἐθαύμασεν, *marvelled*) In fact, it was not the mere cross that deprived Jesus of life. [*Those crucified sometimes used to protract life for a considerably longer time. Pilate had permitted the breaking of the legs; but the fact, that Jesus had died before the breaking of the legs (of the other two), came to Pilate's knowledge through Joseph, and not until then.*—V. g.]—πάλαι) Eustathius has showed that this word is used of even a rather short interval of time.

45. Γνούς, *having ascertained* the fact) that Jesus was really dead.—ἐδωρήσατο, *he gave it*) The body of Him who was crucified had been at the disposal of the judge. [*Therefore the body, which was ordained to be kept free from corruption, was subject to the disposal of a man who was a heathen. Marvellous! Joseph, it is to be supposed, would have paid for it no small sum of money.*—V. g.]

---

[1] Omission of the copula between ἐλθών and τολμήσας.—ED. and TRANSL.

CHAPTER XVI.

1. 'Ηγόρασαν, *they [had] bought*) On the day before the Sabbath they prepared the sweet spices, Luke xxiii. 56, xxiv. 1. Therefore it must have been then also that they had bought them: for on the day following the Sabbath they could not have bought them so early in the morning. Accordingly, either διαγενομένου τοῦ σαββάτου must, by Hyperbaton [the transposition of words contrary to the natural order.—See Append.], be joined with *they come* [ἔρχονται], ver. 2; or else the sense is, *the Sabbath having been kept in the interim*, viz. between the preparation and the first day of the week.—ἀρώματα, *sweet spices*; —ἀλείψωσιν, *they might anoint*) There is a Synecdoche [see Append.] in both words.[1] They were wishing to sprinkle the body with *the sweet spices*, and to *anoint* it with ointments, or else to mix together the sweet spices and ointments.

2. Λίαν πρωΐ, *very early in the morning*.—ἀνατείλαντος τοῦ ἡλίου, *the sun having arisen*) The one [the first] clause applies to Mary Magdalene, John xx. 1; the other clause to the rest of the women.

3. 'Εκ, *from*) Therefore the sepulchre had been very securely guarded. The women, however, were not aware that it had been also sealed [Matt. xxvii. 66].

4. Γὰρ, *for*) The particle intimates both the reason why the *women* were in anxiety [ver. 3], and the reason why they perceived that *the stone* must have been rolled away with an unusually great power.

5. Νεανίσκον, *a young man*) A style of appearance appropriate to angels. For the most part, they appeared in the form of a man, and that a youthful human form in this case [Matt. xxviii. 2].—ἐν τοῖς δεξίοις, *on the right side*) The minister [attendant angel] is thus ready at hand to his Lord, fitly ministering to Him.

---

[1] The ἀρώματα, *sweet spices*, including also *ointments*: the ἀλείψωσιν, *anoint*, including also the *mixing together* of sweet spices and ointments.—ED. and TRANSL.

7. Ἀλλ' ὑπάγετε, *but go your way*) in antithesis to [ver. 6] *He is not here*; [ver. 7] *there shall ye see Him.*—καὶ τῷ Πέτρῳ, *and Peter*) who subsequently proclaimed this testimony in his Acts and Epistles. [*How great must have been the refreshment of spirit, as we may suppose, afforded by this to that disciple, overwhelmed as he was by sorrow!*—V. g.]

8. Τρόμος, *trembling*) of body. Comp. 1 Cor. ii. 3, note.—ἔκστασις, *stupor* [amazement]) of mind.

9. Πρωΐ, *early in the morning*) Construe with ἐφάνη, *He appeared.* Comp. ver. 12. However, it was on that very day the Lord arose, before the dawn.

12. Ἑτέρᾳ, *another* [*different*]) This is the intermediate step of His revelation between His announcement of the fact by messengers, and His manifest appearance: just as the number *two* [viz. of those to whom He here appears] is intermediate between the one single female messenger and the many witnesses.—[εἰς ἀγρὸν, *into the country*) towards Emmaus.—V. g.]

13. Ἀπήγγειλαν) *They brought back word.*—οὐδὲ ἐκείνοις, *not even them*) Luke, xxiv. 34, affirms they did believe. Both statements are true. They did believe: but presently there recurred to them a suspicion as to the truth, and even positive *unbelief.* The faith suddenly arising in them, and entertained at first with a joy which had still in it something of an unwonted and ecstatic character blended with it, was not faith, as compared with the faith which followed, cleared as the latter was of all dregs of unbelief, and fully satisfied as to all difficulties, and suitable to the exigencies of the apostleship. Luke xxiv. 37, 38; John xx. 25; Matt. xxviii. 17.

14. Ὕστερον, *lastly*) The last of His appearances, not absolutely, but of those which Mark describes; [*and which occurred on the very day of the resurrection. For Mark adds:* When the eleven *sat at meat; and therefore he does not speak of the appearance on the mountain of Galilee, which He Himself touches on most briefly,* in ver. 7, and Matthew, xxviii. 16, *expressly records.*—Harm., p. 604.]—ἀνακειμένοις, *as they sat at meat*) At the time when men are most exhilarated by the coming of those whom they were earnestly wishing for.—αὐτοῖς, *themselves*) together.—ὠνείδισε, *He upbraided*) This takes for granted that the proofs of the resurrection were undoubted. [*A wholesome putting of them to*

shame.—V. g.]—*καὶ σκληροκαρδίαν*, *and hardness of heart*) Faith and a tender heart are always conjoined.

15. Κόσμον, *the world*) Jesus Christ, the Lord of all, [is the fitting Giver of this command to preach in *all the world*].—*πάσῃ*, *all*), ver. 20 [*everywhere*]. This is said without limitation. If all men, of all places and ages, have not heard the Gospel, [the blame lies with] the successors of the first preachers, and those whose duty it was to have heard it, [who] have not answered the intention of the Divine will.—*κτίσει, creature*) to men primarily, ver. 16; to the rest of creatures secondarily. As widely extended as was the curse, so widely extended is the blessing. The creation of the world by the Son is the foundation of its redemption and His [coming] kingdom [reign] over it.

16. Πιστεύσας, *he that believeth*) the Gospel. The close of this Gospel corresponds to its opening: ch. i. 15.—*καὶ βαπτισθείς, and that is baptized*) Whosoever once believes, is wont to receive baptism.—*σωθήσεται, shall be saved: κατακριθήσεται, shall be condemned*) There is a Synecdoche in both verbs: *shall have righteousness* [the antithetic term to *κατακρίμα* involved in *κατακριθήσεται*], and *salvation; shall be condemned*, and perish [the antithesis of *σωθήσεται*].—*ἀπιστήσας, he who believeth not*) Those who did not believe, did not receive baptism. The want of baptism does not condemn, unless it be through *unbelief* [that baptism is refused]. The penalty of neglecting circumcision is more expressly indicated, Gen. xvii. 14.

17. Τοῖς πιστεύσασι, in the case of *them that believe*) by the instrumentality of that very faith, of which ver. 16 treats: comp. Heb. xi. 33, etc. The state of mind [faith] whereby Paul was saved, was not different from that whereby he performed miracles. Even in our day, faith has in every believer a hidden power of a miraculous character: every effect resulting from our prayers is really miraculous, even though that miraculous character be not apparent; although in many, both on account of their own feebleness, and on account of the unworthiness of the world,—not merely because [as some say] the Church, being once planted, needs not the continuance of miracles, though no doubt the early miracles of the New Testament have 'made' for the Lord Jesus "an everlasting name" (comp. Isa. lxiii. 12),—that power does not exert itself in our day. Signs were

in the beginning the props and stays of faith: now they are also the object of faith. At Leonberg, a town of Wirtemberg [A.C. 1644, thirteenth Sunday after Trinity], a girl of twenty years of age was so disabled in her limbs, as hardly to be able to creep along by the help of crutches; but whilst the Dean [Raumeier was his name] was, from the pulpit, dwelling on the miraculous power of Jesus' name, she suddenly was raised up and restored to the use of her limbs.[1]—ταῦτα, *these*) Miracles are here alluded to of a most palpable kind, and such as are altogether removed from every suspicion of trickery.—παρακολουθήσει, *shall follow in the train of*) The word and faith precede the signs, ver. 20.—ἐν τῷ ὀνόματί Μου, *in My name*) which believers call upon.—καιναῖς, *new*) Such as they themselves had not previously known: or even such as no nation had previously spoken: 1 Cor. xii. 10. For in Acts ii. 4, the tongues of the Parthians, Medes, etc., are called *other tongues*, not *new* tongues. Ἕτεραι, *other* tongues, were such as were used before, viz., by the various nations: but καιναί, *new* tongues: for instance, as at Corinth, where one spake in the tongue, and another had to interpret it, although there was no one present who used the foreign tongue; a proceeding which was as it were a kind of prophetical exercise.

18. Θανάσιμον, *deadly*) The resurrection of dead men is not here mentioned: Jesus Christ performed more than He promised. But we read of only Tabitha being raised by Peter, and Eutychus by Paul: for now that the Saviour has entered His glory,

---

[1] This happened in the presence of Duke Eberhard III. and his courtiers, and was committed to the public records, which are above all suspicion. However D. Ernesti, *Bibl. Theol.* T. ii. 416, regards the whole affair as not worthy to be dignified with the name of *miracle*. The very words of the Dean are given by E. B. in his Ed. of Beng. Gnom., which the curious reader can consult. The girl had been for nine years continuously disabled. E. B. tells a marvellous tale in addition. At Lavingen, in the year 1606, Nov. 26, Joseph Jenisch was born of the noble stock of the Kellers; he was destitute of a tongue from his birth, but in consequence of the earnest prayers of his parents and family, when he had not yet finished his first year, he was able to name distinctly the several members of the family, and was, therefore, dedicated to the service of the ministry, which for forty years he discharged at Böblingen and Münchingen: he died on the 10th of April 1675.—ED. and TRANSL.

it is more desirable [more to be wished for] to wing one's flight by faith out of this world into the other, than to return to this life.

19. Ὁ Κύριος, *the Lord*) A magnificent and suitable appellation, ver. 20 [ch. xii. 36].—μετὰ τὸ λαλῆσαι αὐτοῖς, *after He had spoken to them*) He furnished them with His instructions, not only on the very day of the resurrection, which has been so copiously described by Mark, but even throughout the succeeding days [*Comp. note on Matth.* xxviii. 19, 20].

20. Πανταχοῦ, *everywhere*) ver. 15. At the time when Mark wrote his Gospel, even then already the apostles had gone forth into all the world; Rom. x. 18: on this account it is that, excepting Peter, James the Elder, John, James the Less, and Jude, we read no mention in the books of the New Testament of any apostle, save Paul, after the second or fifteenth chapter of the Acts. Each one became most known in that place and country where he preached. The name of no apostle was celebrated throughout the whole world, but the name of Jesus Christ alone.

END OF VOL. I.

T. and T. Clark's Publications.

MEYER'S
Commentary on the New Testament.

MESSRS. CLARK beg to announce that they have in course of preparation a Translation of the well-known and justly esteemed

CRITICAL AND EXEGETICAL
COMMENTARY ON THE NEW TESTAMENT,

By Dr. H. A. W. MEYER,

OBERCONSISTORIALRATH, HANOVER,

Of which they hope to publish in October—

ROMANS, Vol. I.
GALATIANS, One Volume.

The Subscription will be 21s. for Four Volumes Demy 8vo.

By arrangement with Dr. MEYER, Messrs. Clark have obtained the sole right of translation into English, and they will also have the very great advantage of Dr. Meyer's latest emendations. In order to secure perfect accuracy, the Publishers have placed the whole work under the editorial care of Rev. Dr. DICKSON, Professor of Biblical Criticism in the University of Glasgow.

The Volumes will vary in number of pages according to the size of the original, but an average of about 400 pages may be assumed. Each Volume will be sold separately at (on an average) 10s. 6d. to Non-Subscribers.

It is obvious that the Series cannot be published with the regularity of the Foreign Theological Library, as in many cases the Publishers must wait for Dr. MEYER's Notes.

Intending Subscribers will be kind enough to fill up the accompanying Form, which may be returned, either direct to the Publishers at 38 George Street, Edinburgh, or through their own Booksellers.

*Mr.*_____

BOOKSELLER,

Will please enter my Name as a Subscriber, and forward, as published, the above Translation of

MEYER'S COMMENTARIES.

T. and T. Clark's Publications.

LANGE'S
COMMENTARIES ON THE OLD AND NEW TESTAMENTS.

MESSRS. CLARK have now pleasure in intimating their arrangements, under the Editorship of Dr. PHILIP SCHAFF, for the Publication of Translations of the Commentaries of Dr. LANGE and his *Collaborateurs* on the Old and New Testaments.

There are now ready (in imperial 8vo, double columns), price 21s. per Volume,

OLD TESTAMENT, Six Volumes:

COMMENTARY ON THE BOOK OF GENESIS, in One Volume.
COMMENTARY ON JOSHUA, JUDGES, AND RUTH, in One Volume.
COMMENTARY ON THE BOOKS OF KINGS, in One Volume.
COMMENTARY ON THE PSALMS, in One Volume.
COMMENTARY ON PROVERBS, ECCLESIASTES, AND THE SONG OF SOLOMON, in One Volume.
COMMENTARY ON JEREMIAH AND LAMENTATIONS, in One Volume.

The other Books of the Old Testament are in active preparation, and will be announced as soon as ready.

NEW TESTAMENT, Ten Volumes:

COMMENTARY ON THE GOSPEL OF ST. MATTHEW, in One Volume.
COMMENTARY ON THE GOSPELS OF ST. MARK and ST. LUKE, in One Volume.
COMMENTARY ON THE GOSPEL OF ST. JOHN, in One Volume.
COMMENTARY ON THE ACTS OF THE APOSTLES, in One Volume.
COMMENTARY ON THE EPISTLE OF ST. PAUL TO THE ROMANS, in One Volume.
COMMENTARY ON THE EPISTLES OF ST. PAUL TO THE CORINTHIANS, in One Volume.
COMMENTARY ON THE EPISTLES OF ST. PAUL TO THE GALATIANS, EPHESIANS, PHILIPPIANS, and COLOSSIANS, in One Vol.
COMMENTARY ON THE EPISTLES TO THE THESSALONIANS, TIMOTHY, TITUS, PHILEMON, and HEBREWS, in One Volume.
COMMENTARY ON THE EPISTLES OF JAMES, PETER, JOHN, and JUDE, in One Volume.
COMMENTARY ON THE BOOK OF REVELATION, in One Volume (*in the press*).

The price to Subscribers to the Foreign Theological Library, St. Augustine's Works, and Ante-Nicene Library, or to Purchasers of Complete Sets of the Commentary (so far as published), will be

FIFTEEN SHILLINGS PER VOLUME.

Dr. LANGE's Commentary on the Gospels and Acts (without Dr. SCHAFF's Notes) is also published in the FOREIGN THEOLOGICAL LIBRARY, in Nine Volumes demy 8vo, and may be had in that form if desired. (For particulars, see List of Foreign Theological Library.)

CLARK'S
FOREIGN THEOLOGICAL LIBRARY.

ANNUAL SUBSCRIPTION:
One Guinea (payable in advance) for Four Volumes, Demy 8vo.
When not paid in advance, the Retail Bookseller is entitled to charge 24s.

N.B.—Any *two* Years in this Series can be had at Subscription Price. *A single Year's Books* (except in the case of the current Year) *cannot be supplied separately.* Non-subscribers, price 10s. 6d. each volume, with exceptions marked.

1864—
Lange on the Acts of the Apostles. Two Volumes.
Keil and Delitzsch on the Pentateuch. Vols. I. and II.

1865—
Keil and Delitzsch on the Pentateuch. Vol. III.
Hengstenberg on the Gospel of John. Two Volumes.
Keil and Delitzsch on Joshua, Judges, and Ruth. One Volume.

1866—
Keil and Delitzsch on Samuel. One Volume.
Keil and Delitzsch on Job. Two Volumes.
Martensen's System of Christian Doctrine. One Volume.

1867—
Delitzsch on Isaiah. Vol. I.
Delitzsch on Biblical Psychology. 12s.
Delitzsch on Isaiah. Vol. II.
Auberlen on Divine Revelation.

1868—
Keil's Commentary on the Minor Prophets. Two Volumes.
Delitzsch's Commentary on Epistle to the Hebrews. Vol. I.
Harless' System of Christian Ethics. One Volume.

1869—
Hengstenberg on Ezekiel. One Volume.
Stier on the Words of the Apostles. One Volume.
Keil's Introduction to the Old Testament. Vol. I.
Bleek's Introduction to the New Testament. Vol. I.

1870—
Keil's Introduction to the Old Testament. Vol. II.
Bleek's Introduction to the New Testament. Vol. II.
Schmid's New Testament Theology. One Volume.
Delitzsch's Commentary on Epistle to the Hebrews. Vol. II.

1871—
Delitzsch's Commentary on the Psalms. Three Volumes.
Hengstenberg's History of the Kingdom of God under the Old Testament. Vol. I.

1872—
Keil's Commentary on the Books of Kings. One Volume.
Keil's Commentary on the Book of Daniel. One Volume.
Keil's Commentary on the Books of Chronicles. One Volume.
Hengstenberg's History of the Kingdom of God under the Old Testament. Vol. II.

MESSRS. CLARK have resolved to allow a SELECTION of TWENTY VOLUMES (*or more at the same ratio*) from the various Series previous to the Volumes issued in 1869 (*see next page*),

At the Subscription Price of Five Guineas.

They trust that this will still more largely extend the usefulness of the FOREIGN THEOLOGICAL LIBRARY, which has so long been recognised as holding an important place in modern Theological literature.

T. and T. Clark's Publications.

In Twenty-four Handsome 8vo Volumes,

SUBSCRIPTION PRICE, £6, 6s.,

Ante-Nicene Christian Library.

A COLLECTION OF ALL THE WORKS OF THE FATHERS OF THE CHRISTIAN CHURCH PRIOR TO THE COUNCIL OF NICÆA.

EDITED BY

ALEXANDER ROBERTS, D.D.,
Professor of Humanity in the University of St. Andrews,

AND

JAMES DONALDSON, LL.D.,
Rector of the Royal High School, Edinburgh, and Author of 'Early Christian Literature and Doctrine.'

MESSRS. CLARK are now happy to announce the completion of this Series. It has been received with marked approval by all sections of the Christian Church in this country and in the United States, as supplying what has long been felt to be a want, and also on account of the impartiality, learning, and care with which Editors and Translators have executed a very difficult task.

Each work is supplied with a good and full Index; but, to add to the value of the completed Series, an Index Volume is preparing for the whole Series, which will be sold separately to those who may desire it, at a moderate price.

The Publishers, however, do not bind themselves to *continue* to supply the Series at the Subscription price.

Single Years cannot be had separately, unless to complete sets; but any Volume may be had separately, price 10s. 6d.,—with the exception of ORIGEN, Vol. II., 12s.: and the EARLY LITURGIES, 9s.

'The series of translations from Ante-Nicene Fathers, for which not professed scholars and divines only, but all the educated class, have to thank Messrs. Clark, is now completed. We cannot allow that series to come to a close without expressing marked satisfaction . . . that there should be so high a standard of real scholarship and marked ability sustained throughout the whole undertaking. It is really not too much to say that Messrs. Clark have fairly established a claim for themselves to be enrolled in that goodly list of great printers who have made a mark in literature by large and enlightened enterprise.'—*Guardian.*

The Homilies of Origen are not included in the Series, as the Publishers have received no encouragement to have them translated.

ANTE-NICENE CHRISTIAN LIBRARY—*continued.*

The Works are arranged as follow :—

FIRST YEAR.

APOSTOLIC FATHERS, comprising Clement's Epistles to the Corinthians; Polycarp to the Ephesians; Martyrdom of Polycarp; Epistle of Barnabas; Epistles of Ignatius (longer and shorter, and also the Syriac version); Martyrdom of Ignatius; Epistle to Diognetus; Pastor of Hermas; Papias; Spurious Epistles of Ignatius. In One Volume.

JUSTIN MARTYR; ATHENAGORAS. In One Volume.

TATIAN; THEOPHILUS; THE CLEMENTINE RECOGNITIONS. In One Volume.

CLEMENT OF ALEXANDRIA, Volume First, comprising Exhortation to Heathen; The Instructor; and a portion of the Miscellanies.

SECOND YEAR.

HIPPOLYTUS, Volume First; Refutation of all Heresies and Fragments from his Commentaries.

IRENÆUS, Volume First.

TERTULLIAN AGAINST MARCION.

CYPRIAN, Volume First; the Epistles and some of the Treatises.

THIRD YEAR.

IRENÆUS (completion); HIPPOLYTUS (completion); Fragments of Third Century. In One Volume.

ORIGEN: De Principiis; Letters; and portion of Treatise against Celsus.

CLEMENT OF ALEXANDRIA, Volume Second; Completion of Miscellanies.

TERTULLIAN, Volume First: To the Martyrs; Apology; To the Nations, etc.

FOURTH YEAR.

CYPRIAN, Volume Second (completion); Novatian; Minucius Felix; Fragments.

METHODIUS; ALEXANDER OF LYCOPOLIS; PETER OF ALEXANDRIA; Anatolius; Clement on Virginity: and Fragments.

TERTULLIAN, Volume Second.

APOCRYPHAL GOSPELS; ACTS AND REVELATIONS, comprising all the very curious Apocryphal Writings of the first Three Centuries.

FIFTH YEAR.

TERTULLIAN, Volume Third (completion).

CLEMENTINE HOMILIES; APOSTOLICAL CONSTITUTIONS. In One Volume.

ARNOBIUS.

DIONYSIUS; GREGORY THAUMATURGUS; SYRIAN FRAGMENTS. In One Volume.

SIXTH YEAR.

LACTANTIUS. Two Volumes.

ORIGEN, Volume Second (completion). 12s. to Non-Subscribers.

EARLY LITURGIES AND REMAINING FRAGMENTS. 9s. to Non-Subscribers.

The Works of St. Augustine.

EDITED BY THE REV. MARCUS DODS, M.A.

SUBSCRIPTION

Four Volumes for a Guinea, *payable in advance*, as in the case of the ANTE-NICENE SERIES (24s. when not paid in advance).

MESSRS. CLARK have much pleasure in announcing the publication of the following Volumes of Translations of the Writings of ST. AUGUSTINE, viz. :—

FIRST YEAR—

THE 'CITY OF GOD.' Two Volumes.

WRITINGS IN CONNECTION WITH THE DONATIST CONTROVERSY. One Volume.

THE ANTI-PELAGIAN WORKS OF ST. AUGUSTINE. Vol. I.

The First Issue of SECOND YEAR—

'LETTERS.' Vol. I. And

TREATISES AGAINST FAUSTUS THE MANICHÆAN. One Volume.

They believe this will prove not the least valuable of their various Series, and no pains will be spared to make it so. The Editor has secured a most competent staff of Translators, and every care is being taken to secure not only accuracy, but elegance.

The Works of ST. AUGUSTINE to be included in the Series are (in addition to the above)—

> The Treatises on CHRISTIAN DOCTRINE; the TRINITY; the HARMONY OF THE EVANGELISTS; the SERMON ON THE MOUNT.
>
> Also, the LECTURES on the GOSPEL OF ST. JOHN; the CONFESSIONS, a SELECTION from the LETTERS, the RETRACTATIONS, the SOLILOQUIES, and SELECTIONS from the PRACTICAL TREATISES.

All these works are of great importance, and few of them have yet appeared in an English dress. The SERMONS and the COMMENTARIES ON THE PSALMS having been already given by the Oxford Translators, it is not intended, at least in the first instance, to publish them.

The Series will include a LIFE OF ST. AUGUSTINE, by ROBERT RAINY, D.D., Professor of Church History, New College, Edinburgh.

The Series will probably extend to about Eighteen Volumes. The Publishers will be glad to receive Subscribers' names as early as possible.

It is understood that Subscribers are bound to take at least the books of the first two years. Each Volume will be sold separately at (on an average) 10s. 6d. each Volume.

LANGE'S
COMMENTARIES ON THE OLD AND NEW TESTAMENTS.

MESSRS. CLARK have now pleasure in intimating their arrangements, under the Editorship of Dr. PHILIP SCHAFF, for the Publication of Translations of the Commentaries of Dr. LANGE and his *Collaborateurs* on the Old and New Testaments.

There are now ready (in imperial 8vo, double column),

COMMENTARY ON THE BOOK OF GENESIS, One Volume.

COMMENTARY ON JOSHUA, JUDGES, AND RUTH, in One Volume.

COMMENTARY ON THE BOOKS OF KINGS, in One Volume.

COMMENTARY ON THE PSALMS, in One Volume.

COMMENTARY ON PROVERBS, ECCLESIASTES, AND THE SONG OF SOLOMON, in One Volume.

COMMENTARY ON JEREMIAH AND LAMENTATIONS, in One Volume.

Other Volumes on the Old Testament are in active preparation, and will be announced as soon as ready.

Messrs. CLARK have already published, in the FOREIGN THEOLOGICAL LIBRARY, the Commentaries on St. Matthew, St. Mark, St. Luke, and the Acts of the Apostles, but they may be had uniform with this Series if desired.

They had resolved to issue that on St. John only in the imperial 8vo form; but at the request of many of their Subscribers they have published it (without Dr. Schaff's Additions) in Two Volumes, demy 8vo (uniform with the FOREIGN THEOLOGICAL LIBRARY), which will be supplied to Subscribers at 10s. 6d.

COMMENTARY ON THE GOSPEL OF ST. JOHN, in One Volume.

COMMENTARY ON THE EPISTLE OF ST. PAUL TO THE ROMANS. In One Volume.

COMMENTARY ON THE EPISTLES OF ST. PAUL TO THE CORINTHIANS. In One Volume.

COMMENTARY ON THE EPISTLES OF ST. PAUL TO THE GALATIANS, EPHESIANS, PHILIPPIANS, and COLOSSIANS. In One Volume.

COMMENTARY ON THE EPISTLES TO THE THESSALONIANS, TIMOTHY, TITUS, PHILEMON, and HEBREWS. In One Vol.

COMMENTARY ON THE EPISTLES OF JAMES, PETER, JOHN, and JUDE. In One Volume.

The New Testament is thus complete, with the exception of the Commentary on the Book of Revelation, which is in progress.

Each of the above volumes (six on the Old and nine on the New Testament) will be supplied to Subscribers to the FOREIGN THEOLOGICAL LIBRARY and ANTE-NICENE LIBRARY, or to Purchasers of complete sets of Old Testament (so far as published), and of Epistles, at 15s. The price to others will be 21s. each volume.

T. and T. Clark's Publications.

New and Cheaper Edition of Lange's Life of Christ.

Just published, in Four Volumes, Demy 8vo, price 28s. (Subscription price),

THE LIFE OF THE LORD JESUS CHRIST:

A COMPLETE CRITICAL EXAMINATION OF THE ORIGIN, CONTENTS, AND CONNECTION OF THE GOSPELS.

Translated from the German of J. P. LANGE, D.D., Professor of Divinity in the University of Bonn. Edited, with additional notes, by the Rev. MARCUS DODS, M.A.

EXTRACT FROM EDITOR'S PREFACE.

'The work of Dr. Lange, translated in the accompanying volumes, holds among books the honourable position of being the most complete Life of our Lord. There are other works which more thoroughly investigate the authenticity of the Gospel records, some which more satisfactorily discuss the chronological difficulties involved in this most important of histories, and some which present a more formal and elaborate exegetical treatment of the sources; but there is no single work in which all these branches are so fully attended to, or in which so much matter bearing on the main subject is brought together, or on which so many points are elucidated. The immediate object of this comprehensive and masterly work was to refute those views of the Life of our Lord which had been propagated by Negative Criticism, and to substitute that authentic and consistent history which a truly scientific and enlightened criticism educes from the Gospels.

'We have arrived at a most favourable conclusion regarding the importance and ability of this work—the former depending upon the present condition of theological criticism, the latter on the wide range of the work itself; the singularly dispassionate judgment of the author, as well as his pious, reverential, and erudite treatment of a subject inexpressibly holy. . . . We have great pleasure in recommending this work to our readers. We are convinced of its value and enormous range.'—*Irish Ecclesiastical Gazette.*

THE COMMENTARIES, ETC., OF JOHN CALVIN,
IN 48 VOLUMES, DEMY 8vo.

MESSRS. CLARK beg respectfully to announce that the whole STOCK and COPYRIGHTS of the WORKS OF CALVIN, published by the Calvin Translation Society, are now their property, and that this valuable Series is now issued by them on the following very favourable terms:—

Complete Sets of Commentaries, etc., 45 vols., £7, 17s. 6d.

A *Selection* of Six Volumes (or more at the same proportion) for 21s.; with the exception of PSALMS, vol. 5; and HABAKKUK.

Any Separate Volume, 6s.

The Contents of the Series are as follow:—

Tracts on the Reformation, 3 vols.
Commentary on Genesis, 2 vols.
Harmony of the last Four Books of the Pentateuch, 4 vols.
Commentary on Joshua, 1 vol.
" on the Psalms, 5 vols.
" on Isaiah, 4 vols.
" on Jeremiah and Lamentations, 5 vols.
" on Ezekiel, 2 vols.
" on Daniel, 2 vols.
" on Hosea, 1 vol.
" on Joel, Amos, and Obadiah, 1 vol.
" on Jonah, Micah, and Nahum, 1 vol.
" on Habakkuk, Zephaniah, and Haggai, 1 vol.
Commentary on Zechariah and Malachi, 1 vol.
Harmony of the Synoptical Evangelists, 3 vols.
Commentary on John's Gospel, 2 vols.
" on Acts of the Apostles, 2 vols.
" on Romans, 1 vol.
" on Corinthians, 2 vols.
" on Galatians and Ephesians, 1 vol.
" on Philippians, Colossians, and Thessalonians, 1 vol.
" on Timothy, Titus, and Philemon, 1 vol.
" on Hebrews, 1 vol.
" on Peter, John, James, and Jude, 1 vol.

www.ingramcontent.com/pod-product-compliance
Lightning Source LLC
Chambersburg PA
CBHW021229300426
44111CB00007B/473